Supercharging
Performance Handbook

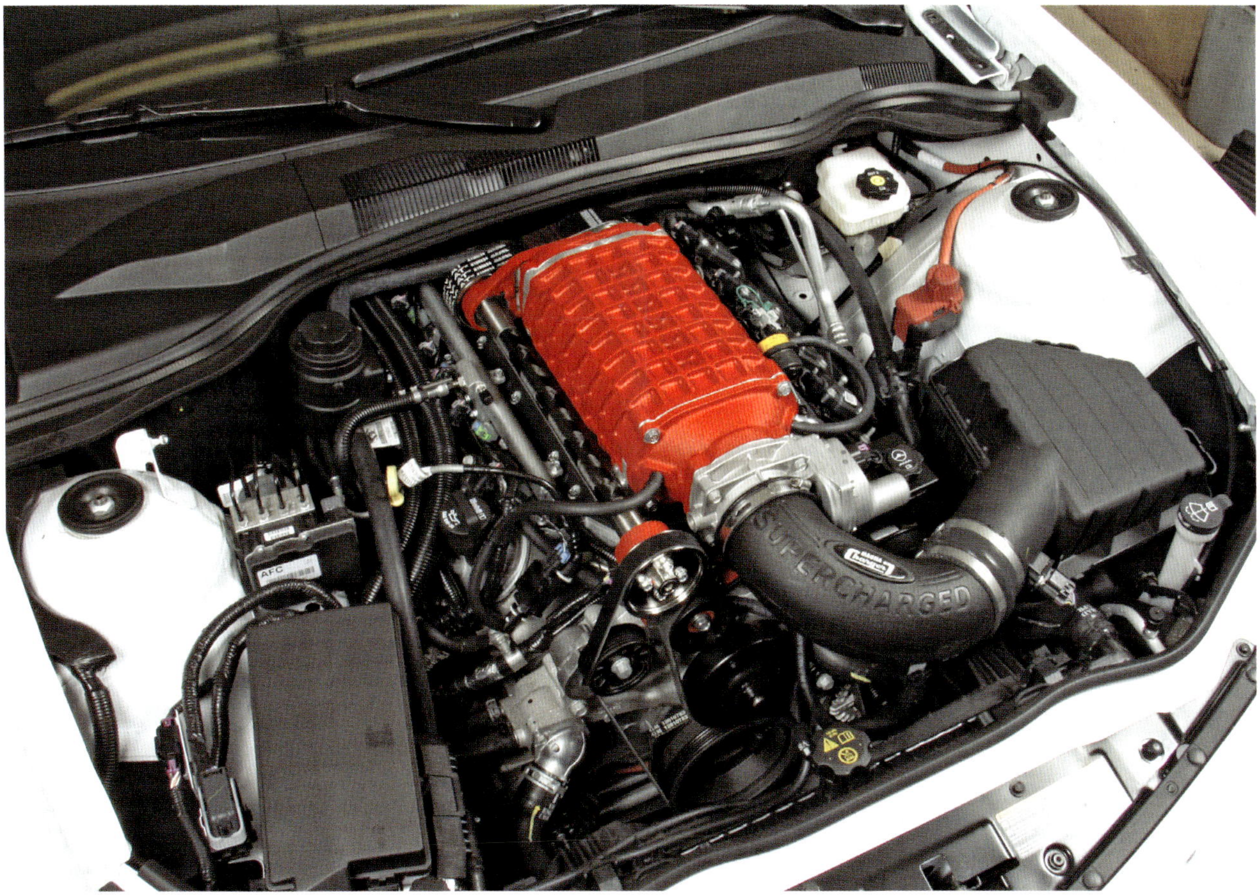

By Jeff Hartman

First published in 2011 by MBI Publishing Company and Motorbooks, an imprint of MBI Publishing Company, 400 First Avenue North, Suite 300, Minneapolis, MN 55401 USA

© 2011 Motorbooks
Text © 2011 Jeff Hartman

All photographs are from the author's collection unless noted otherwise.

All rights reserved. With the exception of quoting brief passages for the purposes of review, no part of this publication may be reproduced without prior written permission from the Publisher.

The information in this book is true and complete to the best of our knowledge. All recommendations are made without any guarantee on the part of the author or Publisher, who also disclaims any liability incurred in connection with the use of this data or specific details.

We recognize, further, that some words, model names, and designations mentioned herein are the property of the trademark holder. We use them for identification purposes only. This is not an official publication.

Motorbooks titles are also available at discounts in bulk quantity for industrial or sales-promotional use. For details write to Special Sales Manager at MBI Publishing Company, 400 First Avenue North, Suite 300, Minneapolis, MN 55401 USA.

To find out more about our books, visit us online at www.motorbooks.com.

ISBN-13: 978-0-7603-3938-1

Editors: Peter Bodensteiner and Jeffrey Zuehlke
Design Manager: James Kegley
Layout by: Kathleen Littfin

Printed in China

10 9 8 7 6 5 4 3 2 1

On the front cover: © Ron Kimball/Kimball Stock

About the author
Jeff Hartman is the author of *How to Tune and Modify Engine Management Systems*; *Fuel Injection: Installation, Performance, Tuning Modification*; *Turbocharging Performance Handbook*, and *Nitrous Oxide Performance Handbook*, all from Motorbooks. He lives in Austin, Texas.

Contents

CHAPTER 1	The Prehistory of Supercharging	4
CHAPTER 2	Normal Versus Super Charging: Volumetric and Thermal Efficiency	28
CHAPTER 3	Choosing the Engine	41
CHAPTER 4	Supercharger Architecture	61
CHAPTER 5	Supercharger Selection and System Modeling	80
CHAPTER 6	Blower Engine Management	106
CHAPTER 7	Heat Management: Combustion, Engine, Blower, Oil, Charge, Exhaust	135
CHAPTER 8	Buying and Installing a Supercharger Kit	169
CHAPTER 9	Designing and Building a Supercharger System	177
CHAPTER 10	Overboosting	200
CHAPTER 11	Extreme Supercharging	206
Index		220

Chapter 1
The Prehistory of Supercharging

A hundred years ago, at the dawn of the automotive age, piston engines universally had poor specific power. The peak output of an early 2.9-liter Model T Ford was a miserable *20 horsepower at 1,600 rpm*, which is about 6.9 horsepower per liter—or about 190 horsepower per liter *less* than modern motorcycle, like Honda's 118-horsepower, 600cc CBR600RR. Back then, the solution to delivering more power was increasing engine displacement to enormous levels. Early John Deere Model A tractors were equipped with huge, two-cylinder engines displacing 5.26 liters that were capable of 19 to 34 horsepower, depending on the fuel, which could be as low as 30 octane. The problem is large-displacement engines tend to be large, heavy, and impractical for many vehicular applications, particularly aircraft.

The search was on for ways to improve the *specific power* of engines, that is, the horsepower per cubic inch. Engineers, inventors, and early racers looking for ways to improve specific power confronted a fact of life that is still true today: Even the most efficient normally charged piston engines eventually smack into an insurmountable oxygen famine at full throttle, which defines peak power.

It takes air to burn fuel, and air is scarce. Or, at least it is inside a spark-ignition internal-combustion engine. By weight, you need at least 12.5 times as much air as gasoline to optimize combustion pressures in a piston engine; burning a single gallon of gasoline requires nearly 10,000 gallons of air at atmospheric pressure. Throwing additional gasoline into an engine starving for air is worse than useless: the excess fuel will not make more power, but it will make black smoke and pollution, and then *diminish* power. When the mixture reaches rich flammability limits (which means the mixture is too rich to ignite), the engine will gasp and stall.

It's all about the air. In fact, the heating value of tiny amounts of hydrocarbon fuel is so extreme that fuel is almost never the critical constraint when it comes to increasing power. A 20-gallon tank of gasoline contains 746-kilowatt hours of heating energy, equivalent to 2,000 horsepower for nearly a half hour. An engine delivering 1,000 continuous horsepower could require as little as a few cups of gasoline a minute, depending on its thermal efficiency.

Early piston engines were entirely dependent on atmospheric pressure to force air into their cylinders. The most you could possibly expect would be to fill or charge each cylinder with one atmosphere of air pressure, but even that virtually never happened. Early internal combustion engines had poor cylinder-filling volumetric efficiency, mainly because of poor induction system design. This was one reason one could not make horsepower by simply running the engine at higher speeds.

But the fundamental problem of any piston engine charged with air in the normal way—then or now—is that the mechanism that produces the power is the same mechanism that charges the engine with air and fuel. An ordinary piston engine must gulp whatever air-fuel charge it can in one intake stroke and burn it immediately on the next power stroke. With this system, it is a fact of life that the charging mechanism can never run faster than the combusting mechanism. A normal four-cycle piston engine can never take, say, two or three gulps of air and then combust it all.

It soon becomes clear that the trick to increasing horsepower in a piston engine, without resorting to greater displacement or speed, is to charge the cylinders with a greater mass of oxygen than could be accomplished using normal means. Once this is done, it would be trivial to richen up the charge mixture with additional gasoline.

One obvious way to increase charge-gas oxygen is to force-feed the powerplant air at higher-than-atmospheric pressure. Shortly after the turn of the 20th century, a number of inventors realized that pump designs previously used to supply air or water for mines, forges, and foundries could be modified to augment the intake airflow systems of internal combustion engines.

The genius of supercharging (originally called overcharging) is the concept of divorcing—or at least partially divorcing—the engine's charging system from its power-making system. Rather than depending on pistons to *suck* in air by creating a vacuum that could only be filled by ambient atmospheric pressure pushing air through narrow twisting intake air passages past restrictive throttles and carburetors to reach the combustion chambers, supercharging employs a compressor module to the front end of the engine intake system. The compressor turns much faster than engine rpm—at whatever speed is required to *force* the required amount of air into the cylinders.

As is so often the case throughout history, the cutting edge of this new technology was found in racing and warfare.

EARLY SUPERCHARGING

Almost all modern superchargers evolved from pumping devices that predated the automotive age and were invented to move large volumes of fluid gas or liquid from Point A to Point B at ambient pressure. For example, the rotary-lobe Roots design—employed by GM starting in the 1930s to scavenge exhaust gases from the clearance volume of two-stroke Detroit Diesels and later by Top Fuel race teams and more recently by GM to supercharge the Corvette ZR1—grew out of a pre-Civil War effort by Philander and Francis Roots to improve the efficiency of the waterwheel powering their textile mill.

Although it turned out that the Roots brothers' intermeshing bi-rotor invention was inferior to the traditional paddle wheel when it came to transforming the potential energy of falling water into shaft horsepower capable of running the machinery in a woolen mill, the Roots design turned out to be quite good at blowing large volumes of air through a foundry blast furnace. The Roots design consisted of twin, interlocking rotors, with at least two lobes per rotor, that meshed with each other a little like gears encased in a housing. This design prevents backflow and moves pockets of air trapped between the lobes and around the circumference of the housing from the inlet port to the discharge.

The Roots is a so-called positive-displacement pump, in that it moves essentially the same volume of fluid each revolution regardless of speed. The Roots brothers patented their device in 1860 and updated the design over the following 24 years with 16 additional patents. The rotary-lobe (Roots) design has been used over the years in a wide variety of industrial pumping applications.

Over the years, engineers have attempted to overcharge engines using centrifugal, axial, rotary sliding vane, scroll, diaphragm, reciprocating piston, rotary twin-screw, and eccentric-rotor Wankel pumping technologies. All of these have their advantages and disadvantages, but only the centrifugal, rotary-lobe, vane (to a lesser extent), and rotary twin-screw compressors have achieved widespread application for automotive forced induction.

The first practical application of a pump to force-feed air into the cylinders of a piston engine occurred in 1901, when experiments by Sir Dugald Clerk proved conclusively that whatever the basic volumetric efficiency of an engine-induction system, increasing the pressure of air entering the throttle would enhance engine horsepower. Clerk, a Scottish engineer who developed the world's first two-stroke engine in 1878, installed the compressor on his engine in a misguided attempt to lower maximum combustion temperature on the theory that additional air molecules in the combustion chambers would cool or moderate combustion. This could have worked had Clerk been using a diesel engine for his experiments, but supercharging a spark-ignition powerplant inevitably requires adding fuel to maintain the air-fuel ratio within the a fairly narrow acceptable range for combustion, which invariably *raises* the temperature and pressure of combustion. Clerk's experiments had the completely unintended consequence of increasing engine power by 6 percent.

In 1902, in France, Louis Renault patented a supercharging system that used a centrifugal compressor to pressurize air entering the mouth of a carburetor. A few years later, in the United States, Lee Chadwick—who had been building "Chadwick" automobiles since about 1900—succeeded in pressurizing an entire carburetor. He also used a centrifugal compressor, which is a high-speed device that moves air using an impeller consisting of a dozen or so curved paddles attached to a conical disk at the end of a shaft that resides in a containment housing. Air enters the inducer section of the compressor wheel and turns 90 degrees to be flung into the compressor housing at tremendous velocity by the exducer section of the paddles. The diffuser section of the housing is carefully designed to decelerate high-speed air with minimal turbulence. This converts velocity into pressure. Slower moving compressed air exits through the discharge port of the housing. Depending on the design, a centrifugal compressor can supply pressurized air efficiently over an extremely wide range of speeds, pressure ratios, and mass-airflow rates. Unfortunately, it does not begin making measurable pressure until it is spinning more than about 20,000 rpm, at which point the airspeed can be nearly supersonic.

The obvious way to drive a screw, Roots, vane, or piston-type compressor was to employ belts, chains, gears, or some combination thereof, driven from the crankshaft. But centrifugal compressors remain a special challenge because of the high speeds involved and the great differential between crankshaft and compressor speed. Chadwick initially used a flat leather belt to drive a single-stage centrifugal compressor at nine times the engine speed from the flywheel. A later version deployed a wider, 2-inch belt to drive a three-stage compressor consisting of three 12-blade impellers 10 inches in diameter arranged by their decreasing width in the second and third stages.

Chadwick was onto something. Centrifugal compressors are extremely efficient, pressurizing air without overheating it as badly as some other types of compressors, delivering excellent thermal and pumping efficiency and low parasitic drag. However, because centrifugal pumping efficiency increases exponentially with speed, to achieve any measurable boost pressure at low engine rpm, a single-stage *mechanically* driven centrifugal compressor would have to be overdriven enough to have the impeller turning 20,000-plus rpm off-idle, which would tend to generate unmanageable mass airflow at redline.

This was less of an issue on early automotive engines with narrow powerbands that redlined at modest speeds and on piston aero engines that are typically governed to a maximum speed in the 1,000- to 3,000-rpm range. But in practice, mechanically driven centrifugal superchargers on most engines must be overdriven to produce safe boost at *peak-power rpm* and are thus ineffective at making boost at low engine speeds.

In 1908, Chadwick entered his supercharged 1,140-cid *Great Chadwick Six* in the Wilkes-Barre, Pennsylvania, hill climb—and won! This was not only the first supercharged car entered in competition, but it was the first to win. Chadwick campaigned the car extensively over the next two years with much success. Its most notable win was a 200-mile road race in Philadelphia's Fairmount Park in 1910. Chadwick's racer was the first car in history to officially exceed 100 miles per hour, and replicas of it were sold to the public. Despite his success in racing, Chadwick was less successful as a car builder. He discontinued production of the Chadwick in 1911 after building 260 cars. It would be another 12 years before anyone in the United States continued with further development of the supercharger.

In the meantime, a young Swiss engineer named Alfred Buchi had been attempting to perfect a revolutionary type of centrifugal supercharger driven by a gas turbine. In 1905, while researching turbines for a Belgian outfit, Buchi realized that it might be possible to drive a centrifugal compressor with a turbine that was powered by exhaust gases supplied by the engine being supercharged. A radial-inflow exhaust turbine is a high-speed device like the centrifugal compressor; a properly sized turbine matched to the correct compressor could share an elegantly simple shaft drive with extremely low torque-loading requirements due to the high speed.

Buchi received a patent from the Imperial Patent Office of the German Reich in November 1905 for the sequential arrangement of a centrifugal compressor, piston engine, and exhaust turbine where the compressor and turbine are mounted on a common shaft. The radial-inflow exhaust gas turbine half of Buchi's device was more or less the opposite of the device's centrifugal compressor: Hot combustion gases entered the turbine containment housing through a nozzle at the circumference. The gases were directed under pressure at high speed against the outer curved inducer section of the turbine blades, channeled inward along the turbine blades and, after giving up heat and kinetic energy to rotate and drive the turbine wheel, were directed out through the turbine housing and into an exhaust system. Buchi's design is still the basis of all but the largest modern turbochargers.

With patent in hand, Buchi focused on building a practical turbo-supercharger suitable for increasing the performance of a diesel engine, with the goal of tripling manifold absolute pressure to three atmospheres. In 1909, he installed a prototype turbo-supercharger on a diesel powerplant and began running tests. Diesel engines, it would turn out, are especially compatible with turbochargers for many reasons, including the fact that diesels have no throttle to stall airflow through the compressor. In testing, Buchi demonstrated that the faster his supercharging compressor turned, the more power the engine made, and, in turn, the more combustion gases entered the turbine. The more exhaust gases entered the turbine, the faster it turned the

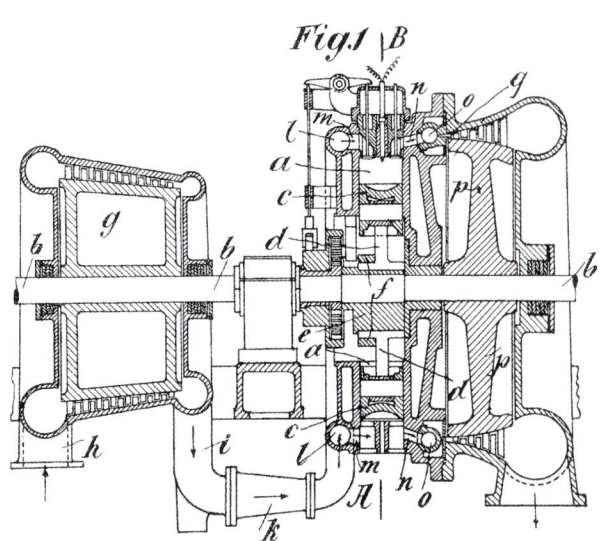

Alfred Buchi's 1905 inspiration was to combine a high-speed centrifugal compressor with an equally high-speed exhaust turbine to supercharge a piston engine, which had terrible volumetric efficiency in the early days. Buchi's initial focus was on diesel engines, which had lower exhaust temperatures and could not detonate like spark-ignition engines. *Patent Office of the German Reich, circa 1905*

NACA (the predecessor to NASA) scientists used this truck rig to dyno-test the performance of a turbo-supercharged Liberty V-12 in the thin air of Pikes Peak at 14,100 feet circa 1920. Supercharging enabled the Liberty to make more power at nearly 3 miles high than a stock Liberty could achieve at sea level. *NASA*

compressor, making more horsepower, more exhaust gases, and so on in an endless cycle that continued until the system choked or the engine blew up. Because the turbocharger was untethered from engine speed, within limits the more power a turbo-supercharged engine made, the more it *could* make—in some cases to a fault. The feedback cycle of increased boost stimulating yet more boost would be an issue that all future turbocharged powerplants would have to manage one way or another.

Buchi's turbine-driven centrifugal supercharger was a great idea for a variety of reasons, beyond the fact that it promised to solve problems related to mechanical drive systems. The thermal efficiency of the compressor was excellent and the parasitic drag was low, a happy situation that would make the device a very efficient power-adder. In fact, all mechanically driven superchargers inevitably rob power from the crankshaft to drive the compressor, typically wasting at least 30 percent of the horsepower produced by the supercharger. The power to drive an exhaust turbine is not free either, but 80 percent of the energy required to drive an exhaust-gas turbine is provided by heat that would otherwise be wasted out the exhaust. The other 20 percent of the energy cost is seen in reduced engine-pumping efficiencies caused by increased exhaust back pressure. Under the right circumstances, Buchi's device would prove itself to be the most efficient type of supercharger for boosting the power of a piston engine in both thermal and mechanical terms.

Unfortunately, the turbocharger was *way* ahead of its time in 1905. On the way to mass production and future deployment in consumer automotive applications, decades of development were needed before exhaust turbines had sufficient longevity and cost-effectiveness to be practical for nonexperimental use, particularly in the metallurgy required by the "hot side" of the device. Additional development issues were related to the "cold-side" centrifugal compressor, center-section lubrication and cooling, boost control, and engine management.

In the meantime, people continued to race engines with mechanically driven superchargers, and intensive development of the centrifugal compressor proceeded for both turbine and crank-driven applications. In 1911, while Buchi worked to perfect his invention as chief engineer at Sulzer Brothers Research Department, Maurice and Georges Sizaire experimented with centrifugal superchargers in France. In 1912, Marc Birkigt built an interesting but unsuccessful six-cylinder engine for a Hispano-Suiza racer competing in the Coupe de l'Auto that dedicated two cylinders to pumping air that supercharged the other four.

World War I ended all racing in Europe in 1914 for at least five years and diverted virtually all automotive engineers and manufacturers into projects supporting the first war in history with significant mechanization.

AIR POWER

As military aviation expanded during the war it quickly became apparent that piston engines became progressively less efficient as altitude increased and atmospheric pressure dropped—to the point that peak power was down by 50 percent at 18,000 feet above sea level. Reduced performance at altitude might create problems for civilian aviation, but inferior engine performance in aerial combat could be fatal.

In addition to supercharging's promise to compensate for altitude-based power losses in aerial combat, it quickly became apparent that supercharging had the potential to boost takeoff power, permitting heaver payloads when fuel tanks were full. Supercharging also promised to increase an aircraft's efficiency and range by increasing its service ceiling enough to permit cruise flight in the thin, low-drag air of extreme altitudes of more than 20,000, 30,000, or even 40,000 feet—altitudes that put reconnaissance aircraft above the range of anti-aircraft weaponry. Aviation quickly became a driving force in the development of super-high output piston engines and high-octane fuels, and would remain so until shortly after the end of World War II, when turbojets abruptly made piston engines obsolete for powering all but the smallest aircraft.

Engineers working to supercharge early military aero engines initially experimented with positive-displacement Roots-type blowers but soon focused on perfecting high-speed centrifugal compressors with their inherently superior thermal efficiency. It added the potential for reliability problems, however, with the complexity of a supercharging

A Curtis P-5 Hawk equipped with early turbo-supercharged, 18.8-liter Curtis D-12F V-12 powerplant. The turbine housing was installed in the open airstream to eliminate persistent turbine blade-burning. *NASA*

NACA Roots-type supercharger installed on Pratt and Whitney Model A Wasp engine. The bypass valve, lower right, controls inlet pressure. In 1927, Lieutenant C. C. Champion Jr., U.S. Navy, in a Wright Apache airplane equipped with a supercharged Wasp, established a new official altitude record. Aviation use of the Roots-type supercharger is virtually unheard of. *NASA*

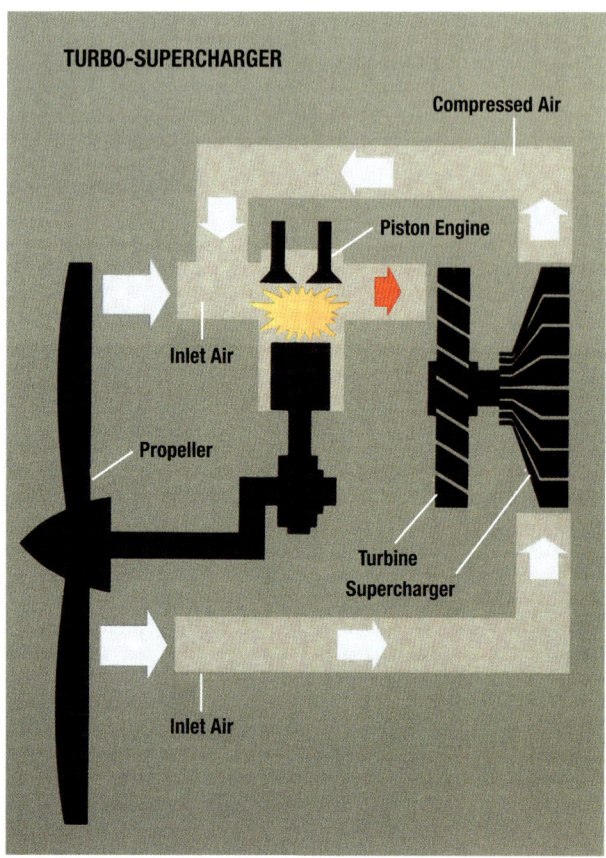

GE Aviation turbine-driven supercharging system schematic *GE*

system that ran at tens or even hundreds of thousands of rpm. The catastrophic failure of an aviation supercharger had the potential to destroy the aircraft and kill the pilot. Engineers devoted considerable effort to developing robust centrifugal gear drive assemblies with aviation reliability.

The high operating speed of centrifugal superchargers was not the only problem. Scientists developing mechanical drives for centrifugal superchargers faced additional reliability and engine management issues related to changes in centrifugal supercharger speed, i.e., supercharger acceleration. Although aircraft engines aren't required to accelerate as quickly as car engines, it was nonetheless true that the high-ratio drive required to spool centrifugal compressors to functional operating speed—and the consequent substantial rotational inertia of the high-speed compressor wheel—caused engineers to face the challenge that relatively small changes in engine rpm inevitably multiply to produce large changes in centrifugal supercharger rpm, potentially delivering unacceptable loading to the internal mechanical gear-up mechanism.

There were additional problems that related to altitude. If designers drove the supercharger with a gear ratio high enough to provide sufficient boost for efficient, low-drag, high-power operation at high altitude, the engine would overboost and detonate to the point of serious engine damage on takeoff runs at the higher atmospheric pressure of sea level. Fifteen psi of boost at 18,000 feet, for example, becomes 30 psi at sea level.

Engineers on both sides of World War I experimented with various types of fluid couplings, centrifugal clutches, flexible drives, spring drives, and variable-speed drives to power centrifugal superchargers. By the time piston-engine aviation reached its apogee, military aircraft powered by supercharged engines, like the Rolls-Royce Merlin, were equipped with two-stage centrifugal compressors and complex multi-speed gear-drive systems that could be deployed at higher altitude to maintain boost pressure.

In 1917, General Electric began experimenting with turbine-driven superchargers using licensed French turbocharger technology patented by Auguste Rateau, which had seen limited testing during the war.

GE assigned a scientist named Sanford Moss to pioneer the development of a practical GE turbo-supercharger. Dr. Moss is sometimes referred to as the "father of turbocharging," because he was largely responsible for advancing the turbocharger from a finicky, short-lived, experimental trick prone to blowing up to a functional, reliable, *manufacturable* power-adder.

Supercharger development resumed for high-performance automotive applications after World War I and grew to dominate motor racing over a 30-year period that would be the heyday of supercharged race cars. During this period, American supercharging efforts focused on the centrifugal compressor and European supercharging efforts focused on the Roots blower, which is ironic given the later renown of big GMC Roots-type superchargers mounted horizontally on growling *American* hot rods and Top Fuel "Hemi" dragsters in the second half of the 20th century.

In 1921, a supercharged 28/95 Mercedes developed by a Daimler team with assistance from Ferdinand Porsche achieved victory for a supercharged engine in competition for the first time since the days of the Chadwick. The car won the 1921 Coppa Florio using a vertically mounted Roots blower driven off the front of the crankshaft by a bevel gear with cone clutch. The supercharger, which only came into play at full throttle, pressurized the carburetor, achieving an alleged 50 percent power increase using 6 to 7 psi of boost pressure. In the years between the two world wars Mercedes-Benz would acquire extensive automotive experience with competition Roots supercharger technology, but the company also worked to develop centrifugal supercharging technology that would be put to use in the Daimler-Benz DB600 inverted V-12 aircraft engine that saw action in World War II in the infamous ME-109 Messerschmitt Nazi fighter plane.

Fiat's earliest supercharging effort in motor racing used a Wittig vane-type supercharger attached to the company's 1923 eight-cylinder Grand Prix racer using a full-throttle-only blow-through arrangement similar to Daimler's. The fact that the vane supercharger required oil injection into the airstream to lubricate the mechanism certainly increased the octane number requirement (ONR) of the fuel required to prevent detonation. This may have been a determining factor in Fiat's decision to switch to a Roots-type supercharger later in the year, resulting in first- and second-place finishes at the Italian Grand Prix at Monza and a new lap record of nearly 100 miles per hour.

Sunbeam's 1924 Grand Prix engine also joined the Roots bandwagon, introducing the innovation of sandwiching the supercharger between the carburetor and intake manifold, thereby sucking a "wet" mixture through the supercharging mechanism. This draw-through layout thrashed air and fuel through the supercharger, which improved fuel atomization and cooled the supercharger. It permitted tighter rotor lobe clearances that improved supercharger pumping efficiency with less risk of damaging rotor interference caused by thermal expansion. Vaporizing fuel in the supercharger produced an intercooling effect that increased the density of the compressed charge and improved power beyond what was available from the basic supercharging effect. Comparison testing by Sunbeam showed that the beneficial effects of the draw-through design combined to increase power 20 percent over an otherwise identical engine with a supercharger arranged in a blow-through configuration.

In 1924, the U.S. luxury auto manufacturer Duesenberg installed a centrifugal supercharger on the company's already-successful inline-8 racing engine in a draw-through arrangement. The experiment was so successful in delivering power for Indianapolis-type racing that Duesenberg subsequently supercharged all of its racing engines.

General Electric aviation turbo-supercharger circa 1920. Note that the compressor is driven by an axial- rather than radial-inflow turbine. The compressor blade inducer section is bent sideways to cut into the intake air like a fan, but the exducer section of the blades that fling air outward are straight rather than curved like modern centrifugal superchargers. *GE*

General Electric turbo-supercharger installed on a Liberty V-12 engine in a LePere biplane. *GE*

Responding to Duesenberg, competitor Harry Miller introduced a straight-8 racing engine designed and built by Leo Goosen and Fred Offenhauser that used a centrifugal supercharger with improved aerodynamics driven off the rear of the engine by a large-circumference flywheel. During the 1920s, race cars with gear-driven centrifugal compressors were achieving as much as 300 horsepower from 90 cubic inches, that is, more than 200 horsepower per liter.

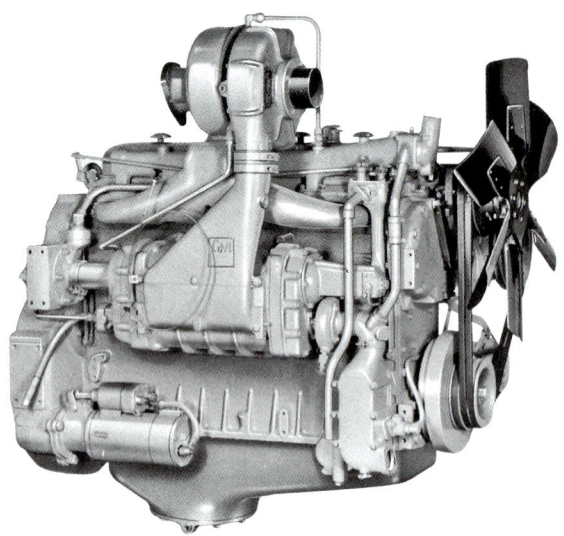

Detroit Diesel with 6-71 Roots blower for cylinder scavenging and Elliot turbocharger providing forced induction. *GM Media Archive*

The supercharged Bentley 4 1/2 Litre—a.k.a., the "Blower Bentley"—was built by Bentley Motors between 1927 and 1931. Of the 720 cars built, 55 of the inline-four powerplants were equipped with a Roots-type supercharger driven from the front of the crankshaft. Walter Owen Bentley, famous for saying, "There's no replacement for displacement," had increased displacement of the I-4 from 3.0 to 4.5-liter in 1926. Oops. In an effort to make even more power, in 1929 the firm contracted supercharger development to Henry Birkin's racing skunkworks. Supercharging increased power from 110 (or 130, tweaked for racing) to 175 horsepower, but lowered fuel consumption at 100 miles per hour from 14.7 miles per gallon to 2.8 miles per gallon. Unfortunately, the supercharged version was not reliable enough to win any major races.

As superchargers began to dominate motor racing, Sanford Moss' West Lynn GE turbocharger lab was a demolition derby of turbines and compressors exploding in wood-lined "blast pits" as engineers and scientists worked to improve the reliability of high-speed spinning components overdriven to ridiculous speeds. The good news was that turbochargers were beginning to prove themselves especially suitable for aviation applications. Because turbine speed is largely determined by the pressure differential between turbine inlet and exhaust, as ambient atmospheric pressure declines at higher altitude the increasing pressure differential between the exhaust manifold and atmospheric pressure at the turbine discharge tends to automatically compensate for reduced compressor efficiency in the thinner altitude. The response is increased turbine speed that, in turn, automatically increases engine boost pressure in the intake manifold, thus maintaining power as an aircraft climbs.

In 1927, the first mass-production aircraft engine with a supercharger went into production when the British Bristol Jupiter was upgraded with a mechanically driven centrifugal compressor. At about the same time, Rolls-Royce began supercharging aircraft engines using twin centrifugal compressors. These were staged in series to achieve very high pressure ratios while absorbing less power than a single supercharger sized to produce an equal amount of boost, a practice known as two-stage supercharging.

With engineers pushing the envelope ever harder with high-pressure supercharged powerplants, excessive compression heating of charge air at high boost levels led to the development of "aftercoolers" (eventually called *intercoolers*), which were air- or liquid-cooled heat exchangers designed to return a charge as close as possible to ambient temperature following compression, thus improving engine power output and limiting problems caused by increased combustion temperatures and spark knock.

Meanwhile, scientists discovered that injecting water (or water with alcohol) directly into the intake charge to lower charge and combustion temperature was an effective anti-knock countermeasure. The cooling effect of water changing from liquid to gas subtracted large amounts of heat from the surroundings during vaporization (a trick that had been patented in 1920 for use in refrigeration systems).

In 1928, Duesenberg leveraged supercharging experience from racing when it introduced the now-famous J and SJ series production cars. The supercharged engines were equipped with centrifugal compressors mounted horizontally above the engine and shaft-driven from the crankshaft. Auburn, Cord, and Hollywood Graham also released vehicles with engines that had similar centrifugal supercharging systems. All had large displacement engines with good low-end torque, relatively narrow rpm ranges, and peak horsepower that could easily be upgraded using an efficient centrifugal supercharger.

Despite tenacious early problems with turbine longevity, GE's supercharger division continued its commitment to

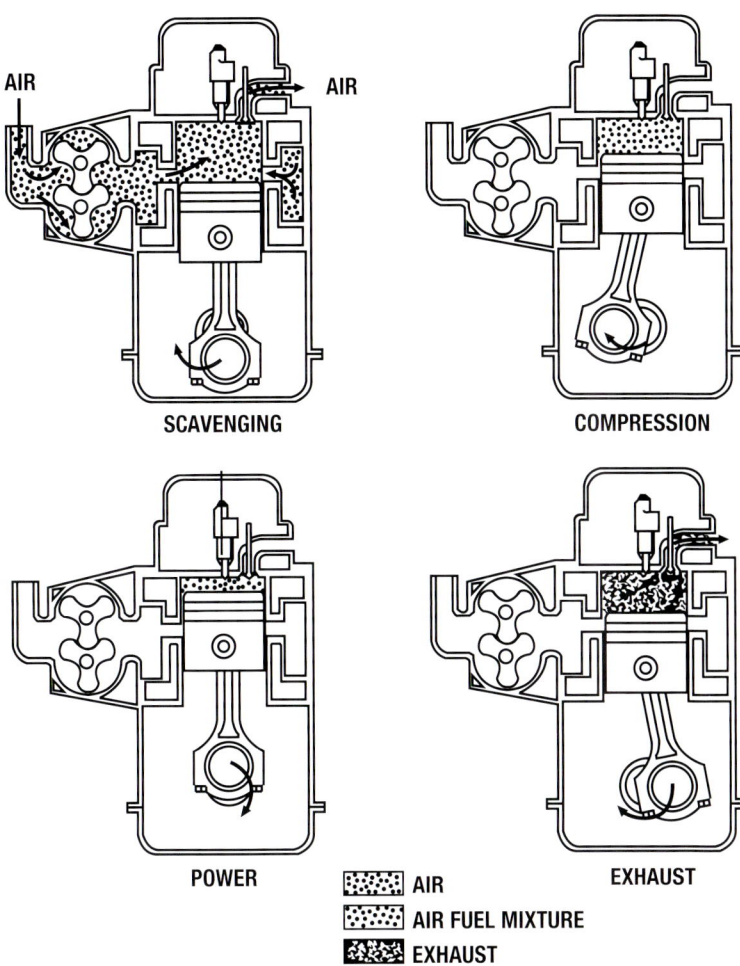

Here is a description of the two-stroke diesel cycle. (1) Scavenging: Intake ports and exhaust valve open, Roots blower pushes fresh air into the intake ports and simultaneously pushes remaining exhaust gases past the still-open exhaust valve. (2) Compression: all ports and valves are closed. (3) Power: Following diesel injection, expanding gases drive the piston toward the crankshaft, making power. (4) Exhaust: Exhaust valve opens and combustion pressure blows down to atmospheric pressure.

developing and building aviation turbochargers for military aircraft into the 1930s. Turbine-driven superchargers and turbo-compound engines were created that converted exhaust heat into shaft horsepower and returned it to the crankshaft via hydraulics, and these were feasible for maintaining power at altitude or increasing fuel efficiency by the onset of World War II.

In 1935, Alf Lysholm, chief engineer at the Swedish turbine manufacturer Ljungstroms Angturbin AB, received a patent for an advanced asymmetric rotary twin-helix screw compressor that was, conceptually, an evolution of expired 1878 patents obtained by a German named Heinrich Krigar. Krigar had described a twisted-lobe screw-type compressor that was not manufacturable using 19th-century technology. Ljungstroms Angturbin would change its name to Svenska Rotor Maskiner AB in 1951, and nearly every modern screw-type compressor would be based on technology licensed from SRM.

Unlike the Roots blower, Lysholm superchargers discharged internally compressed air, giving superior thermal efficiency compared to positive-displacement designs like the Roots. The Lysholm design also reduced parasitic loses and rotor leakage; however, it was extremely difficult to manufacture and thus unacceptably expensive for automotive supercharging applications.

In 1938, GM launched the Detroit Diesel division, which developed a modular family of two-stroke diesel engines. These were initially available with inline configurations ranging from one to six 71-cid cylinders. These were scavenged at the end of the power/exhaust stroke by a gear-driven Roots-type blower. Engines so equipped, but that were not also turbocharged, were considered to be naturally aspirated engines: Their Roots pumps were sized with the appropriate displacement at a 1-1 drive ratio to deliver fresh *ambient-pressure* charge air to the cylinders at all engine speeds. The sole purpose was not to supercharge the cylinders but to scavenge exhaust gases and simultaneously deliver fresh intake air, without which the engine could not function. Until diesel emissions requirements decimated them in the late 1990s, two-stroke diesels with rotary-lobe Roots-type blowers were installed in legions of trucks, ships, locomotives, tractors, combat vehicles, and industrial applications.

Although GMC blowers were not used to produce positive manifold pressure in two-stroke diesels, vintage Roots-type blowers had the potential to be *overdriven* when installed on smaller spark-ignition engines such that they delivered more air than the engine could ingest at ambient pressure. In this application, a GMC blower could build up about a half-atmosphere or so of positive manifold pressure, at which point charge-heating became so severe that additional boost pressure, without some kind of powerful intercooling effect, provided little additional oxygen mass.

The supercharged J-Series Duesenberg was equipped with a 420-cid powerplant and a centrifugal supercharger that raised horsepower of the 5.2:1 compression inline-8 from 265 horsepower to 400 horsepower @ 4,200 rpm. The centrifugal blower, mounted vertically, directed compressed air over the engine to the intake ports.

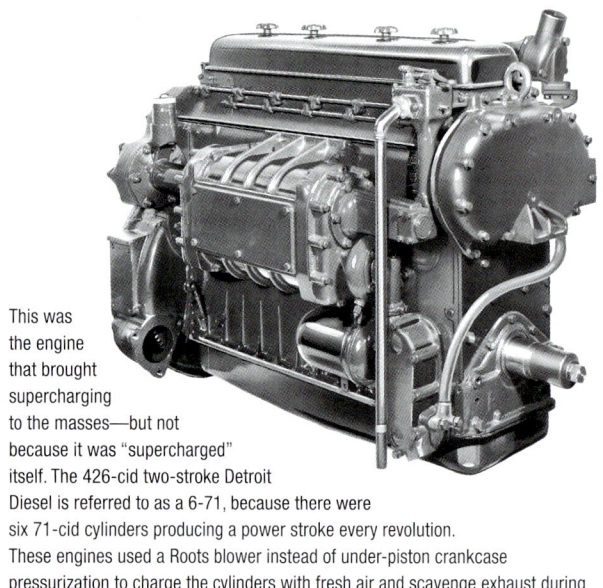

This was the engine that brought supercharging to the masses—but not because it was "supercharged" itself. The 426-cid two-stroke Detroit Diesel is referred to as a 6-71, because there were six 71-cid cylinders producing a power stroke every revolution. These engines used a Roots blower instead of under-piston crankcase pressurization to charge the cylinders with fresh air and scavenge exhaust during the intake cycle. The Roots improved volumetric efficiency but provided little or no actual supercharging, but some later versions were supercharged by installing upstream turbochargers that pressurized the Roots blower. *GM Media Archive*

FORCE-FED WARBIRDS

During the war, the American firms General Electric, Allis-Chalmers, and The Elliot Company manufactured more turbine-superchargers than the production of the entire world from 1923–1940. With the war came intensive new R&D efforts at GE. Expertise gained developing high-speed compressors and exhaust turbines for large turbochargers would evolve directly into participation in the development of experimental military turbojet engines. This in turn would and lead directly to GE's post-war role as a leading supplier of turbojet and fanjet engines for civilian and military aircraft, which continues to the present.

GE's wartime research led to some interesting evolutionary cul-de-sacs on the way to a working turbojet that were neither pure turbojets nor turbocharged piston engines. One of these was a complex and weird ducted-fan hybrid powerplant nicknamed "Jakes Jeep," which was more or less an after-burning piston engine—a "missing link" between the turbine-supercharged piston engine and the turbojet. Jake's Jeep was named for GE engineer Eastman Jacobs, developer of an 8-stage axial compressor that was originally conceived as a

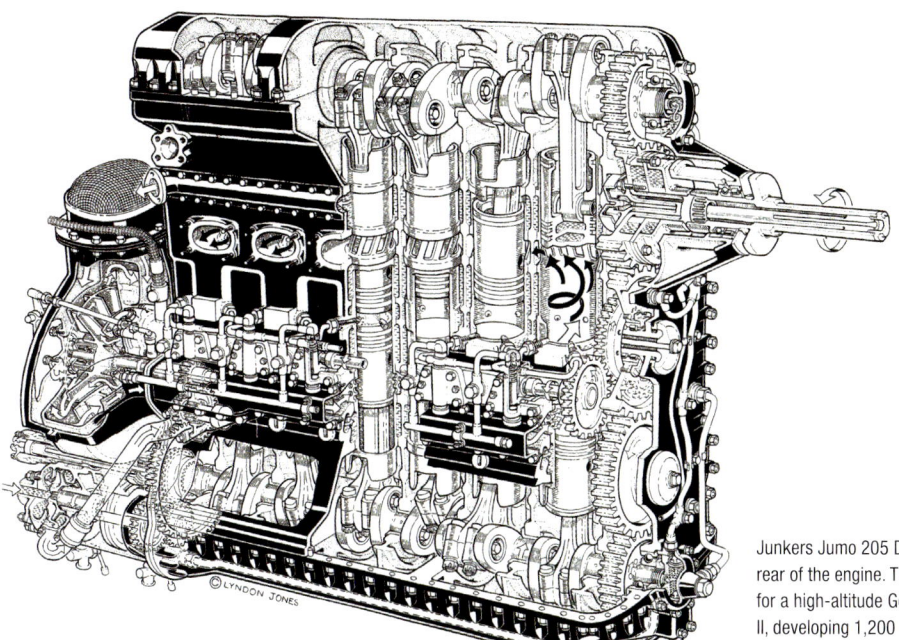

Junkers Jumo 205 Diesel. Note the centrifugal supercharger on the rear of the engine. The engine was equipped with a supercharger for a high-altitude German reconnaissance airplane in World War II, developing 1,200 horsepower at 3,000 rpm, and weighing in at 1,430 pounds, a 170-pound reduction.

A Rolls-Royce Merlin 1,650-cid V-12 equipped with a two-stage supercharging system that operates at low-high drive ratios between 5.5:1 and 10:1, depending on the application. An automatic gear-change shifts to high-speed operation between about 15,000 and 19,000 feet, depending on air speed and ram-air effect. Ambient air enters through a ram-air scoop under the belly of the aircraft and flows through a dual-throat *updraft* SU carburetor before entering the centrifugal supercharger. *Rolls-Royce Heritage Trust*

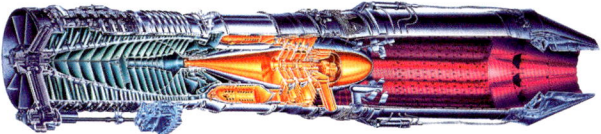

Despite the superior performance of centrifugal compressors (which can achieve pressure ratios of more than 5.0:1 from a single compressor), most turbojet engines make do with axial compressor fans. Axial compressors deliver a maximum pressure ratio of only about 1.2:1 compression, but use as many as 12 fan stages to boost supercharged pressure to ratios over 40:1. By contrast, centrifugal-compressor turbochargers can achieve pressure ratios as high as 65–125:1 in just three stages. *General Electric*

PUMPING UP THE VOLUME POST-WAR

Following the war, people went back to motor racing. After dominating Grand Prix racing for decades, rule changes in 1952 forced tiny supercharged powerplants to compete with naturally aspirated engines with three times the displacement and better fuel economy. This essentially factored supercharged engines out of existence as a viable competitive option, at which point mechanically driven superchargers essentially disappeared from glamour-class racing. With piston engines going or gone from military aircraft and superchargers gone from most organized motor racing, the focus of air-supercharging shifted in to grassroots racing, hot rodding, and diesel trucks.

Hot rodding had taken off in the years following World War II. Standards of living increased in the 1950s, which meant more Americans had money for luxuries like making a car faster. The steep learning curve in engine design

supercharger for very large piston-engine aircraft powerplants. Unlike centrifugal compressors, which accelerate air by flinging it outward using centrifugal force, axial compressors push air directly through the blades like a fan, a process that requires multiple stages to build the type of pressure a centrifugal compressor can achieve in a single stage.

meant that the engines available to hot rodders were a lot of suboptimal factory engine designs that had a lot of headroom for individual car enthusiasts and racers to modify or "soup up" (a horseracing term) to produce significant power gains. The bolt-on performance-racing aftermarket was in its infancy, so early hot rodding involved a lot of do-it-yourself experimentation, fabrication, and machining. Fortunately, large numbers of soldiers had been trained in technical and mechanical skills during World War II, plus plenty of people had grown up on farms or in other circumstances in which knowing how to be self-sufficient and skilled with tools and building was a fact of life. When it came to superchargers, everyone understood the dramatic power-adder potential, though superchargers were generally way too expensive for most young hot rodders, who had more stars in their eyes than money in their pockets.

When the war ended in late 1945, a census of superchargers would have shown (a) thousands of giant centrifugal superchargers installed on giant combat engines that were too large and heavy to be of any use in automotive applications, (b) a sprinkling of Roots-type and centrifugal superchargers that had been manufactured for older race cars and luxury cars from the late 1920s and 1930s, and (c) a steadily increasing supply of blowers installed on two-stroke diesel engines that could be salvaged and converted for use in spark-ignition hot rodding or racing projects.

Organized motor racing may have been heavily regulated, but there were no laws to prevent enthusiasts from installing superchargers on the mass-market Model T or Model A Fords that were growing older and becoming available as inexpensive raw-material for stripped-down hot rods. The most significant engine for such soup-up projects was the Ford flathead V-8. The most important supercharger was the Roots-type GMC blower, but again, superchargers were expensive. This meant that the arrival of supercharged hot rods began slowly.

A few people with money managed to install centrifugal superchargers, salvaged from production luxury cars like the Duesenberg or Graham, onto Ford V-8s, though the

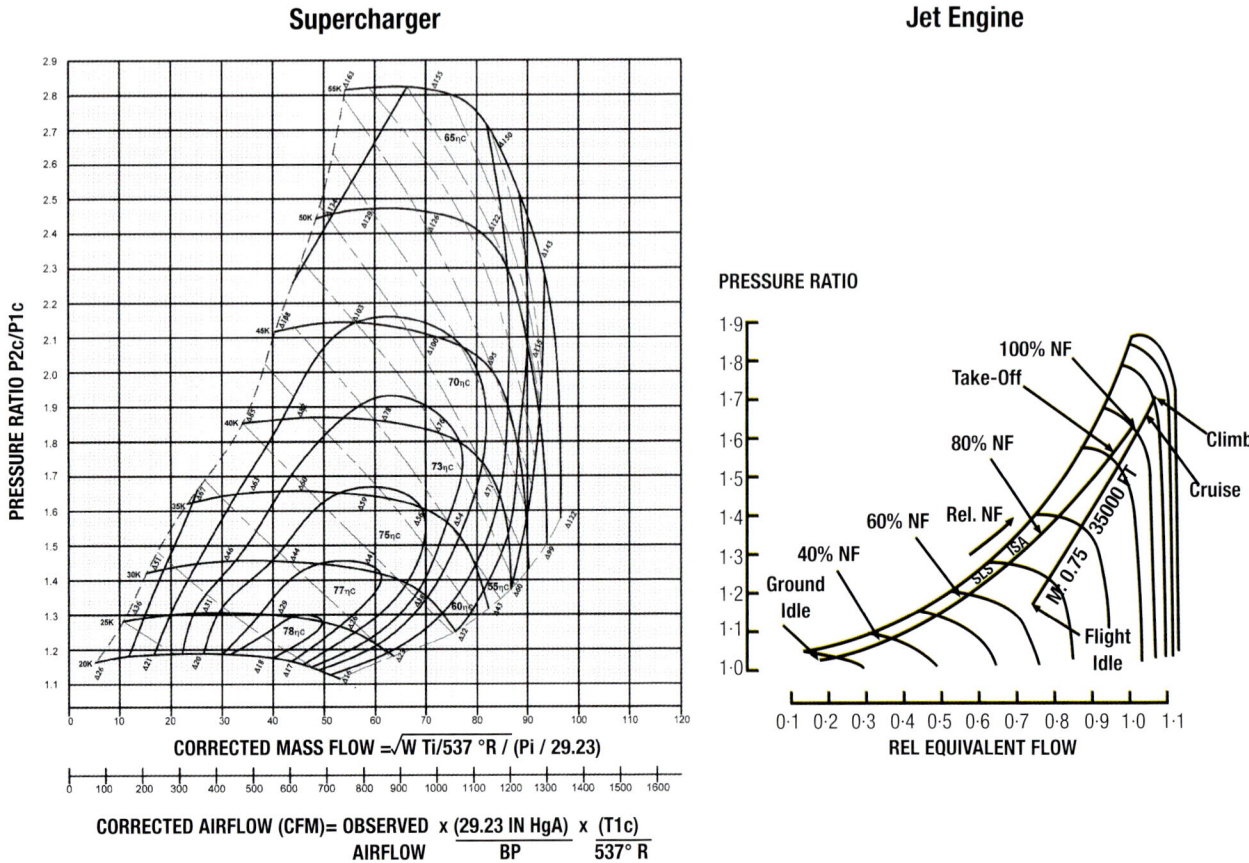

Centrifugal supercharger and jet engine compressor maps, plotting pressure ratio versus airflow. Turbo-supercharger development preceded jet engine development, with the earliest American jet engine architectures assuming the "supercharger" section of the turbojet would require external power from a large, powerful piston engine. As it turned out, power to turn the jet engine's supercharger could be extracted from the turbine, and with proper design, the jet engine could be turned into a kind of "shaped charge," with unidirectional flow and self-sustaining continuous combustion, and tremendous thrust directed exclusively out the rear of the engine. Supercharging, followed by turbo-supercharging, made GE a major player in the jet engine business. The company remains a manufacturer of large turbochargers used in applications such as locomotive and ship diesel engines. *Vortech*

mechanical drive and the drive ratios often made it difficult or impossible to make much boost. One particular Roots-type supercharger migrated from its original home on a Mercedes to a flathead Ford V-8 owned by the Spalding brothers and later onto an Unlimited-class alcohol-fueled roadster owned by Don Blair, who installed it with a dual V-belt drive. In the late 1940s, Blair achieved a top speed of 141 miles per hour with this setup breathing through twin Stromberg carbs.

In 1948, Barney Navarro built the first "classic" Roots-type blower system in which a large Roots-type blower towered above the intake manifold of a V-8 engine, with the blower driven by a belt on the front of the crankshaft. Navarro acquired a 3-71 GMC Roots-type blower from a military landing craft and bolted it on top of a modified version of one of his aftermarket Flathead Ford intake manifolds. He constructed a custom blower drive system consisting of four crank-driven V-belts that supposedly spun the blower fast enough to deliver 16 pounds of boost in a 221-inch Ford V-8 de-stroked to 176 cubic inches. The car managed to achieve a top speed of 146.9 miles per hour at the dry lakes, and the engine's alcohol fuel system was undoubtedly critical in lowering what had to be savagely hot compressed air coming out of the blower. Navarro installed four Stromberg carbs atop the blower case in a suck-through arrangement that provided significant cooling for the twin-lobe rotors, which turned in a blower case remachined to provide additional room for thermal expansion and high-rpm flex. It wasn't long before Tom Beatty adapted the Navarro system to mount a 4-71 blower on an overhead-valve Oldsmobile and began manufacturing manifolds and blower drive systems for Olds racing engines.

Meanwhile in 1949 the first experimental European Volvo and Scania turbo-diesel trucks took to the highways using Elliot and Eberspacher turbochargers. With their lower EGT, diesels were much easier on turbochargers than spark-ignition powerplants. In 1950, Cummins began installing

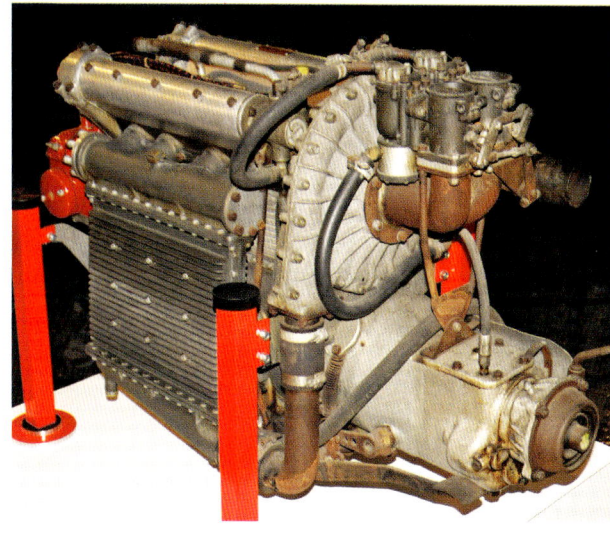

This supercharged 111-cid Offenhauser I-4 ran in the late 1940s and early 1950s in a AAA championship car developed by Murrell Belanger of Crown Point, Indiana, with Tony Bettenhausen driving. A Paxton centrifugal compressor provides forced induction, blowing through an air-cooled intercooler on the side of the engine. The engine had some reliability problems and Belanger switched to a normal-charged 270-cid Offy in 1951. He won the Indy 500 that year with Lee Wallard driving. The Offenhauser Indy engine design received a new lease on life when Drake Engineering added a turbocharger to the 4.2-liter 420-horsepower at 6,600 rpm inline-4 powerplant, producing an engine easily capable of more than 1,000 horsepower. A tremendously boosted Drake had no problems with blowing head gaskets, because the cylinders were cast as part of the head. *Robert Mays Smith Collection*

Buchi-designed turbochargers on American-built trucks (by this time the Swiss engineer and entrepreneur was in his seventies). These early attempts at turbocharging road-going vehicles were not completely successful, given the sluggish spooling performance of the large, heavy turbochargers of the day, but increasing availability of reasonable-cost high-heat metallurgy in the early years of the decade definitely helped make turbo engines more economically viable.

Supercharging systems for the flathead Ford. Note the centrifugal, Roots-type, and Vane-type superchargers. *Robert Mays Smith Collection*

SUPERCHARGERS ON THE STREETS

McCulloch (yes, the chainsaw company!) introduced what was probably the first aftermarket bolt-on supercharger kit around 1950, a package for the Ford V-8 that used a centrifugal compressor driven by a variable-speed belt drive system. The VS-57 used oil pressure to exert variable tension on the outer races of the drive, allowing engine speed to influence how fast the VS-57 impeller turned, but its ball-and-race drive stood in the way of anyone interested in overboosting the unit beyond 7 psi.

Robert Paxton McCullough's kit was too expensive for proletarian rodders, but a few people ran the package at the California dry lakes, and McCullough kits began to appear on the street cars of a relatively few affluent hot rodders. Besides the Ford V-8, McCullough aftermarket centrifugal kits (eventually marketed as *Paxton* superchargers) were available in the 1950s for the Chevrolet Corvette, Chrysler 300C, and certain Cadillac, Buick, and Oldsmobile models. A half-dozen or so Roots-type street supercharger kits arrived on the scene that were based upon reworked 3-71 and 4-71 GMC blowers.

This 1937 Harley-Davidson "knucklehead" V-twin chopper was equipped with a Detroit Diesel Roots supercharger and side-draft Weber DCOE dual-throat carburetion. Hmm. Rigid-frame bike, uneven-firing 45-degree V-2, large two-rotor supercharger with much pulsation and airheating, no air cleaner. Yeah, but it had cold, ram-air intake—unless the springer front-end got in the way. Anyway, it's a beautiful museum piece. *Motorcycle Hall of Fame*

Early Chevrolet 265-cid small-block V-8 with rare Latham axial supercharging system. Axial compressors can only achieve low pressure ratios in the 1.2:1 range, so axial superchargers like the Latham (and most modern jet engines) gang multiple compressor stages together to build combined pressure ratios as high as 40:1. *Robert Mays Smith Collection*

THE CENTRIFUGAL SUPERCHARGER: THE MODERN SUPERCHARGER

"What the Roots-type blower is to street rods and muscle cars, the centrifugal supercharger is to late-model EFI machines, and Paxton blowers brought centrifugals into the mainstream. Innovator Robert Paxton McCulloch introduced the original McCulloch centrifugal supercharger, a giant pancake-looking device that mounted horizontally directly to the intake manifold, in 1937 for Ford flatheads. He introduced an all-new blower in 1953. The revolutionary new design featured a step-up ratio and a V-belt system that altered pulley diameter (much like a modern CVT transmission) to help boost bottom-end performance. Automakers like Kaiser, Packard, and Studebaker used them on production cars, and in 1956, McCulloch set up a separate Paxton Superchargers division dedicated strictly to the supercharger program. That year he introduced the VR-57 supercharger, which made its way to victory on the NASCAR circuit and onto some production '57 Thunderbirds. Two years later, the Granatelli brothers purchased the company and further refined the blower design for greater rpm and boost, calling it the SN60. The company worked on several projects with Carroll Shelby through the '60s but fell off the map during the '70s smog era. In the early to mid-'80s, as OE performance began to return, Paxton reintroduced the SN60 as a bolt-on kit for the 5.0-liter Mustang, which became the first 50-state smog-legal supercharger system. That formula caught on quickly, ushering in a new era of centrifugal supercharging."

—Stephen Kim, from the article, "Greatest Speed Parts of All Time," *Hot Rod Magazine*

The first factory-installed, street-car supercharger since the 1930s arrived in 1954 when Kaiser offered a McCullough centrifugal supercharger option for the inline-six powerplant in the Kaiser Manhattan. The power increase may have been too much for the six, as it caused reliability problems. Kaiser built 5,440 supercharged Manhattans before the company shifted to building Jeep utility vehicles exclusively in 1955.

Ford offered a factory supercharger option in 1957 as a response to Chevrolet's new 265-cid "small-block" V-8, which severely out-performed Ford's 312-cid Y-block V-8 at Daytona, Pike's Peak, and NASCAR tracks. Ford contracted McCullough to build a special competition supercharger for Y-block V-8 racers; simultaneously, it offered the standard McCullough Ford kit as a dealer-installed "Power Pack" option on the Thunderbird, Fairlane, and Edsel, some of which were equipped with dual 4-bbl or triple 2-bbl carburetion. Supercharged Fords dominated racing in 1957 until NASCAR banned fuel injection and supercharging midway through the racing season.

At the same time Studebaker offered McCullough superchargers as an option on Packard and Golden Hawk models. Studebaker still offered a supercharged engine in the Avanti when the company went bankrupt and ceased production at the end of 1963.

WHAT A DRAG!

Through the 1950s, innovative racers worked feverishly to develop successful GMC-based supercharged drag-race engines. Although GMC diesel blowers had dreadful thermal efficiency when used as a supercharger, the positive-displacement architecture that moved essentially the same volume of air every revolution regardless of speed gave a rotary-lobe Roots-type blower the virtue of delivering significant torque increases across the rpm range. This made it ideal for improving the critical 60-foot time, which has a disproportionate impact on the potential to win drag races.

Navarro's top-mounted supercharger configuration ultimately proved to be the arrangement that would dominate drag racing, but mounting a large supercharger on top of a V-8 made it difficult to package the engine in an aerodynamically efficient way within a race car. A number of racers designed front-mount direct-drive systems for the GMC blower that put the blower in front of the crankshaft. This arrangement eliminated the potential for drive belt slippage or failure but made it impossible to quickly tune supercharger boost by altering the size of a drive-belt pulley.

Once high-end drag racers understood how to build supercharged V-8s that stayed together on alcohol or gasoline, elite racers worked on building supercharged engines that could survive burning nitromethane. Nitromethane is a nasty, partially oxygenated fuel that is prone to detonating in an engine, and its one virtue as a power-adder is that it requires little or no air to combust. This means that so much noncompressible liquid fuel is injected that a supercharged nitro engine can hydrolock in some cases (bringing pistons to a catastrophic dead stop!) if the volume of liquid fuel injected accidentally exceeds the clearance volume of the combustion chamber—an unhappy situation that can rip high-strength head bolts and studs out of a block and blow the cylinder heads clean off the engine.

Mickey Thompson built the first supercharged Chrysler Hemi engine in 1953 when he mounted a 4-71 GMC blower atop a new 331-cid "FirePower" V-8, which had Chrysler's new big-valve cylinder heads that used hemispherical combustion chamber architecture developed for aircraft engines to improve high-rpm airflow. This was the progenitor of the engine that would come to dominate Top Fuel drag racing. Thompson, Bruce Crower, and others began bringing blown Hemi racers to the land-speed record trials at Bonneville, Utah, in the mid-1950s, and a '32 Ford roadster powered by one set a record of 189 miles per hour in 1956.

Racers began supercharging Chevrolet's new 265-cid OHV "small-block" V-8 within a year or so of its introduction in 1955, with 4-71 GMC superchargers providing the boost.

The supercharged Hemi completed its ascension to "standard" dragster powerplant after Don Garlits arrived on the West Coast in 1959 with a normal-charged nitro Hemi dragster, only to discover that every one of his competitors was already running a supercharger. Garlits immediately installed a 6-71 GMC on his eight-carb 392 Fire Power Hemi and went on to conquer the world. Blown-fuel Hemis with large Roots-type blowers have dominated glamour-class drag racing ever since, in part due to highly developed technology, and in part due to rules that have prevented Top Fuel dragsters from running turbochargers or multi-valve overhead-cam engines.

In the late '50s, engineers at Chevrolet and Oldsmobile secretly began working on turbocharged engines for gasoline-fueled street cars. It was not until the mid-1950s that manufacturing engineering could begin to mass-produce tiny, intricate high-strength compressor and turbine wheel assemblies with good enough structural quality to make turbochargers practical for small-displacement gasoline-fueled street vehicles. The first factory-turbo car appeared in showrooms in 1962 in the form of the Oldsmobile F-85 "Jetfire Turbo Rocket" Sport Coupe. A month or so later, a turbocharged engine appeared as an option on the Chevrolet Corvair Spyder. By modern standards these turbo-supercharging engine systems were very primitive, equipped as they were with electro-mechanical ignition timing and heavy, sluggish turbochargers sucking through carburetors.

Multi-stage axial compressor fans and stators from a Latham supercharger. Each axial stage increases compression by a factor of up to 1.2 by accelerating air and crushing it against fixed (stator) blades.

The high-compression 10.25:1 Jetfire with 1-barrel carburetor was equipped with an auxiliary fluid injection system that sprayed small amounts of water and alcohol into the intake air stream to cool combustion as an anti-knock countermeasure (which required that the owner remember to fill up a reservoir with special "Turbo Rocket Fluid" and incorporated a complex double-float and valve assembly in the fluid injection system that would close an auxiliary

Eddie Hill's late-1990s Pennzoil Top Fuel dragster, circa 1996. Hill is famous for, among other things, making the first sub-5-second quarter-mile drag time with a damaged supercharged engine that accomplished the feat running on only seven cylinders.

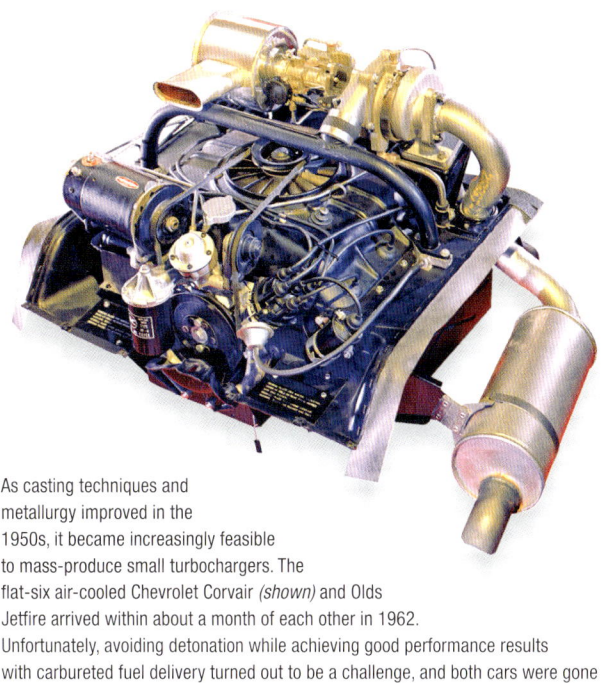

As casting techniques and metallurgy improved in the 1950s, it became increasingly feasible to mass-produce small turbochargers. The flat-six air-cooled Chevrolet Corvair *(shown)* and Olds Jetfire arrived within about a month of each other in 1962. Unfortunately, avoiding detonation while achieving good performance results with carbureted fuel delivery turned out to be a challenge, and both cars were gone within five years. *GM Media Archive*

Paxton's centrifugal blower kit for carbureted 289/302 Ford engines. Carroll Shelby's similar Paxton supercharger option for the 1966 Shelby GT-350 Mustang was rated at 440 (gross) horsepower. *Paxton*

throttle butterfly positioned between the primary throttle and the turbocharger to limit boost if the owner allowed the Rocket fluid reservoir to run dry). To lower the turbo Corvair engine's octane number requirement under boost, the powerplant's static compression ratio was designed quite low (8.0:1). The heavy turbos of both cars spooled slowly, so the Corvair's low-rpm performance both before and after the turbo kicked in more or less sucked. The Jetfire and Corvair reportedly both struggled with reliability problems, and the turbo option for both cars was abandoned after a few years.

In the meantime, a number of street-tuner cars with superchargers were kicking ass. In 1965, Carroll Shelby teamed up with Paxton to build a prototype blown 289 Shelby Mustang and a prototype twin-supercharged 427 Cobra (which Shelby personally sold to comedian Bill Cosby). The blown Cobra never made it into production, but Shelby did market a Paxton supercharger option in limited quantities for 1966–68 Shelby GT 350 Mustangs. The same supercharger package was available over the counter through Ford as a dealer-installed option on standard small-block V-8 Mustangs from 1965 to 1972. Shelby built a prototype GT 500 coupe in 1968 that was equipped with a 500-plus horsepower, Paxton-supercharged super-duty 428 big-block. Rumored to be capable of breaking the tires loose at 80 miles per hour, the car inspired Ford's Southern California district sales manager Lee Grey to successfully lobby Lee Iacocca into building the normally aspirated 1968 California Special Mustang, of which thousands were built and sold.

Throughout the 1960s and most of the 1970s, *Hot Rod* and other car magazines featured a good number of cars and trucks that tuners or grassroots rodders had equipped with modified GMC blowers. The sight and sound of a whining 6-71 GMC blower with dual-quad carbs towering above the intake manifold of an exposed big-block V-8, or flashing through a modified muscle car hood, was nothing less than awesome, but such a project required significant resources as well as serious fabricating and tuning skills. In the days before electronic port fuel injection, many of these setups were marginally streetable, unable to start in cold weather or function well in traffic or heavy rain, and the rich mixtures required to start, idle, and cool the Roots lobes meant that many would today be considered "gross polluters."

Following the experience with the Corvair and F-85 it would be a decade before the next factory turbo car would reappear in American showrooms. Not so in racing. In the late '60s, wildly turbocharged versions of the Offenhauser Indy powerplant and Porsche's air-cooled Can Am boxer engine debuted to spectacular effect.

In 1974, Porsche's 930 Turbo arrived like an earthquake at the Paris Motor Show, giving powerful new life to the 10-year-old air-cooled 911 and immediately establishing Porsche's bragging rights to having the fastest car on the planet at a time when many automakers were retrenching in the face of fuel shortages and stringent new U.S. emissions standards. Turbo engines began to dominate Le Mans starting in 1976, a winning streak that would continue until 1994.

THE PREHISTORY OF SUPERCHARGING

A BDS-supercharged version of John Kaase Racing Engines' blown "Boss Nine." This was a reproduction of the classic Boss 429 Ford, a hemi-head version of the Ford 385-series 370-429-460 powerplants made from 1968 to 1997, later versions of which were found exclusively in trucks. Kaase's crate motor was available with up to 1,500 supercharged horsepower. *John Kaase Racing Engines*

Turbochargers invaded Formula One in 1977 when Renault introduced turbo engine technology that was expensive but so dominant it quickly forced other F1 engine manufacturers to follow the leader. Turbochargers ended the Cosworth DFV era and culminated in Nelson Piquet dominating the series in 1983 powered by a modified cast-iron BMW 2002 block capable of qualifying with as much as 1,400 horsepower from 1.5 liters (approximately 15.5 horsepower per cubic inch!). The Formula One "turbo era" would last from 1977 to 1994 when the rules eliminated turbochargers as a viable engine strategy in the racing series.

Crucial to the ultimate success of gasoline-fueled, forced-induction street cars, port fuel injection began arriving on cars in the mid- to late 1970s in the form of constant mechanical (Bosch K-Jetronic) injection and electronic (Bosch L-Jetronic) injection, with digital engine management controls arriving a few years later. Although Bosch is a European company, its electronic-injection technology was actually licensed from the American firm Bendix, which had invented and patented the original pulse width-modulated "ElectroJector" port-EFI technology back in the 1950s.

Starting in the late 1970s, a number of aftermarket performance shops began to cast special blower intake manifolds that made it easy to bolt on 4-71 or 6-71 GMC blowers to common performance V-8s, along with belt-drive

A 1956 Chevy with Whipple twin-screw supercharged big-block Chevrolet. Yeeeeehaw! *Whipple Superchargers*

20

systems and other accessories that made streetable GMC supercharger conversions. Blower Drive Service, Dyer's Machine Service, Hampton Blowers, Littlefield Blowers, and Mooneyham Blowers provided the basis for a surge in Roots-type V-8 blower conversions. Most of these companies are still in the business of building industrial-strength GMC-type supercharger systems up to and including race-strength blower cases and huge 8-71 or 14-71 performance and race superchargers used in glamour-class drag racing.

Meanwhile, Buick introduced a 3.8-liter V-6 turbo engine in the 1978 Regal based on the turbocharged 1976 Buick Indy pace car—an engine with so much hot rodding headroom that later versions of the powerplant helped fuel a new horsepower war for the first time in a generation. Ford's 2.3-liter turbocharged Mustang arrived in 1979 with a less-than-thrilling 132 *carbureted* horsepower. The Mustang was soon followed by Pontiac's 4.9-liter V-8 Turbo Trans Am Firebird (also, unfortunately, carbureted). Neither car was a poster-child for excellent forced-induction design, but the existence of these turbocharged cars was an indication that the automakers were getting serious again about performance. It wasn't long before virtually every automaker had at least one flagship model equipped with a turbo-supercharged gasoline engine. Within a few years performance enthusiasts could choose from the Nissan 300ZX Turbo, the Buick Regal Turbo, the Merkur XR4TI, various Dodge and Chryslers with a 2.2-liter turbo engine, the Mustang SVO Turbo, the Maserati Bi-Turbo, the Lotus Turbo Espirit, and others. The notorious "pocket rocket" Dodge Turbo Colt sleeper looked like an econo-box but had the turbocharged cajones to humble cars costing vastly more. The FWD 2.2-liter turbo Colt and Shelby Charger foreshadowed the sport compact craze of the 1990s and beyond, when a new generation of young Honda and small import fans ripped apart their factory econo-wagons and hot rodded them.

In the early 1980s, the British company Sprintex introduced the first modern automotive twin rotary-helix screw supercharger (based on patents developed by Alf Lysholm in the years before 1935, which had expired). The Sprintex was a small mechanically driven positive-displacement compressor that moves a fixed amount of air per revolution regardless of speed. It contains high-tolerance left- and right-hand helical lobed rotors that mesh together to form chambers that shrink progressively as they carry air through the supercharger, compressing air within the rotor assembly. The two asymmetrical rotors do not actually touch. They are precisely timed by gears at the end of each rotor, which mesh in a lubricated chamber adjacent to the main rotor housing.

Southern California performance guru Ken Dutweiler with Magnuson-supercharged versions of the classic Flathead Ford V-8 (right), small-block Chevrolet V-8 (center), and fuel-injected GM LS-series V-8 (left). Note the architecture change of the newest Eaton blower on the LS, which inducts air from the rear rather than the top of the blower. Substantial internal architecture changes permitted substantial increases in Roots-type thermal and volumetric efficiency. *Magnuson Products*

The performance of the Sprintex compressor raised the bar for positive-displacement superchargers with respect to thermal efficiency, parasitic loses, and rotor leakage. But machining complex twin-screw rotors was difficult and expensive, which mandated a price point that hampered the device's marketability for both OE and aftermarket applications. Over the next 20 to 30 years a somewhat incestuous group of companies, including Sprintex, Whipple, SRM, Opcon Autorotor, Lysholm Technologies, Kenne Bell, and Opcon Group would collaborate, compete, merge, license, engineer, and scheme in the effort to make a buck. All tried to turn the Lysholm supercharger into a device that could be mass-produced as a cost-effective original-equipment power-adder option for automakers—a potential gold mine if you could pull it off.

At about the same time, Paxton became the first aftermarket supercharger manufacturer to release a 50-state street-legal supercharging kit for the 5.0-liter Mustang V-8. It used an updated version of the company's reciprocating ball-drive centrifugal supercharger. Comparable in size to a large alternator, the centrifugal supercharger had a tremendous advantage over a Roots-type blower when it came to fitting within the crowded engine compartment of a modern vehicle with electronic fuel injection, sophisticated emissions controls, and electronic engine-management systems controlled by digital computers. It wouldn't be long before Paxton centrifugal kits had plenty of competition from outfits like Vortech, ATI, Powerdyne, and Procharger.

A year or two later, B&M Automotive introduced an all-new compact, low-profile Roots-type supercharger with two-lobe, Teflon-sealed aluminum rotors similar in displacement to the GMC 3-53, the smallest of the old GMC diesel blowers, only lighter and more compact. This 144-cid supercharger was about half the displacement of a GMC 4-71 and a third that of a 6-71. The new supercharger was designed to be low enough, using a low-profile EFI throttle body conversion, to fit under the hood of carbureted small-block V-8 ponycars like the 5.0-liter Mustang. The concept was so successful that B&M expanded the product line to include larger displacement versions. B&M and competitor Weiand sold thousands of units within a few years, most installed on street cars and light trucks. The Weiand and B&M supercharger lines would eventually be acquired by Holley Performance Products and combined into a single product line under the Weiand Air Systems brand (one of a number of acquisition deals that eventually drove Holley into bankruptcy when it was unable to service the debt).

Unfortunately, like most traditional Roots-type superchargers, the new compact B&M blowers required a wet mixture to cool the rotors, mandating a draw-through carburetor or injectors delivering fuel upstream of the supercharger. Unfortunately for B&M, the automotive world was already in the midst of a massive conversion to electronic port fuel injection. The relatively complex port-EFI fuel and air-induction systems that arrived on performance V-8s in the mid-1980s, which had front or side-facing throttle bodies, had no facility for cooling supercharger rotors without adding an auxiliary gasoline-injection system upstream of the supercharger. Also, the air-induction systems of these new engines were less able to accommodate sandwiching a Roots-type supercharger (let alone an intercooler!) into the airflow stream.

Some supercharger vendors developed Roots-type aftermarket blower kits for specific performance cars and light trucks, but these only became feasible after Eaton had developed a new generation of rotary-lobe superchargers that didn't require wet-mixture cooling. Such supercharger conversion kits tended to be somewhat complex and expensive. Most late-model kit-builders began building their supercharger systems around compact centrifugal compressors that mounted easily, remote from the intake manifold, with brackets like an alternator and easy incorporation of front-mounted air-air intercoolers for "aftercooling" compressed charge.

TURBO COLOGNE

By the mid-'80s the word "turbo" had become fashionable, even sexy. Buick's GN Turbo arrived for 1986 with more horsepower than the V-8 Corvette. By 1986, Ford's Special Vehicle Operations had pumped the Ford 2.3-liter from 130 to 205 fuel-injected, intercooled horsepower in the Mustang SVO—which could be hot rodded to 355 horsepower by running race gasoline and plugging a performance-calibration auxiliary PROM module into the EEC-IV onboard computer diagnostic port.

Toyota's mid-rear-engine MR2 arrived in 1984 with a 1,587cc inline-4 capable of 112 horsepower in the U.S. version. In 1987, Toyota introduced a supercharged engine for the MR2 with 145 horsepower built around the same 4A-GZE powerplant (with strengthened transmission) equipped with a small Roots-type supercharger and a Denso intercooler. The belt-driven supercharger was actuated by an electromagnetic clutch when needed, for increased fuel economy. In some markets the car had a fuel selector switch to allow the car to run on regular unleaded if required.

The Buick Grand National used turbocharging to boost the power of its 3.8-liter V-6 to equal or exceed the horsepower delivered by performance V-8s in the late 1980s, including the Chevrolet Corvette, which actually had 5 horsepower less than the GN for one model year. In the 1990s Buick used supercharging to boost power of what was then called the 3800 V-6.

By this time the performance aftermarket finally had a good handle on hacking electronic engine-management systems using various electronic and mechanical tweaks to provide timing modifications and fuel enrichment for power-adder conversions and upgrades to factory systems, and hot rodders and racers began to achieve unprecedented levels of streetable power from the combination of forced-induction and port electronic fuel injection.

A cult of young performance enthusiasts in Southern California began demonstrating that you really could use forced induction to boost the performance of, say, a front-wheel-drive late-'80s Honda CRX from a 0–60 time in the high-8s to the mid-5s, which put it on the level of some well-known ponycars.

MODERN SUPERCHARGERS

In the late 1980s, a Danish firm called Rotrex developed a new type of mechanical-drive system for centrifugal superchargers that greatly increased the maximum feasible final-drive ratio. It allowed the use of smaller centrifugal compressors that ran at speeds similar or identical to the turbine-driven centrifugal compressors found in turbochargers. Given that centrifugal superchargers essentially consist of belt-driven, turbo-like compressors, it was inevitable that someone would work with an actual turbo compressor and apply a planetary-gear system of the type used to provide torque multiplication in automatic transmissions to increase the maximum step-up ratio of a mechanically driven centrifugal compressor from 5x crankshaft speed up to as much as 13x. Rotrex's planetary system increased the maximum feasible speed of a centrifugal impeller from 50,000–60,000 into the range of 90,000 to more than 200,000 rpm, allowing various compressors literally designed for turbochargers to

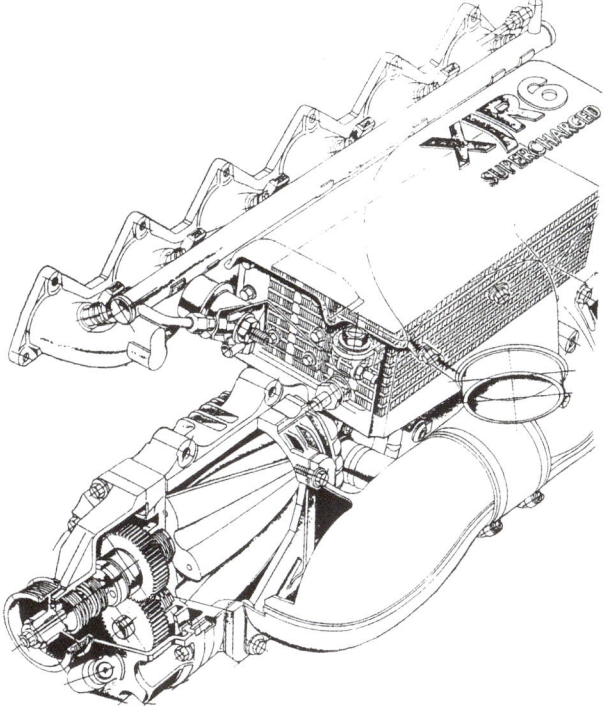

Cutaway drawing of the Jaguar XJR-6 supercharger assembly, including integral water-cooled intercooler core. The car arrived in 1995 with a 4.0-liter inline six producing 321 horsepower, the first supercharged Jaguar in history. The engine was blown with an Eaton M90 supercharger. *Eaton*

be mechanically driven from the crankshaft. Compared to old-school centrifugal superchargers that max out at 60 to 65 percent efficiency and typically employ noisy internal gear-drive systems, Rotrex claimed quieter operation and turbo-like thermal efficiency as high as 80 percent. What's

THE PREHISTORY OF SUPERCHARGING

23

When Acura's NSX rear/mid-engine sports car arrived in 1990, 270 horsepower represented extremely high specific power. In the final year of production, 2009, 290 was still good specific power for a normal-charged engine, but the overall horsepower was less than its competitors'. CT Engineering's blower kit was designed to provide a substantial power boost for the 3.0–3.2-liter V-6 with an Autorotor twin-screw supercharger. *CT Engineering*

more, assuming there was no drive belt slip, Rotrex's Traction Drive totally eliminated turbine spooling lag—though not necessarily centrifugal pumping lag, which exists due to the exponential nature of converting airspeed into pressure in centrifugal compressors.

In 1988, Art Whipple introduced a rebadged version of the Sprintex supercharger to the North American marketplace. The technology was attractive but the small compressor size of the "Whipplecharger" was a problem on large performance V-8s, and the manufacturing cost of the unit made marketing Lysholm superchargers a challenge when other good options were available in the form of turbochargers and centrifugal compressors.

The first modern factory-installed supercharger option arrived in 1989 when Ford introduced the 3.8-liter V-6 Thunderbird Supercoupe, which used forced-induction to upgrade the power of the base V-6 from 140 to 210 horsepower. The Supercoupe used a new-generation, three-lobe, Roots-type supercharger with 60-degree lobe twist. It was developed by Eaton Corporation in a significant R&D effort designed to upgrade the poor thermal efficiency of rotary-lobe superchargers, which had previously had the unfortunate disadvantage of vastly overheating intake air at high levels of boost.

In 1990, Eaton teamed with GM to supercharge the Park Avenue Ultra, and Eaton rotary-lobe superchargers

Saturn produced the supercharged Redline version of the Ion from 2004 through 2007. This factory tuner car featured a 205-horse version of the 2.0-liter Ecotec I-4 with an Eaton M62 Roots-type supercharger and an air-to-liquid intercooler coupled to a stronger F35 five-speed manual transmission. This engine/powertrain combination was also shared with the Chevy Cobalt SS Supercharged Edition. GM Performance Parts has marketed 93-octane premium-fuel upgrade kits for this engine that increase power to 230 horsepower with large Stage 1 fuel injectors and a computer recalibration, or 245 horsepower with Stage 1 plus an overboosting package of supercharger pulley and blower belt. *GM Media Archive*

would eventually become available as a power-adder option on at least 59 production vehicles, including a variety of performance vehicles such as the Jaguar XKR, various Mercedes "Kompressor" models, the Corvette ZR1, the Ford Mustang Cobra, and others. Other Eaton-charged vehicles include the following:

- Ford Festiva S/C 1.0-liter I4
- VW Golf GT ScTc 1.4-liter I4
- BMW-Mini Cooper S S/C 1.6-liter I4
- Mercedes M271 S/C 1.6L/1.8-liter I4
- Cobalt SS S/C 2.0-liter I4
- Saturn Ion Redline S/C 2.0-liter I4
- Audi S4/A6 S/C 3.0-liter V-6
- Pontiac Grand Prix GTP S/C 3800 V-6
- Range Rover Sport S/C 4.2-liter V-8
- Cadillac STS-V S/C 4.4-liter V-8
- Jaguar XFR S/C 5.0-liter V-8
- Ford GT S/C 5.4-liter V-8
- Ford SVT Lightning S/C 5.4-liter V-8
- Ford GT500 S/C 5.4-liter V-8
- Cadillac CTS-V S/C 6.2-liter V-8
- GM ZR1 Corvette S/C 6.2-liter V-8

In the 20-year period following the arrival of the Eaton supercharger, the company would manufacture more than 4 million superchargers. Eaton licensed the right to distribute the company's superchargers for aftermarket use to Magnuson Products and later Edelbrock and Roush Performance Products.

In 1995 Opcon Autorotor of Sweden introduced an automotive rotary twin-screw supercharger based on the designs created by Alf Lyshom in the 1930s (but not the same ones as the Sprintex).

By 1996, the first heavily modified FWD turbo Honda broke into the tens at the drag strip. Sport compact racers would be running in the 7's by the end of the millennium.

The factory turbo craze had lasted over 10 years when it began to fade in the mid-1990s, but before that happened, the world saw various affordable factory "near-supercar" sports cars like the 320-horse Nissan 300ZX Twin Turbo and the "Sequential Twin Turbo" Supra—or the 200-horse MR2 Turbo, with its exotic Mid-engine, Rear-drive, 2-seat layout. Meanwhile, tuners proved that the Turbo Supra 3.0-liter six could be pumped up to double stock horsepower with external-only modifications, and that triple stock power was possible with better connecting rods and head gaskets and TONS of turbo boost from huge turbochargers.

The golden age of turbo cars was killed by a combination of adverse publicity from car owners (who couldn't manage to change the oil on schedule, and therefore fried out-of-warranty turbos) and the arrival of high-output four-valve engines with extremely sophisticated engine management electronics that that could make as much specific power as automakers needed or wanted for most applications without the complexity, expense, or added-maintenance of a turbo system. Nonetheless, factory turbo cars did not go extinct a second time. Exciting sports cars like the Porsche 911 Turbo never stopped selling well (considering their price). Lotus introduced a 3.5-liter V-8 Twin-Turbo Espirit. Volkswagen-Audi introduced multiple successful models based on various versions of the 20-valve "1.8T" turbocharged powerplant making between 150 and 225 horsepower, with the headroom for tuner versions capable of much more. Automotive engineers had more to work with by this time. Fueled by turbochargers' ability to make power AND improve engine efficiency, throughout the '80s and '90s, automotive engineers at Garrett-AiResearch, IHI, KKK, and other turbo manufacturers had worked intensively to develop really responsive turbochargers that would spool very fast, building lightweight turbine wheels from light stainless steels, super-light ceramics, and even titanium.

At the same time, gasoline-direct injection (GDI) began arriving on some engines. The ability to inject fuel directly into the cylinders at 200 atmospheres of fuel pressure independently of prevailing volumetric efficiency as throttle angle changed created the possibility of "shaped" injection events consisting of multiple tiny multiple bursts of fuel that conditioned combustion so as to allow higher static compression ratios, stratified charge combustion, and

Eaton TVS superchargers achieve unheard-of volumetric efficiency for Roots-type superchargers by greatly increasing blower intake volumetric efficiency. They use a 160-degree rotor angle for extremely long rotor charging time, and greatly increase thermal efficiency by eliminating turbulence during the compression process with dedicated ports that pre-compress air pockets that move toward the intake manifold more gradually. This is the supercharger used on the Corvette ZR1. *GM Media Archive*

other tricks that allowed turbo engines to "have it all" with improved torque, reduced brake specific fuel consumption (BSFC), improved drivability, and reduced emissions.

Engine and turbo manufacturers were beginning to experiment with two-stage turbochargers for delivering very high pressure ratios with modest-sized turbochargers. The variable nozzle (VATN) turbo was back again as well, this time on the Porsche 997, allowing the Carrera to deliver stunning low-end performance coupled with very high peak power.

"Twincharging"—first used on military aircraft in the 1940s—arrived in the new millennium on a production VW 1.4-liter powerplant. This engine used a Roots-type blower for instant off-idle boost, fortified with an upstream turbocharger-amplifying boost to meet the requirement for serious performance at high rpm. The goal was a tiny engine that felt like a big V-6 or V-8, and the system delivered.

In the early years of the new millennium, Mercedes-Benz, Ford, and Mercury Marine torture-tested Lysholm superchargers and then incorporated them into their product lines: the AMG tuner division in the case of Mercedes; the midengine Ford GT supercar in the case of Ford; and Mercury Marine began marketing a twin-Lysholm, supercharged big-block V-8 capable of delivering 1,200 continuous horsepower on race gasoline.

In 2008, Eaton introduced a significantly modernized sixth-generation Roots-type supercharger. It delivered peak thermal efficiency above 75 percent across a broad range at pressure ratios ranging from 1.25 to 2.0 bar in the 400 to 1,400 cubic meters per hour mass airflow range, and peak pressure ratios as high as 2.5 bar. Parasitic constant supercharger input power ranged from .67 to 6.7 in the target of 70-plus percent thermal efficiency range. The Eaton Twin Vortices Series (TVS) supercharger was still technically a blower, in that there was no internal compression ratio. Pockets of ambient-pressure air moving through the housing were compressed only when they encountered resistance to airflow through the engine itself, rather than by compression between the rotors of the supercharger. The TVS supercharger incorporated many advanced features designed to improve thermal efficiency, including a four-rotor design with 160 degrees of twist (versus the previous three-rotor, 60-degree twist), much larger supercharger intake ports, and special auxiliary discharge ports that pre-compress air pockets moving through the housing prior to final discharge for reduced backflow turbulence. Eaton predicted that 3.0 bar absolute pressure (ABS) boost would be available in near-future Eaton designs.

In the meantime, there had been a fair amount of recent aftermarket activity related to electric superchargers. Thomas Knight, for example, offered several electric superchargers, including an Eaton Roots-type supercharger converted to be driven by three relatively small 24-volt electric motors and powered by two 12-volt automotive batteries wired in series to dramatically reduce the current required to drive the supercharger, which can require 20 horsepower. Recharge requirements were fairly substantial, but the battery reserve capacity of the supercharger power supply meant that there was zero parasitic loss from driving the supercharger in between boost episodes. Besides the lack of parasitic losses during boost, an attractive feature of electric superchargers is that they do not require complex mechanical drives or exhaust plumbing to a turbine, only wiring, so there is more freedom when locating the electric supercharger in the engine compartment or under the vehicle. A number of outfits have experimented with superchargers driven by a hydraulic drive, i.e., an oil turbine powered by oil pressure. By this time Garrett had designed an electrically assisted turbocharger, with an electric rotor assembly built into the basic turbocharger rotating assembly. It could kick in under computer control to improve engine response by pre-spooling the turbocharger to effective speed prior to when the exhaust energy was sufficient by itself to deliver boost. Garrett appeared to be waiting to release electric turbos, pending the arrival of higher voltage 24-, 36-, or 48-volt electrical systems on factory automobiles to avoid tremendous current requirements.

THE PRESENT

The state of the art for factory street cars boosted with mechanically driven superchargers is represented by the production Corvette ZR1, with 638 horsepower from 6.2-liter displacement, about 103 horsepower per liter. A prototype 2.0-liter Chevy Cobalt SS street car equipped with an Eaton R900 TVS sixth-generation supercharger was designed to make roughly 270 horsepower at about 15-psi boost, which translates to 135 horsepower per liter. Hennessey Performance markets an upgrade package for the supercharged Ford GT that squeezed 850 horsepower from the 5.4-liter Ford V-8, a per-liter figure of 157. Hennessey's 1,000-horse package for the Ford GT abandoned pure mechanical supercharging in favor of a two-stage twin-charging system in which twin turbochargers pump into the engine's positive-displacement supercharger. Mercury Marine's dual-fuel 556-cid (9.1-liter) 1200 SCi V-8 used twin Lysholm superchargers to deliver 1,025 continuous horsepower on 89-octane "pump" gasoline, or 1,200 horsepower on high-octane racing gasoline, with specific power ranging from 113 to 132 horsepower per liter.

For comparison, the state of the art for performance factory turbo-supercharged cars at the time of this writing was about 150 horsepower per liter in a car like the 523-horsepower Porsche 911 turbo, compared to a maximum of 120 horsepower/liter from a state-of-the-art normal-charged street powerplant like the 4.5-liter Ferrari 458 Italia. The state of the art for refined tuner cars with warranties was about 180 horsepower per liter, and for crazy, cost-no-object one-off hot rod street turbo cars running on gasoline was about 325 horses per liter

Of course, the ultimate state of the art for supercharged powerplants would have to be a Hemi-engine Top Fuel dragster burning 90 percent nitromethane and running a 14-71 Roots-type supercharger capable of delivering 2.8–3.5 bar boost (40–50 psi) at full howl. For 4.5 seconds these monsters develop an estimated 8,000 to 10,000 horsepower from the 8.3-liter powerplant, or at least 965 horsepower per liter. Top speed in the quarter-mile is now more than 333 miles per hour in less than 4.5 seconds.

Hennessey Performance upgrades to the factory Ford GT twin-screw supercharging system can deliver up to 850 horsepower from the factory-supercharged 5.4-liter 550-horse powerplant. Hennessey's twincharging package for the Ford GT boosts top speed to 245 miles per hour by increasing the power of the factory-supercharged 5.4-liter DOHC V-8 to 1,000 horsepower with twin turbos that blow into the supercharger. *Hennessey Performance*

For years outfits such as Whipple Superchargers have provided a boost and airflow upgrade for the supercharged 5.4L powerplant found in the Ford GT and various versions of Mustang with giant twin-screw superchargers. *Whipple Superchargers*

Chapter 2
Normal Versus Super Charging: Volumetric and Thermal Efficiency

If you drive a vehicle from Denver, Colorado, to Death Valley, California, you're effectively supercharging your engine along the way. Standard atmospheric pressure in the "Mile-High City" is only 12.2 psi, but in Death Valley—282 feet below sea level—atmospheric pressure is 14.85 psi, which is more than 20 percent greater than in Denver. The additional 5,562 feet of Earth's atmosphere over Death Valley pressurizes the surface air to a greater degree, and this additional 2.65 psi of "boost" pressure forces more air into the cylinders each time an engine turns over. This allows the engine to burn more fuel and make more power. The thicker air it breathes in Death Valley delivers 20 percent more torque and power, at idle, at peak-power rpm, and everywhere else in between.

Installing a supercharger on an engine creates higher atmospheric pressure in the engine's air intake, like driving to a lower elevation. However, predicting the performance increase from a supercharger is complicated by such factors as (1) divergence between the pumping efficiency of the engine and the supercharger as rpm changes, (2) inevitable adiabatic heating during compression with consequent nonlinear changes to charge density and engine octane number requirement as compressor speed changes, (3) power-robbing drag required to turn the compressor, and so on. Truly understanding and predicting the dynamic performance of a power-adder like a supercharging system can be a little tricky. The place to start is with the engine.

Roush Performance's 402IR, a 6.6-liter "all-motor" powerplant was designed to deliver 500 horsepower and 500 pound-feet torque breathing through eight port-injection Weber DCOE-bolt pattern throttle bodies. High-revving all-motor technology is usually more expensive than making power with a blower. At this time of writing you could buy a complete 402IR for about $21,000. *Roush Performance*

A carbureted Magnuson Gen1E "Magnacharger" system installed on a classic Chevrolet small-block V-8 with Vortech-style cylinder heads. The system included an MP112 Roots-type supercharger, lower manifold, lid with optional intercooler, inlet-to-throttle body adapter, complete drive system with dynamic tensioner, with the option of using MEFI 4 fuel-injection systems. *Magnuson Products*

28

The Roush 428R supercharging package for the 4.6-liter Mustang was designed to boost power into the 435–450-horse range with 400 pound-feet of torque. Core components include a ROUSHcharger, intake manifold, air-water intercooler and radiator, air-induction system, and Roush-calibrated ECM. *Roush Performance*

How many supercharging systems do you see for the 273-318-340-360 small-block Mopar V-8? Paxton's centrifugal-based system puts the blow-through carburetor in a pressured housing that allows the carb and induction system to remain in essentially stock location. *Paxton*

THE TRUTH ABOUT PISTON ENGINES

A piston engine is a machine that converts the chemical energy in fuel into thermal energy (heat), and thermal energy into kinetic energy that's capable of doing work. Heat comes from the exothermic reaction of oxygen burning a fuel such as gasoline, propane, natural gas, methanol, ethanol, nitromethane, nitropropane, hydrogen, or diesel. Pressure rises in the cylinders because combustion gases and nonreactive air gases like argon and molecular nitrogen are heated and expanded by the energy released in combustion. Cylinder pressure against pistons turns the crankshaft, which can then do work such as pushing a motor vehicle up a hill. If you define efficiency as horsepower produced per quantity of fuel consumed, piston engines are dreadfully inefficient. The efficiency of an ordinary piston engine is usually about 30 percent at best, meaning only 30 percent of the fuel's chemical energy actually gets converted into useful work such as moving a vehicle. The rest warms the environment.

Most supercharged engines are even worse—in the range of 25 percent thermal efficiency. To understand why this is so—and get a handle on the physics of hot rodding with forced induction—you have to know a little about engine volumetric and thermal efficiency. Return for a moment to automotive kindergarten. A running four-cycle piston engine endlessly repeats the following events in each cylinder:

Intake stroke, during which a cylinder is charged with air (or air and fuel) as the piston moves toward the crankshaft with the intake valve(s) open.

Compression stroke, during which the charge is compressed by the piston moving away from the crankshaft with all valves closed. Fuel is introduced and then ignited by the time the piston is close to top dead center (TDC), causing reactants and inert gases in the combustion chamber to heat and expand, building positive pressure in the combustion chamber.

Power stroke, during which combustion continues for a time and cylinder pressure pushes the piston toward the crankshaft, causing it to rotate and deliver torque that can do work.

Exhaust stroke, during which the piston moves away from the crank with the exhaust valve(s) open, expelling the gaseous products of combustion into the exhaust system (usually water vapor, CO_2, and nonreactant gases). Due to engine inefficiencies, exhaust gases may retain some positive pressure at the moment when the exhaust stroke begins and typically retain large amounts of heat.

If there is a supercharger front-ending the engine, intake air usually arrives in the cylinders hotter than ambient temperature because of the inevitable heating of air caused by its compression by the supercharger. The engine itself heats the charge air in two stages: First, by squeezing it into a very small space during the compression stroke at a ratio that usually ranges between 6:1 and 20:1. Second, by combusting fuel, at which point temperature skyrockets into the 1,200- to 1,800-degree range and cylinder pressure jumps tremendously, from perhaps 180 psi to as much as 1,000 psi or more.

Cylinder pressure drops rapidly as soon as a piston begins accelerating away from the cylinder head on the power stroke, so to achieve maximum power it is crucial that peak pressure occur at the optimal crank position. Because each piston is effectively stopped for about 15 degrees on either side of TDC, it turns out that optimal power results when combustion pressure peaks not at top dead center but somewhere in the 14- to 18-degree range after top dead center (depending on the ratio of rod length to stroke length; longer rods require less timing advance because the piston remains longer at TDC, providing more time for fuel to burn before a piston accelerates away from top dead center, meaning less timing advance is required to achieve peak power). Optimal timing delivers maximum pressure against the piston when it can actually begin to move (in the region of TDC, the piston, rod, and crank throw are lined up such that no amount of pressure exerts any twisting force against the crankshaft).

As long as full-cylinder pressure is available when the piston begins moving downward, slightly delayed combustion maintains greater cylinder pressure farther into the power stroke, when the rods have increasing leverage against the crank. Combustion may still be underway beyond 14 to 18 degrees after TDC, depending on the burn rate of the fuel, the effective compression ratio, the efficiency and size of the combustion chamber, and the number of spark plugs per cylinder or diesel injection pressure.

The length of the connecting rods has an effect on optimal combustion timing because pistons depart TDC more rapidly on engines with shorter connecting rods. This causes the chamber volume to increase more rapidly than in a longer-rod motor, and this affects engine breathing characteristics.

Honda S2000 with Rotrex-based centrifugal supercharging system on the Kraftwerks chassis dyno for tuning development. Chassis dyno development is critical to making a supercharging system into a *great* supercharging system. *Kraftwerks*

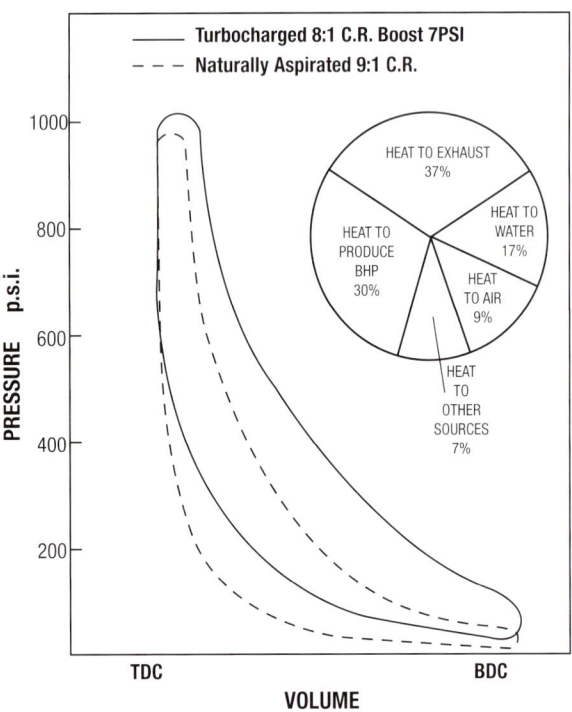

Cylinder pressure versus volume in the engine cycles of a 9:1 compression normal-charged powerplant, and a 7-psi turbocharged powerplant running 8:1 compression. Note that supercharged peak cylinder pressure is only slightly higher, but cylinder pressure later in the expansion cylinder is tremendously higher in the forced-induction powerplant. Although peak torque is only slightly higher, average torque throughout the expansion cycle of the power stroke is much higher nearly everywhere.

The optimal point for maximum cylinder pressure on engines equipped with power-adders like supercharging tends to be on the late side. Because the maximum performance of most supercharged or nitrous-injected spark-ignition engines is knock limited, the optimal combustion point may occur late enough that peak cylinder pressure is reduced by the retreating piston expanding combustion chamber volume. This strategy permits higher levels of boost and higher *average* cylinder pressure by avoiding detonation from excessive *peak* cylinder pressure. The need to optimize cylinder pressure at the correct time is a critical reason why detonation makes less power than normal combustion even though the spike of pressure is somewhat higher during detonation than normal combustion. The spike of combustion pressure from explosive detonation occurs too soon—in some cases even before the piston reaches top dead center—and often with destructive results.

Despite the drop in pressure as the piston accelerates away from TDC, cylinder pressure continues to remain an important factor in making torque deep into the power stroke. This is the key reason supercharged engines make much better torque than normal-charged powerplants despite the fact that *peak* cylinder pressure is typically only a little higher with forced induction. The impact of a supercharged engine's superior post-peak cylinder pressure is amplified by the fact that a piston's *leverage* against the crankshaft continues to increase after TDC until the crank throw is positioned at a 90-degree angle to the connecting rod.

The average torque produced by a piston engine over a given four-stroke cycle is a function of the *average* cylinder pressure multiplied by the area of the piston it's pushing against (force), multiplied by the piston's leverage against the crankshaft (stroke). Average torque must be multiplied by the number of combustion events per minute to get horsepower, which rates an engine's ability to move a certain amount of weight a certain distance in a certain amount of time. For a four-stroke engine, the number of combustion events per minute consists of the engine rpm multiplied by *half* the number of cylinders (since only half the pistons make a power stroke each engine revolution), with a fudge factor (5,250) thrown in to convert rpm to *radians*.

In reality, since torque is a measurement of instantaneous force acting against the crankshaft, instantaneous piston-engine torque fluctuates in overlapping waves according to the number of cylinders and the crank position—which is the reason piston engines need a heavy flywheel and crank damper to smooth things out. Horsepower is essentially torque acting over time, with 1 horsepower defined as the ability to move 550 pounds 1 foot in 1 second.

To get an idea of what happens to cylinder pressure as a piston starts moving downward in the power stroke,

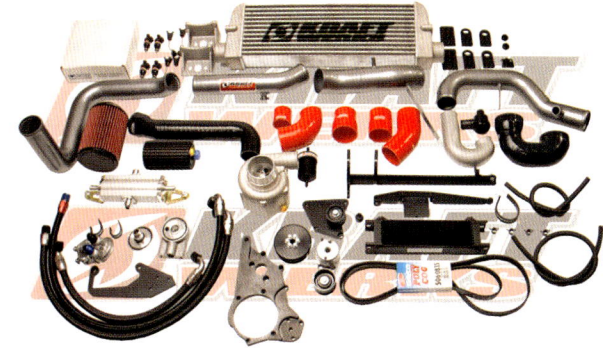

Kraftwerks S2000 system uses air-cooled intercooling, which can increase the effective thermal efficiency of a centrifugal supercharger from a maximum of 75 to 80 percent into the 80 to 90 percent range for increased power and cooler combustion. *Kraftwerks*

consider that if there were, say, 1,000-psi pressure exerted against a 10-square-inch piston at 15 degrees ATDC, this configuration delivers 10,000 pounds of downward force against the piston, albeit initially with very poor leverage against the crank. If the initial combustion space available

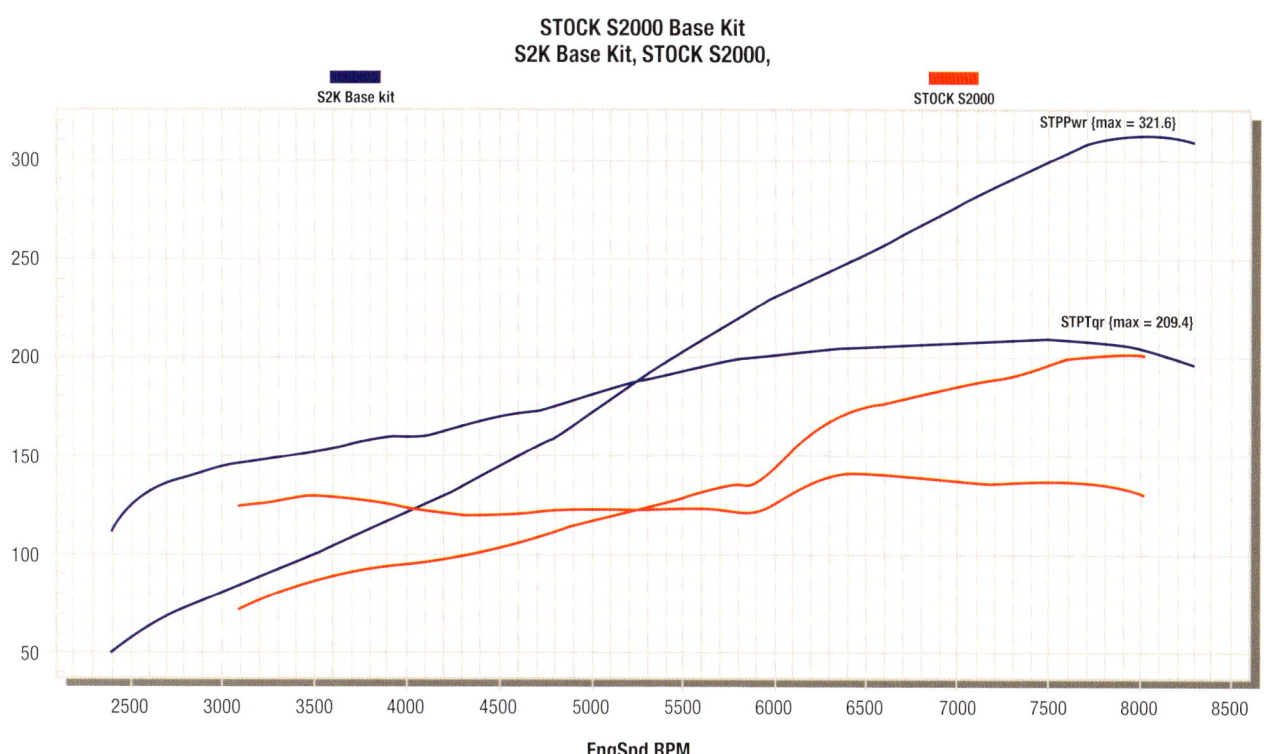

Base kit Kraftwerks S2000 supercharger kits boosts the *rear-wheel* horsepower of a stock 2.0L S2000 from 209 to 312 horsepower at 8,000 rpm. *Kraftwerks*

at 15 degrees after TDC is, say, 5.0 cubic inches, in a mere half inch of piston travel the combustion space doubles to 10.0 cubic inches, dropping combustion pressure to 500 psi (assuming combustion is completely finished by 15 degrees ATDC; normally it would not be). Total force pressing down on the piston a half-inch down would now be 5,000 pounds. The next inch of piston travel drops pressure to 250 psi, with a total force of 2,500 pounds. In terms of actual instantaneous torque delivered to the crankshaft, force against the piston must be corrected for the increasing leverage available as the crank throw moves away from the piston centerline.

To understand the thermodynamics of power creation in a piston engine, it is important to get the following concept: Each time a piston descends through its power stroke and the combustion gases are expanded, a portion of the thermal energy in the combustion gases converts into kinetic energy or motion at the flywheel—a process that cools combustion gases in accordance with the engine's expansion ratio (the same principle produces a spurt of chilled CO_2 when you open a carbonated soda bottle that was under pressure). Expansion ratio is kind of (but not exactly) the reverse of compression ratio. The expansion process creates torque at the flywheel in direct proportion to heat *loss* from combustion gases into the piston. The heat of combustion that is not converted to horsepower at the flywheel (70 to 75 percent!) is mainly wasted out the exhaust pipe as heat or exhaust pressure, with some heat wasted into the atmosphere through the radiator and hot engine components.

GET A HORSE: HORSES, LOCOMOTIVES, HORSEPOWER, TORQUE, AND "5250"

Everyone knows that the power-torque conversion formula is *horsepower = (torque × rpm) / 5,250*.

The purpose of the formula is to derive horsepower (1 horsepower is defined as the ability move 550 pounds 1 foot in 1 second) from torque (pounds of force times leverage in feet)—at a specific engine speed in revolutions per minute.

And then there's the "5,250."

The 5,250 in the formula lumps together several conversion factors and is based on something called *radians* per second. But why do we need conversion factors?

Let's start at the beginning. A horsepower is defined as the ability to lift 550 pounds 1 foot in 1 second, or 33,000 pounds 1 foot in 1 minute.

Torque is normally a measurement of instantaneous force—usually twisting power, represented as force in pounds available to rotate an object—multiplied by the leverage in feet from the center point of the object against which the force is being applied (say against a lever, or maybe a crankshaft, or a torque wrench). This is why torque is represented as *pound-feet*.

In James Watt's original experiments comparing a steam engine to a workhorse pulling in a circle against a 12-foot lever attached to a central capstan (used, for example, to pump water from mines in pre-industrial-revolution England), Watt calculated a typical horse could pull with about 180 pounds of force at just over 3 feet per second. At the center of the 12-foot lever, the horse's force will be multiplied to roughly *2,187 pound-feet of torque*, and the shaft is thus capable of lifting 550 pounds 1 foot in 1 second. The horse's forward rate added up to 2.4 revolutions around the circle per minute. By contrast, pulling against, say, a plough, with no leverage, is simply the force with no multiplication factor; the horse would only have 180 pound-feet of torque (though still 1.0 horsepower).

Horsepower is defined in feet per second. Piston-engine speed is normally represented in revolutions per minute. Getting from one to the other is not perfectly straightforward.

First we will need to convert from minutes to seconds, but that is a trivial division by 60.

Beyond that, because engine speed is measured in *revolutions*—rather than *distance*—per time, and the definition of a horsepower is represented in *distance* rather than *revolutions*, we need a "dimensionless" conversion factor that doesn't involve "feet." We'll need to convert horsepower away from feet per second to something per second that is not a distance. That something is called a *radian*.

If you take the radius of a circle (distance from the center to the outside) and superimpose this length around the arc of the circumference of the circle, it turns out there are 2-pi (pi is 3.14159) radians per circle, such that a radian is about 57.3 degrees. To convert a revolution per minute to radians per second, we divide 1 revolution by 2 × 3.14159 and divide that by 60 seconds. One revolution per minute is thus 0.10472 radians per second, *no dimension involved*. Dividing 550 pound-feet by 0.10472 radians per second yields the conversion factor 5,250.

Therefore, using the conversion formula, in the case of the horse:

((180 pounds force × 12 feet of leverage) × 2.4 revolutions per minute) / 5,250 is approximately 1.0 horsepower, exactly what you'd expect.

A horse plowing a field with a force of 180 pounds—straight ahead, no revolutions involved—and able to move 3 feet in 1 second still moves a total of 550 pound-feet per second, or 1 horsepower. If the horse could move farther in the same time, say *5* feet, it would have 1.6 horsepower! On the other hand, if it could pull with 200 pounds of force and still move 3 feet in a second, it would be capable of 1.09 horsepower, a strong horse. However, it is easy to see that increased speed or distance with a fixed amount of torque vastly multiplies the work that can be done per time, i.e., greatly increasing horsepower, which is why an automotive engine with "only" 500 pound-feet torque at 5,000 or 6,000 rpm (a *lot* of radians or many, *many* feet per second) can do so much more work than a horse on a 12-foot capstan that's producing 2,187 pound-feet torque *at* 2.4 rpm.

A 5,000-horsepower railway locomotive will lift 2.75 million pounds 1 foot in 1 second. If it did this at 5,250 rpm, torque would also be 5,000 pound-feet. If it was rated at 5,000 horsepower at, say, *1,000* rpm—like a typical turbo-diesel locomotive engine—the torque output is 26,250 pound-feet. Yikes!

Stock 2.2-liter GM Ecotec powerplant, circa 2004. Without forced induction the engine was good for about 160 horsepower. Note the plastic intake manifold and electronic throttle body. At the time, the Ecotec was available in 1.8, 2.0, 2.2 versions. The design was "protected" for direct injection and forced induction. *GM Media Archive*

Supercharged Ecotec, as found in the Saturn Ion Redline and Chevrolet Cobalt, good for 205–245 horsepower. Supercharged versions of the engine were built with upgrades such as stronger rods and pistons to handle the increased thermal and mechanical loading of up to 12-psi supercharger boost. *GM Media Archive*

The turbocharged Ecotec I-4, found in the Pontiac Solstice, delivered 260 horsepower and 260 pound-feet from 2.0 liters of displacement. By this time, lessons learned in drag racing had prompted the creation of stronger die-cast cylinder heads (in place of the lost-foam casting used in original versions of the powerplant) and a stronger block, reinforced in the lower bulkhead crankshaft support structure. The turbo Ecotec incorporated oil-jet piston cooling, upgraded connecting rods, and forged pistons with ceramic thermal coating, and engine management used gasoline direct injection with fuel injected at pressures up to 200 bar (3000 PSI). *GM Media Archive*

ADDING POWER

From the point of view of a hot rodder or engineer scheming to increase the power of a particular engine, there is bad news and there is good news. The bad news is that the number of cylinders, bore, stroke, and maximum rpm are essentially a given. The number of cylinders is a given, and the bore and stroke cannot normally be changed without a great deal of difficulty and expense, and even then not usually by very much. Engine speed is similarly constrained. Significantly increasing maximum engine speed without drastically shortening engine life is normally impossible without replacing all major reciprocating components, because the load on the reciprocating components of a piston engine increases exponentially with increases in engine speed. You can increase power a little with a bigger cam, bigger valves, and port work.

But the serious potential for increasing power (say, 50 percent more torque, everywhere) lies in boosting the *average cylinder pressure* during the power stroke. Happily, not only is this completely feasible with supercharging, but boosting the power this way is easier on the engine than you might think. In fact, peak cylinder pressure, and, therefore, rod stress, in a powerplant supercharged to two atmospheres of manifold pressure is only moderately higher (perhaps 25 percent) than a normal-charged engine, because less than a quarter of the charge mixture will have burned at the time of peak pressure.

THE CHARMED LIFE OF A BOOSTED ENGINE

It is no longer uncommon to see street supercharged engines boosted to 200 percent or more of stock horsepower. How do the internal components survive such a mechanical onslaught?

In the first place, sometimes they don't. These days automakers have computational tools that have eliminated the need to over-design engines as much as in the old days. In 2001, GM Racing set about to find the mechanical limits of its new 2.0-liter I4 Ecotec the old-fashioned way—by (1) progressively blowing increasing amounts of nitrous and fuel through the engine on a dyno until something broke, (2) repairing the engine with stronger parts, and (3) pushing on until the next weakest link died. Damaged parts were sent to a lab for forensic analysis. When technicians cranked up the power from the baseline 168 horsepower all the way to 283 screaming horsepower, all four connecting rods abruptly failed simultaneously, with virtually identical mid-beam compression fractures that smashed broken rods through the block and utterly totaled the engine. The Ecotec's powdered metal rods simply could not live at nearly 170 percent of stock power, where horsepower loading per rod had increased from 42 to 71 at the time of the catastrophic failure. Subsequent turbo and supercharged versions of the Ecotec were equipped with stronger forged rods and pistons.

This was quite different from the early 1980s, when a low-compression Ford 4.2 V-8 engine, de-stroked from 5.0 liters and making only 119 horsepower, could be boosted to 336 horsepower with supercharging (minus the power wasted driving the supercharger) before horsepower loading per rod would equal that of the stock four-cylinder Ecotec.

Blower-boosted power is easier on an engine than you might expect given the power gains. For one thing, most of the gain in power from forced induction occurs by increasing the force exerted against the crankshaft at times of sub-peak stress during the four-stroke cycle. Under heavy loading at higher rpm, the charge mixture in the cylinders of a modern piston engine typically ignites at 20 to 30 degrees before top dead center, with ignition timed to achieve peak cylinder pressure at the optimal point 14 to 18 degrees after top dead center. At that time only about 20 percent of the charge mixture has burned, but now the piston begins to accelerate hard away from the cylinder head such that even though gas volume is still increasing from combustion, the size of the combustion chamber is increasing even faster. Inevitably, cylinder pressure is dropping in this portion of the power stroke, and is thus a decreasing factor when considering stress on the various engine components. Although the *average* torque of a supercharged engine is heavily enhanced by gains in this portion of the power stroke, cylinder pressure and mechanical stress are considerably below the peak.

So let's analyze peak cylinder pressure. If an engine is supercharged to the extent required to deliver double the charge mixture in the combustion chamber, the maximum cylinder pressure achieved will be higher than that of an equivalent normal-charged engine. But how much higher? Less than you might think. Suppose normal-charged compression results in 185 psi and a supercharger adds an additional 15 psi of boost pressure. The total compression component of cylinder pressure would be 200 psi. Say this is exerted against a 4-inch piston of 12.57 square inch area. Multiplying the 200 psi by 12.57 indicates a total compression loading on the connecting rod of 2,514 pounds at TDC for the supercharged engine. This is only *8 percent higher* than the 2,324-pound loading of a similar normal-charged powerplant.

Obviously, this is small compared to the change in combustion loading, which could easily quadruple pressure in the combustion chamber to, say, 740 psi in the normal-charged engine and 800 psi in the boosted engine, resulting in total loading of 9,301 versus 10,056 pounds for the two powerplants. But while one atmosphere of boost will double the power output, the supercharged engine's peak combustion pressure is nonetheless only 8 percent higher. And because the supercharged engine need turn no faster to achieve its performance goals, 100 percent of the added load is *compressive* through the connecting rods against the crankshaft.

This last point is significant. Let's compare the increased rod loading of supercharging to the rod stresses that result from increasing the engine redline. This increases the inertial resistance of the mass in the reciprocating assembly and subjects it to extremely rapid changes in piston and rod velocity during the engine cycle. Calculating the period of worst-case tensile rod loading (when the rod bolts alone must bear the entire load of decelerating the piston-rod assembly because the crankshaft is yanking the piston to a halt toward the end of the exhaust stroke and there is no compression and combustion pressure to offset the tensile loading), we find that the loads generated by reciprocating motion increase at the *square* of engine rpm. If redline increases from, say, 6,000 rpm to 7,000 rpm, loading increases not 17 percent—like engine speed—but 36 percent! Compare this to the 8 percent increased rod loading from 15 psi of supercharger boost.

Bottom line, considering the nature of the way supercharging increases cylinder pressure versus the exponential nature of increased rod-loading from higher engine speeds, supercharging is clearly far easier on an engine than power-boosting tricks that increase the redline.

Additional combustion after peak cylinder pressure is precisely why *average* cylinder pressure is considerably higher in a forced-induction powerplant. Midway through the power stroke with the piston at 90 degrees after top dead center (ATDC), supercharged cylinder pressure can easily be three to four times that of a normal-charged engine, with torque over twice as high. True, supercharging does load the rods and pistons somewhat more for a longer time, but the loading from higher cylinder pressure is almost always dwarfed by the far greater stress imparted to reciprocating components at redline. The most critical stress is imparted to the rods as they are stretched when the crankshaft is yanking a piston away from top dead center at extreme acceleration during the early part of the intake stroke, at which time 100 percent of the tensile stress is absorbed by the weakest link, the rod bolts.

Assuming an engine is correctly tuned, average cylinder pressure is mostly dependent on the volumetric efficiency (VE) of the engine—that is, the percentage of atmospheric pressure in a given cylinder at the end of its intake stroke. You might assume VE should be 100 percent at wide-open throttle, but most normal-charged piston engines cannot achieve more than about 80 percent VE at peak torque due to inevitable pumping inefficiencies related to the air intake, clearance volume, compression, and crankcase windage. A typical engine cannot ever pump an air mass equal to the full displacement of the cylinders at full atmospheric pressure because of: (1) intake restrictions from the intake valves, ports, and throttle that prevent full cylinder filling in the available time, (2) exhaust restrictions from the exhaust valves and pipes that cause pressure to back up in the combustion chambers late in the exhaust stroke, and (3) hot combustion gases remaining in the clearance volume (the unswept portion of the combustion chamber) that cannot be completely expelled by the exhaust stroke. Charge heating, as we shall see, can also affect charge density, and, thus, VE.

It is worth noting that by using heroic measures, racing engine designers are able to construct highly specialized competition engines capable of achieving VE above 100 percent. They do this by harnessing inertial and pressure-wave resonation effects at high engine speeds to achieve positive pressure at the intake valves (sometimes as high as 10 psi!). The trick is in tuning intake and exhaust pipes to precise lengths and installing oversized valves, precisely shaped ports, and optimized camshafts. Unfortunately, the results are only applicable to a particular narrow rpm band, which makes such engines suboptimal for street cars (though you do commonly find roadgoing superbikes equipped with these Formula One-type engines). Modern variable valve timing and lift systems (such as Honda's twin-cam iVTEC) improve VE over a somewhat wider range, but for typical normal-charged street engines, a 2.0-liter engine is, in reality, a 1.6-liter engine when it comes to the amount of air it can actually breathe.

HOW TO COMPUTE THE HEATING EFFECT OF A SUPERCHARGER

Squeezing air always increases its temperature even under ideal adiabatic conditions when no heat is added or lost due to inefficiencies in the method of compression. The adiabatic compressor outlet temperature rise is only theoretical, because it's never fully achievable, but it is an important component of boost-heating, so it's the place to start:

$T_{ideal} = T_1 \times PR^{.283}$

Where:

T_{ideal} = Ideal (adiabatic) absolute outlet air temperature (degrees R)
T_1 = absolute inlet air temperature (degrees R)
PR = Pressure Ratio (outlet absolute pressure / Inlet absolute pressure)

To perform this calculation, you'll need a calculator with a Yx key or Y tables or Google: Calculate + y + to + x + power. It is actually not necessary to work with temperature in the Kelvin scale; absolute temperature in degrees Rankine will work just as well (Degrees R = Degrees Fahrenheit + 460).

Assume inlet air temperature is 70 degrees F, i.e., then 70F + 460 = 530R (absolute pressure in degrees F). Assume Intake Pressure is standard barometric pressure for one atmosphere, i.e., 14.7 psia (which reads 0 psig on a boost gauge). If compressor outlet boost pressure is 20 psi gauge pressure, then 20 psig + 14.7 psia = 34.7 psia. This results in a pressure ratio of 34.7 / 14.7 = 2.36.

Plugging in the numbers, ideal outlet temperature (Tideal) from adiabatic compression would be:

$T_{ideal} = T_1 \times PR^{.283}$
$= 530 \times 2.36^{.283}$
$= 530 \times 1.275$
$= 675.78$ degrees R

Theoretical adiabatic air temperature after 20-psi compression is 675.78R, or, rounding and converting to ordinary Fahrenheit, **675.8R − 460 = 215.8F**.

Since the air temperature was already 70F before compression, the ideal temperature *rise* ($T_{IdealRise}$) would be:

$T_{IdealRise} = 215.8F - 70F = 145.8F$

Unfortunately the most efficient automotive centrifugal compressors, optimized to deliver the least heating at the cost of a relatively narrow peak-efficiency range, have only about 80 percent thermal efficiency, meaning that a compressor always adds some extra heat by thrashing the air. Adiabatic compression is not achievable in the real world.

The following formula corrects adiabatic compressor outlet temperature for real-world compressor inefficiencies:

$T_{ActRise} = T_{IdealRise} / CE$

Where:

$T_{ActRise}$ = actual temperature increase
$T_{IdealRise}$ = ideal (adiabatic) temperature rise from compression
CE = compressor thermal efficiency

Assuming a compressor had 78 percent thermal efficiency, the actual temperature *rise* would be:

$T_{ActRise} = T_{IdealRise} / CE$
$= 145.8F / .78$
$= 186.9F$

To compute the actual compressor-out discharge temperature:

$T_{CO} = T_{ActRise} + TCI$

Where:

T_{CO} = compressor-out temperature (degrees F)
$T_{ActRise}$ = Actual temperature increase (degrees F)
T_{CI} = compressor inlet temperature (degrees F)

$T_{CO} = T_{ActRise} + T_{CI}$
$= 186.9F + 70F$
$= 256.9F$

We conclude 70F air boosted to 20 psig whistles out of a 78 percent efficient compressor at **256.9 degrees F**.

Putting this all together to short-circuit our way directly to a single equation for the temperature of air T2C leaving a compressor of a certain efficiency at a certain boost pressure based on a certain inlet air temperature (T1C):

$T_{2C} = T_{1C} + (((T_{1C} \times (PR^{.283})) - T_{1C}) / CE$

Plugging in the numbers for 20-psig boost (pressure ratio of 2.36), inlet air temperature of 70F (530R), and a 78 percent efficient compressor:

$T_{2C} = 530 + (((530 \times 2.36^{.283})) - 530) / .78$
$= 716R$
$= 716 - 460 = 256F$

Supercharging, of course, has no such inherent VE limitations. Forced-induction diesels have achieved as much as *1,000 percent* volumetric efficiency using many atmospheres of boost pressure. The bottom-line effect of most low-pressure street supercharging systems, however, is simply to boost power into the neighborhood of what it *would have been* had the engine been able to breathe in its full displacement of charge air. Contrast the performance of a 1990s-vintage 16-valve 2.0-liter Toyota MR2 Turbo powerplant capable of up to 241 horsepower at 6,000 rpm with an almost dead-flat torque curve to the millennium-vintage normal-charged 2.0-liter Honda S2000 VTEC powerplant, which achieved 240 horsepower 8,300 rpm without supercharging, but with a decidedly peaky torque curve.

The weight or mass of air actually arriving in the cylinders of an engine is not simply a function of the volumetric efficiency of the engine, which can be modified with supercharging. Let's say an engine's VE is 80 percent of ambient atmospheric pressure. How dense is atmospheric pressure? Well, that depends on the elevation, the temperature, and even the weather. At sea level at standard temperature and pressure weather conditions, atmospheric pressure is 14.65 psi; at 18,000 feet, it's half that. If the temperature is 100 degrees F instead of 70 degrees, density is down 5 percent.

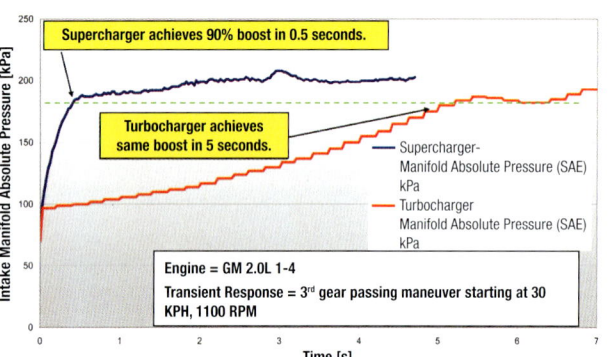

0 RESPONSE: SUPERCHARGER VS. TURBOCHARGER: Making the case for supercharging as a fuel-economy improver, this Eaton graph compares the time to achieve boost for an Eaton TVS Roots-type positive-displacement supercharger and an unknown turbocharger. A great strength of Roots-type blowers is nearly instantaneous boost. *Eaton*

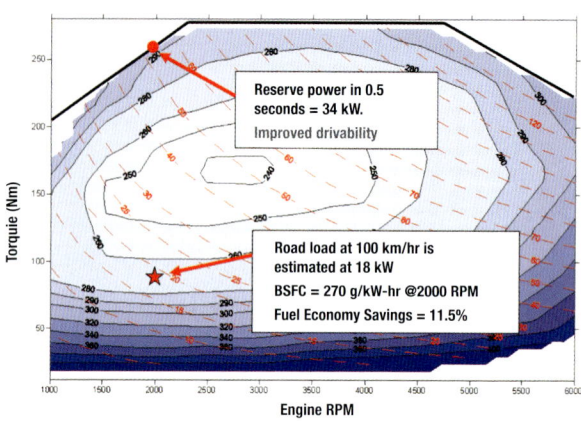

2 DOWNSIZING – 2.0L SUPERCHARGED: Smaller engines with fewer cylinders usually gain efficiency from reduced friction and wider throttle angles that improve pumping efficiency through the engine at less than full throttle. In this case, downsizing a normal-charged V-6 to a smaller GM 2.0-liter I-4 maintained reserve power of 34 kW for passing while improving fuel economy 11.5 percent. *Eaton*

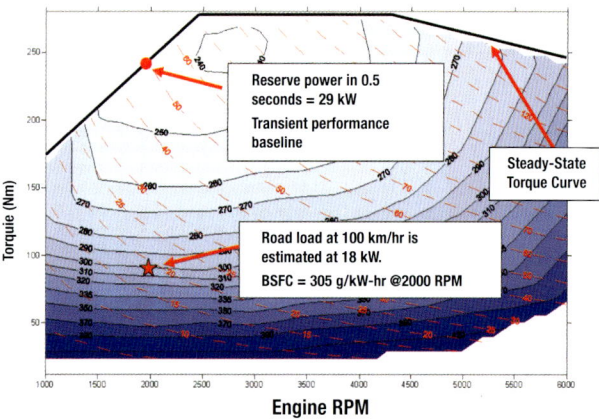

1 2.8L V-6 NATURALLY ASPIRATED BSFC MAP: Suppose you were looking to improve the efficiency of a vehicle powered by a normal-charged 2.8-liter V-6 powerplant. It takes torque to pass. In this Eaton slide, the base V-6 powerplant could deliver 29 kW power (about 39 horsepower) for passing within 0.5 seconds, with the vehicle requiring 18 kW power required to maintain cruise speed. Fuel economy was 305 grams per kilowatt-hour. *Eaton*

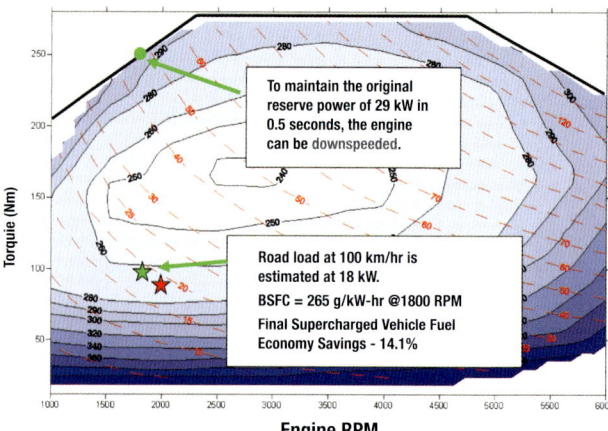

3 DOWNSPEEDING – 2.0L SUPERCHARGED: Since supercharging has provided more passing torque and power than the 2.8-liter V-6 in the original configuration, the 2.0-liter supercharged I-4 could be down speeded to the point where the engine equaled the original 29 kW V-6 reserve power, which boosted fuel economy 14.1 percent. *Eaton*

A supercharger's airflow must significantly exceed the nonsupercharged breathing capacity of the engine in order to be able to force-feed the engine a significant mass of additional air, but the pumping capacity of the supercharger itself is subject to the laws of physics and is thus affected by the density of the ambient air. A supercharger operating at high altitude breathes less dense ambient air and will need to turn faster to boost engine manifold pressure to the same absolute pressure specification that was achievable at sea level. Turbochargers tend to be somewhat self-correcting in this aspect because the pressure differential through an exhaust turbine is greater in lower ambient pressure, causing the turbine to run faster at higher altitude. But for a supercharger, the need to run faster at altitude to maintain manifold pressure has a cost: The more you have to thrash the air to achieve a given level of manifold pressure, the hotter the air becomes. And hotter air at a specified pressure has lower density compared to cooler air at the same pressure. In other words, the mass of a cubic foot of air at a given pressure is less when the air is hotter, thus the engine gets less oxygen even if boost pressure is the same. Viewed in this context, charge heat is the enemy of volumetric efficiency and therefore horsepower.

It is interesting to note that besides delivering the required mass of additional oxygen to burn the fuel required to increase horsepower, supercharging delivers substantial power gains from the higher *effective* compression ratio that results when a super-normal charge mass is stuffed into a fixed-size combustion chamber. This results in a super-dense charge that burns faster and hotter with less thermal leakage into the cooling jacket. This is good heat, and it really makes power, assuming the engine survives without a meltdown and doesn't knock.

Unfortunately, supercharging an engine does not mean that a higher percentage of heat energy can be extracted from the expansion phase of the four-stroke cycle compared to a normal-charged version of the same powerplant. In fact, the opposite is true. To understand why this is so, consider that in a normal-charged engine, increasing the compression ratio not only increases power during combustion due to the increased charge density; it simultaneously gains thermal efficiency from the increased expansion ratio, which extracts the power as combustion gases cool and the cylinders lose pressure.

Modern Atkinson Cycle engines found in high-efficiency hybrid vehicles such as the Toyota Prius take this a step further, in the direction of improved efficiency, by *lowering* the compression ratio relative to the expansion ratio. This is done by holding the intake valves open far into the compression stroke (as much as 20 to 30 percent), which pushes some of the charge air back out of the cylinders into the intake manifold. The pumping efficiency of the powerplant suffers, but the greater expansion ratio of a normal-duration power stroke means *all* combustion pressure can be extracted before the exhaust valves open, resulting in higher thermal efficiency and lower brake specific fuel consumption (BSFC).

By contrast, supercharging an engine increases the density of the compressed charge in the combustion chamber at the time of ignition by increasing the *effective* compression ratio rather than the real compression ratio. The result is that the *expansion ratio* of a supercharged powerplant remains essentially unchanged compared to an equivalent normal-charged engine. Therefore, supercharging increases the pressure and heat delivered to a power stroke in a situation where the expansion ratio is less than the effective compression ratio.

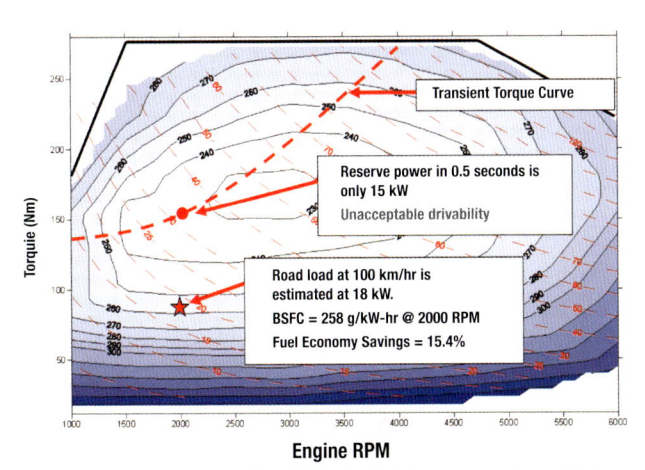

4 DOWNSIZING – 2.0L TURBOCHARGED: In this Eaton comparo slide, a 2.0-liter turbocharged engine equaled the ultimate power of a much larger normal-charged V-6 with fuel efficiency improvement of 15.4 percent, but was unable to maintain passing performance due to a serious boost lag. *Eaton*

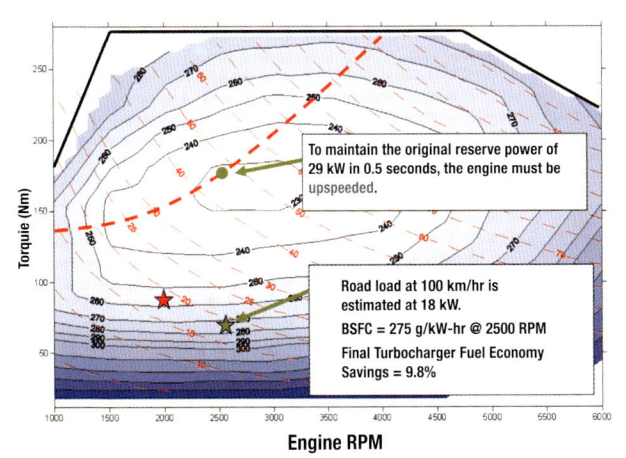

5 UPSPEEDING – 2.0L TURBOCHARGED: In order to retain normal-charged passing performance, the example turbo engine in this Eaton slide had to be upspeeded with a higher gearing, which reduced the turbo's fuel economy improvement from 15.4 percent to 9.8 percent, which compared unfavorably to the supercharged powerplant's 14.1 improvement. *Eaton*

NORMAL VERSUS SUPER CHARGING: VOLUMETRIC AND THERMAL EFFICIENCY

Norwood Autocraft

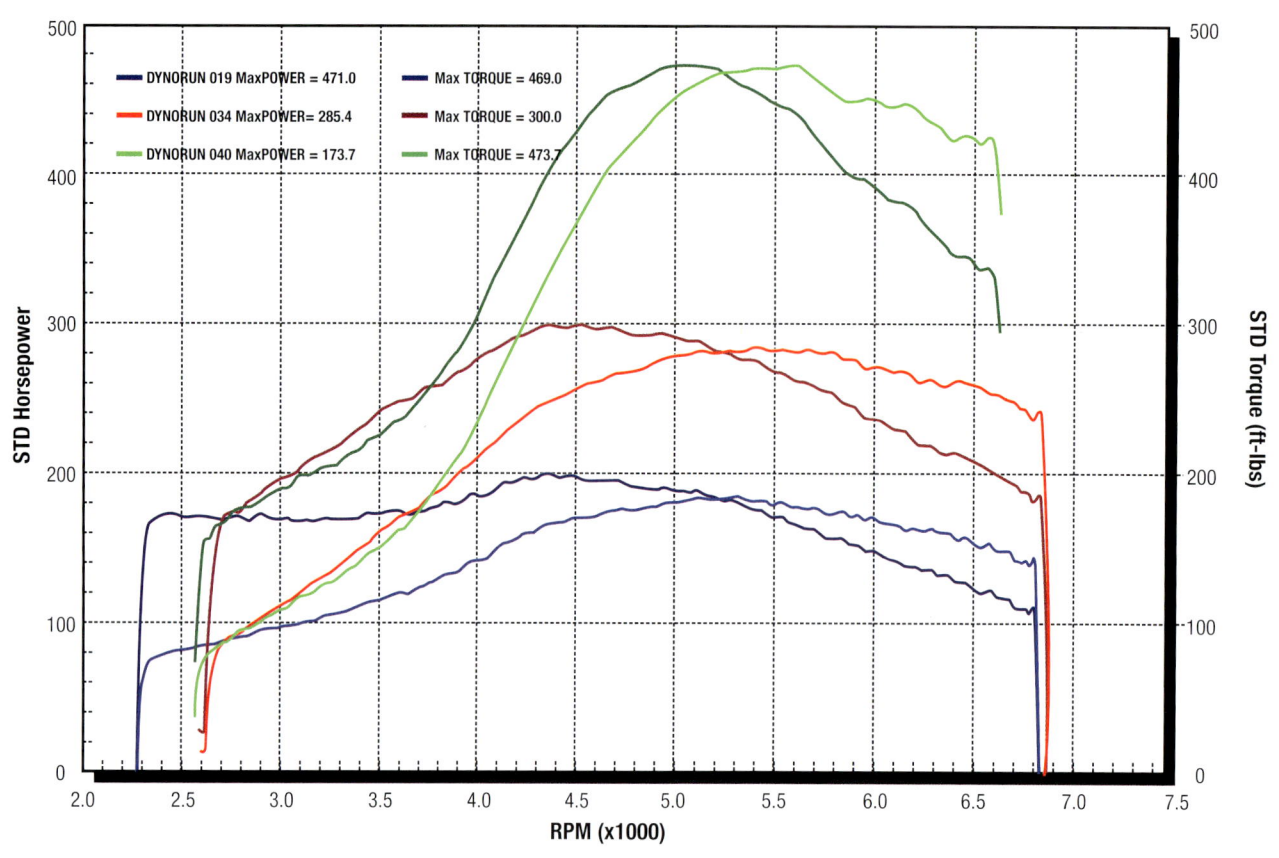

DYNORUN 019 MaxPOWER = 471.0	Max TORQUE = 469.0
DYNORUN 034 MaxPOWER = 285.4	Max TORQUE = 300.0
DYNORUN 040 MaxPOWER = 173.7	Max TORQUE = 473.7

OEMs have often used forced induction to improve engine efficiency, but hot rodders add blowers for pure horsepower and torque. Here we see wheel horsepower generated by a 3.0-liter Toyota V-6 when: (1) normal-charged (Dyno Run 040), (2) supercharged (Eaton Roots-type blower) (Dyno Run 034), and (3) turbocharged (Dyno Run 019).

Jaguar's 5.3-liter V-12 delivered 282–295 normal-charged horsepower. Dodge-Maxwell added an Eaton supercharger with air-water intercooling. Dual Electromotive engine management computers mount on the outboard side of the air-cooler units.

If exhaust valves open before cylinder pressure has reached ambient levels, some of the pressure and heat generated by combustion cannot be recovered in time and gets wasted into the exhaust—kind of the opposite of the Atkinson-cycle situation. The overall efficiency of a supercharged powerplant is further reduced because of the parasitic losses incurred by driving the supercharger during boost.

The result is that a supercharged engine is likely to be *less* efficient than a normal-charged version of the same engine. Turbocharged engines are able to reclaim some of the waste heat energy in the exhaust and use it to drive the compressor. Turbines tend to reduce exhaust pumping efficiency, however, as exhaust pressure upstream of the turbine backs up into the exhaust ports and prevents complete combustion chamber exhaust scavenging. In fact, turbocharged engines gain efficiency almost exclusively from their increased dynamic range, which permits smaller engines with fewer cylinders and reduced internal friction; they deliver high specific power only when it's required for hard acceleration, towing, or maximum performance hill climbing. During nonboosted operation, a turbocharger is freewheeling, and the engine functions as a small, low-output, normal-charged powerplant with a slight exhaust restriction.

Some modern mechanical superchargers eliminate the parasitic drag of driving the compressor during light engine loading by disengaging the supercharger drive with an electrical clutch or by relieving or "scramming" boost pressure with a bypass valve.

The negative consequences of charge heat make the thermal efficiency of a supercharger very critical on any high-pressure boosted engine. Even an imaginary compressor with perfect 100 percent adiabatic efficiency would heat charge air by an amount proportional to the pressure ratio of pressure increase; compressing any gas into a smaller space *always* adds thermal energy. It's a simple law of physics. This is true even if you do it really carefully and slowly—and superchargers do *not* compress air carefully and slowly. They whip the air around furiously in a tremendous hurry and thus heat it much more than the theoretical minimum.

Magnuson Products' supercharger kit for the Dodge Hemi was designed to jack power of the stock 370-horse engine by 30 percent and stock torque by 40 percent with the use of an Eaton Gen-6 4-lobe Roots-type blower pumping out 6-psi boost. *Magnuson Products*

Porsche tuner Alois Ruf developed this "Kompressor" centrifugal supercharger conversion system for late-model liquid-cooled normal-charged Porsche 911s. The system added 80 to 100 horsepower, enough to *really* wake up the stock engine. The rush of power from a centrifugal blower can be truly thrilling to drive.

NORMAL VERSUS SUPER CHARGING: VOLUMETRIC AND THERMAL EFFICIENCY

39

There are many types of compressors, but all range in thermal efficiency from as low as 50 percent to a maximum of about 80 percent. The imaginary compressor with 100 percent thermal efficiency would heat 70-degree F air an additional 65 degrees on the way to making a half-atmosphere (7.5 psi) of boost. In the real world, the best you'll see from a state-of-the-art centrifugal compressor with 80 percent thermal efficiency is a 100-degree rise to 170 degrees F. This translates directly into a 100-degree increase in combustion temperature. This is why all modern forced-induction engines should be equipped with intercoolers, which are capable of improving even the least efficient supercharger's effective thermal efficiency by cooling the charge air *after* it leaves the compressor.

Given the stakes, this is a good time to take a look at the various types of compressors and their pumping and thermal efficiency.

Mr. Norm 6.1-liter Hemi Challenger features Kenne Bell's "Mammoth" twin-screw positive-displacement supercharger. Note the chrome air intake that sucks fresh air from outside the engine compartment. *Kenne Bell*

This wheel-standing 1956 Chevy leaps off the line with boost by twin-screw "Whipplecharger." *Whipple Superchargers*

Chapter 3
Choosing the Engine

You name it, it's been supercharged: cars, diesel trucks, boats, jet-skis, motorcycles, go-karts, snowmobiles, aircraft, dragsters, speed-record cars, road-racers, industrial engines, farm tractors, heavy equipment, locomotives, large ships, hybrid automobiles, air-cooled spark-ignition engines, Wankel engines, and even lawnmowers. Any type or brand of internal combustion engine of any age with a target output of at least 15 horsepower can be supercharged with existing technology. The boost can begin at whatever rpm the designer wants, and maximum boost can increase until the engine destroys itself. No kidding.

Any engine *can* be supercharged. But *should* it be?

Some engines are MUCH more blower-ready than others right out of the box—the most obvious example being an engine that was factory-turbocharged or supercharged. The fact that you already own a specific engine or vehicle is not necessarily a good justification for plowing money and sweat into a supercharger conversion—although this sort of upgrade can make all the sense in the world if you're a car company with a lot invested in a certain platform and drivetrain and you know that a high-output option will sell cars—or if you're a tuner and can leverage R&D over dozens, hundreds, or even thousands of engines and vehicles. If you're a hot rodder, the existence of a reputable kit chargeable to your Visa card can make the math look good compared to the cost of building a roll-your-own system (particularly if you factor in the sweat equity of designing it, installation, parts-chasing, mistake making, mistake fixing, and so forth). If there's no kit, yes,

With 430 stock horsepower at 5,900 rpm, the 2010 Camaro SS is difficult to hot rod using all-motor parts without destroying street legality. Procharger's intercooled blower kit was designed to increase horsepower 40 to 45 percent with 7-psi boost. There are several supercharger choices (with optional helical internal step-up gears for noise reduction), as well as 8- or 12-ribbed, or cogged drive belts. Obviously, the underhood air cleaner shown in this system is not going to provide the coolest temperature intake air, but almost all supercharger systems have some compromises. *Procharger*

anything can be done, given time and money, but then again, it's going to take time and money and patience and above-average engineering and mechanical skills: There are plenty of people who could do a good job installing a supercharger kit who would have trouble building a custom system. And there are people who could build a good supercharger system by subcontracting some of the fabrication or design work.

In spite of the fact that this book is about superchargers, it's worth pointing out that there are sometimes better ways of going faster or increasing power than installing a supercharger. If you have a certain vehicle with a certain engine and you're dissatisfied with the performance and thinking about doing a supercharger conversion, there is always the option of selling it and buying a faster vehicle, or installing a turbocharger or nitrous injection system. These options should probably be exercised much more than they are. On the other hand, some people love a challenge, or just need to have something totally unique.

It is critical that a supercharger's size and speed are properly matched to the engine being supercharged across the required operating range for the intended application. An engine and a supercharger are both air pumps, and for the engine to receive boost at a particular speed, the supercharger must be pumping at a faster rate than the engine. A certain application may not require that the engine be supercharged across the entire operating range (no engine is supercharged at idle, and most engines need not be boosted at all below 1,500 rpm—at which point supercharger boost can actually be harmful to a "lugging" engine). Many engines do not need to be boosted below 2,000 or even 2,500 rpm, but the dynamic range of the engine and supercharger must be compatible. In fact, meeting torque requirements will require not only that the engine and supercharger are well-matched, but also that both are correctly matched to the final drive ratio in various gears.

It is wise to keep in mind that even if the supercharging system is initially a good match, plenty of engines have been incrementally over-boosted to levels beyond (or *far* beyond) what's optimal for the design—because there is always a hot rodder willing to pump up the boost a little more, and then a little more, and then a little more, and so on. Many hot rodders are not going to be permanently satisfied with the status-quo levels of boost and power, so any aftermarket supercharging system designer should consider "protecting" the design by providing headroom for future modifications that may occur.

The raw characteristics of the engine are critical. Two engines of identical peak power may have entirely different operating characteristics at other engine speeds and while accelerating. Everyone knows (don't they?) that there is a difference between the personality of a 210-horsepower, factory supercharged 2.3-liter four-cylinder with a centrifugal supercharger and a 210-horsepower normal-charged factory 5.0-liter V-8 of more than twice the displacement. Despite peak horsepower numbers equal to the V-8 and regardless of the ability of sophisticated electronic powertrain management (engine and transmission) to get wonderful performance out of supercharged engines, a supercharged 2.3-liter I-4 and a 5.0 V-8 are very different powerplants with different personalities.

But why?

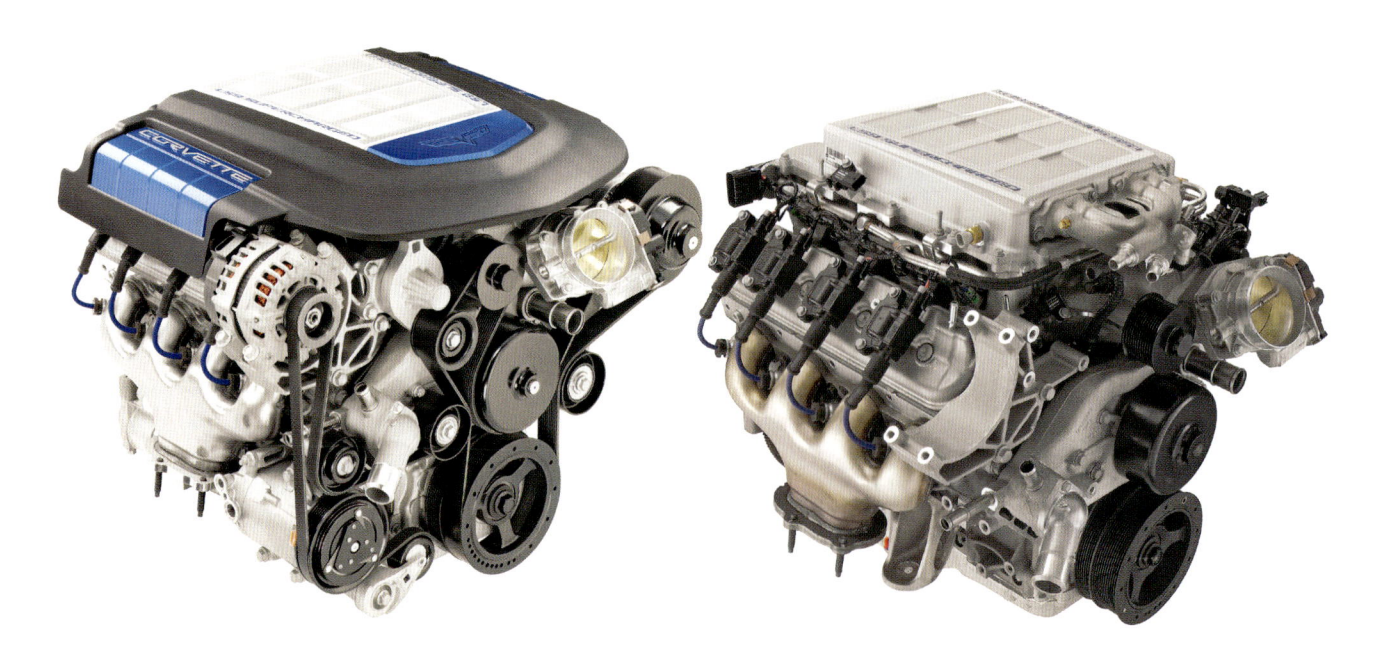

Covered and naked shots of the 2009 ZR1 Corvette LS9 powerplant reveal the water-cooled intercooler section above the virtually invisible blower. The engine featured one-per-bank, dual-brick, Behr air-water intercoolers in order to improve hood clearance to the extent required to avoid changes to the hood. *General Motors*

In the first place, the shapes of the torque curves of the two engines will almost definitely be different, requiring different ratios in various gears to effectively multiply torque for street driving or various kinds of racing (such as a first gear specifically designed to "upspeed" the engine to produce more torque until the supercharger begins to make boost). This is particularly true in low gear, much of which, for various reasons, will effectively be normal-charged on most powerplants with centrifugal superchargers or turbos.

The reciprocating parts of a bigger normal-charged engine may have more inertia, which will affect how fast it can accelerate or even rev itself with no load. Engine designs that require heavy counterweights on the crankshaft have even more inertia. For example, free-revving flat-plane crank V-8s require smaller counterweights than cross-plane cranks, which is one reason Ferrari uses a flat-crank design (which also delivers evenly spaced exhaust pulses to the two headers for improved exhaust tuning without having to collect exhaust tubing from two different cylinder heads at opposite sides of the powerplant).

When operating in the normal-charged range, a small-displacement powerplant with a centrifugal supercharger will simply have less torque than a larger-displacement normal-charged engine. A tall first gear will amp up the torque, but then you've got a bigger drop in rpm when shifting into second gear.

The cam specs, valve size, and intake and exhaust runners of the two engines are probably different, because (1) the I-4 powerplant may have a higher redline and (2) the I-4 will have a greater dynamic range of operation, which

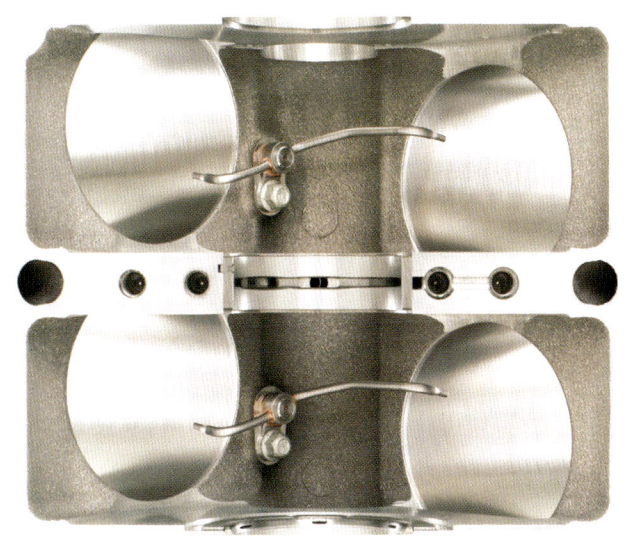

The supercharged 4.4-liter Cadillac Northstar V-8 had to deal with much higher thermal loading than the 4.6-liter (normal-charged) version of the engine. The supercharged powerplant was equipped with piston-cooling oil-squirters to keep piston crown temperatures safe. *GM Media Archive*

is the difference between air and fuel (charge) consumption at idle versus peak power. Peak power and peak torque may occur at a significantly higher rpm in the smaller centrifugally supercharged engine, depending on whether the personality of the two engines is a technical issue or whether they are engineered a particular way for marketing to different groups of customers.

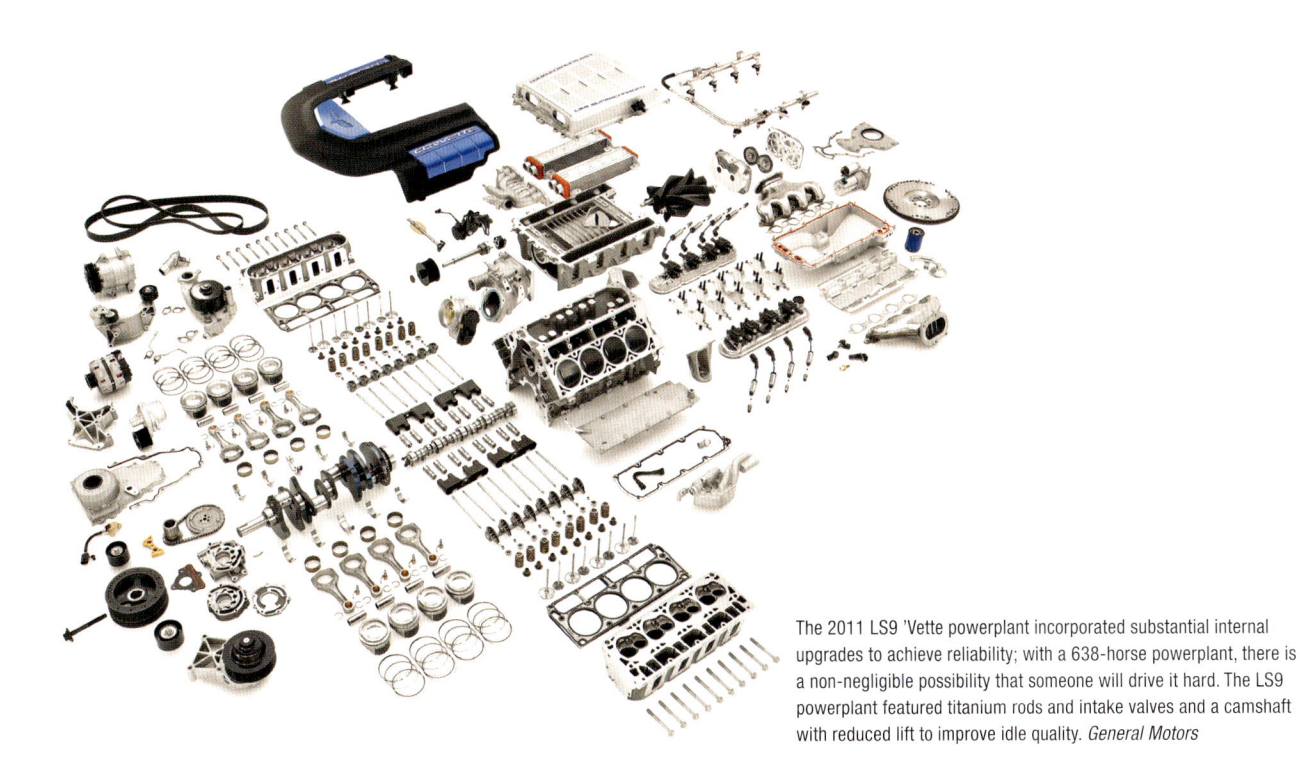

The 2011 LS9 'Vette powerplant incorporated substantial internal upgrades to achieve reliability; with a 638-horse powerplant, there is a non-negligible possibility that someone will drive it hard. The LS9 powerplant featured titanium rods and intake valves and a camshaft with reduced lift to improve idle quality. *General Motors*

A modern normal-charged engine is likely to have a flat torque curve; whereas, a centrifugal-supercharged engine's torque will rise noticeably with the onset of boost. The supercharged engine will probably be unable to achieve peak boost at low rpm in first gear (or even second) gear.

In addition to the obvious factors that affect observable drivability, torque, and power, a supercharged engine requires differences under the skin that do not affect performance but are related to what it takes to make any boosted engine survive and thrive. This is one reason why—considering the basic preexisting infrastructure of a supercharger system and more robust engine internals—it is typically much less expensive to overboost a factory forced-induction engine than it is to hot rod a normal-charged engine. And when you're finished, the overboosted factory engine would normally have no trouble passing a tailpipe emissions test or a visual inspection, which could be a nightmare for a normally charged powerplant that has been extensively modified with power-adders or other hot-rodding modifications.

In many or even most cases, engine manufacturers have developed forced-induction and normal-charged versions of the same basic engine block. It can be highly enlightening to "peek under the skirts" and see the hidden differences. Beneath the surface—even on a light road-going vehicle—the differences between a 140-horsepower normal-charged engine and a 200-horsepower forced-induction version of the same basic automotive powerplant go beyond the obvious fact that one has a supercharger and the other doesn't, or that one has more peak power and the other has less. Usually the forced-induction engine has forged pistons, stronger rods, moly rings, improved head gaskets, engine oil coolers, and so on. Manufacturers always engineer factory forced-induction engines with super-duty parts not found in the normal-charged version of the engine, more so the heavier the vehicle.

But why? Almost any engine can survive the additional thermal and mechanical loading of a low-pressure supercharger conversion to 5 or 6 psi without internal changes—in normal street driving—for a while. But any time you increase power and boost, you are eating into the factory-provided margin of safety and reducing the life of the engine. If you put the pedal to the metal in top gear and hold it there for a long time at the vehicle's maximum speed, a forced-induction powerplant will see tremendous thermal loading that would kill many supercharger-conversion engines. On the other hand, all factory engines are designed to survive an impressive amount of abuse. For hot rodders, the bottom line is that whatever thermal and mechanical margin of error exists in the normal-charged version of an engine *cannot* be maintained in a supercharged version without upgrading parts directly impacted by the increased mechanical and thermal loading.

YOU CAN'T BEAT THE FACTORY—OR CAN YOU?

It's difficult and expensive to beat factory reliability. This is just as true when superchargers are involved.

These days, the federal government forces auto- and truckmakers to warrant all systems that are involved in meeting federal emissions standards for 120,000 miles—which amounts to warranting nearly everything having anything do to with any engine system (the failure or degradation of anything, which could impact engine exhaust emissions and could even result in a hellishly expensive product recall). The result is that modern factory supercharged engines are always made stronger internally in critical ways than lower output normal-charged versions of the same powerplant, with additional upgraded external systems to improve or modify engine cooling, lubrication, fuel supply, and engine management.

Procharger's Harley supercharging system was based upon a centrifugal supercharger and designed to add 50 to 65 percent power to a big twin. *Procharger*

The great thing about supercharging a marine powerplant is that you don't usually have to worry about frying the clutch or transmission. Note the backward-facing blower hat on this supercharged big-block lake racer.

Blown head gaskets can quickly become an issue for supercharger-conversion or overboosted factory engines. This 3.0-liter V-6 Toyota 1MZ-FE from the author's twin-charged 1991 Toyota MR2 is being outfitted with custom annealed-copper head gaskets and underlying wire O-rings as a significant anti-blow countermeasure during the rebuild process. In this case, problems with coolant leakage eventually forced a fallback to stock composition gaskets combined with the O-rings, which got the job done on both accounts.

But there are countervailing forces that impact what's possible with aftermarket supercharging. These days, engine manufacturers balance reliability versus cost using sophisticated computational modeling and simulation tools with names like Finite Element Analysis and Failure Mode Effects Analysis to predict exactly what heavy-duty parts and special engine management strategies are required to achieve the required reliability. Manufacturers then torture-test sample parts with specialized machines to verify reliability, often under abusive situations, such as unusually high thermal loading, unusually infrequent oil changes, or substandard regular fuel instead of premium. Given a better understanding of the failure mode effects of engine parts, manufacturers no longer have to overbuild parts as much as they used to achieve the required reliability plus a margin of error.

Obviously, the factory strategy of precisely analyzing the strength requirement of all engine parts is not within the scope of possibility for many tuners or hot rodders planning a supercharger or turbo conversion. Most specialty equipment manufacturers—many of whom are *not* automotive or mechanical engineers—want to build good stuff but some do not have the expertise. Hot rodders cannot usually afford much in the way of failed parts, which can instigate collateral damage that destroys other parts and multiplies the cost of catastrophic failure. To achieve factory-type reliability, hot rodders and turners have two choices: (1) Install a high-quality kit developed by someone else that has torture-tested it and upgraded parts that they broke, or (2) build in reliability the old-fashioned way using parts with a *large* safety margin of strength. When it's just one vehicle, a highly overbuilt part can be the most affordable solution.

Pity, however, the poor aftermarket kit manufacturers who are caught between the high price of building really robust components and the high-price elasticity of many performance enthusiasts. There is a tremendous incentive to cut corners when expensive parts simply will not sell.

In the case of aircraft engines, where power loading is high and an engine failure can kill you, any forced-induction engine must be equipped with exotic super-duty parts and metallurgy, such as sodium-filled exhaust valves (which can cost as much as $275 each), robust engine oil coolers, Inconel turbine housings (rather than automotive-type ductile-iron housings), oil pumps designed to scavenge drain-back oil from the supercharger at unusual aircraft attitudes, and everything constructed to aircraft standards of quality. Even with super-high-octane 100LL aviation gasoline, the compression ratio on turbocharged air-cooled aviation powerplants is usually between 6.5 and 7.5:1—a wise precaution on air-cooled engines with cylinder head temperatures ranging up to 250 degrees hotter than liquid-cooled engines, where exhaust gas temperatures are under manual control.

Some automotive engines can unquestionably handle a low-pressure supercharger conversion without needing any internal modifications for the sake of longevity. Good examples are the low-compression, low-specific power engines with relatively large displacement built during the pre-EFI emissions era from about 1973 to 1982–1987, many of which were detuned versions of older high-output engines. On many of these engines, adding forced induction simply puts

Some crate motors almost beg for supercharging. GM's 454-type 502 HO long block consisted of a cast-iron four-bolt block, forged steel crankshaft, shot-peened forged steel connecting rods, and forged pistons for a final compression ratio of 8.75:1 (which is low enough for supercharging with premium fuel and the right engine management). A high-lift roller camshaft controlled airflow through rectangular-port cast-iron cylinder heads. High valve lift is fine, but you don't want much overlap with supercharging, which can blow unburned charge straight out the exhaust ports when both valves are partly open. *GM Media Archive*

CHOOSING THE ENGINE

45

the VE and power back to where they used to be circa 1970, before the addition of early, crude, power-robbing emissions controls and lowered compression ratios. Many performance engines from the 1980s are also quite robust relative to their output, coming from the years immediately before factory engine designers could safely reduce production costs by reducing the degree of engine "over-design."

As factory engineers acquired new computational tools that allowed them to shave built-in OEM safety margins, the differences between factory forced-induction and normal-charged powerplants increased. An example is the late-1990s liquid-cooled Porsche Turbo Carrera, which employed an entirely different engine than the normal-charged 911; this was not the case with older air-cooled turbo models. The basic engine simply could not be boosted enough to achieve the output people expect from a turbo Porsche without unacceptable compromises to reliability. Forced-induction conversions for the basic normal-charged engine from high-end aftermarket tuners like Ruf were low-pressure supercharger ("Kompressor") packages that added about 80 to 100 horsepower to the 325-horsepower Porsche 911, using 8- to 9-psi boost.

PLUSSES AND MINUSES

To understand the consequences and implications of a supercharger conversion, let's compare the advantages and disadvantages of normal-charged and supercharged powerplants:

Things Supercharged Engines Do Better Compared to Normal-Charged Powerplants...

1. Superchargers enable engines with fewer cylinders and smaller displacement to make as much peak torque and power as larger displacement engines with more cylinders.
2. With fewer cylinders, a supercharged-engine represents a smaller package for a given power output, typically enabling it to weigh less and to fit in a smaller engine compartment—for improved handling and better acceleration.
3. If supercharged engines have computer-commanded boost-control (usually by bleeding off boost, as is the case with some supercharged Mercury Marine powerplants, but in some cases where using a variable-

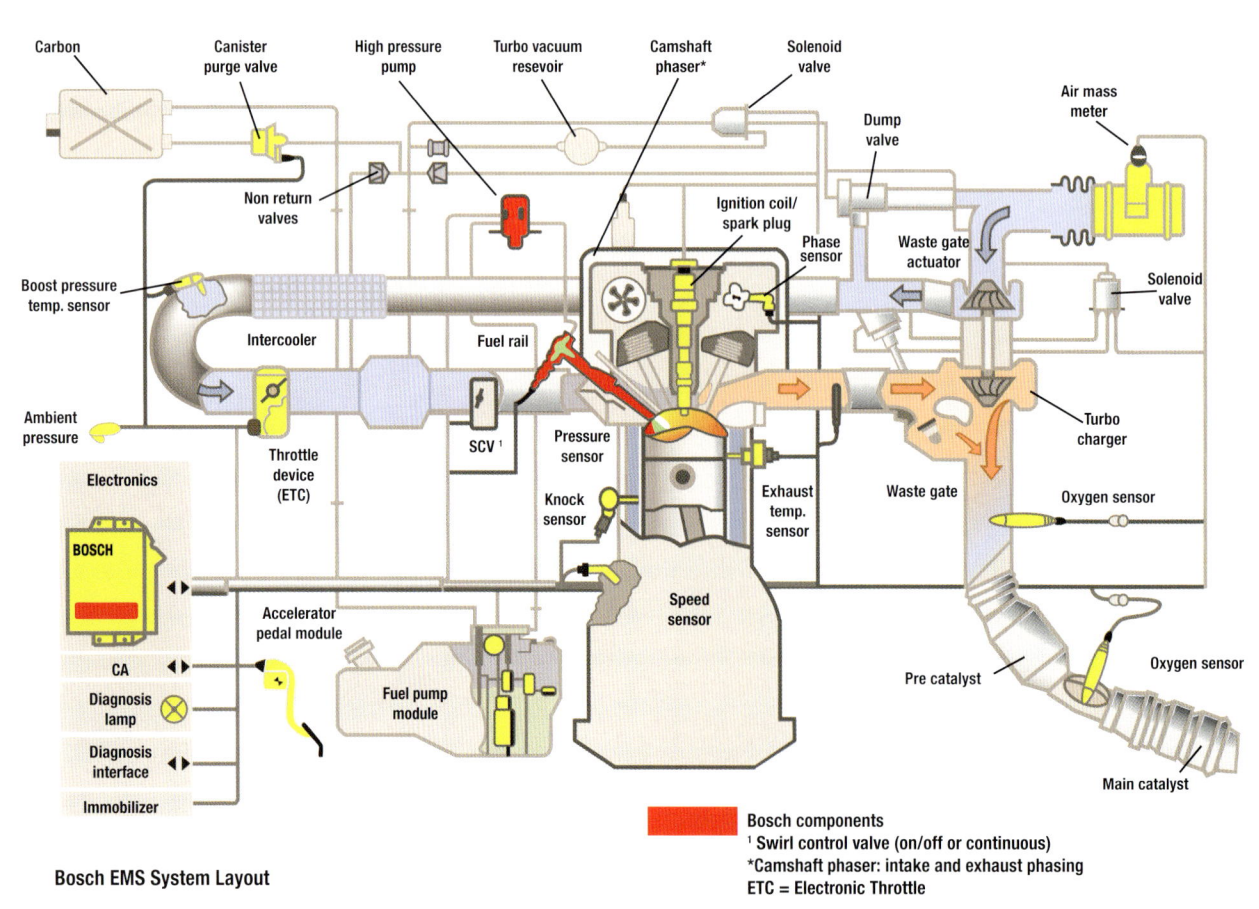

Bosch EMS System Layout

A schematic of Bosch Gasoline-Direct Injection (GDI) engine management components (turbocharged). Some types of engine management are much more compatible with supercharging than others, and some are much easier to modify. GDI systems are more complex, for example, than carburetion, but in some cases fuel enrichment for supercharging can be handled with GDI using an interceptor circuit that misreports fuel rail pressure, causing the system to automatically increase fuel pressure and increase injected fuel. *Bosch*

speed drive—or a turbine drive, as is the case with turbo-superchargers), this can provide dynamic adjustment of maximum boost. This may enable the engine to safely "overboost" for brief periods of super-high-output performance while avoiding internal damage from excessive thermal or mechanical loading, or to lower maximum boost under heavy-load, high-temperature conditions, or if fuel octane does not meet the normal specification. Maximum boost and torque could be dynamically adjusted under computer control according to gear, engine temperature, air temperature, altitude, or other factors in order to protect the transmission from damage, provide traction control, maintain full performance at altitude, or to achieve other performance goals.

4. To some extent positive-displacement supercharging systems can help to flatten the engine's torque curve, compensating for poor volumetric efficiency in certain parts of the torque curve by automatically cramming in boost. It is common for supercharger boost to increase somewhat at very high rpm as the induction system becomes more of a performance bottleneck, forcing the supercharger to create more boost to maintain airflow in the face of decreasing engine VE.

5. Factory supercharged engines typically have a certain amount of supercharger and engine system "headroom" to pump up the boost by overdriving the blower with undersized or oversized supercharger or crankshaft pulleys, typically to 110 to 135 percent of rated power. Of course, as you crank up the boost you're eating further into the factory margin of safety.

6. Compared to some normal-charged high-output engines with traditional hot cams and a lumpy idle, a well-designed forced-induction engine of similar or greater power output can be smooth and tractable, with good drivability in city driving. Many supercharged engines are equipped with relatively small intake ports and mild cams for optimal cylinder-filling below the boost threshold, and to prevent boosted air-fuel mixture from being pushed straight through the combustion chamber and out the exhaust valve during cam overlap, when intake manifold pressure is higher than exhaust/atmospheric pressure. Instead of radical VE tricks, supercharged street engines often rely on the blower to make the power and torque at higher rpm ranges by stuffing in the boost for peak power.

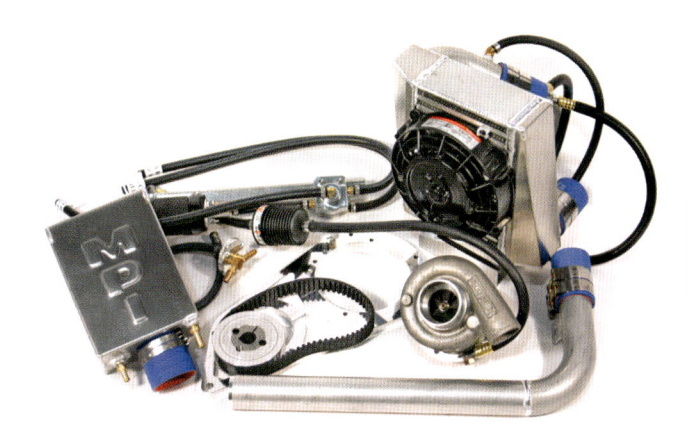

A 1999–2005 GM Hydra-Matic 5L40/50 automatic transmission. Supercharging a powerplant will massively increase stress on the transmission by significantly amplifying torque. A strong stock automatic transmission may be okay with low-boost supercharging if you are able to foil boost during shifts. One way to do this is to electronically open a bypass valve to foil boost during the shift, as Toyota Racing Development accomplished in its Eaton-based supercharging system for the 3.0-liter V-6 Toyota 1MZ-FE by using the built-in bypass within the supercharger assembly. Manual transmissions are often okay unless you're running insane levels of boost, but unless the driver is careful, many clutches will not live to enjoy the torque boost of supercharging for very long. *GM*

Mountain Performance supercharged Yamaha Rhino ATV delivers 52 rear-wheel horsepower, up from the stock Rhino's 22 rear-wheel horsepower (37 horsepower at the crank), which is approximately a 135 percent power boost. Mountain recommends premium 92- or 93-octane fuel, an electric water pump, a high-pressure radiator cap, and a gauge package for extreme use. *Mountain Performance*

CHOOSING THE ENGINE

47

Problematic Aspects of Supercharged Engines…

1. The ability to rely on a smaller-displacement powerplant comes with it the need to extract more power from a given displacement engine, which increases the thermal and mechanical loading on virtually all engine systems, from cooling and lubrication to pistons, rods, crankshaft, rod and main bearings, exhaust valves, and so on. Even using expensive super-duty parts, forced-induction engines tend to take more abuse, and in the best case boosted powerplants tend to have at least a slighter, shorter engine life than equivalent normal-charged engines. Check out the statistical Time Between Overhauls (TBO) for aviation piston engines, where reliability is critical: Actual TBO—determined by the inspection of an airframe and powerplant mechanic—is shorter for boosted aviation engines in general and, in particular, compared to forced-induction versions of the same powerplant.

2. Boosted engines typically require more maintenance than similar normal-charged engines. Even equipped with an engine oil cooler, the oil change interval of a boosted engine is shorter than normal because of higher oil thermal loading from the engine at high power levels. Motor oil for boosted engines can be more expensive, as many engine builders and manufacturers recommend or require fully synthetic oil, which has better stability and resistance to oxidation in a hot engine. Underhood temperatures of a supercharged engine tend to be at least a little higher, which can degrade plastic and rubber components.

3. Hot rodding projects built around very small boosted engines with very high specific power can encounter unusual design problems related to the engine's extreme dynamic range that increase the complexity and expense of the engine systems. An example would be the need, in some cases, for staged multiple fuel injectors per cylinder. This solution could be required because of the need to balance the requirement for injectors big enough to supply sufficient fuel for rich best torque at extreme levels of peak power and the requirement for injectors small enough to permit a sufficiently long injection pulse width at idle for excellent repeatability and fine granularity of adjustment to achieve a high-quality idle. Staging injectors normally requires unusually sophisticated engine management electronics, or an auxiliary injector electronic controller. In general, very high output boosted engines will require complex, sophisticated, expensive engine electronics.

4. Boost pressure raises the effective compression ratio of an engine, which is the ratio of the charge mass volume at ambient pressure versus the clearance volume of the combustion chamber. This tends to increase the octane number requirement (ONR) of the powerplant. Preventing engine damage from spark knock thus typically requires some combination of higher octane fuel, specific countermeasures to lower engine ONR such as high-efficiency intercoolers or a reduced static compression ratio, and engine management tricks such as boost-based ignition retard strategies combined with aggressive fuel enrichment to cool combustion during boost. Any engine without intercooling and more than 2- to 3-psi boost will require better fuel or special tuning to prevent detonation (which can add expense and hurt drivability, power, and fuel economy). Because virtually all forced-induction street engines are knock-limited in terms of maximum boost, these engines are never designed to run on regular-octane fuel—though modern factory engines with knock sensors can tolerate misfueling at the cost of the computer aggressively retarding ignition timing to fight knock.

For years Honda's S2000 had the highest specific power of any non-supercharged automotive production engine in history. With the ability to handle the FAR greater mechanical loading of a 9,000 rpm redline, the powerplant has no trouble handling the slightly greater additional cylinder pressure of an intercooled blower conversion kit like this Vortech. Keep in mind that most of the additional combustion pressure of a supercharger occurs after peak cylinder pressure, deeper into the power stroke. *Vortech*

Yamaha Phazer stage I snowmobiles with Mountain Performance blower kit 10-11 psi boost increases power from 137.5 to 231.1 horsepower. *Mountain Performance*

5. The torque curve of centrifugal-supercharged engines can be peaky, with tricky or even unpleasant drivability. With no torque-enhancing boost available at all below a threshold engine rpm, an engine built with low static compression as an anti-knock countermeasure for high-boost operation may have awful low-end torque in the normal-charged operating range below the boost threshold. Once boost begins to build, particularly on maximum-effort racing or speed-record engines with large centrifugal superchargers configured to deliver high levels of boost pressure, the exponential nature of the centrifugal compressor's boost delivery can produce extremely large and rapid torque gains at mid- and upper-range engine speeds.

THE EXTREME EVOLUTION OF GM'S BOOSTED 2.0-LITER ECOTEC

What does it take to convert a mild-mannered stock engine into a high-boost terror?

It is hard to find a more interesting scenario than GM's methodical approach to boosting the 2.0-liter Ecotec four-cylinder powerplant for drag racing and speed-record trials. Using gasoline and methanol, engineers and racers at General Motors and GM Racing incrementally hot rodded the Ecotec through every possible stage of horsepower and torque increase, from stock to the far outer reaches of hot rodding hell. This effort is indicative of the sorts of tricks required to make an engine live as you boost it to insane limits.

The Ecotec arrived in Y2K in some models of Saturn automobiles as a 140-horse, normal-charged powerplant. Within a few years, GM offered the 1.8-2.0-2.2-liter engine in street versions of cars and SUVs around the world from Pontiac to Saab, ranging from normal-charged 140- horsepower versions seen in garden-variety GM vehicles, to bigger displacement, normally charged engines with 15 to 25 percent more power, to a 205-horsepower supercharged Chevy Cobalt, to a 260-horse turbocharged version in the Pontiac Solstice GXP. GM eventually began marketing Stage 1 and Stage 2 upgrade kits for supercharged engines that boosted power to 235 horsepower and 205 pound-feet, or to 241 horsepower and 218 pound-feet.

Starting in 2001, GM Racing developed the Ecotec for an all-out crash drag racing program that eventually boosted power to nearly 1,400 horsepower, an order-of-magnitude increase.

As raw material, the Ecotec was reasonably impressive. Although the original iteration of the aluminum-block powerplant was not boosted, it was "protected" for future forced induction (as well as gasoline direct injection and variable cam phasing). It was built to be strong, with features such as six-fastener main caps (four studs plus cross-bolting) integrated into a die-cast girdle structure and buttressed by a structural aluminum oil pan. The semi-floating block deck was designed with pressed-in, cast-iron cylinder sleeves. The block was manufactured with lost-foam casting and included oil gallery passages machine-able for piston-cooling oil jets ("oil squirters") and a provision for the installation of an oil cooler. GM's design employed extra-thick main bearings to resist the differential expansion of the nodular iron crankshaft and aluminum block. Eventually, based on lessons learned from the racing effort, GM would enlarge the block bulkheads that act as attachment points for the main bearing caps, as well as the bore walls. This "Gen II" version of the Ecotec was used in the Pontiac Solstice GXP's 2.4L, 260-horsepower factory turbo package.

Bob Norwood swapped a high-performance Chevy LT1 into his personal Jaguar XJ6 and then bolted on a Vortech LT1 centrifugal supercharger kit originally designed for the F-Body Firebird. The wonderful thing about Chevrolet V-8s of almost any vintage is that there is a tremendous amount of performance gear available off the shelf to do almost anything.

CHOOSING THE ENGINE

49

Most people consider closed-deck engines of the sort found in traditional American iron-block engines to be stronger than the open-deck engines of a design like the Ecotec. Though the Ecotec used a modified open deck, the block deck was considered very strong. The stock composition head gasket that rode on the open deck was, well, stock, and theoretically not designed to seal at super-duty levels of cylinder pressure. The stock normal-charged Ecotec used high-silicon, cast pistons and relatively wimpy powder-metal connecting rods, which in theory would not be appropriate for a boosted factory powerplant. You never see ordinary cast pistons on a factory supercharged engine, but you do sometimes find boosted factory engines using pressure-cast or hypereutectic high-silicon pistons (which have fewer issues with thermal expansion and require less piston-cylinder clearance than forgings). No cast piston can survive anything more than superficial spark knock, but serious detonation will kill forged pistons fairly quickly as well. You virtually never find anything less than forged rods in a seriously boosted factory powerplant. In 2001, GM personnel said they were interchangeably using both power-metal rods and forged rods in various versions of the Ecotec. They assured me that the power-metal rods were just as strong, but it is interesting to note that the Solstice GXP Turbo was equipped exclusively with forged connecting rods. Obviously upgrading the pistons, rings, and rods for a boosted version of an engine is a trivial change on the engine assembly line.

With the goal of building an 800-horse, 10,000-rpm Ecotec powerplant that could survive 20 to 40 drag runs at 800 horsepower, a GM Racing team working in an advanced southern California skunkworks set about to find the limits of the brand-new Ecotec. They progressively added more and more nitrous through the powerplant on a dyno until something broke. They then repaired the engine with stronger parts (and sent the damaged pieces to a lab for forensic analysis), and pushing on until the next weakest link died and went to hell. When the engine's intake and exhaust systems became too constipated to make more power, the team would abandon nitrous and switch exclusively to turbo-supercharging as the power-adder, constructing new intake and exhaust plumbing.

With a racing turbocharger system in place, they would push on, replacing destroyed parts and removing bottlenecks until they made at least 800 horsepower. Engineers began making bets about what was going to break first as the GM Racing team geared up to begin breaking engines.

GM's team set up a stock Ecotec on a Hienen-Freud water-brake engine dyno and wired the powerplant for engine management using a DFI/Accel programmable system that controlled fuel, spark, and a cold spray of nitrous and enrichment fuel entering the induction system from a single point near the throttle body, delivered by a three-stage nitrous system. With a crew standing by with fire extinguishers, GM Racing began a rigorous series of tests. They would certify that the Ecotec had survived a given level of power if and only if the engine had lived through a set of 8 to 10 full-power dyno "sprints" from peak torque to maximum power in rapid 50-rpm steps. Each test concluded with at least six seconds at full power—a total of at least 20 seconds of an engine-raping flog-per-dyno run.

The stock-block Ecotec—running premium fuel, a custom free-flow exhaust, and no accessories but the

GM Racing's flogged 2003 2.0-liter turbo Ecotec was good for 1,200-horsepower drag passes and 700 to 800 horsepower land-speed record attempts. The engine was designed from day one to be strong enough for forced induction, but all things are relative. What was left here was a hollowed-out block with massive pressed-in steel sleeves embedded in a layer of epoxy and a reinforced cylinder head casting. Both turbocharged and supercharged versions of the Ecotec have found their way into production GM street cars. GM Media Archive

In the late 1990s, Norwood Autocraft installed this centrifugal kit on a C5 Corvette, which has very little space for power-adders. The advent of efficient Eaton superchargers that work fine without a wet mixture, combined with more recent blower-in-manifold air-water intercooling systems, made it relatively simple to supercharge an LS Corvette.

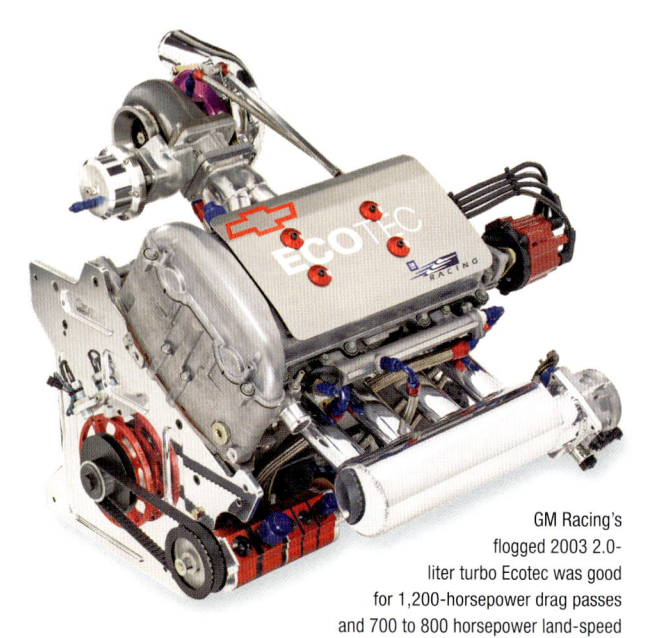

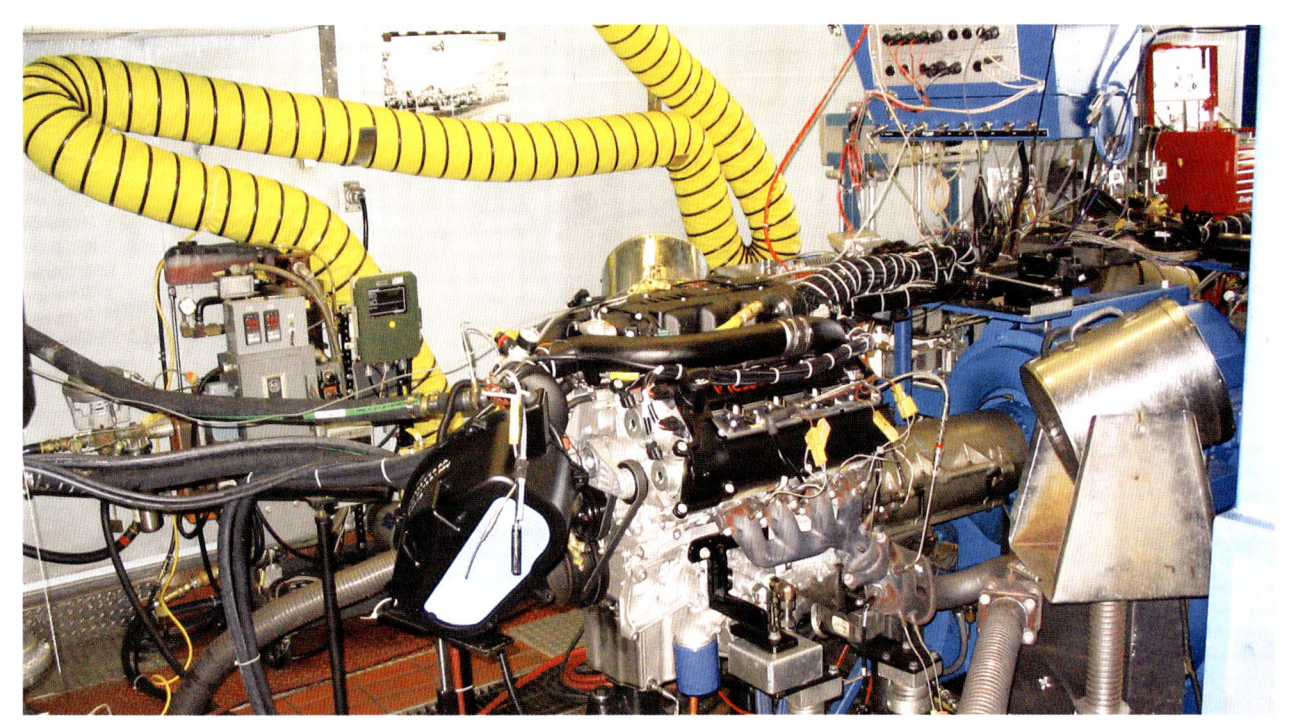

Dyno-testing the supercharged and liquid-intercooled 4.4-liter Cadillac V-8. All 4.4-liter Cadillacs were supercharged. Cadillac decreased the bore size of the 4.6-liter engine to increase block strength to augment the margin of safety during boost. *General Motors*

alternator—immediately ripped off a 168-horsepower baseline run without nitrous (up from the stock advertised 140 horsepower). Boosted with nitrous, the engine survived happily at 200, 225, and 250 horsepower—at which point the Ecotec was making 80 percent more power than stock.

The bet at GM Racing was still that the first thing to fail would be the head gasket. Not so. As the Ecotec pushed through 283 horsepower at 4,400 rpm (twice stock power as installed in early USA-spec cars), all four rods failed simultaneously and smashed though the side of the block, totaling the engine. Forensic analysis subsequently revealed a mid-beam compression fracture of all four powder-metal connecting rods. This was *not* a high-rpm stretch failure, *not* a fastener failure, and *not* a lubrication failure. And all the rod bearings, wrist pins, and ring packs checked out fine.

News You Can Use

What's the conclusion? With proper engine management, premium fuel, and good engine cooling, you can figure conservatively on boosting a healthy, modern engine at least 50 percent above stock power without killing anything right away. The Ecotec's stock components tolerated a 110-horsepower nitrous boost from the stock 140-horsepower output to 250 horsepower—an 80 percent increase—without incident. The rods failed when GM pushed output to 200 percent of stock. Of course, without upgraded components any increase in maximum power can be expected to shorten the life of a stock engine.

Starting over again with a brand-new engine, GM Racing installed a package of parts typical of what any serious performance enthusiast or racer would use when taking the trouble to open the engine to upgrade the connecting rods: Super-duty X-beam Crower rods, 10:1 JE forged pistons with thicker (4.5 millimeter versus 3.0 millimeter) top ring lands, and moly ring packs.

The 10-to-1 pistons are about as high as you'd normally see on any gasoline-fuel forced-induction engine, and much higher than ever found on older boosted engines from the 1970s and 1980s (the 1976 930 Porsche Turbo ran less than 6.5:1!), but modern four-valve pentroof engines running street premium fuel are knock-resistant enough to run 10- to 15-psi boost with 93 octane premium fuel and excellent engine management. GM, in its testing, was running super-high-octane racing fuel. The GM team also installed larger fuel injectors, and then continued to lean on the engine.

With the new parts installed, and before anything else could break, the engine ran out of breathing room on the exhaust side at 350 horsepower. Keep in mind that in terms of engine gas flow, nitrous produces an extremely high ratio of products to reactants, constipating the exhaust long before the intake. The stock exhaust manifold became so restrictive at 350 horsepower that without careful tuning, more nitrous would actually make less power. "We actually made 370 to 375 horsepower on nitrous," said team leader Stephen Bothwell, "but the engine was really pissed off."

So far, the head gasket had not failed.

At this point, the GM team set out to build a serious forced-induction motor. "The stock crankshaft would've clearly worked through 400 horsepower—maybe a short while at 500 horsepower—before it cracked," said Bothwell. In fact, given the ability of most good forged crankshafts to live when boosted—intermittently—to three times stock power, it is unusual for boosted street engines to run a custom crankshaft.

But with loftier performance goals in mind than 400 to 500 horsepower at stock redline, Bothwell put Crower Cams and Equipment to work building a de-stroked, super-duty, forged billet crankshaft with the durability to withstand radically serious horsepower numbers. Of course, engine builders working with common performance engines like the Chevy small-block V-8 will have access to off-the-shelf super-duty forged cranks at reasonable prices, which is certainly the way to go if you're building a high-boost competition or street engine from scratch. When GM released the factory Pontiac Solstice GXP turbo, it was equipped with a factory steel crankshaft.

Meanwhile, although the Ecotec's scroll-type plastic intake manifold was deemed capable of flowing enough air for at least 500 horsepower (given enough boost!), Bothwell decided this was the time for something better.

Because larger intake runners won't usually help much on a supercharged engine unless the head ports are enlarged, most people design street supercharger conversions around stock manifolds, often using larger throttle bodies. An oversized throttle body can never hurt peak power, but it can screw up drivability if a huge throttle body has much more airflow capacity than the engine can ever use. The throttle will be really twitchy at small throttle angles and then completely ineffective at modulating power delivery in higher ranges of throttle opening. A larger intake plenum can add power at high rpm or perhaps reduce the amount of boost that's required to pack a certain amount of air in the engine; sometimes small street plenums are removed with a band saw, to be replaced with a larger custom plenum built from thick aluminum pipe and welded to the stock intake runners. Such a manifold would be illegal from an emissions point of view, but if there is no aftermarket street-legal upgrade manifold available, extrude-honing or otherwise modifying the stock manifold can be a good option. Well, unless the stock manifold is made of plastic. Like the Ecotec's.

GM Racing fabricated a straight-port aluminum "sheet metal" manifold with a high-volume plenum capable of flowing more than 1,000 horsepower worth of air at 35- to 50-psi boost and pilfered a huge LS1 Corvette throttle body from Chevrolet to regulate airflow.

On the exhaust side, GM Racing trashed the stock cast-iron exhaust manifold and fabricated an equal-length, stainless-steel tube header assembly with thick stainless flanges to collect exhaust pulses. Five years down the line, high-output factory-boosted versions of the Ecotec would be equipped with stainless-steel exhaust headers.

The super-duty 8.0-liter Dodge Ram was fully capable of handling a supercharger conversion and the Carroll Supercharging Company was more than happy to provide the weapons of mass destruction in the form of 8- and 12-psi centrifugal supercharger kits. Stage 1 and 2 kits amped up the stock V-10's 310-horsepower output to 424 or 475 horsepower, with 12- or 16-hour installation times, and a Stage 3 kit was good for 500 horsepower but required an estimated 40 hours to install! Carroll kits included a SuperPumper electronic fuel pump controller that regulated rail pressure from 20- to 100-psi in response to manifold pressure. *Carroll's Superchargers*

Meanwhile, GM Racing fabricated a custom intercooler unit using an air-water design that also was capable of acting as a dry ice heat sink.

Even if you ran the supercharger at a very high pressure ratio, in order to make truly prodigious power, the Ecotec engine would still need a LOT of power pulses per minute and Godlike volumetric efficiency. In practical terms, on a maximum-effort engine with a final minimum power goal of 500–600 percent of stock, this cannot be done with boost alone. For one thing, by definition, it's not "maximum effort" if you're leaving power on the table with suboptimal engine airflow. What's more, there are unfortunate second-order inefficiencies related to intake manifold heat and exhaust manifold back pressure that degrade maximum power and drivability if you're trying to do it all with "excessive" boost, particularly on a drag car. Just because you're changing the intake manifold pressure doesn't mean the laws of gas flow downstream of the compressor no longer apply. The engine itself must allow the maximum possible airflow under boost at extremely high rpm.

To increase both the intake and exhaust flow rates for a 10,000 rpm powerplant, GM ported the stock cylinder heads and installed the largest possible narrow-stem stainless-steel valves and small-diameter valve guides. In order to put maximum valve lift over .460 on both intake and exhaust, GM would eventually remove the valve stem oil seals in order to keep huge-lift cams from smacking the valve retainers into the seals. Both intake and exhaust duration were slightly over

221 degrees, but overlap was kept conservative to keep the supercharger from blowing air-fuel mixture straight through the combustion chambers.

GM Racing deployed a proprietary solution to eliminate valve float at high speed, but we can assume that this included strong valve springs given the high rpm target and the need to fight the tendency of boost pressure in the intake manifold to push open the intake valves. Any supercharger conversion engine—stock cams or not, stock redline or not—running much more than one atmosphere of boost will need stronger valve springs to avoid valve float at high boost and high rpm. When GM released the 260-horsepower turbo Ecotec used in the Solstice GXP, the company also upgraded the valvetrain to include sodium-filled exhaust valves.

To prevent the Ecotec head from lifting under extreme cylinder pressure, GM equipped the boosted powerplant with upgraded engine fasteners. Head studs (and main studs, which the Ecotec already had) are a common modification for high-output street supercharger and turbo conversions and race engines, but GM went one step further with special oversized head studs that required drilling the head and block to a larger size, then tapping the block for the larger studs. GM Racing installed a stock Ecotec head gasket, a good, modern-composition piece with wire rings embedded in the fire ring around each cylinder.

GM Racing installed an oil cooler and multi-stage pump cluster equipped with a mechanical fuel pump and multi-stage dry-sump oiling system that could create a partial vacuum in the crankshaft. The oil pump on most engines, if healthy, is fully capable of providing the relatively modest amount of oil required to lubricate a supercharger or turbo (if required); GM wanted the power gains available from reducing the aerodynamic drag on the crankshaft, rods, and the bottoms of the pistons from flying oil and windage in the crankcase, and it wanted a super-high volume mechanical fuel pump available to meet the requirements of methanol fueling.

The Ecotec immediately cranked out 350 horsepower at 7,000 rpm at 2-psi boost. With additional boost it rapidly closed in on 450 horsepower with no failures, using the tuning technique of gently approaching rich best torque (RBT) from the rich side based on air-fuel ratio data from a wideband O_2 sensor.

At 450 horsepower and 8-psi boost, the Ecotec began blowing head gaskets, mainly in the outboard regions of cylinders one and four, at the ends of the block. A high-output supercharger conversion without improved head fasteners would definitely be at risk for encountering cylinder head lifting no later than 200 percent normal-charged power and torque, but with super-duty head studs already installed, head lifting should not have been a factor.

Based on problems sometimes seen in boosted, open-deck Honda powerplants, some GM Racing personnel were concerned that there might be a core shift occurring in the block, which can literally drop floating cylinders away from the head-block interface when the supporting internal engine main bulkheads and crank support structure warp under the stress of much higher-than-stock cylinder pressures and rpm.

This turned out not to be the case. GM Racing lost some time converting several Ecotec blocks to a closed deck, welding in a precisely shaped section of billet aluminum, similar to the "block-guards" still used on some boosted Hondas. The aluminum piece is designed to precisely fill the narrow, open water jacket surrounding the cylinders like a precise piece in a jigsaw puzzle, followed by resurfacing the welded deck. Despite multiple tries, the closed desk conversion consistently resulted in warped cylinder bores after a single cycle of thermal expansion and cool-down.

GM Racing eventually decided that the problem causing the blown gaskets was cylinder head flexing. For the time being the group solved the gasket-blowing problem by installing jam studs machined to screw into the upper head structure and through the water jacket. These studs reinforced weak sectors of the outboard combustion chambers that would flex and lift off the block surface under severe combustion pressures, permitting the stock Ecotec gasket to blow out. At this point the engine happily made 500 horsepower. GM Racing's modifications eventually fed back into design changes to the Ecotec cylinder head to improve the strength and rigidity of the outer regions of the end combustion chambers.

A hot rod Integra GSR engine with Jackson Racing supercharger system. The Integra GSR with twin-cam VTEC architecture was the hero of the sport compact set in the early years of the new millennium, and Jackson's high-boost system included a Roots-type supercharger with three different boost pulleys designed to deliver 6-, 8-, or 11-psi boost, a Hondata S300 Honda ECU reprogrammed to handle up to 12-psi boost, and RC 440cc injectors. *Jackson Racing*

As power moved upward toward 600 horsepower (roughly four times stock power!), the entire blockhead interface began leaking, indicating that the head was starting to "flutter" everywhere from extreme combustion pressures. At this point the GM team O-ringed the head with diamond-cut, stainless-steel, continuous wire-type rings that pressed into a groove cut around each combustion chamber in the head. This solution was designed to produce tremendous clamping force against a special annealed-copper head gasket. Many engines, at considerably less cylinder pressure than four times stock power, require either steel-shim head gaskets, O-ringing of the fire-ring area in the head or block combined with copper head gaskets, individual nitrogen-filled fire-ring gaskets (which expand with heat to increase the effective clamping pressure in the fire-ring area), or similar gasket-blowing countermeasures. On the other hand, it is often surprising how well stock-composition head gaskets will work combined with wire O-rings and improved head fasteners.

At 600 horsepower, the extreme torque and high crank speed began distorting and flexing the piston wrist pins, which would eventually tear out the pin towers below the wrist pins. Simultaneously, the moly ring packs began failing. GM Racing converted to thicker H11 wrist pins and changed over to Total Seal rings—parts in the realm of "as good as it gets." At this point, the modified Ecotec was consistently capable of 650 horsepower at 19 pounds of boost and 8,500 rpm.

Between 650 and 800 horsepower on the Ecotec drag engine project, GM Racing encountered a whole new world of problems. Rings that sealed well at 650 horsepower failed to seal with acceptable blowby as power approached 700. Pistons scuffed on cylinders, wrist pins encountered binding problems, and rod bearings began to go away. Spark plugs needed more power to ignite the super-dense mixtures of 6 horsepower per cubic inch, which required new, better coils. Anti-detonation countermeasures became critical, requiring super-cold spark plugs that were simply not manufactured in a size that would fit the Ecotec, necessitating machining the plug bosses in the Ecotec heads to accept 3/4-inch thread-length spark plugs, which were available in colder ranges. With better coils, colder plugs, and methanol fuel, the stock-block Ecotec managed 750 horsepower at 9,000 rpm: more than five times stock power!

Even with detonation under full control, when pushing above 750 horsepower the thin-wall stock iron cylinder sleeves began to warp and go out-of-round, unable to handle the extreme combustion pressures and thermal expansion. Piston-cylinder scuffing became a problem. By this time there was so much fuel going into the cylinders that the GM team began worrying about hydro-locking cylinders with the high volume of noncompressible fuel, should there be a misfire.

In order to achieve 800 reliable horsepower, GM had to gut the stock cylinder sleeves and aluminum core support structure, installing super-thick, full-floating, custom bottom-flanged steel cylinder sleeves that pressed into receiver bores machined into the floor of the water jacket above the crankshaft. The new sleeves were reinforced by a layer of epoxy compound surrounding the lower cylinder sleeves, which effectively raised the floor of the water jacket around the base of the cylinders. As an anti-scuff countermeasure, GM Racing increased the new cylinder bores by 0.001 inch and shot-peened the piston skirts to help retain oil.

The final package enabled GM Racing to crank up the power to much higher levels in the 1,200-plus horsepower range that would enable the engine to remain competitive in glamour-class four-wheel-drive drag racing as competition pushed power above 1,000 horsepower in future years. Three years later, GM decreased the drag engine to 700 horsepower for much longer competition runs at the land-speed record trials at Bonneville. The company test cycled the Bonneville engines to peak power in three-minute cycles for nearly an hour in testing before proceeding to set several new land speed records in four vehicles.

BOTTOM LINE
Engine Health

A supercharger conversion will only magnify symptoms of a sick or worn engine. It should go without saying, but it is critical that any candidate for a forced-induction conversion be verified not just as healthy, but very healthy lest the stresses of supercharging accelerate an engine's downfall.

Chevy 502 Rat with Vortech supercharger kit. This is an evil system (in a good way), but keep in mind that big-block, big-bore engines are more susceptible to detonation than smaller engines because the additional flame travel distance slows the total time of combustion enough that there is more time for detonation before combustion can complete normally.

ID Software, which popularized "first-person-shooter" computer games, sponsored the Doom Norwood Autocraft Porsche racer, which was designed with a hybrid monocoque spaceframe that housed a flipped transaxle that converted the powerplant from a rear-engine to mid-engine configuration. The Porsche 3.8-liter flat-six was boosted with a cogged Vortech centrifugal supercharger that sucked massive quantities of air through a giant scoop at the center of the vehicle to deliver nearly 20-psi boost.

These days, with extremely good motor oils, port fuel injection under computer control, and unleaded fuel, engines can last an extremely long time (more than 200,000 miles) without significant wear. Nevertheless, if a candidate engine for a supercharger conversion has more than 30,000 miles, you should verify the health of internal engine systems, including cylinder head and valves, pistons and rings, cylinder bores, and the crankshaft assembly. Good health means excellent compression that's close to the ideal specification, and it means cylinder leakdown at less than 6 percent. Anything less than 10 percent leakdown is usually considered acceptable on a factory engine, but not for a supercharger conversion.

Because an engine can have decent compression but poor leakdown, you need to test both. Both tests involve installing special gauged fittings in the spark plug holes; the compression test measures accumulated pressure as the engine cranks with the ignition disconnected, while the leakdown test involves sequentially moving each piston to top dead center on the compression stroke and adding compressed air while observing two gauges that display the difference between the source pressure and pressure in the cylinder after any leaking effects are factored in. Any competent hobbyist can perform compression and leakdown tests, and many repair shops will perform such tests for a reasonable price (usually in the $50 to $100 range).

If you're worried about internal engine wear, there are special labs that can analyze engine oil for unusual amounts of various metals in the oil without even opening the engine. Superchargers—even ones that require an external source of lubrication—do not require super-stock oil pressure or volume. But engine oil pressure should meet stock specifications, the testing of which, these days, usually means attaching a test gauge in place of the stock oil pressure sending unit, as few vehicles have enumerated oil pressure gauges anymore.

It is surprisingly difficult to do a truly great engine rebuild, which is why a known-healthy used factory stock motor is often preferable to a rebuilt engine. It's also why a factory performance crate motor—typically available with a selection of blower-ready super-duty internal parts—is probably better than what you can build yourself, even if you know what you're doing. Engineering experts at GM specifically claim that even wizard aftermarket engine builders cannot equal factory quality, and they have evidence to back up this opinion.

These days, for example, factory engine-building robots deploy DC electric gang drivers and "torque to turn" controls that simultaneously tighten all the head fasteners on an engine at once to the correct torque, delivering perfectly even clamping force and improved head-block sealing that GM says is beyond the capability of even good professional engine builders. Today's factory-machined cylinders are bored and honed with a sophisticated stress plate torqued in place on the block to simulate the block warping that stress head fasteners impart to the block to make sure that cylinder machining will produce bores that are stretched perfectly round when the head is torqued in place.

Keep in mind that the cylinder head itself will warp when torqued in place (and not necessarily with perfect linearity). Except with the most common performance engines, it can be difficult for aftermarket machine shops to build or obtain stress plates that accurately simulate cylinder head give-and-take on clamp-down, resulting in less-than-round cylinders and increased blowby. Nonetheless, really round cylinders spell "power."

Difficult Engines

When it comes to the engine choice for a supercharger conversion, some engines present special problems.

Air-cooled engines tend to run hotter cylinder head temperatures than liquid-cooled engines, but can also generate colder temperatures, particularly in the case of aviation engines. Shock-cooling an air-cooled aircraft powerplant can warp heads and even cylinder barrels via uneven cooling in the freezing temperatures of high-altitude. This can happen if the pilot throttles back too much for a fast descent at a high rate of speed at little or no engine loading—and can compound the problem with sudden application of high power at lower altitude. Overheated combustion chambers can quickly lead to detonation and pre-ignition, either of which can kill an engine in a matter of seconds.

On the other hand, Porsche built a supercar using a turbo-supercharged version of the air-cooled 911 flat-six, and many people have successfully supercharged or turbocharged air-cooled VWs. Air-cooled aircraft are routinely turbocharged, and the FAA recently certified a Vortech-based centrifugal supercharger conversion for the 310-horsepower 550-cid Continental flat-six. In fact, Porsche converted and briefly marketed the automotive 911 flat-six powerplant for aviation use as the "Porsche Flugmotor." However, it can be difficult or impossible for aftermarket tuners to upgrade air-cooled cylinders or heads for improved cooling, and it's worth noting that Porsche actually converted the cylinder heads of some super-high output engines to liquid cooling for some high-pressure turbo applications. Eventually, Porsche phased out the old air-cooled flat-six automotive powerplant in favor of a 100-percent liquid-cooled, flat-six powerplant.

Boosted air-cooled engines under heavy load will generally require richer-than-normal air-fuel mixtures to cool combustion, so the brake-specific fuel consumption of a boosted air-cooled powerplant tends to be higher. Beyond this, the oil temperatures of air-cooled engines tend to be hotter than liquid-cooled powerplants even when normal-charged. Because it is critical that oil temperature remain within specifications, high-efficiency engine oil coolers are critical on some air-cooled engines with supercharging.

Street engines with a lot of static compression in the 9.5–10 and above range can be a challenge to supercharge because positive manifold pressure raises the effective compression ratio and, therefore, the absolute compression pressure of the engine. To avoid catastrophic engine damage when supercharging a high-compression powerplant, detonation must be prevented using some combination of (1) higher octane fuel; (2) reduced combustion temperatures; (3) special engine management countermeasures such as fuel-cooling, retarded ignition timing, or water injection; (4) diminished maximum boost pressures; (5) intercooling; or (6) reducing static compression ratio via internal engine changes. Competition engines like GM Racing's Ecotec drag-race and Bonneville engines, running three or four atmospheres of boost pressure, have effectively used alcohol fuels, with their high-octane ratings and evaporative cooling effects.

Thirty years ago, forced-induction experts used the rule of thumb that each pound of supercharger boost raised an engine's octane number requirement (ONR) by one point. Keep in mind, those were the bad old days of single-carbureted engines with ubiquitous mixture distribution problems and mechanical ignition-timing systems. If such an engine required 87 octane unleaded regular fuel in normal-charged stock form, the rule said that 8 psi of boost would require 95-octane leaded premium, which was unavailable in America after the lead phase-out was complete in 1986. In those days experts recommended 8.5:1 as a maximum static compression ratio for a supercharged engine, and many ran less compression than that. Such low ratios caused sluggish off-idle performance before the boost kicked in.

ONR requirements changed with the advent of (1) modern four-valve pentroof combustion chambers; (2) smaller bore sizes requiring less flame travel during combustion; (3) port fuel injection; (4) ubiquitous installation of high-efficiency charge-cooling intercoolers on virtually all boosted engines; and (5) sophisticated computer-controlled engine management strategies. These factors dramatically increased the amount of boost pressure that's feasible with premium pump gasoline. My own 24-valve Toyota 3.0-liter V-6 project car with 10:1 compression proved capable of handling 15-psi boost without detonation, using 93-octane Texas street gasoline and programmable engine management controls.

Porsche 911 boosted with a Roots-type supercharger. Given the lack of intercooling and the hot-air intake, this is obviously not a high-boost package, but this supercharger is discharging compressed air upward, and systems with similar architecture from TPC Racing have incorporated inline water-cooled intercoolers into the air space above the engine, with a remote heat exchanger. As is always the case when you're making more than 4- to 5-psi boost, heat management is critical, particularly with an air-cooled engine.

Emission-compliant engines can be a challenge. To be street-legal, all late-model automotive engines and vehicles must comply with federal or state emissions requirements, but there are technical issues that can be difficult to overcome in the case of a supercharger conversion. Superchargers that increase combustion temperatures will tend to raise NOx levels. Fuel enrichment that provides combustion cooling to fight detonation will increase exhaust emissions, though usually only at wide-open throttle.

Some states require that a vehicle pass a tailpipe sniff test on a rolling road, plus an underhood inspection to verify that the original engine and emissions equipment are in place and that no untoward add-ons—such as a supercharger—are present. Obviously this can be an insurmountable obstacle even if the engine is perfectly compliant from an emissions point of view. There are specified procedures to get aftermarket supercharger kits approved for street use, but the expense of getting a vehicle through the federal test procedure (FTP) is simply prohibitive for most individuals, because the FTP was designed as a rigorous and expensive procedure conducted at a special testing laboratory with the goal of forcing the professional performance aftermarket to demonstrate that exhaust and crankcase emissions are not degraded from stock by performance modifications. The good news is that as of this writing, vehicles more than 30 years old are not usually required (even in California) to pass emissions testing (nor are diesels, electric vehicles, hybrids, motorcycles, or heavy vehicles over 14,001 pounds fueled by natural gas). This explains the popularity of old vehicles for hot rodding in California.

Increasingly, the newest late-model engines have been designed with engine-management systems (EMS) logic that makes it difficult or impossible to successfully modify the air-fuel ratio or ignition timing in ways that may be required to permit performance modifications—such as supercharging—without damaging the engine. In some cases this includes full-time, 100-percent closed-loop engine management in which O_2-sensor feedback gets factored into the injection air-fuel calculation under control of a target air-fuel ratio table. Some recent engine-management systems may be unhappy with anything higher than a couple pounds of boosted manifold pressure, and, even more serious, some engine-management systems will fight back with performance-killing countermeasures if the engine's slew rate (rate of acceleration) is higher than predetermined value representing the maximum plausible performance of the stock powerplant plus a small margin.

The bottom line these days is that there is a lot to be said for installing a supercharger kit or starting with a common performance engine in a supercharger conversion project. Many super-duty parts will be available and much will be known regarding pushing the envelope in terms of power, longevity, and engine management. In the case of performance cars like the Chevrolet Corvette, the aftermarket has decoded the engine-management system to the point that downloadable software like LS1-Edit can be used to modify essentially anything in the factory powertrain control module (PCM) calibration. For "off-highway" use, closed-loop air-fuel controls can be entirely deactivated.

CHOOSING THE ENGINE

Edelbrock's eForce supercharger system was designed to pump up the volume on the 2005–09 Ford Mustang using a Gen-6 TVS supercharger that delivered 469 street-legal horsepower with 5-psi boost (and as much as 70 to 800 horsepower for off-road competition). The street blower kit included the supercharger/manifold assembly, air inlet with 85 millimeter throttle body, upgraded fuel injectors, air-to-water intercooler, spark plugs, coil covers, handheld flash programmer to properly tune the factory ECU for the added power, and an optional three-year/36,000-mile warranty. *Edelbrock*

Two-Stroke Engines

These can be supercharged, but it's tricky. Two-stroke performance is extremely sensitive to the design of the exhaust system. Improvised exhaust designs (including "passive" exhaust systems without expansion chambers) can destroy exhaust resonances, greatly degrading two-stroke performance. For good performance the expansion chamber must be left in place. Careful R&D would test the effect of various modifications to maintain beneficial exhaust resonation effects.

Head-Block Sealing

As GM found out with the Ecotec racing project, with conventional engines at certain power levels you need to beef up stock-type sealing between the block and head or the head gaskets will blow out at high-boost or any time the engine knocks under boost. Knock produces pressure spikes that challenge any stock-type head-block sealing strategy and quickly defeat even the best super-duty solutions.

Head sealing can be such a serious problem on super-high-output engines that some racing engine manufacturers have implemented extreme measures. The old Offy-Drake Indy engine was designed with the cylinder sleeves integral to the cylinder head so that no gasket existed in the combustion chamber that could blow. Access to the combustion chamber in this engine was through the cylinder bores, which detached from the block with the head. In other cases, racers have actually gone to the extreme of *welding* the head to the block. These welds would need to be ground away to remove the cylinder head.

The most important aspect of head-block sealing is the strength of the fasteners holding down the head. If the head lifts under high-combustion pressure, no gasket system can seal it. Beyond that, the ability of the gasket material to resist blowing out is important, with solid-metal gaskets having much greater strength than organic gaskets with metal reinforcing. Unfortunately, copper and steel gaskets have a much greater tendency to leak water from the cooling jacket, and therefore require extremely flat deck surfaces. This necessitates special head-milling techniques that eliminate even the normal machining marks left behind by a cylinder mill or belt-sanding device.

If you pump up the boost enough, you will probably want to O-ring the cylinders of a boosted engine. O-ringing consists of machining a shallow groove into the fire-ring area of the block or head around each cylinder bore and then installing gapless machined-steel rings or steel wire into the groove (with the ends sanded flat using a special tool designed to produce a virtually nonexistent end gap). The correct O-ring is slightly tall for the groove and therefore bites hard into the head gasket when the head is torqued.

In extremely high-output powerplants, engine builders have sometimes used two concentric O-rings around each bore. Where adjacent cylinder sleeves are siamesed together, the O-ring groove may form a "figure-8" around two cylinders, with a single long piece of wire sealing both bores. O-ringing serves the purpose of providing extremely high clamping pressure in the area of the wire, creating a strong combustion chamber seal. Perhaps more important, by biting deeply into the gasket (and thus deforming it) in such a way as to provide a physical interlock between the O-ring and the gasket, the O-rings provide an immovable barrier that physically prevents the head gasket from pushing sideways and blowing out of the head-block interface.

If the head has never been off a healthy factory-boosted engine, the stock, layered gasket will often be "glued" to both the block and head to the extent that its gasket tears apart internally before the head will come off either deck surface. The glued gasket and strong head fasteners will usually prevent the head from lifting until the combustion pressures are quite high (or until the engine starts knocking). Once you've replaced the stock gasket, however, my experience is that without additional measures it will blow more easily because the head is no longer "glued" to the block.

Compression Ratio

Raising compression increases the thermal efficiency of combustion and increases the expansion ratio as well. Except for the fact that the higher heat of increased compression increases NOx emissions in the exhaust, more static compression is a good thing for several reasons, one of which is that it gives an engine the crisp, torquey feel all driving enthusiasts like off-idle. Unfortunately, higher static compression and the added combustion pressure of supercharger boost increase the likelihood of the charge mixture auto-igniting before normal combustion smoothly burns its way through the air-fuel mixture. Detonation is precisely what higher-octane fuel helps prevent. But if you can't run higher octane fuel, and none of the other anti-knock countermeasures mentioned above are sufficient, there is no choice but to lower compression. The right way to lower compression is to increase the combustion chamber volume by installing new pistons with a lower crown. Piston manufacturers like Wiseco, JE, Venolia, and others can punch a few numbers in a computer and build custom pistons designed to achieve the exact compression ratio you want on your engine.

Some people have machined pockets in the stock pistons to reduce the compression, or even machined the combustion chambers to add to the clearance volume. Neither is a good idea because this weakens the piston crown or the combustion chamber, which reduces their strength. New custom pistons can be surprisingly affordable (in the case of some luxury performance cars, significantly cheaper than factory stock pistons). If you absolutely can't afford custom pistons, you should consider whether you may be in over your head with your power-adder conversion project. If the stock pistons have thick crowns, or you only need to remove a tiny bit of compression, machining the piston crown can be viable—if you know what you're doing and don't touch the squish ring area.

All modern overhead-valve and overhead-cam pistons and combustion chambers are designed with flat "squish rings" around the circumference of the piston and combustion chamber surface opposite it such that when pistons are at top dead center, the two ring surfaces are virtually touching. As a piston nears top dead center, the proximity of the two squish rings forces the charge mixture toward the center of the combustion chamber, violently mixing and churning the burning air-fuel mixture. This greatly decreases the likelihood of any homogeneous "end gas" pockets remaining that might explode as combustion temperatures and pressures increase in normal combustion. *It is critical that any compression-lowering strategy not mess with the squish ring.* Adverse changes to the squish ring may result from thicker head gaskets, machined stock pistons, shorter-than-stock connecting rods, relocated wrist pins, or shorter-than-stock pistons. Don't do it.

Another questionable procedure is installing thicker-than-stock head gaskets. If you are already buying copper head gaskets for other reasons, the manufacturer will ask you what thickness you want, and it might be tempting to grasp for thicker gaskets as the solution to lowering compression. The trouble is, a thicker head gasket could adversely change the geometry of the head-block interface on the intake manifold of a Vee-type engine. It could also subtly alter cam timing on an overhead-cam engine. Worst of all it will degrade the "squish" effect in the combustion chambers (which can be a more powerful pro-knock factor than a little more compression).

Cylinder Head Preparation

In a forced-induction conversion, the head itself is one of the last areas that could need attention.

If all you are trying to do is pump up a supercharger-conversion engine's power and torque with stock engine internals, you almost definitely do not need to change anything about the cylinder head that affects airflow. Boost alone will do the job up to the limits of the physically weakest engine parts. Even if you've installed improved pistons and perhaps better rods, and the goal is to push the power envelope as far as possible within the limits of a super-stock street engine and reasonable supercharger boost (say 15 psi), you do not need to modify the cylinder head beyond beefing up the valve springs or perhaps installing sodium-filled or other super-duty exhaust valves.

Many aftermarket supercharger conversions retain the stock valves and live for a long time. On the other hand, GM installed sodium-filled valves in the 260-horse Pontiac Solstice, which was boosted 100 horsepower above the normal-charged base engine. If you want factory-type reliability, know that GM is not spending that money for better exhaust valves for no reason. What else is there to say?

To run much more than an atmosphere or so of boost in a supercharger conversion, you will probably need stronger valve springs. These will help keep boost pressure upstream of the intake valves from increasing the tendency of the valves to float at higher rpm. Overboosted factory engines (particularly turbocharged engines, which have tended to run more boost than factory-supercharged powerplants) are already equipped with better parts and will not usually run into trouble with valve springs until somewhat higher boost (say, 20 psi).

If you are trying to make astronomical levels of horsepower, you will need to have the engine making a lot of torque with high efficiency at high rpm. It takes a lot of high-efficiency "putts" per minute to make huge power. Although stuffing boost in an engine will increase torque and power across the rpm range, once a supercharger has spooled to full boost, the addition of a little more or a little less total boost does not change the *shape* of the engine's basic VE curve. Torque will fall off above the engine's maximum volumetric efficiency rpm just the way it did when it was normal-charged. True, boosting an engine tends to push up the peak torque rpm a little, but only a little. To make piles of power in a maximum-effort supercharging project, you are going to want to increase the engine's basic, normal-charged ability to breathe at higher rpm.

All the standard head flow tricks will work on a supercharged engine, including porting and polishing the runners, increasing the valve size, running more cam lift and duration, and installing valve springs that will keep the valves from floating at super-stock rpm. The exception is increasing the intake-exhaust valve overlap, which in a supercharged engine can defeat the whole purpose, as it allows the pressurized charge mixture to blow in the intake valve and escape right out the exhaust valve during overlap, to the degree that boost pressure is higher than exhaust back pressure. (Boost pressure being greater than exhaust back pressure will not happen some of the time on certain turbocharged engines but should *always* be the case with a mechanically supercharged powerplant.)

Optimizing an engine's high-speed volumetric efficiency can seriously degrade the engine's torque curve below the point at which boost kicks in. If an engine has variable cam phasing or variable valve timing and lift, maximum-effort supercharger conversions should only change the profile or phasing of the *high-speed* cam lobes, exactly as would be the case if the engine were not supercharged.

Block Preparation

If you are working with an iron-block powerplant with a closed-block deck, or a modern alloy performance block with closed deck, you should not need to modify the block at all for a supercharger conversion unless you are also increasing the redline (in which case you'll want the typical super-duty screamer upgrades like block girdles, crank studs, cross-bolted main caps, and so forth). If you want to work with a lightweight normal-charged powerplant with an open deck, you should choose an engine that has already been heavily hot rodded by experts or you will find yourself undertaking your own private R&D project. Honda engine builders know that some open-deck engines are subject to core-shift if you lean on them too hard, and there are off-the-shelf parts available to convert some blocks to a closed deck. The time to figure this out is before the block is damaged in the first place, because once the cylinders begin to move around, they won't want to stop, and the block is probably a write-off.

GM's Ecotec drag engine could not be converted to a closed deck, but it actually didn't need to be. When it was 800-plus horsepower time, GM Racing did eventually bore out the open deck and press massive steel cylinder sleeves into the floor of the block above the crank, pouring epoxy around the bases to add strength. At the time of this writing, resleeving has become the modern (but expensive!) solution for strengthening open-deck blocks—not just for 1,200-horse superfreaks but also for semi-pro racers and *Fast and Furious* street cars making power in the 500-plus horsepower range. Some cars purpose-built for short-duration drag racing are equipped with engines in which the block water jacket is completely filled with epoxy and cement. GM Racing tried and abandoned that tactic for the Ecotec engine.

Supercharger Pistons and Rings

Most stock pistons and rods will work fine to about 6-psi boost, though, of course, no automaker would ever sell a 6-psi boosted engine without better pistons and rods. Beyond 6 psi, it's anyone's guess for a particular engine. Unless you have GM's ability to waste blocks to find out when the pistons and rods fail, you'll need to plan on upgrading to forged pistons and rods as you push a supercharger-conversion engine that was previously normal-charged past half an atmosphere or so of boost. A 6-psi manifold pressure boost can typically increase peak torque by about 50 percent, with the rule of thumb being a 10 percent torque boost per 1-psi pressure increase.

Factory turbo and supercharged engines typically have some headroom to pump up the boost without immediately killing the stock rods and pistons. You can usually assume that a 50 percent torque increase is safe on a robust factory forced-induction engine. For example, assuming there is never detonation, a stock 2.0-liter 1991 MR2 Turbo, which made 200 horsepower and 200 pound-feet of torque at the stock 7.5-psi boost, will live a long time with the stock rods and pistons, even with boost pumped up enough to make at least 300 pound-feet of torque. GM Racing found out the hard way that the Ecotec destroyed its rods at twice stock power. But sometimes you get lucky; with stock rods and JE forged stroker pistons, my MR2 Turbo project car survived hundreds of dyno runs in the 400 to 550 horsepower range, two to three times stock power.

Chapter 4
Supercharger Architecture

There are at least a dozen distinct designs of superchargers. What they all have in common is that if the supercharger is sized such that the airflow capacity at an appropriate speed is greater than that of a particular engine in the required rpm range, the supercharger will force more charge air into the powerplant than it could ingest if normal-charged. This allows the engine to burn more fuel and make more power.

Supercharging systems fall within the general classes of (1) those driven mechanically by the engine via gears or belts; (2) those driven by an exhaust-gas turbine; (3) those driven by electric or hydraulic motors; and (4) pressure-wave superchargers (a strange fish-nor-fowl hybrid powered by exhaust energy but also requiring a mechanical drive system). Mechanically driven superchargers fall within the two basic classes of (1) positive-displacement and (2) dynamic compressors.

Specific compressor types include centrifugal, axial, traditional Roots (straight lobe), modern Roots (lobes twisted as much as 160 degrees), Vane, sliding-vane, rotary (Wankel-type), Lysholm-type (twin-screw), reciprocating-piston, rotary-piston, spiral, and pressure-wave (Comprex). Some of these are more commonly used for nonsupercharging automotive pumping tasks, like compressing refrigerant in an air conditioning system or powering a smog pump, and many have been scaled for use in large pumping applications that have nothing to do with engines, such as scavenging explosive gases from coal mines. By far the most common compressors applied to modern supercharging systems are the Roots (Eaton, Weiand, and so on), centrifugal (Vortech, Procharger, and so on, plus all turbochargers), and Lysholm (Autorotor, Whipple, and so on).

All modern automotive-type turbo-superchargers consist of a high-speed centrifugal compressor sharing a common shaft with a radial-inflow turbine. High-speed *axial* compressors and axial turbines have sometimes been installed for supercharging extremely large aircraft, marine, railway, and industrial engines (all diesel except for World War II–vintage spark-ignition pistons and modern jet aircraft powerplants) where it is not cost-effective to cast sufficiently large one-piece centrifugal compressors or radial-inflow turbine wheels. And yes, except for (rare) ramjets and scramjets, the combustion chambers of all turbojets, fanjets, turboprops, and turboshaft engines require supercharging to pressures as high as 40:1, which is 575 psi at sea level!

There is no inherent reason a turbine couldn't be used to drive a positive-displacement supercharger rather than a high-speed centrifugal compressor (after all, turbines are sometimes used to recover power from exhaust heat and add it back to the crankshaft). The trouble is, the main advantage of positive-displacement superchargers is their effectiveness at low engine rpm—which is precisely where exhaust turbines lack the exhaust energy to deliver any useful torque, meaning you'd need an expensive and complex back-up electrical or mechanical drive system at low engine speeds. You'd also have to eat the expense and inefficiency of a gear-down drive system or torque converter to link devices with such dissimilar operating speeds. A high-speed gas turbine operates in the 25,000-to 300,000 –rpm range while a Roots or Lysholm supercharger operates at 2,000–15,000 rpm. And then there's the fact that centrifugal compressors have historically had better thermal efficiency than most other types of superchargers. All of this adds up to the

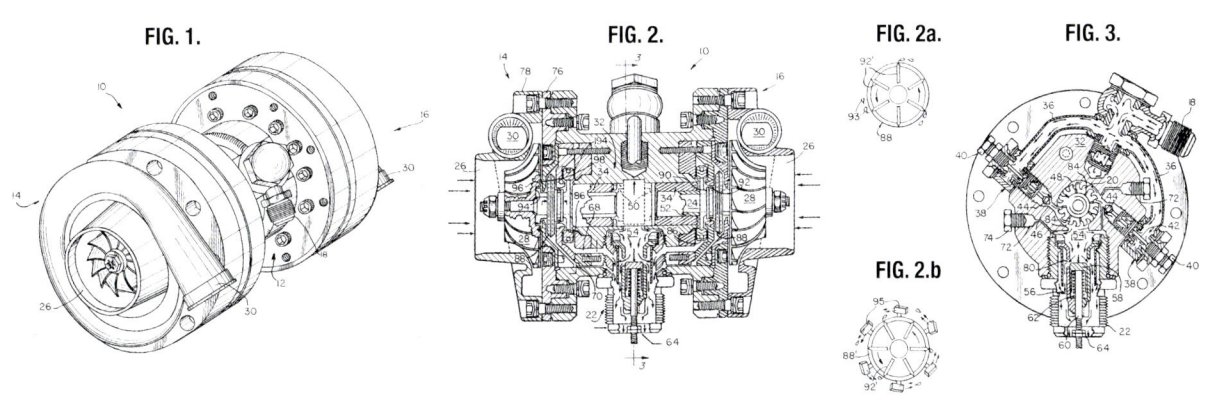

FIG. 1. **FIG. 2.** **FIG. 2a.** **FIG. 3.**

FIG. 2.b

Patent drawings for a hydraulically driven supercharger that depends on an external pump to supply pressurized fluid to a hydraulic motor in the compressor assembly. The availability of high-pressure fluid at idle to redline, combined with a fluid-control valve, gives this system the potential to act as a variable-speed transmission to provide appropriate boost at all engine speeds. *U.S. Patent Office*

SUPERCHARGER ARCHITECTURE

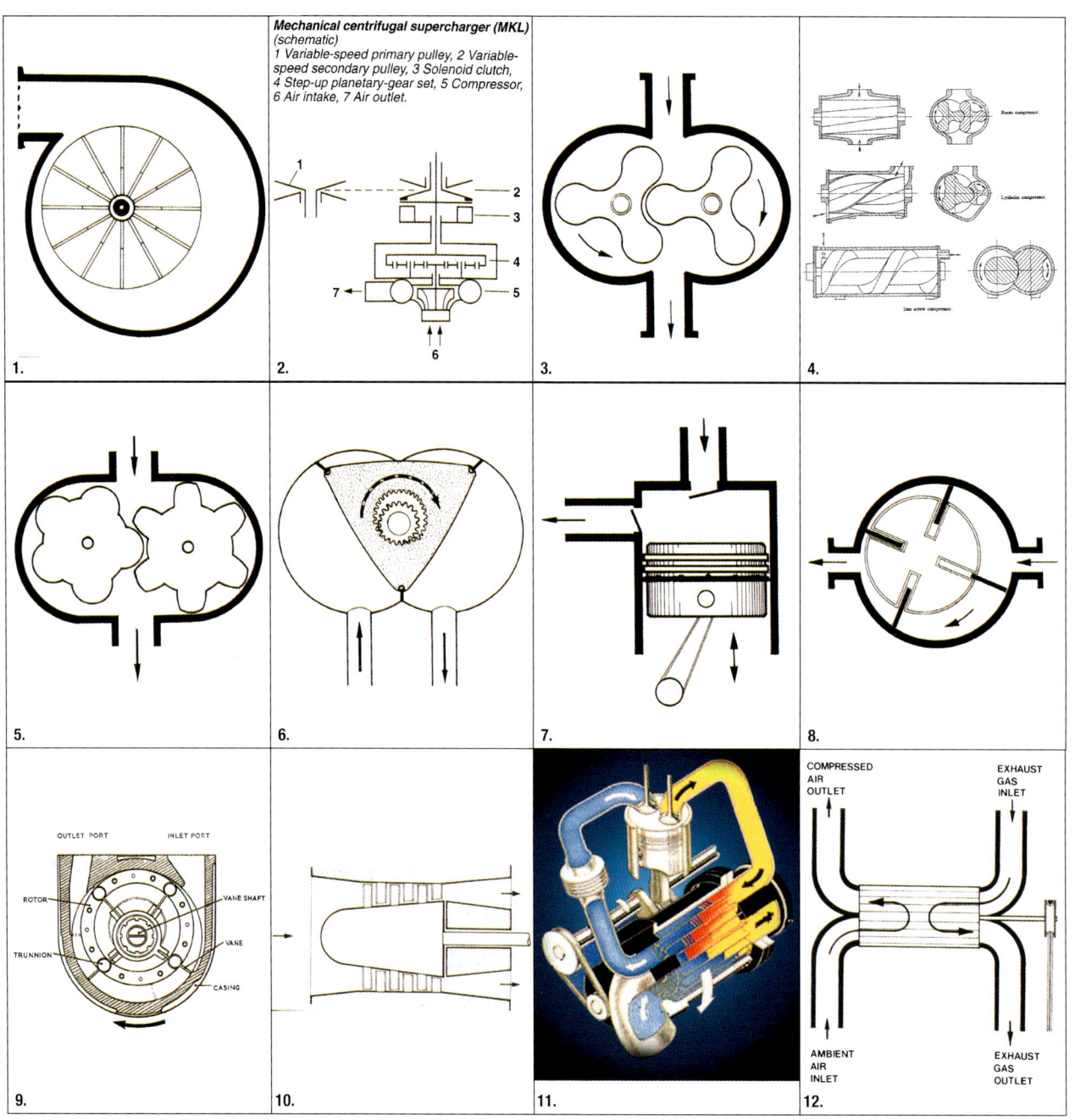

Mechanical centrifugal supercharger (MKL) (schematic)
1 Variable-speed primary pulley, 2 Variable-speed secondary pulley, 3 Solenoid clutch, 4 Step-up planetary-gear set, 5 Compressor, 6 Air intake, 7 Air outlet.

Common types of compressors used in supercharging engines:
1. Centrifugal compressor
2. Mechanical variable-speed drive system for centrifugal compressor
3. Positive-displacement Roots type "blower," 3-lobe design
4. Three different styles of positive-displacement Lysholm superchargers
5. End view of common Lysholm (screw-type) supercharger
6. Rotary (Wankel-type) supercharger
7. Reciprocating-piston supercharger
8. Sliding-vane supercharger
9. Vane-type supercharger
10. Axial compressor
11. Comprex flow diagram
12. Comprex supercharger

62

Look Ma, no carb! Here's the classic old-school supercharger, based on the Roots blower architecture originally used to "blow" air at near atmospheric pressure into a two-stroke Detroit Diesel truck/bus engine. These superchargers originally had two-lobe rotors with extremely poor thermal efficiency, and many still require a "wet" mixture in which fuel introduced upstream by carburetion or fuel injection cools the rotors enough to maintain safe internal rotor clearances. Note that although you can see an auxiliary injector at the rear of the blower hat that provides fuel cooling for the rotor assembly, what you can't see is the custom Norwood Autocraft port fuel injection system located *inside* the intake manifold below the supercharger.

reality that exhaust turbines have been used almost exclusively used to drive centrifugal compressors. In other words, they have been turbochargers.

Mechanically driven superchargers have advantages and disadvantages compared to turbochargers. The most obvious advantage is that superchargers cannot lag behind engine speed (unless the belt slips!), though they also cannot surge ahead of engine speed when an engine is lugging. The most obvious disadvantage of any mechanically driven supercharger is that it is exclusively driven by mechanical energy robbed directly from the crankshaft, whereas the exhaust-turbine drive systems used in turbochargers and the power-recovery systems used to improve fuel economy in an increasing number of modern powerplants ranging from Scania trucks to Ferrari racers make use of heat that would otherwise be wasted out the exhaust system.

POSITIVE-DISPLACEMENT SUPERCHARGERS

This category of supercharger includes reciprocating, lobe, and vane compressors. All are driven directly from the crankshaft by gears, chains, or belts. This class of supercharger is referred to as "positive displacement" because they pump essentially the same amount of charge air per compressor revolution regardless of speed, with the pumping capacity depending on the displacement per revolution of the supercharger.

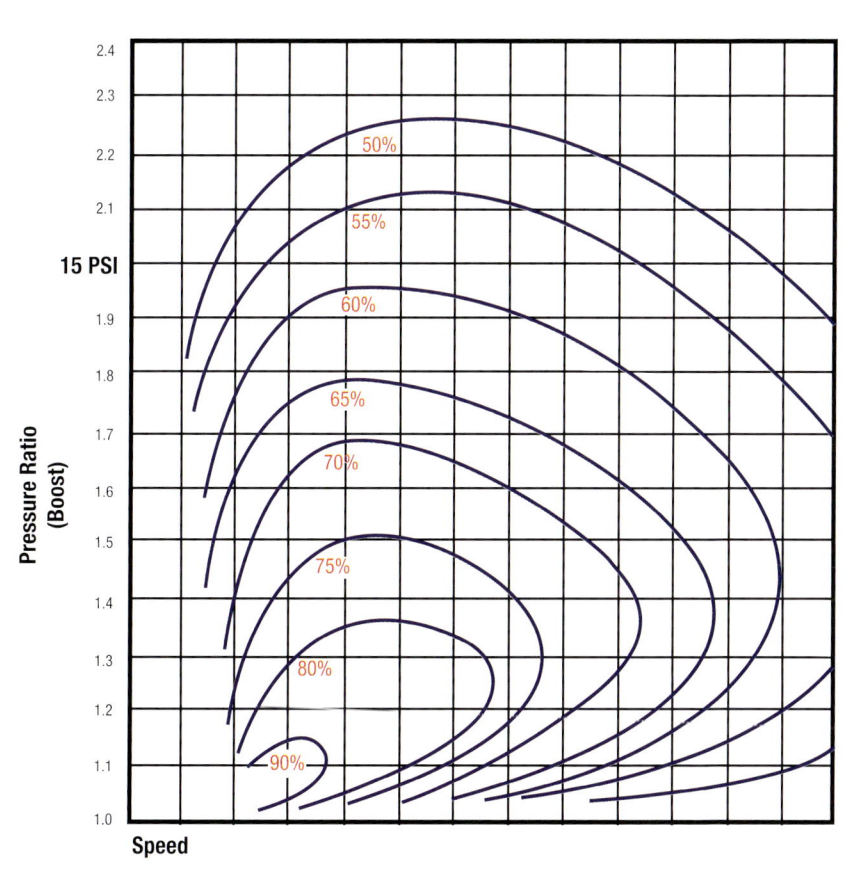

This old-school Roots-type supercharger flow map is similar to a centrifugal compressor map, though it is conventional to show airflow in volumetric terms (cfm) rather than mass airflow. The speed lines are perfectly linear and correlate well with volumetric airflow, indicating that this is a positive-displacement supercharger that pumps essentially the same volume of air at all speeds. Thermal efficiency (and, hence, mass airflow in pounds per minute) and the drive power requirement do vary with speed, pressure, and cfm airflow. Note that peak thermal efficiency is much lower than a centrifugal compressor (63 vs. 78–80), and that efficiency drops below 60 percent (raginglyinefficient) at .3–.4 bar boost in the 3.5–6.5K speed range. This type of supercharger is not good for more than 5- to 7-psi boost without really good intercooling or tons of fuel cooling, preferably with a fuel like methanol, which absorbs a lot of heat when it vaporizes. *Wikipedia*

SUPERCHARGER ARCHITECTURE

63

BDS "Huffer" Roots-type supercharger. This classic-looking blower uses three-lobe rotors with a small amount of twist to improve thermal and volumetric efficiency, and weighs in at about 70 pounds. *BDS*

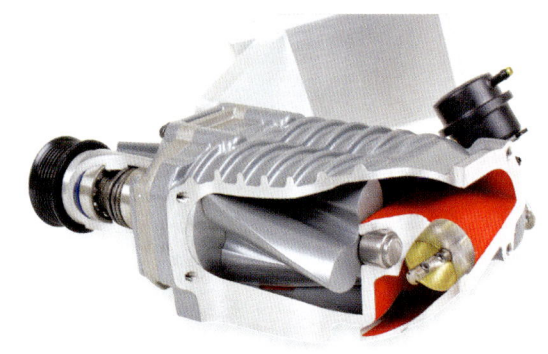

Jackson Racing supercharger with Gen 5 "modern-roots" Eaton architecture incorporates a bypass valve opened by manifold vacuum at idle and very light cruise to scram all boost by permitting charge air to bypass the rotor assembly entirely. Note that Eaton Roots-type superchargers discharge from the side like the old Roots, but breathe through the end of the blower case for lower hood clearance and improved compatibility with EFI engine layouts. In this case, the supercharger case is incorporated with the intake manifold. A combination of relatively good thermal efficiency and adequate rotor clearance allows this type of supercharger to safely compress dry air without fuel. Note that the latest Gen 6 TVS technology differs in significant ways. *Jackson Racing*

The air path through a positive-displacement supercharger is irreversible. This means that 100 percent of the air pumped by the compressor *must* go through the engine. Think of it conceptually as an air lock where doors open, air is sucked in, the doors close, and the air is forced out through doors that open on the other side. Because the pressure ratio of a positive-displacement supercharger is not dependent on rpm, relatively high pressure ratios can be generated even at low volumetric flow rates, with the flow rate of the supercharger independent of the pressure ratio. In fact, some positive-displacement "blowers" can be used to move air with no compression at all.

Positive-displacement superchargers are stable throughout the operating range: They cannot surge or stall, and backflow is impossible at all speeds. A positive-displacement supercharger is going to pump a certain amount of air each revolution, regardless of whatever pressurizing happens along the way. Consequently, if an engine with such a supercharger backfires into the intake, this may be handled with a pop-off valve in the case of a small backfire, but a *large* backfire can blow the supercharger clean off the engine.

If the displacement of a positive-displacement compressor is twice that of the engine being supercharged, intake manifold pressure *must* rise to whatever degree is required for the engine to ingest the entire airflow delivered by the supercharger—though the boost pressure required to do this will *not* be anything as simple as, say, two atmospheres of boost if the supercharger has twice the displacement as the engine's. Unless the engine has a peaky normal-charged torque curve, maximum supercharged manifold pressure at wide-open throttle will be roughly the same across the rpm range. In practice it is common to see boost rise a bit as engine VE falls off in the upper rpm ranges above peak torque. The result is that a supercharged engine's peak torque is not only greater but occurs at a higher engine speed. Higher peak torque at a higher rpm boosts the maximum horsepower figure much more than you might otherwise expect, versus if the entire torque curve were simply shifted directly upward.

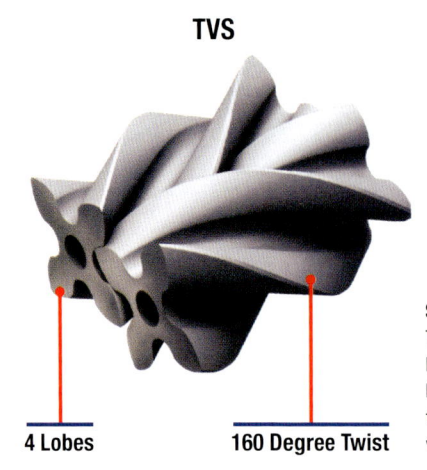

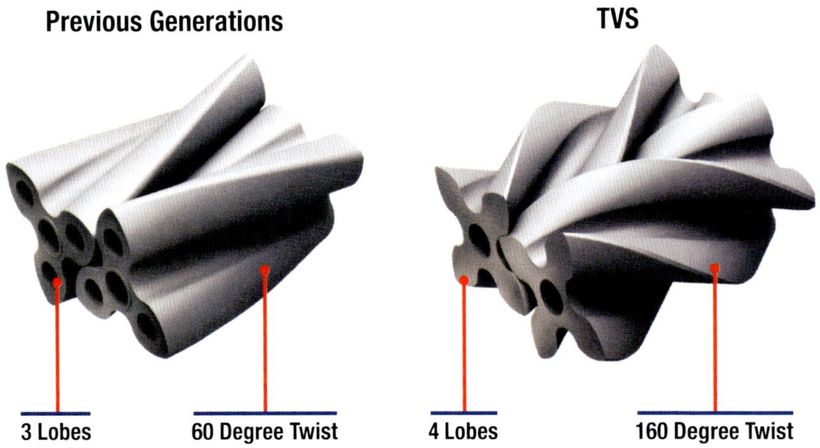

Previous Generations

TVS

3 Lobes | 60 Degree Twist | 4 Lobes | 160 Degree Twist

SUPERCHARGER ROTOR DESIGN: Eaton TVS vs. pre-TVS rotor architecture revealing four rather than three lobes and 100 more degrees of helix angle. The greater helix angle and redesigned TVS intake port exposes half the length of the rotor in the intake phase for improved volumetric efficiency and noise control. *Eaton*

Cadillac Northstar supercharger assembly with integral water-cooler charge cooler. Note built-in bypass valve and Gen 5 backflow slots, designed to reduce noise by permitting a controlled leak for rotor cavity equalization. *GM Media Archive*

Toyota Racing Development's FJ Cruiser blower assembly cleverly incorporates a pre-TVS Gen 5 Eaton rotor assembly into the intake manifold in a way that allows a stock throttle body and air intake to remain in the stock location. *Toyota Racing Development*

Note that although a positive-displacement supercharger has approximately linear airflow delivery, overdriving the blower to higher speeds to increase airflow can severely overheat the air if the compressor is forced to run at a pressure ratio too far above its optimal thermal efficiency envelope (with all the attendant problems of overheated charge air).

At very low and very high compressor speeds, when leakage past rings or seals becomes more significant compared to the total supercharged airflow, the volumetric efficiency of a positive displacement supercharger can degrade to the extent that the blower's ability to maintain equal airflow per revolution breaks down. This is a function of pressure ratio,

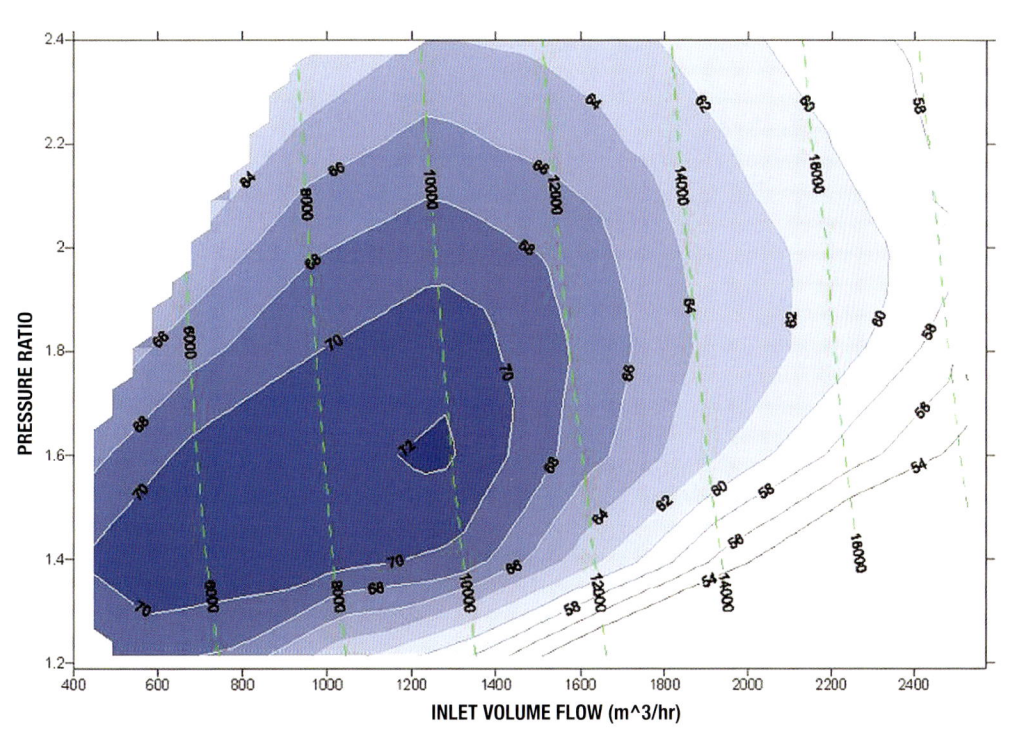

R2300 PERFORMANCE MAP: Corvette ZR1 Eaton R2300 supercharger performance map. Note that this supercharger will flow 450 to more than 1,800 cfm at more than 64 percent thermal efficiency at pressure ratios between 1.2 and 2.4. *Eaton*

time, and the gap seal clearance (or Teflon sealing strips) and is not simply a function of supercharger rpm.

Roots superchargers are not, technically speaking, compressors at all, in that they do not actually compress air internally in the supercharger. Rather, they push air into the intake manifold, where it backs up against the restriction of closed engine valves and restrictive intake and exhaust plumbing, producing pressure. That is why this type of supercharger is sometimes called a "blower" rather than a compressor.

There is a lot of turbulence on the discharge side of a traditional straight-lobe Roots blower, which results in extremely poor thermal efficiency at high levels of boost. Traditional Roots superchargers are not suitable for street applications of more than 5- to 7-psi manifold pressure because of the fierce charge heating—to the point that most require a "wet" fuel-air mixture moving through the supercharger to cool the rotors enough to prevent overheating, thermal expansion, and consequent rotor clash and damage.

The twin rotary pistons (a.k.a. rotors) of a Roots-type supercharger are meshed tightly together with a narrow clearance. The lobes on each rotor engage each other something like gears and spin in opposite directions at speeds up to 14,000–15,000 rpm. One at a time, the rotors capture air sucked into the supercharger intake port in chambers that form dynamically between the blower casing and the hollow trough located between adjacent lobes of a rotor each time a lobe rotates past the intake port and subsequently forms a seal with the blower housing. The two rotors move the trapped charge in opposite directions around the periphery of the blower casing, at ambient pressure, toward a plenum at the opposite (discharge) side of the housing. In the discharge plenum, air emerges from the rotors in a rapid-fire series of noisy, flatulent pulses as positive pressure in the throttle and intake manifold resonates backward to compress the ambient-pressure pulses of new charge.

The length and diameter of the rotors determines the amount of air displaced by a Roots blower each revolution. Displacement, lobe profile, and port shape combine to define a 2D map of flow rates across the operating range of the supercharger. Although Roots-type blowers are known for providing low-rpm boost, the pumping efficiency at very low speeds can suffer significantly because of relatively high-charge leakage around the rotors.

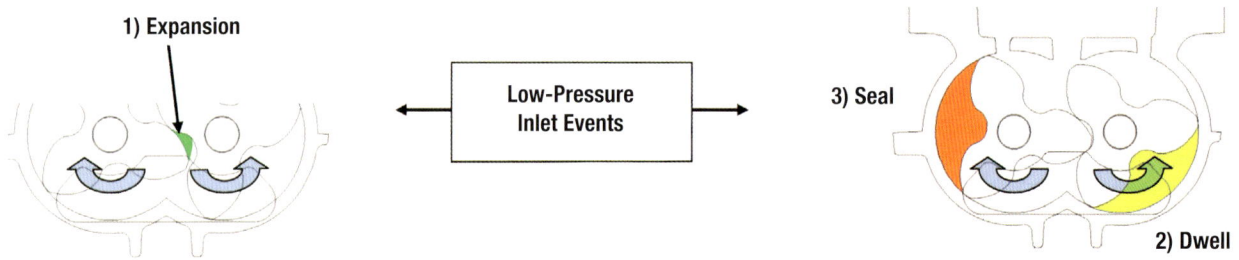

5th Gen	Event	Degrees Rotation	TVS
210	1	Inlet (Expansion)	280
50	2	Dwell	20
40	3	Seal	10
40	4	Backflow (Compression)	80
200	5	Outlet (Exhaust)	220

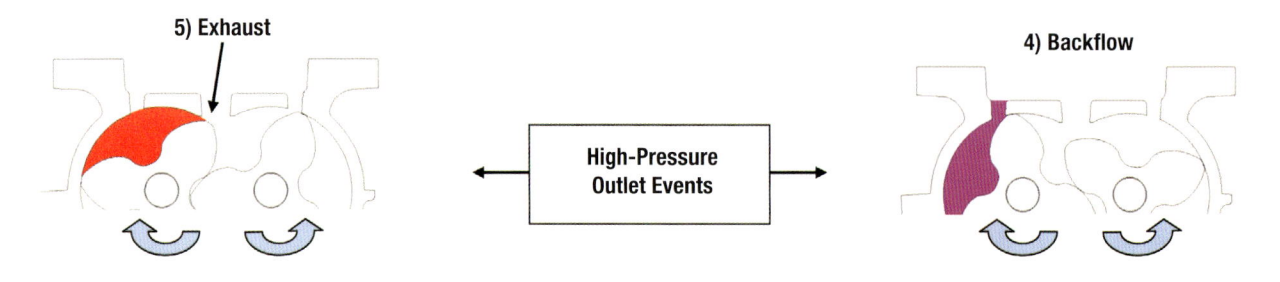

FUNDAMENTAL CYCLES OF EATON ROOTS TYPE SUPERCHARGER: The fundamental cycles of Eaton Roots-type supercharger: (1) inlet (expansion), (2) dwell, (3) seal, (4) backflow (compression), and (5) outlet (exhaust). *Eaton*

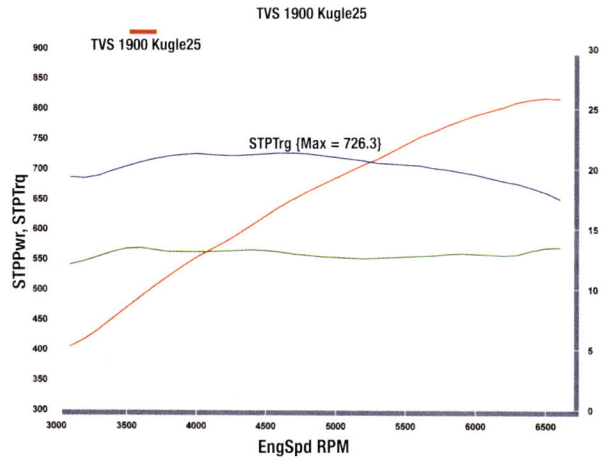

STANDARD CORRECTED POWER: A Kugel '32 Hiboy Roadster with Magnuson R2300 TVS supercharger waiting for completion and the land speed-record trials at the Bonneville Salt Flats. Engine is a Ken Dutweiler LS1 Chevrolet V-8 that made 817.4 horsepower on the Magnuson Superflow engine dynamometer. *Magnuson Products*

Edelbrock eForce TVS Gen 6 Roots-type supercharger assembly with integral charge-cooler is designed to bolt to a Ford 5.4-liter V-8 in place of the stock intake manifold. The eForce package is capable of flowing enough air for 700 to 800 horsepower. *Edelbrock*

The rotors of a Roots supercharger are precisely synchronized with each other and prevented from clashing by meshing external gears that maintain a narrow but precise gap between the two rotors at all times. The size of the sealing gap between the rotors and the blower casing in a Roots blower—critical in determining pumping efficiency at the extremes of very low and very high airflow—is essentially mandated by the choice of materials used to manufacture the rotors and housing, the available manufacturing tolerances, and the basic design. The twin rotors of a Roots blower should never actually contact each other except in unusual cases such as the monster Roots-type superchargers used on Top Fuel dragsters. These are faced with Teflon sealing strips that must be replaced following the ruinous levels of boost, rpm, and thermal-loading encountered in the course of a single Top Fuel drag run.

Historically, Roots superchargers had notoriously poor maximum thermal efficiency, in the 50 to 55 percent range, due in part to the fact that the spinning rotors were delivering incremental gulps of *nonpressurized* air into a *pressurized* manifold. This situation produces turbulence, backwash, and pulsation, which is noisy and thrashes and heats the air far beyond the inevitable adiabatic heat of compression. The original Roots blowers were designed for scavenging the cylinders of heavy, slow-turning two-stroke Detroit Diesel engines on 18-wheeler trucks with 3, 4, 6, or 8 cylinders of 71-cid (hence the designation of the various sizes of Roots superchargers as 3-71, 4-71, 6-71, and 8-71). Low noise, compact size, and high thermal efficiency were not required for this application, whose main purpose was to provide a forceful blast of fresh charge air at *very* low boost pressure, which entered a diesel cylinder through the two-stroke intake port that was exposed when the piston was near bottom dead center (BDC). The charge air would blow residual exhaust gases out through open overhead exhaust valve(s) while modestly improving the engine's volumetric efficiency.

Later, when hot rodders of the 1960s were adapting Roots-type blowers to purpose-built V-8 blower manifolds, the fact that the Roots superchargers roared and growled—and gobbled air through massive in-your-face chrome blower hats on top of 4-barrel carburetors, standing up through the hoods of beautiful but crude jacked-up muscle cars—was undoubtedly a plus to some people. When boosting gasoline-fueled engines instead of diesels, the usual trick with these old blowers was to tighten up the blower's internal clearances a bit and suck a wet charge mixture through carburetors, using

SUPERCHARGER ARCHITECTURE

67

BDS competition blower showing apex seal strips used in Top Fuel and other radical competition for improved rotor sealing at boost pressures as high as 70 psi. *BDS*

Gibson-Miller Mark II Top Fuel blower. This Top Fuel supercharger had to meet stringent NHRA rules that prohibit high-helix rotors with a lot of twist. Mark II design goals included excellent airflow performance with reduced rotor flex at extreme speeds and pressure to increase the number of drag passes between apex rotor seal replacements. *BME*

fuel to lubricate and cool the supercharger, which would otherwise run hot and require looser clearances.

Starting in the 1980s, engineers at Eaton Automotive began devoting considerable research to modernizing and upgrading the traditional Roots blower design, which had serious deficits as a supercharger. Eaton's new design used three lobes per rotor rather than the two found on traditional Roots blowers. They added a 60-degree twist to the rotor lobes to form a helix that added some internal air compression. The design reduced pulsation by staggering each air delivery pulse across a greater percentage of blower rotation. The resulting supercharger was more compact, quieter, and had less pulsation than old-style Roots blowers. All boost at idle or other low-load, high-vacuum manifold situations was diverted using a vacuum-actuated bypass valve that recirculated air back into the intake manifold, simultaneously reducing blower noise at idle. The new design was capable of 60 to 65 percent thermal efficiency, which is extremely good for this breed of supercharger; many of the older designs had thermal efficiency below 55 percent in the bad old days.

Beginning in the 1980s, Eaton-type superchargers were installed on a variety of OE factory cars and other automakers, and in a variety of aftermarket or dealer-installed supercharger kits and street-legal new-vehicle packages. Newer versions of the Eaton three-lobe superchargers were manufactured with a special rotor coating designed to erode to improve rotor-case sealing as the supercharger wore in. Eaton's M62—still sold—was good for boosting a 3.0-liter V-6 from 180 to 200 horsepower to about 275 at 3- to 5-psi pressure. The M62 was capable of spinning to about 14,000 rpm before the lobes of the twin rotors begin flexing enough to clash with each other or contact the housing (to the detriment of future sealing).

More recently, Eaton research developed the sixth-generation Eaton TVS (Twin Vortices System), a revolutionary four-rotor Roots supercharger with 160-degree rotor twist and advanced geometry to minimize turbulence during compression. It is capable of delivering more than 20-psi boost with good efficiency and peak thermal efficiency—as high as 80 percent. This supercharger was used to great effect, for example, in the 2009 and newer 638-horse ZR1 Corvette.

Perhaps the most interesting application for Roots superchargers is Top Fuel drag racing, where monster oversized Roots-type superchargers of 10-71, 12-71, and 14-71 displacement, which consume as much as 900 horsepower at full howl, have been developed by companies such as Weiand for pressurizing monster 500-plus-cid Hemi drag motors to 8,000 horsepower on nitromethane.

Like all superchargers, the Roots requires power to compress air, meaning that a percentage of the crankshaft horsepower developed under boost is always lost driving the supercharger. Assuming that 5,000 to 6,000 horsepower of the peak rating of a Top Fuel engine comes from supercharging, 900 horsepower easily represents a 15 percent power loss just from driving the blower. Parasitic losses of supercharging are covered in detail later in this book.

Twin-screw Lysholm superchargers have been marketed by Autorotor, Lysholm, Whipple, Kenne-Bell, and others. Lysholm-type superchargers are a positive-displacement design and have occasionally been lumped in with twin-rotor lobe-type designs as a "Roots-type" supercharger, but the twin-screw design is so unique in its difficulty of manufacture and operating characteristics that it is usually considered to be in a class of its own.

The twin-screw supercharger is a bit like a vastly twisted set of Roots lobes with a conical taper. The two rotors mesh together like a set of worm gears to push air longitudinally through channels that decrease in size as air moves through the supercharger toward the discharge port (versus the Roots design, which paddles air sideways as the rotors turn away from each other, moving air transversely from one side of the two rotors to the other).

The result is a high amount of internal compression that gives this supercharger much more adiabatic efficiency throughout the operating range than the traditional Roots design. It makes the design viable for higher levels of boost at and above an additional atmosphere of pressure. Manufacturers typically tweak the Lysholm design to increase thermal efficiency for specific applications based on the required pressure ratio. Until recently the twin-screw design was clearly superior to all Roots superchargers for boost applications above about 7-psi boost, but the improved thermal efficiency of the latest Eaton TVS compressors calls into question the twin-screw's advantage for many high-performance street supercharging applications.

Twin-screw superchargers have excellent low-end boost capability, but unless an electrical clutch is incorporated to allow the supercharger to stop turning under conditions when positive manifold pressure is neither required nor desirable (such as idle), the work required by the supercharger's internal compression ratio will rob power from the crankshaft under all operating conditions, including idle—even if a bypass valve is open to prevent the supercharger from boosting the engine. Another disadvantage of the design's internal compression ratio is that the twin-screw produces a characteristic "popping" noise as compressed air exits the compression channels between the twin-screw rotors. In the absence of noise-suppression countermeasures, such popping sounds can merge to produce something between a whistle, whine, and scream, depending on the frequency. Yet another disadvantage of the twin-screw design is that the close tolerances required have made this type of supercharger relatively expensive to manufacture.

Most twin-screw superchargers are designed with four "lobes" on each rotor rather than the two or three seen on

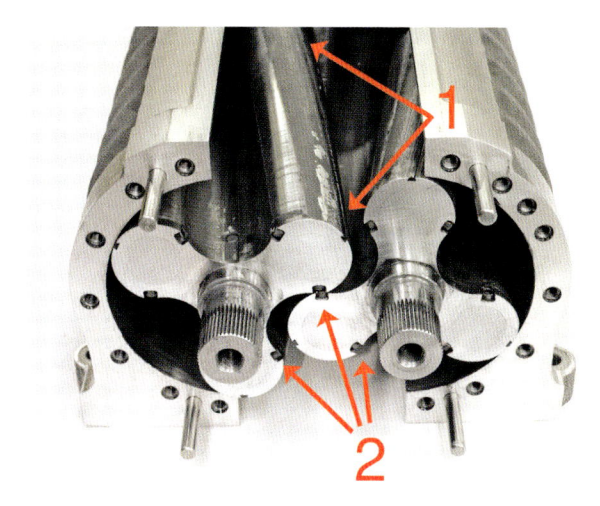

Each rotor lobe in the Gibson-Miller Mark II Top Fuel supercharger has an apex seal (1) made of Nylatron and two side seals (2) made of carbon-impregnated Teflon. These strips seal off the cavities formed by the rotor lobe and the blower case, preventing the air trapped inside the cavities from leaking away and reducing the supercharger's efficiency. Apex seal durability is so problematic in Top Fuel drag racing that G-M touts the ability of the Mark II to survive as many as 10 drag passes before restripping. *BME*

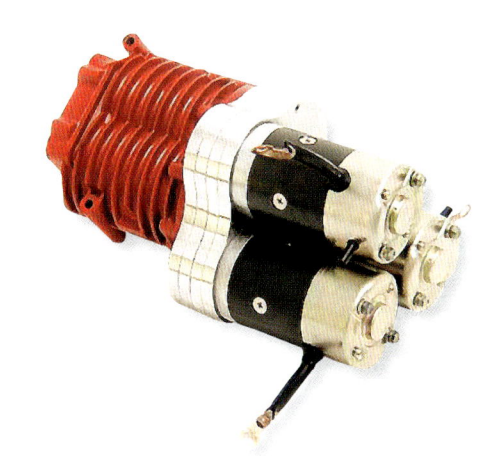

Roots-type supercharger with electric drive. The downside of 13.7v (low-voltage) automotive electrical systems is that tremendous current is required to deliver the 5 to 25 max horsepower required to drive a street supercharger. Here we see three automotive starter motors deployed to turn the blower. *Thomas Knight*

Cutaway of the Kenne Bell twin-screw supercharger *Kenne Bell*

SUPERCHARGER ARCHITECTURE

69

all but the newest Roots superchargers. The two meshing rotors in a Lysholm supercharger are not a mirror image of each other: One has bulbous, teardrop-shaped lobes with a narrower "fin" rising off the top of the lobes, whereas the second rotor has thinner, blade-style lobes with a fat ridge on top. These profiles form a nearly airtight mesh with each other.

Although twin-screw superchargers have long had obvious efficiency advantages compared to other positive-displacement designs and have been built in very large sizes to supercharge big-block V-8s in racing boats and similar applications, entities with a vested interest in the status quo prevented Lysholm-type superchargers from being legalized for use in glamour-class NHRA Top Fuel and blown-alcohol drag racing.

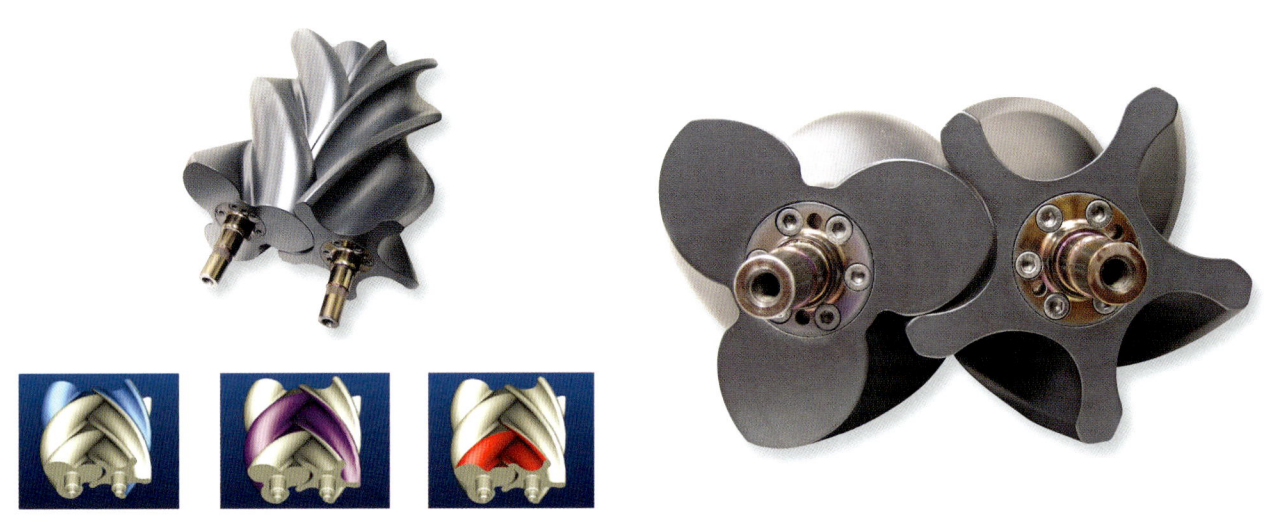

Twin-screw supercharger rotors mesh to push air along the length of the "screws," simultaneously squeezing the air such that charge emerges from the supercharger already pressurized. This is a fairly efficient compressor, but because of the internal compression ratio, unless there is a pulley clutch, the Lysholm will waste energy compressing (and heating!) air even at idle. It is common to optimize twin-screw architecture depending on target boost pressure. Note the male and female rotors, which, unlike Roots superchargers, are not symmetrical. *Whipple Superchargers*

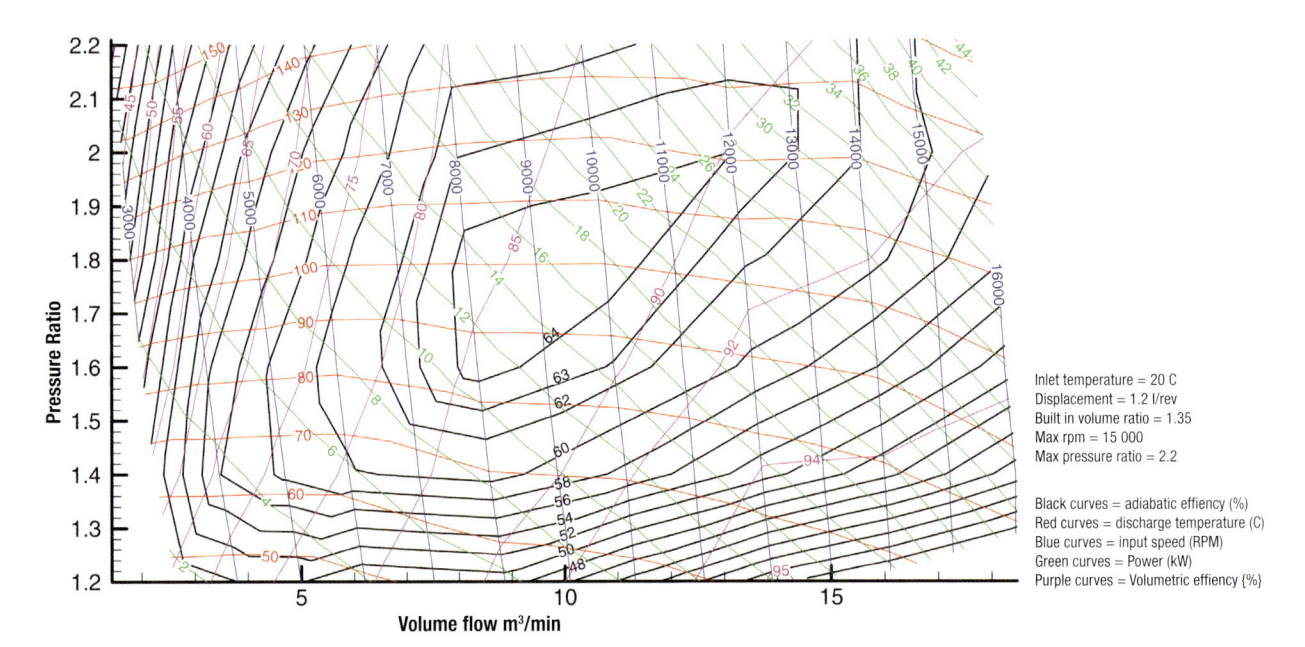

Inlet temperature = 20 C
Displacement = 1.2 l/rev
Built in volume ratio = 1.35
Max rpm = 15 000
Max pressure ratio = 2.2

Black curves = adiabatic effiency (%)
Red curves = discharge temperature (C)
Blue curves = input speed (RPM)
Green curves = Power (kW)
Purple curves = Volumetric effiency (%)

FULL LOAD PERFORMANCE CHARACTERISTIC FOR LYSHOLM SUPERCHARGER LYS1200A: Lysholm LYS1200A twin-screw compressor map. This is a small supercharger good for about 550 cfm. This map is wonderfully complete, with data revealing adiabatic efficiency, discharge temperature, rpm, power requirement, and volumetric efficiency for various combinations of pressure ratio and volumetric airflow.

Lysholm twin-screw 3300 supercharger system provides 14- to 15-psi boost for 2007–09 Shelby GT500 Mustangs. The 3300AX compressor can flow up to about 1,100 cfm. *Lysholm*

A BEGi supercharging system for a BMW M3. Note the Opcon Autorotor twin-screw supercharger.

Ultimately, the twin-screw design is less efficient than the centrifugal compressor, and, like all superchargers, it can benefit from an intercooler to upgrade the thermal efficiency. Like the Roots, intercooling a twin-screw can be a more difficult packaging challenge than intercooling a turbocharger or centrifugal supercharger. It usually requires a compact liquid-cooled inline "charge-cooler" unit with an additional, remote-mounted, air-liquid cooler (to cool the liquid that cools the intake charge) to work in most applications.

A number of production engines have been equipped with twin-screw superchargers, including the Mazda Millenia S, Mercedes-Benz SLR McLaren, the Koenigsegg CC8S and CCR, and some Mercury Marine racing V-8s.

Reciprocating-piston compressors are commonly found in shops and factories pumping air to paint guns and pneumatic air tools, though they have been used to supercharge large stationary engines. Because this type of compressor uses auxiliary pistons to move air (which must have greater displacement than the engine they're supercharging), reciprocating-piston compressors are too large to be practical for most motor vehicle applications. In the extreme, it's like having a second engine to supercharge the first.

Sliding-vane compressors employ an eccentric rotor to push air around the circumference of the compressor housing from an intake port to an exhaust port. Sealing is provided by spring-loaded vanes that scrape the housing, extending and retracting throughout each revolution as required to maintain the seal for the eccentric revolution. This design may or may not provide internal compression. Sliding-vane compressors have a serious liability for supercharging performance engines, in that oil misted into the charge to lubricate the friction surfaces of the sliding vanes increases the likelihood of detonation, effectively raising the engine's fuel octane number requirement.

Smog pumps often use *eccentric-vane compressors*, which do not require vane lubrication. This design, like that of the Lysholm compressor, tends to be expensive in sizes large enough to supercharge an automotive engine, though Bendix did build one with enhanced mechanical efficiency by eliminating internal compression, so that the device consumed less power when the engine was not under much load.

DYNAMIC SUPERCHARGERS

Dynamic compressors are intrinsically high-speed devices because they compress air by accelerating it to a high velocity and then diffusing it, converting velocity into pressure. Unlike positive-displacement superchargers, dynamic compressors vary tremendously in the volume of air pumped per revolution as speed and pressure ratio change. Dynamic compressors that have been used to supercharge engines include axial, centrifugal, and Comprex designs.

Axial compressors normally consist of a staged array of multi-bladed fans, each of which is designed to increase pressure by accelerating air as it moves longitudinally through the compressor housing along the axis of the shaft. The high-velocity air is then crushed against a row of stationary vanes to build pressure. Because it is impossible to obtain pressure ratios higher than about 1.1–1.2 with a single-axial fan, axial compressors typically gang multiple fans and stators in a series of stages, each of which builds upon the pressure increase of the last. Multi-stage axial compressors are not particularly compact but are capable of achieving extremely high pressure ratios. This type of compressor is used in large sizes to supercharge the combustion chambers of modern fanjet engines to pressure ratios as high as 40:1. Axial compressors are large and expensive, and therefore have been used mainly to supercharge continuous-flame turbojet and large piston engines of the sorts used in ships and railway locomotives. They have no advantages, and numerous disadvantages, for automotive use compared to centrifugal compressors.

The *Comprex pressure-wave supercharger* is a fascinating device that uses pulsating high-energy exhaust pressure waves to compress intake charge air. A rotating cylinder or "cell rotor" is divided into multiple cells arranged around the circumference of the cylinder (kind of like the chambers in a revolver handgun) that run the length of the cylinder as pie slice-shaped tubes. These are irregularly spaced to reduce noise. One end of the cell rotor is sealed inside a charge-air housing and the other is sealed inside an exhaust housing.

The housings are designed so that each cell rotates sequentially past strategically placed intake and exhaust ports located in each of the housings. The "cold side" charge-air housing has an intake port that draws in ambient air and a discharge port that supplies compressed air to the engine intake. The "hot side" exhaust housing has an intake port that receives high-energy exhaust pulses from the engine exhaust manifold and a discharge port that routes "depleted" lower-energy exhaust gases into the vehicle's muffler system after some of the exhaust energy has been harnessed to pressurize the charge air. The cold-side charge air housing is made of cast aluminum; the hot-side exhaust gas housing is made of NiResist materials capable of surviving in exhaust gases that retain the majority of the heat from combustion.

What is really interesting is that despite the fact that there is no barrier between the hot and cold ends of each Comprex cell, pressurized charge air leaving the supercharger does not become contaminated with exhaust (more on this in a moment). The intake and discharge ports of the cold-side housing and the intake and discharge ports of the hot-side housing of the Comprex supercharger are positioned such that the two ends of an individual cell are periodically open or closed at certain times during the revolution as the cells rotate sequentially past the four ports. A pulley from the crankshaft rotates the cell rotor in order to synchronize rotor rpm with engine speed, and the Comprex system incorporates an integral governing mechanism that allows the Comprex to deliver boost pressure according to engine demand.

The Comprex pressure-wave supercharger uses high-energy exhaust pulses to pressurize fresh charge in rotating barrels and suck fresh charge into the rotating assembly. The placement of cold- and hot-side intake and exhaust ports and clever timing prevent fresh charge air from being contaminated with exhaust. Pressure waves traveling at the speed of sound provide excellent low-end boost even when exhaust energy is low. *Sport Compact Car magazine*

Paxton Novi SL centrifugal supercharger. Mechanically driven (versus turbine-driven) centrifugal compressors are optimized for producing boost at the lowest possible rpm due to the difficulty in achieving blower speeds above about 55,000 to 60,000 rpm with conventional belt- or gear-based internal speed-multiplication systems. *Paxton*

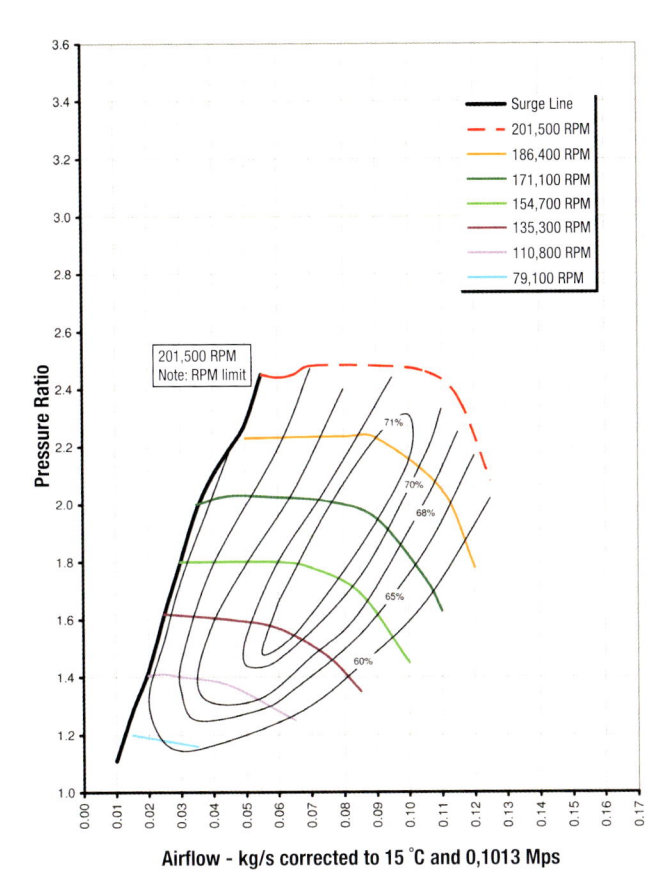

A Rotrex C15-16 compressor map. The Rotrex is basically a gear-driven turbocharger, which is why mechanical limitations essentially amputate the upper end of the compressor flow map. It is amazing that an engine crankshaft can drive a supercharger at speeds up to 201,500 rpm! *Rotrex*

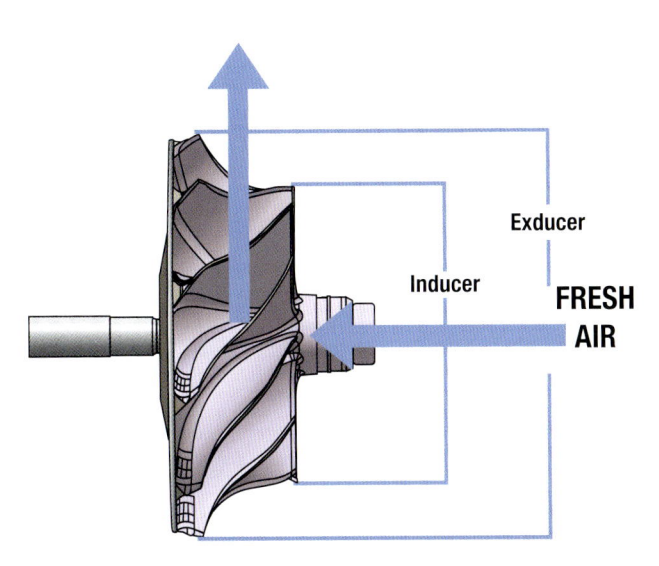

Centrifugal compressor wheel, indicating inducer and exducer. Compressor trim refers to the ratio of the two sizes, although some centrifugal compressor suppliers do not supply trim numbers but code the trim as a letter (i.e., "X-trim," as opposed to say "50-trim.") *Honeywell Garrett*

Here is the Comprex sequence: (1) Fresh charge air at ambient temperature and atmospheric pressure rushes into the low-pressure environment of a Comprex cell through the cold-side intake port as a cell rotates past the port. (2) As the cell rotates away from the cold-side intake port, the fresh charge air becomes trapped (neither end of the cell is adjacent to a port in either housing). (3) Subsequently, the hot end of the cell rotates past a port in the exhaust housing that is plumbed to the engine's exhaust header, permitting a high-energy pressure wave of exhaust to enter the Comprex cell and crash into the fresh charge air at the speed of sound, instantly compressing it to as much as two or three atmospheres. (4) The cell rotates away from the hot-side inlet port, trapping the pressurized charge and exhaust gas. At this time, cold fresh charge air is stratified at the cold end of the cell and hot exhaust is concentrated at the hot end of the cell, and there is a boundary layer of partially contaminated charge in the middle. (5) The rotating cell arrives at the cold-side compressor discharge port, permitting pressurized fresh charge to escape into the cold-end compressor discharge and from there into the engine's intake system. (6) Just in time to prevent the pressure wave of high-speed exhaust gas at the hot side of the cell from escaping into the cold-side compressor housing and contaminating the fresh charge air, the cell rotates away from the compressor discharge port. The pressure wave of exhaust gas and partially contaminated "boundary air" just ahead of it crash into the now-closed cold end of the cell and instantly reflect back toward the hot end at high speed. (8) By this time, the hot-side end of the Comprex cell has arrived at the exhaust discharge port, which permits the exhaust pressure wave (and boundary air) in the cell to exit through the port at high speed, leaving behind negative pressure trapped in the cell (a vacuum) as the cell rotates away from the exhaust port. (9) The negative pressure is shortly relieved when the cell arrives again at the compressor intake port, at which time high-momentum ambient-pressure fresh charge air rushes into the low-pressure cell (repeating step no. 1). (10) The process continues in an identical manner for the other Comprex cells as the cell rotor cycles around its axis.

On the cold side, the Comprex system ingests a steady flow of ambient charge air into the compressor inlet, which emerges from the compressor discharge as pure compressed air. On the other hand, exhaust gas flows into the Comprex hot-side housing and, having done its work, exits from the hot-side discharge into the exhaust system depleted of heat and energy and contaminated with a certain amount of fresh charge air. The Comprex belt-drive mechanism is designed to ensure the cylinder rotates at the optimal speed to satisfy the engine's boost requirements with the currently available exhaust energy.

Because Comprex cell rotor rotation does not compress the charge, little crank energy is wasted turning the rotor.

The Comprex process is driven by exhaust gas pressure waves and therefore dependent on exhaust gas temperature, making compression a function of engine torque rather than speed. Thus, the Comprex compressor is highly effective even at low engine rpm, with boost available immediately. To get around the constraint that a constant drive ratio between engine speed and cell rotor speed essentially tunes the system for only one operating point, special "pockets" are designed into the Comprex compressor housing to provide a much wider range of operation and a good boost curve. Ferrari tested a pressure-wave supercharger during the development of the 126C Formula One racer, rejecting the system in favor of twin turbochargers when Comprex system packaging became an issue. Mazda manufactured more than 100,000 examples of the 1988 626 Capella sedan with an RF-series diesel engine boosted with a Comprex supercharger, and Peugeot and Mercedes-Benz also have utilized pressure-wave superchargers. Greenpeace's SmILE concept car was equipped with a Hyprex pressure wave supercharger developed by the Swiss company Wenko AG.

The *centrifugal compressor* is still without question the most compact and efficient mass-production automotive supercharger. This is the compressor used in all automotive-size turbo-superchargers as well as some mechanical superchargers.

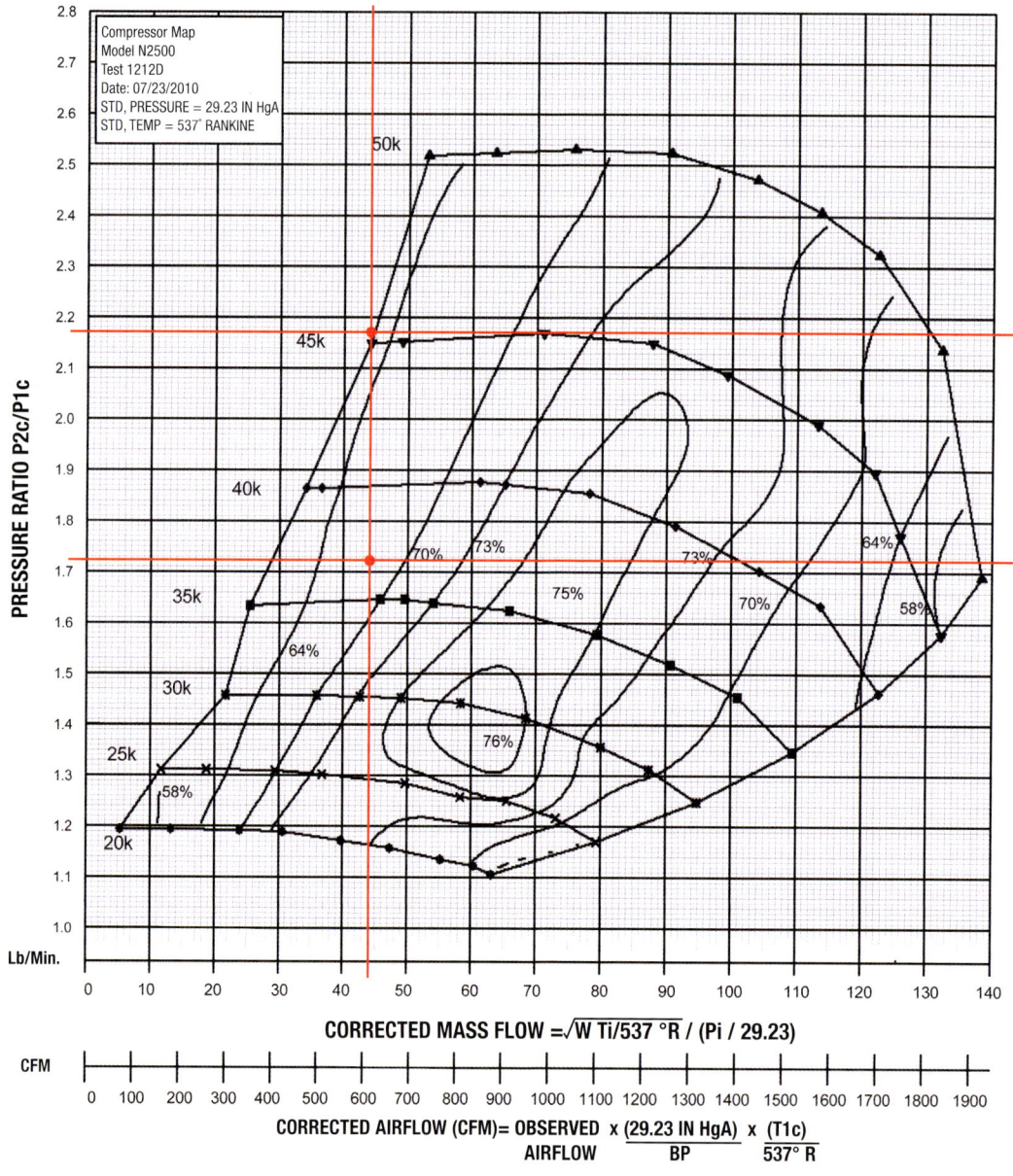

Paxton's N2500 centrifugal compressor is capable of delivering enough air to make 1,300–1,400 horsepower ! It is too big to efficiently deliver 44 lb/min air at a pressure ration of 1.73 (as shown in red). *Paxton*

Large centrifugal compressors are commonly used to pressurize the turboshaft engines found on turbine-powered helicopters. The primordial turbojet developed by Frank Whittle used a large centrifugal compressor. This type of compressor is basically a high-speed air centrifuge that sucks in air through an impeller section located in the center of the compressor housing, where a dozen or so curved paddles, cast as part of a conical disk, attach to a high-speed shaft delivering power from a turbine, gear-drive, or pulley mechanism.

A centrifugal compressor wheel looks a bit like a multi-bladed paddle wheel attached to a flat disk with the paddles (vanes) widening and bending sideways toward the direction of rotation at the center to improve efficiency by biting into the air like a fan (vintage centrifugal compressors used straight paddles). Air is sucked inward along the paddles toward the disk and flung outward along the larger-diameter "exducer" region of the paddles (which may bend toward or away from the direction of rotation, depending on the application) and into the compressor housing at tremendous velocity using centrifugal force. The tip speed of some centrifugal compressors can approach twice the speed of sound.

Centrifugal compressors have a scroll-type outer housing that provides a discharge with a continuously expanding flow path. This housing is wrapped around the circumference of the compressor wheel a bit like a snail shell. The compressor housing is carefully designed to aerodynamically diffuse high-velocity air in such a way as to convert velocity into pressure and disgorge slower-moving compressed air.

Unlike the straight-through axial fan compressor used in many jet engines, which moves air directly through the fan(s), centrifugal compressor gas flow turns approximately 90 degrees during the compression process. Because of the extreme exducer velocities required to generate significant boost pressure, small centrifugal compressors may operate at speeds as high as 200K to 300K rpm. The compressor wheel design ensures that charge air stays in contact with the impeller

Helical internal step-up gears in Vortech centrifugal supercharger. Centrifugal blower gear systems must multiply input speed as much as reasonably possible, as quietly as possible, and as reliably as possible. Internal step-up systems survive better teamed with external ribbed drive belts that can slip under hard acceleration to limit overstressing the internal gears. *Vortech*

COMPRESSOR TRIM

What is the mathematical definition of compressor trim? Compressor trim is a number, not some esoteric-sounding title like "Q-trim." It is a number relating to the ratio of the size of the compressor wheel inducer, which gobbles air, to the size of the compressor wheel exducer, which slings air into the compressor housing at tremendous speed. The rigorous definition of compressor trim is thus:

Trim = (inducer diameter / exducer diameter)^2 × 100

Therefore, Garrett's GT2871R centrifugal compressor with wheel 743347-2 (53.1 mm inducer and a 71.0 mm exducer) has a 56 trim as follows:

Trim = (53.1^2 / 71.0^2) × 100 = 56

On the other hand, Garrett's GT2871R centrifugal compressor with wheel 743347-1 (49.2 mm inducer and a 71.0 mm exducer) has a 48 trim as follows:

Trim = (49.2^2 / 71.0^2) × 100 = 48

If we know trim is 48 and inducer is 49.2 mm, we can deduce the compressor wheel's exducer as follows:

Trim = (inducer diameter / exducer diameter)^2 × 100
Exducer^2 = Inducer^2 × (100 / Trim)
Exducer = Inducer × Square Root [100 / 48]
        = 49.2 × 1.44337
        = 71.0

A Vortech Maxflow Race bypass valve. Because they can, centrifugal superchargers normally blow into the throttle body or carb, allowing the throttle to remain in the stock location on a supercharger conversion. When the throttle suddenly closes, pressure will back up and surge backward through the compressor wheel with a noticeable chuffing noise. The bypass valve opens with manifold vacuum to eliminate surge by routing pressure back to the inlet side of the supercharger (or turbo). *Vortech*

blades for a relatively long time, which provides a much higher acceleration of charge air than a single axial fan. While individual-stage axial fans are limited to a maximum absolute pressure ratio of about 1.2:1, some centrifugal compressors achieve pressure ratios as high 4:1 in a single stage.

Under ideal conditions centrifugal compressors are capable of peak thermal efficiencies above 80 percent, though the actual thermal efficiency varies widely, depending on the compressor wheel design, the pressure ratio, and airflow. This is as good as it gets in the real world but still represents considerable heating. Getting air to enter the engine at ambient temperature is impossible with any type of compressor without "aftercooling" the compressed charge air using cold water, ice, or refrigerant coolant; centrifugal compressors make the intercooling job much easier than most other types of compressors, through their flexible mounting options, simple means of expelling compressed air, and their relative efficiency. Centrifugal compressors are normally sized to the application to make sure the compressor never operates at any combination of pressure ratio and mass airflow that delivers less than 60 percent thermal efficiency.

Depending on the design, a centrifugal compressor can efficiently supply pressurized air over quite a broad range of compressor speeds, airflow rates, and pressure ratios, but the design cannot begin making any pressure at all until it is spinning quite fast. In fact, the biggest disadvantage

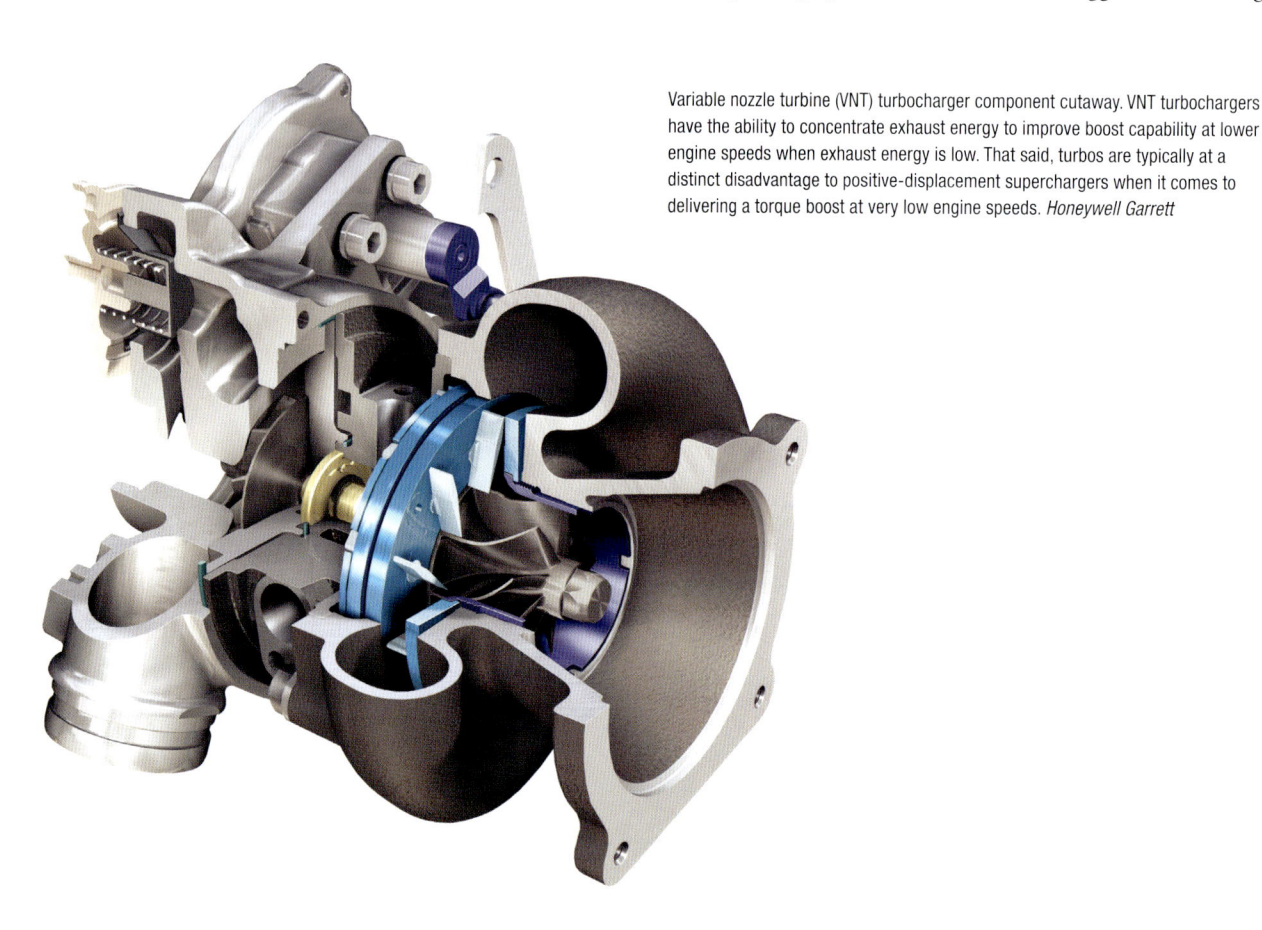

Variable nozzle turbine (VNT) turbocharger component cutaway. VNT turbochargers have the ability to concentrate exhaust energy to improve boost capability at lower engine speeds when exhaust energy is low. That said, turbos are typically at a distinct disadvantage to positive-displacement superchargers when it comes to delivering a torque boost at very low engine speeds. *Honeywell Garrett*

of centrifugal compressors is the fact that mass airflow per revolution varies tremendously with compressor speed. Because airflow from a centrifugal compressor increases at the *square* of compressor rpm, modern automotive-sized centrifugal compressors must spool to a threshold of 25,000 or more rpm to achieve measurable boost pressure. It follows, however, that once boost becomes available, the mass airflow increases rapidly with additional compressor speed. For example, assume a mechanically driven centrifugal compressor driven at an engine speed of, say 3,000 rpm is making 5-psi boost at 50K rpm for an absolute pressure ratio of roughly 1.3:1—that is, 1.3 atmosphere of total pressure above nothing at all. Doubling engine rpm to 6,000 doubles the compressor speed to 100K rpm and doubles the absolute pressure ratio to 2.6, which represents more than a fourfold increase in boost pressure, to 24 psi!

To achieve sufficient centrifugal compressor wheel tip speed for effective pumping, mechanical centrifugal supercharger drive systems typically couple an overdrive ratio of 2:1 at the crank pulley with single-stage internal planetary gearing providing a 15:1 step-up ratio, thus driving the supercharger at 30 times crank speed.

In addition to the extreme drive ratio, mechanically driven centrifugal superchargers for street automotive applications are typically designed with oversized compressor wheels optimized to deliver the lowest possible boost threshold, at the cost of significantly increased compressor wheel inertia. The result is that an aluminum compressor wheel in a mechanically driven centrifugal supercharger can be turning at 50K rpm and have considerable momentum. Because high drive ratios are prone to converting sudden changes in engine speed into extreme, gear-wrecking quantum leaps in compressor speed, it is critical that centrifugal superchargers be equipped with slip-clutches, noncogged drive belts, or other cushioning devices that will slip before excessive acceleration or deceleration damages the supercharger.

Early 1950s Paxton superchargers mitigated the mathematical drive liabilities of centrifugal compressors by employing a variable-speed drive based on a V-belt system. Paxton's effective pulley size changed according to throttle position, effectively decreasing the supercharger pulley's size at full throttle to run the compressor faster and produce more boost, while driving the supercharger at a slower speed during ordinary cruise conditions, like a turbocharger.

Centrifugal compressors have not been installed on any modern factory-supercharged engines as a result of centrifugal supercharger drive issues and pressure-ratio considerations. OE manufacturers have found good alternatives available to increase engine torque, particularly at low rpm. Tuners—with a different set of priorities—have used modern mechanical-drive centrifugal superchargers to dramatically boost the high-rpm performance of medium and large displacement engines that are not in need of enhanced low-rpm torque (or where intermittent nitrous injection does the job).

Turbine-Driven Centrifugal Superchargers

A centrifugal compressor driven by a radial-inflow exhaust gas turbine rather than the crankshaft of an engine would accurately and descriptively be referred to as a "turbine-supercharger," but the name was long ago shortened to turbo-supercharger, turbocharger, and finally just turbo. Unlike the Comprex pressure-wave supercharging system, the turbine and centrifugal compressor assemblies of a turbocharger are entirely separate assemblies sharing a common shaft. The intake and exhaust gases do not mix in any way except through the engine. The fact that centrifugal compressors on turbochargers are not driven mechanically from the crankshaft as are centrifugal superchargers allows the compressor design to be optimized for operation at much higher speeds than most mechanically driven centrifugal superchargers, allowing reduced size, lower inertia, and higher thermal efficiency.

A turbocharger's radial-inflow gas turbine is more or less the opposite of a centrifugal compressor: Hot combustion gases enter the turbine housing through a tangential turbine inlet nozzle located at the periphery of the housing such that exhaust blasts against the larger curved *outer* inducer section of the turbine paddles at very high speed to amplify exhaust energy. Having given up heat and kinetic energy to rotate the turbine wheel, lower-energy exhaust gases are funneled inward along the turbine blades toward the central (exducer) section of the blades, where it turns 90 degrees sideways and dumps out the center of the turbine housing into an exhaust pipe (or, occasionally, the turbine inducer of

Big-block drag-race engine with The Supercharger Store's gear-driven competition centrifugal supercharger. As was the case with the Merlin aviation engine, gear-drive systems are not subject to drive belt failure or slippage. Note the belt-driven fuel/scavange pump just above "charger" in the sign. *The Supercharger Store*

SUPERCHARGER ARCHITECTURE

77

another turbocharger). This difference in gas-flow direction means the inducer and exducer sections of radial-inflow turbines and centrifugal compressors are in essentially opposite places, with the central inlet of the compressor and the tangential inlet of the turbine referred to as the "inducer," and the "exducer" being the peripheral "flinging section" of the compressor blades and the central discharge section of the turbine blades. Although axial (fan-type) turbines of the sort used in modern jet engines have been used in large, heavy-duty engine applications when the turbocharged power output is above 2,500 horsepower and a sufficiently large radial-inflow wheel is too big to cast in one piece, a one-piece radial-inflow turbine casting is far more cost-effective.

A turbocharger turbine requires a threshold amount of exhaust pressure and heat energy before it can deliver enough torque to spool up the centrifugal compressor to a high enough speed to produce any positive boost pressure. This defines the minimum engine speed and loading required to make turbo boost. In an effort to lower the boost threshold or reduce or eliminate turbo lag, turbocharger compressors have been equipped with electric motors integral to the rotating assembly that pre-spool the rotating assembly. For similar reasons, some turbocharger turbines have been equipped with variable geometry turbine nozzles that replace the conventional fixed-size turbine nozzle with a series of vanes and an electro-pneumatic controller that optimizes the effective nozzle size according to available exhaust energy and engine loading as conditions demand.

When a turbocharged engine is idling or lightly loaded in cruise operation, the throttle opening is small, exhaust energy is minimal, and the engine is operating with low volumetric efficiency. Under such conditions, a turbocharger is freewheeling and at idle may even be stopped or turning very slowly, such that the turbine nozzle has no effect on engine-pumping efficiency. Properly sized turbochargers with large turbine wheels and nozzles designed to optimize maximum power can achieve exhaust back pressure that's significantly *lower* than the intake boost pressure—a happy condition known as *crossover* that delivers extremely good power per psi boost. In a worst case scenario, however, turbine-generated exhaust back pressure can be *several times* that of intake manifold boost pressure. This occurs in poorly designed or low-rpm turbo systems under heavy engine loading, when the compressor is making boost and large amounts of exhaust gases are entering the turbine, which can be a severe constraint on peak power.

The bottom line is that *any* exhaust back pressure will tend to reduce engine pumping efficiency such that any turbocharged engine delivers somewhat less power under boost than it would if the compressor could be driven completely by an external power source that did not constrain engine exhaust flow.

The full extent of horsepower wasted driving an exhaust turbine will depend on the sizes of the turbine housing, wheel, and nozzle, with bigger turbines and larger turbine nozzles degrading power less. The goal of automotive engineers designing original-equipment engines is to achieve a target amount of horsepower rather than the *maximum* feasible horsepower from an engine package. Early factory turbo cars like the Chevrolet Corvair were intentionally designed with high back pressure at peak power precisely to control maximum boost by choking the turbine and eliminating any need for a wastegate or blow-off valve. Typically 80 percent of the energy to drive a turbine comes from harnessing heat that would otherwise be wasted out the exhaust system,

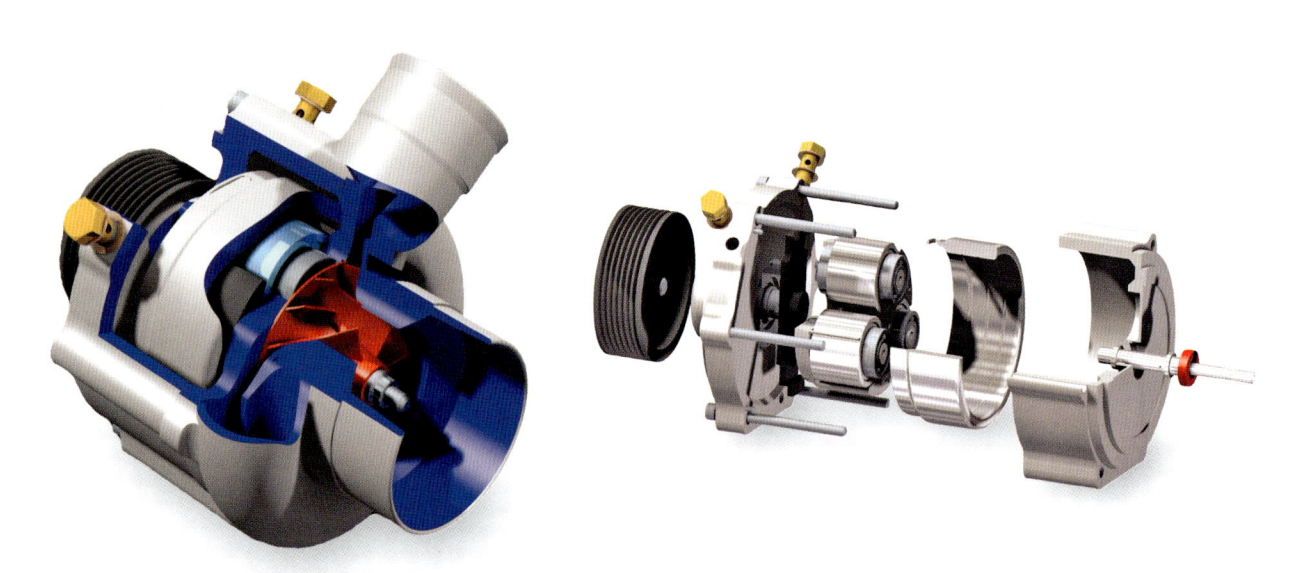

Solids-modeling rendering of the Rotrex centrifugal supercharger. This is basically a turbo-sized compressor that is mechanically driven using a planetary drive system that enables much higher drive ratios than conventional internal belt or gear step-up systems.

with the other 20 percent coming from pumping pressure. This may be a little difficult to imagine, but suffice it to say that exhaust exits the turbine having been significantly cooled, and that pressure resulting from exhaust heat has been harnessed to accomplish work and dissipated. It is not necessary or desirable to have tremendous amounts of exhaust back pressure. Harnessing waste exhaust heat can extract about 10 percent more energy from motor fuel. Recovering exhaust heat provides up to 2.5 percent increase in thermal efficiency for a piston engine, but the additional efficiency is not typically available on street turbo engines partly because forced induction is virtually always optimized on gasoline-fueled automotive engines to increase horsepower rather than fuel economy, but also due to the implicit inefficiencies in forced-induction engines discussed earlier in this chapter related to effective compression ratio versus actual expansion ratio. Supercharged engines—including superchargers driven by a turbine—are designed to make power, and most of this is accomplished by burning additional fuel.

Within limits, the more boost a turbocharged engine makes, the more it *can* make, due to the feedback cycle of boost burning more fuel, which generates more exhaust pressure and heat, which spins the turbine faster, which has the compressor make more boost, which generates more exhaust energy, and so on until the gas flow chokes somewhere or the engine fails from detonation or other problems of extreme overboost become a constraint.

If you spin a centrifugal compressor fast enough, it will eventually reach compressor choke, a point at which thermal efficiency degenerates to the degree that no more air will flow no matter what the additional compressor speed or pressure ratio. Under some circumstances, a turbocharger operating near its upper airflow limitations can actually be damaged by over-speeding. Modern turbocharged engines require a method of controlling boost, which is typically a wastegate between the exhaust manifold and turbocharger to bypass exhaust gases around the turbine, or a spring-loaded valve in the intake tract to blow-off excessive charge air, or a variable geometry turbine nozzle (VGTN). If centrifugal compressor output is restricted to the point that too much pressure develops with too little mass airflow, compressor airflow can become unstable as potentially dangerous surges of air intermittently flow backwards through the compressor wheel to dissipate pressure.

To get a handle on the performance characteristics of a turbocharger, engineers test the centrifugal compressors by driving them to speeds not safely achievable with mechanical drive systems using high-speed turbines powered by combustion gases or pressurized room-temperature inert gas to develop *compressor maps* that chart the range of mass airflow versus pressure ratio that a particular design of compressor wheel and housing can achieve at various levels of thermal efficiency and compressor rpm.

The intercooled Rotrex compressor is key to Mountain Performance's Yamaha Rhino ATV supercharging system. The Rotrex boosts the Yamaha ATV power from 22 to 52 wheel horsepower. Rotrex compressors are wonderfully compact, which makes them great for bikes, snowmobiles, or automotive engine compartments where space is tight. *Mountain Performance*

The advantages of forced induction from a turbine-driven centrifugal compressor include the following:

- A 3 to 4 atmosphere pressure ratio is available from a single-stage compressor.
- The compact, lightweight design allows installation on a wide range of engines and vehicles.
- It has an acceptable-to-great thermal efficiency over a wide range of mass airflow and pressure.
- There are low levels of parasitic drag vs. boost.
- It has a wide range of compressor and turbine sizes available to match a powerplant's airflow requirements.
- The turbocharger need not be located close to a mechanical drive on the crankshaft or bell housing.
- The compact "inline" aspects of a turbocharger make plumbing air-to-air intercoolers simpler than most positive displacement superchargers.

The disadvantages of a turbine-driven centrifugal compressor include the following:

- Negligible exhaust turbine energy at low engine speeds combined with exponential compressor airflow characteristics provides no boost pressure below a threshold engine rpm.
- Extremely high rotational speed makes clean, fresh oil critically important, raising the standards for acceptable preventative maintenance.
- Operating speeds mandate precision tolerances and balance, requiring professional rebuilding and assembly.

Chapter 5
Supercharger Selection and System Modeling

It is critical to select the correct supercharger before you lay out the larger supercharging system because the size and type of compressor will constrain other decisions in the design process.

Modeling a supercharger system is a process by which you calculate and test the effects of various assumptions about the basic system operating parameters, evaluate tradeoffs, and iteratively correct the model to hone in on a compressor (and intercooler, if necessary) that will meet your performance requirements with the fewest compromises.

This is an iterative process in which you start with a basic model and then make a series of corrections to make the model's predictions more realistic. Keep in mind that if you are going boldly where no man has gone before with a supercharging project—that is, you're doing research and development on an engine that has not commonly been supercharged—you can expect that the initial performance results will not work out exactly as predicted when you build the system, and you may have to make adjustments to the supercharger drive ratio or possibly even change to a different supercharger or intercooler to meet the performance goals for the project.

If you are lucky, the model will do a good job and the project will exceed the expected performance. If you are unlucky, it may be impossible to meet the predicted performance goals on street fuel without detonation, and you'll discover unexpectedly weak engine parts when they fail catastrophically.

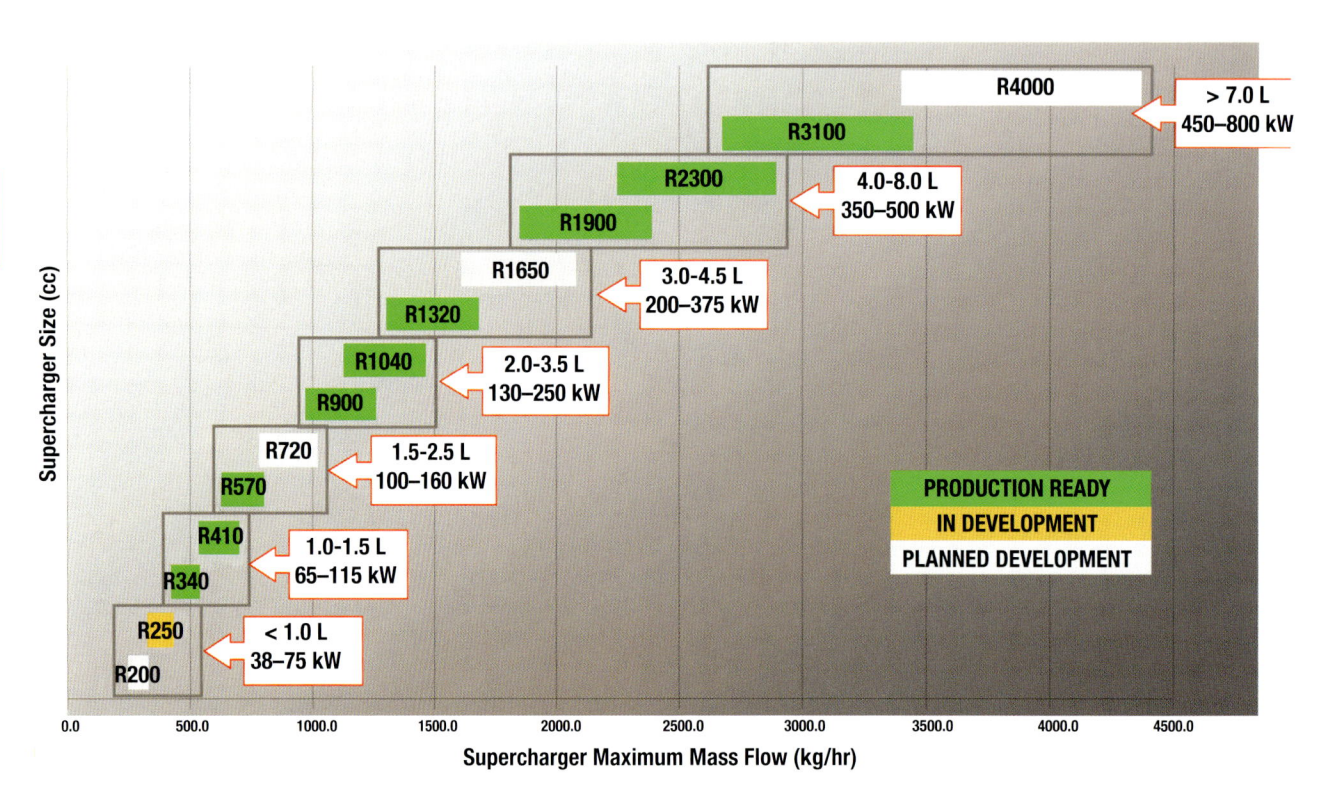

TVS® SUPERCHARGER FAMILY TABLE: The Eaton TVS family tree shows TVS superchargers providing airflow for 51–1,072-horsepower (38–800 kW) engines. At this time of writing, some superchargers were still in the planning or development stage.

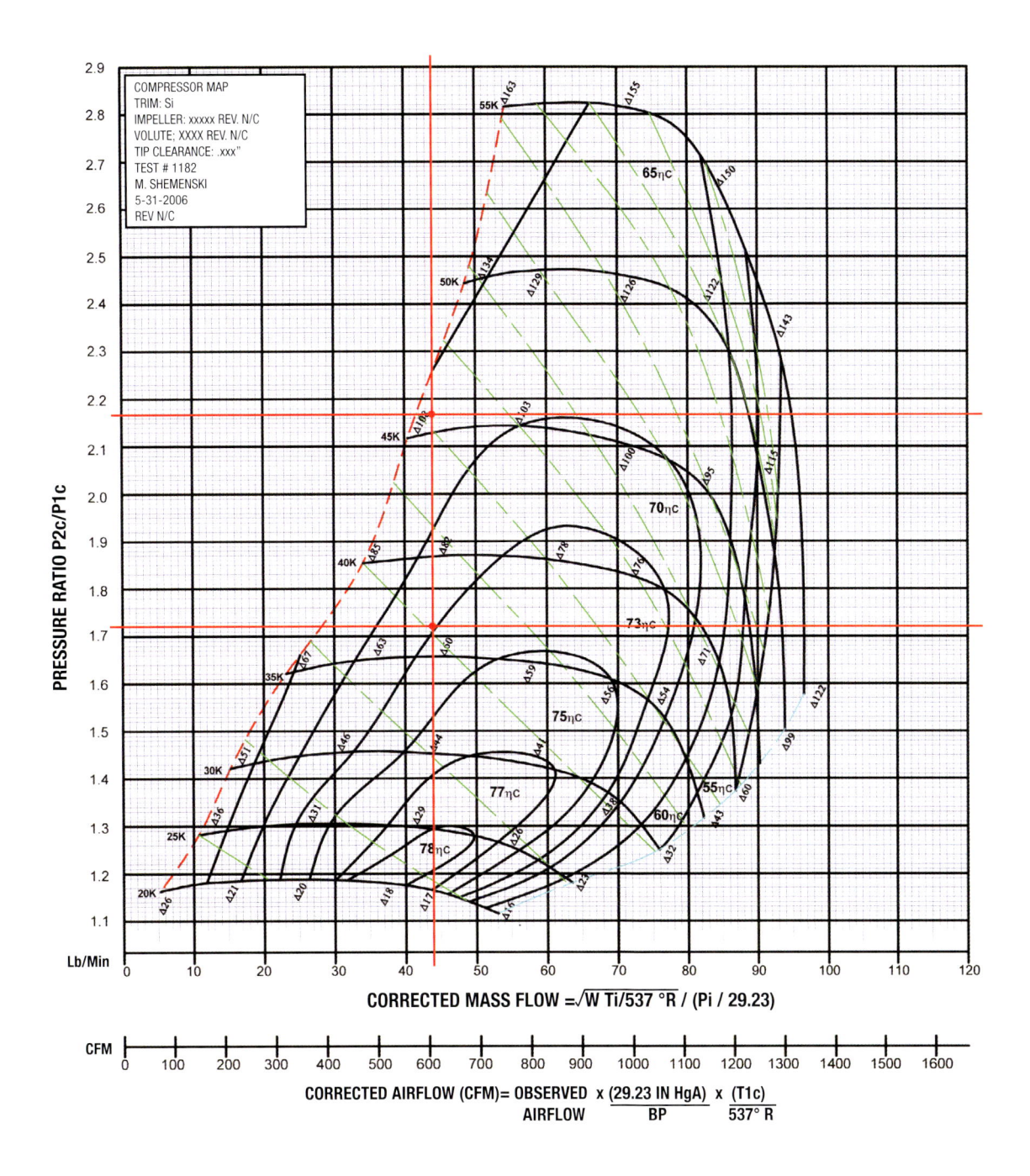

Compressor Map — TRIM: Si, IMPELLER: xxxxx REV. N/C, VOLUTE: XXXX REV. N/C, TIP CLEARANCE: .xxx", TEST # 1182, M. SHEMENSKI, 5-31-2006, REV N/C

$$\text{CORRECTED MASS FLOW} = \sqrt{W\, T_i / 537\,°R} \,/\, (P_i / 29.23)$$

$$\text{CORRECTED AIRFLOW (CFM)} = \text{OBSERVED AIRFLOW} \times \frac{29.23\ \text{IN HgA}}{BP} \times \frac{T_{1c}}{537°\ R}$$

Modeling a supercharger conversion using compressor maps consists of the following steps:

- Determine the ideal target horsepower increase for your vehicle.
- Determine the engine rpm range of the application, which will impact the target rpm for maximum compressor efficiency.
- Make an initial calculation of the mass air flow that will be required to achieve the target horsepower.
- Estimate the initial supercharger pressure ratio required to achieve the target mass airflow based on an assumed or "standard" intake manifold air temperature.
- Based on the magnitude of the pressure ratio, reexamine the manifold air temperature and if necessary recalculate the pressure ratio.
- Model the effect of intercooling.
- Correct for a pressure drop upstream and downstream of the compressor, altitude, unusual weather environments, power required to drive the supercharger, and plausible supercharger thermal and volumetric efficiency.

SUPERCHARGER SELECTION AND SYSTEM MODELING

81

- Calculate the final pressure ratio to use in evaluating compressor performance maps.
- Optional: Recalculate the final pressure ratio using the *power-ratio* model.
- Select "ballpark" viable superchargers.
- Revisit the manifold inlet temperature for specific "real-world" compressor-intercooler thermal efficiency.
- Verify that mechanical and thermal loading demands are realistic without detonation and without overloading mechanical parts when relying on available fuel.
- Determine the required supercharger drive ratio (after adjusting blower rpm for compressor volumetric efficiency in the case of positive-displacement superchargers).
- Determine the belt-loading requirement.
- Verify that the supercharger will not over-speed at engine redline and, if necessary, reduce de-facto engine redline.
- If necessary, evaluate supercharger performance at subpeak blower and engine rpm.

Supercharger selection begins with defining peak horsepower and torque goals; you'll eventually want to evaluate the impact of boost on torque requirements at lower engine speeds and redline, but the place to start is peak power. Some supercharging system designs (and all turbochargers) offer a tuner the potential to warp the shape of an engine's basic normal-charged torque and power curves by varying boost pressure electronically at various points in the engine's operating envelope, though most mechanical drive systems make it difficult or impossible.

Mechanically driven superchargers are far less flexible with regard to electronic boost control than the exhaust-driven

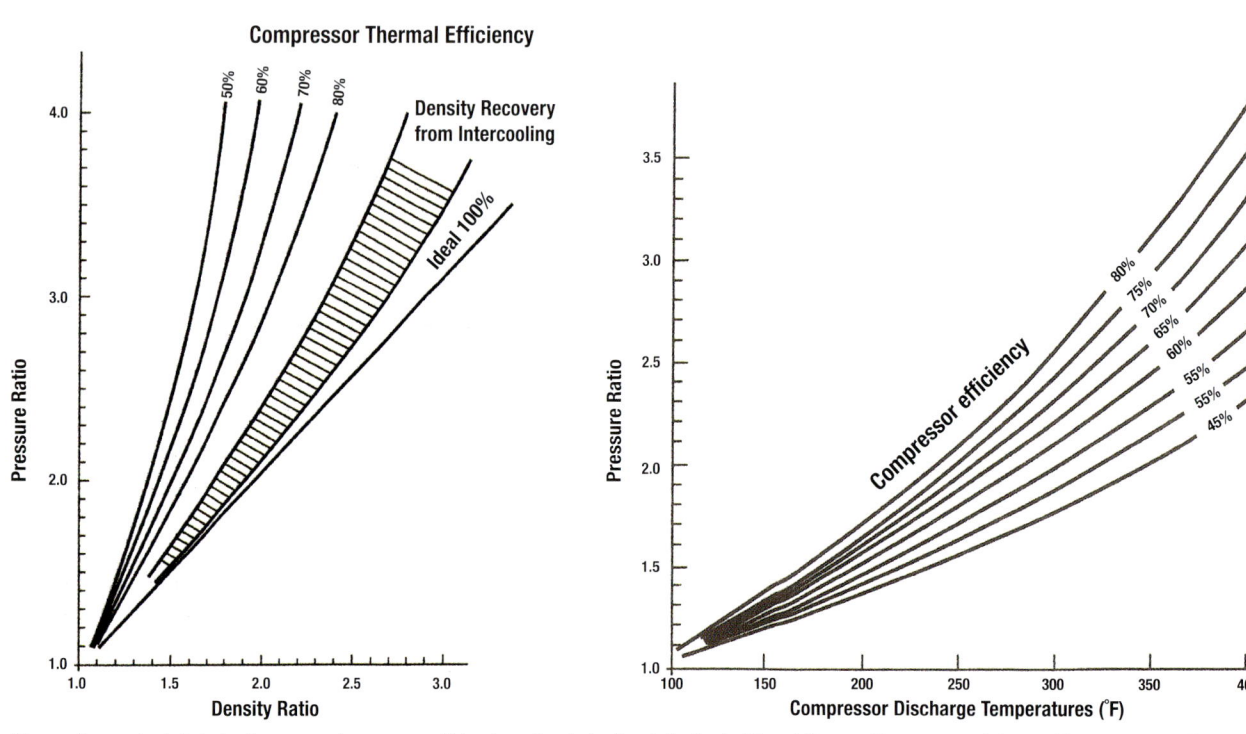

Honda's 2.0-liter S2000 typified a modern powerplant with extremely high volumetric efficiency. Such an engine makes the job of a supercharger easier, as it takes less work to force a given amount of air through the engine. The S2000 made use of extremely high redline and variable valve timing to achieve 240 crankshaft horsepower at 8,000 rpm without supercharging. That said, 240 is only 240, and there are plenty of S2000s driving around with supercharger conversion systems.

All superchargers heat air during the compression process, which reduces the air density relative to what it would be were the compressed air at ambient temperature. The greater the thermal efficiency, the less heating occurs during compression. A good intercooler will lower air temperature after compression, increasing air density and lowering combustion temperature enough to run more boost pressure without detonation. These tables translate the ratio of compressor discharge pressure to inlet pressure into the ratio discharge air density to compressor inlet density, which takes into account both pressure and temperature. It is the density ratio that determines the maximum power boost possible from supercharging. *Bell Intercoolers*

turbines used to drive centrifugal compressors in turbo systems (an exception is with the continuously variable transmission that has been used in a few historic centrifugal supercharger systems). The bottom line is that if you want to do a lot of fancy torque manipulation that cannot be approximated with a deft combination of (1) the basic VE curve of the engine, (2) the superimposed VE map of a particular type and size supercharger, (3) careful selection of the blower drive ratio, and (4) torque multiplication from the right gears (perhaps with custom gear ratios), you should seriously consider abandoning traditional supercharging in favor of turbocharging, two-stage twincharging, or supercharging combined with pulse width-modulated nitrous injection. That said, supercharger systems from outfits like Mercury Marine have used electronic blow-off valves to bleed off boost to provide a low-boost mode. This allows marine engines (inherently under heavy load in most cruise operations) to function on reduced-octane fuel when necessary. However, boost bleeding can introduce inefficiencies if heated boost air is recycled back into the compressor intake and reheated, or if crankshaft power is wasted to achieve compressure discharge pressure that is partially wasted. You may decide to increase horsepower by a percentage of the stock normal-charged peak power, or you may want to work backward from, say, a required quarter-mile time for a certain weight vehicle to the horsepower that will get the job done. Or you may identify a required top speed for a vehicle with a certain coefficient of drag and rolling resistance.

You'll need to know or estimate some things about your application before you can crunch the numbers to select the right supercharger by plotting required pressure ratio and mass airflow on a compressor performance map.

Things you need to know:
- Target horsepower
- Engine displacement (it is good to know peak torque rpm as well)
- Engine redline, peak power, and peak torque rpm
- Ambient conditions (temperature and barometric pressure)
  Note: Barometric pressure is usually given as inches of mercury and can be converted to psi by dividing by 2.

CALCULATING INTAKE MANIFOLD TEMPERATURE

Intake manifold temperature can be predicted on the basis of compressor inlet temperature, compressor pressure ratio, compressor thermal efficiency, and the effectiveness of the intercooling system (which is 0 if there is no intercooler).

The pressure ratio of a supercharger is relative rather than absolute, a number greater than or equal to 1.0 that represents the percentage increase of absolute air pressure leaving the compressor discharge versus that of absolute air pressure entering the compressor inlet, which is about 14.7 psi, or 1 atmosphere, at sea level in standard weather conditions. The thermal efficiency of a particular compressor is an indication of how much worse the compressor is than the "ideal" heating that's an inevitable result of the physics of squeezing a gas into a smaller space.

If compressor discharge pressure is a bit less than, say, 25.5 psiabs, and compressor intake pressure is standard atmospheric pressure, the pressure ratio is **25.28 / 14.7 ≈ 1.72**.

Assuming compressor thermal efficiency is 70 percent (a fairly good number), the temperature gain of 70 degrees F ambient air will be:

Temp Gain = ((PR$^{0.28}$ -1) × T$_{ABS}$) / CE

where...
PR = Pressure ratio
T$_{ABS}$ = Compressor inlet temperature (absolute) = degrees F + 460
CE = Compressor efficiency between 45 and - 80 percent = > 0.45-.80
PR$^{0.28}$ = The pressure ratio to the .28th power (use Y^x key on a calculator), which defines the relationship between pressure ratio and temperature increase as a function of the ideal gas law.

Assuming air inlet temperature of 70 degrees F, compressor thermal efficiency of .7, and pressure ratio of 1.72,

Temp Gain = ((1.72$^{0.28}$ -1) × (70 + 460)) / 0.7
= 124.2

Thus:
Intake manifold temperature = 70F + 124.2F
= 194.2F

The 194.2 degrees F is not the end of the story, however, since there can be an intercooler between the compressor and the intake manifold. Installing an 85 percent efficient intercooler, the temperature gain of compression can be reduced from 125.6 degrees F to **124.2F × (1 − 0.85) = 18.63F**. When added to the compressor-in temperature of 70 degrees F, the intercooled intake manifold temperature becomes **70F + 18.63F = 88.63F ≈ 89F**.

A fact of life is that the best thermal efficiency you can achieve in a practical air-cooled intercooler doing its work in the fraction of a second available as high-speed charge air rushes from the compressor to the intake manifold is usually not much above 85 percent.

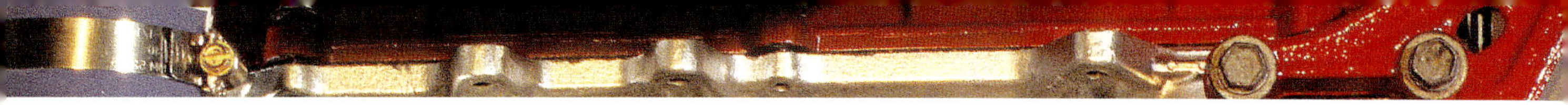

S2000 with Comptech centrifugal supercharger system (located in front of yellow cam cover). Most S2000 supercharging systems have used centrifugal compressors. Space for a positive-displacement supercharger was tight, and many people seem to have been loath to mess with violating the basic VE of the S2000 by attempting to redesign the Honda intake manifold to mount a twin-screw or Roots-type supercharger.

Other parameters you need to know or estimate:

- *Engine volumetric efficiency.* Typical numbers for peak normal-charged engine volumetric efficiency (VE)—i.e., percentage of cylinder filling—typically range from 88 to 95 percent for two-valve designs, and 95 to 99 percent for modern four-valve heads. On a well-tuned engine, the VE will peak at the torque peak (*not* peak power). Fully developed multi-valve Formula One-type race engines have achieved VE as high as 115 percent, but if you want a conservative number that will definitely not leave you disappointed with a supercharger conversion, go with 80 to 85 percent or less for two-valve engines, and 88 to 92 percent or less for four-valve designs. If you have a torque curve for your engine, you can use this to estimate VE at various engine speeds. If you know the flywheel horsepower at a certain rpm, a simple calculation will tell you the VE, as we shall see. A four-valve engine will typically have higher VE over more of its rev range than a two-valve engine.

- *Brake-specific fuel consumption (BSFC).* BSFC describes the fuel-flow rate required to generate each horsepower for a particular engine and state of tune. BSFC for supercharged gasoline engines typically ranges from 0.55 to 0.65. Well-designed turbo engines, which harness exhaust energy to drive the compressor, can be a bit lower, ranging from 0.50 on up. Really efficient normal-charged gasoline engines like the Honda S2000 achieve BSFC in the .44 to .45 range. The units of BSFC are **pounds / horsepower-hour (lb/hp-hr)**. Lower BSFC means that the engine requires less fuel to generate a given horsepower and therefore less air at a given air-fuel ratio. Race fuels and aggressive tuning are required to reach the low end of the BSFC range described above.

- *Pre-supercharged horsepower @ rpm* (alternative to VE and BSFC). Modern advertised (net) horsepower is accurate. Older advertised figures—particularly from the pre-1972 muscle car era—may not be accurate, and keep in mind that pre-1972 advertised power was

Toyota's 2.0-liter 3S-GTE with its Yamaha-designed cylinder head was capable of 7,250 rpm but made maximum power at 6,000 without variable valve timing and lift. A normal-charged version of the engine made between 138 and 209 horsepower at rpm ranging from 6,200–7,500. In the MR2 turbo, Toyota relied on forced induction to make 200–256 horsepower at 6,000–6,200 rpm. This steel-crank, aluminum-head, iron-block powerplant is extremely strong and has proven capable of surviving at horsepower levels in the 500 to 700 range with relatively small internal changes.

typically *gross* horsepower as measured on an engine dyno, with open headers and no power-robbing accessories installed. Gross horsepower says something about the basic engine design but is not an accurate measure of flywheel horsepower available to do work in a particular vehicle, and it does not accurately predict BSFC. Wheel horsepower measured by a chassis dyno is not the same as net crankshaft power because of drivetrain losses. Many tuners assume a 15 to 20 percent drivetrain loss, while others work from a known stock power loss and assume supercharging will not change this, resulting in lower estimated losses in percentage terms when supercharged and thus less impressive estimated crankshaft horsepower. The second approach is more conservative in estimating the crankshaft horsepower of an engine that has had a supercharger conversion system installed because you are assuming that power losses remain fixed at the stock normal-charged level rather than increasing as a

FLYWHEEL VERSUS WHEEL HORSEPOWER

When it comes to horsepower, beware the difference between inertial chassis dynamometer *wheel* horsepower and *crankshaft* horsepower measured by an engine dynamometer. Not all the crankshaft horsepower arrives at the driving wheels of a vehicle because of power absorbed in the act of rotating the drivetrain components, such as driveshafts, transmission and rear end gears, and axles.

Therefore, measuring a certain amount of measured "wheel horsepower" on a chassis dyno is an indication that the engine is actually producing more horsepower at the crankshaft. Most tuners adjust chassis dyno numbers upward by 15 to 20 percent to arrive at an estimate of flywheel horsepower. Some tuners—not many, because the numbers look worse—assume there is a fixed power loss in the drivetrain that does not change when you load the drivetrain more heavily with large power increases from supercharging. For a certain measured wheel horsepower, smaller assumed losses between the engine and the wheels implies lower horsepower at the crankshaft because of lower assumed parasitic losses in the drivetrain. A good yardstick of power loss in the drivetrain of a particular vehicle is to compare the wheel horsepower of a bone-stock factory vehicle with the factory horsepower rating so you can apply the loss information to an identical vehicle with a heavily boosted engine.

Be aware that forced-induction calculations related to BSFC and so forth are based on crankshaft horsepower, which is almost always computed from torque measured on a water-brake engine dyno. Keep in mind that the supercharger is serving the power requirements of the engine at the flywheel, not at the tires. In the case of an engine with a mechanically driven supercharger, flywheel horsepower is still not the whole story of the power actually being generated in the cylinders, because a significant percentage of the supercharged horsepower actually being generated is wasted driving the supercharger itself. Ten percent or more is not uncommon. Thus, if you are seeing 100 horsepower at the wheels, a supercharged engine is perhaps delivering 121.2 horsepower to the transmission and burning the fuel to deliver 142.6 horsepower at the blower pulley.

Calculations:
Working from the wheels to the crankshaft: $\frac{100 \text{ (wheel) hp}}{(1 - 17.5 \text{ percent})} = \frac{100}{.825} = 121.2121$ hp available at the transmission input.

$\frac{121.2121 \text{ hp}}{(1 - 15 \text{ percent})} = \frac{121.2121}{.85} = 142.60$ hp available at the blower pulley.

Working the other way from horsepower seen at the blower pulley to the wheels:
142.60 (blower pulley) hp − 15 percent = 142.60 hp − (142.60 × .15) = 142.6 − 21.39 hp = 121.209 hp seen at the transmission input shaft.
121.21 (flywheel horsepower) − 17.5 percent = 121.21 − (.175 × 121.21) = 2121.21 − 21.21 = 100 (wheel horsepower).

---

percentage of horsepower. When supercharging pumps up the volume, the lower drivetrain power loss estimate means you do not correct wheel horsepower upward as much to arrive at crankshaft horsepower. Let's say that a stock 2.0L engine made 170 horsepower on a wheel dyno, and that the engine was known to make 200 horsepower at the crankshaft. The power loss is therefore 30 horsepower out of 200, which is 30 / 200 = 15 percent. Going in the opposite direction, 170 / (1 − 0.15) = 200. Now let's say a supercharger conversion doubled wheel horsepower to 340. If you assume that the power loss is still 30 horsepower, the engine would be making 340 + 30 = 370 estimated crankshaft horsepower. However, if you assume power loss is 15 percent, 340 / (1 − .15) = 340 / .85 = 400 estimated crankshaft horsepower.

- *Intake manifold temperature.* Compressors with higher thermal efficiency deliver lower intake manifold temperatures by heating the air less during the compression process. According to Garrett, manifold temperatures of intercooled aftermarket turbo systems are typically a disappointing 100 to 130 degrees F, while non-intercooled manifold temperatures can reach from 175 to 300 degrees F—and typical supercharged systems are certainly not any better. That said, it is certainly possible to do better than average. An extremely well-designed air-cooled intercooler system, with good insulation where required to prevent heat-soak, can remove 85 percent of the temperature increase of supercharging.

Naturally, intake manifold temperature is heavily dependent on the temperature of air entering the compressor, which could be a 100 degrees Fahrenheit cooler on a cold winter day than on a hot summer day (or more, if the air intake is inside the engine compartment and breathing hot air). Intake manifold temperature is critically important when modeling a supercharger system to select the right compressor and intercooler, but you won't really know what it is until you know the pressure ratio and supercharger efficiency. But you have to start somewhere. The trick is to assume a certain manifold temperature—say, 80, 100 or 130 degrees F—and after you home in on a candidate supercharger-intercooler combination and pressure ratio, remodel the system with improved data. In the end, you'll need to calculate the actual heat of compression of a certain supercharger operating at particular boost pressure and speed and compute the actual effectiveness of a particular intercooler at recooling the compressed air to reclaim charge density lost in the heat of compression. From there you can home in on the boost pressure required to compensate for compressor and intercooler deficiencies and meet the power goals.

When it comes to collecting data to use in modeling a supercharger system, keep in mind the old acronym GIGO: Garbage In, Garbage Out.

STEP-BY-STEP SUPERCHARGER SIZING

1. Determine the ideal horsepower gain for your vehicle.
You probably already know this if you are racing. If not, there are simulation programs that can help you decide how much power it will take to win in your class of drag racing, land-speed record trials, or other types of racing.

The following formula provides a rough estimate of the horsepower required to achieve a certain quarter-mile drag time:

Power = Weight × (5.825 / elapsed time)^3

...where 5.825 is a constant derived experimentally

For example, if the vehicle and contents weighs 2,750 pounds and you want to do the quarter-mile in 11.1 seconds...

Power = 2,750 × (5.825 / 11.1)^3
= 2,750 × 0.1445
≈ 397.4 hp

You can also use the reworked formula below to determine the quarter-mile drag time achievable for a certain weight vehicle, given a certain amount of horsepower:

ET = 1 / ($\sqrt[3]{\text{horsepower / weight}}$ / 5.825)

= 1 / ($\sqrt[3]{400 / 2750}$ / 5.825)

= 1 / (0.5259 / 5.825)

≈ 11.08 seconds

You can also look at the horsepower needed to reach a top speed requirement based on the vehicle's coefficient of drag and rolling resistance.

For the purposes of illustration we're going to be assuming the goal of our supercharging project is 400 flywheel horsepower, because 400 horsepower is achievable for street-type usage in almost any size engine with forced induction, yet it is still above the stock horsepower of most normal-charged engines. Also, 400 is within the capability of some superchargers for both the low-to-moderate boost required to achieve target power with a V-8 powerplant and the medium-to-high boost required to do the job with a much smaller I-4.

2. Target the engine rpm range for your application.
For competition or nonautomotive engines, you'll want to select a supercharger with a maximum thermal efficiency rating that is at or near the most useful part of the engine's rpm range. For a street vehicle it is a good idea to target the supercharger's maximum thermal efficiency at a range

As legions of hot rodders have discovered, the relatively low horsepower per cylinder (15 horsepower and up) of the low-deck pushrod Ford Windsor V-8 makes the 4.2–5.0-liter engine excellent raw material for supercharging. Shown here with a simple but effective Paxton Novi blower kit, non-intercooled.

A classic carbureted Chevrolet pushrod small-block V-8 with the Paxton centrifugal blower kit. The original engine arrived in 1954 with 4.3-liter displacement and grew as large as 6.6L, making as little as 13.75 horsepower per cylinder in the mid-1970s. As with the 5.0-liter Ford, the classic Chevy small-block is a fruitful platform for supercharging.

Small-block Mopar V-8s have not been released with 5.0-liter displacement since the 1950s, but 5.2-liter Mopar A-block engines were manufactured by the gazillions from the mid-1960s onward, and 3x2bbl versions made as much as 315 to 325 horsepower (although Chrysler advertised 290 or less to keep the insurance companies at bay). A 5.9-liter (360-cid) version survived into the new millennium equipped with electronic fuel injection (after which it was replaced by the new Hemi), but a market remains for A-block carbureted supercharging, as evidenced by this Paxton Mopar kit. *Paxton*

about 25 percent above the engine's peak torque rpm (peak torque is also peak volumetric efficiency) so that supercharger efficiency increases as engine volumetric efficiency decreases going from peak torque to peak power.

For example, the peak torque of a stock 1990 Mustang GT 5.0 occurs at 3,200 rpm, so you'd place the peak thermal efficiency target of the blower at 4,000 rpm, which also happens to be the engine's peak power rpm, where it makes 225 horsepower.

Targeting the engine RPM for peak blower efficiency requires some judgment. If you're trying to maximize peak power, keep in mind that forced induction may shift peak engine volumetric efficiency (peak torque) upward to a slightly higher rpm (which will raise horsepower more than you'd predict simply from the effect of boost alone).

For the purposes of example, we're going to assume that boosted peak power rpm stays what it was prior to supercharging, though in actual practice it might increase a bit.

Keep in mind that *transition* performance during acceleration is usually more important than peak power in maximizing street performance. With this in mind, rather than simply modeling maximum horsepower at the peak-power rpm, you may want to evaluate the effect of engine boost at lower rpm points as well.

3. Model airflow and pressure required to achieve target horsepower

A rough rule of thumb is that each pound of air per minute delivered to the intake manifold of a well-tuned spark-ignition gasoline engine will make somewhere between 9 and 11 horsepower. Accordingly, we can expect that a 400-horsepower piston engine running on gasoline will require somewhere between 36 and 44 pounds of air per minute when operating at maximum power. Oxygenated fuels like methanol and nitromethane require far less air to burn than gasoline because they are already, in a sense, partially burned (4:1 is the common air-fuel ratio for best power with methanol; nitromethane can actually "burn" as a monopropellant without any oxygen at all, but will make more power at an air-fuel ratio of 1.7:1). The reduced stoichiometric air-fuel ratio is the reason why methanol and nitromethane have a much higher fuel consumption per horsepower and will always make more power than an equivalent gasoline-fueled engine where volumetric efficiency is limited by the ability of atmospheric pressure to charge the cylinders (i.e., not supercharged).

A more sophisticated way of modeling airflow and boost pressure requires that you have data regarding the specific energy of the fuel, e.g., the horsepower the fuel can make for a given mass of air (fuel heating value divided by the stoichiometric air-fuel ratio). The airflow calculation does not require that you know engine size or rpm or volumetric efficiency, which makes the model especially valuable if you want to evaluate the effect of changing the fuel type or the air-fuel mixture on your supercharger selection. The manifold pressure (boost) calculations in this model do not even require that you know the existing horsepower of an engine prior to supercharging. We'll also look at another method of modeling that works from existing horsepower to the supercharging pressure required to achieve a target horsepower.

Note: It is human nature to be optimistic when plugging numbers into a mathematical model. One way to avoid trouble is to calculate "best case" and "worst case" numbers to see if the same equipment could handle both cases.

To model airflow purely as a function of the target horsepower requirement, plug in the estimated air-fuel ratio and the brake specific fuel consumption (BSFC) of a particular type of engine burning a particular type of fuel into the following equation:

$$MAF = HP \times AFR \times BSFC / 60$$

Where:
MAF = Mass airflow rate in pounds per minute
HP = Target horsepower (at the flywheel)
AFR = Air-fuel ratio
BSFC = Brake specific fuel consumption (pounds fuel per horsepower-hour)
60 = Hours-to-minutes conversion

To illustrate, let's assume we're working with a spark-ignition engine fueled with gasoline. **Our goal is 400 horsepower, and we'll assume an air-fuel ratio of 12.0 and a BSFC of 0.55.**

Logic: A 12.0:1 ratio of air to gasoline is richer than the basic mean best torque air-fuel ratio, thus providing some additional gasoline that cannot be burned but will cool combustion and fight detonation. BSFC is .55 (.55 pounds gasoline per horsepower per hour) because the engine is supercharged, and supercharged engines are in general less fuel-efficient per cubic inch displacement at full, boosted power than turbo engines, which are in turn less fuel efficient at full power per cubic inch than the most efficient normal-charged engines. That said, keep in mind that the overall fuel economy of forced-induction engines may exceed that of normal-charged engines of the same peak output because a normal-charged engine of a certain power output would typically have greater internal friction from increased displacement and additional cylinders (and might deliver peak power at a higher rpm); whereas, forced-induction engines with equal power output would be smaller powerplants with less inherent internal friction (possibly geared to cut friction even more by down-speeding the engine). This efficiency is partially offset by the increased BSFC during boosted operations but is reinforced at idle and light cruise by de-clutching the compressor or opening bypass valves to allow the compressor to freewheel at no load. Supercharged BSFC can sometimes be as high as .60 or even .65 if large amounts of fuel are wasted to cool combustion in order to prevent spark knock.

Applying these numbers to the formula:

$$MAF = HP \times AFR \times BSFC / 60$$

$$= 400 \times 12.0 \times 0.55 / 60$$

$$= 44 \text{ lb / min of air}$$

Any engine with BSFC of .55 and air-fuel ratio of 12.0:1 needs to flow about 44 lb/min of air to make 400 horsepower.

If, on the other hand, BSFC were .60, we'd need more air at the 12.0:1 air-fuel ratio—just over 48 lb/min—to make 400 horsepower:

MAF = 400 × 12.0 × 0.60 / 60 = 48 lb / min

If BSFC were .65, we'd need 52 lb/min air.

In terms of the airflow requirement, it is fascinating to note that, assuming the air-fuel ratio remains constant, a 400-horsepower engine with BSFC of just more than .6 is roughly equivalent to a 440-horsepower engine with .55 BSFC:

MAF = 440 × 12.0 × 0.55 / 60 = 48.4 lb / min

The reason why this is increasing is that BSFC is precisely the mechanism by which this model seamlessly accounts for the drag of mechanically driven superchargers that typically waste 5 to 15 percent of the power they generate driving the blower—power you'll never see at the wheels or even the flywheel, but power that nonetheless requires burning more fuel and air. A "400 horsepower" supercharged engine may actually be generating an additional 40 horsepower you never see because it is wasted driving the blower.

Meanwhile, let's say we're considering fueling an engine with alcohol or an alcohol-gasoline mixture instead of neat gasoline. A typical best-power air-fuel ratio (AFR) and BSFC for methanol would be 4.0:1 AFR and 1.2 BSFC:

MAF = HP × AFR × BSFC / 60

= 400 × 4.0 × (1.2 / 60)

= 32 lb / min of air

Any motor fuel with BSFC of 1.2 and 4:1 AFR needs only 32 lb/min mass airflow to make 400 horsepower (rather than 44 lb/min as is the case with gasoline).

Alternatively, given 44 pounds per minute of airflow, switching to methanol instead of gasoline would allow you to make 550 horsepower instead of just 400:

HP = 44 lb/min / ((AFR × BSFC) / 60)

= 44 / ((4.0 × 1.2) / 60)

= 550

GM's replacement for the Offenhauser-like Quad-4 was the Ecotec, a fully modern powerplant designed by an international GM team. The initial Y2K version was strong, smooth, and conventional, but exciting tricks came in subsequent years, when the powerplant became available with variable valve timing, supercharging, turbocharging, and gasoline direct injection. In the meantime, GM decided to generate excitement in competition, targeting drag racing and then various land-speed records. This glamour-class Cavalier drag car eventually made more than 1,200 horsepower and won many races in NHRA competition. *GM Media Archive*

ALTERNATE SCENARIOS

Suppose we're looking at how much boost it takes to get to 400 horsepower when the raw material is an "old-school" 5.0-liter V-8? 14.3 psi will do it, assuming the following:

MAF = 44 lb / min (as calculated previously from formula using target power, AFR, and BSFC)
T_m = 105 degrees F (say you're running a K&N filter drawing warm engine-compartment air)
VE = 80% at peak power (it's an old-school pushrod V-8)
RPM = 4,000 rpm (peak power rpm in a stock 1990 Mustang GT)
CID = 302 ci (4.942 liters × 61.02)

MAP = (44 × 639.6 × (105F + 460)) / (.80 × 4000 × .5 × 302)
= 32.9 psi_{abs}

Boost = 32.9 − 14.7
= 18.2 psi

Alternate scenario 1: Plugging in different numbers, we see that if the intake air temperature were not 105 degrees F but 70 degrees (colder air of a given pressure is more dense), less pressure is required to push 44 pounds of air per minute through the engine:

MAP = (44 × 639.6 × (70F + 460)) / (.80 × 4000 × .5 × 302)
= 30.9 ps_{iabs}

Boost = 30.9 − 14.7
= 16.2 psi boost

Continued on page 89

ALTERNATE SCENARIOS *Continued from page 88*

Alternate scenario #2: If the engine could achieve the same VE at higher engine speed—say 5000 rpms—the extra combustion events per time mean that even less manifold pressure is required to make 400 horsepower:

MAP = (44 × 639.6 × (70F + 460)) / (.80 × 5000 × .5 × 302)
= 24.7 psi$_{abs}$

Boost = 20.6 – 14.7
= 10 psi

Alternate scenario 3: If the engine could achieve higher VE at even higher engine speed with .85 VE, the extra combustion events per time mean that even less manifold pressure is required to make 400 horsepower:

MAP = (44 × 639.6 × (70F + 460)) / (.85 × 6000 × .5 × 302)
= 19.37 psi$_{abs}$

Boost = 19.37 – 14.7
= 4.7 psi

Alternate scenario 4: If the engine had better than 85 percent VE of the sort easily achievable with four-valve heads and high-speed cams at still higher engine speed (say .95 VE at 7,250 rpm), even less pressure is required to push 44 pounds of 70 degrees F air per minute through a 5.0-liter powerplant:

MAP = (44 × 639.6 × (70F + 460)) / (.95 × 7250 × .5 × 302)
= 14.34 psi$_{abs}$
≈ 0 psi boost

Atmospheric pressure will make 400 horsepower under these circumstances, no supercharger required!

Alternate scenario 5: On the other hand, we could specify a much smaller engine—say 122 cubic inches (2.0L) instead of 302—in which case the model reveals we'll need a ton of boost pressure to force 44 pounds of air per minute through the engine:

MAP = (44 × 639.6 × (70F + 460)) / (.95 × 7250 × .5 × 122)
= 35.5 psi$_{abs}$
= 20.8 psi boost

A 2.0-liter engine running at 7,250 rpm with .95 VE requires more than 2.4 atmospheres of manifold pressure to make 400 horsepower: (35.5 psi$_{abs}$ / 14.7 = 2.415)

Alternate scenario 6: A 2.0-liter engine in more need of supercharging than a 7,250-rpm screamer would be an ordinary 2.0-liter street engine with nonphasing overhead cams like the Toyota's 135–177 horsepower 3S-GE—a powerplant whose Yamaha cylinder head was good for .91 VE, with peak power occurring at 5,400–6,000 rpm. If you can keep the manifold air temperature at 70 degrees F, the 400 horsepower equation for this type of powerplant looks like this:

MAP = (44 × 639.6 × (70F + 460)) / (.91 × 6000 × .5 × 122)
= 44.8 psi$_{abs}$
= 30.1 psi boost

Unfortunately, 30-plus psi boost calls into question the viability of achieving 70 degrees F manifold temperature. We have not so far addressed inlet manifold temperature beyond assuming manifold air temperature is 105 degrees F or 70 degrees F. In fact, we cannot know the final air temperature for a given supercharged manifold pressure until we know (in addition to the pressure ratio and airflow): (1) precisely which compressor will be doing the work and the speed required for it to deliver the target manifold pressure and airflow, (2) ambient air temperature, (3) the thermal efficiency of an intercooler, if there is one, and (4) pressure drop upstream or downstream of the compressor.

Because compressor speed, pressure, and airflow are interrelated, changing one parameter forces you to recalculate the others until successive iterations produce little or no further change. It is critical to precisely model manifold air temperature in realistic ways when designing a supercharger system because temperature rise from compression is a fact of life. Higher temperature reduces air density for a given pressure, with the result that virtually all compressors must be forced to work somewhat harder to build additional pressure to compensate for the adverse effect of compression heating on the compressor's relative mass airflow delivery to the intake manifold.

Looked at another way, forcing an inefficient positive-displacement supercharger to deliver a particular mass airflow will automatically cause the supercharger to deliver higher pressure than you would otherwise expect, and correcting for inefficiencies in compressor design and compressor inlet or outlet plumbing, or unusually sparse inlet air due to temperature or altitude, requires extra work to overcome the deficit, causing the compressor to heat the compressed air even more.

Compressing air always heats it and the unfortunate fact is that supercharging intake air to more than 3 atmospheres of pressure results in the most thermally efficient centrifugal superchargers heating air almost 250 degrees F above compressor inlet temperature when boosting air pressure to 30-psi boost. A compressor with relatively poor peak thermal efficiency—or one that is not operating in a range with good thermal efficiency—could heat air by 325 degrees F or more! Which is why they have intercoolers.

Even if you manage to remove as much as 85 percent of the 250-degree temperature rise with an air-cooled intercooler cooled by 70 degrees F ambient air, at 3 atmospheres of pressure you're still going to be pushing air into the intake manifold at a temperature approaching 110 degrees. You'll then need some extra boost pressure to achieve 44 lb/min airflow to compensate for the decrease in air density from heat.

Alternate scenario 7: Forcing 110 degrees F rather than 70 degrees F charge air into the intake manifold, you're going need even more supercharger boost than you did with 70 degrees F air to make the 44 lb/min airflow required to make 400 horses in a 2.0-liter powerplant.

MAP = (44 × 639.6 × (110F + 460)) / (.91 × 6000 × .5 × 122)
= 48.1 psi$_{abs}$
= 33.4 psi boost

At this point, it becomes clear that manifold absolute pressure may be distinct from compressor discharge pressure. When you're

Continued on page 90

SUPERCHARGER SELECTION AND SYSTEM MODELING

89

ALTERNATE SCENARIOS *Continued from page 89*

using an intercooler, there is typically at least some pressure drop through the intercooler and plumbing between the compressor discharge and the intake manifold. If there is a 2.0-psi pressure drop in this part of the system, we will need to increase the required compressor discharge pressure by the same amount so that air arrives at the intake manifold at the correct pressure after having lost 2.0-psi pressure.

$P_{CD} = MAP_{req} + PR\ Drop_{IC}$

Where:
P_{CD} = Corrected compressor discharge pressure
P_{Drop} = Pressure drop through the intercooler and plumbing

In this case, corrected compressor discharge pressure is:

$P_{cor} = 48.1 + 2.0 = 50.1\ psi_{abs}$
$= 35.4\ psi\ boost$

Alternate scenario 8: But let's say this is a street car. You need an air cleaner. Even the best streetable air cleaner intake systems typically reduce compressor intake pressure by at least 0.5 to 1.0 psi. Although pressure drop on the inlet side of a compressor does not change the required compressor discharge pressure, some additional work will be required when you're starting with air that's below atmospheric pressure to boost the pressure to the required 50.1 psi_{abs} compressor discharge pressure.

Corrected compressor intake pressure is equal to atmospheric pressure minus intake pressure drop (absolute pressure, of course). In this case, 14.7 psi_{abs} – 1.0 psi = 13.7 psi_{abs} at sea level. And let's say you're not at sea level but instead at the Bonneville Salt Flats, an elevation of nearly 4,300 feet? Barometric pressure decrease from the altitude alone is about 2 psi. Total pressure drop at the compressor inlet is thus 3.0 psi, producing air pressure at the compressor inlet of (14.7 – 2.0) – 1.0 = 11.7 psi_{abs}.

Thus, corrected boost pressure is calculated as follows:

Boost = $P_{CD} - P_{CI}$

Where:
P_{CD} = Compressor discharge pressure
P_{CI} = Compressor inlet pressure

Boost = 50.1 psi_{abs} – 11.7 psi_{abs}
= 38.4 psi boost

To achieve the required manifold absolute pressure in the intake for the required 44 lb/min airflow, we would need 38.4-psi boost.

Yikes! A powerplant breathing 110 degrees F air at 38.4-psi boost would detonate itself to pieces on gasoline, but that's academic because at the time of this writing there were *no currently available mechanically driven superchargers that could deliver that kind of pressure.*

How do we know? Every compressor has a compressor map that shows airflow performance as a function of pressure—not absolute pressure or boost pressure, but *relative* pressure. Compressor maps use something called pressure ratio, which expresses the relationship between compressor discharge pressure and compressor inlet pressure, that is, the ratio of compressor discharge pressure divided by inlet pressure.

PR = P_{CD} / P_{CI}

Where:
PR = Pressure ratio
P_{Cd} = Compressor discharge pressure
P_{Ci} = Compressor inlet pressure

Assuming the compressor discharge pressure upstream of the intercooler is 50.1 psiabs and the compressor inlet pressure is 11.7 psiabs (to compensate for pressure drop through the intercooler plumbing and pressure drop through the air cleaner and elevation of 4,300 feet),

PR = P_{CD} / P_{CD}
= 50.1 psi_{abs} / 11.7 psi_{abs}
≈ 4.28

Pressurizing air by a factor of 4.28 was way off the map of all commercially available crank-driven superchargers at this time. Here are typical current maximum pressure ratio for commercially available superchargers at the time of this writing:

Compressor Type	Current Max Pressure Ratio
Centrifugal	2.8
Twin-screw	2.2
Roots TVS	2.5
Traditional Roots	1.5–1.8
Turbocharger	4.5–5.0
Axial (multistage)	40.0

Yes, you could deliver such a pressure ratio and airflow with a two-stage supercharging system consisting of two compressors arranged in series—one compressing charge air part of the way with a realistic achievable pressure ratio and then forcing the partially compressed air into the second-stage compressor for final pressurization at another realistic achievable pressure ratio.

Multi-stage compressors are common in the gigantic superchargers front-ending civilian-aviation turbofan or turboshaft jet engines, which boost air pressure entering the constant-flame combustion chamber(s) to as much as 40 atmospheres. In the automotive universe, supercharging pressure ratios over 4.0 with thermal efficiency as high as 74 percent are actually achievable using a modern centrifugal compressor optimized for operation far above 100,000 rpm driven by a *direct-drive* shaft from an exhaust turbine. That is, a turbocharger.

Interestingly, Rotrex centrifugal superchargers like the C38-61 have the *compressor capacity* to achieve pressure ratios as high as 4.6 atmospheres (they're basically belt-driven turbocharger compressors with internal planetary gears delivering an unusually high step-up ratio), but Rotrex compressors are rpm-limited by the internal mechanical planetary drive to a compressor speed that's below the maximum pumping envelope of the compressor, which effectively decapitates a significant portion of the upper region of the compressor performance map.

The model tells us that for a given airflow, methanol fuel makes almost 40 percent more power than gasoline—and this leaves out the fact that vaporizing alcohol has a powerful cooling effect that significantly increases air density and typically allows more boost without detonation.

Anyway, assuming we're running gasoline, it is a realistic assumption that 44 lb/min of air will make 400 supercharged horsepower.

Next, model the manifold pressure required force 44 lb/min air through an engine as a function of engine size, speed, volumetric efficiency, and manifold air temperature. It turns out we do not need to know the normal-charged horsepower of an engine prior to being supercharged in order to design a forced-induction system. Working with the previously calculated mass airflow required for the target horsepower and fuel, we factor in manifold air temperature, engine volumetric efficiency, rpm, and displacement in the following equation:

$$MAP = \frac{(MAF \times 639.6 \times (T_m + 460)}{(VE \times RPM \times .5 \times cid)}$$

where…
MAP = Manifold absolute pressure (psi_{abs}) required to deliver target horsepower
MAF = Airflow (lb / min)
639.6 = Gas constant (ideal gas law)
T_m = Intake manifold temperature (degrees F)
460 = Conversion from °F to absolute temperature (°R)
VE = Engine volumetric efficiency
RPM = Engine rpm
.5 = Correction for four-stroke cycle engines that only fire cylinders every other revolution
CID = Engine displacement in cubic inches (cid = liters × 61.02)

Suppose we're looking at how much boost it takes to get to 400 horsepower when the raw material is a 4.2-liter (256 cid) V-8?

Assume:
MAF = 44 lb / min (as calculated previously from formula using target power, AFR, and BSFC)
T_m = 105 degrees F (it's a hot summer day in Texas or you're running a K&N filter drawing warm engine-compartment air)
VE = 80 percent at peak power (It's an old-school pushrod V-8.)
RPM = 4,000 rpm (peak power rpm)
CID = 256 cubic inches (4.2 liters * 61.02)

Therefore:

$$MAP = \frac{(44 \times 639.6 \times (105F + 460)}{(.80 \times 4000 \times .5 \times 256)}$$
$$\approx 38.8 \; psi_{abs}$$

We can convert manifold absolute pressure to gauge pressure as seen on a normal boost gauge, where pressure reads 0 at ordinary ambient atmospheric pressure by subtracting one standard atmosphere (14.7 psi_{abs} at sea level) from manifold absolute pressure (a boost gauge shows pressure *above* ambient atmospheric pressure (which varies with temperature and altitude):

Boost = 38.8 psi_{abs} – 14.7
= 24.1 psi_{gauge}

Thus, we discover that 44 pounds per minute of 105 degrees F air entering the intake manifold of a 4.2-liter engine at 24.1 psi boost pressure should make 400 horsepower on gasoline if the engine powerband peaks at 4,000 rpm with 80 percent volumetric efficiency. Keep in mind that this model does not take into account real-world powerplant, fuel, and manifold air-temperature characteristics that might make it impossible to achieve the specified horsepower at the required manifold pressure because of detonation.

For the purposes of a supercharger selection, we'll work through two examples of two very different engines boosted to 400 horsepower.

Example 1: The first is an "old school" 5.0-liter pushrod V-8 with the following parameters:

MAF = 44 lb/min (as calculated previously from equations using target power, AFR, and BSFC)
T_m = 88 degrees F
VE = 80% (at peak-power rpm, where VE is less than it is at peak torque)
RPM = 5,900 rpm (peak power rpm)
CID = 302 cid

$$MAP = \frac{(44 \times 639.6 \times (88F + 460))}{(.8 \times 5900 \times .5 \times 302)}$$
$$= 21.6 \; psi_{abs}$$

In the case of the 5.0—assuming a 1.0-psi pressure drop through the air-cleaner system and a 2.0-psi drop through the intercooler—21.6 psi_{abs} transforms into the required pressure ratio as follows:

$$PR_{cor} = (P_{CD} + \Delta P_{ICLoss}) \; psi_{abs} \; / \; (P_{amb} - \Delta P_{ACLoss}) \; psi_{abs}$$

where,
P_{CD} = compressor discharge pressure (psia)
ΔP_{ICLoss} = pressure drop through intercooler between the compressor and the intake manifold (psi)
P_{amb} – = ambient air pressure (standard pressure at sea level is 14.7 psi_{abs})
ΔP_{ACLoss} = pressure drop between the air intake air cleaner and the compressor (psi)

$$PR_{cor} = (P_{CD} + \Delta P_{ICLoss})\, psi_{abs} / (P_{amb} - \Delta P_{ACLoss})\, psi_{abs}$$

$$= (21.6 + 2.0)\, psi_{abs} / (14.7 - 1.0)\, psi_{abs}$$

$$= 23.6\, psi_{abs} / 13.7\, psi_{abs}$$

$$\approx 1.72$$

Boost = $(1.72 \times 14.7) - 14.7$
= $25.28\, psi_{abs} - 14.7$
$\approx 10.6\, psi_{gauge}$

We'll target 10.6 psi boost.

Example 2: The second example is a modern, high-revving 2.2-liter (134 cid) twin-cam inline-four with variable valve timing and lift under electronic control:

MAF = 44 lb/min (as calculated previously from equations using target power, AFR, and BSFC)
T_m = 88 degrees F
VE = 97%
RPM = 8,000 rpm
CID = 134 cid

$$MAP = \frac{(44 \times 639.6 \times (88F + 460))}{(.97 \times 8000 \times .5 \times 134)}$$

$\approx 29.7\, psi_{abs}$

In this case, assuming an air-intake pressure drop of 0.5 psi and pressure drop through an intercooler of 1.0 psi (this is a maximum-effort system with a lot of attention given to pressure-drop reduction), the initial corrected pressure ratio for the 2.2-liter powerplant is:

$$PR_{cor} = (P_{CD} + \Delta P_{ICLoss})\, psi_{abs} / (P_{am} - \Delta P_{ACLoss})\, psi_{abs}$$

$$= (29.7 + 1.0)\, psi_{abs} / (14.7 - .5)\, psi_{abs}$$

$$= 30.7\, psi_{abs} / 14.2\, psi_{abs}$$

$$\approx 2.16$$

To be conservative, since standard atmospheric pressure is actually slightly lower than 14.7 psi (14.65), we'll round the required pressure ratio up slightly to 2.17.

Boost = $(2.17 \times 14.7) - 14.7$
= **17.2 psi**

At this point—equipped with mass airflow (MAF) and manifold absolute pressure (MAP) numbers for the 5.0-liter and 2.2-liter applications—we are almost ready to look at a selection of real-world compressor maps to get an idea about which are the possible solutions to get the job done in our two sample applications.

Compressor maps represent real-world data gained from rigorously controlled scientific experiments that measure how much air a compressor will actually pump at various pressure ratios and speeds, and how much temperature rise will occur. Compressor maps graphically illustrate thermal efficiency across the range of achievable airflow and pressure and the required compressor speeds. The horizontal axis represents volumetric or mass airflow (compressor inlet airflow volume per time, or compressor discharge airflow weight per time at a standardized temperature and barometric pressure). Pressure is not specified as pounds per square inch of absolute pressure at the compressor outlet—which depends in part on the temperature and absolute pressure of air entering the compressor—but as the ratio of compressor discharge pressure to compressor inlet pressure, which is unaffected by compressor inlet temperature and pressure.

Alternative: Model pressure ratio based on "before" horsepower

A real-world alternative to the practice of modeling supercharged engine performance using airflow and pressure calculations based on acceleration, BSFC, and air-fuel ratio is to start with non-supercharged "before" horsepower and calculate (1) the density change required to get to the target horsepower and (2) the pressure ratio required to get there.

The best way to know pre-supercharged horsepower is to have a dyno sheet from an engine brake dynamometer that shows power and torque across the range of engine speed. The second-best way to know "before" power and torque at all engine speeds is to get a dyno sheet from a chassis dyno and correct the wheel horsepower to crankshaft numbers using published peak-power numbers from the factory that designed and built the vehicle (assuming it's stock), or if not, using "standard" aftermarket drivetrain-loss assumptions to estimate crankshaft horsepower. A similar method would be to get wheel power and torque numbers based on acceleration numbers from an in-car Gtech- or accelerometer-type device programmed with the precise vehicle weight (including all fluids and payload, including the driver) and then make corrections to crankshaft horsepower as above. The advertised peak factory torque and power numbers by themselves can work to model what's required to get to *peak* boosted power (though you're more or less in the dark when it comes to predicting the effect of various types of superchargers and drive ratios at engine speeds at less than peak power). The most problematic way to estimate existing horsepower is to calculate pre-supercharged horsepower based on engine size, peak power rpm, and assumptions about volumetric efficiency (VE) for the type of engine at a selection of engine speeds. You are making a lot of assumptions, and, as the old saying goes, "Garbage In, Garbage Out."

In any case, the percentage increase in manifold pressure or "boost" required to achieve a particular target horsepower is strongly correlated to the ratio of "After" versus "Before" horsepower, and would be exactly the same were it not for compression charge heating, horsepower losses driving the supercharger, and pressure drop through the air cleaner or intercooler. It is possible to design a supercharging system where the pressure ratio is exactly the same as the horsepower ratio, but it is usually not practical.

In this model we start with the horsepower ratio and make corrections where required to convert it to the pressure ratio of compressor discharge to inlet pressure that will suffice to achieve the required power boost. Assume that the pre-supercharged horsepower of a the high-performance factory 5.0-liter V-8 we modeled earlier in this chapter is advertised to be 290 horsepower at 5,900 rpm, and that the goal is 400 horsepower.

$$HP\ ratio = HP_{After} / HP_{Before}$$
$$= 400\ hp / 290\ hp$$
$$\approx 1.38$$

$$PR = HP\ ratio$$
$$= 1.38$$

This is a decent first guess of the required pressure ratio the supercharger must deliver to push 400 horsepower worth of air through the engine, but it will require a number of corrections to be realistic.

ABSOLUTE TEMPERATURE

Absolute temperature, in case you're curious, is a temperature scale derived from the laws of thermodynamics, as opposed to being relative only to the properties of substances like water. Thus, absolute zero (0 degrees Kelvin) is the lowest possible temperature a substance can be, beyond which nothing can be colder, since there is no heat energy remaining in the molecules.

Absolute temperature degrees Kelvin are of the same magnitude increment as degrees centigrade. Absolute zero is approximately -273.15 degrees C, which is -460 degrees F. The rest of the Kelvin scale technically relates to the "triple point" of water, a thermodynamic point 1/100th of a degree above 0 degrees C at which water vapor, liquid water, and ice can co-exist in equilibrium when the pressure is about 6 percent normal atmospheric pressure.

You can convert any temperature in Fahrenheit to absolute temperature by adding 460, which then expresses the temperature in degrees F above absolute zero, also known as degrees Rankine or R.

Adding 460 to the 212 degrees F at which water boils, for example, equals 672R.

$$Boost = (PR \times 14.7\ psi) - 14.7\ psi$$
$$= (1.38 \times 14.7) - 14.7$$
$$\approx 5.6\ psi$$

Unfortunately, in the absence of strong countermeasures, the supercharger will heat the charge air as it increases manifold pressure by 38 percent, meaning that some portion of the pressure increase will be a function of temperature rather than increased air density. But how much?

To determine the air density increase from a 38 percent increase in pressure, begin by calculating the temperature gain at the compressor discharge:

Temp gain = $((PR^{0.28} - 1) \times T_{ABS}) / CE$

Where:
PR = Pressure ratio
T_{ABS} = Compressor inlet temperature (absolute) = degrees F + 460
CE = Compressor efficiency (typically 45-80 percent = 0.45-.80)
$PR^{0.28}$ = The pressure ratio to the .28th power (use Y^X key on a calculator), which defines the relationship between pressure ratio and temperature increase as a function of the ideal gas law.

Assuming air inlet temperature of 70 degrees F, compressor thermal efficiency of .7, and pressure ratio of 1.38,

$$Temp\ Gain_{CD} = ((PR^{0.28} - 1) \times Tabs) / 0.7$$
$$= ((1.38^{0.28} - 1) \times (70F + 460F)) / 0.7$$
$$\approx 71.5F$$

Actual compressor discharge temperature is thus the temperature gain plus compressor inlet temperature, which we're initially assuming is 70 degrees F:

$$Temp_{CD} = 71.5F + 70F$$
$$= 141.5F$$

But we're going want to re-cool charge air with an intercooler as much as possible. Assuming a top-quality air-cooled intercooler with 85 percent thermal efficiency, temperature gain at the intake manifold will have lost 85 percent of the heat that was present at the compressor discharge:

$$Temp\ Gain_{IM} = Temp\ Gain_{CD} \times (1 - IC_{EFF})$$
$$= 71.5 \times (1 - .85)$$
$$\approx 10.7F$$

$$Temp_{IM} = Temp\ gain_{IM} + Temp_{CI}$$
$$= 10.7 + 70$$
$$= 80.7F$$

Knowing the temperature at the compressor inlet and intake manifold, we can now calculate a number that tells us what percentage of the pressure ratio delivered by a supercharger results from greater air density and how much is "hot air." In this equation temperature must be converted to absolute temperature, i.e., temperature above *nothing at all*. Since the lowest possible temperature is –460 degrees F, we convert degrees F to absolute by adding 460, giving degrees R (Rankine). Thus, the freezing point of water, 32F, becomes 32 + 460 = 492 degrees R.

Next we compute the density ratio.

$$DR = T_{CI} / T_{IM}$$

Where:
DR = Density ratio
T_{CI} = Compressor-inlet temperature (absolute)
T_{IM} = Intake manifold inlet temperature (absolute)

$$DR = (70F + 460) / (80.7F + 460)$$

$$= 530 / 540.7$$

$$= .98$$

At a 1.38 pressure ratio, a compressor breathing 70 degrees F ambient air and compressing it with 70 percent thermal efficiency backed up by an ambient air-cooled intercooler that is 85 percent efficient at removing heat, 98 percent of the pressure increase is the result of increased air density.

We may also need to correct supercharger pressure ratio, however, because—like almost all piston engines almost all of the time—positive-displacement superchargers cannot usually manage to pump 100 percent of the air you'd expect based on the volumetric displacement of the supercharger. Of course, neither can the engine. A positive-displacement supercharger like the 1.9-liter Eaton TVS Roots-type supercharger will usually not pump 1.9-liter of air per rotation, particularly at lower speeds, and will have to turn a little faster (heating the charge a little more) to deliver the expected boost pressure.

The volumetric efficiency ratio (VE ratio) is a ratio of the pumping efficiency of the supercharger divided by the pumping efficiency of the engine. The VE ratio could be thought of as the efficiency of the compressor-engine pair at making boost. Keep in mind that a very efficient positive-displacement supercharger of a certain size will make less boost pushing air through an engine that breathes really well than it will through an engine of the same displacement that does not breathe as freely. A high VE ratio indicates that the compressor-engine pairing will require less manifold pressure to shove a certain mass of air through the engine. This means that charge air will be thrashed around less and heated less, and less gratuitous pressure increase is necessary, such that a lower pressure ratio will get the job done. Keep in mind that because supercharger and engine VE do not remain constant across the speed range of either the blower or the powerplant, the VE ratio does not in reality remain constant, which is one reason why boost pressure may not remain constant across the rpm range.

Volumetric efficiency has no meaning with respect to centrifugal compressors, which do not have fixed volume of air ingested per revolution. The VE ratio is assumed to be 1.0 for centrifugal compressor.

Assuming the VE of the supercharger is 88 percent (this is *not* thermal efficiency) and the VE of the engine is 80 percent at peak power,

VE ratio = supercharger VE / engine VE
= 88% / 80%
= 1.1

We'll also need to adjust the pressure ratio to compensate for the fact that we're going to need some extra air to burn fuel to drive the supercharger itself. The supercharger uses some horsepower and wastes some horsepower, and the supercharger drive belt (or gear drive, found on some modern drag engines and a few old aviation powerplants like the Rolls Royce Merlin) wastes a little additional power. Typically the total waste of driving a blower is 5 to 15 percent of the power generated by the supercharged engine. A typical drive power efficiency would be 90 percent. Some supercharger manufacturers publish actual drive power numbers on the compressor map. Drive power is low or nil at low airflow and pressure but rises with increases in pressure and/or airflow. On a graph, drive power lines are warped by nonlinear changes in thermal efficiency. Published numbers do not reflect drive belt inefficiencies, which are typically 2 to 3 percent.

At this point we are ready to recalculate the horsepower ratio with these required compensations:

$$PR = \frac{HP_{After}}{(HP_{Before} \times DR \times VE\ ratio \times drive\ efficiency)}$$

Where:
HP_{After} = Target horsepower "after" supercharging
HP_{Before} = Pre-supercharged horsepower
DR = Density ratio (T_{CI} / T_{IM})
VE_{ratio} = Volumetric efficiency ratio ($VE_{Blower} / VE_{Engine}$)
$Drive_{Eff}$ = Drive efficiency (typically 85–95 percent)

Assuming target horsepower is 400, existing horsepower is 290, density ratio is 98 percent (at PR of 1.38), VE ratio is 110 percent, and drive efficiency is 90 percent), corrected pressure ratio becomes:

PR = 400 / (290 × .98 × 1.1 × .9)

≈ 1.42

Boost is therefore (1.42 × 14.7) - 14.7 ≈ 6.2 psi,

However, we're still not there because the final required pressure ratio is impacted by any pressure drop in the air cleaner and plumbing, or the intercooler and plumbing to the intake manifold. Pressure drop depends on the mass airflow rate, intercooler design and size, plumbing size and the number, quality, and angle of bends, throttle body location and size, and so forth. Pressure drop through a well-designed intercooler system could be as low as 1.0 psi or less, but might be as much as 4 psi or more in overboosted stock forced-induction systems with small intercoolers. We can correct as follows, beginning by converting pressure ratio to compressor discharge pressure:

P_{CD} = PR × 14.7
= 1.42 × 14.7
≈ 20.9 psi_{abs}

The corrected pressure ratio becomes:

PR_{cor} = (P_{CD} + ΔP_{ICLoss}) psi_{abs} / (P_{amb} – ΔP_{ACLoss}) psi_{abs}

Where:
P_{CD} = Compressor discharge pressure (psi)
ΔP_{ICLoss} = Pressure drop between the compressor and the intake manifold (psi)
P_{amb} – = Ambient air pressure (standard pressure at sea level is 14.7 psi_{abs})
ΔP_{ACLoss} = Pressure drop between the compressor and the intake manifold (psi)

For the 5.0 V-8, assuming a **2.0 psi drop** through the intercooler and **1.0 drop** in the air cleaner:

PR_{cor} = (20.9 + 2.0) psi_{abs} / (14.7 – 1.0) psi_{abs}

= 22.9 psi_{abs} / 13.7 psi_{abs}

= 1.67

Boost is now (1.67 × 14.7) – 14.7 ≈ 9.9 psi (versus the uncorrected 6.2 psi!), which is an indication of the importance of avoiding pressure drop.

Okay, having adjusted the target pressure ratio upward for the various compensations, we are now squeezing the charge air harder, which means we are heating it more than we'd planned. Do we need additional pressure to compensate for the heating from the added compensation pressure? Let's look.

Recalculate the temp gain at the compressor discharge:

Temp gain$_{CD}$ = (PR$^{0.28}$ - 1) × Tabs) / 0.7

= (1.67$^{0.28}$ - 1) × (70F + 460F) / 0.7

≈ 116.9F

Compute temp gain at the intake manifold after intercooler effect (.85)

Temp gain$_{IM}$ = Temp gain$_{CD}$ × (1 – EFF$_{IC}$)
= 116.9 × .15
= 17.5F

Temp$_{IM}$ = Temp gain$_{IM}$ + Temp$_{CI}$
= 17.5F + 70F
= 87.5F

Next, recalculate density ratio in light of recalculated intake manifold temperature:

Density Ratio = T$_{CI}$ / T$_{IM}$

Where:
T$_{CI}$ = Compressor-inlet temperature (degrees R)
T$_{IM}$ = Intake manifold inlet temperature (degrees R)

DR = (70F + 460)/ (87.5F + 460)

= 530 / 547.5

≈ .97

DR is less than 1 percent different, so we'll stick with a pressure ratio of 1.67. (One iteration is usually enough for intercooled blowers.)

Preliminary Conclusions

Comparing the results from the horsepower-based model with the BSFC and VE-based model, we see that there are discrepancies. The first model predicted we'd need a pressure ratio of 1.72 (10.6 psi), but the second predicts only 1.67 (9.8 psi).

Why the discrepancy? Well, we trusted advertised horsepower in the second model, and perhaps the horsepower number was wrong. The example engine is essentially a 1970 Ford Boss 302 Mustang, and 1970 engines were rated in gross horsepower with the test engine installed on an engine dyno with open headers and no accessories installed. Real crankshaft horsepower of an engine installed in a car was usually less (well, unless the car company intentionally underreported horsepower to keep customer's insurance affordable). The before and target horsepower establish the initial pressure ratio estimate in the model, which would be higher if Before horsepower is less, which would affect the density ratio later in the model, and so on.

On the other hand, perhaps we underestimated the fuel consumption in the first model, assumed to be 0.55. As reported earlier in this chapter, an engine with BSFC of 0.65 would need as much as 52 lb/min air in the first model.

To be safe we'll assume the required pressure ratio to boost the example 5.0-liter V-8 to 400 horsepower is 1.72. We'll stick with 44 lb/min airflow, but keep in mind that it could be optimistic if the engine's fuel consumption is higher than 0.55 BSFC.

4. Plot the operating data points for the modeled engine applications on plausible compressor maps.

Note that that there are compressor maps available that categorize various applications and compressors to make it easier to hone in on compressors that are worth considering.

Once again, for our example 400-horsepower application, both the 5.0-liter and 2.2-liter powerplants require 44 lb/min of airflow. Under the conditions we modeled, the 2.2-liter powerplant will require a pressure ratio of 2.17, which is 17.2-psi pressure on the boost gauge. The 5.0-liter engine requires a pressure ratio of 1.72, which is 10.6 psig boost pressure.

Having calculated that a generic forced-induction gasoline engine running at a 12.0 air-fuel ratio with BSFC of .55 requires 44 pounds per minute of air (or 33 kilograms per second) to make 400 horsepower, we look for compressors capable of achieving this airflow at a 1.72 or a 2.17 pressure ratio. We discover a range of types and brands of superchargers that look feasible for one or both applications. At this point we should have enough information to plot these operating points on the candidate compressor maps.

But alas, we don't, because positive displacement supercharger compressor maps typically plot *volumetric* compressor inlet air flow on the horizontal axis instead of compressor discharge mass air flow in pounds per minute (or kilograms per second or whatever) as is typically the case with centrifugal compressors. Volumetric air flow may be in cubic feet per minute (CFM) or in cubic meters per hour or per minute.

How do we convert mass airflow to volumetric airflow so we can evaluate positive displacement maps? As they say, very carefully. For one thing, like the engine itself, a positive displacement supercharger always ingests the same volume of air every revolution, but the volumetric efficiency of the supercharger varies with speed and pressure when there is not time for the supercharger to fill properly with air at high speeds or where a significant amount of air leaks around the rotors at lower speeds or at higher pressures.

How do we convert from volumetric airflow to mass air flow? A cubic foot of air weighs 0.075 pounds at 68 degrees at sea level, which means a pound of air takes up 13.33 cubic feet. Under these conditions, in order to deliver 44 lb/min of mass airflow a supercharger would need to breathe 585 cfm, which is the same as 994 cubic meters per hour on Eaton Roots-type compressor maps, or 16.4 cubic meters per minute on Lysholm maps. Of course, higher ambient temperature or higher altitude would mean that more cfm of air must be ingested to deliver the required mass flow, since each ten degree increase in temperature decreases air density about 2 percent. Delivering 44 pounds per minute requires 596 cfm (1013 m3/hr;16.9 m3/min) of 77 degree sea level air, and 610 cfm (1036 m3/hr; 17.3 m3/min) of 88 degree air.

To be conservative, this discussion assumes that we are interested in a positive displacement compressor that can ingest 620 cfm or a centrifugal compressor that can deliver 44 lb/min airflow—in either case at a pressure ratio of 1.72 or 2.17, 620 cfm is about five percent more than 585 cfm.

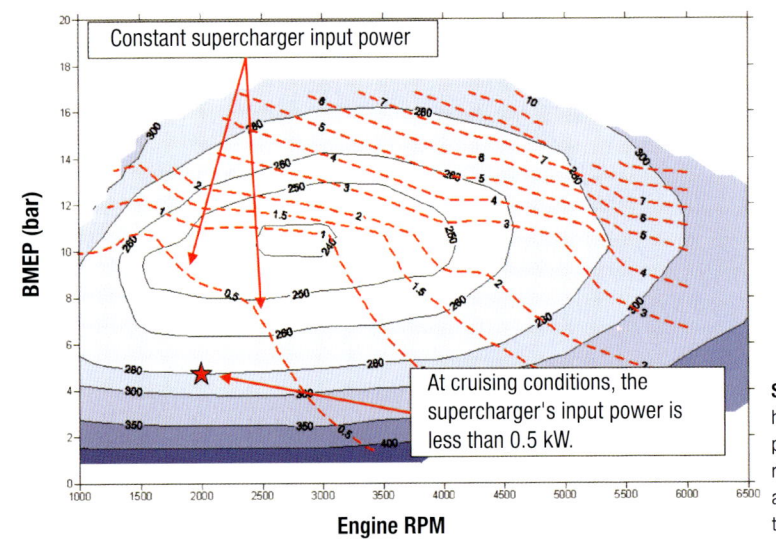

SUPERCHARGER INPUT POWER REQUIREMENT: The horsepower required to drive a supercharger is a function of the pressure ratio, airflow, and compressor efficiency. Drive power required to drive a supercharger increases with higher pressure and airflow, but not in a perfectly linear fashion because of thermal and volumetric efficiency fluctuations. *Eaton*

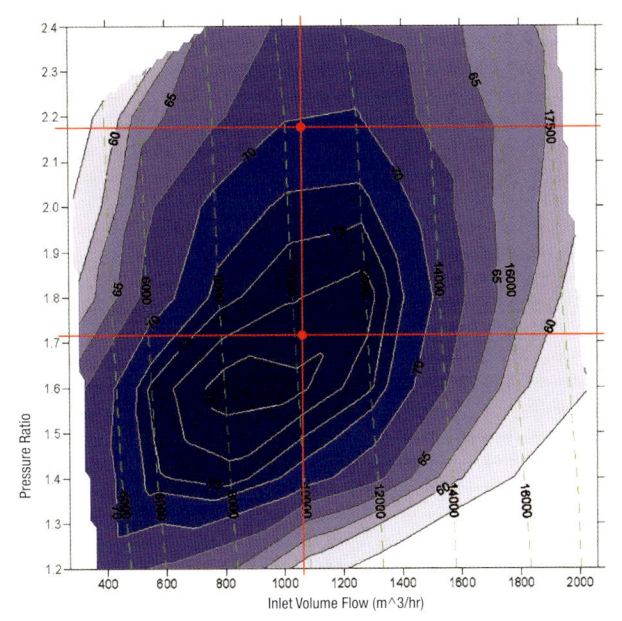

R1900 TVS SUPERCHARGER PERFORMANCE MAP: An *Eaton R1900 TVS Roots* four-lobe supercharger—a bit smaller than the R2300 supercharger used in the 2010 Corvette ZR1—will ingest 1053 m3/hr (620 cfm) of air at a pressure ratio of up to about 2.5, with thermal efficiency as high as .75, with blower VE in the range of 85–90 percent near 10,000 rpm compressor speed).

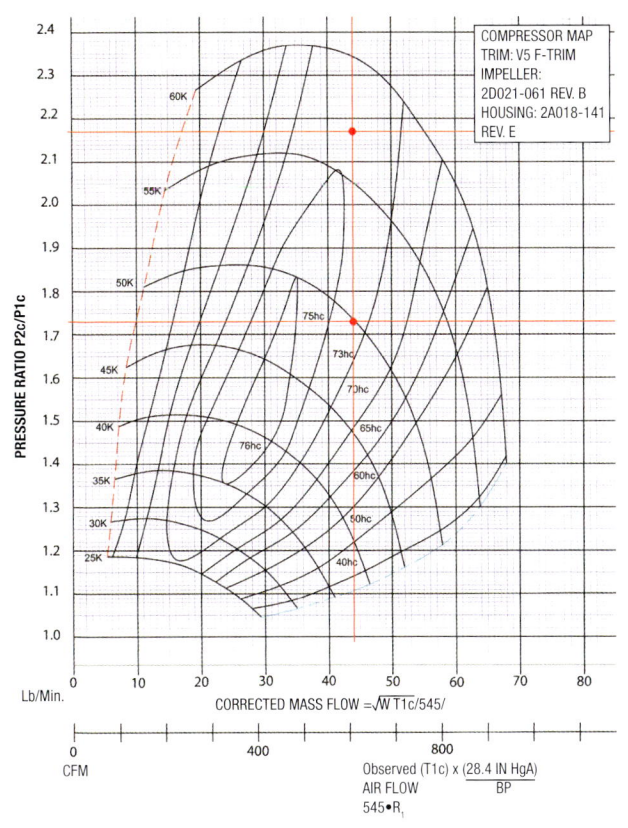

The *Vortech V-5 G-trim* will pump 44 lb/min at 1.72 PR with .69 thermal efficiency at 50,000 rpm, and 2.17 PR with .73 efficiency at 56,500 rpm.

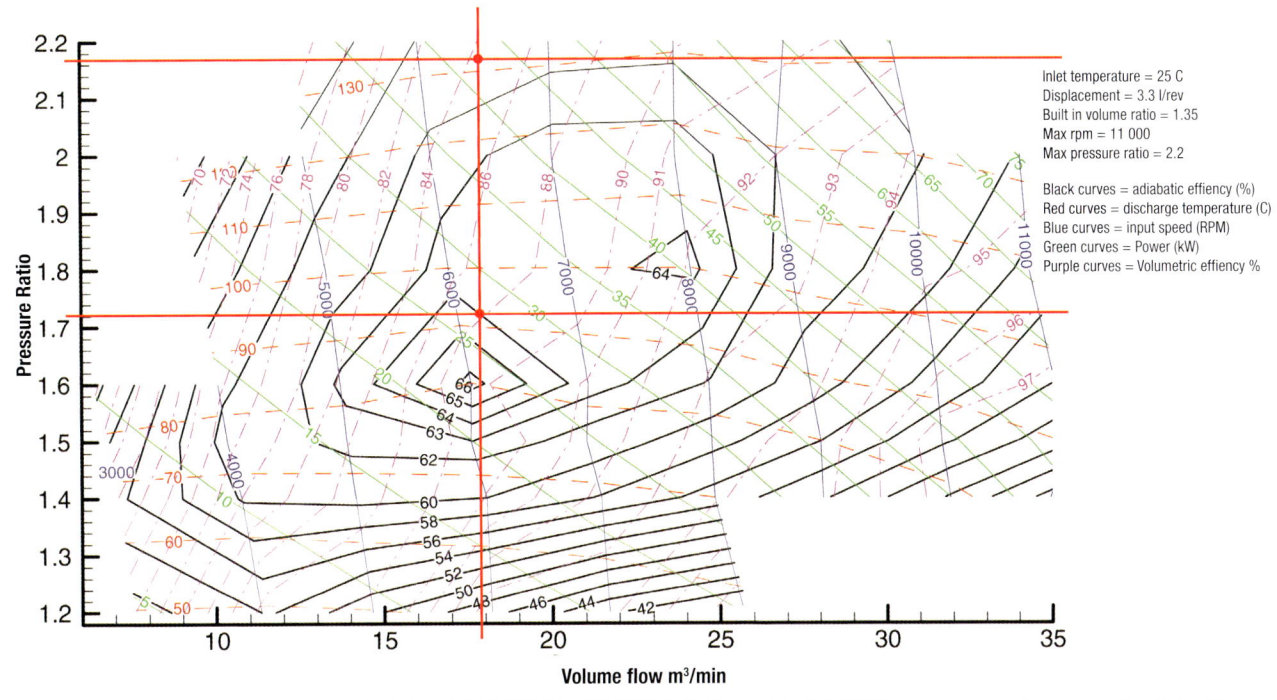

FULL LOAD PERFORMANCE CHARACTERISTICS FOR LYSHOLM SUPERCHARGER LYS3300AX: The *Lysholm LYS3300AX* twin-screw supercharger can deliver 17.6 m3/min (620 cfm) and pressure ratios up to 2.2 without over-speeding with .6 to .64 thermal efficiency at 6,100 to 6,400 compressor rpm.

SUPERCHARGER SELECTION AND SYSTEM MODELING

97

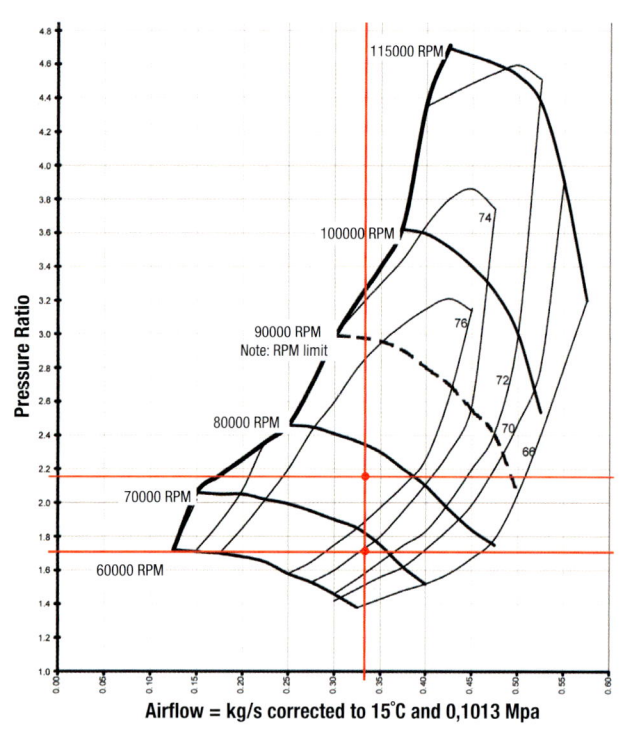

The *Rotrex C38-61-trim centrifugal with planetary gear drive* delivers pressure ratios up to 3.0 without over-speeding, and easily makes a pressure ratio of 2.17 at 44 lb/min with at least .76 efficiency at 75,000 rpm, and 1.72 PR with .74 efficiency at 66,500 rpm.

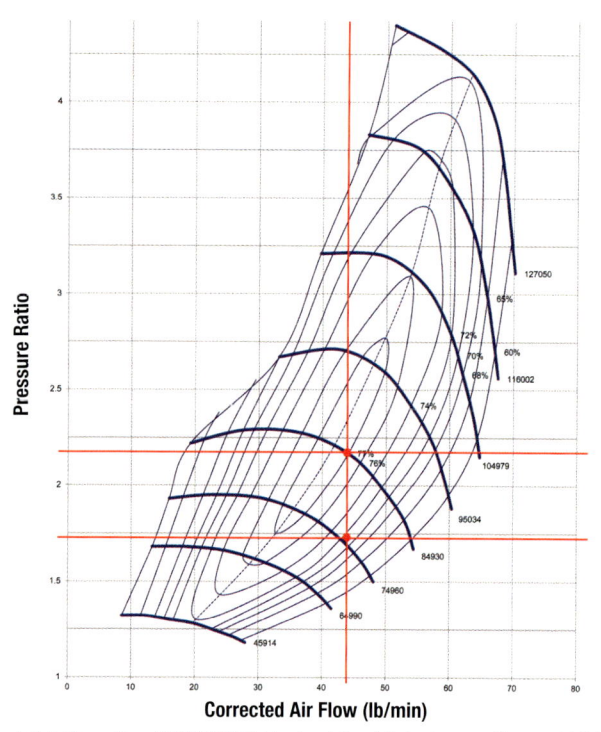

Just for fun, a *Garret GT3788R 52-trim (centrifugal) turbocharger* will pump 44 lb/min at a 2.17 pressure ratio at 83,500 rpm with over .78 efficiency, or 44 lb/min at a pressure ratio of 1.72 PR with .75 efficiency at 74,000 rpm.

This is the time to calculate actual intake manifold temperature in light of specific compressor performance and recalculate pressure ratio in light of adjustments to temperature. The assumptions behind intake manifold temperature of 90 degrees F for both the high- and low-pressure ratio were excellent intercooling and compressor thermal efficiency above 0.70—which may not be the case. Unexpectedly high manifold temperature means unexpectedly low air density, which requires a recalculated higher pressure ratio to compensate (which may then increase the manifold temperature enough to require another round of pressure and temperature compensation).

Before going further into the details of compressor maps and intercooler selection, however, it's worth remembering that the mass airflow rate used in the manifold pressure calculations in this model is based on assumptions not only about target horsepower but air-fuel ratio and brake-specific fuel consumption, which are generic and questionable. BSFC changes in relation to (1) the fuel (and power) wasted driving a supercharger, (2) the fuel wasted cooling combustion to fight detonation at higher levels of boost, or (3) the still-burning fuel and pressure wasted out the exhaust due to spark retard required to fight detonation in knock-limited supercharged engines, and so on. The manifold absolute pressure calculations are based on assumptions about engine volumetric efficiency that are also generic and therefore questionable. Target horsepower itself is based on a "racer math" formula that computes power required to deliver the acceleration required to achieve a certain ET in a certain weight vehicle.

5. Verify that the target boost pressure is realistic.

On a street car, target boost will be the lesser of the boost needed to make target power or—more likely—the engine's boost-detonation limit. Increase boost enough and the air-fuel mixture in the combustion chambers will begin to explode instead of burning smoothly, which can kill the engine faster than you think.

Obviously, there is no point in having a supercharger capable of boosting an engine to stratospheric levels that are beyond the boost-detonation limits of the engine on available fuel. Anti-detonation strategies and fuels are covered in other sections of this book (and in greater detail in my books *How to Modify Engine Management Systems* and *High Performance Automotive Fuels and Fluids*). Definitely do a reality check regarding the risk of spark knock at the target boost pressure and run this through the chart in this book that takes you from static compression and target boost to the effective compression ratio.

Depending on the static compression ratio of the engine, with premium street gasoline, figure a maximum of 10-psi boost without an intercooler, and 15-psi boost with intercooling. The highest viable boost is available on engines with pentroof combustion chambers, really efficient intercooling, the highest-available octane fuel, and excellent engine management with a high-quality calibration that takes advantage of the best anti-detonation countermeasures.

In many cases supercharger selection will actually work backward from a known-tolerable boost pressure that a certain engine can survive without knocking under certain conditions. With the boost pressure converted to a pressure ratio on a particular candidate compressor with a certain thermal efficiency and a certain intercooler of a certain effectiveness, density ratio can be computed to determine the expected density and power gain.

A .70 compressor with .85 intercooling would add approximately 18.6 degrees F to the charge temperature at 10.6-psi boost. The 5.0-liter Boss 302's compression ratio is 10.5:1, which raises the temperature on the compression stroke.

$$\begin{aligned} \text{Temperature} &= CR^{0.28} \times T_{abs} \\ &= 10.5^{0.28} \times (530F + 18.6F) \\ &\approx 1060F \end{aligned}$$

According to forced induction expert Corky Bell, a plausible assumption for detonation threshold is 1,075F. We should be okay with the 5.0-liter engine supercharged to 10.6 psi boost.

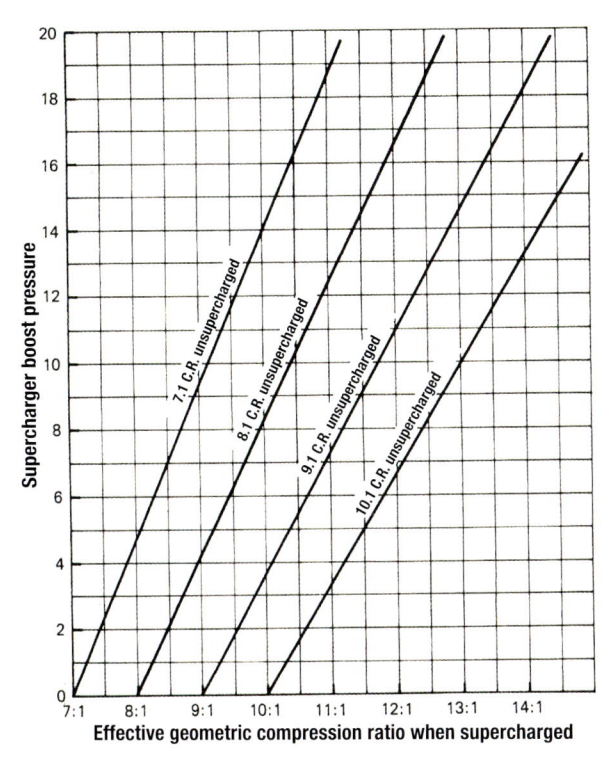

Effective compression ratio combines the effect of static compression ratio and supercharger boost to describe how much ambient air is compressed at top dead center on the compression stroke. Both cylinder compression and supercharger compression contribute to the ratio of maximum pressure in the combustion chamber before ignition to ambient pressure.

6. Select the supercharger and determine rpm.

You'll notice compressor maps resemble a topographical contour map of a hill, but instead of describing elevations above sea level at various combinations of latitude and longitude, compressor maps describe levels of compressor thermal (and sometimes mechanical) efficiency at various combinations of airflow and boost pressure. A centrifugal compressor map also demarcates "danger zones" on the "east" and "west" side of the map, beyond which the compressor may surge or choke. Sloping lines plotted across the topography indicate a representative selection of compressor speeds required to achieve various combinations of boost and airflow.

Start by analyzing compressor maps with peak airflow in the right ballpark at a reasonable pressure ratio, using 60 percent efficiency as the lower limit the compressor should ever see in your application.

You'll discover that some compressors with much greater maximum airflow than you can use may appear feasible at *peak power*. But selecting a really oversized compressor is usually a terrible idea, because oversized centrifugal compressors are prone to surging at low airflow and high boost, and large positive-displacement superchargers will lose pumping efficiency at low speeds as the percentage of air leaking around the rotors becomes more significant.

It is true that larger centrifugal compressors typically begin slinging air at a lower compressor rpm, but this isn't saying much, as automotive-sized centrifugal compressors do not make any boost at all until they are turning at least 25,000 to 30,000 rpm. A *moderately* oversized compressor driven relatively slowly could work well to meet present boost needs with more headroom for future power upgrade *as long as you can stay away from the surge line*.

Do the math and plot your engine's airflow requirements at various representative rpm points on candidate compressor maps. Again, make sure that a centrifugal compressor can never operate on the wrong side of the surge line under any circumstances, *which can include part throttle*.

Once in a while supercharger system designers have elected to install twin superchargers operating in parallel. Although it is fairly common to run twin turbochargers, this is done mainly to eliminate miles of plumbing required to route exhaust from Vee-type or horizontally opposed engines to a single turbocharger, and to reduce turbine inertia and improve compressor spooling time, neither of which is relevant to a mechanically driven supercharger. These days, superchargers exist with tremendous airflow and fairly high pressure-ratio capabilities, so there is seldom any technical reason for installing multiple superchargers except in very large automotive-type marine engines. But twin superchargers do look cool.

The maximum practical volumetric airflow rate of a 1.9L (115 cid) positive displacement supercharger like the Eaton TVS R1900 can be calculated as follows, in this case assuming a maximum speed of 15,000 rpms (below which the R1900 still has fairly good thermal efficiency), at which point the blower is capable of at least 92 percent volumetric efficiency at 18 psi boost:

Airflow rate = (115 × 15,000 × .92) / 1728

= 918 cfm

This translates to mass airflow as follows:

918 cfm × .075 = 68.85 lb/min

The Eaton TVS R1900, for example, will do the job of supplying 44 lb/min of air with plenty of headroom for future horsepower increases.

The required blower rpm for the R1900 to meet the airflow requirement of 400 horsepower is . . .

Blower rpm$_{req}$ = (620 cfm / 918 cfm) × 15,000 rpm

= 10,134

The remaining "headroom" pumping capability for future power increases is more than **918** cfm - **620.6** cfm = **297.4** cfm, or **297.4** / **620.6** = **32%**.

Keep in mind that when all is said and done, there is the question of what will fit in the engine compartment, and where you need power, and your financial and temporal resources to deal with a really difficult installation.

7. Revisit supercharger/drive parasitic drag.

Magnuson Products' published drive power chart for the Eaton R1900 indicates less than **27.5** horsepower is required to drive the supercharger at 10,400 blower rpm at a pressure ratio of 1.6, about 9 psi. At 1.44 pressure ratio, drive power will require less power.

Adiabatic loss, which occurs inside the blower, is accounted for when reading from the graph. Belt loss, which is external to the blower, is not. To find the power required at the crankshaft, we must divide by belt efficiency. Assuming 97 percent belt efficiency:

27.5 hp / 0.97 = 28.4 hp

The final drive-power loss should be below 28.4 horsepower.

If a graph is not available, the power required by the supercharger can be calculated as a simple function of boost and airflow:

Drive Power ft-lb/sec = **Boost** lb/in^2 × **Airflow** ft^3/min

To get drive power in horsepower rather than pound-feet per second, we make use of the fact that 1 horsepower will lift 550 pounds 1 foot in 1 second and convert minutes to seconds and cubic feet to cubic inches as follows:

Drive power (ft-lb/sec) =
$$\frac{((\textbf{Boost } \text{lb/in}^2) \times (\textbf{Airflow } \text{ft}^3/\text{min}) \times 144 \text{ in2/ft}^3))}{(60 \text{ sec/min} \times 550 \text{ ft-lb / hp-sec}))}$$

Simplified, at 10.6 psi boost this works out to:

Drive power = Boost × Airflow / 229 hp

= (10.6 × 620 cfm) / 229

= 28.7 hp

This calculated number represents the horsepower required to turn the supercharger at the required pressure ratio and airflow (higher flow and pressure independently require more power). To find horsepower drag at the crankshaft driving the belt and supercharger, we must divide by belt efficiency and adiabatic efficiency. A typical figure for belt efficiency is 97 percent, and 60 percent is a safe guess for adiabatic efficiency. Dividing by these numbers, **28.7** / (.97 * .6) ≈ **50** hp. However, we also note from the graph that the thermal efficiency of the TVS R1900 at 10,130 rpm is 74 percent at a 1.72 pressure ratio rather than the generic figure of 60 percent suggested when no blower-specific thermal efficiency number is available. Dividing by 74 percent instead of 60 percent brings the drive power down to:

28.7 / (.97 × .74) = 39.98

≈40 hp

This is slightly more than Eaton's published figure of 32 hp, but Eaton should know, so we'll go with 32 drive horsepower as the minimum.

However, it makes sense to design a drive system with some headroom to crank up the boost further. Let's say we decide we might someday want to pump up the volume to 500 horsepower. Assuming we need 50 lb/min airflow, or about 650 cfm, and that we think we'll need at least 16-psi boost to do the job, we notice that Eaton publishes drive power numbers for 18 psi boost of about 51 drive hosepower.

We should design a drive system that could easily be upgraded to deliver 50 horsepower to the supercharger.

8. Determine supercharger pulley ratio.

Now we can calculate the pulley ratio needed to achieve 10,130 rpm compressor speed.

$$\text{Pulley ratio} \leq \frac{\text{Blower rpm}}{\text{Blower integral step-up ratio} \times \text{Engine rpm at redline}}$$

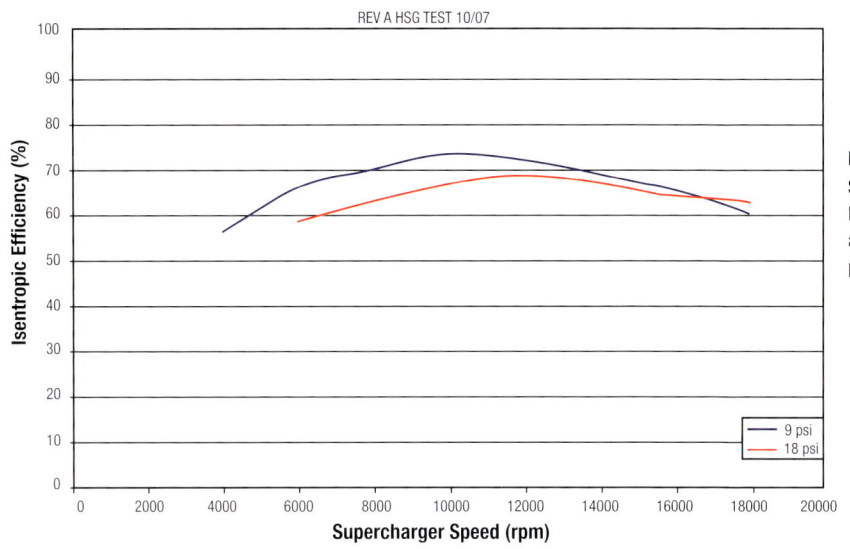

MAGNUSON PRODUCTS 6TH GENERATION 1900 SUPERCHARGER ISENTROPIC EFFICIENCY:
R1900 TVS supercharger isentropic (thermal) efficiency as a function of supercharger speed at 9 and 18 psi boost pressure. *Magnuson Products*

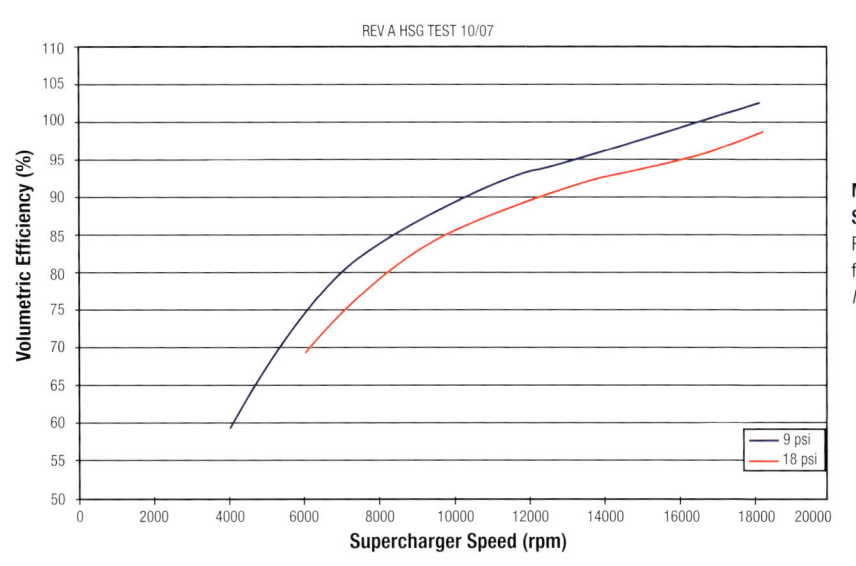

MAGNUSON PRODUCTS 6TH GENERATION 1900 SUPERCHARGER VOLUMETRIC EFFICIENCY:
R1900 TVS supercharger volumetric efficiency as a function of supercharger speed at 9 and 18 psi boost. *Magnuson Products*

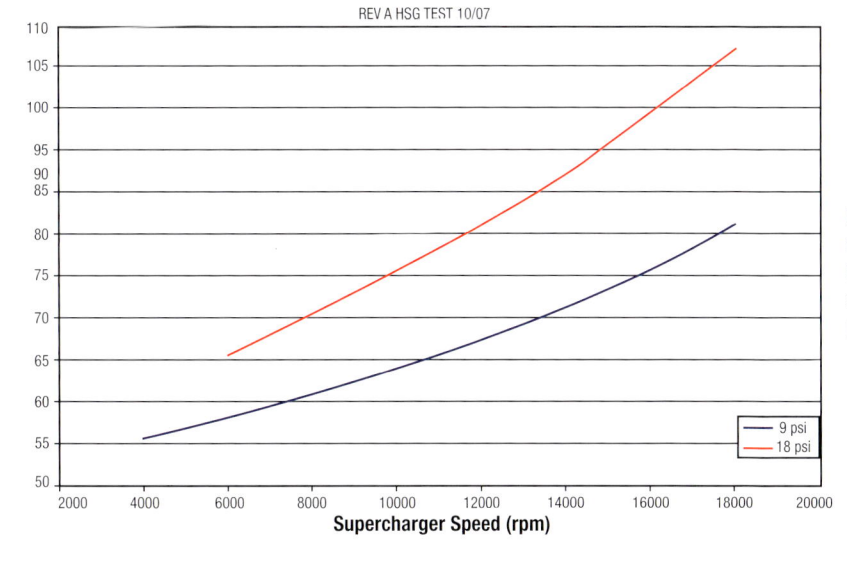

MAGNUSON PRODUCTS 6TH GENERATION 1900 SUPERCHARGER DRIVE POWER:
R1900 TVS supercharger drive power requirement as a function of supercharger speed at 9 and 18 psi boost pressure. *Magnuson Products*

SUPERCHARGER SELECTION AND SYSTEM MODELING

101

The Eaton TV R1900 supercharger has no internal step-up ratio like a centrifugal supercharger, so the internal blower step-up ratio is 1. Assuming the engine redline rpm is 6,800,

$$\text{Ratio}_{req} = 10{,}130 / (1 \times 6{,}800 \text{ rpm})$$
$$\approx 1.49$$

The crankshaft drive-pulley diameter must be 1.49 times the supercharger pulley diameter. If the Eaton TVS R1900 supercharger is supplied with the (minimum) 72-millimeer diameter pulley, the crank drive pulley must therefore be:

Crank pulley diameter = **1.49 × 72** mm
= **107.28** mm
= **4.22** inches

9. Determine belt loading.

Determining the belt load is critical to sizing the idler pulley bearing and, therefore, idler pulley. Assuming the crankshaft pulley diameter is 4.22 inches and the crankshaft speed is 6,800 rpm,

$$\text{Belt velocity} = \frac{\text{Crankshaft pulley diameter} \times \text{crankshaft rpm}}{229 \text{ ft/sec}}$$

$$= (4.22 \times 6{,}800) / 229 \text{ ft/sec}$$

$$\approx 125.3 \text{ ft/sec}$$

Convert drive horsepower to pound-feetpound-feet per second using the conversion factor of 1 horsepower = 550 ft-lb/sec. The initial supercharging system will only require 32 horsepower to drive the blower, but we've decided the drive system should be built to tolerate 50 horsepower to allow future hot-rodding. Therefore:

50 hp × **550** ft-lb / hp-sec = **27,500** ft-lb/sec

and

Force = Power / velocity
= **27,500** ft-lb/sec / **125.3** ft-sec ≈ **219.5** lb

This 329.25 pounds represents the load on the drive belt. In the worst case, the loading on a pulley bearing would be double this if the belt is perpendicular to a pulley on both sides. Typically, though, the total force on a pulley bearing would be more like 150 percent of the belt load, given that it is unusual to have a belt wrap *exactly* 180 degrees around a pulley. Assuming 150 percent, total loading would be

(219.5 / 2) + 219.5 = 109.75 + 219.5 = 329.25 lb

10. Determine Intercooler and Air Ducting Size

Obviously, many good supercharging systems have been built without intercooling systems, but intercoolers will make "free" power and enable more boost pressure without knock and reduce the thermal loading on the engine. It is important to build or select an intercooler that is up to the job. An entire chapter of this book is devoted to the subject of heat management, of which a large portion is a section about charge cooling that includes information on intercooler sizing for good cooling performance and minimal pressure drop.

Regarding air ducting to and from a supercharger or intercooler, assuming turbulent air flow (normal in intercooler plumbing), the following formulas are useful to determine the effects of changing intercooler piping diameter and flow rates. These are rough estimates because they actually require that the plumbing is smooth on the inside without sharp bends. If you Google engineering + tool + box, you will find many formulae that can be used to model the gas flow systems used in supercharged engine systems.

$$\Delta P = (\text{Flow}_2 / \text{Flow}_1)^2$$

where,
ΔP = pressure loss in the same pipe with different flow rates
Flow_1 = initial flow rate
Flow_2 = new flow rate

At the same flow rate in pipes of two different diameters, pressure loss in the pipe with Diam_2 as compared to the pipe with Diam_1 is approximated by $(\text{Diam}_2/\text{Diam}_1)^{-5.2}$.

$$\Delta P = (\text{Diam}_2 / \text{Diam}_1)^{-5.2}$$

where,
ΔP = pressure drop in pipes with different diameters
Diam_1 = initial diameter
Diam_2 = new diameter

In the same pipe with same flow rate but with different total pressures at different times, pressure loss at Pres_2 compared to Pres_1 is approximated by $(\text{Pres}_2/\text{Pres}_1)$.

$$\Delta P = (\text{Pres}_2 / \text{Pres}_1)^{-5.2}$$

where,
ΔP = pressure loss in pipes with equal flow rates but different total pressures

Pres_1 = initial pressure
Pres_2 = new pressure

MODELING STAGED COMPRESSORS

Staged superchargers—with the compressor of one supercharger feeding the inlet of another, with it possibly feeding the inlet of a third in some wild classes of tractor-pulling—can achieve tremendously high boost pressures in the 200-psi-plus range, and with much better thermal efficiency than would be possible in fewer stages. Modern jet engines routinely achieve an operating pressure ratio in the 40:1 range, with multi-stage axial or axial/centrifugal compressors.

In the case of jet engines, "intercooling" is not an option. The only possible way to cool supercharged inlet air is to dilute it with bypass air from the main compressor fan, which can be between -30 degrees F and -140 degrees F at altitude, since temperature typically drops 3.5 degrees F per 1,000 feet. Because detonation is not a factor in a continuous-flame powerplant, the priority is to keep the combustion chamber(s) and turbine section from burning up in the high heat. This is accomplished using cold bypass air as a coolant.

Intercooling between stages is critical on a piston engine to keep combustion temperatures under control. Let's say the goal is to run 60-psi boost pressure on a spark-ignition methanol engine. This is actually 74.7-psi absolute pressure, which is a pressure ratio of roughly 5.1, which is off the map of virtually all off-the-shelf automotive superchargers (although one, Garrett's GT5533, can deliver about 130 lb/min air at a pressure ratio over 5.5, which is *66-psig boost*, though this is available in the most extreme upper corner of the compressor map where surge, choke, and over-speed are all way too close for comfort). Even 45 psi, a PR of roughly 4.0, is barely within the outer limits of the operating envelope for many large automotive racing superchargers like Garrett's GT4508R. At or very near over-speed, the GT4508R can deliver a maximum of about 45-psi boost at 95 lb/min airflow with a thermal efficiency of about 70 percent.

But 60 psi could also be achieved with *staged superchargers* teamed with *staged intercoolers*. Two superchargers, each delivering a pressure ratio of 2.3, could deliver 5 atmospheres of charge pressure, which is 63-psi boost as shown on the gauge. Simplified, the first-stage compressor essentially delivers 33.81-psi inter-stage absolute pressure by raising atmospheric pressure 2.3 times, or 2.3 * 14.7 = 33.81 psia. The second-stage compressor boosts the 33.81 inter-stage absolute pressure by 2.3 times to 77.76 psia.

When staging superchargers, the output of the first stage must be matched to the input of the second stage, and the matching must factor in the effects of intercooling between the stages. Modeling a multi-stage supercharging system requires working "backward" from the engine to the second-stage supercharger, to the first supercharger, and then forward from the Stage 1 supercharger to the Stage 1 intercooler to the Stage 2 supercharger, to the Stage 2 intercooler, to the engine.

Start by computing the airflow requirements of the engine.

Again, the goal is 60 psi boost (77.76 psi_{abs} manifold pressure) on methanol. Assume we have a 2.0-liter (122 cid) engine running at 8,000 rpm with 85 percent volumetric efficiency (VE) that will consume air according to the following:

$Airflow_{cfm}$ = cid × rpm × 0.5 × VE / 1,728

Where:

$Airflow_{cfm}$ = Volumetric airflow in cfm
CID = Displacement in cubic inches = liters × 61.02
RPM = Engine speed in revolutions per minute
VE = Volumetric efficiency (xx percent would be .xx)
Note: Volumetric efficiency is the ratio or percentage comparing the volume of charge gases that actually enter a cylinder during induction to the actual capacity of the cylinder under static conditions.

$Airflow_{cfm}$ = (cid × rpm × 0.5 × VE) / 1,728

= (122 × 8,000 × 0.5 × .85) / 1,728

= 240 cfm

Many modern compressor maps show airflow in pounds per minute. There are 0.076 pounds of air per cubic foot at standard temperature and pressure (STP), which is 68 F at sea level, so:

240 × 0.075 = 18.24 lb/min

We assume the normal-charged version of the engine is capable of breathing 18 lb/min air.

Choose the Stage 2 supercharger.

The second-stage compressor (closest to the engine) must be capable of delivering 18.24 pounds per minute of air at a pressure ratio of 2.3. Assuming compressor efficiency of 75 percent at a 2.3 PR, the density ratio is:

$DR = (T_{1c} / T_{2c}) \times PR$

Where:

T_{1c} = Original (inlet) absolute air temp (degrees R)
T_{2c} = New (outlet) temp in degrees R for a certain compressor
       = $T_{1c} + (((T_{1c} \times (PR^{.283})) - T_{1c}) / CE)$

PR = Pressure ratio = P_{2c} / P_{1c}

Therefore:

$DR = (T_{1c} T_{2c}) \times PR$
$= (T_{1c} / (T_{1c} + (((T_{1c} \times (PR^{.283})) - T_{1c}) / CE))) \times PR$
$= (530 / (530 + (((530 \times (2.3^{.283})) - 530) / .75))) \times 2.3$
$= 1.70$

Continued on page 104

For example, consider a forced-induction engine sucking air at 360 cfm through each of two compressors and compressing a 200 F hot charge at 15 psig boost through two separate, ten-feet sections of 1.5-inch smooth tubing. The pressure loss would be roughly 1.2 psi in each half of the twin-turbo, twin-intercooler plumbing. Increasing plumbing diameter to 2 inches, the pressure drop declines to 0.26 psi. Increasing plumbing diameter to 2.5-inches, the pressure drop is now 0.090 psi; and with 3-inch plumbing, pressure loss declines to 0.034 psi. Bottom line, a 2-inch tube has a pressure drop that is about 22 percent that of the 1.5-inch pipe pressure drop as follows:

$$\Delta P = (Diam_2 / Diam_1)^{-5.2}$$
$$= (2/1.5)^{-5.2}$$
$$= 1.3333^{-5.2}$$
$$= 0.224$$

11. Determine the strategy to increase fuel flow.
The increased airflow resulting from supercharging will require additional fuel by increasing one or more of the following:

- Injector pulse duration
- Nozzle size
- Fuel pressure
- Number of injectors

See Chapter 6 of this book about supercharger engine management, and for additional detail read my book *How to Tune and Modify Engine Management Systems*.

MODELING STAGED COMPRESSORS *Continued on from page 103*

So the Stage 2 compressor must flow:

1.70 × 18 = 30.6 lb/min

Or, if you like cfm:

1.70 × 240 = 408 cfm

Looking over some compressor maps, we see a Garrett GT2871R central compressor will do the job with at least 75 percent thermal efficiency. This is actually a turbo compressor, but it is nearly identical to the type of compressor found in Rotrex superchargers.

Choose the Stage 1 supercharger.
Choosing a Stage 1 compressor is complicated by the fact that the charge air from Stage 1 must be intercooled before it is delivered to the Stage 2 compressor. Let's assume that the air from the Stage 1 compressor is also delivered at a pressure ratio of 2.3 at 75 percent efficiency.

Assuming that ambient air is 70 degrees F, the compressor-out temperature from the first stage (TCO1) will be approximately:

$$T_{CO1} = T_{1C} + (((T_{1C} \times (PR^{.283})) - T_{1C}) / CE)$$

Where:
T_{CO} = Absolute compressor-out temp (degrees R)
T_{1C} = Compressor inlet temp (degrees R)
CE = Compressor efficiency

Then:
$$T_{CO1} = T_{1C} + (((T1C \times (PR^{.283})) - T_{1C}) / CE)$$
$$= 530 + (((530 \times (2.3^{.283})) - 530) / .75)$$
$$= 717.84R$$

Converting back to Fahrenheit, the compressor-out temperature is

717.84R - 460 = 257.8F

Now, assume the charge from Stage 1 is cooled by a large air-cooled intercooler cooled with ambient 70 degree F air at 80 percent efficiency. Such an intercooler will cool the 257.8 degree F charge from Stage 1 by 150.2 degrees F to a compressor-out temperature of 107.6 degrees F, at which point it will enter the GT2871R compressor.

If we assume that the Stage 1 intercooler has a negligible pressure drop, the required mass airflow in lb/min from it must be:

$$AF_{ST1} = AF_{ST2} \times T_{CO1} / T_{IO1}$$

Where:
AF_{ST1} = Airflow from the Stage 1 compressor (lb/min)
AF_{ST2} = Airflow from the Stage 2 compressor (lb/min)
T_{CO1} = Compressor-out temperature (degrees R)
T_{IO1} = Intercooler-out temperature (degrees R)

Therefore:
$$AF_{ST1} = AF_{ST2} \times T_{CO1} / T_{IO1}$$
$$= 30.6 \times ((257.8F + 460) 107.6F + 460)$$
$$= 30.6 \times (717.8R 567.6R)$$
$$= 30.6 \times 1.26$$
$$= 38.56 \text{ lb/min}$$

Correcting airflow for the same density ratio of 1.7,

38.56 × 1.70 = 65.56 lb/min

65.54 lb/min airflow must be delivered at a PR of 2.3 by the Stage 1 compressor.

Garrett's GT4508R centrifugal compressor can easily deliver this airflow without breaking a sweat at 79 percent thermal efficiency (which is actually better than our assumed 75 percent thermal efficiency).

Of course, the output of the Stage 2 compressor must also be intercooled.

Having selected the actual equipment, let's add up how this will play out:

1. Ambient air enters the GT4508R at 70 degrees F, departing the compressor boosted to a pressure ratio of 2.3, which at this stage means 19.11-psi gauge pressure or 2.3 × 14.7 = 33.81 psia. When air leaves the compressor, it has actually been heated from 70 degrees F (530R) ambient temperature to compressor-out temperature (T_{CO1}) to 248.3 degrees F by the .79-efficient GT4508 as follows:

$$T_{CO1} = T_{1C} + (((T_{1C} \times (PR^{.283})) - T_{1C}) / CE)$$
$$= 530 + (((530 \times (2.3^{.283})) - 530) / .79)$$
$$= 708.3R$$

Converting back to Fahrenheit, the compressor discharge temperature is

708.3R - 460 = 248.3F

2. Previously, the density change from air at atmospheric pressure (14.7 psi) being pressurized 2.3 times to 33.81-psi absolute pressure (19.11-psi boost pressure) had been assumed to represent a density increase of only 1.70 times because of the heat of compression, but the GT4508 is a bit more efficient and the Stage 1 Density Ratio is actually 1.72 as follows:

Contiued on page 105

MODELING STAGED COMPRESSORS *Continued on from page 104*

$$DR = (T_{1c} / T_{2c}) * PR$$
$$= (T_{1c} / (T_{1c} + (((T_{1c} \times (PR^{.283})) - T_{1c}) / CE))) \times PR$$
$$= (530 / (530 + (((530 \times (2.3^{.283})) - 530) / .79))) \times 2.3$$
$$= 1.72$$

The hot air leaving the Stage 1 compressor at 19.11-psig boost pressure (33.81 psia) at a pressure ratio of 2.3 PR is 172 percent more dense than ambient air.

(Note: Pressure ratio-to-density ratio tables are a quick, rough way to convert a pressure ratio to the density ratio for a compressor of a particular thermal efficiency.)

3. The 248.3-degree F Stage 1 charge from the Garrett GT4508R now enters an air-cooled intercooler we've assumed to have 80 percent thermal efficiency. Intercooler-induced density changes occur as follows:

$$\Delta D = (T_{co1} / T_{i01}) - 1$$

Where:

ΔD = Density change resulting from Stage 1 intercooling
T_{co1} = Original temperature (degrees R) of air leaving the Stage 1 compressor
T_{i01} = New temperature (degrees R) of air leaving the Stage 1 intercooler

$$\Delta D = (T_{co1} / T_{i01}) - 1$$
$$= (708.3 / (248.3 - ((248.3 - 70) \times .8) + 460) - 1$$
$$= (708.3 / 565.76) - 1$$
$$\approx 1.25 - 1$$
$$= 0.25$$
$$\approx 25 \text{ percent density increase}$$

4. Stage 1 supercharging has multiplied air density by a factor of 1.72, and Stage 1 intercooling has now increased *that* density by 25 percent, which increases the overall density ratio to $1.72 \times 1.25 = 2.15$. Air density exiting the zero-pressure-drop intercooler at 19.11-psi boost (33.81 psia) is now 215 percent of normal ambient air pressure.

5. Charge air from the Stage 1 intercooler now enters the Stage 2 Garrett GT2871R compressor at 565.7 − 460 = 105.7°F, at 19.11 psi boost. Physically, the GT2871 is a smaller compressor than the GT4508, but charge air entering the GT2871 is already compressed to 2.15 times atmospheric density. The GT2871 now boosts the already-compressed air further with an identical pressure ratio of 2.3, from 33.81 psia to 77.76 psia, which is 63-psi boost gauge pressure.

6. When air leaves the GT 2871, it has been heated by the .75 compressor from 105.66 degrees F inter-stage temperature (565.7R) to Stage 2 compressor-out temperature (T_{co2}) as follows:

$$T_{co2} = T_{1c} + (((T1C \times (PR^{.283})) - T_{1c}) / CE)$$
$$= 565.7 + (((565.7 \times (2.3^{.283})) - 565.7) / .75)$$
$$= 766.2R$$

Converting back to Fahrenheit, the hot compressor-out temperature is

$$766.2R - 460 \approx 306F$$

The charge leaves the Stage 2 compressor at 306 F, of which 105.7 F was already in the air ingested from Stage 1 compression and intercooling and 200.3 F was added by the additional compression.

7. At this point, the density change to air at inter-stage pressure (33.81 psi) being further pressurized 2.3 times to 77.76-psi absolute pressure (63.1-psig boost) represents an additional density increase of only 1.70 times due to the heat of compression effect on density ratio (1.70 for the slightly less efficient .75-efficient GT2871). Therefore, following Stage 2 compression, the density ratio is increased by

$$DR = 2.15 \times 1.70 = 3.66$$

The combined density increase is 3.66 times ambient atmospheric pressure. Though *pressure* has increased from supercharging by 2.3 times to 77.76 psia for a total pressure ratio of 5.28, once again more than 25 percent density has been lost because of charge heating in the Stage 2 compressor, and the total air mass or weight per cubic foot only increases to 366 percent, i.e., approaching 4 atmospheres.

8. The 306-degree F (766R) Stage 2 charge air exiting from the Garrett GT2871R is then cooled by a second Stage 2 intercooler cooled with 70-degree ambient air at 80-percent thermal efficiency by 188.8 degrees F to 117.2 degrees F (577R). This increases the density as follows:

$$\Delta D = (T_{co2} / T_{i02}) - 1$$

Where:

ΔD = Density change resulting from Stage 2 intercooling
T_{co2} = Original temperature (degrees R) of air leaving the Stage 2 compressor
T_{i02} = New temperature (degrees R) of air leaving the intercooler

Plugging in the numbers:
$$\Delta D = (T_{co2} / T_{i02}) - 1$$
$$= ((306 + 460) / (306 - ((306 - 70) \times .8) + 460)) - 1$$
$$= (766 / 577.2) - 1$$
$$= 1.327 - 1$$
$$= 0.33$$
$$= 33 \text{ percent density increase}$$

Stage 2 supercharging has increased air density by a factor of 1.7, and Stage 2 intercooling has now increased *that* density by 33 percent, which increases the total Stage 2 density ratio to

$$1.7 \times 1.33 = 2.35$$

But the air leaving the Stage 1 intercooler was already at a density ratio of 2.34, which was then increased by the Stage 2 density increase as follows:

$$2.34 \times 2.35 \approx 5.5 \text{ density ratio}$$

9. Air density leaving the Stage 2 intercooler at 63-psi boost (77.76 psia) will be 550 percent of atmospheric density. This means that if the engine could make, say, 200 horsepower without supercharging, 63-psi boost from two-stage intercooled supercharging would increase power by 5.5 times to at least 1,100 horsepower, and probably more by raising the peak torque rpm above the normal-charged peak. In addition, this engine would almost certainly require methanol fuel, and methanol would provide additional charge-cooling due to the high heat of vaporization of alcohol, lowering the 156-degree F air temperature considerably.

Chapter 6
Blower Engine Management

Bolting a supercharger to an engine, improvising a mechanical drive, and piping pressurized air from the compressor to the throttle body is certainly not trivial, but it is a straightforward mechanical task. However, the basis of a *great* supercharger system is great engine management, which can be quite a bit more esoteric. Great engine management is more important to successful supercharging than almost any other factor, and this is true whether you are using modern electronic fuel injection and engine management, or traditional carburetion. The goals of supercharged engine management are the same regardless of the fuel delivery system, but the goals and issues related to carbureted supercharging are unique enough that there is a special section dedicated to carburetion later in this chapter.

The marriage of electronic fuel injection with forced induction provided a quantum leap in the practicality of street vehicles with outrageous power in the range of 250 to 500 horsepower per liter. Unfortunately, an engine-management system designed for a normal-charged factory engine will not work well if you install a supercharger, and it is likely to require significant changes to spark timing and fuel delivery that may require changes to the internal calibration tables that drive digital engine management. In some cases it may require modifications or additions to the electronic control logic and hardware, as well as the sensor and actuator systems that deliver spark, fuel, boost control, and other engine management functions. The necessary solution might be as simple as retarding static timing and installing a variable-rate-of-gain fuel pressure regulator to increase fuel pressure during boost, or it might be as complex as installing an entire aftermarket engine-management system, larger fuel injectors, a more powerful fuel pump, and so on.

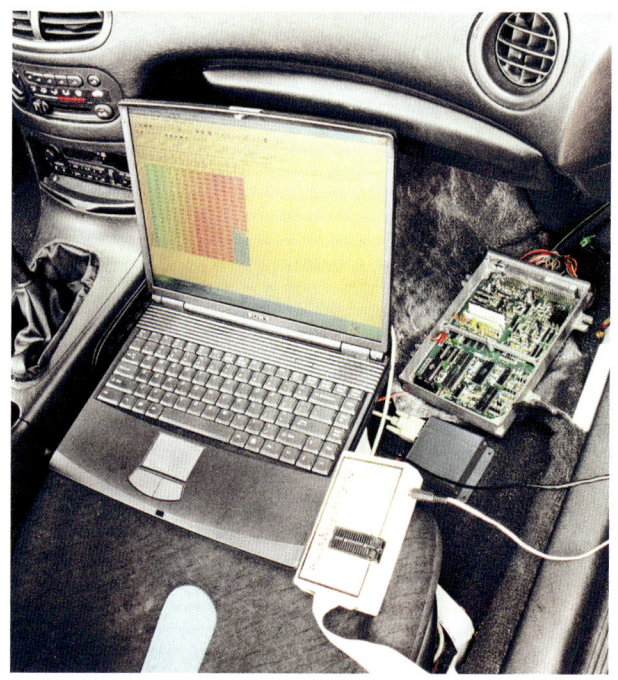

Author's forced-induction Honda del Sol during dyno recalibration process. Graphing power, torque, and air-fuel ratio at full throttle on an inertial chassis dyno, the trick is to recalibrate the fuel and retest over and over until you achieve best torque at all points at wide open throttle at the leanest settings achievable without detonation.

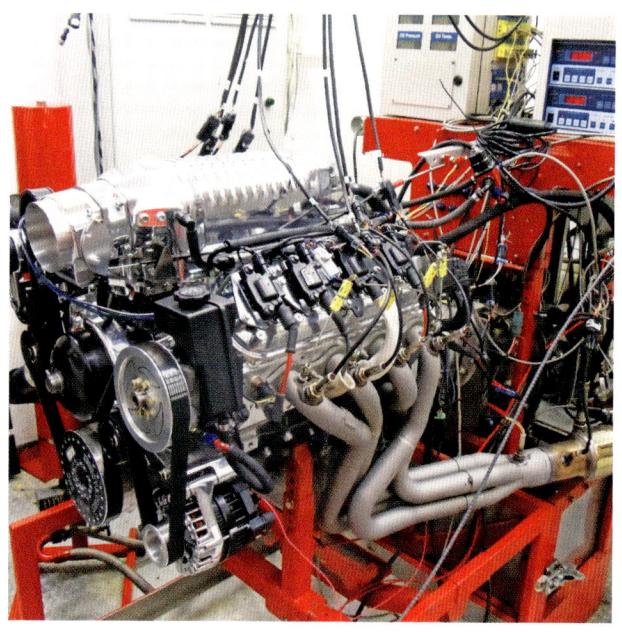

The GM LS3 V-8 on the Whipple torque-cell engine dyno. Load-holding dynos allow tuners to hold the powerplant at discrete breakpoints of rpm and load to optimize power and fuel economy. Note the EGT probes in the individual header tubes, which, in many sophisticated aftermarket engine management systems, enable a tuner to optimize the fuel and timing for individual cylinders as if you were optimizing eight separate engines. *Whipple Superchargers*

Virtually any modern engine that came from the factory equipped with a turbo or supercharger can be *overboosted* by 3 to 5 psi or more without requiring radical changes to engine management—or even any at all, in some cases—but the same most definitely cannot be said when it comes to adding 3- to 5-psi boost to a normal-charged spark-ignition EFI engine with a supercharger conversion. Boosting a normal-charged engine more than 1 or 2 psi without important enrichment changes to the air-fuel ratio, or more than 3 psi without commensurate ignition timing retard, will certainly not deliver good performance increases and will almost definitely damage the engine if excursions into boosted territory last more than a few seconds.

The difficulty of modifying a stock normal-charged engine-management system so that it's *capable* of delivering proper fuel and spark when manifold pressure goes into boost can vary considerably depending on the design of the stock engine-management system. It may require both hardware and software changes or an external electronic interceptor or piggyback device. Even if a supercharger conversion does not confuse or disrupt the stock spark-ignition engine management procedures under heavy load in ways that deliver timing and air-fuel ratios under boost that are seriously dysfunctional if not totally non-operable, a supercharger conversion without EMS calibration changes is likely to produce air-fuel ratios and ignition timing that would be suboptimal on *any engine*, supercharged or not. For reliability and high power under boost, supercharged engines require unique engine management procedures for two basic reasons:

1. The higher effective compression ratio of supercharging results in denser charge mixtures in the combustion chambers of a spark-ignition powerplant, leading to hotter, higher combustion pressures that are prone to exploding (detonating) the charge before normal combustion can complete (diesel engines normally run *cooler* with forced induction).
2. The additional power being generated increases thermal and mechanical loading on various engine and vehicle systems, which may require sophisticated engine management countermeasures to protect the engine from damage.

Both of these factors tend to significantly increase the octane number requirement (ONR) of an engine when it's converted to supercharging. Compared to an otherwise identical but nonboosted engine, a supercharged spark-ignition powerplant will require one or all of the following:

- Higher octane fuel
- Physical design countermeasures to *lower* the engine's ONR back down as much as possible (such as lower-compression pistons)
- Engine management or supercharger system design tricks to cool combustion or lower peak combustion pressures (such as retarded ignition timing and fuel enrichment during boost, intercooling, and so on)

WHY YOUR EMS CALIBRATION IS WRONG FOR PERFORMANCE SUPERCHARGING

When it comes to air-fuel ratio, regardless of whether an engine is supercharged, in the presence of sufficient air, gasoline and air react chemically in a ratio of 14.65 pounds air to 1 pound of gasoline during the burn, totally consuming the fuel and the oxygen in air and producing water and carbon dioxide. The chemically perfect air-fuel charge mixture is referred to as *stoichiometric*. Nongasoline fuels like methyl alcohol have their own stoichiometric air-fuel ratio that can vary considerably from gasoline. For this reason, the stoichiometric air-fuel ratio of any fuel is often referred to a *Lambda* 1.0, which is the ratio of the actual air-fuel ratio to the stoichiometric air-fuel ratio. The stoichiometric ratio of methanol is about 6.4:1, and that ratio is therefore Lambda 1.0. The stoichiometric ratio for nitromethane is 1.7:1. The ratio for diesel is roughly 15:1 (but no one ever runs a diesel at stoichiometric mixtures due to the fact that, unlike spark-ignition combustion, an air surplus *cools* diesel combustion).

Unfortunately, because air and fuel can never be perfectly mixed in the real world, a stoichiometric air-fuel mixture will always result in (1) some residual fuel in the exhaust that didn't burn, (2) some partially burned fuel in the form of carbon monoxide, and (3) some residual oxygen that found

Dyno-testing a blown truck on the Magnuson Products' Mustang chassis dynamometer. Dyno-testing tells you if you are going in the right or wrong direction with engine modifications and changes to fuel and spark delivery. Experienced Dyno tuners can almost always find power that was left on the table by amateurs, who would gain a lot if they put as much effort into perfecting the calibration as they did into building the supercharging system. *Magnuson Products*

nothing to burn. Exhaust gas oxygen is rare in spark-ignition engines. If there is a surplus of fuel, and therefore insufficient oxygen available to produce complete combustion, exhaust will contain high levels of unburned waste hydrocarbons and partially combusted carbon monoxide gas (a fuel that burns with a hot blue flame).

Nonetheless, richer-than-stoichiometric air-fuel mixtures are required on any spark-ignition engine to optimize torque and power. Why is this? The reason a spark-ignition engine needs richer mixtures to maximize torque than you'd expect from a mathematical point of view stems from the persistent air famine in a spark-ignition engine, and the fact that real-world internal combustion in a piston engine is "messy." Rather than being some neat, perfect thermodynamic or chemical equation, real-world combustion is a swirling, turbulent mixture of high-speed fluids and gases of varying temperatures and chemical composition, high-speed flame fronts, sparking electrical energy, and even, on occasion, explosive detonations.

Air tends to be scarce in the combustion chamber(s) of a spark-ignition engine at wide-open throttle, particularly when it's a normal-charged engine. This is because you need a lot of air by weight to burn gasoline (nearly 15 times as much!) and even more by volume. Only about 21 percent of air is the oxygen that's really needed for combustion; the rest is nitrogen gas that is nearly inert. At higher engine speeds there is little time available to charge the cylinders, and the pathway into the combustion chambers is through twisting, complex, restrictive plumbing, with various obstacles in the way (closed valves, throttle bodies, and so on) that completely block the airway a high percentage of the time and partially block it all the time.

The air famine in piston engines is the raison d'être for superchargers. But, for a variety of reasons, supercharged engines are boost-limited most of the time, and the goal is virtually always to make maximum use of the available air supply.

Which brings us back to the reason for running richer-than-stoichiometric mixtures to maximize power. Because air is relatively scarce and fuel is easily abundant and the charge mixture can never be entirely homogenous, the strategy that optimizes power on any spark-ignition engine is to make sure that every molecule of oxygen that does make it into the combustion chambers has fuel to burn. For gasoline fuel, it turns out the way to accomplish this is to richen the air-fuel mixture from the chemically ideal 14.7:1 to something in the range of 13:1 (13/14.65 ≈ .89 Lambda). It's a little like inviting extra girls to a dance to increase the odds every guy can always find a partner.

Depending on engine speed, gasoline fuel will produce best torque over a range of mixtures, with lean best torque (LBT) as lean as 13.3:1 (.91 Lambda), rich best torque (RBT) as rich as 11.5:1 (.78 Lambda), and mean best torque (MBT) in the 12-12.5:1 area (.84 Lambda). The width of the range of air-fuel mixtures over which an engine will make

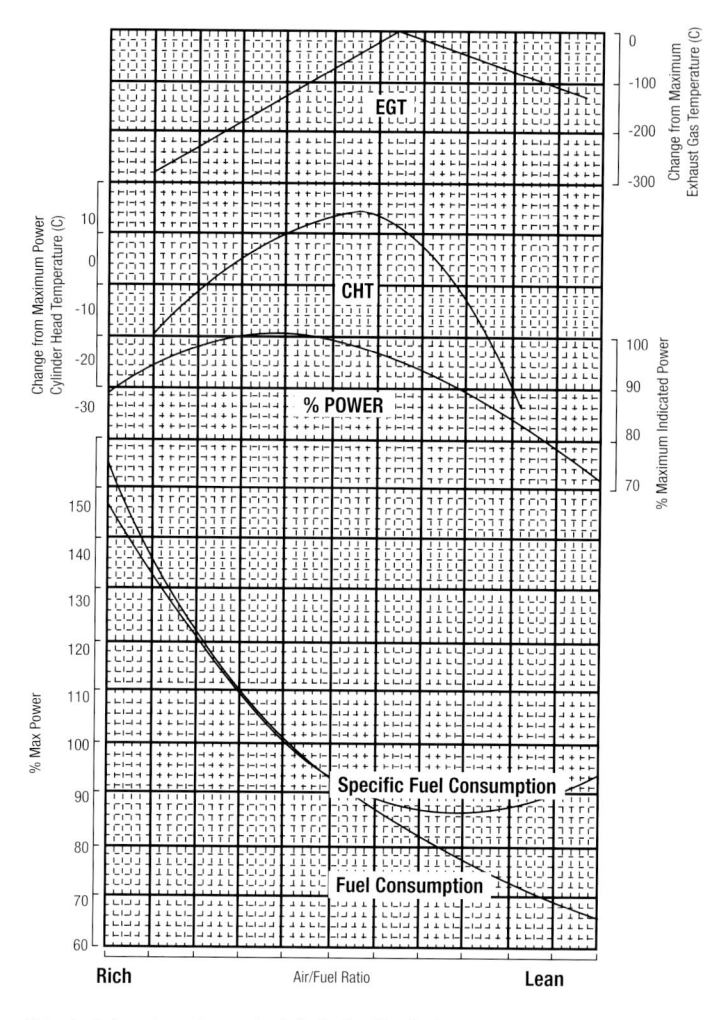

This chart shows how changes to air-fuel ratio affect fuel consumption, specific fuel consumption (the amount of fuel required to produce a unit of power), power, cylinder head temperature (CHT), and exhaust gas temperature (EGT). Note that best fuel economy occurs slightly lean of peak EGT, while best power occurs in a range rich of EGT. Gasoline-fueled engines are insensitive enough to air-fuel ratio that peak power is achievable over a fairly wide range if the engine is turning slowly enough that it is not necessary to achieve the highest possible flame speed.

maximum torque is referred to as the fuel's *sensitivity*. The sensitivity of gasoline narrows at high engine speeds, which require the highest possible flame speed so that combustion can be completed in the tiny amount of available time.

It turns out that the difference between available power at stoichiometric mixtures and at richer MBT mixtures is often substantial. Many normal-charged street engines with a moderate compression ratio work well with a 13.3:1 air-fuel ratio that delivers maximum torque with best fuel economy on street gasoline. Low-pressure forced-induction engines will safely make more power at 12.5:1 or richer because cooler combustion permits more ignition advance without knock, which is critical to achieving peak cylinder pressure at the optimal time for delivering maximum torque.

Paxton's 351-Windsor system brings supercharging to classic raised-block Windsor Fords. Special carb housing keeps fuel in the float chambers during boost without carb modifications. *Paxton*

A Vortech blower kit for a carbureted big-block Chevys. As always, cool intake air is critical to fighting detonation, particularly on non-intercooled supercharging systems. *Vortech*

A marine big-block Chevrolet with mechanical fuel injection above the blower. Marine racing could be extremely challenging for carbureted engines due to fuel agitation in the carb float chamber. This is old-school mechanical injection where you tune fuel delivery by swapping "pills" in the fuel return line. Boats, of course, do not require nearly as sophisticated transient performance, since prop speed and engine rpm are not tied to forward speed in a fluid drive system.

Alas, high-pressure supercharged engines running on gasoline need mixtures even richer than .84 Lambda. True, air-fuel ratios richer than .84 Lambda are increasingly inefficient from the point of view of producing the highest combustion energy per weight of fuel. And, as mixtures move rich of RBT, you eventually get less torque per weight of air. As boost increases on high-pressure blown engines, however, thermal loading from the enhanced horsepower of supercharged combustion eventually becomes a critical problem that can cause severe high-power detonation that limits maximum boost pressure.

On a knock-limited engine, an excellent strategy for maximizing power turns out to be the use of fuel enrichment to produce a super-rich combustion environment in which excess fuel that cannot be burned due to the oxygen shortage is present in the combustion process solely to lower high-combustion temperatures with the powerful cooling effect of fuel vaporization. In this odd environment, excess gasoline absorbs large amounts of heat as drops of fuel vaporize and slow combustion. The rich mixture acts exactly like water or water-alcohol injection (which was commonly used to fight knock in the old days before EFI and electronic engine management, and has made something of a comeback recently as states like California have reduced the octane of premium street gasoline). Without fuel enrichment, the higher boost pressures of radical supercharged engines would result in uncontrolled knock and burned pistons. Keep in mind, the excess fuel doesn't directly make power (in fact, in a way it makes *less*), but it permits additional boost, which *does* make more net power (even as you're burning fuel and spewing pollution at a furious rate).

So the required air-fuel ratio of a supercharged engine tends to increase in a relatively linear fashion as boost rises from 0, first to maximize torque and then more steeply as surplus fuel is introduced for charge-cooling as an anti-knock countermeasure. The fuel-cooling requirment of high-pressure supercharging is why significantly overboosting a factory forced-induction engine will eventually demand fuel enrichment that is beyond the scope of the stock engine-management system, even if the EMS can continue delivering air-fuel ratios equal to those that worked well to deliver mean best torque at lower boost.

A supercharger conversion can adversely affect stock tuning even when the engine is not making any boost at all. For example, the power needed to drive the supercharger at idle can load the engine enough that the engine-management system fuels the engine from a different cell in the speed-density tables, which calls for a different injection pulse width or timing. The supercharger can alter tuning anywhere in an engine's operating range, from idle on up, where the supercharger is not making positive boost pressure but is enhancing intake airflow enough to change manifold pressure on an engine equipped with a speed-density engine-management system.

Such systems deduce engine airflow based on engine speed and manifold pressure and then deliver fuel delivery and ignition timing based on look-up numbers in calibration tables. In a speed-density EMS, the correlation between manifold pressure and airflow can be thrown off by changes to the intake volumetric efficiency in the normal-charged operating envelope of the engine, and positive boost pressure may be invisible to the engine-management system if the manifold pressure sensor sensitivity range ends at or near ambient atmospheric pressure, a.k.a., zero vacuum in the intake manifold.

When a supercharged engine *is* making boost, the blower warps the effective volumetric efficiency (VE) of the engine upward in a way that can be (a) simple and linear or (b) radical, complex, and even unpredictable, depending on the type of compressor and drive system. A supercharger conversion engine under boost commonly operates at combinations of airflow, manifold pressure, and rpm that were not achievable without the blower and thus usually cannot be handled correctly with the engine-management system's stock fuel and ignition tables.

A conversion-engine's rate of acceleration, airflow, or manifold pressure can increase relative to an rpm slew rate or MAP or MAF sensor value in a way that is known by the factory onboard computer to be suspiciously high, out of range, or otherwise implausible. The consequences may range from nothing at all to a temporarily set check engine light, to the ECU permanently storing a malfunction code (which could create warranty problems), to the ECU commanding immediate special engine-management operating countermeasures such as harshly retarded timing or hard rev-limiting, to the ECU implementing full-blown limp home mode operation until the ECU is reset.

Holley aftermarket electronic controllers for managing Pro-Jection throttle-body injection system with Holley four-barrel bolt pattern and multi-port add-on fuel-injection systems. The simplest controllers involve choosing fuel parameters on a dedicated remote-control-type box, with more sophisticated systems providing complex calibration from programmer software on a laptop computer. *Holley*

A big-block engine with Procharger centrifugal supercharging system and blow-through C&S Aerosol Billet Carburetor. C&S specializes in blow-through race-type gas or alcohol carburetors that can handle boost pressures of more than 40 psi and power levels over 2,500 horsepower. C&S touts power increases of 30 to 150 percent—with intercooling provided exclusively by fuel vaporization. *Procharger*

DI-Motronic

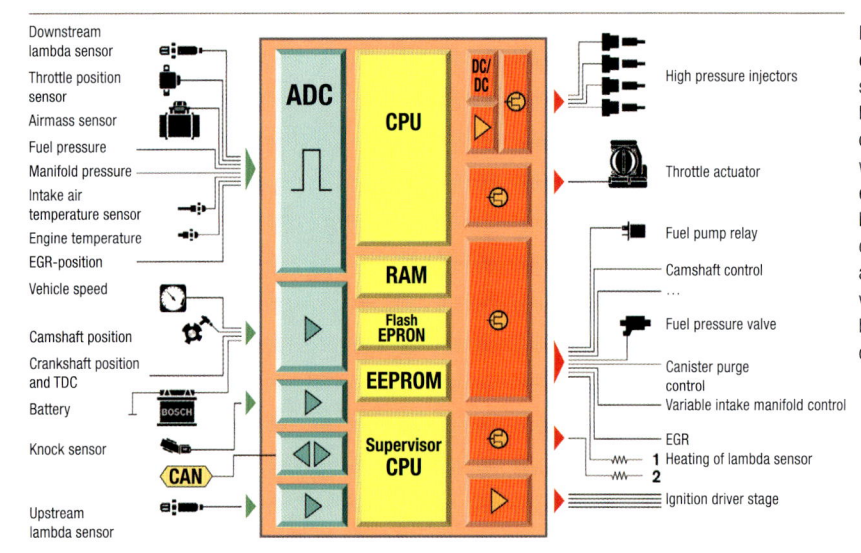

Hardware subsystems in a Bosch Motronic Direct Injection engine-management system. This is a multi-processor system similar in some ways to a personal computer, but because an engine management system needs to operate in real time across a wide range of temperatures with extremely high reliability, the clock speed of the electronics is much slower than a typical PC. Note the hardware's ability to transmit and receive both analog and digital data between the onboard computer and a large array of vehicle and engine sensors and actuators. New vehicles use a controller area network to communicate between multiple vehicle computers that share the load of controlling increasingly robotic vehicles. *Bosch*

110

BLOWER ENGINE MANAGEMENT

Bill Miller Engineering's "blower dyno" tests all Gibson-Miller Top Fuel superchargers on a blown-alcohol 502 Hemi to verify performance without subjecting the supercharger and engine to the savage beating of nitromethane combustion. *Bill Miller Engineering*

If boost gets high enough, engine airflow and manifold pressure arrive at a point where the MAP and MAF sensor electrical output maxes out at the highest achievable voltage or frequency. At this point additional manifold pressure or airflow will not result in higher readings being reported to the ECU.

It is common (but not universal!) engineering practice to equip an engine with airflow sensors that are limited to measuring the narrowest range of manifold pressure or airflow that's wide enough to encompass the expected operating range of the engine. This provides the most accurate sensor readings by dedicating the entire available resolution of the circuit to the expected range of airflow or pressure. For example, normal-charged engines typically have "1-BAR" MAP sensors good for measuring about 1 atmosphere of air pressure, because a normal-charged engine (except under rare environmental conditions) should never see manifold plenum pressure greater than ambient pressure at sea level.

A typical GM 1-bar MAP sensor actually reports up to 108 kPa, and the stock MAP sensor on some normal-charged Honda engines will actually report up to 1.8 bar, which is over 10-psi boost pressure. Unfortunately, the Honda computer will freak and set a trouble code at any manifold pressure above 1- or 2-psi boost. In any case, there are good reasons why automakers maintain arctic, desert, and mountain test facilities where they calibrate factory engine-management systems to start well and run well at extremes of temperature and air density.

Certain combinations of rpm and engine loading that *are* correctly defined in the stock normal-charged calibration tables of some engine-management systems may not work right for a supercharged version of the engine. This is because the engine-management needs for supercharged and normal-charged engines are different enough to require very different fuel and timing delivery even as they produce the same combination of engine sensor data. An engine-management system that estimates engine airflow based solely on engine rpm, cylinder head temperature, and throttle angle cannot deliver required additional fuel when a turbo or supercharger is making boost. This is much more of an issue when the supercharger is driven by a variable-speed mechanical or turbine drive. Most sophisticated aftermarket engine-management systems now support "nested tables" that can be factored into the air-fuel calculation to take into account the rate of change in throttle angle, manifold pressure, and engine speed, as well as the differential between manifold pressure and compressor discharge pressure, and so on.

IGNITION TIMING

Supercharged engines making boost virtually always require special ignition timing compared to an otherwise identical normal-charged version of the same powerplant.

In the first place, the denser charge mixtures arriving in the combustion chambers of a forced-induction powerplant under boost at wide-open throttle will burn faster than less dense mixtures, meaning less time will be required for the burn. To maximize cylinder pressure at the optimal 14 to 18 degrees after top dead center that's required for the maximum recovery of work from the expanding combustion gases, ignition only needs 20 to 25 degrees of advance on a high-pressure blown engine at high rpm, versus as much as 30 to 35 degrees when the engine is normal-charged. Engines with high *effective* compression ratios simply need less timing advance to optimize combustion pressures and therefore torque.

Unfortunately, depending on the octane of the fuel and the air-fuel ratio, the highest achievable cylinder pressure may be too high for combustion to complete normally. If heat and pressure get too high as combustion proceeds, the remaining unburned air-fuel mixture will auto-ignite and explode all at once, rather than the flame front burning smoothly through the unburned charge mixture like a fire burning progressively through a field of dry grass. If higher octane fuel that's more resistant to explosive detonation is not available or practical and the air-fuel ratio is already dead rich to cool combustion, a successful supercharger conversion may require additional tricks to reduce the ONR of the engine, such as intake charge cooling (intercooling), upgraded cylinder head cooling, cooler spark plugs, piston-cooling oil-squirters, or water/alcohol injection.

If all else fails, the ultimate anti-knock countermeasure is to retard ignition timing, but there will be a cost in terms of reduced engine efficiency. Retarding ignition timing beyond what would be optimal for delivering peak torque from a particular engine using a particular fuel with a particular burn rate fights detonation by lowering peak combustion pressure. By 14 to 18 ATDC, a piston is accelerating away from top dead center. Combustion continues but the combustion chamber size is increasing in size faster than continuing combustion can make pressure against the piston, and combustion chamber pressure and, therefore, force delivered drops rapidly. On the other hand, an offsetting factor that tends to slow the decline in crankshaft torque is that the *arm* of force exerted against the crank by the piston improves dramatically as the piston moves downward, giving the piston increasing leverage against the crank until the crankshaft throw reaches 90 degrees ATDC, at which point leverage begins to decline. Retarding timing beyond what would be optimal if the engine were not knock-limited does not simply delay peak cylinder pressure, it lowers overall pressure. If you lower peak combustion pressures with retarded timing to fight knock, you are simultaneously dialing down the torque, which is why excessively retarded timing is a weapon of last resort.

Nevertheless, retarded ignition timing is an important weapon to fight knock in forced-induction engines. The OE strategy of dynamically and aggressively retarding ignition timing in the presence of spark knock as detected by a knock sensor is dramatically effective in killing knock quickly.

WIDE-RANGE CLOSED LOOP

In the case of very modern engines operating under the control of engine-management systems with wide-range or even *full-authority* closed-loop algorithms that trim fuel delivery based on the feedback from one or more fast wideband exhaust gas oxygen sensor(s), the ECU dynamically adjusts fuel-injection pulse width on an ongoing basis, even during heavy engine loading, according to the data in a speed-density table of target air-fuel ratios for various segments of the engine operating envelope. A full-authority ECU will work to maintain the correct air-fuel ratio (AFR). But unless the computer was specifically calibrated for factory forced-induction engine, the air-fuel ratio table will be dysfunctional if you install a power-adder like supercharging. Let's take a closer look to understand why.

Like older ordinary narrow-band closed-loop systems that used exhaust gas-oxygen feedback to trim fuel delivery at idle and light cruise in order to keep emissions as low as possible, a wide- or full-range EMS "learns" over time by tracking required fuel trim so it can be saved and folded back into the basic fuel calculation on a semi-permanent basis. The correction table (sometimes called a "block learn" table) will evolve over time as the engine gradually wears out in ways that affect engine volumetric efficiency, unless the "learning" system is reset by various means such as disconnecting the battery, in which case the engine-management system will start over again to relearn required fuel trim and rebuild the correction table. On some vehicles, a full-authority or wide-band feedback system has produced endless heartache for tuners who have achieved great initial results with performance modifications and tricks that alter the air-fuel ratio, only to discover down the line at the next dyno session that the EMS has been working patiently over the miles to return air-fuel ratios to where *it* wants them, erasing some or all of the beneficial effect of power-tuning.

With full-authority engine-management systems, fuel delivery is no longer deterministic in such a way that boosting the engine with a supercharger conversion produces completely dysfunctional air-fuel mixtures during boost. Such dysfunctional mixtures occur with many older speed-density engine-management systems that only operate in closed loop mode during idle or light cruise to trim fuel delivery to achieve stoichiometric mixtures that work well with catalytic converters. Nevertheless, from a tuning point of view, wide-range closed-loop systems have their own air-fuel agenda that may not be designed for boosted operation, and they aggressively interfere much more of the time to achieve it. What's worse, you cannot count on a wide-range system to *stay* consistently in closed-loop mode. In fact, some wide-range closed loop systems switch over to open-loop after a couple of seconds of hard acceleration (after the closed loop system has made sure the air-fuel ratio stayed lean enough to keep emissions low).

If you can hack such a system and bring it over to the dark side with your own target air-fuel calibration data, wide-range closed-loop can be helpful to dial in blower-friendly alternate air-fuel ratios and get them in the block learn table. But if not, you'll probably need to deal with this type of EMS by deploying a sophisticated piggyback computer to create an alternate reality that beguiles the EMS into doing your bidding with clever lies about engine status, or by intercepting stock computer commands to engine actuators and substituting alternate commands that work well with a supercharger.

The authority of a wide-range closed-loop system to implement large levels of fuel correction will almost definitely be clamped to a certain percentage of the expected value of the fuel-injection pulse width, at which point the EMS may disbelieve wideband oxygen sensors to the extent of disregarding them entirely and entering into some version of "limp-home" mode with fueling based on some subset of sensor data. This may or may not reduce engine performance; for example, some engine-management systems are more tolerant of forced-induction conversions with the MAF sensor disconnected, such that the ECU is forced to run the engine on MAP data alone. Again, if you've hacked your way into the EMS, the authority range of the closed-loop system is itself a configuration parameter.

Bottom line: Because factory full-authority or wide-range closed-loop systems operate under the control of target air-fuel ratio tables that encompass the *expected* airflow range of the various possible combinations of engine speed and loading, closed-loop fuel corrections on factory normal-charged powerplant—even if they're in the direction of adding fuel—will be suboptimally lean for supercharger-conversion engines running street-premium fuel, which will almost always require fuel-cooling during boost to prevent knock. Yes, the EMS will strive to increase fuel delivery if the exhaust gas oxygen gets too high for normal-charged conditions, but the *target* air-fuel ratios will almost definitely not be rich enough for high-pressure supercharging.

WHY YOUR EMS HARDWARE MAY BE WRONG FOR SUPERCHARGING

There are a variety of potentially problematic issues related to a vehicle's engine-management hardware or hard logic that, without modifications, could be fatal to a blower conversion or factory-supercharged overboosting project.

In the days when essentially all engines were carbureted with breaker-point ignition, engine management was implicit in the design of certain mechanical parts. Tiny progressively wound springs connected to weights associated with ignition breaker points in the distributor determined the amount of "centrifugal" advance in spark timing that the ignition delivered as engine speed increased. Mechanical plumbing and tiny valves and orifices in the carburetor deterministically modified and shaped the amount of fuel misting into intake air roaring through the carb on the basis of subtle differences in air and fuel pressure in several overlapping segments of the engine's operating envelope as the engine's volumetric efficiency and rate of acceleration changed with rpm and throttle angle. The "calibration" of mechanical engine management controls is intrinsic to the fuel and spark delivery hardware.

What goes on in the onboard computer of a modern EFI engine is somewhat removed from the physical hardware side of fuel and spark delivery, but not completely. Yes, electronic engine management has significant flexibility to modify engine operation on the basis of a few changed numbers in computer memory, but when conditions exceed certain limits, the physical limitations of fuel and spark delivery can and do bite tuners badly. Some hardware deficiencies or limits can be corrected with electronic means, but in other cases equipment must be replaced entirely, or supplemented with auxiliary hardware.

Making power with superchargers takes fuel, and at maximum duty cycle the stock *fuel injectors* may be too small to deliver the required fuel in some parts of the engine operating range. Electronic injectors have a finite maximum flow at rated fuel pressure, but the realistic maximum flow will be less because injectors can overheat when held open continuously, and if you wisely decide to avoid driving the injectors all the way to 100 percent duty cycle, there is a minimum "turnaround" time for closing and opening events: It takes a finite time for the electronic injector to spring closed and then reopen under electromagnetic power. This limitation takes a chunk of time out of the available time for the fuel delivery pulse, which, in a four-stroke engine is the time it takes for two engine revolutions. As engine rpm increases, there is a declining maximum amount of time available to inject fuel. At 6,000 rpm, an engine is rotating 100 times per second, so the four-cycle internal combustion process that takes place over two revolutions allows a total of only 20 thousandths of a second (20 milliseconds) for injecting fuel.

To increase fuel delivery, electronic injectors can be run at higher-than-rated pressure, which is normally about 40 psi at full throttle on a normal-charged engine with port fuel injection, with an additional 1 psi increase per pound of boost on forced-induction powerplants. Electronic port injectors almost never run at pressures above 55 psi on factory engines, because there are a large number of different sizes and types of port fuel injectors, and it's easy to upsize the injectors for supercharged versions of an engine.

When it comes to over-pressuring, all electronic injectors have a maximum pressure capacity, beyond which the spring-loaded electromagnetic system that opens and closes the injector valves will no longer function properly. Many experts have suggested running a maximum of 80- or 90-psi fuel rail pressure, but actual maximum operable pressure will vary, depending on injector design, the electrical characteristics of the driver circuitry, and the manifold pressure into which the injectors are squirting. Some electronic injectors have been

Multi-port Fuel Injector assembly from a 2005 VVT 2.4-liter GM Ecotec inline-4. Fuel delivery is a function of injection pulse width (injector open time) and fuel rail pressure, both of which may be under electronic control, and both of which may be modifiable by aftermarket interceptor computers to synchronize stock fuel and ignition algorithms with special add-on recalibration data during boost to provide correct engine management for supercharger conversions. *GM Media Archive*

113

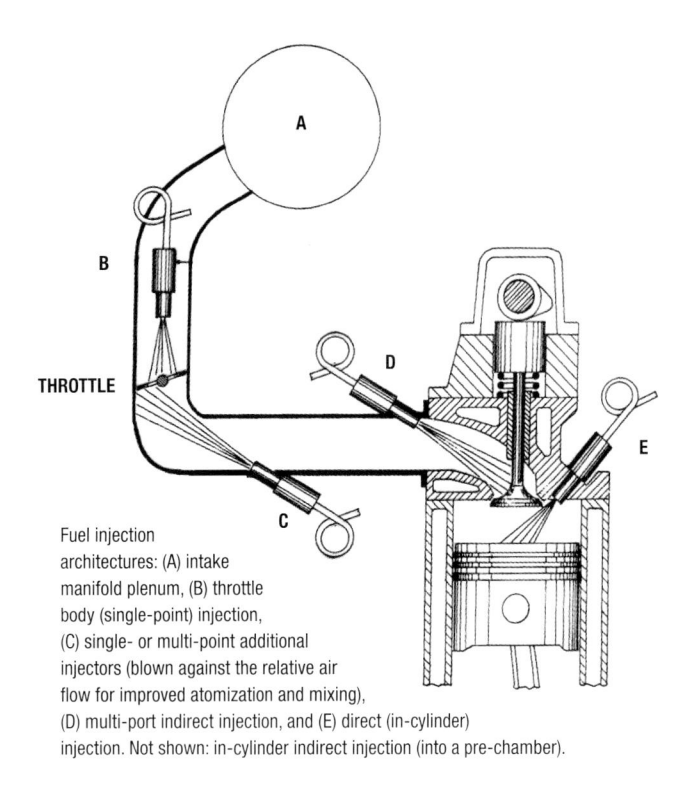

Fuel injection architectures: (A) intake manifold plenum, (B) throttle body (single-point) injection, (C) single- or multi-point additional injectors (blown against the relative air flow for improved atomization and mixing), (D) multi-port indirect injection, and (E) direct (in-cylinder) injection. Not shown: in-cylinder indirect injection (into a pre-chamber).

successfully run (at least for a while) with more than 100 psi of fuel pressure. And, of course, the latest electronic injectors for gasoline direction injection powerplants inject fuel directly into the cylinders at more than 100 atmospheres (roughly 3,000 psi), and the engine-management system dynamically regulates fuel pressure under computer control according to engine conditions and internal calibration tables. Some of the latest "common-rail" electronic diesel injectors operate up to 24,000 psi.

Electronic injectors can also be too *large* for an engine. In fact, injector selection is a balancing act on engines boosted to high specific power because injectors big enough to deliver the fuel for big power on the high end may be so large that the required injection pulse width at idle is too short to be fine-tuned accurately. In some cases, such short durations may not be repeatable within the minimum pulse width resolution of some ECUs. Staged multiple injectors per cylinder could be required to achieve a good idle and maximum power, with one injector per cylinder fueling idle and lighter loading and a second or third injector per cylinder kicking in as fuel requirements increase as the supercharger makes boost.

Stock injectors on factory vehicles are typically selected so that they are oversized to the extent that at maximum duty cycle they would be capable of delivering perhaps 25 percent more fuel than the actual stock fuel requirement at peak horsepower. Increasing injection pulse width time to hold the injectors open longer will thus fuel up to 25 percent more horsepower on a supercharger-conversion powerplant. Increasing the fuel pressure (commensurate with boost pressure or as a multiple of it) will deliver still more fuel per injector squirt. Even using both tricks, a set of stock injectors on an engine will probably be physically unable to deliver much more than about 50 percent additional fuel above stock. Beyond that, electronic injectors must be upgraded to a larger size or supplemented with additional fuel injectors and a control system capable of driving auxiliary injectors.

The electric *fuel pump* on a vehicle supplying fuel to electronic injectors can become a constraint on fuel delivery if you modify the injection system to deliver more fuel for a blower conversion or overboosted supercharger. The fuel pump on an EFI engine has a rated fuel-flow volume that varies inversely with pressure, such that the higher the head of pressure it's pumping against, the less fuel volume it can deliver. If the total combined flow rate of all fuel injectors is higher than what the fuel pump can supply at a given pressure, the fuel pressure regulator will lose control of fuel pressure and pressure at the injector rail will drop until fuel flow reaches an equilibrium flow rate that the pump *can* deliver at the reduced pressure. The result is that each injector squirt will deliver less fuel than it should, resulting in reduced power and lean mixtures.

Besides fuel pressure, another variable affecting fuel delivery to the injector rail is the amplitude of electrical voltage driving the fuel pump. Most modern electrical systems work at 13.7 volts when the alternator is running, but increases above design voltage will force the pump to run faster and with greater power, such that it can deliver more fuel at a given level of fuel pressure. Conversely, if voltage drops below the design standard, *less* fuel than the rated pump capacity is delivered.

Add-on power-supply devices may be installed that overdrive a fuel pump (stock or aftermarket) with super-normal voltage when fuel demand is high, to maintain or increase the fuel delivery during periods when supercharger boost is making horsepower. Another common practice is to increase the fuel delivery capacity of an in-tank fuel pump by adding a second-stage inline pump in series to boost pressure. Alternately, fuel supply may be doubled using two fuel pumps operating in parallel. Obviously the fuel supply plumbing itself can become a restriction to fuel delivery. If the fuel line to or from the tank is too small, it must be upgraded.

The fuel pressure on EFI systems is normally determined by a mechanical or electronically controlled *fuel pressure regulator*, also known as a *fuel control valve* on direct-injection systems. The regulator's job is to ensure fuel delivery to the injectors occurs at a conditioned pressure by maintaining a target fuel pressure within the fuel rail. Historically, this was accomplished by throttling the fuel flow that exits the fuel rail to return to the fuel tank. Some aftermarket mechanical fuel pressure regulators are adjustable to a limited degree by turning a bolt that alters preload against the internal diaphragm spring, which will then hold the regulator closed to a somewhat higher pressure. A port-EFI regulator is also typically—but not always—referenced to manifold pressure.

This allows the fuel pressure at the injectors to stay a fixed amount above manifold pressure by using it to supplement the power of the regulator spring as manifold pressure increases toward atmospheric pressure and above when a supercharger is making boost.

Some modern port-EFI engine-management systems now have an embedded ability to manage fuel pump speed to maintain required injection pressure—and no more—via voltage changes that are calculated based on internal demand tables and feedback from a fuel rail pressure sensor.

In the case of supercharger-conversion engines, tuners sometimes deploy a special aftermarket *variable-rate-of-gain (VRG) fuel pressure regulator* (sometimes called a fuel management unit or FMU) *downstream* of the standard port-EFI fuel pressure regulator in the fuel tank return line. The goal of using such a device is to enrich air-fuel ratios under boost by increasing fuel pressure as a multiple of manifold pressure increases that occur after the blower kicks in and manifold pressure becomes positive. Typically a 5- to 7-psi increase in fuel pressure per pound of boost will deliver acceptably correct fuel enrichment if the stock EMS is unable to command additional fuel delivery beyond the normal-charged requirements of the powerplant via increased injection pulse width. This means there is a ceiling of about 7- to 8-psi supercharger boost for this enrichment technique, before fuel pressure becomes too high for port injectors to function correctly. During normal-charged operation when the VRG regulator is inoperative, the standard regulator manages fuel pressure as always.

Gasoline direct injection (GDI) engines, which inject fuel straight into the cylinders rather than the intake runners, run radical injection pressures, typically in the 100- to 200-bar range (1,500 to 3,000 psi). GDI piezo *hydraulic* injectors open and close using an electrical current that slightly changes the *volume* of a substrate surrounding a microscopic fuel channel such that it functions as a valve. This tiny valve is much too small and weak by itself to supply the fuel for a full-blown injector squirt, so fuel pressure from the Piezo orifice is used to hydraulically actuate a larger servo valve in the injector that opens and closes to spray fuel into the engine at extreme pressure. This is similar to the way a backhoe operator uses the various hand-control valves to control the high-pressure hydraulic system that moves the shovel. Some GDI systems work under a constant high pressure. Other "demand control" GDI systems dynamically manage fuel pressure to the injectors under computer control based on feedback from a fuel-pressure sensor. This enables a tuner to install an electronic interceptor to manipulate fuel pressure during supercharger boost by under-reporting fuel rail pressure to the main electronic control unit managing the engine.

GDI systems are not exactly hacker-friendly, equipped as they are with modern OBDII security and complex engine management algorithms that deliver lean-burn economy-mode combustion under very light loading using a stratified charge (while keeping the electronic throttle wide open!), stoichiometric combustion during normal operation, or peak-torque combustion under heavy loading and high boost. The good news for hot rodders is that GDI fuel systems are extremely robust, and GDI demand-control systems provide the possibility for tuners to increase fuel pressure under electronic control during open-loop fueling conditions at high engine loads (i.e., when a supercharger is making boost). Intercepting the fuel pressure sensor signal and reporting a falsely low signal to the ECU causes the ECU to reduce the bleed rate of the control valve, raising pressure in the fuel rail such that the system delivers forced-induction fuel enrichment.

Airflow sensors include manifold absolute pressure (MAP), mass airflow (MAF), and vane airflow (VAF) sensors that enable an engine-management system to directly measure or to deduce engine airflow. These sensors are normally selected to map the highest and lowest pressure or airflow measurements within the expected range and translate that information into voltages or frequencies that are conveyed to the ECU. In other words, a 1-bar pressure sensor designed for a normal-charged engine typically maps manifold pressure measurements from vacuum to a little more than 1 full atmosphere of pressure across nearly the entire 0- to 5-volt range of the typical input circuit. A 1-bar sensor, therefore, would be unable to distinguish any pressure over 1 atmosphere, since the sensor would be maxed-out reporting 5 volts at 1 atmosphere.

Unfortunately for hot rodders, there is sometimes a small amount of reporting range above the maximum expected pressure that enables the ECU to detect overpressure or "out-of-range" conditions and cause trouble. A 2-bar sensor, on the other hand, maps pressure from 0 to 2 atmospheres absolute (14.7-psi boost) across the same 0- to 5-volt range. Boost-control failures on turbocharged engines that are wastegate-limited to less than 1 bar of boost can result in higher boost pressure, so the sensor on such an engine is normally selected to be able to measure a certain amount of overboost so that the EMS can provide fail-safe engine management and activate countermeasures designed to prevent engine damage and expensive warranty claims. MAP sensors with 3-, 4-, 5-, or even 10-bar capacity extend the measurement range even farther—at the cost of decreasing resolution within each atmosphere of airflow range. MAF sensors also typically map a moderate superset of the finite range of expected airflow across the range of the circuit.

In order for a factory ECU to provide accurate fueling across the extended airflow range of a blower conversion or a significantly overboosted factory supercharged powerplant, the EMS would require a replacement MAP or MAF sensor with a greater range of sensitivity. Of course, the internal ECU air-fuel and timing maps then have to be completely recalibrated, as sensor output from a new, wider-range sensor will translate to different, increasingly inaccurate airflow rates in the stock calibration tables as engine airflow increases from 0.

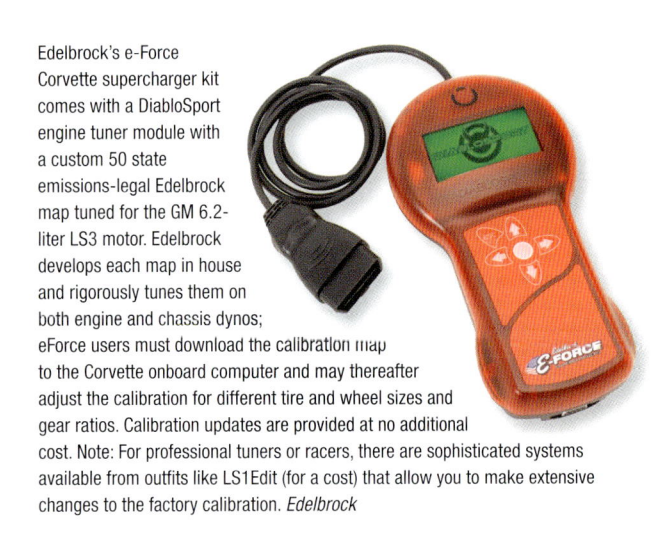

Edelbrock's e-Force Corvette supercharger kit comes with a DiabloSport engine tuner module with a custom 50 state emissions-legal Edelbrock map tuned for the GM 6.2-liter LS3 motor. Edelbrock develops each map in house and rigorously tunes them on both engine and chassis dynos; eForce users must download the calibration map to the Corvette onboard computer and may thereafter adjust the calibration for different tire and wheel sizes and gear ratios. Calibration updates are provided at no additional cost. Note: For professional tuners or racers, there are sophisticated systems available from outfits like LS1Edit (for a cost) that allow you to make extensive changes to the factory calibration. *Edelbrock*

The *electronic control units* of primitive, normal-charged EFI engines (based on analog computers) cannot be hacked and recalibrated, as the logic is completely hardwired into the circuitry. The good news is that these systems—most of which controlled fuel only—typically have no concept of manifold overpressure or out-of-range airflow all the way to the limits of the sensor, making it simple for tuners to supply boost fuel enrichment outside the EMS. This can be done using a variable-rate-of-gain fuel pressure regulator, an auxiliary injector controller, or perhaps a piggyback auxiliary computer that extends, truncates, or otherwise modifies signals to the EMS actuators or from the sensors. It is rather simple and straightforward to replace these ancient ECUs with a modern aftermarket digital engine-management system that's programmable from a laptop computer and will do forced-induction engine management the way you want it done.

Newer *pre-OBDII factory digital engine-management systems* designed for normal-charged engines or low-pressure forced induction are smarter about detecting failed sensors or unauthorized hot rodding modifications. But most can be hacked and recalibrated, or fooled into acceptable behavior for a supercharger conversion using a basic piggyback computer that intercepts sensor and actuator signals to alter EMS behavior by lying to the computer about engine conditions, or modifying outbound EMS commands to the injectors, and so forth. These pre-1996 (in a few cases, pre-1994) digital engine-management systems may set a trouble code and turn on the check engine light if airflow or manifold pressure get too high, and may set a flag that activates a fuel cut if pressure or airflow get high enough (until reset by means that may be as simple as turning off the ignition one or more times). But these ECUs are not particularly smart, and it is still common hot rodding practice to employ simple tricks to fool them—for example, installing a simple voltage clamping device to limit airflow or pressure sensor voltages to a value that will not cause the EMS to freak out, and then providing boost fuel enrichment and ignition retard using add-on auxiliary equipment to supplement fuel. ECUs of this vintage still mostly do only engine management (as opposed to *vehicle* management), so they are fairly easy to de-install and replace with an aftermarket programmable EMS.

Some *early OBD-II engine-management systems* were prone to setting trouble codes if engine sensor values deviate even slightly from expected values. But as required misfire-detection techniques improved and wideband oxygen sensors made wider range closed-loop air-fuel operation feasible, modern engine-management systems were given the slack to tolerate a wider range of engine (sensor) signals. The good news is that an impressive array of performance-oriented OBD-II engine-management systems have been hacked for the purpose of facilitating recalibration of fuel and ignition tables or substituting larger fuel injectors without ruining idle and low-end performance and so forth. Even though OBD-II makes it harder to hot rod an engine without pissing off the ECU, if you've learned the system Security Seed and hacked your way in, OBD-II ironically made it easier than ever to modify the calibration and configuration tables from a laptop computer interfaced to the OBD-II diagnostic port by simply overwriting the internal calibration tables the EMS keeps stored in nonvolatile flash memory.

Lately, because power-adders such as blowers or turbos can damage an engine if improperly installed, tuned, or overboosted beyond reason—potentially resulting in expensive bogus warranty claims if the "abuse" goes undetected—some engine manufacturers have gotten serious about antihacking countermeasures with the newest *OBD-II+ engine management computers*. BMW, for example, seems to have had its fill with tuners hacking, hot rodding, and damaging late-model Bimmers. Some 2007 BMW engine-management systems arrived with the ability to report unusual sensor values to a central factory management information system (MIS) database in real time over a satellite or other communications network. Such systems require one-time remote approval to tolerate certain engine conditions. Some sophisticated piggybacks soon had the ability to impersonate the MIS database and communications protocol.

Obviously, forced-induction conversions or overboosting projects built around complex modern engines require extremely sophisticated piggyback computers to create a virtual reality good enough to keep a sophisticated EMS happy and fool it into playing nice with a forced-induction conversion. But in practical terms there is usually no good alternative, because even sophisticated aftermarket programmable engine-management systems are not usually designed to handle the onslaught of vehicle management tasks like electronic stability control (ESC) that are now intrinsic to the stock vehicle management network of onboard computers. And even if the hardware and processor logic can be configured to handle complex vehicle management in an aftermarket EMS, reinventing and calibrating the entire factory vehicle management system would be a nightmarishly huge task. With respect to supercharging, complex factory engine-management systems have a range of tricks to prevent or neutralize out-of-range manifold pressure/airflow or enrichment air-fuel mixtures. The good news for hot rodders is that sophisticated piggyback computers exist that are every bit their equal. You will not need to discard your 2005 BMW 7-series EMS unless you are building a full-bore road-race competition car.

High-voltage ignition components designed for a normal-charged or low-pressure boosted engine will sooner or later prove inadequate to spark properly through the dense charge mixtures of high boost levels. Stock heat range spark plugs can contribute to knock or pre-ignition, and should be replaced with plugs at least one or two ranges colder than stock for street supercharged engines. If colder stock-type plugs are not available for a high-boost powerplant, you might have to machine the head surface deeper into the spark plug threads or otherwise machine the head to accommodate foreign plugs with shallower threads that are cold enough. In some cases, tuners have resorted to modifying spark plugs by machining them to fit an engine application.

PowerCard Pro, developed by Dobeck Performance, is a highly configurable piggyback interceptor system designed to meet the needs of professional Miata tuners. The controller can be programmed to modify factory engine management to work with boost, supplemental injectors, and nitrous oxide injection. The PowerCard Pro builds upon the stock ECU calibration while giving you an expansive set of tuning tools for optimizing performance of power-adders like superchargers. *Dobeck Performance*

If the *ignition* is too weak to fire reliably through the super-dense charge mixtures of high-boost supercharging, the engine will begin to misfire under heavy loading, though this may not be immediately obvious, particularly if the engine has a lot of cylinders. Common first-aid when the high-side ignition voltage becomes problematic is to decrease the spark plug gap to .020 inches or even less. A better solution is to upgrade coils and coil drivers, though this can be challenging on modern coil-on-plug engines where the coil and driver reside in one package sitting directly on each plug. If you do install upgraded ignition coils, some aftermarket engine-management systems provide the capability to configure the coil charge time (dwell) in the ECU with a laptop. Unfortunately, the downside of extensive on-board diagnostics embedded in really modern factory engine-management systems is that such systems are sensitive to downstream electrical changes in the ignition system, with the EMS measuring the electronic "ring" in ignition and injector circuits to distinguish the electrical characteristics of normal ignition events versus misfires or failed components. This can make upgrading high-voltage ignition components problematic.

You never see *knock sensors* on race engines, which are always tuned and maintained carefully and run on excellent, high-octane fuel, but knock sensors are good engine insurance for street-going forced-induction powerplants. All premium-fuel spark-ignition factory production automotive engines—supercharged or not—use knock sensors to prevent engine damage from overboosting or something as simple as filling up the tank with substandard regular fuel. A knock sensor is essentially a microphone of sorts, threaded into the block, that listens for spark knock. The sensor contains a sensitive crystal selected to resonate to the particular frequency range of vibration known to be characteristic of knock on the particular engine.

The factory knock sensor system, however, can be problematic on a supercharger conversion or overboosted factory-supercharged engine. Engine performance modifications sometimes introduce noises or vibrations that are mistaken as detonation by the EMS knock-control system. Any vibration suspected of being knock will trigger aggressive EMS ignition-retard strategies designed to indiscriminately kill knock. Factory anti-knock countermeasures typically retard timing harshly on all cylinders, for example, even if only one or two are knocking. And they bring back full timing at a leisurely, conservative pace.

Some modern piggyback computers are capable of synthesizing the output signal a factory knock sensor produces when the engine is running normally. This effectively enables knock control to be disabled entirely or offloaded from the stock EMS to the piggyback/interceptor computer or other auxiliary control system. Some piggybacks provide a user-definable listening mode for detecting detonation (perhaps with a more tolerant threshold), combined with user-definable knock-retard strategies managed entirely in the piggyback that use

Carbureted turbo 4.2-liter Jaguar I-6 with pressurized SU carburetion. It was once reasonably common to see Weber and SU constant-velocity carburetors modified for forced induction. This is an early pre-injection version of the author's turbocharged Jaguar XKE. Note the hoses that pressurize the carburetor float chambers with reference to boost pressure upstream of the throttles. To maintain correct airflow with minimal complexity, SU carbs were equipped with free-floating slides that automatically rise and fall to maintain constant air velocity through the carbs as engine airflow changes. Not visible are the jet needles with modified profiles that richen air-fuel mixtures as the slides rise with increased airflow. Fuel injection was a great improvement. These days, what remains of carbureted forced-induction is largely in the form of the Holley four-barrel.

normal interception methods to tamper with stock timing (such as misreporting crankshaft position to the ECU). Assuming the factory knock-retard system is disabled by the piggyback, a less aggressive aftermarket knock algorithm could increase engine performance when things get noisy, through the application of more subtle knock-retard strategies. Alternately, a standalone aftermarket knock-sensor system with individual cylinder retard could control knock more efficiently by retarding only the cylinders actually experiencing detonation—a capability that may someday become common in piggybacks.

The *stock emissions-control hardware* on a road-going vehicle may be on your own private search-and-destroy wish list. Where a factory ECU cannot realistically be recalibrated to manage a blower conversion engine, it is tempting to think about installing a standalone aftermarket EMS—particularly if you are planning to make radical power—because a standalone programmable EMS provides straightforward, direct control over all aspects of engine management. Usually, that is, with the exception of complex emissions controls, which may only be manageable using an aftermarket EMS by cobbling together miscellaneous user-defined control algorithms. In fact, modern OBD-II-plus engines have sophisticated emissions-control systems that use electronically managed components. Many basic standalone aftermarket engine-management systems are not really designed for controlling EGR valves, charcoal canister purge valves, cat air injection, and all the rest.

Fine, junk all that stuff and go aftermarket, right? The trouble is, anything that can affect exhaust emissions—such as aftermarket engine management—is patently illegal for gasoline-fueled street-driven vehicles unless the system has passed the Federal Test Procedure (FTP) and proven that emissions are no more than 10 percent worse than stock. But late-model vehicles will definitely not pass even casual,

no-load inspection-station-type emissions testing without the stock emissions-control equipment in place and functioning. What's more, the FTP is too expensive to be practical for most individuals, and to pass it, you'll need the emissions equipment and a *great* EMS calibration. Sooner or later, in any state with emissions testing and inspection requirements, you're going to regret removing or disabling stock emissions equipment in a way that makes emissions controls unavailable for emissions testing and legal highway usage when you're done playing at the track.

The good news is, in states and cities where emissions testing via exhaust sniffer is required to pass inspection—in some cases on a rolling road—the test usually consists of a driving cycle that is too mild-mannered to load the engine enough to cause a forced-induction engine to make much or any boost. Any power-adder conversion system that leaves the stock engine management and emissions control devices in place should have no trouble passing a light-load sniff test. Engine management during moderate-to-high boost can be modified using add-on auxiliary equipment such as an electronic interceptor/piggyback or a variable-rate-of-gain fuel pressure regulator. Of course, even if the vehicle makes the HC, CO, and NOx numbers to pass emissions, some test stations will look under the hood for illegal hotrodding equipment, like a supercharger that doesn't have FTP approval or a California exemption order, but that's a separate issue.

The *vehicle management* functionality of many newer vehicles requires onboard computing capabilities that go far beyond immediate engine management, integrating traditional engine management with subsystems that on first glace might seem unrelated to running the engine. GPS location, microwave proximity warning systems, and engine throttle position factor into intelligent cruise-control systems. The vehicle speed sensor and navigation system user interface factor into whether you will be allowed to ask your car for directions; this will not be permitted on some systems if the vehicle is moving at all or moving faster than a walking pace. Airbag status, GPS position, OnStar-type communications, engine status, and remote diagnostics will be factors in your car computer's ability to effectively "phone home" for help in case of a breakdown or crash.

Vehicle management functionality may include:

- Electronic stability control (with dynamic braking effort, brake standby, active-steering-on-brake
- Traction control
- Powertrain shift and control
- Airbags
- Sound system
- A/C
- Lane departure warning (LDW)
- Anti-lock brakes
- OnStar-type communications
- Remote diagnostics
- Camel-mode and other limp-home strategies
- Speech recognition
- Anti-theft/entry
- Intermittent alternator on during braking
- Electric water pump control
- Stratified-charge and other gasoline direct injection functionality

Managing all of the above tasks with a standalone aftermarket EMS would be extremely difficult, though there are now a few massively powerful and sophisticated modular programmable engine-management systems that might have the I/O hardware and processing power to handle the job, or to communicate with auxiliary computers to handle the job over a controller area network (CAN). There are a few aftermarket supertuners in the world who have the skills to handle the complex engineering required to handle such a job, and more who could give you a reasonable subset of factory tricks using sophisticated aftermarket engine-management hardware. So if you're a millionaire, find one of these guys and have at it.

Even if you have money to burn, why bother? There are now extremely sophisticated and powerful piggyback computers (some more powerful than a standalone engine-management computer) that can lie so convincingly to the stock EMS, disobey it so creatively, and manage auxiliary fueling and functionality so effectively and seamlessly that they are able to create their own "virtual reality" bubble around the stock EMS. When required, it becomes possible to effectively hijack the stock calibration, add a few auxiliary tricks like direct piggyback-based boost control, and put the stock EMS to work on the dark side of The Force—the hot rodding side. If you want to retain all the factory vehicle and engine management amenities, it makes no sense to replace the stock EMS. A better trick is to whisper sweet lies in its ear and go crazy behind its back.

There are a range of innovations that tend to raise the stakes for blower-conversion or overboosted vehicle tuners working with interceptor or piggyback computers to manipulate stock tuning for power-adder conversions. These include:

- Torque-based engine management
- Transmission torque sensors
- Online wide-area networking with real-time vehicle telemetry to dealers, automakers, or government agencies)
- Vehicle data recorders that compute and record horsepower, torque, and all sensor values for the life of the vehicle, ready and able to void the vehicle warranty for illegal tampering
- Enhanced full-authority, closed-loop engine management
- Drive-by-wire speed and acceleration controls
- Gasoline direct injection fuel pressure management
- Calculated slew rate, horsepower, and torque based on the rate of acceleration.

STRATEGIES FOR SUPERCHARGED ENGINE MANAGEMENT

There are a number of strategies that can be used to tune and manage blower-conversion engines:

- Standalone aftermarket programmable EMS
- Hacked and reprogrammed factory EMS
- Factory EMS plus auxiliary piggyback/interceptor computer
- Factory EMS with standalone aftermarket ECU taking over some EMS tasks
- Factory EMS with auxiliary EMS modifiers (programmable sensors or actuators, VRG regulators, boost-retard black boxes, and so on)
- Carburetion with adaptations for supercharging

Each of these has its advantages and disadvantages under various circumstances.

BDS's "Xcelerator" adaptor plate is specially engineered to provide more air-fuel volume on top of Roots-type blowers to increase the ram-air effect into the supercharger for increased horsepower. The adaptor is 2 inches tall and O-ringed for a total seal on the top and bottom. It is drilled and tapped for four mechanical-injection nozzle bodies on each side and adds a cutting edge advantage by offsetting the blower hat location 4 5/8 inches on competition systems with mechanical injection. It can be custom fitted to fit all blowers with a standard GM top opening and can be used with either a mechanical or electronic bug catcher or bird catcher injector. *BDS*

Standalone Aftermarket "Programmable" EMS

For supercharged racing applications you want the ability to quickly and easily modify any and all aspects of the engine management configuration and calibration as track conditions or installed equipment change. You also want the capability of interfacing the ECU to a wide variety of aftermarket sensors, actuators, data-acquisition, and telemetry equipment.

Although modern factory engine-management systems are powerful and can, to some extent, be extensively recalibrated and reconfigured from a laptop like an aftermarket programmable system (given access to proprietary tools or the right hacking software), such systems are not primarily designed to accommodate interactive modification on the fly. They are designed for cost-effective mass production, for ultimate reliability under the harshest climatic conditions, and for doing a fabulous job, endlessly, of executing a fixed-engine-management calibration with great drivability, efficiency, and power while simultaneously meeting California emissions standards. In fact, some factory engine-management systems require that changes to the calibration be made offline with the engine stopped and then batch-uploaded to the ECU. It is not unheard of for factory teams to race using recalibrated off-the-shelf factory EMS hardware, but most factory teams junk the factory EMS and run aftermarket programmable systems.

There is a good reason. High-end programmable engine-management systems from outfits like Motec, Zytek, and EFI Technology are designed for easy adaptation to a large variety of engine applications. From a laptop PC user interface these systems allow you to easily configure a large number of parameters that define functionality as basic as the number of cylinders or as complex as hardware device definition and management for various types of auxiliary I/O ports.

Typically, the laptop interface provides a powerful set of mathematical functions with the facility to effortlessly modify individual cells or various large subsets of the fuel and ignition tables—in a hurry. Most programmable engine-management systems have a rich graphical and tabular user interface that runs under Windows. Virtually all have extensive built-in boost-control management capabilities. They have extensive acquisition, logging, and reporting capabilities. A second-tier group of ECUs offers a subset of these same functions at reduced cost, often without the most powerful tuning tools (they are designed to manage the engine with a great calibration rather than create the great calibration). In some cases, these de-rated ECUs are based on the same hardware with the same internal software—with certain functions programmatically disabled.

The user interface software on a modern standalone EMS is highly interactive in real time, with virtually all of the calibration functions taking effect immediately while the engine is running—essential functionality for interactive tuning on the dyno or track. Configuration functions—including actuator device hardware definition and management—normally take effect following an ECU reset. High-end standalone ECUs employ powerful logic and hardware to provide functionality not found on road-going factory engine-management systems, but that can be critical for rule-driven racing in which every last horsepower is pursued with relentless zeal. An example is individual-cylinder fuel and ignition trim tables, which enable tuners to optimize the EMS calibration on an *individual cylinder basis* as if each cylinder were a separate engine, to compensate for minor differences in cylinder thermal loading and VE. Another example is multi-level nested recursive control tables that provide tuners the building blocks to implement complex user-defined control logic if something special is required to perfect an esoteric or unusual aspect of engine management.

The boost-management capabilities of a system like the Motec M800 include three-dimensional control, which allows the M800 to manage maximum boost by controlling a pulse width–modulated (PWM) electro-pneumatic valve as a function of three user-defined parameters at once. Combinations of control parameters might include engine rpm, torque, and gear. Or perhaps rpm, coolant temperature, and a driver-adjustable in-cockpit boost-control potentiometer. And so on.

Programmable engine-management systems are not actually "programmable," in the traditional sense of providing tuners the ability to modify or enhance the source code of the EMS software to modify the overall scope of the logic and functionality of the system using logical objects or subroutines compiled into the main source code. These systems are programmable in the sense that the (inaccessible) logic of the proprietary control software is highly table-driven, with much of the system logic explicitly designed to be vastly conditional at a million places in the operating software, depending on what data is stored in various tables or parameters. No, you can't write your own software to implement completely new functionality that was not built into the ECU's operating software, but there is a lot of embedded logic that can be conditionally activated to handle various situations, and a lot of power in the tables that drive the existing logic, with many, many possible paths through the logic that produce very different engine control.

If the ultimate goal is raw power in competition-type conditions—no more, no less—a standalone programmable system is the obvious choice. Of course, none of these aftermarket systems are really street legal for gasoline-fueled vehicles in the United States. Not that there aren't a fair number of outlaw systems loose on the streets, kicking your ass.

Hacked and Reprogrammed Factory EMS

If you will be driving on the street, there are good reasons to retain the factory engine-management system, even if the objective is an ultra-high-output blower conversion or overboost project. On the face of it, a stock ECU offers the significant advantage that it is legal. And it will look exactly the same from the outside to inspectors, whether or not someone has hacked the internal data tables that define the EMS calibration.

Beyond that, stock ECUs are powerful and reliable, and the newest ones are often packed with vehicle management and computer-to-computer controller area network multi-processor capabilities that are way beyond the scope of simple engine management and are difficult or impossible to duplicate with aftermarket computers. The stock EMS is also priced right; you already have one installed on the vehicle, so it's free. The good news for supercharger mavens is that while some factory ECUs are, for all practical purposes sealed, inaccessible "black boxes," many can be hacked and recalibrated or reconfigured to make them workable for performance supercharger conversions or significant overboost projects for factory-supercharged powerplants.

The earliest fuel-only ECUs built in the 1960s, 1970s, and early 1980s to manage electronic fuel injection were hardwired analog computers with the logic intrinsic to the circuitry, meaning they absolutely cannot be reprogrammed (like any ECU, however, their behavior can potentially be modified using a piggyback computer by intercepting and modifying data to or from the sensors and actuators to manipulate the behavior of the ECU). The continuous injection systems of the same vintage (Bosch CIS/K-Jetronic, GM/Rochester) were not electronic fuel injection. They were (brainless) mechanical injection systems with port injectors that squirted constantly, relying on mechanical door-type airflow meters to modify injection pressure and flow to keep fuel delivery from the continuous injectors consistent with engine load. The K-Jet airflow meter was linked to a plunger in a barrel-valve that covered or uncovered fuel-delivery slits to the degree required to deliver target fuel pressure and volume through the fuel injectors; later versions were enhanced with electro-mechanical closed-loop fuel trim at idle. The Porsche 930, Porsche 924 Turbo, and the Ferrari 308 Turbo are examples of vehicles from the late-1970s and 1980s that used CIS injection calibrated for turbocharging, and it worked well enough. Tweaking K-Jet systems to provide fuel enrichment on turbo or supercharger conversions was once fairly common, and though the results obtained were better than you could get with carbureted turbo engines, CIS forced-induction conversions were somewhat problematic. Anyone seriously considering supercharging an old K-Jet/CIS vehicle these days should probably think better of the project, or convert the engine to EFI (saving the original parts in case it becomes desirable to return a collector car to stock condition).

Digital EFI is a different story. Digital computers separate the operating programmatic logic and data from the hardware electronics, running general-purpose, real-time engine management software that operates on real-time sensor data and memory-resident tables of calibration data specific to a particular engine or model of engine to dynamically manage fuel delivery, ignition timing, and other factors as the engine runs. Digital EMS calibration data is stored in various types of nonvolatile memory devices that will not lose data if the ECU loses battery power.

Modern OBD-II-plus ECUs store the calibration data in nonvolatile (flash) memory, which can be modified in part or whole through the diagnostic port using special OBD-II commands that change the data in specified memory locations—if, and only if, you know the password or "security seed." This process, commonly available to dealers through restrictive factory tools that are available to fix minor problems or bugs via minor reconfiguration, is called "flashing."

BEGi twin-screw supercharging system on the BMW 318ti inline-4. Note the BEGi variable-rate-of-gain fuel pressure regulator (next to the air cleaner). This type of fuel management unit installs downstream of the OE fuel pressure regulator and pinches off fuel return flow during boost to increase fuel pressure as a multiple of boost pressure. Not all FMUs are user-adjustable, but BEGi's allows you to adjust both onset pressure (from slight vacuum to several pounds of boost pressure) and the rate of gain in fuel pressure from about 4 up to 7 psi per pound increase in boost pressure. Stock engine management is unaffected during nonboosted operations. Because higher pressure reduces fuel pump fuel flow capacity, it is common to upgrade the fuel supply system when using an FMU.

Most racers and tuners are not qualified to hack into factory ECUs on their own, but many common factory ECUs have been hacked by automotive-electronics wizards who *are* qualified, and who can then tell you or sell you a method to recalibrate the EMS, or even provide a significant turnkey recalibration. In the case of some popular performance vehicles—the LS-engine Corvettes, for example—hackers have reverse-engineered the system and developed extensive graphical laptop software able to modify specific elements of the calibration and configuration, including the main fuel and ignition tables.

The calibration data—tables of ignition advance values, injector open times, air-fuel ratios, maximum boost pressures, and so forth—span the range of expected possible engine rpm and loading, temperature, and various other conditions, and tells the ECU exactly how to manage the engine under all circumstances that could occur with a stock factory engine.

On older engine-management systems, digital EMS calibration data is stored in a PROM that is sometimes soldered to the ECU's motherboard, or in other cases is removable and easily unplugged from a socket for replacement with another PROM containing different calibration data. Replaceable PROMs simplified inventory problems for car companies by enabling a generic corporate ECU to receive a last-minute "just-in-time" personality, enabling it to handle a particular vehicle and engine application simply with a different PROM. In addition, this approach permitted EMS bug fixes and upgrades without having to swap out the entire computer. In some cases, instead of swapping PROMs to recalibrate, there is a way to force the ECU to read alternate calibration data from an alternate memory location on the motherboard or from a memory device connected to a special diagnostic port in the ECU.

Tuning a PROM-based ECU by burning and swapping new PROMs for each iteration of tuning is feasible though cumbersome, but recalibration is much easier using a PROM emulator. An emulator is a small microcomputer with an extension cable that plugs into the PROM socket in the ECU in place of the usual stock PROM. The stock PROM plugs into a socket in the emulator so that existing calibration data can be uploaded into working storage in the emulator's random-access memory. From here out, calibration data can be tweaked or replaced interactively using a laptop connected to the emulator. The data can be changed to tune the engine while it is running or to reconfigure system parameters while it is not. When the emulator-resident data is where you want it, you offload the data to a PROM-burner, burn a PROM, remove the emulator, plug in the new updated PROM, and rock and roll.

Some modern OBD-II-plus factory ECUs with flash memory are equipped with general purpose operating software that has a fair amount of configurability (though not as much as a modern aftermarket programmable system). For example, you may be unable to reconfigure the factory ECU to change really basic stuff like the number of cylinders,

as you can with most aftermarket EMS. Most really modern OBD-II EMS systems were designed to manage entire *families* of engines, so the internal table entries of the EMS must be configured with data that tells the ECU the engine displacement, the installed fuel injector size, the airflow or pressure range of the MAF and MAP sensors, redline rpm, target idle speed, whether or not to implement a boost or "overpressure" fuel cut and at what pressure, and more. This table-driven configuration facility allows tuners who gain access to the system and reconfigure these variables to seamlessly upsize the injectors and install a wider-range airflow or pressure sensor for a supercharger conversion.

Until recently, however, most ECU calibrations were designed to work with a particular version of ECU operating software that assumed the airflow range, injector size, and displacement of a particular engine. Older, more primitive, engine-management systems used digitized and rounded MAF or MAP sensor data as an index into the appropriate cell in each of the various load-oriented internal calibration tables, with the ECU control software assuming that the sensor data represented a certain airflow. The EMS reads data from the indexed table cell and generates a weighted average ignition timing and injection pulse width from this and surrounding table cells for the next cylinder's engine cycle.

So what are the implications on this type of system if you swap, say, a 1-bar MAP sensor for a 2-bar MAP sensor capable of measuring the full range of a 13-psi blower conversion? Unfortunately, almost all of the stock calibration data must be trashed, relocated, or built from scratch. The reason is that after installing the 2-bar sensor, all speed-density table cells above 0 airflow in the internal tables indexed from particular sensor voltages no longer represent the same engine airflow as they did when the 1-bar sensor was installed. With the 2-bar sensor, since the EMS's speed-density table remains the same size but must now approximate an operating range covering twice the airflow, the normal-charged operating airflow range is now approximated with only half as many rows or columns in the speed-density table. Everything except the 0-load numbers must be redone.

Depending on the airflow sensor design, transferring data from the old normal-charged table to the normal-charged *section* of the new table may not be as straightforward as you'd hope, particularly where identical loading ranges do not exist for the new sensor. For example, suppose various 1-bar sensor voltages represented 0-, 15-, 30-, 45-, 60-, 75-, 90-, and 110-kPa manifold pressure with the stock calibration (this is straight out of a Motec EMS connected to a 1-bar GM MAP sensor). Now, suppose you replace the 1-bar MAP sensor with a 2-bar sensor where the exact same sensor voltages now represent 0, 33, 66, 100, 133, 166, 200, and 233 kPa? You could discard the old 15-kPa data from the old calibration and copy the old 30-kPa data straightforwardly into the second row of the table, which previously represented 15-kPa fuel or ignition data but now represents 33 kPa with the new sensor.

How well will this work is not clear without testing, particularly since 33 is not equal to 30, and the 30–33 kPa airflow range is fairly close to idle manifold pressure, where really precise ignition timing and air-fuel ratios are critical to good idle and good off-idle performance. But ignoring the 30 versus 33 disconnect, there are other potential problems. Let's say the engine is running with the new 2-bar MAP sensor and the sensor reports that manifold pressure is 25 kPa, which does not correspond precisely to any table data. This sort of thing happens all the time, and the ECU routinely computes a weighted-average interpolation for data that falls between table cells to generate spark or fuel calculations between ranges where actual sensor voltages and rpm data do not round exactly to one particular cell in the table. In this case, the EMS would look up 0- and 33-kPa table entries for injection pulse width and average them, with added weight given to the 33-kPa entry because it is much closer to the 25-kPa sensor data. In effect, the system is drawing a straight line between 0 and 33 and using this linear interpolation to derive fueling data for airflow that falls in the middle.

Compare this to the situation with the 1-bar sensor, where a 25-kPa data interpolation would have fallen in the range between 15- and 30-kPa cells rather than between 0- and 33-kPa, with the 15-kPa value potentially defining an entirely different linear interpolation at 25 kPa. The weighted-average fuel data might be close to the old tuning, but it might not, so you're probably going to have to test –and tune every cell in the fuel and ignition tables, even within the normal-charged section of the operating range, most of which should require essentially identical tuning. Of course, to complicate things further, a supercharger installation might alter normal-charged volumetric efficiency enough to require different tuning even when the supercharger is not making boost, as could the drag of driving the supercharger.

This sort of factory EMS recalibration task is not for the faint of heart, because you're building a whole new calibration for a high-output supercharged engine, and with an older factory EMS it may not be feasible to tune cells while the engine is running. In this case, recalibration will be an exhaustive iterative process of test-tune-upload/burn, test-tune-upload/burn, repeat, and so on. This could be worth it if you've got time to burn or you're building a turnkey boost kit for a common engine or vehicle and will sell multiple kits.

The upside of a recalibrated factory EMS is that it's an elegant, robust solution that does not require a lot of new onboard hardware, and should seamlessly retain auxiliary computer functionality like A/C control and so forth. And the hardware is legal.

Bottom line: You can't expect a calibration designed for normal-charging to work well on a blower conversion without major changes.

In the case of a factory-supercharged EMS, things are often much simpler. Modifying a few stock settings to turn off the overboost fuel cut, for example, in many cases will free up the stock EMS to happily manage a significant amount of additional boost.

Factory EMS and Piggyback/Interceptor

If a vehicle will ever be driven on the street, there are good reasons to retain the factory engine-management system, not the least of which is legality. However, in contrast to a hacked and recalibrated factory ECU (which will not be running the factory calibration on a blower conversion!), installing a piggyback/interceptor auxiliary computer between the factory ECU and its sensors—or sensors and actuators—retains perfect, bone-stock engine management during no-boost engine operation, manipulating factory engine management with external tricks only when the blower begins making boost.

Aside from its legality advantages, the stock EMS has the overwhelming advantage that it provides unbeatable drivability in ordinary driving on the street. Wizard calibration engineers at the car companies have spent many months or even years

You need fuel to make power, and that's not going to happen if fuel pressure drops. There are some humongous fuel pumps out there these days. Paxton's 1,100-billet fuel pump will deliver 500 pounds per hour at 45 psi for EFI-type fuel-return type systems that have also been used effectively with carbs by adding a branch line from the fuel loop to a deadhead-type regulator and carb. Keep in mind that you may also want to amp up the electrical power with a Boost-A-Pump type boost-activated voltage boosting power supply. *Paxton*

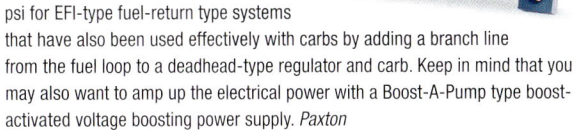

The BEGi fuel management unit provides the fuel for low-boost supercharger conversions by transiently increasing fuel rail pressure as a multiple of boost pressure. Note the fuel inlet, outlet, boost reference ports, and adjustment screws for base pressure and rate of gain. *BEGi*

The Vortech fuel pressure regulator permits adjustment of diaphragm preload spring pressure to set base fuel pressure, which is modified on the fly by supplying manifold pressure to the reference port on the side. *Vortech*

optimizing the calibration for best power, efficiency, and drivability within the engine's stock operating envelope—an effort justifiable in part because it's required to meet emissions standards and in part because the cost will be leveraged across many thousands of vehicles. The best supertuners in the country cannot do as well because they don't have the time. Even if you have the skills, you probably don't have the time either. Nor do you have the freezing arctic, baking desert, or high-altitude test facilities to get the calibration perfect under all conditions. I have seen wicked-expensive tuner cars with aftermarket engine management refuse to start under unusual conditions, such as the morning after a nice drive the previous evening from the palm trees of L.A. to a Sierra Nevada ski area. There, one car proved it had never been calibrated in such freezing-cold, high-altitude conditions.

Beyond the quality of the calibration, modern factory ECUs are powerful, reliable, and (these days) packed with vehicle management or even controller area network multi-processor communications capabilities way beyond the scope of what would be called "engine management," which are virtually impossible to duplicate with off-the-shelf aftermarket computers.

The purpose of a sophisticated piggyback computer is to create a false virtual reality around the stock EMS during boost conditions within which *stock EMS algorithms*, (i.e., the stock onboard computer logic and calibration data tables) deliver excellent blower-conversion or overboost engine management as a result of having the piggyback lie about the status of certain engine sensors, or having the piggyback modify stock EMS commands to certain engine actuators (such as electronic fuel injectors). Within the scope of EMS changes that are achievable with a particular piggyback or interceptor, the laptop user interface of the piggyback is typically similar to that of a standalone aftermarket EMS, complete with fuel, timing, boost, and various other calibration maps—except that timing and fuel numbers may represent *offsets* from stock engine management. Exactly how a piggyback manages to retard the timing for selected engine rpm-loading breakpoints when you tweak cells in the piggyback's timing table, for example, is determined by the architecture and the way it's wired into the stock EMS. On some older engines with a single coil driver, piggyback installation might involve cutting the ECU's coil-driver output wire and connecting the two open ends to input and output channels on the piggyback, whereupon the timing retard strategy would involve simply intercepting the timing pulse input from the stock ECU and recreating it after a suitable delay as an output to the coil driver. On modern multi-coil engines with sophisticated EMS diagnostics that are constantly looking for subtle changes in the electronic "ring" of an ignition circuit to detect the telltale signs of misfire (which might be problematic if you cut the wiring and intersperse the piggyback's electronics into the ignition circuitry), the piggyback might instead intercept and delay data from the crank position sensor such that stock EMS ignition commands are generated late in relation to actual engine position (which, by the way, might produce the unintended consequences of also delaying variable-cam advance and injection-timing events).

What tricks are available to a piggyback/interceptor?

- Delay crank trigger signal to ECU (retards ignition, variable-cam, and injection timing)
- Delay coil trigger signal(s) from ECU (retard spark timing)
- Generate "anticipatory" early crank trigger signal (advances timing of everything)
- Modify coolant or air temperature sensor data (provides warm-up fuel enrichment by simulating a cold or cool engine)
- Modify MAF/MAP sensor data (increase or decrease the air-fuel ratio by simulating alternate engine airflow. This might trigger "out-of-range" EMS countermeasures and also change timing if the cell for the bogus airflow in the ignition table commands different timing. It could also change fuel pressure if pressure is electronically controlled.)
- Modify injection pulse width duration (change air-fuel ratio by truncating or extending the length of time electronic injectors are open)
- Modify fuel pressure sensor data (modifies the air-fuel ratio by tricking the EMS into raising or lowering fuel pressure—or increasing or decreasing injection pulse width to compensate for the false fuel pressure. This is usually available on gasoline direct-injection or diesel powerplants. Alternately, false fuel pressure data can be used to keep the EMS happy if the piggyback or other device has directly modified fuel pressure.)
- Modify PWM command to the fuel pressure control valve to raise or lower rail pressure by trimming rail bleed (which modifies air-fuel ratio by increasing or decreasing the fuel injected per time)

Weiand/Holley 950-cfm carb designed for suck-through supercharging applications. Modified power valve reference keeps the fuel flowing during boost, and special jetting provides boost fuel enrichment. *Holley*

- Modify data from the wideband O2 sensor during closed-loop fueling to manipulate the ECU into changing fuel delivery or to conceal changes in the air-fuel ratio to prevent the EMS from implementing fueling countermeasures in response to nonstock air-fuel ratios instigated by the piggyback or other external equipment.
- Modify EMS PWM commands to an electronic boost controller to deliver overboost
- Control additional injectors (provide boost fuel enrichment)
- Control fuel pressure via auxiliary electronic pressure regulator (modify air-fuel ratios across the board or under select conditions)

Auxiliary Engine Management Modifiers

Another class of tricks for modifying engine management for a blower conversion or overboost project is to "Band-aid" auxiliary physical or electronic devices onto the basic EMS.

A VRG fuel pressure regulator or fuel management unit (FMU) radically jacks up fuel pressure as a multiple of boost pressure to provide fuel enrichment. The FMU is usually mechanical device, but it can also be electro-mechanical and under computer control, similar to the closed-loop fuel-pressure management of some modern engine-management systems, particularly gasoline direct injection. FMUs work great, but limitations in injector maximum fuel pressure constrain this method of fueling supercharger-conversion up to about 1/2 atmosphere of boost. FMUs can also be useful for delivering addition fuel in overboost situations when injector duty cycle is at or near 100 percent.

Boost-retard electronic black boxes are essentially single-purpose interceptors. They work well as an anti-knock countermeasure on low-pressure blower conversions where fuel enrichment alone is not sufficient and where stock timing control is a simple rpm-manifold pressure algorithm that lacks the subtlety to optimize torque across the operating range in high-pressure boost situations. Boost-retard boxes provide an easy way to customize ignition timing for supercharger conversions to eliminate detonation under boost without degrading normal-charged performance by retarding static timing. Replacement dual-ported vacuum-advance/boost-retard canisters for distributors have been sold in the past to deliver mechanical timing retard on GM distributor ignitions and have been adapted to other applications, but these were rendered obsolete by the electronic boost-retard interceptor.

Given sufficient fuel-pump capacity, larger fuel injectors will deliver more fuel. A combination of the right larger injectors and tuned fuel pressure can richen up the air-fuel mixture to optimize maximum torque power for a boosted engine. But this simplistic method of fuel enrichment is likely to enrich the air-fuel ratio in dysfunctional ways everywhere else (subject to the ameliorating ability of closed-loop or wide-range or full-authority closed-loop systems to trim fuel delivery to achieve target air-fuel ratios in the operating range over which they have authority). You'll need to combine big injectors with a piggyback to pull fuel in at lighter engine loading, or you'll need to recalibrate the EMS for upgraded injectors. Or you'll need a programmable MAF sensor.

Programmable MAF sensors are a neat trick. Let's say you install injectors with 10 percent more fuel capacity to fuel a blower conversion at full boost. If the MAF sensor were to report 10 percent less air, the engine would automatically shorten the injection pulse width, and the air-fuel ratios would remain exactly the same, exactly as it should if you had driven up into the mountains where the air is thinner. You still don't have any additional boost fuel enrichment, but if you program tell the MAF to make a smooth transition to reporting full airflow above a certain manifold pressure or airflow. This would do the trick, providing 10 percent additional fuel under heavy load.

Carburetion

Due to the advantages of electronic engine management, and the fact the carburetors have been extinct on roadgoing American factory automotive vehicles since the early 1990s, supercharging with carburetion has become a niche that is not included in some mainstream discussions of supercharging. However, a big carbureted V-8 with a big supercharger in your face still has appeal, and carbureted supercharging remains.

Once upon a time, if you wanted fuel in an engine, you did it with a carburetor—a mechanical device that uses an induced pressure drop in the inlet airway air to suck fuel out of a reservoir kept filled with fuel by a float valve (remarkably similar in concept to the device in home toilet tanks). The float valve opens or closes to admit fuel from a low-pressure source in order to maintain fuel at a constant level in the reservoir (typically known as the float bowl or float chamber). Ambient pressure pushes fuel out the bottom of the reservoir through a metering jet, and then through a passage to an atomizer nozzle located in the reduced pressure of a venturi that is located above the float level to prevent gravity from draining the reservoir when the engine is stopped. A venturi is a slight aerodynamic bottleneck or narrowing in the airway above the throttle that briefly accelerates air to produce locally reduced static pressure according to the Bernoulli effect. Fuel sucked from the reservoir into this low-pressure area mists into the intake air stream in a precisely metered volumetric air-fuel ratio that can be tuned by changing the metering jet size to approximate the optimal mass air-fuel ratio at a certain elevation and temperature. (Because air mass changes according to air pressure changes related to elevation and temperature, and fuel mass changes with temperature according to the fuel's coefficient of thermal expansion, mechanical carburetors have no intrinsic way to compensate for altitude or weather changes.)

BLOW-THROUGH VS. SUCK-THROUGH CARBURETED SUPERCHARGING

Property	Suck-through	Blow-through
Supercharger size	Inlet pressure may be below ambient, so slightly larger or faster compressor is required	Inlet pressure is ambient (minus air cleaner), so full compressor capacity is available
Compressor surge (centrifugal blowers only)	Not usually applicable, but not usually a problem	Can be a problem on deceleration
Supercharger swirl or turbulence	Could interfere with good mixture distribution, could improve fuel atomization.	Not usually a factor
Intake manifold	Custom blower manifold could affect unboosted VE and mixture distribution	No change
Carburetor location and linkage	Carb must be relocated, which could require a longer cable or a different linkage	No change
Fuel pump	No change	Pump/booster must compensate for boost by providing increased fuel pressure
Carburetor inlet temperature	Constant regardless of MAP. Carb icing is possible. Could require carb heat source.	Temperature increases during boost, proving carb heating
Positive crankcase ventilation system	No change	Must move to compressor inlet
Fuel EVAP system	No change	Requires one-way check valve to prevent pressurizing the fuel tank
Distance from carburetor to cylinders	Wet mixtures must be handled over a much greater distance	No change
Carburetor leakage or misting	No change, carb is always under vacuum	Pressurized carb must be fully housed or all vents and shafts sealed
Carburetor float	No change	Metal usually okay, plastic could potentially collapse unless filled with closed-cell plastic
Carb size	Larger carb required to handle 40 to 50 percent cfm airflow increase through carb	No change (boost air is compressed, leaving cfm through carb unaffected)
Vacuum source for pneumatic vehicle systems such as brake booster	Vacuum source must be located between the carb and supercharger inlet	Check valve required to avoid pressurizing (vacuum is intermittent)

Note: Over the years people have developed workable blow-through alternatives to the "carb-in-a-box" architecture, and I have personally converted a number of carbureted engines with Weber or constant-velocity carburetors to forced induction by modifying the carburetors to seal and pressurize the float chambers, allowing them to maintain fuel flow through the jets during boost conditions. Due to the collector value of some such vehicles and the availability of EFI throttle bodies with Holley and Weber bolt-patterns that vastly outperform carburetors in forced-induction applications, it typically no longer makes sense to undertake such a project. No matter what the application (including the classic large V-8 with a big Roots-type blower), there are always excellent technical reasons to consider electronic fuel injection, but if you are determined to proceed with custom carbureted supercharging, there is an excellent chapter on vintage carburetion and forced induction in Hugh MacInnes's excellent but dated book Turbochargers, last updated in 1984 but still available new and used from Amazon.com.

By the time the carburetor was completely superseded by electronic fuel injection on new roadgoing automotive vehicles in the United States, it had been around in one form or another for nearly 100 years. There has not been a carbureted automotive vehicle sold in the United States since the 1994 Isuzu pickup, or in a domestically manufactured vehicle since the 1991 Jeep Grand Wagoneer with the 360 V-8, but at the time of this writing carbs were definitely not extinct. Twenty years later, they are still installed on a variety of motorcycles and are still required in certain classes of racing such as NASCAR. They can still be found on many older vehicles on the road, and new aftermarket carburetors are still installed fairly commonly by people building classic-style V-8 hot rods based on chassis and engines more than 30 years old. Carbs were still fueling small air-cooled engines powering everything from chainsaws to weed-eaters to generators, lawn mowers, garden tractors, and ATVs. Although more and more performance motorcycles, snowmobiles, and watercraft are equipped with fuel injection as performance and emissions standards increased, fuel injection is still not cost-effective on lower-cost models at the time of this writing, and many of these vehicles are still fueled with single or multiple carburetion.

Although production single-point carburetion installed on variable-speed multi-cylinder automotive engines cannot provide fuel distribution and air-fuel ratio accuracy that's up to the standards of performance of modern electronic fuel injection, carburetors are well-developed and extremely reliable, and they will do the job if you're okay with 1970-style performance and drivability. You can still buy new four-venturi carburetors (a.k.a., "4-barrel" or "4-bbl" carbs) from aftermarket companies like Holley, that once sold them by the millions to the car companies for installation on new vehicles. And you can still buy carbureted supercharger kits from companies like Vortech.

There was a time when supercharged engines were (like everything else) fueled by carburetors, but carburetion depends on a pressure differential existing between ambient pressure in the float chamber and the reduced pressure of a venturi to suck fuel into the airstream. Without special modifications for forced induction, simply pressurizing the intake passage(s) through a carb will instantly eliminate the lower pressure required for fuel delivery to the venturi. This instantly halts fuel delivery and blows air backward through the main jet into the float chamber and out the float chamber vent(s) into the engine compartment. And although carbs are equipped with complex, overlapping fuel-delivery systems designed to correct the main-jet fuel delivery system so the engine will run during idle, midrange, transition, acceleration, warm-up, and wide-open-throttle, carburetors do not have specific systems to provide additional fuel enrichment during boost or to fight detonation.

Because carbureted supercharged engines have never been built in large volumes, it has not been cost-effective to develop special carburetors purpose-built for forced induction. So carburetors employed to fuel production forced-induction engines are modified versions of devices that were never designed to deliver fuel enrichment when manifold pressure exceeds 14.7 psi absolute ambient pressure. Because of the nature of single-point production carburetion and the tradeoffs involved in handling a wet mixture in the supercharger or intake manifold, many factory forced-induction vehicles with carburetion were infamous for being inefficient and ornery, with questionable drivability at least some of the time.

Over the years, people have developed many different carburetor and supercharger configurations, but these days the carburetor of significance is the venerable Holley 4-barrel. At this point there remains essentially only two carbureted engine-blower configurations available as turnkey solutions or universal kits that require some adaptation to work on less-common engines. Both involve American V-8s and Holley 4-barrel carbs.

The first is the classic "old-school" Roots supercharger sucking through one or two 4-barrel carbs that provide the "wet" air-fuel mixture essential to cooling this type of supercharger enough to limit rotor thermal expansion during boost to prevent metal-to-metal contact and rotor damage or seizure. Because of the potential for intake backfires where you've got a large Roots-type supercharger case and an intake manifold packed with explosive fumes, such engines are equipped with backfire valves that blow open to prevent an explosion from turning the intake and supercharger into a pipe bomb that literally blows apart the engine. Large, old-school Roots blowers with gasoline carburetion are normally limited by their poor thermal efficiency and primitive engine management to fairly low boost, in the 5- to 7-psi range.

The other viable carbureted configuration is the "carb-in-a-box," where you have a centrifugal supercharger pressurizing a comparatively smaller 4-barrel carburetor housed in an air

With no carb to provide wet mixtures through the Roots blower, a single auxiliary electronic injector sprays fuel into the supercharger from the back of the blower hat. Port injection occurs below the supercharger *inside* the intake manifold. A Motec aftermarket EMS controls the show.

BLOWER ENGINE MANAGEMENT

127

box. A bolt-on access panel surrounds the carb entirely so that boost pressure automatically pressurizes the float chamber without the need to seal unusually shaped vents (or, say, the throttle shafts) to eliminate all possibility of deadly air-fuel mixture misting into the engine compartment. Centrifugal superchargers can function in a blow-through configuration without requiring a fail-safe pressure relief valve because they will tolerate the throttle abruptly slamming shut by permitting a backward surge of air without damage to eliminate the pressure spike. Many of these blow-through systems incorporate an inexpensive blow-off valve to eliminate surging noises and to reduce side-loading on the compressor wheel when the throttle closes suddenly, but eliminating boost pressure on throttle closure is not as critical as it would be on a positive-displacement supercharger, which requires the throttle to be upstream of the blower to eliminate savage pressure spikes due to the one-way air path. Because air is being forced through the carb under pressure rather than being sucked through at subatmospheric pressure, the blow-through configuration can get by with a smaller cfm carb than an engine of the same horsepower with suck-through carburetion.

There are excellent supercharging systems based on both suck-through and blow-through architectures. A minor advantage of blow-through architecture is that the pressure ratio required from a compressor to deliver a target mass airflow is a bit less, because there is no throttle-based pressure drop upstream of the compressor that must be compensated for with increased boost. Breathing through a carb rather than into a carb (with all the adverse consequences of added thermal loading) could require spinning the supercharger at a less efficient, higher speed, or in a worst case require a larger compressor. The most significant advantage of a blow-through system—whether EFI or carbureted—is that there's no need to modify the stock intake system, including manifold, throttle body, fuel lines, accelerator linkage, and so on. By contrast, when carburetors are installed upstream of the compressor in a suck-through architecture, it is important to make sure that the blower intake manifold does not compromise normal-charged volumetric efficiency and mixture distribution among the cylinders to a dysfunctional extent, and that swirl or turbulence from the supercharger does not interfere with mixture distribution when the compressor is making boost.

A common practice in suck-through architectures is to construct a square-cornered plenum between the compressor and intake runners to foil swirl that interferes with air or fuel distribution, but it is still probable that that fuel distribution will change when you convert to a suck-through carbureted supercharging system. Unfortunately, you will not know what is going on unless you carefully read the spark plugs or log data from individual-cylinder EGT or wideband AFR sensors, which is likely to be expensive and impractical for many people who are interested in carbureted supercharging. Even if you are aware of mixture distribution problems, making modifications that cure fuel and air distribution problems in wet-mixture plenums and manifolds requires sophisticated scientific flow test equipment and instrumented engine dynamometers, and knowledge that is vastly out of reach for most people—a great reason to use forced-induction intake systems developed by professional supercharging specialists with the ability and resources to develop and test until they get it right.

Like all carburetors, Holley 4-barrel carbs are designed with multiple overlapping air-fuel delivery systems that work together to overcome the fact that pressure reduction in a venturi is proportional to the square of the increase in air speed (or the square root of the decrease). This meaning that an imaginary 1-jet carb on a high-speed powerplant with a lot of dynamic range with fuel-metering calibrated for good idle would deliver grotesquely rich mixtures at maximum airflow, or fuel starvation at idle if fuel metering were calibrated for maximum airflow. In real-world carbs, there are overlapping auxiliary fuel systems that deliver supplemental fuel at idle, midrange, high-rpm, wide-open-throttle, and during sudden-acceleration that work together to approximate the correct air-fuel curve across the range of engine operating conditions. Except for warm-up enrichment, these are basically auxiliary jetting systems (jets, needle jets, jet needles, booster venturis, power valves, and so forth) that come into play as the throttle opens, airflow increases, or manifold pressure increases. For warm-up enrichment an auxiliary throttle-type blade closes at colder temperatures to restrict air entry into the carb throats, greatly increasing vacuum in the main venturis and thus pulling in extra fuel through the main jets. Unlike EFI, carbs do not have any automatic ability to compensate for air pressure changes due to altitude, requiring pilots flying carbureted piston-engine aircraft to manually lean the mixture in aviation carbs as altitude increases. Some carburetors have additional systems such as constant-velocity slides or variable venturis that have their advantages under certain conditions.

What's relevant to carbureted supercharging is that Holley 4-barrel carbs address fuel enrichment required during wide-open throttle with a spring-loaded power valve. The power valve opens an auxiliary main jet by unseating a spring-loaded needle valve controlled by a diaphragm that senses engine load through a reference to the intake manifold immediately downstream of the throttle. The reference supplies engine vacuum to hold the valve closed when the engine is lightly loaded. As the throttle opens and loading increases, vacuum decreases in the intake and a spring opens the valve to let more fuel into the main circuit.

Problems arise with suck-through carbureted supercharging because a partially closed throttle during boost will produce vacuum between the carburetor and the supercharger that closes the power valve while the engine is still supercharged, potentially causing a lean condition and detonation. The power valve system can be modified for suck-through supercharging by plugging the stock power valve manifold reference and connecting the diaphragm to an external metal pipe routed to the intake manifold downstream of the supercharger, thus providing the correct signal to the power valve and permitting it to open under heavy loading. A number of outfits such as Weiand, a sister company to Holley, sell "supercharger carburetors" already equipped with this modification and advertised as "100 percent wet-flowed, equipped, and calibrated for the special needs of a supercharged engine."

Reworking the power valve reference prevents a suck-through carburetor power-valve system from being confused about manifold pressure, which is a good start. Unfortunately, there is still no facility that intrinsically provides fuel enrichment during boost. The same is true with a "carb-in-a-box" blow-through setup, where the relationship between venturi pressure and "ambient" (box) pressure is unaffected by boost, allowing all fuel systems to remain functional with no power valve modification required. When the supercharger pressurizes the box with boost it is like driving to a lower elevation.

But here's the rub: As volumetric (cfm) rather than mass-airflow (lb/min) devices, carburetors do nothing to compensate for air density changes, which is why the carbureted street cars of the 1970s and 1980s ran dreadfully rich when you drove up to the mountains to go skiing. CFM was unaffected; there was just less oxygen mass in a cubic foot of air.

Dealing with air density changes can be problematic with turbochargers, where there is no fixed relationship between engine rpm and boost pressure, and where manifold pressure can be almost anything at any rpm, depending on throttle position, exhaust heat, what gear you're in, the steepness of a hill, and other factors. Which is why carbureted turbo systems are dead and buried except in the case of a few unfortunate souls who own carbureted, turbocharged collector cars like the Corvair Spyder, Olds Jetfire, Maserati Biturbo, or Firebird Trans Am Turbo.

The good news in a book about supercharging is that the fixed, relationship between engine and mechanical supercharger speed means that even though a carb has zero ability to compensate for increases in air density that result from supercharger boost, the relationship between rpm and supercharger boost is fixed at full throttle, making the torque curve as predictable as that of a nonboosted engine. This means that you can treat boost-based increases in volumetric efficiency exactly as you would if they resulted from displacement, cam, or head changes, or anything else that increases normal-charged torque and power—with careful jetting and tuning of the various fuel-delivery subsystems, preferably on a chassis dynamometer.

However, supercharged engines with a lot of dynamic range (exceptionally large difference between the fuel flow at idle and maximum power) can still be difficult to tune well, particular if there are sharp increases required in the air-fuel ratio during boost as an anti-knock countermeasure.

Fueling Your Boost

There are a number of tricks that can be used to provide boost-specific fuel enrichment:

1. The first is to build an auxiliary "electric jet" circuit that's regulated by a solenoid controlled by a pressure switch. It triggers at a designated boost pressure to spray fuel tapped from the fuel line directly into a nozzle aimed straight down one or more barrels of the carb. This is an all-or-nothing system that intrinsically provides more fuel and richer air-fuel mixtures when it opens at, say, 2-psi boost than it does at, say, 8 psi due to the fact that enrichment fuel flow stays constant but airflow increases, and ideal air-fuel ratio at higher boost may be richer to fight detonation. However, the air-fuel ratio *sensitivity* of gasoline supports peak torque across a fairly wide range of air-fuel ratios, as follows:

AFR	Comment
6.0	Rich burn limit (fully warm engine)
9.0	Black smoke/low power
11.5	Approximate rich best torque at wide-open throttle
12.2	Safe best power at wide-open throttle
13.3	Approximate lean best torque
14.6	Stoichiometric AFR (chemically ideal)
15.5	Lean cruise
16.5	Usual best economy
18.0	Carbureted lean burn limit
22+	EEC/EFI lean burn limit

If you don't have to care too much about flame speed as you would at extreme rpm, and if boost pressure is relatively modest, it should be possible to optimize the air-fuel ratio somewhere between lean best torque at maximum boost and not be too rich of rich best torque (RBT) at lower boost. A pressurized carb-in-a-box blow-through supercharging system intensifies the liabilities of this enrichment system because the spray system must overcome boost pressure to inject fuel (meaning that fuel line pressure must significantly exceed boost pressure), which decreases fuel flow precisely when you'd like it to increase. A significant improvement to this type of system involves adding a fuel pressure regulator with an adjustable rate-of-gain. You would reference the regulator to manifold pressure to increase the flow rate of enrichment fuel as boost increases using amplified fuel pressure that increases as a multiple of boost. Another version of this system would deliver alcohol injection during boost to raise octane, massively cool combustion, and boost power. There are now good processor-controlled "water" injection systems that spray water or a water-alcohol mixture into the carb to fight detonation, though it is questionable if this would be considered fuel enrichment.

WEIAND SUPERCHARGER/CARBURETOR SELECTION MATRIX

Blower Size	Engine	Approximate Required CFM	Holley Carb(s) P/N	Holley HP Carb(s) P/N
142	GM Small-block 350	700	0-80572S	0-80576
174	Ford Small-block 302	750	0-80573S	0-80576
177	GM Big-block 454	800	0-80576	-
256	GM Big-block 454	750 (x2)	0-80573S	0-80576
420	GM Small-block 350	600 (x2)	0-80592S	0-80575
420	GM Big-block 454	750 (x2)	0-80573S	0-80576
6-71	GM Small-block 350	600 (x2)	0-80592S	0-80575
6-71	GM Big-block 454	750 (x2)	0-80573S	0-80576
6-71	Chrysler Hemi 392	750 (x2)	0-80573S	0-80576
8-71	GM Small-block 350	750 (x2)	0-80573S	0-80576
8-71	GM Big-block 454	800 (x2)	-	0-80576
8-71	Chrysler Hemi 426	750 (x2)	0-80573S	0-80576

Sufficient carburetor airflow is important to optimizing suck-through supercharging performance, but sufficient fuel delivery is critical because a carburetor that delivers lean mixtures will cause detonation, which will destroy a boosting motor in a matter of seconds. You'll know it's too lean if the engine is surging or you hear audible lean popping noises, or if you see glowing red headers. Again, it is important to read the spark plugs for proper color, which should be a medium to dark tan.

BLOWER ENGINE MANAGEMENT

2. Another boost fuel enrichment trick available on a progressive 4-barrel carburetor is to modify the carb so that the secondary throttles are dedicated to providing air and fuel enrichment during—and only during—boost. Stock progressive 4-barrel carbs are designed to provide high-velocity air to the intake manifold at lower rpm by opening only the two primary throttles until the primaries are mostly open. At higher rpm and heavier loading, a mechanical linkage or a vacuum-controlled diaphragm opens the two secondary throttles to relieve the excessive pressure drop through the throttles at maximum power. The secondary throttles or barrels typically do not have a choke and often have no power system, accelerator pump, or idle system. Set up the secondary throttles to open exclusively during boosted conditions to eliminate pressure drop through the carb, and with the secondary main jets set up rich to deliver correct boost fuel enrichment. A simple mechanical linkage can be used to open the secondaries when the primaries are, say, 75 percent open, depending on how fast and effectively the blower makes boost. A vacuum secondary progressive 4-barrel carb can be reworked by removing the backup primary-secondary interlock. Reassemble the actuator diaphragm with the spring on the opposite side of the diaphragm so that *pressure*, rather than vacuum, opens the secondaries and the actuator spring closes the secondaries when boost is absent.

With this arrangement, the secondaries no longer begin to open when the primaries reach a certain percentage of full throttle but instead when boost reaches, say, 1 psi, at which point the primary throttles are 100 percent open. Then the secondary throttle circuit opens and there is a strong burst of supercharged power. With the primary and secondary mechanical interlock gone, however, removing the driver's foot from the accelerator no longer forces the secondary

Pressurized carburetor? Nope. This Paxton supercharging system was designed to amp-up the power of '80s and '90s Chevy trucks equipped with throttle-body injection. Such systems increase injection pressure during boost to maintain correct mixtures and provide fuel-cooling to fight detonation.

130

throttles closed, potentially allowing a boosted engine with this modification to run supercharged on the secondary throttles as long as there is boost pressure holding open the secondary-throttle actuator diaphragm. The solution is to install a valve that opens to vent the secondary diaphragm to the atmosphere as soon as the primary throttles close, at which point the spring-loaded actuator diaphragm immediately closes the secondaries.

Carburetor Selection

A blow-through, carb-in-a-box supercharging system *does not increase the CFM airflow through the carb* because although air mass increases, air volume ingested by the engine remains unchanged, so there is no reason to install a larger carb unless you've made changes that affect the engine's basic volumetric efficiency.

On the other hand, carb selection is important to a suck-through supercharging system, because volumetric airflow through a suck-through carb can easily increase 40 or 50 percent when the engine is supercharged. Pressure drop through a suck-through carb will adversely impact a positive-displacement supercharger's ability to achieve target boost without having to run faster and hotter.

Proper suck-through carb size depends on engine VE and boost. Weiand recommends the following formula to calculate required carburetor CFM:

Max CFM = ((engine cid × maximum rpm) / 356) × ((maximum blower boost / 14.7) + 1)

The following table lists CFM, recommended Holley carburetion for 1- or 2-carb suck-through supercharging systems, and recommended Weiand (Roots-type) supercharger size for a selection of GM, Ford, and Chrysler V-8 powerplants.

Fuel Supply

You'll need to verify that the fuel supply system is up to the job when you convert to supercharging.

For a suck-through system: Most carburetors need a minimum of 4 to 6 pounds of pressure at the float to keep the fuel reservoir full. If you are using an old-school lever-type mechanical fuel pump driven from a cam in the engine block, you'll need to research the pump capacity to make sure you've got what you need to fuel the target horsepower. A better idea is to install an aftermarket electric fuel pump and fuel pressure regulator known to have sufficient fuel-delivery capacity and then remove the stock fuel pump and install a drilled plate in its place to seal the block.

The best type of fuel supply system is an EFI-type fuel loop, with in-tank or inline high-pressure electric fuel pump building pressure against a fuel pressure regulator that pinches off flow in the fuel loop to whatever extent is required to achieve the target fuel pressure. The diaphragm in such a fuel pressure regulator is usually referenced to the intake system keep pressure regulated a fixed amount above manifold (boost) pressure, allowing excess fuel to return to the fuel tank. You can build a simple fuel return by removing the fuel tank filler tube, *cleaning off all traces of gasoline*, and welding or brazing in a fitting that dumps fuel from the return line back into the tank. If you are running EFI pressure in the fuel loop in a carbureted application, tap into the loop to attach a branch line that supplies fuel for the carb, with a standard deadhead regulator to lower pressure to standard carb pressure. You might be able to find a pinch-type regulator with low enough pressure for a carb, which would allow the use of a low-pressure electric fuel pump.

For a blow-through system: The above system is ideal when the carburetor is pressurized, because blow-through carbs require that fuel pressure that is standard pressure *plus boost pressure* to prevent boost from forcing fuel backward out of the float chamber into the fuel line, which instantly starves the engine of fuel. The loop-type system described above works great, but whichever type of regulator is being used to determine pressure at the float chamber must be referenced to manifold pressure to keep the engine running during boost. Always verify that the fuel pump, fuel lines, and fuel pressure regulators will support the flow rate you need at full boost pressure. As you might expect, the flow rate of fuel pumps is generally inversely proportional to the pressure, with the highest fuel flow available at zero pressure and maximum flow gradually declining to zero as pressure increases. The pump must be able to supply the required flow rate at maximum boost pressure plus the 4 to 6 psi required at all times.

It is worth keeping in mind that carbureted engines are intrinsically more cold-blooded than engines with fuel injection. The intake systems of carbureted engines must handle wet mixtures, and a fact of life is that fuel and air have different mass, and there is always a tendency for fuel to "understeer" in turns in the intake system and condense on the walls of the manifold when cold. This fuel then tears off in sheets and re-enters the air stream at unpredictable intervals. What's more, the venturi-based architecture of carburetors that produces a low-pressure region will increase the likelihood of ice forming in the carb during cold, humid weather. It was once common to heat intake manifolds during warm up with exhaust heat. Carbureted supercharging systems with no intake heating can be miserably undrivable in cold weather until they warm up, or even later if ice forms in the carb. Obviously if you are building or installing a blow-through supercharging system, stock heating systems can remain functional. Suck-through systems that seek drivability in cold weather require spacer plates between the carb and the supercharger that are heated with engine coolant (from the heater system, if applicable). A heated spacer plate can keep carb temperature above 60 degrees F to prevent icing and condensation that can cause stalling, over-speeding, or both.

ALTERNATE/DUAL-FUEL INJECTION

Dual-fuel injection is a special case of engine management that can solve some difficult problems.

Inventors have long recognized the advantages of a vehicle that can run on more than one type of fuel. When I was working on an irrigated family farm 30 years ago in eastern Arizona, the pickup trucks we used frequently had both gasoline carburetors and Impco propane carbs—one mounted on top of the other. Gasoline started the vehicle more easily, made more power, and you could get it at any gas station. But propane or natural gas was much cheaper for use around the huge irrigated farms of Cochise County. A manual dashboard switch activated solenoids to effect fuel changeover. We also used turbo-supercharged big-block V-8 engines, fueled by natural gas piped out to the fields, to drive turbine and centrifugal well and pressurizing pumps. With the high octane of these gaseous fuels, no boost controls were required except maybe an emergency blow-off valve.

Flexible-fuel injection, in which a vehicle's EMS calibrates fuel injection and timing based on the specific gravity of the fuel or other means, is now mainstream, and you can now find U.S.-market vehicles capable of running on pure gasoline or some percentage of alcohol with gasoline. Vehicles in countries like Brazil are often capable of running on undiluted ("neat") gasoline or ethanol—or a mixture.

Meanwhile, the advent of programmable aftermarket electronic fuel injection gave the concept of dual-fuel vehicles new life for high-pressure forced induction with high-compression engines. Dallas car builder Bob Norwood applied the dual-fuel concept to several supercar projects when 93-octane gasoline could not support enough boost pressure to meet the power and boost goals at higher manifold pressures, or where high-octane, clean-burning fuels made it easier to pass emissions testing. In addition to gasoline-alcohol injection, Norwood designed dual-fuel systems that delivered intermittent injection of unleaded race gasoline and nitromethane. Staged dual-fuel injection makes sense for high-pressure supercharging from many points of view, including fuel cost and availability, detonation control, emissions compliance, improved power via the higher specific energy in oxygenated fuels, and increased dynamic range (the smallest injection capability at idle compared to the largest injection capacity at maximum power) via extra staged injectors.

In one project, Norwood Autocraft reworked a boosted Ferrari F50 to run on E85, a common gasoline-alcohol blend that provided sufficient octane (102–106) to run 10-psi boost with the stock 11.3:1 compression ratio without detonation. HC, CO, and NOx emissions improved in all cases.

In another project, Norwood built a 24-injector, flat-12 Ferrari Testarossa forced-induction powerplant with a complete set of 12 additional staged fuel injectors that kicked in at higher levels of boost to inject alcohol fuel. Multiple-injector, dual-fuel architectures like this equip each intake runner with one or more additional injectors fed by segregated fuel rails that provide an entirely independent fuel supply for the secondary injectors. An aftermarket ECU managed both the primary and secondary injectors on the Testarossa. This system provided:

- Ultra-high octane fuel during boost conditions
- Combustion-cooling and charge density increases from alcohol's high vaporization heat
- Conservation of alcohol fuel due to intermittent use
- Lower NOx emissions due to cooler combustion
- Lower HC emissions due to the oxygenated alcohol fuel.

In yet a third project, Norwood used methanol to provide extra fuel enrichment for a high-boost forced-induction Acura NSX with stock 10.2:1 compression. By retaining the stock internal engine configuration, the stock engine calibration and engine management components continued to function under all driving conditions, yielding excellent drivability at

Mountain Performance ProLogger is a data logging system designed to provide Wideband O2 sensor-based air-fuel ratio data for tuning and calibration of electronic fuel injection controllers, carburetors, superchargers, nitrous oxide injection. The ProLogger is designed to accommodate analog and digital input and output devices for mapping or remapping electronic controllers and mechanical fuel delivery systems. *Mountain Performance*

idle and light cruise, with great low-end crispness and torque, plus emissions compliance and the economy and convenience of street gasoline. As boost came on, an auxiliary fuel-only computer activated two huge, 1,600 cc Indycar fuel injectors to add 100-octane methanol for air-fuel mixture enrichment and detonation control, enabling the car to safely run 9-psi boost. The NSX was equipped with an auxiliary 5-gallon methanol fuel tank, supplying fuel to a high-pressure rail that supported the two single-point injectors, each of which fired three times per engine revolution near the throttle body. The auxiliary ECU managing the additional injectors executed fuel calculation based solely on engine speed and manifold pressure. The car appeared normal from the outside and idled normally, but made more than 50 percent more power and torque at 9-psi boost.

The automotive performance aftermarket has always been seriously challenged to build legal add-on or modified parts or parts kits with a legal California emissions exemption order. This is one reason auxiliary computers and injectors enter the picture. It is usually a far simpler task to use a piggyback or standalone auxiliary computer to modify the behavior of the factory engine-management system under the limited circumstances during which power-adder conversions are active and require special engine fueling or spark timing. The alternative is to start from scratch, building an entirely new set of engine-control parameters with the precision required to pass emissions testing. Why reinvent the wheel when the factory has already done all the work to pass emissions? Since many performance modifications only make a difference at full throttle (which is not part of the Federal Test Procedure for emissions compliance) the add-on auxiliary computer is a potent weapon in the hands of tuners. And when you have secondary injectors, it is relatively easy to supply them with a different fuel.

There are definitely power advantages to supplying high-pressure supercharged engines with two fuels. The fact that methanol contains 10 percent oxygen helps support additional combustion—a little like shooting nitrous oxide into a motor. Nitromethane contains even more oxygen, performing as a monopropellant under certain circumstances, meaning it can burn without oxygen. This is one reason nitro can be incredibly dangerous. Some racers and tuners have used as many as three electronic injectors per cylinder for gasoline, Nitro or alcohol, producing prodigious amounts of power on demand while offering precise computer control of both fuels.

Staged dual-fuel injection has the added benefit of extending the dynamic fueling range of the stock injectors to much higher levels of boost while allowing the engine to idle properly at the other end of the scale. Without separate control, however, the EMS is limited to firing additional dual-fuel injectors with the same calibration at the same rate and pulse width as the primary-fuel injectors. The fuel mix of such a system must be tuned by balancing the size of the primary and secondary injector nozzles, or by adjusting the fuel pressure independently for the two fuel systems. An auxiliary computer has no such limitation, firing dual fuel injectors entirely independently.

High-octane fuel availability can be a serious problem for any dual-use vehicle—even if you don't care what it costs. But vehicles like powerboats and club-race cars do not usually require super high-octane fuel except under heavy loading and high-boost conditions. Running on pump gas vastly extends the practicality of such a car or boat, though controlling detonation is critical. For the lunatic fringe that require a dual-use street-mannered vehicle with an ultra-high power boost on demand, dual-fuel injection may be the solution.

TUNING (CALIBRATION)

Optimizing the EMS calibration for a forced-induction powerplant is an exhaustive process that is explored more fully in my book *How to Tune and Modify Engine Management Systems*. It is a process that aftermarket tuners pursue only as far as the point when they achieve acceptable results. As a car magazine writer, I've seen many, many vehicles end up with drivability that would've been completely unacceptable in a factory vehicle. Good professional tuners with chassis dynos, fast, wideband air-fuel ratio meters, infrared gas analyzers, and other critical test equipment can almost always find additional power and fuel economy in a vehicle that has been tuned by a minimally competent hobbyist or a professional who cut corners because there wasn't enough time or money to do it right. In my experience, pro tuners reflexively bad-mouth calibrations that arrive on their doorstep from other tuning shops that should know better. Ironically, it is the hobbyists who have the time to work forever on tuning an engine perfectly, but they often don't have the test equipment or experience or patience to do it really right.

Tuning an electronic engine-management system right always involves dyno work, ideally starting on an engine or torque-cell chassis dyno, where the operator runs the engine at all achievable combinations of engine rpm and loading

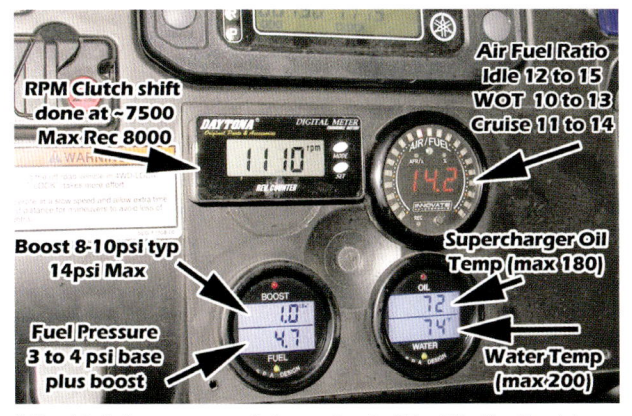

A Mountain Performance gauge cluster on a Yamaha Rhino ATV with a Mountain supercharging system. With wheel horsepower more than doubled from 22 to 52 on a 686-cc single-cylinder, managing the engine correctly is critically important. It makes sense to keep an eye on fuel and boost pressure, oil and water temperature, air-fuel ratio, and rpm. *Mountain Performance*

to optimize the calibration everywhere for best torque or economy. You need a good starting point, which will probably be the stock calibration if you're tuning a factory system for added boost, or better yet, an EMS or interceptor calibration from a similar vehicle that was tuned previously by someone good. In the case of a programmable aftermarket system, the starting point will consist of calibration data borrowed from another vehicle as above, or calculated values generated by modeling software supplied by the manufacturer of the engine-management system (sometimes quite good).

No matter the method, tuning involves holding the engine at scores or hundreds of speed-density breakpoints across the entire operating range of the engine or at least across the boosted range in which operating conditions are not stock. You're always going to start with conservative (late) timing and rich air-fuel ratios at idle, then move to no-load higher speeds, modifying *groups* of table cells in the vicinity of the current speed and loading/airflow. Next, you move to higher engine loads in the nonboosted realm, always tuning rich-to-lean, adding timing gradually, and working back and forth from fuel to timing under heavier load.

Next, the tuner transitions gradually into boost, always keeping in mind that an EMS computes fuel and timing as a *weighted average* of the surrounding defined speed-density cells in the relevant table. Ideally, there will be a way to severely limit maximum boost at first by adjusting the wastegate jam bolt or changing wastegate springs, then adding boost incrementally by adjusting the wastegate. Once the engine is working well at the maximum boost the wastegate can achieve, boost can be added a little at a time with a wastegate controller under electronic control.

An engine torque-cell dyno calibration is perfect for optimizing steady-state torque across the board, but it does little to help transition or acceleration performance. A torque-cell dyno calibration usually ends up too rich for best real-world performance, where *acceleration* performance is the thing people really care about, except in the case of trailer-towing. Even when engine dynos do wide-range pulls across the rpm range, they are actually stepping through the speed range of the pull in tiny increments, holding the engine at each speed in steady state for an instant—which is not the same as real inertial acceleration and is certainly not the same as moving the weight of the vehicle. Acceleration enrichment specifies the fuel required when the throttle position changes quickly and manifold pressure makes sudden swings that affect the ability of fuel to remain atomized well in the intake air stream. As we shall see in the chapter of this book about heat management, the boiling or vaporization point of a liquid changes with pressure. You calibrate the percentage and sustain the acceleration enrichment by trial and error, ideally on an inertial chassis dyno, which is great at simulating acceleration under controlled conditions and timing acceleration precisely.

Eventually you move to tuning while road testing—but always with full data logging capability and test equipment to

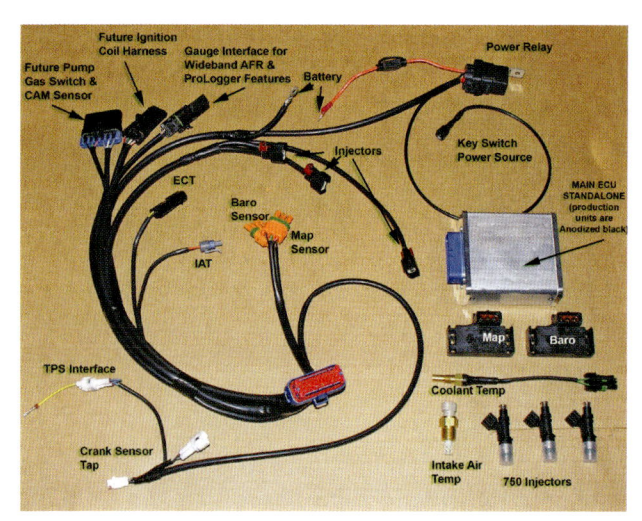

The Mountain Performance standalone engine management system controller, harness, and selected sensors and actuators are designed to plug-and-play on Yamaha R1 engines in bikes and snowmobiles. *Mountain Performance*

identify the air-fuel ratios, the brake-specific fuel consumption, and the torque, which can be calculated based on acceleration and weight data while tuning on the road. If you are building a complete calibration from scratch or improving the computed calibration by EMS modeling software, you'll eventually have to tune the engine during cold-start and warm-up conditions. This involves an exhaustive process of allowing the engine to cold-soak completely, often overnight, and then tuning *fast* while the engine is starting and heating up. And trying again tomorrow, or any time the weather reaches previously unencountered extremes of cold.

Most people who do not own any test equipment would do well to trailer their vehicles to a professional tuner, who should agree to calibrate the vehicle for a flat fee. Alternatively, you could tune it enough on your own so that it runs and drives well enough, and then drive or trailer it to a pro tuner. A top pro tuner should take responsibility for tuning your engine without damaging it, but it is worth remembering that car companies typically devote many months or even years to getting the calibration perfect, implying that a tuner who's only spent a few hours doing the calibration will be delivering out maps that cannot be perfect under all conditions. If you are willing to invest in an acceleration-based, onboard dyno and wideband air-fuel equipment, and if you are meticulous and patient, you can continue to tune the car while driving on the street and track over the long term. This will allow you to work incrementally toward perfection, keeping in mind that it is radically dangerous and stupid to attempt laptop tuning alone while you are on the street. The better course is to log the data from various maneuvers while driving, and then pull over to make changes that correct air-fuel or timing problems.

For more information about engine-management systems and EMS calibration, you may want to read my book *How to Tune and Modify Engine Management Systems*.

Chapter 7
Heat Management: Combustion, Engine, Blower, Oil, Charge, Exhaust

Next to primary engine management, the quality of heat management is literally the make or break of any supercharged engine.

The first thing to know about heat is that horsepower *is* heat in an internal-combustion engine. If you overcool an engine, you're giving away horsepower, which is one reason why NASCAR racers run a minimum of 200 degrees coolant temperature. The higher the temperature of the combustion chamber and cylinders, the more efficiently the engine runs and the more power it makes. Heat is good.

The problem is that the higher the combustion temperature of a spark-ignition engine, the more likely it is to self-destruct during heavy loading from detonation, pre-ignition, or excessive EGT. Diesel engines are normally incapable of knock or pre-ignition, but excessive combustion temperature can overheat and damage diesel pistons and rings exactly as it does in spark-ignition powerplants.

In fact, heat is responsible for most engine problems. Heat breaks down motor oil, weakens and distorts parts, and attacks gaskets and seals, shortening engine life and increasing maintenance expenses. Engines must operate at a safe temperature under the most severe conditions and factory automotive cooling systems are normally built to handle thermal loading under worst-case *street-legal* operating conditions.

Heat management is even more critical when an engine is supercharged. To achieve high performance and reliability, factory engineers, aftermarket tuners, and hot rodders must carefully manage heat in a variety of critical systems:

- Cooling system
- Engine lubrication
- Pistons and other internal engine components
- Air intake and delivery system
- Charge cooler system (intercooler)
- Compressor
- Exhaust manifold and plumbing
- Engine compartment

Modern factory supercharged engines are protected by an engine-management computer intelligently controlling injection pulse width, ignition timing, boost pressure (in some cases), cooling fans, and other equipment that can help prevent a disastrous melt-down. Even so, many factory supercharged automobile engines could not survive at maximum *achievable* engine loading for long without suffering engine damage. Fortunately, light streamlined vehicles accelerate so quickly it is difficult or impossible to maintain maximum engine loading for long unless you push it to vastly illegal high speeds, at which point the exponentially increasing air resistance becomes extreme and you *can* maintain ultra-heavy engine loading for a long time.

It is even worse when a stock normal-charged engine has been converted to supercharging. Stock engine systems and components will not provide the same margin of factory reliability on a blower conversion or overboosted factory-supercharged engine. Unless engine, transmission, and drivetrain weaknesses are adequately protected with backup

Heat: The good, the bad, the ugly. It takes heat to make power, but too much heat in the wrong place can ruin your whole day. This supercharged V-8 makes heat on a Magnuson Products engine dyno. *Magnuson Products*

systems that cannot fail to prevent engine damage, you are depending on the driver to manage the engine manually with his right foot to avoid engine damage.

It is rather common for hot-rodded, forced-induction powerplants running constantly on the ragged edge of trouble to suffer engine damage. In fact, if held at maximum boost on a continuous top-speed banzai run, many hot-rodded, boosted engines will sicken and die rather quickly from a spring-loaded series of thermal overloading events:

- The coolant temperature begins to increase and cannot be controlled even with the fans on high speed.
- As the water jacket heats up, combustion temperatures rise and the entire engine compartment begins to heat-soak.
- Oil temperatures rise and oil-squirters inject hotter oil against the undersides of the pistons (assuming there are piston oil-squirters).
- Pistons heat up and the piston-to-cylinder wall clearance decreases.
- EGT rises.
- Coolant temperatures increase further.
- The supercharger itself heat-soaks more and more.
- Air intake temperature increases.
- Combustion temperatures approach auto-ignition temperature.
- The engine begins to knock.
- Piston temperatures skyrocket.
- Steam pockets form in the water—with the positive void coefficient leading to more steam pockets and overheating.
- The combustion chambers begin to pre-ignite, which makes even more heat.
- Oil begins to oxidize, and hydrodynamic lubrication begins to fail in various places.

CALCULATING HEAT TRANSFER BETWEEN FLUIDS IN A HEAT EXCHANGER

Isaac Newton discovered that the rate of heat transfer Q between two fluids was directly proportional to the overall difference between the temperatures and the heat transfer surface area. Newton's equation can be applied as follows:

$$Q_{rate} = U \times A \times Qm$$

Where:

Q_{rate} = Rate of heat transfer between fluids
U = Overall heat transfer coefficient, determined by the air velocity and geometric coefficient of the radiator core, as well as the water velocity through the tubes
A = Radiator's heat transfer area (dependent upon the length, width, and number of fins and tubes)
Qm = Temperature difference between average water temperature and the air coolant

Assuming a heat transfer area of 150.0 square feet, an overall heat transfer coefficient of 12.2 Btu/hr. per square foot at 30 miles per hour, coolant temperature varying from 192 to 200 degrees F, and 100 degrees F inlet air temperature:

$$Q_{rate} = 12.2 \times 150.0 \times (((200 + 192) / 2) - 100)$$
$$= 174,000 \text{ BTU/hr}$$
$$= 2,900 \text{ BTU/min} <2,928>$$

The example heat exchanger can handle 19.5 BTU/min per square foot of area under the above conditions.

Air temperature rise through the 3.25-square-foot heat exchanger at 2,650 ft/min air velocity (30 miles per hour) with 425 lb/min of airflow can be calculated with a new equation:

$$Q_{load} = W \times Cp \times (T_{out} - T_{in})$$

Where:

Q_{load} = Cooling load
W = Rate of airflow = 425 lb/min
C_p = Specific heat of air = .241 Btu/lb per degree F of air
T_{in} = Inlet air temperature = 100F
T_{out} = Outlet temperature of air exiting the radiator = 128.3F

Then:

$$Q_{load} = W \times Cp \times (T_{out} - T_{in})$$
$$= 425 \times .241 \times (128.3 - 100)$$
$$\approx 2,900 \text{ BTU/min}$$

Assume that an A/C condenser that rejects 300 BTU/min raises the 100-degree air temperature to 110.0 before it reaches the radiator. We can calculate that A/C will raise the temperature of hot water entering the radiator from 200 degrees to 211.5, and the air exiting the radiator from 128.3 to 138.3.

Air-to-boil (ATB) temperature indicates the air inlet temperature at which the coolant will start to boil. An ATB of 112 degrees means that a nonpressurized radiator will start to boil when the inlet air reaches 112 degrees, meaning a radiator running nonpressurized 200-degree top tank water temperature would boil with a 12-degree F air temperature increase. Lower ATB implies lower radiator performance.

In a real world example, a vehicle was tested by Modine in four configurations:

No A/C, standard radiator, four-blade fan, no shroud, no condenser
A/C, standard radiator, four-blade fan, no shroud, A/C condenser
A/C, standard radiator, heavy-duty seven-blade fan w/shroud, A/C condenser
A/C, H-D radiator, H-D fan w/shroud, A/C condenser

The vehicle was heat-soaked at 110 degrees ambient, then run in a wind tunnel with windows closed and A/C on at 20, 30, and 60 miles per hour for 30 minutes, then at idle for 30 minutes.

The non-A/C car generally had the lowest top-tank temperatures, while the standard-cooling car with A/C boiled at 248 degrees after 24 minutes idling. The heavy-duty fan did not do much at speed but radically dropped temperatures at idle. The big radiator by itself did not help greatly at idle, but reduced temperatures 20 degrees F during higher speed runs.

- Knock shatters ring lands and rings.
- Pistons begin melting.
- Finally, a piston seizes, the wrist pin tears out of the piston, and one or more connecting rods smash through the block.
- Game over.

Obviously, it is critically important to manage heat in all of these systems to achieve optimal power and reliability in any supercharged powerplant.

UPGRADING ENGINE COOLING SYSTEMS

Internal combustion engines have terrible thermal efficiency. No more than a third of the potential energy in a gallon of gasoline can be converted into usable mechanical energy. Another third disappears as heat and water vapor out the exhaust—there's typically enough heat energy coming from an automobile engine to heat, in fact, to heat a six-room house in the winter in a cold climate. The final third must be dissipated through the engine cooling system. Engine heat will rapidly destroy the engine unless the cooling system can quickly dissipate heat into the air. Unfortunately, this conflicts with achieving high thermal efficiency for best power and a responsive supercharging system. Heat management can be complex, but there are some tricks to improve the situation without it becoming a zero-sum game.

Maximum power depends on achieving the highest possible cylinder pressure from hot combustion gases, but combustion gases in contact with the cooler metal of the piston and combustion chamber surfaces undergo a "quench" effect, losing heat (and, therefore, pressure) to the cooling and lubrication systems. This reduces power. The more heat that can be kept in the combustion gases without overheating the combustion chambers and piston domes, the higher the power—which is one reason *thermal coatings* are an effective method of making power in a race engine or high-performance street powerplant.

Although it may seem counterintuitive, engine heat management can more effective if you run *hotter* engine coolant. The hotter the coolant is in a liquid-cooled engine compared to the temperature of the ambient air cooling the radiator, the more efficiently the cooling system operates. A 70-degree ambient air stream flowing through the radiator will remove far more heat from 220-degree coolant than it will from 160-degree coolant. A radiator is a heat exchanger, and much more heat gets exchanged as the temperature gap between coolant and air increases.

On the other hand, each 10-degree increase in coolant temperature in the 160- to 180-degree range increases the engine octane number requirement by one number, which then must be lowered by other design countermeasures or the engine will require higher octane fuel (which may not be available or practical). Left unattended, higher combustion chamber temperatures and consequent incipient knock can cause knock sensor systems to retard timing on premium-fuel factory engines and kill power. Retarded timing also tends to further overload the cooling system because fuel is burning longer into the power or even exhaust stroke, thereby delivering additional heating to the water jacket around the exhaust ports and to the exhaust header. Happily, in addition to increasing charge density (which increases power with no adverse side effects), tricks such as cold air intakes, intercoolers, and other charge cooling strategies reduce final combustion temperatures without quenching heat into the cooling system, thus reducing the load on the cooling system and simultaneously reducing the tendency for spark knock. But it's complicated, and many heat-management tactics do have unintended consequences.

A perfect engine cooling system would keep all cylinders and combustion chambers perfectly cooled to the same temperature, but in practice this is rarely possible. This is part of the reason some cylinders run hotter and want to knock more (other common reasons include fuel distribution problems or unequal breathing or volumetric efficiency), which is why really advanced racing engine-management systems provide for individual-cylinder trim of injection pulse width and spark timing.

Modern liquid cooling systems are pressurized by a spring-loaded filler cap that typically maintains up to 22 psi of steam pressure in the system. Pressure raises the boiling point of coolant, helping prevent the formation of steam bubbles and hot spots that reduce thermal transfer properties. When internal pressure exceeds the cap design pressure, coolant escapes into a coolant-recovery tank. Later, when the engine cools and the system loses its pressure, liquid coolant siphons back into the main cooling system. Modified cooling system pressurization specs and coolant recovery system strategies must be carefully designed because loss of hot coolant gases into the recovery system can allow cavitations on the suction side of the water pump.

It can sometimes be a challenge to get enough heat-exchanger real estate for engine radiator, A/C condenser, engine oil cooler, and intercooler water-cooler unit. PES strings together multiple heat exchangers out in front to keep its remote intercooler chilled. *PES*

PES/Setrab aluminum heat exchangers get the heat out of engine oil and air-water intercoolers. Note the cylindrical finned coolers: Every bit helps. *PES*

Radiators

Like many other components on modern passenger cars, the radiator is now carefully designed to meet the performance of a given engine in a given vehicle, and not much more. These days when you hot-rod a factory engine, you may find the cooling system's capacity is quickly used up and the stock cooling system is no longer adequate under critical conditions. Engines that are modified for increased horsepower—with add-on supercharger conversion systems or overboosting tricks—put increased Btu into a cooling system that was not designed for the additional load, so you may have to upgrade the cooling system too. Trucks—even light-duty ones—are typically designed with the reserve capacity to survive greater thermal loading and mechanical stress.

As you might expect, the radiator is the foundation of an engine cooling system. The efficiency of the radiator as a heat exchanger is largely determined by the difference between the air temperature and the temperature of the liquid coolant, though copper radiators are a bit more efficient than aluminum ones. To achieve maximum radiator efficiency, automotive engineers run the highest practical coolant temperature in order to exchange the most heat with the atmosphere, and then run high cooling system pressures and optimized glycol/water ratios in order to keep coolant from boiling when the engine is under heavy load on a hot day.

The mass of air flowing through the radiator is a critical factor in determining its cooling performance. This is a function of (1) vehicle speed through the relative wind, (2) the radiator core's resistance to airflow, (3) the engine compartment's resistance to airflow (if airflow from the radiator continues on through the engine compartment, as is the usual case on front-engine cars), and (4) the efficiency of the fan. Normally, the more air going through the radiator, the better—so cars and trucks have auxiliary fans to improve airflow when the cooling system is stressed.

Any fan consumes power, but thermostatically driven electric fans are now almost universal in cars precisely because an electric fan can be deactivated when coolant exiting the radiator has cooled below a threshold temperature—for example, at cruising speed, or after starting on a cold day. Electric fans do not run when they're not needed, yet they can deliver full airflow even when the engine is idling (or stopped!). Many electric fans move air at 12 to 15 miles per hour, and provide airflow benefits to about 35 to 45 miles per hour, when airflow to the radiator can be hindered by grilles, bumpers, and other obstructions. A typical 12-inch fan draws 10 amps and uses 1/6 horsepower to move 1,000 cfm.

On larger longitudinally mounted engines and in truck applications—where crankshaft-driven fans are still common—fans are designed with built-in viscous clutches that essentially allow the fans to slip or freewheel at higher engine speeds, reducing the power drain. Some engine-driven fans go so far as to deploy a thermostatically controlled fan clutch that ensures the fan never draws more than 1 horsepower or so. Contrast this to an 18-inch engine-driven flex-fan without a clutch, which might draw 1 horsepower at 2,000 rpm, pulling 6,000 cfm, or six times the airflow of an electric fan. At 3,500 rpm, the clutchless flex fan is using 5 horsepower and pulling 30 times the air of an electric fan, and at 5,000 rpm the flex-fan is burning up 9 horsepower!

Radiator designs and materials include copper-brass, aluminum, 1-row core, 2-row core, 3-row core, 4-row core, continuous fin, louvered fin, straight fin, serpentine fin, dimpled tube, cross-flow, down flow, high-efficiency core, 1-pass core, 2-pass core, and so on. Street-machine radiators are constructed from aluminum or copper-brass (many now with plastic end tanks). With excellent thermal transfer capabilities and its light weight, aluminum is the material of choice for race cars.

Good radiator shops and specialty manufacturers can custom-build radiators to your specs for upgraded cooling on over-boosted or blower-conversion engines. Get a 4-row core using 1/2-inch wide tubes spaced at 7/16-inch centers with 14 fins per inch; use the louvered serpentine design with a 2.625-inch core, if possible. If you are willing to hack up the sheet metal of the front bulkhead, it may be possible to install a larger radiator. If you can't increase the frontal area of an existing core, making the radiator core thicker may be the only choice. Most radiator shops have the ability to remove the original core and replace it with a thicker core, often with more rows of tubes. Unfortunately, rearward tubes are cooled with air that has already exchanged heat with the front tubes, so efficiency suffers, and the rear half of the core can only provide 25 percent of the cooling. In some cases, it may be possible to install a second or third auxiliary radiator somewhere on the car.

A simple method of increasing cooling capacity at slow highway speeds is to install more powerful or more efficient fans. It may be possible to install a larger diameter fan or a second or even third electric fan, since factory-original electric fans seldom cover the entire radiator core.

Fans are more efficient when installed on the rear of the radiator. In fact, some experts suggest a 1,000-cfm puller electric fan will out-cool a 1,500-cfm pusher electric fan. Installing *both* front and rear fans can help. Fan blade aerodynamics are important for best efficiency, and in general, the more blades, the better. Curved blades are better, but this design may not be reversible without large efficiency losses. Fans should be mounted with the convex part of the fan blade facing forward, if applicable.

To optimize efficiency, fans should have a close-fitting shroud that ducts air directly to or from the radiator to the fan, preventing the fan from breathing air that did not come through the radiator or allowing a pusher fan's airflow to leak around the radiator. High-performance engines that almost never idle and need maximum cooling at high rpm are an exception. There, a shroud would diminish ambient airflow through the radiator. A shroud covering the entire radiator area may help when cooling power is marginal, although this could hurt airflow through the radiator at high speeds when the fan is not doing much good. Fans with a ring around the outside will give about 3 to 6 percent more cooling; a full shroud delivers about a 5 to 8 percent improvement. The only way to really know what works and what doesn't work is to log data from temperature probes in the inlet and outlet coolant and air streams.

Cars with A/C impose a much greater burden on the radiator. Not only is there additional parasitic drag on the engine, forcing it to work harder, but it has been common practice on many cars to locate the A/C condenser in front of the radiator (though this is less true than it once was). In this case, the A/C condenser not only restricts highway airflow through the radiator but preheats air entering the radiator when the A/C is running (which is the reason why electric fans are automatically activated when you turn on the A/C, with a high-speed "raging" capability for extreme conditions). Where the cooling system is marginal and heavily stressed and you can live without A/C, removing an A/C condenser from in front of the radiator will improve radiator efficiency.

The efficiency of the radiator is further diminished if there is a (hot) intercooler located directly in front of the radiator and A/C condenser, which introduces the double-whammy of diminished ambient airflow through the radiator, and air that has been *heated*. Air-air intercoolers are a more substantial detriment to radiator airflow than A/C condensers, because they are thicker and denser. It can be critically important that the engine cooling system not be degraded at the same time that it must deal with increased thermal loading from the increased horsepower of higher-boost supercharging. Some intercooling systems add a thermostatically controlled fan to improve intercooler efficiency and reduce heat-soak at slower road speeds, but the happiest situation exists where the A/C condenser, radiator, and intercooler are beside rather than in front of each other, or in the case of some rear- or midengine cars, if the intercooler is located far from the radiator, at the rear of the vehicle.

One answer—dealt with in more detail in this chapter's section on intercooling—is to design add-on intercooler systems with a staggered configuration so that there will always be at least some fresh airflow available to the radiator that does not pass through the intercooler (or the water-cooler section of an air-water intercooler). Then upgrade the fans and radiator if necessary so that the engine-cooling system is robust enough to easily handle worst-case conditions. Beyond that, the engine-management system should be designed to handle unusually severe thermal loading by deploying all primary and auxiliary fans at the highest speed, limiting boost, engaging the A/C compressor clutch, and optimizing ignition timing and air-fuel ratios to lower combustion temperatures.

Correctly designed air dams in front of the car tend to help the cooling system by deflecting air upward from the road toward the grille and radiator, increasing the air pressure at the front of the radiator.

Other heat exchangers that provide auxiliary cooling for oil, transmission fluid, and the intake charge all help take heat out of the engine. They will help the radiator do its job as long as these heat exchangers are separate units that do not interfere with the radiator cooling system or use engine coolant as the cooling medium (which will *increase* the thermal loading on the radiator and engine-cooling system).

All these factors must be considered when computing engine-cooling requirements. But what are the cooling requirements of an engine? One horsepower-minute requires 10,686 scientific (not weight loss) calories of energy. A horsepower-second requires 178.1 calories, but due to inefficiencies, multiply this by three in terms of heat yield. A working 1-horsepower powerplant therefore expends three million calories in about 90 minutes, assuming 33 percent efficiency, and two-thirds of this is waste heat. A gallon of gasoline, with roughly 115,000 Btu or 30 million calories, will make 45 horsepower for an hour or 54,000 horsepower for three seconds, at 100 percent efficiency. At 33 percent efficiency, a 100-horsepower engine—or a 100-horsepower increase to an existing engine—expends 7,666,665 Btu of energy in an hour, of which 5,111,135 is waste heat per hour, or 1,420 Btu of waste heat per second. Of this, half must be dealt with by the radiator, indicating the power boost demands an additional additional 710 Btu/sec of radiator capacity. What this translates to in terms of additional radiator capacity for a supercharging conversion project is a judgment call based on the reserve capacity of the stock radiator, the estimated amount of time spent under boost, the type of application, the space available for a radiator upgrade, and so forth. Actual testing will reveal the truth.

Water Pumps

Racers and car builders routinely design or redesign the way coolant moves through a competition powerplant. Most hot rodders, on the other hand, will not ever attempt to modify and upgrade the engine's stock water pump and coolant circulatory system. This is one more reason why many blower-conversion or overboosted vehicles often do not have sufficiently robust cooling system power to maintain thermal homeostasis during boosted conditions in hot weather for more than a brief period.

Installing water pressure gauges in the engine and radiator is a great way to discover how good a job your water pump and thermostat are doing at getting a lot of water into your engine at high pressure. Bonneville land-speed record holder Bob Norwood likes to see 40-psi internal pressure in the cooling system of a serious high-performance engine, because high pressure helps prevent bubbles and scrubs steam bubbles out of the coolant as they form, producing better thermal transfer.

To pressurize the cooling system, the engine *requires* a restriction to permit the water pump to build pressure in the engine water jacket, making the thermostat and thermostat bypass size a critical aspect of the pressurizing strategy. Never remove the thermostat, unless you're replacing it with a restrictor. Removing the thermostat lowers the block pressure, and could lower the water level in the heads or intake, creating serious hot spots. Running without a thermostat also effectively puts the coolant temperature out of control, which is certainly not desirable. NASCAR racers take the thermostat out of an engine and replace it with a 3/8-inch restrictor orifice.

Thermostat bypasses are necessary, but they ultimately reduce the efficiency of the cooling system by allowing a percentage of coolant to circulate that does not go through the radiator at all. Once the engine is up to operating temperature and the thermostat is open or partially open, the bypass becomes superfluous or even detrimental to efficient cooling. If maximum cooling capacity is critical, installing a temperature-controlled valve in the bypass line to close it completely on a warm engine will help (Ferrari does this on some engines).

Water pumps can be overdriven with a smaller pump pulley or a larger crank pulley (which will then overdrive all accessories that are driven from the crank). Although this strategy will consume more horsepower, combined with the right thermostat or restrictor, it could improve cooling. The reverse—underdriving accessories—is a common hot rodding tactic to allow an engine to make additional power by removing parasitic drag.

Racer supply shops sell battery- or alternator-driven electric water pumps for drag racing use or other situations when the goal is to completely eliminate parasitic drag from the water pump. The right electrical control system will allow regulation of water pump speed by regulating voltage to the electric motor, which could be managed under the control of the main EMS.

Engine Coolant

Water has better thermal transfer capabilities than antifreeze or even a mixture of antifreeze and water. For this reason, racers commonly use pure water (or water with an anti-surface tension product like Red Line's Watter Wetter) as the coolant. Watter Wetter is designed to reduce the surface tension of water around steam bubbles, allowing bubbles to be purged faster and more easily from the cooling system.

Street vehicles need the anti-rust, anti-corrosion, and anti-deposit properties of ethylene or propylene glycol antifreeze, and in cold climates you need to protect your block from freezing. The freezing and boiling point curve of various water and antifreeze mixtures is bell-shaped; that is, a mixture of the two is better than either alone at preventing freezing and boil-over. For best cooling, however, it is better to use the *minimum* antifreeze needed to prevent freezing for the best thermal conductivity—and then to pressurize the cooling system to fight boil-over problems.

If you're doing a supercharger conversion on a used vehicle, it is possible that the cooling system may not have been maintained properly or that someone might have abused it with such things as anti-leak additives. If there are any doubts about whether the radiator is operating at full efficiency, remove it and have it flushed by professionals, who will remove the end tanks and push cleaning rods through the cores and then reattach the tanks or replace the core assembly with a brand new one. Life is too short to fuss with cooling problems on a supercharged engine.

Engine Cooling and Detonation

In spite of the thermal transfer advantages of a high-temp cooling system, you may have a knock problem that requires everything you can throw at it (and most gasoline-fueled street powerplants are knock-limited). You may need to run a lower temperature thermostat to fight knock with increased combustion chamber quench (which is usually more efficient than pulling ignition timing). In this case it is critical to install a thermostat that permits the engine to run hot enough to allow the EFI warmup enrichment algorithm to terminate before the engine is as warm as it can get. Alternatively, modify the EMS with recalibration or an interceptor to end warmup enrichment at a cooler temperature.

If you are running high-boost supercharging on a spark-ignition engine and must burn street gasoline, you'll be fighting detonation with all weapons at your disposal. In this case you might want to consider designing a reverse-flow cooling system, which can be a significant anti-knock countermeasure that permits running higher boost, or more timing advance, or a higher geometric compression ratio—or some of all three. On a conventional cooling system, freshly chilled coolant is generally sucked into the block from the bottom of the radiator through a noncollapsible metal-reinforced rubber hose that attaches to the water pump. Coolant flows through the water pump and into the block water jacket, where it flows among the various cylinder barrels and upward through passages in the head gasket and into the cylinder head, exiting the head through a housing containing the thermostat, from which the coolant flows through a hose that dumps into the top of the radiator.

This is all well and fine, but from a performance point of view on boosted spark-ignition engines this is precisely the wrong direction. Ideally, freshly chilled coolant should be pumped from the radiator bottom outlet directly to the cylinder heads, where a cooler water jacket lowers the octane number requirement of the engine by keeping charge gases below auto-ignition temperature as combustion proceeds. From there, partially warmed coolant should flow downward into the block to cool the cylinders, which will make more power when running hotter due to reduced quenching of combustion gases. At this point, hot water exits the block through a thermostat housing for the return to the radiator inlet in the top tank.

Reverse-cooling has been used on some mass-production engines, such as the second-generation port-EFI V-8 engines used in the C4 Corvette and high-performance Camaros and Firebirds built from 1993 to 1997. The LT-1 cooling system has a significantly more complex design and plumbing than traditional flow systems, with rigorous air and vapor venting procedures mandatory on fill-up and during routine maintenance. Because of this, the GM system turned out to be problematic when owner-operators did not follow correct fill-up procedures. GM abandoned reverse-flow cooling in the newer LS1 engine.

Nonetheless, the LT-1 'Vette is an excellent example that illustrates how to implement reverse-flow engine cooling. The biggest challenge in building a roll-your-own system will almost definitely be relocating or replacing the stock belt-driven water pump, but there are now some in-line electric water pumps available that could make this much simpler. It is important to realize that scratch-built reverse-flow cooling is for experts or hot rodders with good fabrication skills, and plenty of time, patience, and money for experimentation.

PISTON COOLING AND HEATING

Pistons are subject to tremendous thermal and mechanical forces in any high-performance engine, and they are the Achilles' heel of a supercharged powerplant, particularly if it's a blower conversion of a stock normal-charged powerplant. Pistons operate at an average piston-crown temperature of about 600 degrees F. Ideally, piston temperature should be no higher on a supercharged engine, but sometimes it will be. Supercharged factory engines are virtually always equipped with more robust pistons than lower-output normal-charged versions of the same powerplant. This is partly to provide (some) insurance against immediate catastrophic mechanical damage if detonation occurs, but also to survive routinely greater thermal loading. Unfortunately, there are some tradeoffs between piston strength and thermal expansion characteristics.

Pistons appropriate for a high-boost forced-induction engine are designed with exceptionally robust ring land geometry and then manufactured from strong aluminum forgings or T6 hypereutectic alloy rather than ordinary cast aluminum. Forged pistons are rough-cast and then, while hot, are compressed under tremendous pressure in a mechanical die using a hydraulic press to build strength by forcing out undesirable porosity and compacting the alloy grains to maximum tightness. The forging process adds to the complexity of manufacturing, making them more expensive. Forged pistons built from 2618 and 4032 aluminum alloys are strong—and thus excellent for application on high-revving engines where lightweight pistons are critical to limiting the tremendous compression and tensile inertial forces to a manageable level.

Unfortunately, forged pistons tend to have increased thermal expansion properties, requiring greater piston-cylinder clearances for the cold-fit, which then results in increased piston-slap until the engine warms up, producing noise, faster wear, and higher HC emissions. This is acceptable for competition engines but makes forged pistons less desirable for mass-production factory powerplants.

A Weiand-supercharged Chevy small-block. There's no intercooler, but the rotors in this type of blower are cooled by a combination of fresh air, vaporizing fuel, and oil cooled by heater-exchanger at lower right. *Holley*

On the other hand, the strength and expansion characteristic of a piston can be heavily modified by adding a portion of silicon to the aluminum alloy. Forged pistons may have varying percentages of silicon melted into the aluminum alloy, which remains a normal *eutectic* alloy until the silicon content goes above 12 percent, at which point the alloy as a whole no longer has the lowest freezing point of any of its constituents. At this point, additional blended silicon will have a higher melting point than the aluminum alloy and thus retain a granular structure that redefines the alloy as "hypereutectic." The strongest forged pistons are built from 2618 alloy, which has only 2 percent silicon, but this alloy requires large piston-cylinder wall clearance to accommodate the high thermal expansion. On the other hand, 4032 alloy contains 11 percent silicon, and thus has less thermal expansion than 2618 but is still less brittle and more flexible than high-silicon hypereutectic alloys. Newer design tricks, such as a slightly "oval" piston profile, with the wider radius 90 degrees from the wrist pin, have mitigated the thermal expansion problems of forgings in some designs.

Hypereutectic pistons, with silicon content in the 12 to 19 percent range, have the lowest thermal expansion and reduced heat transfer properties due to the granular structure of excessive silicon dispersed throughout the aluminum alloy. Hypereutectic pistons are weaker in general than forgings, but can be pressure-cast for added strength. T6 hypereutectic alloys in particular are extremely hard and thus actually have superior strength to forgings in the vulnerable piston ring land areas that are subject to shock damage from detonation—a highly desirable characteristic for spark-ignition supercharged powerplants.

Virtually all modern factory-blown engines provide supplemental piston cooling via pressurized oil squirters aimed at the undersides of the pistons. There are many good reasons for keeping the pistons as cool as possible in a high-performance boosted engine, the most obvious one being that aluminum loses strength as it gets hotter. In some engines, oil squirts upward at each piston from a tiny orifice in the side of the connecting rod. This hole will be a few hundredths of an inch in diameter and is machined straight through to the big-end journal, where oil enters through a matching hole in the bearing shell. In other engines, oil-squirter fittings in the block plumb directly into an oil gallery, with one or two oil jets aimed upward at the underside of each piston. Oil-cooling can lower the temperature of the piston crown significantly, with the secondary effect of lowering combustion temperature and EGT.

Oil squirters are excellent for supercharged street cars, but they are scorned by some expert competition engine builders who do not like anything that increases the power-robbing windage of air, blowby combustion gases, and lubricant flying around the crankcase at high rpm that inevitably exerts a drag on engine movement. The crankshaft weights plow through the storm of fluids and gases inside the engine, and pistons force the airborne contents of the crankcase to surge back and forth between cylinders as they move up and down. Some builders of super-high-output engines also prefer not to compromise the integrity of the connecting rods by machining even tiny passages through them (the simplest way to implement add-on piston oil-cooling). In any case, any engine builder who *is* installing supplemental oil-squirters or a supercharger oil supply must verify there is sufficient surplus oil pump capacity to maintain minimum acceptable oil pressure at idle. A higher-capacity oil pump, or a reworked pump that has had the pressure-relief spring replaced or shimmed to jack up pressure, could be necessary in a few cases.

Many high-tech performance engine builders believe in coating forced-induction piston crowns with a ceramic thermal coating to insulate pistons from damage due to overheating. Coatings reduce engine oil temperatures by reducing the thermal loading on oil being used to cool the pistons. They can make power by keeping the heat in the combustion chambers. If a thermal barrier is used to coat the combustion chamber surfaces of the head, it will help keep heat out of the cooling system by insulating the head from hot combustion gases—which increases the thermal efficiency of the engine. Thermal-coated combustion chambers achieve higher combustion pressure by dramatically reducing the quench effect on combustion gases through the piston crown and other combustion chamber surfaces, which is both good and bad. Higher temperature combustion gases make power by producing higher cylinder pressures, but hotter combustion is a pro-knock factor, since heat that is not quenched into the water jacket stays in the combustion charge, which could auto-ignite and explode if pressure and temperature get too high as combustion proceeds. On the other hand, cooler combustion chamber surfaces reduce the possibility of pre-ignition from hot spots in the combustion chamber.

COOLING THE OIL

Every supercharged engine should have an oil cooler. As long as oil is above 150 degrees F, colder oil performs better as a lubricant and helps protect critical parts from overheating. Should the oil heat exchanger be cooled directly by ambient air (or water in the case of marine engines), or cooled by engine coolant that is, in turn, cooled by the radiator?

Some factory forced-induction engines control oil temperature by routing oil into a liquid-to-liquid heat exchanger that is cooled by radiator coolant (or *heated* during engine warmup, if the cooler is part of the coolant bypass circuit). In such cases, radiator coolant that has already traveled through the engine is typically diverted to a small heat exchanger sandwiched between the oil filter and the engine block, and from there back into the cooling system. In other cases, it is the oil that is diverted out of the engine on its way in or out of the oil filter to an oil cooler siamesed to the coolant tank of the radiator, and from there back to the engine oiling system.

One innovation on later forced-induction GM Ecotec fours was a thermal coating on the piston tops and combustion chambers. This was once an exotic Formula-1-type racing trick, but no more. *General Motors*

The advantages of a coolant-based engine oil cooler is that coolant temperature (and, thus, the oil temperature) is controlled by a sophisticated factory thermostatic system designed to get the coolant heated as fast as possible to operating temperature and keep it within a narrow temperature range under the most extreme conditions using a robust air-cooled radiator system augmented with features like multiple variable-speed fans. If the engine oil is tied into this system with a liquid-cooled heat exchanger, it too will heat quickly and then remain at a moderate equilibrium temperature once the engine is hot. As long as the thermal loading from the engine remains within the performance envelope of the cooling system for the prevailing weather conditions—in other words, as long as the cooling system is not overwhelmed by weather and high supercharged horsepower—radiator-cooled engine oil has a high likelihood of remaining at a dependable temperature specification.

By contrast, oil pumped through its own auxiliary air-cooled heat exchanger will not necessarily have its temperature thermostatically controlled with a cooler-bypass arrangement (though it should!). In this case, the efficiency of oil cooling will vary, depending on ambient air temperature and the temperature of oil as it enters the oil cooler, with a greater temperature differential producing greater cooling efficiency. An unregulated air-cooled oil heat exchanger has the adverse effect of adding to the time it takes engine oil to reach operating temperature, particularly in cold weather, reducing engine efficiency during warmup and possibly increasing engine wear.

Unfortunately, cooling the oil with the engine's cooling system definitely increases the thermal load on the cooling system. In fact, cooling engine oil through the radiator could cause the cooling system temperature to rise to undesirable super-normal levels or even overheat to catastrophic levels at high boost or in hot weather. If the cooling system is already marginal, or if the radiator has diminished power because airflow is pre-warmed by an intercooler, isolating the oil cooling system from the coolant cooling system will not only lower the burden on the main radiator system, but will actually relieve stress on the cooling system by helping to cool the engine with oil via the additional heat-exchanger capacity of the oil-cooler.

Although the thermal transfer properties of a liquid are superior to a gas, even in hot weather ambient air is much cooler than engine coolant, so air cooling the oil can be very effective. Obviously, cooling oil with ambient sea water is tremendously effective for marine applications.

Regardless of whether engine oil is cooled by a dedicated cooler or by dissipation via the surface of the oil pan, greater engine oil capacity is beneficial in giving the oil a longer average "rest" before it is sucked back into the oil pump and heated during the next trip through the engine. This is why large commercial engines sometimes have tremendous engine oil capacities, with some large railway locomotive diesel engines hauling around 500 gallons of oil, which is 11 gallons of oil for each 100 horsepower of capacity on a typical 4,400-horsepower EMD locomotive. A large oil capacity is a great idea when the engine must work hard with high reliability. Unfortunately, many modern factory automotive engines have a stock capacity of only about 1 gallon of oil.

Performance and racing powerplants usually carry more oil, even at the added cost of the additional weight of the oil (a gallon of oil weighs about 7 pounds). If the engine has a dry-sump crankcase, all oil that drains to the bottom of the engine is removed immediately with a special pump all capable of scavenging enough crankcase gases to produce a partial vacuum in the crankcase. Oil scavenged from the sump flows to a remote external oil reserve tank, from which a separate and lower-capacity oil pump constantly draws oil to pressurize the engine with fresh oil. A dry-sump oiling system permits a large oil reservoir, since it does not have to fit in the engine.

The Ecotec engine in Pontiac's Solstice Turbo used piston-cooling oil-squirters to lower the temperature of the piston crown. *General Motors*

Even if the engine has an ordinary wet sump oiling system, there may be aftermarket deep-sump oil pans available with extra oil capacity if it is a common performance engine. If not, if there is space underneath the stock oil pan, increasing the oil capacity simply requires installing a custom spacer plate between the oil pan and block or extending the pan downward (or sideways) through modification by a welding and fabrication shop. Additional oil can then be added until it reaches the proper level on the dipstick. This same method can potentially be used to *lower* the oil level in the sump a few inches if a supercharger with external oiling cannot be elevated enough above the stock oil level to permit proper oil drainage downhill from the supercharger oil drain fitting to the air space in the sump. In this case, the oil capacity would not be increased, so the dipstick would have to be extended and recalibrated to reflect the new oil level. Obviously, it is critical that the oil pickup be extended downward commensurate with the new sump level.

ENGINE COMPARTMENT COOLING AND EXHAUST HEATING

Power is heat, and superchargers make power. As long as the cooling system is effective, a liquid-cooled engine itself will stay at less than 220 degrees, but when the system is making boost, heat pours into the exhaust manifold or headers, radiating heat into the engine compartment at a furious rate. This is not a good thing.

Despite its advantages, insulating exhaust pipes should never be attempted unless the wrapped parts are made from stainless steel or preferably Inconel (a nickel-based austenitic iron superalloy of high-carbon steel used

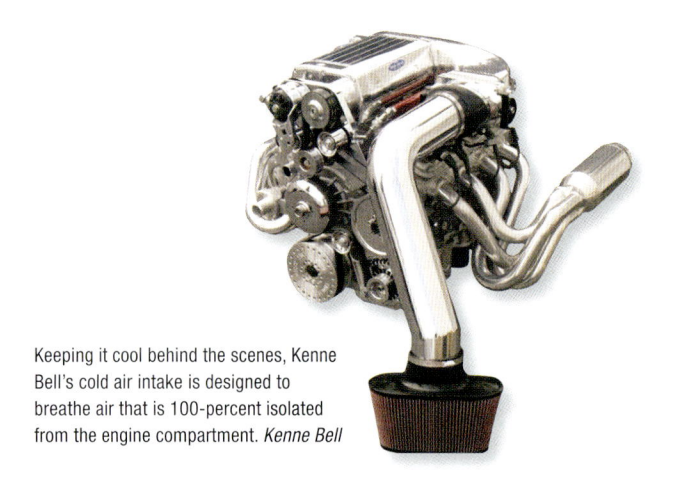

Keeping it cool behind the scenes, Kenne Bell's cold air intake is designed to breathe air that is 100-percent isolated from the engine compartment. *Kenne Bell*

in the space program for rocket and reentry parts that had to survive extreme heat with high reliability). Toyota has installed welded stainless headers on some mass-production engines, with the headers surrounded by a composite package of insulation-inside-molded-sheet-steel stampings that provide an additional thermal barrier and contain and protect the insulation.

The ideal solution is to insulate the *inside* of the exhaust plumbing. Jet-Hot, HPC, and some other outfits have the capability to dip or spray and bake-on ceramic coatings that are robust enough to survive on the exterior of a turbine housing. The insides of exhaust pipes can be dipped and coated, which will provide a significant thermal barrier that insulates the pipe from heat on the inside, keeping the heat inside the exhaust and out of the pipes and engine compartment. Coating the

The BEGi S2000 turbo system makes extensive use of heat shields to keep heat out of the engine compartment and protect vulnerable or heat-sensitive components like the A/C lines near the battery and fusebox.

outside of pipes provides additional insulation at the cost of higher thermal loading.

The best way to prevent heat damage to delicate parts in the engine compartment of street-type supercharger conversions is to build heat shields next to or around hot parts where they are in close proximity to parts that might be damaged or burned by overheating—and then make sure there is a good way for heat to escape the engine compartment—which, in some cases, could mean installing louvers in sheet metal or providing other mechanisms to scavenge hot air from the engine compartment. The OE plastic or sheet-metal panels, scoops, and air dams at the bottoms of some engines are not just there to keep water-splash out of the engine compartment, but also to enhance ventilation through the engine compartment. Some factory cars have used thermostatically controlled electric fans to suck fresh air into the engine compartment *through* an air-air intercooler, which not only enhances cooling power in the intercooler when the vehicle is moving slowly but forcibly ventilates the engine compartment if it starts to overheat.

With up to 900-horsepower worth of heat pouring out of this supercharged speed-record racer, builders of the Kugel '32 Hiboy Roadster insulated things that were hot (headers), and things that should stay cool (hoses). *Magnuson Products*

Heat soak is worse than you think, and you don't want engine heat to turn your charge-cooler into an "inter-heater". The Vortech supercharging system on the author's Chevy LT1 project is kept cool on the Kim Barr Racing Superflow by Vortech insulating jackets that snap around the air-cooler unit and discharge ducting.

Counterintuitively, exhaust plumbing with thicker walls—such as thick castings—has *better* thermal transfer capability than thinner stainless-steel tubing, which, by the way, also happens to have relatively low thermal conductivity, which is always a good thing unless you want to sink heat. Thicker metal transfers heat faster, and the larger outside diameter of thicker plumbing has more surface area in contact with air, giving it greater ability to radiate heat. Header pipes should never be smaller than the exhaust runners, but oversized pipes will leak more heat as well as lower exhaust energy by reducing the velocity of exhaust gases. Collector pipes should never provide a flow area that's greater than the runners being collected for the same reasons. Anything that can be done to improve the internal aerodynamics of the exhaust system via smooth, nonturbulent exhaust flow will not only improve the exhaust flow rate but help prevent hot spots in the exhaust system that leak heat egregiously. Log-type exhaust manifolds that tee exhaust runners into a perpendicular collector pipe that forces exhaust to negotiate sharp 90-degree bends are a particularly flagrant example of what not to do.

The author's turbo Honda Del Sol with turbo heat shield and extensive insulation around the Perkins refrigerated intercooler. Michael Perkins' charge cooling system was designed to deliver 7-psi boost at 45 degrees to the 1.6-liter SOHC VTEC powerplant.

Cold-air versus hot-air intake: They both look great, but there is no getting around the fact that breathing some or all intake air from the engine compartment is going to raise combustion temperatures above what they'd be if you started with cool ambient air—regardless of the effectiveness of the intercooling system. *Magnuson Products*

INTERCOOLER SIZING

Whatever type of intercooler you're using must provide the following:

The intercooler system must be a large enough "pipe," meaning it must have a large enough internal flow area through the air-cooler core to accommodate the maximum mass airflow under-peak conditions so the charge air makes it through with little or no pressure drop.

It must also have enough counter-flow area so enough coolant can move through fast enough to achieve the required thermal effectiveness. The type of coolant will have a large effect; water, for example, has 14 times the thermal conductivity of air.

The coolant-cooler must be large and effective enough to keep the coolant and the air-cooler from heat-soaking.

It must be effective enough to reduce the charge temperature to avoid knock in a spark-ignition engine, given the available cooling medium temperature.

It must be effective enough to reduce the temperature to make the power requirements for the engine.

It must fit in the space available.

These goals may conflict with each other.

1. Start by calculating the airflow requirements for the engine at the required horsepower as follows:

AF = HP × AFR × BSFC / 60

Where:
AF = Actual mass airflow in pounds per minute
HP = Target flywheel horsepower
AFR = Air-fuel ratio
BSFC = Brake specific fuel consumption

Assume the goal is 400 horsepower with an air-fuel ratio of 12.0 and use a BSFC of 0.55. Applying these numbers to the above formula:

AF = HP × AFR × BSFC / 60

= 400 × 12 × 0.55 / 60 = 44.0 lb/min of air

2. Calculate the heat content of the charge coming from the compressor that must be removed to achieve a target intercooler-out temperature.

Btu in the heat from 44 lb/min charge headed toward the engine at 31.5-psi boost at a temperature of 329 degrees F as follows:

T_{2c} = 530 + (((530 × 3.14$^{.283}$)) - 530) / .78)
= 789R
= 789 – 460
= 329 F

Assume that the goal is an intercooler-out charge temperature of 100 degrees F. The heat energy in Btu that must be removed by the intercooler is:

Qload = W × Cp × (T_{out} - T_{in})

Where:
Q_{load} = Cooling load in Btu per hour
W = Rate of airflow = 44 lb/min
Cp = Specific heat of air = .241 Btu/lb degrees F
T_{in} = Inlet air temperature = 329F
T_{out} = Outlet temperature of air exiting heat exchanger = 100F

Then:
Q_{load} = W × Cp × (T_{out} - T_{in})
= 44 × .241 × (100 - 329)
= -2428 Btu/min
= 2428 × 60 = 145,700 Btu/hr

Just so you know, a Btu stands for British Thermal Units (even though the British are now on the metric system, where they talk about joules; BTU are used only in the United States anymore). One Btu is an amount of heat energy that can raise the temperature of 1 pound of water by 1 degree Fahrenheit.

3. Calculate the internal flow area required in any intercooler system air-cooler core to avoid significant charge pressure drop through the intercooler:

Assume that every 10 horsepower requires a pound of air (this typically ranges between 9.5–10.5 hp/lb).

Bell Intercoolers recommends the rule of thumb of a *minimum* of 6 to 7 square inches of internal intercooler flow area for every 100 horsepower, with up to 40 percent more area needed for intercooler cores with really dense internal finning. Assuming 7, and bringing the numbers together, then

A_{req} = (HP / 100) × 7

Where:
A_{req} = area required to flow air with low pressure drop (in2)
HP = flywheel horsepower

The new (combined) formula is thus:

A_{req} = HP × 7/100
= HP × 0.07

Assuming the engine will make 400 horsepower,

A_{req} = HP × 0.07
= 400 × .07
= 28 in^2

The rule thus says there should be a minimum requirement of 28 square-inches of internal intercooler core flow area, but adding a 40 percent margin for dense cores, the requirement could actually be as much as 40 in^2.

If this were a pipe, how big would it be? Not as big as you think, because only 45 percent of the core will be available for airflow (the rest is metal or dedicated to coolant flow). Therefore:

A_{actual} = .45 × 28
= 12.6 in^2 (40 percent margin makes this 18!)

The equivalent pipe size is:

D_{pipe} = 2 × SQR [A_{actual} / π]

Where:
D_{pipe} = Required pipe diameter for airflow
SQR = Square root of [quantity]
A_{actual} = Actual flow area of intercooler core
π = Ratio of circumference of a circle to the diameter, ≈ 3.141592654, use π key

Contiued on page 148

INTERCOOLER SIZING Continued on from page 147

Plugging in the numbers:

$D_{pipe} = 2 \times SQR\ [A_{actual} / \pi]$
$= 2 \times SQR\ [12.6 / \pi]$
$= 2 \times SQR\ [4]$
$= 4.0$ inch

This is a 4-inch diameter pipe. Why so large? Because the intercooler is loaded with fins and turbulators that facilitate thermal transfer but really interfere with airflow. Smooth piping of 2.5 to 3.0 inches inside diameter would certainly suffice for ducting air to and from the intercooler.

If you repeat the same calculations but assume a dense core of 18 in^2:

$D_{pipe} = 2 \times SQR\ [A_{actual} / \pi]$
$= 2 \times SQR\ [18 / \pi]$
≈ 4.8 inch

To summarize, the internal flow area in the core needs to be 28 to 40 square inches.

4. Calculate the air-cooler charge-flow core size that achieves the required charge flow area:

If this is an ordinary air-cooled intercooler, then the core thickness is typically available in 2- and 3-inch sizes.

A 2-inch core typically has better thermal efficiency for a given area. From the estimated area of 28 to 40 square inches we calculate the core width as follows:

Width = Core area / core thickness

$= 28 / 2$

$= 14$ inches

Alternately,

Width = Core area / core thickness

$= 40 / 2$

$= 20$ inches

To flow sufficient hot pressurized charge air with negligible pressure drop, the 2-inch core needs to be somewhere between 14 and 20 inches wide.

For a 3-inch core:

Width = Core area / core thickness

$= 28 / 3$

$= 9.33$ inches

or

Width = Core area / core thickness

$= 40 / 3$

$= 13.33$ inches

To flow sufficient hot pressurized charge air with negligible pressure drop, the 3-inch core needs to be somewhere between 9.3 and 13.3 inches wide.

This is true regardless of the intercooler type or coolant, because it simply represents the minimum area needed to get the charge through without a pressure drop. It is only a rule of thumb.

Let's assume we'll be using the worst-case 2-inch core, which is 20 inches wide.

5. Calculate the frontal area required to remove the calculated charge heat:

This is heavily dependent on the type of coolant, its thermal transfer coefficient, and the volume of coolant moving through the core per unit of time. The thermodynamics can get complicated, and there are always many assumptions: How fast is the coolant moving through the air-cooler? How cold is the coolant? What type of coolant is it? How much heat transfer surface area exits in the air-cooler core per volume of core?

But let's work through an example. Once again, we are trying to calculate the size of the intercooler needed to remove the heat from supercharging a 2.0-liter engine to 400 horsepower, where the air is leaving the compressor at a rate of 44 lb/min at 329 degrees F. We want air to leave the intercooler cooled to 100 degrees F. We are planning to remove 145,700 BTU per hour from the charge.

We'll need estimates for some parameters:

- Heat transfer surface area per volume of intercooler core
- Heat transfer coefficient from the charge air to the coolant

You'll need to get the first from the manufacturer or supplier of the intercooler cores.

You'll need to supply some data to the vendor for them to provide the second: The heat transfer coefficient is available based on the velocities of the charge and coolant through the core, and the geometric coefficient of the heat-exchanger core. The charge mass can be calculated as we did a moment ago (44 lb/min). The charge area through the core we've already calculated for negligible pressure drop (40 in^2). Intercooler vendors such as Bell Intercoolers have computer programs that can calculate the charge speed. If the coolant is road-draft air, that speed will vary all over the place, depending on the speed of the vehicle. If the coolant is water, the flow capacity of the pump and the volume of the air-cooler water jacket determine the water coolant speed through the core as above. In any case, all this will add up to a certain thermal transfer coefficient.

For the purposes of this calculation, I'm assuming the intercooler is an air-water unit, with a thermal transfer coefficient between the two fluids of 12.2 (that assumes 30 miles per hour air).

I'm assuming that the core will have 23 in^2 of thermal transfer surface per in^3 of core volume.

I'm assuming that the water coolant temperature is 70 degrees F.

Intercooler internal surface area required to achieve the required charge cooling can be expressed as:

$$A = Q_{rate} / (U \times Qm)$$

Where:
A = Radiator's heat transfer area (dependent upon the length, width, and number of fins and tubes)
Q_{rate} = Rate of heat transfer between fluids = **145,700 BTU/hr**

Contiued on page 149

INTERCOOLER SIZING *Continued on from page 148*

U = Overall heat transfer coefficient, determined by the air velocity and geometric coefficient of the radiator core, as well as the water velocity through the tubes = **12.2**

Q_m = Temperature difference between average charge and water coolant = **329F − 70F = 259F**

Plugging in the numbers:

$A = Q_{rate} / (U \times Q_m)$

$= 145{,}700 / (12.2 \times 259)$

$= 46.1 \text{ ft}^2$

$46.1 \times 144 \text{ (in}^2/\text{ft}^2\text{)} = \mathbf{6{,}640 \text{ in}^2}$

A suitable intercooler must have 6,640 square inches of internal heat transfer surface.

Since my estimate is that there are 23.0 square inches of internal heat transfer surface per cubic inch of intercooler core volume,

6,640 / 23 = 289 cubic inches of core required.

But we have already decided we need 40 square inches of area for the charge to flow through the core with negligible pressure drop, so

289 / 40 = 7.2

Assuming our assumptions are correct, a 2-inch-thick-by-20-inch-wide water-cooled intercooler needs to be at least 7.2 inches high. We could pick a core 8, 10, or 12 inches high.

This is still rather compact, but an air-air intercooler would have to be much larger, because the heat transfer coefficient would be much less favorable.

(Cores, by the way, are usually available in rather short 6- to 12-inch air-channel lengths, but you wouldn't want them any longer, because air cools as it moves through the channels, and the cooling efficiency degrades tremendously as the charge temperature approaches the coolant temperature as it moves through the air channels.)

7. For an air-air intercooler (or an air-cooled water-cooler unit in an air-water intercooler system) in a moving vehicle, available airflow through an intercooler can be calculated roughly as follows:

$AF_{cfm} = Area_{IC} \times Speed$

Where:
AF_{cfm} = Airflow (cfm)
$Area_{IC}$ = Intercooler frontal area (ft^2)
Speed = Vehicle speed in ft/min

Suppose we installed an intercooler 24 inches wide and 12 inches deep. This is 288 in^2.

Since each square foot is 144 square inches, our 240 in^2 core converts as follows:

$Area_{sqft} = 288 / 144$

$= 2.0 \text{ (ft}^2\text{)}$

Suppose the vehicle is moving at 100 miles per hour. We need to convert that to feet per minute as follows:

$Speed = MPH \times 5{,}280 / 60$

$= 100 \times 5{,}280 / 60$

$= 8{,}800 \text{ ft/min}$

Plugging in the numbers generated from 100 miles per hour speed and 2 square-feet frontal coolers,

$AF_{cfm} = Area_{IC} \times speed$
$= 2.0 \times 8{,}800$
$= 17{,}600 \text{ cfm}$

Compared to still air, which is a rather good insulator, ambient airflow through the engine compartment will suck heat out of hot exhaust components, but it can also prevent heat damage to sensitive components in the engine compartment. In one project car I replaced a melted speedo cable five or six times because the cable was too close to a turbine housing. The cable location was actually fine while the car was moving or in cooler weather, but the plastic sheathing couldn't withstand being stuck in traffic on a hot summer day in Texas. Escalating insulation efforts inevitably failed. Installing an electrical fan to blow air at the cable and turbine housing was a workable solution until I redesigned the turbo system for other reasons and eliminated the problem by relocating the turbocharger.

It is fairly common to see wastegate housings with cooling fins, which dissipate heat like the fins on the cylinders of air-cooled bike engines. Obviously, hot exhaust on its way out the wastegate is no longer precious, but a finned wastegate might act as a heat sink to steal energy from the exhaust even when the gate is closed—and simultaneously heat up the engine compartment.

COMBUSTION COOLING

The combustion temperature of diesel and spark-ignition engines is critically important in making maximum power without damaging the engine. The parameters that affect combustion temperature are (1) charge temperature when air leaves the compressor or intercooler, (2) air-fuel ratio (spark-ignition engines) or air-surplus (diesel engines), (3) ignition timing (spark ignition) or injection timing (diesel engines), (4) compression ratio, (5) piston-cooling techniques, (6) exhaust backpressure, and (7) combustion chamber design (ceramic thermal coatings, coolant jacket design, and so on).

Test 1000

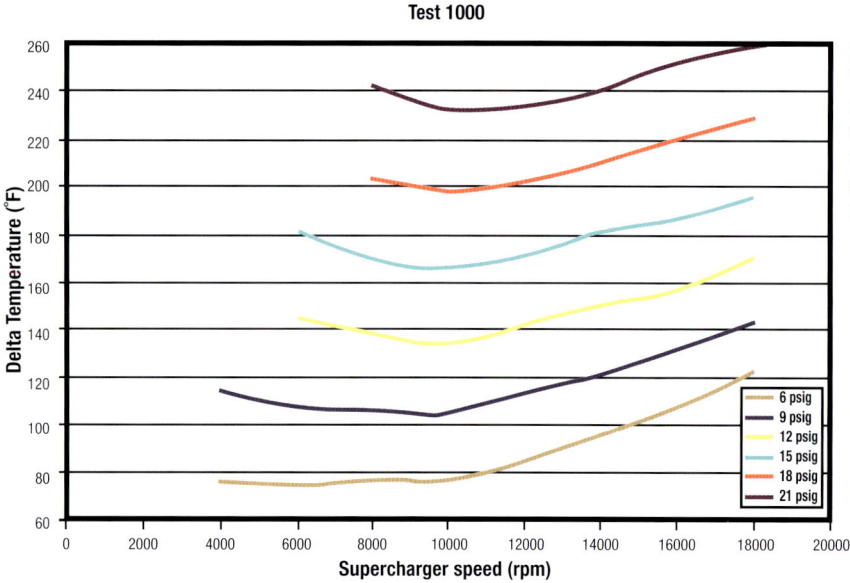

MAGNUSON PRODUCTS 2300 SUPERCHARGER DELTA TEMPERATURE: Magnuson TVS 2300 supercharger discharge temperature increases at 6-, 9-, 12-, 15-, 18-, and 21-psi boost. The increase is dramatic and fairly linear, though you can see that the supercharger gains efficiency between 8,000 and 12,000 rpm, particularly at higher boost. *Magnuson Products*

HOW TO CALCULATE INTERCOOLER THERMAL EFFECTIVENESS

The *effectiveness* of a heat exchanger is a measure of how efficient the heat exchanger is at cooling a hot fluid down to the temperature of the cooling medium. If the hot pressurized air exiting a compressor discharge is 200 degrees F, and the ambient air used as the cooling medium in an air-air intercooler is 100 degrees F, an intercooler with 100 percent effectiveness would cool the hot charge air 100 percent of the way back down to 100 degrees F.

Assume that you measure charge air entering an intercooler at 200 degrees F and leaving it at 130 degrees, which is a drop of 70 degrees F. Ambient air temperature is 100 degrees F. Intercooler thermal efficiency (TE) can be computed as follows:

$$TE = T_{drop} / (T_{charge} - T_{coolant})$$

Where:
TE = Thermal effectiveness of a heat exchanger
T_{drop} = The actual temperature drop achieved through the heat exchanger
T_{charge} = Temperature of the hot pressurized charge air being cooled
$T_{coolant}$ = Temperature of the cooling medium (degrees F)

Therefore:

$$TE = T_{drop} / (T_{charge} - T_{coolant})$$

$$= 70 / (200 - 100)$$

$$= 70 / 100$$

$$= .70$$

This intercooler is 70 percent effective.

Now suppose that you measure charge air entering an ice-water heat-sink intercooler at 200 degrees F and leaving it at 60 degrees F, which is a drop of 140 degrees F. Ambient the ice-water temperature is 32 degrees F. Intercooler thermal efficiency (TE) can be computed as follows:

$$TE = T_{drop} / (T_{charge} - T_{coolant})$$

$$= 140 (200 - 32)$$

$$= 140 / 168$$

$$= .83$$

Although this intercooler cooled the charge 40 degrees below 100 degrees F ambient air temperature, the intercooler is 83 percent effective at reducing charge temperature to the temperature *of the coolant*.

But let's say specifications indicate that a particular intercooler is 75 percent effective. How much will it cool 250-degree F air, if the cooling medium is 70-degree F ambient air?

$$T_{drop} = TE \times (T_{charge} - T_{coolant})$$
$$= .75 \times (250 - 70)$$
$$= 135F$$

The temperature will drop 135 degrees F through the intercooler. Actual intercooler-out temperature will thus be:

$$T_{IO} = (T_{charge} - T_{drop})$$
$$= 250 - 135$$
$$= 115F$$

Charge enters the engine with a 45-degree F rise over ambient 70-degree F air.

CHARGE COOLING (INTERCOOLING)

Intake charge coolers—once referred to as aftercoolers, now typically (for whatever reason) called intercoolers—are designed to remove the heat of compression from supercharged air, which otherwise cancels out some of the benefits of supercharging by making the charge less dense than it would be if compressed to the same pressure but at a colder temperature. Intercoolers make power, and, more importantly, they lower the ONR (octane number requirement) of a spark-ignition engine and the EGT of a diesel powerplant. When deployed between multistage compressors, intercoolers enable a forced-induction system to deliver quite radical boost pressures without exceeding the thermal capacity of the engine.

Supercharged lake racers at San Jose, California, circa 1991. With all that cool water it is a crime there was not a single intercooled engine in sight, but how do you intercool a giant 6-71 or 8-71 Roots blower? With fuel, actually.

Vortech Power Cooler system providing inline charge cooling with remote water-cooler unit. Major components include water-cooled intercooler, pump, reservoir, hoses, and air-cooled heat exchanger. *Vortech*

An intercooler is similar to an automotive radiator, except that the hot fluid moving through the passages of the heat exchanger for cooling is air. The cooling medium surrounding an intercooler core can be one of the following:

- Recirculating water jacket
- Total-loss water jacket
- Fan-driven air
- Road-draft air
- Static air
- Evaporative water spray
- Liquid nitrogen (N2) spray
- Liquid nitrous oxide (N2O) spray
- Water-ice bath
- Dry-ice pellets
- Peltier Effect thermoelectric semiconductors
- Circulated boiling refrigerant
- Something else
- Some combination of the above

Technically speaking, the thermal efficiency of an intercooler relates to its ability to cool charge air down to the temperature of the cooling medium, which is not necessarily the same as ambient air. Certain types of intercoolers, however, have 100 percent or greater *effective thermal efficiency* (i.e., the ability to chill compressed charge air below ambient air temperature). This can be accomplished using coldness stockpiled in water, ice, dry ice, or seawater, or by harnessing the cooling effect of depressurizing a compressed gas or liquid in an expansion chamber or turbine, a strategy that ultimately requires a certain amount of energy to compress the coolant. Most ordinary air-cooled intercoolers struggle hard to remove even 70 percent of boost heat—that is, to achieve 70 percent thermal efficiency.

The most important function of an intercooler is to reduce the combustion temperature of a supercharged engine. Lower temperature combustion decreases harmful thermal

A 5.7 Hemi with air-water intercooler system. The Vortech PowerCooler system looks great but it would not hurt to install an insulating heat jacket around the air cooler and ducting to mitigate engine compartment heat soak. Note the brass fitting in the supercharger, indicating that this centrifugal blower has a self-contained lubrication system. *Vortech*

151

loading on a variety of engine systems and components and acts as a important anti-knock countermeasure on spark-ignition engines. Every bit of heat that can be eliminated from the charge before it enters the engine cuts down on the heat-rejection requirement of the cooling system. That is, unless the engine's cooling system is being used to cool the charge, which was viable when superchargers of all types heated the air tremendously due to poor thermal efficiency, but it is not found in modern performance engines with efficient centrifugal compressors.

One degree of reduction in intake charge temperature typically results in 1 degree of reduction in combustion temperature and 1 degree of reduction in EGT (which, of course, reduces the heat energy available to the turbine, conceivably mandating a smaller turbine housing in some situations to maintain full boost). Any surplus ONR headroom in a spark-ignition engine following intercooler installation potentially permits the use of higher maximum boost, a higher state of tune, or a higher geometric compression ratio than would otherwise be possible—all of which increase engine performance. In diesel engines, reduced EGT permits more fuel to be burned for higher reliable horsepower without overheating pistons and rings. Alternately, rather than increasing power, the reduced ONR from intercooling could potentially be used to permit the use of less expansive reduced-octane fuel or a more efficient state of tune.

The other main benefit of an intercooler is that cooling the charge quiets the thermal activity in the air so that it fits in a given space with less pressure, allowing the compressor to push in more air for a given boost pressure. You could say an intercooler "shrinks" the charge to increase the mass of air entering a powerplant. In any case, higher charge mass permits a spark-ignition engine to inject more fuel and make more power, or a diesel engine to burn more fuel without smoking or burning pistons.

HOW LONG WILL IT TAKE A SUPERCHARGER TO FILL AN INTERCOOLER?

When there is an intercooler installed, the internal volume of the air-cooler must be pumped full and pressurized as you make boost.

One model of how intercooler volume affects lag on a full-throttle roll-on, starting at cruise and continuing to full boost, starts by averaging the airflow to take into account the fact that the cycle begins at 0 boost, when the airflow through the compressor is exactly that of the engine at cruise rpm with the throttle mostly closed, and ends at full-boost airflow:

$T_{fill} = V_{IC} / ((AF_{start} + AF_{final}) / 2)$

Where:

T_{fill} = Time to fill the intercooler
V_{IC} = Volume of the intercooler tanks and core in cubic feet or ft^2
AF_{start} = Starting compressor flow rate
AF_{final} = Final compressor flow rate

The starting compressor flow rate is defined as,

AF_{start} = rpm/2 × displacement / VE

The final compressor flow rate is determined by the usual methods involving engine speed and density ratio.

Let's plug in some numbers.

Assume the intercooler has 1,000 cubic inches of interior space. This is 1,000 / 1,728 = .579 cubic feet.

Volumetric efficiency at idle is typically 20 to 30 percent, so let's assume VE is 40 percent at light cruise.

Assuming the engine has 122 cubic inches (2.0L) of displacement, is turning 2,500 rpm, and has a four-stroke cycle, the airflow in cubic inches per minute at the beginning of the roll-on is:

AF_{start} = rpm/2 × displacement / VE
= 122 × 2500 / 2 × .40
= 61,000 cubic inches per minute
= 35.30 cfm (61,000 / 1,728)

Assuming the engine achieves full boost at 4,000 rpm, and the basic volumetric efficiency of the powerplant there is 80 percent,

Then:

$T = V_{IC} / ((AF_{start} + AF_{final}) / 2)$
$T = 1000 / ((AF_{start} + AF_{final}) / 2)$

At the final flow rate:

AF_{start} = rpm/2 × displacement / VE
= (122 × 4000 / 2 × .80) / 1,728
= 112.96 cfm.

Assuming the intercooled supercharger is capable of delivering a density ratio of 2.15 (pressure ratio of 2.3 with .79 efficient compressor and 80 percent efficient intercooling), airflow at 4,000 rpm and 19.11 psi boost is:

112.96 × 2.15 = 242.86 cfm

Averaging light cruise airflow of 35.3 and earliest full-boost airflow of 242.86 gives 139.1 cfm.

Therefore:

$T_{fill} = V_{IC} / ((AF_{start} + AF_{final}) / 2)$
= .579 / ((35.3 + 260.9) / 2)
= .579 / 148.1
= .0039 × 60 sec/min
= .234 seconds

Filling a 1,000 in^2 intercooler adds about a quarter of a second of lag.

Vortech Marine supercharged and seawater-intercooled Mercruiser 454-502 Magnum big-block was designed to make 570 horsepower with stock engine and fuel system, 620 horsepower with modifications to the fuel system, or 720 horsepower with a modified engine and fuel system. *Vortech Marine*

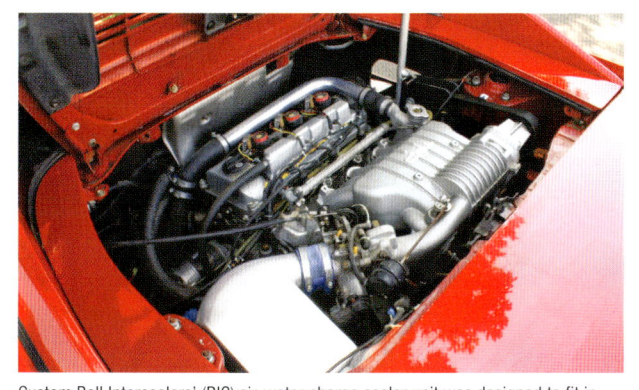

Custom Bell Intercoolers' (BIC) air-water charge cooler unit was designed to fit in the author's twin-charged V-6 MR2 and look good. Although it was impractical to cool the charge leaving the Toyota Racing Development supercharger assembly (integrated into the intake manifold), the pressure ratio of the Stage-2 Roots compressor was a relatively low at 1.33, with a large Stage-1 turbocharger doing most of the heavy lifting to boost manifold pressure from 14.7-psi ambient to 45.7 psia. Extremely effective air-water intercooling prevented hot air from overheating the Eaton rotor assembly.

HPS supercharging system for Mercedes V-8s is similar to the Cadillac Northstar, in that charge air enters the supercharger from the rear and passes upward into the air-water intercooler, before turning downward into outboard intake runners. *HPS*

The charge-density benefit of intercooling—which is fairly negligible on an engine with an efficient compressor running less than about 5- to 7-psi boost—can be viewed as a *byproduct* of other overriding design considerations. Where knock and thermal loading are not a problem on low-pressure supercharger systems, an intercooler wouldn't make much power to speak of in any case, so why have one? Where knock and thermal loading *are* a problem, you already needed the intercooler anyway to lower engine ONR and dump heat, whether it would make more power or not.

That said, when a compressor is seriously cooking the charge because the boost pressure is high or the compressor is operating with poor thermal efficiency, intercoolers can and do make serious power through density increases alone. An intercooler of 80 percent efficiency cooling ambient air that has been boosted 30 psi using a 75 percent efficient compressor (increasing charge temperature from 70 degrees F to 354 degrees F) will reduce the charge temperature to 127 degrees F, increasing air mass by roughly 39 percent, which translates directly to power if the engine is not knock-limited. In any case, no spark ignition engine could function with a 354-degree intake charge, which is within 141 degrees of auto-ignition temperature; it would knock like crazy.

Intercooler Design Tradeoffs

The goal of an intercooler is nothing less than to recool pressurized charge air back down to ambient temperature (or colder) as it screams toward the engine at a velocity that can exceed 400 feet per second. Achieving ambient or lower temps is actually feasible in supercharged marine engines. In such an application, fast throttle response is not usually important, which enables charge air to be cooled to subambient temperatures in summer weather using large, efficient heat-exchanger units chilled with the infinite supply of cold water, which has outstanding thermal conductivity.

Unfortunately, achieving ambient temperatures with intercooling in a road-going automotive vehicle is impossible or expensive and difficult, because the only large supply of coolant that's easily available is ambient air itself, which has less than 10 percent the thermal conductivity of water and is thus not a very good coolant. In fact, under the right circumstances, air actually makes a rather good *insulator*. That said, if you blow enough cold air on something hot it will cool down. But by the time supercharged air has cooled to within even 35 percent of ambient temperature in an air-cooled intercooler, the narrowing temperature differential between charge and ambient air has degraded the cooler's effectiveness tremendously. Automotive intercooler designers are forced to fight hard for every degree of additional cooling by packing as large an air-cooled intercooler as possible beneath the bodywork of the car and then optimizing thermal efficiency using meticulous design, careful attention to detail, careful testing and analysis, and a philosophical acceptance of tradeoffs. In most cases they ultimately settle for about 70 percent-efficient intercooling.

Unfortunately, even if you have the space, simply increasing intercooler size yields diminishing returns. If the original design was 75 percent efficient, making the cooler 10 percent larger will not improve efficiency by 10 percent but will only get you 10 percent of the charge heat you missed with the previous design, bettering the original intercooler's thermal efficiency by 2.5 percent from 75 to 77.5 percent. And that's assuming that the heroic measures required to jam in the larger cooler don't degrade its efficiency, say because airflow through the bigger core cannot be maintained. Size does count, but it is not enough. To achieve really superior intercooling, you need every trick in the book. What's worse, there are problematic aspects of intercooler design that result from inherently contradictory engineering tradeoffs in thermal efficiency, airflow capability, intercooler size, and cooling medium.

Effective charge-cooling begins in the guts of the air cooler core with a large, efficient thermal-transfer surface and appropriate airflow geometry to remove heat from charge air with the highest practical thermal efficiency. The way to facilitate high-efficiency thermal transfer in the air cooler is to have turbulent air moving evenly through intricate, convoluted airways that are loaded with metal fins and baffles. This forces as many air molecules as possible into repeated, direct collisions with hypertrophied thermal transfer surfaces that have a high temperature differential from the air and excellent thermal conductivity. The airways must be designed specifically to prevent smooth (laminar) flow that's insulated from the cooler surface by a layer of stationary boundary air. You could say that intercooler airways are, in effect, designed to interfere with smooth, efficient charge air throughput. This inevitably produces some pressure drop through the intercooler, particularly when air is screaming through at hundreds of feet per second. An intercooler with inadequate airflow at negligible pressure drop *will* drop boost pressure through the intercooler, and this *will* undo some of the density advantage of charge cooling.

An intercooler that is an airflow bottleneck kills horsepower in one of two ways: If the wastegate is referenced to the compressor discharge upstream of the intercooler where pressure is higher, reduced boost pressure in the intake manifold after the pressure drop in the intercooler will reduce mass airflow into the engine. If the wastegate is referenced to the intake manifold in the reduced pressure zone downstream of the intercooler, boost will be where it should be in the intake manifold, but this will force the supercharger to produce higher boost at the compressor discharge in order to force enough air through the intercooler. Achieving higher compressor discharge pressure forces the turbine to work harder, almost definitely producing higher back pressure at the exhaust ports and higher thermal loading in the engine via higher EGT.

Bottom line, efficient intercooler airflow implies a streamlined air path, but this is exactly what you *don't* want if the goal is high intercooler thermal efficiency.

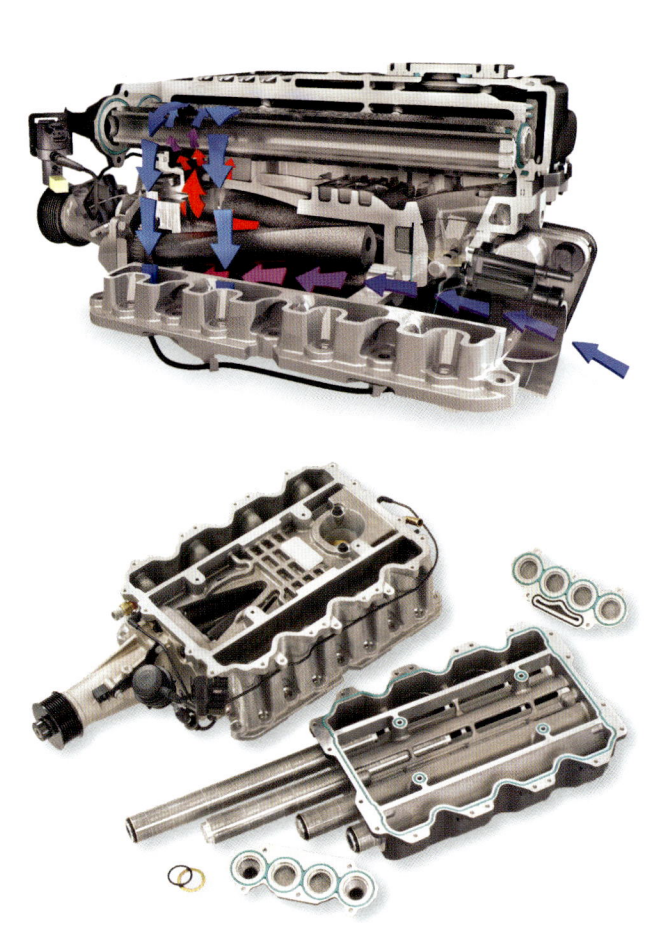

The supercharged Cadillac 4.4-liter Northstar V-8 drew air from a throttle at the rear of the engine, compressed it in a Gen 5 Eaton Roots-type blower, discharged compressed air upward past four finned air-water intercooling tubes, at which point the air turned 180 degrees into outboard runners that led directly downward into the cylinder heads. *General Motors*

Dry ice in a huge drag-car heat-sink intercooler. Dry ice temperature is below 100 degrees F and sublimates directly from a solid to a gas, producing no messy liquid to foul traction at the drag races. What would you call this thing? Supernaturally intercooled? *ARE Cooling (www.are.com/av)*

Unfortunately, attempting to reconcile thermal-efficiency versus airflow tradeoffs by installing an oversized air cooler may not be feasible due to space and packaging constraints in many road-going vehicles. Even when it is feasible, there are problems with oversized air coolers that go beyond the diminishing-returns problem discussed previously.

In the first place, if the air velocity through a cooler gets too low, thermal efficiency can suffer because of uneven airflow through the air-cooler core. This is why all intercooler end tanks, inlets, and outlets must be designed to facilitate uniform air distribution through the cooler and why oversized intercoolers in particular can sometimes require baffling to prevent hot spots. Beyond that, larger intercoolers flow more air because the total area of the airway is larger, which results in a larger internal volume. This air space—plus that of the tubing required to plumb the intercooler to the compressor and engine—is essentially a big air tank that must be pressurized every time the engine makes boost, although even a large, 1,000-cubic-inch intercooler system only delays boost arrival by perhaps a quarter of a second. In addition to these issues, huge intercoolers can cause other unintended negative consequences, such as degrading the performance of the engine cooling system by interfering with road draft through the radiator.

The silver-bullet solution, then, would be to install a smallish air cooler of low internal volume but high cooling power, in which streamlined internal aerodynamics minimize pressure drop. Couple that with a lower temperature cooling medium with improved thermal conductivity to chill the air cooler and maintain thermal efficiency via increased temperature differential between the charge and the internal surfaces of the air cooler. This is the holy grail of intercooler performance. Ambient air won't work as the cooling medium, because ambient air is ambient temperature, and it's air, which doesn't conduct heat particularly well from a metal surface. Even a water-cooled air cooler—with 14 times greater thermal conductivity, high thermal momentum, and the ability to bank coldness in a large heat sink of reserve water, which can be cooled at leisure between the intermittent boost events of a typical street vehicle—is ultimately limited by the need to cool the water, which, onboard a moving vehicle, typically is done with *air*. And air won't do the job.

Achieving or exceeding 100-percent effective thermal efficiency with an intercooler can be done, but it requires brute-force tricks like piped-in cold seawater, or exotic measures that involve harnessing the cooling effects of expanding gases or boiling, thus evaporating liquids with high heat. That said, the performance advantage of these types of "super-coolers" is undeniable, which is why short-duration competition vehicles involved in drag racing, tractor-pulling, and speed-record attempts all use them to be competitive.

This is a good time to point out that an intercooler is not only a heat exchanger but, to some extent, also serves as a heat sink. Because of the inevitable inefficiencies in thermal conductivity, an intercooler has a certain amount of thermal "momentum," meaning there is some tendency to store heat or coldness in the metal structure of the intercooler itself that lags behind the rapid changes in charge temperature as the compressor switches between processing hot compressed air and freewheeling in the (cool) intake airstream. Because the any cooling medium only removes a percentage of heat from the intercooler, a really hot charge from high boost will heat-soak the intercooler structure itself. As the intercooler heat soaks, the temperature differential from the cooling medium increases, making the intercooler more effective at shedding heat, and eventually resulting in equilibrium at a hotter temperature. When the supercharger stops making boost, charge air at atmospheric pressure and temperature continues flowing through the intercooler. If the intercooler is hotter than ambient air temperature, the *charge air* begins helping cool the heat-soaked intercooler, intake manifold, intake plumbing, and compressor—which are now temporarily acting as a kind of "interheater," shedding heat into the charge. In other words, rather than the intercooler cooling the charge, the charge is cooling the intercooler (which is more-or-less fine, because the engine is not making boost). Meanwhile, the intercooler's cooling system is also doing its best to drive the heat-soak out of the intercooler. In the case of a water-cooled system, the coolant itself will probably have sunk some heat that must also be removed before the intercooler regains full cooling capacity.

Once the whole system has reached equilibrium at the coolest achievable temperature for the prevailing weather conditions, the intercooler is ready and able to sink more heat the next time the engine begins making boost. This essentially provides backup cooling capacity for the next squirt of boost. The heat-sink capability of an intercooler can provide a significant amount of charge cooling for intermittent boosting even if the normal cooling medium is completely ineffective.

Procharger's air-air intercooled Harley supercharging system was designed to add 50 to 65 percent power to a big twin. But company literature suggests it is not wise to add more than about 8 to 12 percent more power to an air-cooled Harley motorcycle with a nonintercooled Roots blower, or a 15 to 20 percent power boost with competing nonintercooled centrifugal supercharging systems. Indeed, air-cooled engines run hotter and have less of a safety margin to handle the increased thermal loading of supercharger conversions. Intercooling is always a great idea, and there's plenty of moving air around a fast motorcycle. *Procharger*

Intercooler Architecture
Liquid-Cooled ("Air-Water") Intercoolers

Liquid-cooled intercoolers logically consist of an air-cooler section (which is water-cooled), a water-cooler section (which is often air-cooled), and a fluid reservoir or heat sink. These components may or may not be integrated.

Ice-Water Heat Sink Intercooler: In the simplest case (used for drag racing, speed-record attempts, dyno-testing, and other relatively short-duration, high-power operations) an ice-water or dry ice-alcohol water jacket is combined with a radiator-type heat exchanger to form a giant heat sink. The ice—loaded into the intercooler prior to each competition run—provides high cooling power, while the water eliminates air pockets and conducts heat from the air channels in the air cooler to the ice.

As with any intercooler, charge air enters the air cooler through a tube in the inlet (upstream) end tank, from which air distributes itself into a plenitude of thin channels that route through the water jacket to form the core of the air-water heat exchanger. Each air channel is finned internally with a myriad of tiny "turbulator" fins that substantially increase the metal surface area to improve heat transfer from the charge into the metal air-water interface (or from the metal into the air after boost stops and the charge is helping drive heat-soak out of the cooler). At the far end, air channels dump into an outlet (downstream) end tank, where cooled charge air collects and exits through a discharge tube. The water-filled spaces between the air channels are also finned to increase thermal transfer from the air-water interface into the water, though this is much less of a problem due to the vastly superior thermal conductivity of water.

Commonly, a radial-outflow bilge pump circulates iced coolant through the air-cooler water jacket/reservoir to prevent hot spots. Coolant flow through the core is always perpendicular to the direction of charge-airflow. Because of the high thermal conductivity of water, it is possible to reduce boost pressure drop through an air-water intercooler by sending charge air straight through the core in the short direction, exactly as road-air blows through an engine radiator. Of course, unlike a radiator, the "front" and "back" of the core must be enclosed to contain the pressurized air, and the end tanks should be designed carefully, and possibly baffled to promote even air distribution through the core.

In this kind of intercooler, the coolant reservoir and water cooler are integral, with cooling provided purely by sinking heat into the ice. Melted water coolant flows through a large volume of ice during the course of, say, a land-speed record attempt. For some drag-race applications, the ice-water heat sink directly surrounds the air cooler, forming a single large "inline" heat sink. Waterless heat sinks of this type built for drag racing sometimes use dry-ice pellets to replace the ice-water mixture around the air cooler. The dry ice sublimates directly into carbon dioxide gas as the dry ice melts, thereby eliminating any possibility of water spills contaminating a competition track surface.

IMA Motorsports 993 Porsche with liquid-cooled GT3R engine was intercooled with this giant air-air intercooler located above the powerplant (as is the case on all whale-tale turbo Porsche flat-six vehicles). Careful air circulation is required on any engine-mounted charge-cooler to prevent cooked air from rising off the hot engine and heat-soaking the intercooler. Some air-water charger cooler units are insulated inside a heat blanket for precisely this reason.

An ice-cooled heat sink begins melting the ice immediately when hot charge air starts through the cooler as the boost cranks up. It remains effective in keeping melted water cold until the ice has melted, at which point the temperature rises more rapidly and the cooler rapidly loses effectiveness, which is why this type of cooler is only useful for relatively short duration competition. For example, Banks Power's 700-plus-horsepower Sidewinder Dodge truck set a land-speed record of 213 miles per hour in 2002, making it the fastest pickup truck in the world. The engine's 50-psi boost was intercooled using liquid-cooled marine air-cooler units chilled by 30- to 35-degree F water pumped through a 40-gallon heat-sink tank filled with ice cubes. At full howl, ice water emerged from the air coolers 6 degrees warmer after having cooled 480 degrees charge to 100 degrees F, and immediately returned for another trip through the ice tank at a rate of 120 gallons per minute. The vehicle required about 90 seconds of intercooling each time it ripped through the 7-mile course.

Because the cooling medium can be very cold, the effective thermal efficiency of an *ice-water heat sink* can be much greater than 100 percent (meaning that the intercooler cools compressed air below compressor-inlet temperature), resulting in compressed charge air that is cooled far below ambient air temperature. Of course, real thermal efficiency quantifies the percentage of the temperature differential between the hot charge air and the cooling medium that a heat exchanger is able to eliminate as it cools the charge, which can never reach 100 percent.

To get an idea of the power potential of an ice-water heat sink, if 470 degrees F compressed air enters a heat exchanger cooled with 15 gallons of 32 degrees F ice water, then an 85 percent efficient cooler would cool the charge 85 percent of the 438-degree temperature differential, or 372.3 degrees, from 470 down to 97.7 degrees. This produces a 66 percent density improvement (which translates directly to horsepower) and reduces thermal loading to a manageable level.

But how fast does an ice-water heat sink melt ice? Let's assume the airflow rate for a particular supercharged 2.0-liter engine is 28 lb/min (408.17 cfm) at a high boost pressure. How much ice is required for, say, a speed-record attempt, where the engine is boosting at maximum power for minutes at a time?

Under ordinary conditions the melting rate of ice (m_{ice}) is given by

$m_{ice} = \varepsilon \times w \times (T_{inlet}$ of hot air charge $- 32F) / L$

Where:

T_{inlet} = The temperature of the hot charge entering the air cooler

L = The latent heat of ice = 144 BTU/lb

Q = Heat transfer rate from charge to coolant in Btu/hr = $\varepsilon \times w \times (Tinlet$ of hot gas $- 32F)$.

w = Mass flow specific heat product of the gas/coolant (whichever has the smallest value $m \times c_p$) = $m \times c_p$ [Btu/hr - F]

So:

$w = m \times c_p$ = 28 lb/min × 0.24 Btu/lb - F = 6.7 Btu/min - F

$Q = \varepsilon \times w \times (T_{inlet}$ of hot charge $- 32) = 0.85 \times 6.7 \times (470 - 32) = 2{,}494$ Btu/min

$m_{ice} = Q/L = 2494/144 = 17$ lb/min

Under these conditions, the ice-water heat-sink intercooler will melt about 17 pounds of ice per minute to cool the charge, which is about 2 gallons of water. If the speed record attempt took 2 minutes, a 4-gallon ice tank would do the job.

But there are colder things than ice. I have never seen it tried, but mixing salt with ice water can greatly lower the temperature of the mixture using the principle that rock salt lowers the freezing point of ice and simultaneously steals heat from the water as the salt dissolves—with the result that an ice-brine mixture that started with 32-degree ice can achieve temperatures as low as -4 degrees F. Obviously, saltwater would be hard on the guts of an intercooler, but then again, no guts, no glory, right?

If a cooler were chilled by -115 degrees F dry ice, perhaps in a bath of methanol (freezing point -141 degrees F), equal results are achievable with a heat sink of reduced weight and volume. Since dry ice sublimates directly into CO_2 gas, the payload of dry ice loses weight during competition, which can be a factor in drag racing, where pro racers fight to trim factions of a pound of weight.

Bob Norwood chose air-air intercooling for the supercharged Porsche flat-six that powered his mid-1990s Doom racer. This was a race car, so there was no need to worry about idling in traffic. Ram-air entered the supercharger through a giant scoop directly above the midengine powerplant.

If the temperature of an *ice-water heat sink* is too cold, core-icing can become a problem when the engine is not making boost in cold, humid weather.

Air-Cooled Air-Water Intercooler: A common variety of liquid-cooled intercooler uses an air-cooled heat exchanger instead of ice to chill water recirculating on a continuous basis through the air-cooler unit.

In this system, a water pump located at the bottom of a coolant reservoir pumps chilled water through a water-jacket surrounding the air cooler, where the water heats as it exchanges thermal energy with the charge. From there, the heated coolant flows to a water cooler located where large amounts of ambient air are available to cool the water in a radiator-type heat exchanger, usually at the front of the vehicle. From there, the freshly chilled coolant circulates back to the reservoir.

The larger the reservoir, the greater the system's backup capability to sink heat without large water-temperature increases if the water-cooler is not powerful enough to remove all the heat during high engine loading. In fact, some air-water systems are intentionally designed with a reservoir large enough that it can supply cooling power for a typical boost episode without water having to travel through the air cooler twice. With a high density compared to air, water can absorb a large amount of heat from air with only a small temperature rise, and the large temperature differential between the hot charge and the coolant only improves the cooling power of the air cooler. On the other hand, the cooling effectiveness of the water cooler is rather low, because the temperature differential between charge-warmed coolant and ambient air is small.

This type of intercooler is really an air-water-water-air system—meaning ultimately it is an air-air cooler with a water loop transporting heat between the two heat exchangers. The continuous thermal efficiency of such a system is ultimately limited by the ability of the water cooler to shed heat into the atmosphere, and there are inefficiencies introduced in the process of moving the heat into and out of the water (which can be significant if engine compartment heat is heat-soaking the water-cooling loop).

The fact that the charge cooler and water cooler are two entirely separate units has some tremendous advantages:

- There is a large degree of freedom to optimize the design of each heat exchanger to perform its part of the heat-transfer job with specialized airflow and thermal efficiency characteristics.
- There is increased freedom to optimize the location of each heat exchanger for improved cooling and airflow performance.
- The water cooler can be positioned at the front of the vehicle in the air stream without requiring very large 2- to 3-inch-diameter plumbing to move charge air forward from the compressor to the front of the car and back to the engine. This reduces the system's volume, which must be pumped full of compressed air before the engine sees full boost. This is critical for mid- or rear-engine vehicles, because a water-cooler can be located at the front of the car for maximum cooling efficiency with the coolant transported the length of the car between the rear air-cooler and front water-cooler in 3/4-inch hose or pipe.
- The air cooler can be both small and efficient, and located conveniently in the engine compartment near the throttle body or centrifugal supercharger (preferably insulated to protect it from heat-soaking), or integral to the intake manifold in the case of a positive-displacement supercharger.
- This type of air-water system can be designed so that the coolant reservoir can be packed with ice to provide greater cooling power for short-duration competition events.
- For automotive vehicles operating in street-type conditions where boost is intermittent and of short-duration, a carefully designed and well-insulated air-water system can achieve ever-higher thermal efficiencies by continuously cooling the water over and over with the water cooler, ever colder, ever closer to ambient air temperature, essentially banking coldness to use for intercooling during the next boost event.
- When a vehicle with an air-water intercooler is moving slowly, the reservoir will still provide maximum cooling until the water heat-soaks.

The end-to-end effectiveness of this type of air-water system must be computed in two parts, based on known air cooler and water cooler thermal efficiency. Alternately, the efficiency can be calculated based on measured changes in water and air temperature in the system. The bottom line is that water moving through the air cooler increases in temperature only a small amount, while the air cools a huge amount. By the same token, water moving through the front water-cooler heat-exchanger cools little.

Refrigerant-Cooled Air-Liquid Intercooler A variation of the air-water-water-air intercooler gains enormous cooling power by switching from water coolant to a gas/liquid refrigerant such as Freon or R-134 to move heat out of the air-cooler and then out of the refrigerant with extremely high effectiveness by harnessing the cooling power of evaporation and wide temperature differentials—essentially turning the air-liquid intercooling system into a big air conditioner. Of course, the task of cooling hundreds or thousands of cubic feet per minute of 350-degree-F-plus charge air is a bit more ambitious than simply cooling the interior of a car.

The critical principles behind the enhanced cooling power of this type of intercooler are

- The state change from liquid to gas has a tremendous cooling effect.
- The thermal efficiency of a heat exchanger is much higher when the temperature differential is large.

To escape the molecular forces that hold a liquid together, in order to vaporize it, a particular molecule of the liquid must be at or near the surface, and—depending on the surrounding vapor pressure—must acquire a certain amount of energy to escape the liquid by gaining heat in collisions with nearby molecules—an exchange of momentum that leaves other molecules remaining behind in the liquid with *less* heat energy. When you heat water on a stove, the heating element supplies the energy required for water molecules to vaporize. However, evaporating liquids such as water at ambient temperature may also steal heat from the surrounding water or atmosphere to vaporize, which is why sweat evaporating off your arm in a breeze feels cold. The required heat to escape a liquid is thus called the "heat of vaporization" (non-scientists frequently don't understand why it's called that, since the environment gets *cold* as evaporating molecules steal heat to escape).

Some liquids require more heat than others to vaporize. A good refrigerant has a high heat of vaporization combined with properties that cause it to change state at a convenient temperature and pressure. Actually, the temperature at which a liquid boils into a gas varies considerably with pressure (which is why a campfire at 15,000 feet of elevation boils water at 189.8 degrees F instead of 212 degrees F), a happy fact that enables an A/C system to manipulate the boiling and evaporation temperature of a refrigerant by compressing or expanding it.

An air-refrigerant intercooler works as follows:

- An engine-driven compressor scavenges low-pressure refrigerant gas from the cooling jacket of the air cooler, compressing the gas and pumping it through a condenser, which is an air-cooled heat-exchanger precisely analogous to the water-cooler of an ordinary air-water intercooler (but designed to handle up to 300 psi).
- The condenser removes heat that was previously transferred into the refrigerant when cooling the charge air, plus the heat from compressing the refrigerant. As always, the hotter the refrigerant is, the greater the temperature differential from ambient air, and the greater the effectiveness of the heat-removal process.
- As it cools, the compressed refrigerant condenses into liquid as it gives up its heat into road-draft air or fan-driven ambient air blowing through the condenser.
- Liquid refrigerant flows under pressure out of the condenser and into a reservoir (sometimes called an accumulator) just upstream of the air-cooler unit. When there is plenty of pressurized refrigerant in the accumulator, a pressure switch temporarily disengages the compressor clutch to achieve a certain pressure range. This is analogous to the way a thermostat controls a furnace to keep temperature within certain limits.
- Refrigerant enters the cooling jacket of the air cooler (which is normally called an "evaporator" in air conditioning systems) through an orifice/bottleneck that is sufficiently restrictive that it greatly reduces pressure downstream in the cooling jacket of the air-cooler (which is being scavenged by the compressor pump.
- As refrigerant sprays through the orifice tube into the lower-pressure cooling jacket around the air-cooler core, the boiling point of the refrigerant plummets. Liquid refrigerant sprays against the metal core and through cooling channels in the core perpendicular to the charge airflow, boiling into a fog and leaving behind freezing-cold metal surfaces that have given up heat to the evaporating refrigerant.
- The heat transfer from charge air to the refrigerant occurs with high efficiency because of the temperature differential between hot charge and cold refrigerant, which is enhanced by the ability of refrigeration to achieve temperatures below 0 degrees F.

On a chassis dynamometer, tests reveal that powering a typical cockpit air conditioning system drops engine torque by 8 to 9 pound-feetpound-feet across the rpm range, with some small, efficient A/C compressors requiring even less. Taking a 232-hp 3.0-liter BMW as an example, eight or nine pound-feet equates to about 11 horsepower, or about 5 percent, with the loss increasing at higher rpm as the compressor turns faster. Because passenger-compartment air-conditioning requirements do not increase with engine rpm, while the thermal efficiency

An air-air intercooler plus back-mounted oil-cooler on Mountain Performance's Yamaha Rhino blower kit. *Mountain Performance*

of an A/C condenser increases markedly with vehicle speed as more air becomes available for cooling, most A/C compressors are intentionally designed to have terrible pumping efficiency at higher speeds in an effort to provide relatively constant pumping across the rpm range while avoiding unnecessary increases in parasitic drag at higher speeds.

Obviously, the cooling requirements of an air-refrigerant intercooling system are completely different from those of ordinary cockpit climate control, with little or no cooling requirement whatsoever at idle or cruise. As intake cfm increases during boost, the cooling requirement escalates tremendously. Unlike an A/C compressor, the ideal air-refrigerant compressor should provide minimal cooling during no-boost conditions, but increase steadily in efficiency to keep up with increasing boost and engine airflow during boost events. In practical terms, the easiest compressor solution is adapting a large automotive or RV A/C compressor, which could be hot rodded with typical induction and exhaust flow tricks to increase pumping capacity at higher speeds, or even be equipped with a variable- or multi-speed drive mechanism.

The critical parameters or an air-refrigerant intercooler are

- The throughput and thermal effectiveness of the refrigerant-cooler (the condenser)
- The throughput and thermal effectiveness of the air-cooler (evaporator)
- The heat carrying capacity of a particular refrigerant (and there are many possible choices)

The *compressor* must be able pump and compress enough refrigerant to move sufficient charge heat out of the air-cooler to achieve the required intercooled charge temperature. Refrigerant suppliers can provide the heat-carrying specifications of the various refrigerants. Compressor manufacturers can provide flow maps indicating pumping capacity at various pressures and speeds—exactly like a supercharger.

TWO-STAGE INTERCOOLING

It is asking a lot to expect a *refrigeration* system to remove the heat from a 1,000- or 1,500-horse powerplant running extreme levels of boost in the 40-psi range. But *two-stage intercooling* can be used to remove a great deal of heat in a primary stage, with a more efficient second (refrigerated or Peltier) stage used to achieve greater than 100 percent effective thermal efficiency.

For example, suppose you are running an air-cooled intercooler with 80 percent thermal efficiency to deal with the heat of 30-psi boost pressure on a day when ambient temperature is 70 degrees F. How hot is the charge leaving the supercharger?

$T_{2c} = T_{1c} + (((T_{1c} \times (PR^{.283})) - T_{1c}) / CE)$

Where:
T_1 = absolute inlet air temperature (degrees R)
   = 70F + 460
   = 530R
PR = Pressure ratio (outlet absolute pressure/inlet absolute pressure)

   = (30 + 14.7) / 14.7
   = 3.04

Plugging in the numbers for 30-psig boost (pressure ratio of 3.04), inlet air temperature of 70 degrees F (530R), and a 78 percent efficient compressor:

T_{2c} = 530 + (((530 × (3.04$^{.283}$)) − 530) / .78)
   = 781R
   = 781 − 460 = 321.2F

The charge leaves this compressor at 321.2 degrees F.

The 80 percent air-air intercooler now cools the charge as follows:

$T_{IO1} = T_{charge} - (TE \times (T_{charge} - T_{coolant}))$

Where:
T_{IO1} = Stage 1 intercooler-out temperature
T_{charge} = Temperature of the charge before intercooling (degrees F)
$T_{coolant}$ = Temperature of the intercooler coolant (degrees F)

Plugging in the numbers:

$T_{IO1} = T_{charge} - (TE \times (T_{charge} - T_{coolant}))$
   = 321.2 − (.80 × (321.2 − 70))
   = 120.24F

(The temperature drops 200.96 degrees F through the Stage 1 intercooler.)

Adding a refrigerated second-stage intercooler operating at 80 percent efficiency with 32-degree coolant would cool the charge as follows:

$T_{IO2} = T_{charge} - (TE \times (T_{charge} - T_{coolant}))$
   = 120.24 − (.80 × (120.24 − 32))
   = 49.65F

(The temperature drops 70.59 degrees F through the Stage 2 intercooler.)

The density gain from Stage 1 is:

Density change = $\frac{\text{(Original Temperature ABS)}}{\text{New Temperature ABS}}$ − 1

Density change = $\frac{(425 + 460)}{(141 + 460)}$ − 1

Density change = $\frac{(885)}{601}$ − 1 = .47 or 47 percent gain from Stage 1 intercooling

$\Delta D1 = (T_1 / T_2) - 1$

Where:
$\Delta D1$ = Density change resulting from a temperature increase or decrease
T_1 = Original temperature (degrees R) of air
T_2 = New temperature (degrees R) of air

Plugging in the numbers,

$\Delta D1 = (T_1 / T_2) - 1$

   = ((321.2 + 460) / (120.24 + 460)) − 1

   = (781.2 / 580.24) − 1

   = .35

The density (and horsepower!) increase from Stage 1 intercooling is 35 percent.

Additional density gain from re-cooling the 120.4-degree F air in a second-stage intercooler will be:

$\Delta D2 = (T_1 / T_2) - 1$

   = ((120.24 + 460) / (49.65 + 460)) − 1

   = (580.24 / 509.65) − 1

   = .13

The density (and horsepower!) increase from Stage 2 intercooling is an additional 13 percent.

Total density gain from both stages is:

$D2 = (T_1 / T_2) - 1$

   = ((321.2 + 460) / (49.65 + 460)) − 1

   = (781.2 / 509.65) − 1

   = .53

This is the same as multiplying the Stage 1 density change of 1.35 times the Stage 2 density change of 1.13:

1.35 × 1.13 = 1.53

The power gain from single-stage intercooling of a 400-horsepower engine is 140, for a total of 540 horsepower. The power gain from the two-stage intercooling system is 212 horsepower, for a total of 612 horsepower (which is reduced by the power required to drive the refrigerant compressor). The second-stage intercooler added 50 percent of the additional power!

The *condenser* must have sufficient flow capacity without being a bottleneck, and it must have the capacity to completely transfer this heat into the atmosphere (which is a function of size and thermal efficiency, exactly like any heat exchanger). Manufacturers have this kind of data, or instrumented testing with hot liquid and known airflow will reveal it.

The *air-cooler* must have a large enough orifice tube to flow the required amount of refrigerant at a specified pressure drop, and it must have enough surface area in the core that the thermal efficiency is adequate to do the job, given the refrigerant temperature achievable in the evaporator. These are numbers you get from refrigeration engineers.

But let's consider the implications of refrigerant intercooling compared to ordinary air-water intercooling. Suppose 100 degree F water is available to chill the charge-cooler of an air-water intercooler, versus 32 degree F refrigerant in an air-refrigerant intercooler. Suppose both air-cooler designs have 80 percent thermal efficiency. If charge air enters the cooler at 350 degrees F, the air-water intercooler will reduce the temperature of the charge by 200 degrees [(350-100) × .8] to 150 degrees F. On the other hand, the refrigerant system will reduce temperature by 254 degrees [(350-32) × .8] to 95.6 degrees F.

What is the power difference?

Density-change = (Original temperature ABS / New temperature ABS) -1

Density-change$_{H2O}$ = (350 + 460) / (150 + 460) – 1 = .32, a 32 percent density increase

Density-change$_{Refrigerant}$ = (350 + 460) / (95.6 + 460) – 1 = .46, a 46 percent density increase

If the boosted engine would have made 400 horsepower without intercooling, than the relative power gain is 128 horsepower for air-water versus 200 horsepower for air-refrigerant, resulting in 528 versus 583 supercharged horsepower. If a refrigerant compressor could operate at the cost of 20 horsepower, then it's 128 vs. 163 horsepower, or a gain of a little more than 35 horses from refrigerant intercooling. This might be conservative. If a spark-ignition engine is knock-limited by the fuel, a 55-degree reduction in charge temperature could lower the detonation threshold enough to run a more efficient state of tune with more ignition advance, or perhaps more boost.

Depending on the application, it could make more sense to refrigerate a large water bath between boost events with a small,

HOW TO COMPUTE INTERCOOLING'S EFFECT ON AIR DENSITY AND HORSEPOWER

Assuming appropriate fuel delivery and engine management, any density increase from intercooling will increase horsepower commensurate to the density changes resulting from the temperature drop. If intake air density increases 25 percent, power increases 25 percent. This should be corrected for any offsetting density *decreases* if there is increased pressure drop through the intercooler that results from having to push a greater mass of air through the core.

It is easy to calculate changes in charge density resulting from the temperature drop of intercooling because the density change is a simple ratio of the before and after temperatures of the charge—converted to absolute temperature.

Suppose you are intercooling charge air that has been heated 250 degrees F above ambient temperature during supercharging to about 28-psi boost with a .75 percent efficient compressor? Assume ambient compressor-inlet temperature is 70 degrees F. This means the supercharged air is 320 degrees F leaving the compressor.

If an intercooler is capable of 60 percent thermal efficiency, it will cut the charge temperature increase by 60 percent of 250 degrees F, or 150 degrees F, so that the rise is only 100 degrees instead of 250. This will produce important density changes.

Adding in the inlet temperature of 70 degrees, the non-intercooled air leaves the compressor at 70 + 250 = 320F, which converts to 780R absolute by adding 460. Now let's send the air through the intercooler. The charge air left the compressor at 780R but it departs the intercooler at 70 + 100 (new rise) + 460 = 630R. The ratio of these numbers is the key to the density change according to the following:

$\Delta D = (T_1 / T_2) - 1$

Where:

ΔD = Density change resulting from a temperature increase or decrease
T_1 = Original temperature (degrees R) of air leaving the compressor
T_2 = New temperature (degrees R) of air leaving the intercooler

Plugging in the numbers,

$\Delta D = (T_1 / T_2) - 1$

= (780 / 630) - 1

= .238

The density (and horsepower!) increase from intercooling is 23.8 percent.

Imagine if an intercooler could return the charge temperature all the way back down to 70 degrees F:

$\Delta D = (780 / 530) - 1$

= .471

This approaches a 50 percent power increase from intercooling. No intercoolers are literally 100 percent efficient, but by using a very cold cooling medium (ice water, for example), some intercoolers can certainly get temperature down to or below ambient air temperature.

Unfortunately, this is not the full story because there will typically be at least *some* boost pressure drop due to aerodynamic drag in the intercooler.

efficient A/C compressor, or to use refrigeration in a two-stage intercooling system to remove heat after a primary air-cooled stage has already removed 70 or 80 percent of the charge heat.

As with the ice-water heat-sink intercooler, if the temperature of a refrigerant-cooled intercooler is too cold, core-icing can become a problem when the engine is not making boost in cold, humid weather.

Air-Cooled ("Air-Air") Intercoolers

Air-cooled intercoolers consist of a single integrated heat-exchanger unit, in which charge flows through the core from the inlet to the outlet end tank, and ambient air coolant blows through the core the narrow way from front to back.

Many motor vehicles employ a simplified architecture in which a single air-cooled heat-exchanger directly chills charge air using road-draft or fan-driven ambient air.

Air-air intercoolers have some important virtues that conspire to make them the most widely used charge-cooler for many applications:

- Air-air intercoolers usually cost less than more complex air-liquid systems.
- They are simple and reliable, with many having no moving parts whatsoever—
- though a few applications have dedicated, thermostatically controlled electric fans, and others (Porsche) use electrically operated cowl flaps or spoilers to manage ventilation through the air-cooler in order to provide improve cooling at lower vehicle speeds without having to sacrifice a good coefficient of drag at higher vehicle speeds when there is more than enough road draft available for cooling.
- Air-air intercoolers have relatively good thermal efficiency at high vehicle speeds.
- Most require little or no maintenance.

Air-air intercoolers also have their problematic aspects:

- The thermal conductivity of air is one-fourteenth that of water, which means that neither charge air nor coolant are effective at transferring heat to or from the metal coolant-charge interface of an air-cooled intercooler. Air-air intercoolers have to be large.
- Because air is a poor coolant, the air-cooler must be designed with the emphasis on high thermal transfer, meaning that pressure drop suffers compared to what's typical in a water-cooled intercooler—which can reduce power.
- A pressure drop increases the possibility of compressor surge, since the pressure ratio at the compressor discharge must be higher for a given airflow to maintain full target boost pressure in the intake manifold.
- The relatively large air-cooler volume required for high cooling power—as we've discussed previously—must be pressurized every time the engine makes boost.

Bell Intercoolers-designed air-cooled intercooler on the author's three-turbo Jaguar 4.2-liter I-6. Engine cooling is somewhat marginal on the vintage XKE Jaguar, but, fortunately, Jaguar had enlarged the air-intake in the nose of the car by 1969 from the problematic layout of early 1961+ cars. The engine and systems were arranged here for light run-in of a newly rebuilt version of the engine prior to dyno-testing. The engine was boosted with triple turbochargers and sequential progressive nitrous injection integrated into the EFI Technology engine-management system.

- Thermal efficiency suffers at low vehicle speeds when less coolant (ambient air) is available per unit of time.
- If an air-air intercooler is installed on an engine equipped with a mass airflow (MAF) meter that cannot be pressurized, the MAF must be installed upstream of the compressor, meaning intercooler volume can result in sluggish EMS response to airflow changes.

To minimize the distance charge air must travel to and from the engine, and to limit the volume of the intercooler plumbing, a few factory air-cooled intercoolers have been packaged in the engine compartment, but most front-engine factory and aftermarket systems are located in one of the radiator air-intakes at the front of the car for the ram-air effect—typically ahead of or beside the radiator and A/C condenser unit (appearing superficially like an aluminum radiator). Vehicles as varied as the 2.3-liter Mustang SVO and the Nissan Z had air-air intercoolers located at the top of the engine, below an air scoop in the hood or engine cover. On mid- or rear-engine cars, an air-air intercooler is usually located in an air intake on the side of the vehicle, though Porsche has used air-cooled intercoolers located in the engine cover above the rear-mounted 911 engine.

The amount of ambient air available as a coolant in practical terms is not infinite, but it is massive compared to the charge airflow through virtually any engine; an air-air intercooler encountering ambient road-draft air rammed toward it by the speed of the vehicle will encounter more than 5,000 cfm per square foot at freeway speeds and even more at racing speeds. However, the pressure of air encountering a flat intercooler surface at 60 miles per hour is less than .06 psi.

Streamlined cooling and charge air channels, with an optimized airfoil shape where ambient air enters the core, will help keep excessive amounts of air from being deflected around the cooler by *lowering* air pressure in front of the cooler. Anything that can be done aerodynamically with ducting to increase the ram-air effect of ambient air hitting the intercooler will improve the thermal efficiency of the cooler. The bottom line goal, though, is to maintain maximum airflow through the cooler, *not* maximum pressure in front of it.

Fabricating ducting with priority given to preventing reversion will help ram more cooling air through the intercooler. A funnel-shaped duct is better than no ducting, but—counterintuitively—reversed-funnel ducting, where the inlet is slightly *smaller* than the area of the intercooler, can be even better if you can minimize high-pressure zones that occur at the boundaries of a funnel duct and consequent reversion away from the "mouth" of the intercooler. Auxiliary fans are worthy of consideration if the thermal efficiency of the cooler is marginal and there is any doubt about whether enough coolant (air) is penetrating the core.

Because of the huge quantity of ambient air available as a total-loss coolant, and the fact that any coolant gets hotter as it moves through a heat-exchanger (becoming less and less effective as it penetrates deeper in the core as the narrowing temperature differential between the coolant and the charge), air-cooled intercoolers achieve higher thermal efficiency when they are built with the largest possible frontal area and a thin core. In the real world, the rear half of an air-cooled core delivers only about 25 percent of the cooling. The extra inch of a 3-inch thick core increases cooling only about 10 to 15 percent above that of a 2-inch core.

Real estate in the core of an air-cooled intercooler is scarce. You need as much space as possible to move charge air vertically through the core without a pressure drop, but you also need all the space you can get to move ambient air through the core from front to back in order to achieve the highest possible thermal efficiency.

In terms of volume, air-cooled heat-exchanger cores compromise by dedicating approximately half the core to charge air and half to coolant air, but in terms of available airflow *area*, ambient air gets vastly more frontal area for throughput than does the charge flow—and it needs to, as we shall see in a moment. Coolant mass airflow occurs at ambient pressure (or, on occasion, a few percent more from the ram effect of speed), while the charge mass-airflow is boosted significantly above ambient any time the blower is making boost.

Cores are available in rectangular modules of various sizes, and these can be cut or stacked in various ways to achieve the ideal size for a particular application. Typical air-cooled cores are available from intercooler specialists like Bell Intercoolers and Spearco in thicknesses of approximately 2, 3, 3.5, 4.5, and 6 inches, with charge air-channel lengths available in a

The Paxton air-cooled intercooling system for late-model Ford Mustang GTs is actually two side-by-side intercooler cores with an end-tank crossover, which allows hot compressed air and cooled charge to enter and exit the intercooler in close proximity. *Paxton*

163

variety of sizes, from 5 to 26 inches long. Core widths are available from Spearco in sizes ranging from 5 to 32 inches, but can be shortened prior to end-tank installation. Unneeded or unwanted charge air channels can be eliminated by cutting through the adjacent cooling channel/fins with a band saw and welding on a section of sheet metal for appearance. A core can be lengthened by stacking additional core modules side-by-side and welding them together at the end seams before installing end tanks of the appropriate length.

Water-cooled air cooler cores—which need not have a large frontal area for effective air-cooling—tend to be more compact and square, with cores ranging in size from about 2x5x7 to 12x12x13.5 inches. Because of the need to divide space in the core between charge air and coolant (whatever the medium), 50 percent of the area in each open face of the core is not available for airflow. Another 5 percent of the open space in a core is lost to additional structural metal forming the boundaries of the air channels, leaving about 45 percent of the area available for actually moving air. Charge air flows vertically up or down through an air-cooled core, and cooling air moves straight through it like air through a radiator. A 12x24x2-inch core thus provides 24 × 2 = 48 square inches of charge flow area, minus 55 percent, or 48 – 26.4 = 21.6 square inches, which is equivalent to the flow area of a pipe with 5.24 inches of inside diameter. Meanwhile, the core provides 12 × 24 = 288 square inches of frontal area, minus 55 percent, or 288 – 158.4 = 129.6 square inches of coolant flow area (which is the size of a fan duct about 13 inches in diameter). In either case the actual flow rate will vary, depending on the density of internal cooling fins or turbulators.

To estimate appropriate air-air intercooler core size, the trick is to start with a cfm requirement for the engine at full boost. Assume, for example, that the engine requires 1,000 cfm. This, according to published charts from Bell Intercoolers, typically requires an average of about 53 square inches of intercooler flow area. Since less than half of the core is actually

AIR-WATER VERSUS AIR-REFRIGERANT INTERCOOLING

Assume the water coolant available to cool the charge-cooler of an air-water intercooler is at 90 degrees F. Suppose that a refrigerant intercooler could deliver refrigerant coolant to the air cooler at 32 degrees F. Assume the air-cooler units of both intercoolers are 80 percent efficient. How does the cooling power of the two intercooler systems compare?

If charge air enters each air-cooler at 306 degrees F, the air-water system will reduce the temperature of the charge by:

$(306-90) \times .8 = 173F$

Therefore, the intercooled charge will exit the air-water intercooler at:

$306 - 173 = 133F$

On the other hand, the air-refrigerant system will reduce temperature by:

$(306 - 32) \times .8 = 219.2F$

Therefore, the intercooled charge will exit the air-refrigerant intercooler at:

$306 - 219.2 = 86.8F$

Okay, so how much power will the two different intercoolers make?

$\Delta D = (T_1 / T_2) - 1$

Where:
ΔD = Density change resulting from a temperature increase or decrease
T_1 = Original temperature (degrees R) of air leaving the compressor
T_2 = New temperature (degrees R) of air leaving the intercooler

Converting the number to absolute temperature:

$T_1 = 306F; 306F + 460 = 766R$

$T_2 = 133F + 460 = 593R$ (air-water intercooler-out temp)
or,
$T_2 = 86.8F + 460 = 546.8R$ (air-refrigerant intercooler-out temp)

Therefore, plugging in the air-water numbers,

$\Delta D = (T_1 / T_2) - 1$

$= (766 / 593) - 1$

$= .29$

The density (and horsepower!) increase from air-water intercooling is 34 percent.

Plugging in the air-water numbers,

$\Delta D = (766 / 546.8) - 1$

$= .4$

The density/power increase from air-refrigerant intercooling is 43 percent.

If the engine could have theoretically have made 400 horsepower without intercooling, than the air-water power increase is 136 horsepower versus 172 horsepower.

But the air-refrigerant system will rob power to drive the compressor (the air-water system also has an electric water pump, but that's a negligible parasitic loss). Published tests from one chassis dynamometer found that running a standard A/C system dropped torque by 8 to 9 pound-feet across the rpm range in a 3.0-liter BMW. This equated to about 11 hp out of 232, or about 5 percent, with the loss increasing at higher rpm as the compressor turned faster.

If an A/C-type compressor could cool an intercooler at a cost of 15 horsepower, then it's 136 vs. 157 horsepower, or a gain of 21 horses from refrigerant intercooling. The break-even point would be if the compressor robbed 36 horsepower.

available to flow air (again, typically 45 percent), then 53/.45 indicates you'll need 117 square inches of core. The same charts predict that cores with low-density finning may require as little as 42 square inches of flow area (in a 93-square-inch core), while high-density cores could require a worst case of 68 square inches (in a 151-square-inch core). Taking the average case, and using a 2-inch thick core, the core needs to be 117 / 2 = 58.2 inches wide (which is almost 5 feet wide!). If it's a 3-inch core, 39 inches wide will do the job.

Obviously, there is a limited amount of space to locate to an intercooler in a factory-built street vehicle without getting into serious sheet-metal modifications, particularly if it's a sports car with a small nose. In some cases it may be possible and necessary to split an air-cooled intercooler into two or more entirely separate cooling units, which might, for example, be located in front of the front radiator *and* somewhere in or near the two front wheelwells. Charge air should always be routed in *parallel* to the various air-cooled cooling units, since thermal efficiency is higher when the temperature differential between charge and coolant is highest, which would not be the case if the charge were successively staged in series through multiple intercoolers of equal thermal capacity.

In some cases, it may be possible to gain additional intercooling power by installing more than one intercooler unit in the same place—say, in the nose of the car in front of the radiator—with one core farther forward than the other and the two cores partially overlapping such that there is space for significant cold ambient air to bypass the frontal cooler and reach the rear unit without being pre-heated. There may also be space for exhausted warm air from the frontal unit to evacuate without having to pass through the rearward cooler unit. Obviously such a system is too complex to realistically be modeled with high confidence, so it must unfold as an R&D project—an experiment that must be instrumented, then tested, analyzed, developed, and proven.

Spray-Cooled Intercooler: The efficiency of an air-air intercooler can be improved by spraying water, alcohol, or various nonflammable expanding compressed gases or liquids, such as nitrous oxide or liquid nitrogen, against the exterior of the core. This enhances the cooling power of the intercooler with latent heat of vaporization of the spray liquid to the thermal transfer abilities of air. A few limited-production factory rally cars have been sold equipped with auxiliary water-spray intercooler systems. Auxiliary liquid sprays work.

According to some published, instrumented road testing, well-designed pro-built aftermarket water-spray systems that are carefully installed, tested, and optimized can typically reduce charge-air temperature as much as 25 degrees F, which will typically produce a 5 percent increase in air density. The best spray systems use a microcontroller to manage water-delivery so that water is not wasted when it's not needed. This would include when the intercooler is not hot, or when it is hot but the vehicle is idling in traffic, when there's rainy weather and the intercooler is already wet, and so forth.

The downside of enhancing intercooler cooling power with fluid spray is that the fluid reservoir must be refilled frequently, and a heavy reservoir of water must be tankered around. Water spray is illegal on some drag strips if the spray wets the track in a way that interferes with traction or safety.

Water-Injection Intercooling: Injecting water into the charge air—or better still, injecting a 50-50 fluid mixture of water and methanol—will cool charge air with the latent heat of vaporization of the injection fluid as it evaporates or turns into steam—which can be very effective in fighting

The Kraftwerks Honda Fit high-boost upgrade package allows the base Kraftwerks supercharging system to run at 10-psi boost for off-highway use for a 75 percent power increase over stock. The upgrade includes a cowl air-air intercooler designed to return charge to near-ambient temperature, larger fuel injectors, and Hondata reflashed Honda ECU to handle the big injectors. *Kraftwerks*

detonation. Water-injection intercooling is not usually considered to be a power-adder in and of itself, since the injection fluid vapor displaces a certain amount of air, which will negate some or all of the increase in charge density. Windshield-washer fluid—containing water and methanol—makes a great injection fluid, or you can make your own brew from water and methanol, ethanol, or iso-propanol alcohol, all of which love combining with water.

Water injection originated as a critical anti-knock countermeasure for World War II piston-engine combat aircraft engaged in maximum-performance climb maneuvers, and it moved into mainstream automotive use when Oldsmobile used "Turbo Rocket Fluid" injection to fight detonation in its early-1960s high-compression, factory-turbocharged Olds Jetfire. Water injection was a common anti-knock countermeasure for carbureted turbo engines in the 1970s and early 1980s, but it fell out of favor when electronic injection and programmable aftermarket engine-management systems allowed tuners to conquer detonation with fuel, timing, and intercoolers.

Water-injection has made something of a comeback in recent years, particularly as California reduced the octane of street premium fuel, because it combines well with most other anti-knock countermeasures to lower the octane number requirement of an engine. As tuners have pushed "streetable" boosted performance to levels that would once have been considered pure fantasy, water injection has once again become a valuable tool to consider in heat and knock control.

And water injection is much better than it used to be. In recent years aftermarket companies have released products with names like Aqua-Mist. These improved systems don't simply pee liquid into the intake charge using a modified windshield-washer system, but actually deliver 50-psi-plus injection under electronic control. This provides accurate quantities of injection fluid and the excellent atomization required to maximize the cooling effect by producing tiny drops of injection fluid with a large surface area. A modern water-injection system precisely injects water or injection fluid in a ratio that's typically 10 to 25 percent of the engine fuel requirement.

Some older racers and forced-induction specialists hate water injection, which they remember as being unreliable from the old days when it had to function with electric or mechanical controls rather than computer logic controlling the system. There is nothing as effective as a knocked-to-death, expensive race engine to sour you on unreliable water injection. But the problems of electro-mechanical water injection are about as relevant to modern engines as the problems of magneto ignitions and carburetors. Today's modern aftermarket programmable engine-management systems have the capability to manage water injection as reliably as any other complex engine system.

Water injection is effective in preventing spark knock in gasoline engines, and some water-injection vendors claim it is effective in lowering EGT in diesel engines, thus facilitating overfueling diesel engines for more power without flaming the engine (though GM Research did not find EGT reductions when it studied fluid injection—see sidebar on pg. 167). But since water injection fights knock by lowering combustion temperatures in a spark-ignition powerplant (the GM study confirmed that it does do that with high effectiveness), it is unclear why fluid injection would not reduce EGT in a diesel.

One of the biggest problems with water injection is that the required amount of water is quite small, requiring a small orifice that can easily become blocked with dirt or corrosion. But that is not much different from electronic fuel injection, which also must be protected with in-line fuel filters and fine screens upstream of each injector. Another problem is that you have to keep the system filled with injection fluid or water.

Instead of installing a big-block FE Ford V-8, the builders of this Cobra kit car decided to keep the front end light for improved handling. They installed a lightweight, ultra-high-boost SVO 2.3-liter turbo powerplant with refrigerant intercooling to cool charge temperatures below ambient temperature. Freon was injected into an evaporator chamber surrounding the air-cooler unit.

GM L18 8100 8.1-liter (496-cid) big-block (454-type) truck V-8 with Whipple twin-screw supercharging system. Note the large, black air-water intercooler above the rear of the engine: Stock 8100s had 225 to 450 stock horsepower and super-duty truck engines with supercharger conversions that pull continuous heavy loads up long hills need massive intercoolers. *Whipple Superchargers*

Either way, if you're depending on water injection and it stops, unless you've got a functioning automatic knock sensor ignition-retard system, the engine will begin knocking the next time you hit the gas and make real boost. Water injection permits more timing advance or more boost without knock, but it produces diminishing returns in power gain as water vapor displaces charge oxygen in increasing amounts and eventually begins to cause misfiring in spark-ignition engines.

True, water injection is one more thing to go wrong, one more complex system that must be maintained and kept full and worried about. But there is actually no reason that water injection can't be as reliable as fuel injection (particularly if you're willing to spend the money to build a robust, fail-safe, fluid-injection system). Water injection can be made to work, and it is ultimately one more thing in the bag of tricks for managing heat in a supercharged powerplant.

Air-Peltier Junction Intercooling: Michael Perkins patented a practical electronic intercooler (U.S. patent No. 7,171,955) that uses Peltier Junctions to create an electronic heat pump powerful enough to cool engine charge to 35 degrees F.

The Peltier effect, which was first seen by Jean Peltier in 1834, creates a heat difference from an electric voltage. When a current passes through two dissimilar metals (or n/p-type semiconductors) that are connected to each other at two junctions, the current drives a transfer of heat from one "Peltier junction" to the other. The result is that one junction cools off while the other heats up, and if the two junctions are thermally isolated from each other, the effect can be used for thermoelectric cooling.

The Peltier-effect cooling unit requires fairly significant electrical power, so it is not desirable to run it constantly. Perkins' trick was to send charge only through the thermoelectric cooler unit during actual boost events and otherwise divert intake air along a path that bypasses the intercooler to keep the heat exchanger surfaces from being continuously warmed by normal ambient charge air. This keeps the cooler ready for immediate action when the boost hits.

Perkins' original prototype used a 225-watt junction array and consumed roughly 27 amps at 12 volts. The unit ran a water-cooled heat sink block and copper exchanger with heat pipes to speed the cooling. A double-insulated "thermos" housed the exchanger, which was kept out of the charge air stream except during boost conditions. Although a Peltier intercooler is somewhat complicated, other active "chilling" methods, such as using a refrigerated air cooler, are considerably more plumbing-intensive and vulnerable to failure.

The Peltier-effect technical explanation goes as follows:

When a current (*I*) is made to flow through the circuit, heat is exuded at an upper junction (T_2), and absorbed at a lower junction (T_1). The Peltier heat absorbed by the lower junction per unit time Q, is equal to

Kenne Bell—fanatics about heat management—introduced the liquid-cooled twin-screw supercharger, designed to minimize charge heating in the supercharger and reduce thermal loading on the internal bearings. *Kenne Bell*

$$Q = \Pi_{AB} I$$
$$= (\Pi_B - \Pi_A) I$$

Where:

Π = The Peltier coefficient Π_{AB} of the entire thermocouple

Π_A = The coefficient of material A

Π_B = The coefficient of material B

I = Current flowing through the circuit

The Peltier coefficients represent how much heat current is carried per unit charge through a certain material. Because charging current must be continuous across a junction, the associated heat flow will develop a discontinuity if Π_A and Π_B are different.

This causes a nonzero divergence at the junction, causing heat to accumulate or deplete there, depending on the sign of the current. But when electrons flow from a high-density region to a low-density region, they expand and cool—like a refrigerant gas. The conductors attempt to return to the electron equilibrium that existed before a current was switched on by absorbing energy at one connector and releasing it at the other.

Individual couples are connected in series to enhance the thermal power. The polarity of the current controls the direction of heat transfer, which means reversing the polarity will change the direction of transfer and thus the direction of the heat that's absorbed and exuded. A Peltier intercooler is thus a kind of solid-state active heat pump that transfers heat from one side of the device located in the charge air stream into the other side, which is an air-cooled heat sink.

New technologies being developed for constructing Peltier-type junctions, by companies such as CoolChips and NanoCooler, promise more efficient and cost-effective devices, which could lead to broadened use of this active technology to make increased boost levels possible with safer, lower charge-air temperatures.

GM'S FLUID INJECTION RESEARCH

GM Research studied the impact of water injection into the intake air upon the combustion process. Testing examined the anti-knock characteristics of water, minimum advance for best torque (MBT) spark requirements, engine power and efficiency, volumetric efficiency, lean operating limits, smoke, exhaust gas temperature, engine cooling requirements, drivability, and exhaust emissions. The studies ignored engine durability, lubricant degradation, catalyst deterioration, and long-term deposit accumulation.

The studies found:

Water has definite anti-knock characteristics. Adding water at a mass flow rate of up to 40 percent fuel weight increased the research octane linearly by roughly 10 numbers, from 90 to 100. Motor octane increased in a linear fashion from 82 to 87 at 20 percent water (due to the heat of vaporization of the water, it was not possible to obtain a motor octane number with 40-weight water addition).

Alternatively, without increasing fuel octane, 40 percent water addition allowed the knock-limited engine compression ratios to be increased one full ratio (in the testing, from 8:1, to 9:1), which increased engine power and efficiency. This increased engine efficiency approximately 3 percent. Other than this, the effects of water injection on engine efficiency (reduced compression workload due to the water's heat of vaporization reducing the gas pressure by lowering temperature, versus reduced peak combustion pressure, which decreased the work done during the combustion cycle) essentially balanced each other out.

MBT increases with water injection. Forty percent water increased MBT requirements by 5 to 15 degrees because the water addition slowed down the combustion process.

The addition of water to the inlet charge had little or no effect on thermal efficiency, volumetric efficiency, lean operating limits, smoke, exhaust gas temperature (EGT), and engine cooling requirements. Water addition to the engine slightly reduced the coolant system load.

Exhaust emissions were affected, with oxides of nitrogen decreasing by up to 40 percent with 40 percent water, while hydrocarbon emissions increased about 50 percent with direct manifold water injection—and this in spite of the fact that GM determined that water was not decreasing the efficiency of the catalytic converter. Carbon monoxide emissions essentially stayed the same.

Scientists testing water injection concluded that water injection offers tuners the following:

- The ability to use lower octane fuels safely without detonation in an otherwise unchanged engine
- The ability to increase compression or boost without engine octane requirements increasing, with the benefits of increased power or efficiency
- Reduced oxides of nitrogen, by lowering combustion temperatures

Other findings included the following:

1. HC emissions increased with water injection, but these can be reduced to acceptable levels with other technology.
2. Water injection tends to contaminate the lubrication system (which can reportedly be eliminated by direct injection of water into the cylinder near the end of compression).
3. Water injection may corrode internal engine surfaces.
4. In cold climates, injection water freeze protection can be achieved by the addition of methanol.

Aqua-mist water-alcohol injection systems brought modern electronic controls to charge cooling. Water injection can be extremely effective as a supplemental anti-knock countermeasure in difficult circumstances where premium street gasoline is less than 93 octane (in California, for example) and detonation is a serious problem.

Perkins "Blizzard Booster" installed on a 24-valve Ford SHO engine. The hot side of the Peltier junction electronic intercooler is liquid-cooled by an air-cooled heat exchanger/heat sink located in the air stream at the bottom of the grille air intake. The cold side of the Peltier junction is located in the charge air stream below the hot-side junction in the form of a copper-finned heat-exchanging air cooler. In order to prevent ambient air from warming the air cooler when the electric centrifugal supercharger is not boosting the engine, the Perkins system bypasses charger air around the Peltier intercooler through a separate air path to the throttle body (to the left of the cooling-path). This cooler is normally able to cool moderately supercharged air 45 degrees below ambient air temperature.

Chapter 8
Buying and Installing a Supercharger Kit

There are plenty of aftermarket supercharger conversion kits out there. For some common performance vehicles you'll find multiple supercharging options, both in terms of competing vendors offering kits for the same vehicle or engine, as well as multiple packages from the same vendor that offer various "stages" of increasing levels of supercharged performance.

Because of consolidation in the performance industry, some brands that were formerly competitors are now part of the same company. Vortech, Lysholm, and Paxton are now one company, with Vortech and Paxton offering centrifugal superchargers and kits, Lysholm offering twin-screw units and kits.

Leaving aside the intrinsic performance differences of the various supercharging technologies discussed in Chapter 4, Supercharger Architecture, it is important to compare apples to apples when you consider power-adder options, particularly when it comes to price. Some supercharger kits are very complete when it comes to including all the forced-induction components you'll need but do not include essential engine-

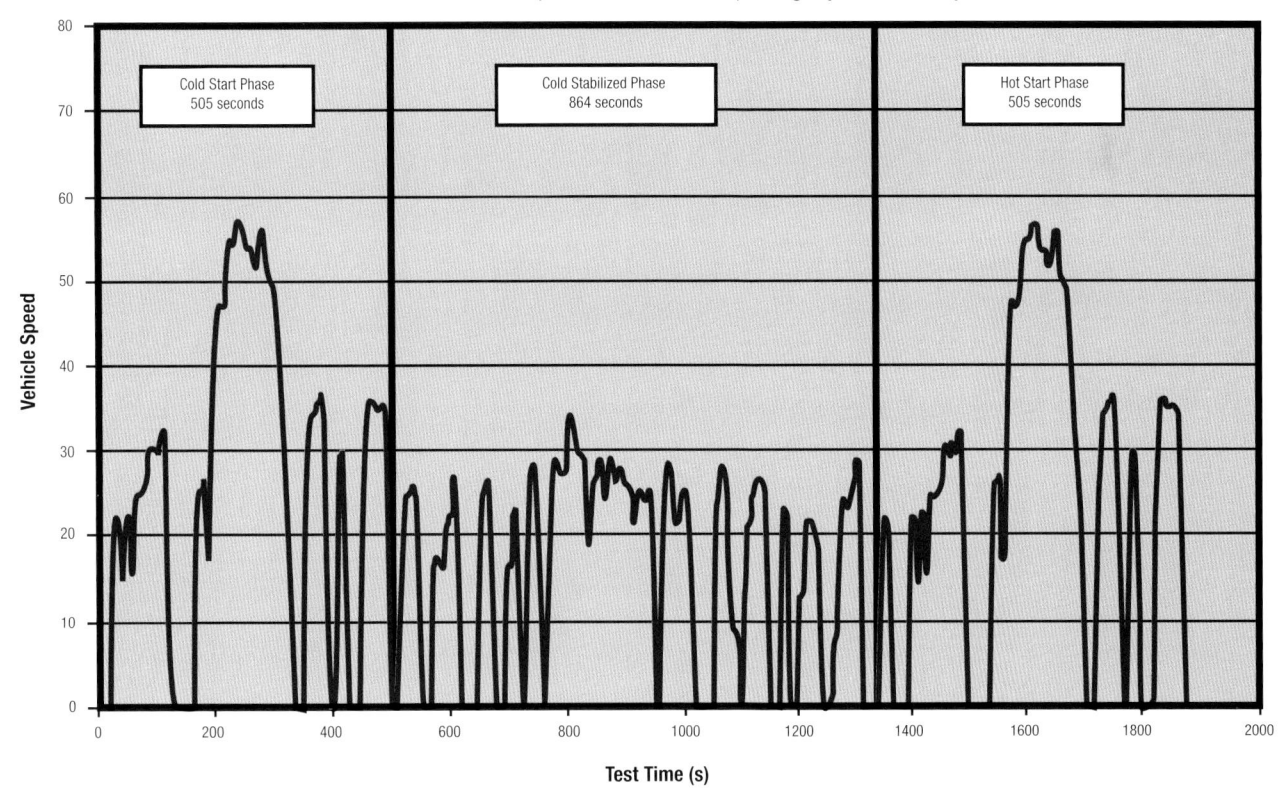

Data log of EPA Federal Test Procedure. For 50-state legality for on-highway use, suppliers of supercharger kits must prove that installation does not degrade stock engine emissions more than 10 percent in a pre-determined test procedure on a rolling road chassis torque cell dyno. Note that the test took a little more than 31 minutes, including idle time, and covered a bit more than 11 miles, with average speed of 21.19 miles per hour and maximum speed of about 55 miles per hour. Since power-adders mainly affect operation at wide-open throttle, the FTP has allowed approval of hundreds of aftermarket supercharger conversion systems.

169

management components, without which the kit cannot perform well and might damage your engine. Read the fine print: There is nothing wrong with buying a kit that you know needs additional parts, but no one likes expensive surprises.

In fact, a kit with unbundled engine-management components is desirable because you can have it your way. You can manage fuel and spark with a primo standalone aftermarket engine-management system, if, say, you plan to maximize power across the board and go racing. Orr perhaps an ECU recalibration or a much less expensive variable-rate-of-gain fuel pressure regulator with static timing changes is all you need if you're not running too much boost and want to save money or need a package that will pass emissions. Most supercharger kit suppliers will tell you their kit has the best numbers, at least in some area, but in fact it is great engine management—not the highest horsepower numbers at some subset of the dyno graph—that is critical to achieving the kind of drivability that makes a car really perform and genuinely fun to drive.

CONSIDERATIONS

Does the kit include engine-management modifications that will provide proper fuel and spark across the range of the engine's performance envelope under boost conditions? There is no way to do a supercharger conversion without engine management changes.

Is boost fuel enrichment and engine management sophisticated and perfect at all breakpoints of engine speed and loading? Some supercharger kits throw a bunch of fuel at the engine under boost conditions that are only really correct some of the time—like a stopped clock that is right twice a day.

Will the kit require super-premium fuel to avoid detonation on your vehicle? Is the kit design conservative enough that you will not be fighting endemic detonation problems if you install the kit correctly and operate the vehicle the way people operate vehicles when they install supercharger conversion kits?

Are the instructions complete and well written, with good supporting drawings, photography, and videos?

Does the kit vendor offer high-quality telephone tech support and hand-holding from people who are polite and articulate and know what they're doing? In advance of a sale, will the vendor supply references of customers who made use of tech support?

How good is the manufacturing quality assurance? Some kits contain components that are difficult to manufacture.

Is the kit emission-legal in all 50 states? Supercharger kits are *never* legal for street use in the United States unless the vehicle is quite old or the supplier has obtained an EPA or CARB exemption order. Such an order can be granted to certify aftermarket specialty equipment that are able to pass muster with the Environmental Protection Agency or the California Air Resources Board in a rigorous test procedure that proves installation of the product does not degrade emissions more than 10 percent when operated in a specific driving cycle on a chassis dynamometer. A recent check of the CARB database found 285 exemption orders under the classification "Supercharger System/Supercharger Modification," some of which covered a large numbers of vehicles.

How much power and torque does a supercharger conversion kit really make as installed? Does the manufacturer provide dyno graphs? Are the graphs realistic for your vehicle in precisely the configuration you are buying? What corrections have been made for weather and altitude? Are there dyno graphs available from customers who have installed the product and tested the power and torque? Are there boost and air-fuel ratio numbers on the graph? Keep in mind that there is normally nothing on a dyno graph to prove it was generated by the vehicle and engine it is purported to be from. And if it is, unless the dyno graph includes data-logger information, there is no way of knowing what boost pressure and fuel octane the engine required to achieve the numbers shown on the dyno graph. Sad but true, temperature correction can make a large difference in the reported power numbers, but there is nothing to prevent unscrupulous dyno operators from heat-soaking the dyno weather station before a run. As they say, *caveat emptor* (let the buyer beware).

INSTALLING A SUPERCHARGER KIT

Here's what's involved in installing a "typical" supercharger conversion kit, in this case Magnuson Products' Eaton TVS-based modern Roots-based package for the 2010 Camaro V-8.

When the kit arrives:

- Make a parts check to make certain the kit is complete.
- Take a look at exactly what you are going to need in terms of tools, time, and experience.
- Review the limited warranty with care.
- When unpacking the supercharger kit, *do not* lift the supercharger assembly by the black plastic bypass actuator. This is pre-set from the factory and can be altered if used as a lifting point!

Before installation:

- Run the vehicle nearly out of (regular) fuel and fill up with premium gasoline of at least 91 octane.
- Relieve the fuel system pressure before servicing fuel system components in order to reduce the risk of fire and personal injury. After relieving the system pressure, a small amount of fuel may be released when servicing the fuel lines or connections. In order to reduce the risk of personal injury, cover the regulator and fuel line fittings with a shop towel before disconnecting. This will catch

any fuel that may leak out. Place the towel in an approved container when the job is complete.
- Magnuson recommends installing a new GM fuel filter at the time of supercharger installation. Use stock spark plugs with stock plug gap.

Keep in mind:

- Magna Charger systems are manufactured to produce about 20 raw horsepower per pound of boost at sea level. High altitudes will produce different numbers.
- The kit is designed for engines in good mechanical condition only. Installation on high-mileage or damaged engines is not recommended and may result in engine failure.
- Magna Charger is not responsible for the engine or consequential damages.
- Aftermarket engine recalibration devices that modify fuel and spark curve (including, but not limited to programmers) are not recommended and may cause engine damage or failure.
- Use of non-Magna Charger approved programming will void all warranties.

Tools required:

- Metric wrench set
- 1/4–3/8-inch and 1/2-inch-drive metric socket set (Standard and Deep)
- 3/8-inch and 1/2-inch-drive ft-lb and in-lb torque wrenches
- Phillips and flat-head screwdrivers
- Fuel line quick disconnect tools (included in kit)
- Small or angled 3/8-inch drill motor
- Drain pan
- Hose cutters

- Hose clamp pliers
- Safety glasses
- Metric Allen socket set 3/8-inch drive
- Shop vacuum cleaner

Helpful tool:

- Air or electric impact wrench

ACTUAL INSTALLATION PROCEDURE

Basically, you are going to disconnect some stuff around the front and top of the engine, remove the intake manifold and valley cover, remove the fan shroud and disconnect the top radiator support brackets, and remove the serpentine belt. After that, you'll begin modifications: Drill and pin the harmonic balancer, install a replacement valley cover with added clearance, install the supercharger-intercooler-intake assembly, install the intercooler water-cooler heat exchanger in front of the radiator, and install the intercooler pump and reservoir. Move some OE parts like the throttle body from components that will not be needed like the stock intake manifold to the supercharger. Finally, you're going to reinstall some stock parts such as the airbox/MAF assembly, and then you can rock and roll.

The installation manual is detailed and exhaustive, but the specific procedures are:

1. Drive the car until it is virtually out of fuel and fill up with premium fuel.
2. Reflash the stock onboard computer.
3. Disconnect the battery, remove the fuel cap and engine cover.
4. Drain the radiator and save the fluid for screening and recycling back into the engine.
5. Remove the airbox and air inlet tube, vent tube, and heater hoses.
6. Disconnect engine electrics: the EVAP solenoid, MAP sensor, eight fuel injectors, and throttle body.
7. Disconnect certain vacuum, PCV, and emissions hoses.
8. Disconnect the fuel line with the provided special tool.
9. Remove the OEM intake manifold after removing 10 8-millimeter bolts.
10. Vacuum the valve cover, clean cylinder heads with solvent, and tape intake ports.
11. Disconnect MAF connector and remove the airbox.
12. Remove the radiator overflow, steam vent hose, and fan shroud assembly.
13. Remove the harmonic balancer bolt and use the guide tool to drill the harmonic balancer and install two pins that positively prevent additional load on the crank pulley from twisting the balancer; then install the new harmonic balancer bolt.

Magnuson MP2300 supercharger, manifold, and intercooler assembly for the GM LS3 V-8. *Magnuson Products*

14. Release the belt tensioner and serpentine belt.
15. Remove the oil pressure sensor from the valley cover.
16. Replace the OE valley cover with the new unit with the OE gasket and O-rings, and reinstall and clock the oil pressure sender and connector the electrical plug and locking clip.
17. Remove the upper radiator mounting brackets and assemble the intercooler heat-exchanger unit with hooks, hose barbs, and hoses and adhesive foam, and slide into place in front of the radiator.
18. Replace the air-deflector strip and upper radiator brackets and bolts and the fan shroud, reconnect coolant-recover hoses, and reattach the upper radiator hose to the water pump and radiator.
19. Attach the electronic throttle control extension harness to the stock ETC harness connection.
20. Remove direct-fire coil brackets with four coils and each side of the engine for modifications. Remove the wire loom covers.
21. Remove the heater hoses and clamps. Cut and install new hoses.
22. Remove the MAP sensor, electronic throttle, throttle O-ring, and brake boost valve from the stock intake manifold and install them on the supercharger-intake assembly. Fit the intake manifold gaskets to the supercharger manifold.
23. Install the supercharger assembly on the block and torque in place.
24. Install the MAP sensor extension harness and connect the engine wiring harness to the MAP sensor and fuel injectors.
25. Install the modified coil brackets and coils on the valve covers, connect the stock plug connectors, and connect the extended ETC harness to the throttle.
26. Connect the replacement fuel line to the supercharger manifold fuel rail and stock fuel supply.
27. Plug in various EVAP, PCV, and brake booster hoses, add-on check valves, and connections, and secure with cable-ties.
28. Connect replacement intake air temp (IAT) connector by amputating the stock connector and splicing new wires to the stock IAT wiring with heat-shrink insulation.
29. Remove the stock belt tensioner pulley and install replacement (smaller) pulley in its place.
30. Install the replacement (extended) serpentine belt and tighten the tensioner pulley with (temporary) pivot bolt installed.
31. Reinstall the airbox/MAF unit and plug in the harness connector.
32. Clamp the intercooler pump to the vehicle frame rail.
33. Attach the reservoir bracket to the passenger-side coil bracket and install the reservoir bottle in the bracket.
34. Cut the intercooler hose to length, route the hoses to the various hose barbs on the heat exchanger, intercooler, heat exchanger, and pump. Install the clamps on the hoses and push on the hose barbs and clamp in place.
35. Attach the various intercooler pump harness wires to the stock electrical system in the engine compartment fusebox and attach the harness to the intercooler pump.
36. Attach the replacement air inlet tube to the airbox and throttle body and tighten the clamps.
37. Cut a piece of 3/8-inch PCV to attach the PCV fitting on the passenger-side valve cover to the hose barb on the bottom of the air inlet tube and push both end on the hose barbs.
38. Reattach the battery.
39. Fill the intercooler system with 50-50 antifreeze.
40. Refill the engine-cooling system with the (recycled) water-antifreeze solution.
41. Affix the replacement vacuum hose diagram and belt routing diagram in a conspicuous place and attach the "Use Premium Fuel Only" decal to the gas tank fill cap or door.
42. Run the engine for a short time and check for leaks, topping off fluids as necessary.
43. Test drive the vehicle for the first few miles under ordinary driving conditions, listening for any abnormal noises, vibrations, misfires, or anything whatsoever that does not seem normal. Expect the supercharger to make a (slight) whining noise under boost conditions. Retension the serpentine belt after the initial test drive.
44. Work gradually up to full-throttle runs, *listening carefully for detonation*, and if there is any *get out of the throttle immediately*. Low-octane fuel left in the tank could cause detonation.
45. Recheck fluids regularly over the first 1,000 miles.

A Magnuson 2010–2011 Camaro SS supercharger kit. *Magnuson Products*

172

PROJECT 1
Installing the Magnuson Products 2010–2011 Camaro SS Supercharger Kit

Photos by Magnuson Performance Products

1 A Camaro engine cover before removal.

2 Removing the stock Camaro intake manifold.

3 Installing the air-water intercooler heat exchanger in front of the stock radiator.

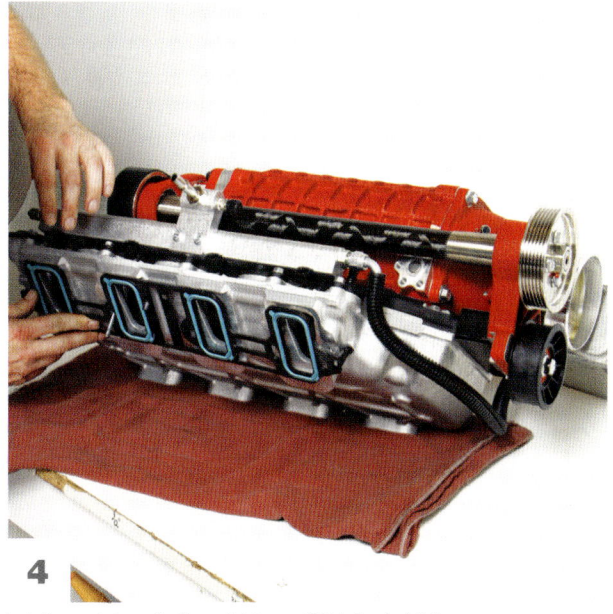

4 Installing gaskets on the blower intake manifold before installation.

5 Lowering the supercharger assembly into place on the Camaro engine. Get help to maneuver the heavy assembly.

6 Bolting down the supercharger manifold.

7 A ribbed supercharger pulley drive (top), idler pulley (left), and tensioner.

8 A Camaro SS with installed Magnuson supercharger kit is ready to rock and roll.

BUYING AND INSTALLING A SUPERCHARGER KIT

174

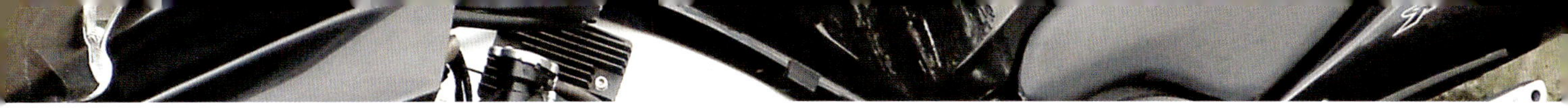

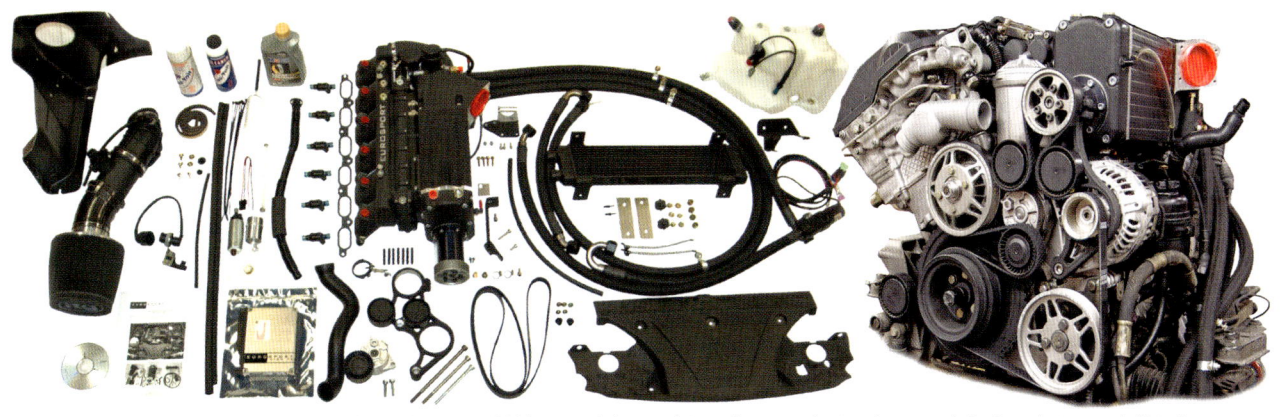

Eurosport's twin-screw blower kit for the BMW M3 with intake manifold-integrated air-water intercooler, remote heat exchanger, and plastic coolant reservoir. Note the replacement upgraded fuel injectors, replacement mass airflow sensor, and high-flow fuel pump. *Eurosport*

The 2003–06 Dodge SRT-10 Viper 8.3-liter V-10 with installed dual-pass air-water intercooled Novi supercharger kit was good for a 200-horsepower increase over the stock 500-horse powerplant. *Paxton*

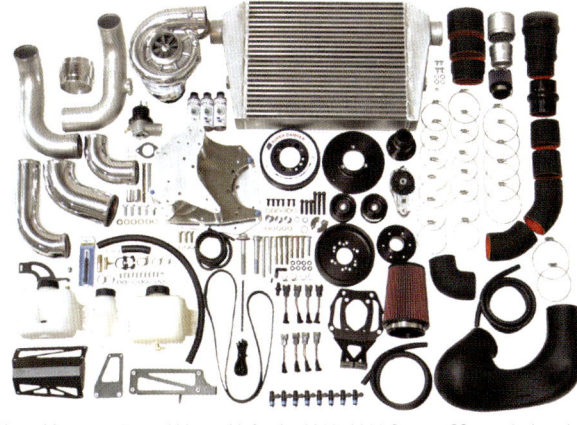

Vortech's 6.5- to 7.5-psi blower kit for the 2010–2011 Camaro SS was designed with V-3 Si-trim centrifugal supercharger, air-air intercooling system, supercharger driver system, and air intake. Standard power increase is 47 percent. Tuner kits with the V-7 YSi supercharger support up to 1,200 horsepower. *Vortech*

CT Engineering's supercharger kit for front-wheel-drive TSX and RSX inline-4s is a straightforward blower-on-intake, Roots-type architecture. *CT Engineering*

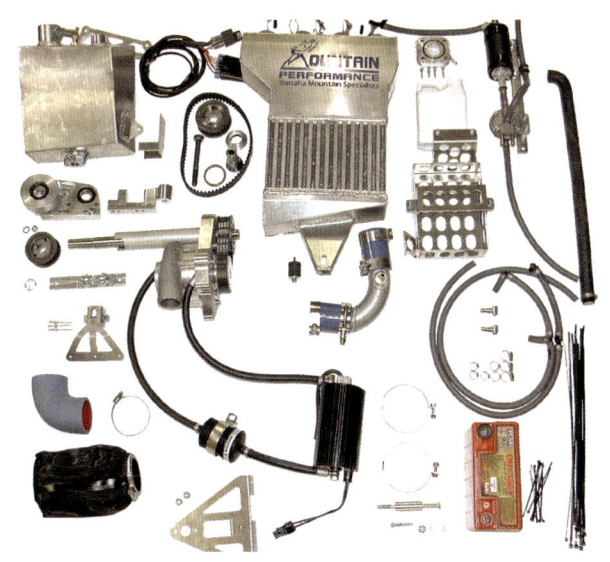

Mountain RX-1 snowmobile dual-belt supercharger kit. Note the replacement battery (lower right) and tank (upper left) that are used to create space for the supercharger. *Mountain Performance*

BUYING AND INSTALLING A SUPERCHARGER KIT

The base Kraftwerks Honda Fit blower kit passed FTP/CARB emission testing for legal on-highway usage in all 50 states. The 10-psi intercooled version of the kit shown here is for off-highway use only. *Kraftwerks*

Honda's 1998+ VFR800 bike made 110 stock horsepower at 10,500 rpm. This A&A performance supercharger kit was designed to add 50 to 60 percent more power with boost from a Rotrex centrifugal blower with no internal engine changes. As always on a bike, the trick is to find a power-takeoff source to drive the supercharger. On the other hand, some modern performance bike engines turn faster than superchargers, so there's probably no need for a huge drive ratio. Note the upgraded fuel pump and fuel pressure regulator at lower left. *A&A Performance*

Tork Tech intercooled kit for the 1999–2004 Mustang GT included Magnuson TVS 1900 positive-displacement Roots-type supercharger with self-contained synthetic lubrication, good for up to 750 rear-wheel horsepower. Note that the 8-rib supercharger drive system is independent from the stock accessory-drive system, which permits crankshaft drive pulleys up to 11-inch diameter for increased boost pressure. *Tork Tech*

The great thing about snowmobiles is that you can count on plenty of cold ambient air for charging the engine and intercooling. Mountain's blower kit for the Yamaha RX-1 provides an air-air intercooler with a cold-side plenum that distributes air to the sled's four carburetors. Note the Rotrex supercharger below the forward intercooler tank and cogged drive belt at lower left with polished transfer shaft that moves power to the drive side of the blower (hidden). *Mountain Performance*

Chapter 9
Designing and Building a Supercharger System

Suppose there's no turnkey supercharger conversion kit available for your vehicle-engine combination? If you're a competent mechanic with good fabrication skills, you may want to design and build your own supercharger system.

Keep in mind that if a supercharger kit exists for a similar engine or vehicle, it may be feasible and perhaps simpler or cheaper to adapt some or all of the alien supercharger kit to your engine and vehicle, with modifications or replacement components where required. Perhaps "universal" supercharging components are available that could be assembled into a supercharging system more easily or cheaply than building new components from scratch. If there was a factory supercharging option available for a similar engine, OE supercharging components—or perhaps the entire engine—might be transplanted into your engine compartment with relative ease.

BEGi's supercharger kit for the RAS Miata mounts a twin-screw on the intake manifold, but the kit makes use of a front-mounted air-air intercooler system (not visible). Air enters the air filter at lower right but rather than immediately entering the intake manifold, compressed air travels through air ducting (underneath the supercharger pulley) to the intercooler before returning to the engine. Note the relocated throttle body behind the supercharger. What's invisible is the stock intake manifold, which has been replaced with a custom Bell intake that delivers air to the cylinder head and also mounts the supercharger.

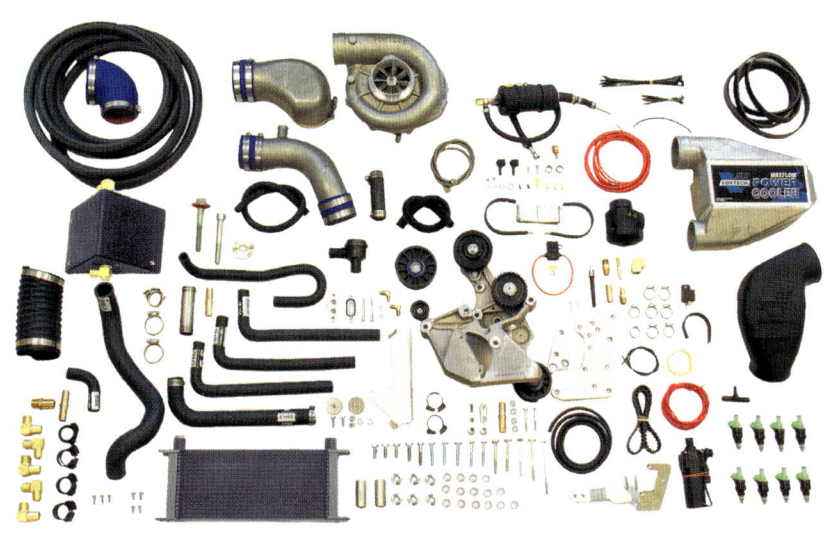

Vortech's Z06 Corvette supercharging system takes the modern approach of in-line water-cooled intercooling with remote heat exchanger. Surveying these parts, this is the magnitude of the task of designing a supercharging system using a centrifugal blower. What you don't usually have to do with a centrifugal supercharging system is relocate the throttle body and replace or reconstruct the stock intake manifold to locate a bulky positive-displacement supercharger. *Vortech*

GENERIC SUPERCHARGER CONVERSION COMPONENTS

- Supercharger
- Supercharger belt
- Supercharger belt tensioner
- Supercharger belt drive pulley (attaches to crankshaft or accessory drive)

- Supercharger mounting assembly or mountable intake manifold
- Supercharger mounting plate, brackets, spacers, stanchions, support braces, and so on

- Air cleaner interface and ducting
- Supercharger intake housing or intake housing with throttle mount

- Miscellaneous hardware: nuts, bolts, lock washers, spacers, hose clamps, cable ties, hoses, hose barbs, wiring, connectors, fuses, gaskets, check valves, banjo bolts, adaptors, wiring connectors, wiring adaptors

- Supercharger belt idler pulley(s)
- Supercharger shaft drive assembly
- Electric supercharger clutch and controller
- Replacement crank damper
- Supercharger manual belt tensioner

- Supercharger oil supply hose and fittings
- Supercharger oil drain hose and fittings
- Supercharger auxiliary lubrication system, reservoir, and fittings
- Supercharger lubricant

- Air cleaner
- Air cleaner housing
- Air intake ducting
- Cold-air intake system
- Supercharger discharge plenum or ducting
- Silicon boost hoses (straight, angle, reducer, and so on)

- Intercooler charger-cooler heat exchanger and mount (air-air or air-water)
- Intercooler water-cooler heat exchanger and mount
- Intercooler coolant reservoir tank, pump, hoses, and fittings
- Intercooler-engine ducting and hoses
- Intercooler cooling fan(s)
- Carbon or metal intercooler tanks and covers

- Closed-throttle blow-off valve
- Supercharger idle boost-recirculation system

- Fuel injectors (upgrade)
- Fuel injectors (auxiliary fuel enrichment)
- Carburetor (replacement)
- Carb pressurization and jetting kit
- Carb pressurization airbox enclosure
- Fuel filter
- Fuel rail(s)
- Throttle body replacement
- Throttle linkage parts (Heim joints, levers, rods, cables, and so on)
- Fuel pump (electric, replacement, or booster) and mounting brackets

- Fuel pump (mechanical)
- Fuel supply hoses and pipes (upgrade)
- Ignition upgrade components (coils, high-tension wiring, and so on)

- Variable-rate-of-gain fuel pressure regulator (FMU providing injection pressure increase for boost fuel enrichment)
- Electronic interceptor to modify fuel injection pulse width
- Boost ignition retard interceptor
- EMS (standalone)
- Piggyback programmable interceptor
- Water-alcohol injection system
- EMS Reflash/recalibration device and software
- Auxiliary fuel-injector systems
- Knock sensor and control system
- Emissions components (replacement/upgrade, including high-flow CAT)
- Nitrous injection and control system
- Engine sensors (replacement or upgrade multi-bar MAP sensors, cold-start enrichment, and so on)
- Fuel pressure regulator (upgrade/adjustable)
- Fuel pressure regulator (electronic)
- Fuel pump voltage booster system (Boost-a-Pump)
- Colder or redesigned spark plugs
- Boost controller (PWM bleed valve, CVT, and so on)

- Supercharger intake manifold adaptor
- Supercharger replacement intake manifold
- Supercharger-in-intake manifold
- Upgrade throttle body

- Alternator

- Oil filter (remote)
- Oil cooler system

- Muffler and exhaust piping
- Heat shields

- Upgrade radiator
- Auxiliary/upgrade radiator cooling fans
- Replacement/upgrade radiator fan shroud

- Replacement engine cover (motorcycle, sled, ATV, and so on) for blower drive power take-off

- Battery (compact or relocation)
- Battery cables (relocation)

- Engine water pump
- Brake fluid reservoir (replacement)
- Windshield washer reservoir (replacement)
- Coolant recovery tank
- Power steering hose(s) (replacement)
- Motor mounts (replacement)
- Strut mounts (replacement)
- Vacuum tank

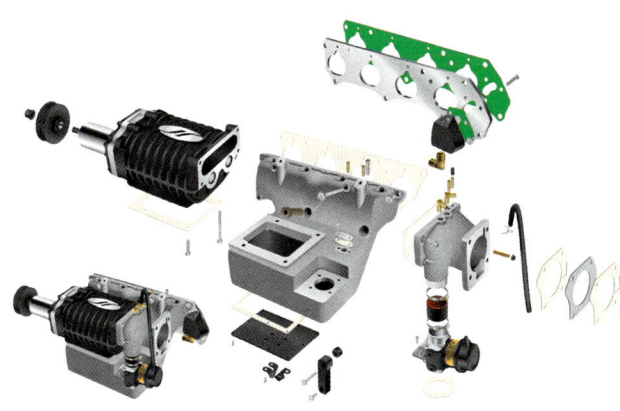

Jackson Racing supercharger assembly components. The Eaton supercharger mounts on a custom intake manifold and sucks air through a custom throttle body mount. *Jackson Racing*

If you are starting from scratch and you are not a fabricator or don't have access to special fabrication tools, you may still be able to put together a "roll-your-own" supercharger conversion system using custom parts that you design and subcontract out to be fabricated by professional performance/racing shops, machine shops, and welders. Designing a supercharger system this way can be rewarding and relatively straightforward—assuming you have the patience and the skills for careful planning and a backup support structure of professionals able to fabricate or complete custom parts and provide back-up consulting if you run into difficulties.

If you are not buying a kit or copying what someone else has already proven successful, you are taking on an R&D project, and it is up to you to decide whether you have the resources and skill to explore strange new worlds—including *learning from your mistakes*. It may be harder than you think if you're the first person on the planet to do a blower conversion for some really unusual engine and vehicle. Keep in mind that some types of engines are more suitable than others for forced induction, and some engine-management systems are *much* easier to recalibrate or hack for supercharging (read my book *How to Tune and Modify Engine Management Systems*.)

If you are an enthusiast building your own system for fun, your advantage is that you are not in it to make a profit and can therefore absorb whatever time and resources are required to build a really elegant system that might not be profitable for a pro-tuner to manufacture and sell as a kit. If you are considering the possibility of developing your supercharger system into a manufacturable kit that could be marketed to other people with the same vehicle, designing a supercharger kit imposes additional constraints on the design:

1. A kit must be manufacturable at a cost that allows it to be sold at a profit.
2. It must be sufficiently straightforward that ordinary mechanics or enthusiasts can do the job successfully in a reasonable time.
3. Installing the kit does not degrade serviceability of other engine systems to an extreme extent such as engine removal required to change the spark plugs.

A custom supercharging project will involve some or all of the following:

- Model the system mathematically.
- Select a supercharger.
- Select or design an intercooler.
- Mount the supercharger.
- Build a mechanical drive system.
- Construct an air inlet system for the supercharger (which may or may not involve relocating the throttle body or carburetor upstream of the supercharger).
- Construct compressor discharge plumbing from the blower to the intake manifold or throttle body. Note: (1) Compressor discharge plumbing may comprise all or part of the supercharger mounting system, if, for example, the supercharger discharge bolts directly to the intake manifold (which may be custom-built for mounting the supercharger). (2) Discharge plumbing or may not include an intercooler to lower compressed charge temperature. (3) In some cases, the supercharger case might be cast as an integral part of the intake manifold, which contains the supercharger rotor set.
- Construct high-pressure lubrication plumbing that connects the engine oiling system to the supercharger and plumbing for oil drain-back to the sump (not required if the supercharger has a self-contained lubrication system).
- Modify the engine's fuel delivery system to provide additional fuel during boost for increased horsepower.
- Modify the spark delivery system to prevent detonation and provide the least-compromised optimal timing for supercharged power.
- Modify critical engine, drivetrain, and suspension components to handle heavier thermal and mechanical loading.

Keep in mind that proper tuning is critical to unlocking the potential of forced induction. Improper engine calibration is another way that people end up with blowers that are really too big for their needs: If they had put as much thought into the calibration and integration of the engine controller (fuel, spark, and boost control) as they did the forced-induction components themselves, they would not only have more power, but better boost response and drivability. It is amazing how much "free power" chassis dyno operators find is typically available by optimizing tuning and fuel delivery. After you model the system and acquire the supercharger and build the supercharging package, plan on testing the car rigorously. Data-log all parameters from the supercharged engine on a chassis dyno and later on the street and track to optimize tuning.

THE SCOPE OF A SUPERCHARGER CONVERSION

If you are thinking about designing a custom supercharger conversion system, it is instructive to consider the scope of what you are taking on, and a great way to do that is to look at what is included in a "typical" supercharger conversion kit. The list on page 177 is an organized compilation of the contents of some popular commercially available automotive, bike, and marine supercharger kits, and if you are designing and building a supercharger system you will have to fabricate or buy a subset of these components. The elements of a commercially available centrifugal supercharger kit for the Dodge Viper V-10 are highlighted. No single kit would comprise all of these components, some of which are redundant, though some high-quality, high-boost systems for difficult vehicles with complex engine-management systems targeted at luxury brands, whose owners demand and can afford factory-type reliability, have a large number of components—particularly tuner kits from outfits like Ruf that are commonly installed by authorized professional dealers.

Some of the components listed have nothing to do with supercharging beyond enabling something to be relocated in the engine compartment to make room for a core supercharging component. Many supercharger kit vendors keep the cost down by unbundling "optional" components that are actually essential to the safe functioning of a supercharged powerplant. The best example of this are parts required to modify the behavior of engine management components that must be modified to deliver good performance and prevent a supercharging system from damaging the engine. It is rarely the case that a supercharger kit includes internal engine, clutch, and transmission components, without which the supercharger conversion could dramatically reduce the reliability of the vehicle if driven hard.

FATAL ERRORS

There are a number of classes of strategic errors you can make designing a supercharger system. The first is that you head down the wrong road in the design and hit a dead-end serious enough that the supercharger system literally cannot be finished or cannot work at all without starting over, or at least undertaking a major redesign. For example, you discover too late that your drive system turns the supercharger backward. Or there is no way to install an air cleaner at all (the compressor inlet is a half inch from the firewall). Or you're forced to choose between installing an air cleaner that sucks really hot engine air and causes detonation or violating the sheet metal of your expensive mid-engine sports car to build a cold-air intake. Or clearances are so tight that you have to redesign the engine mount subframe unless you're willing to put up with a horrible vibrating noise every time the engine makes enough torque to twist the engine and transaxle to the extent that the air intake contacts a bulkhead.

A similar situation would be that the supercharger system works, but the engine or the vehicle itself must be significantly reworked before the supercharging effort can be considered successful. An example of this would be the case that you build a great supercharging system, but the combination of a high-compression engine and a supercharger system raises the engine octane number requirement to the extent that you are forced to choose between running $10-per-gallon racing gasoline or pulling the engine to install custom pistons that lower the static compression ratio.

Another class of error is that you design the system around a supercharger that cannot achieve the performance required for the application and discover the supercharger cannot be replaced without a major supercharger system redesign or even a complete redo. An example of this would be if you built the system using a large centrifugal supercharger with air-air intercooler and realize too late that the centrifugal

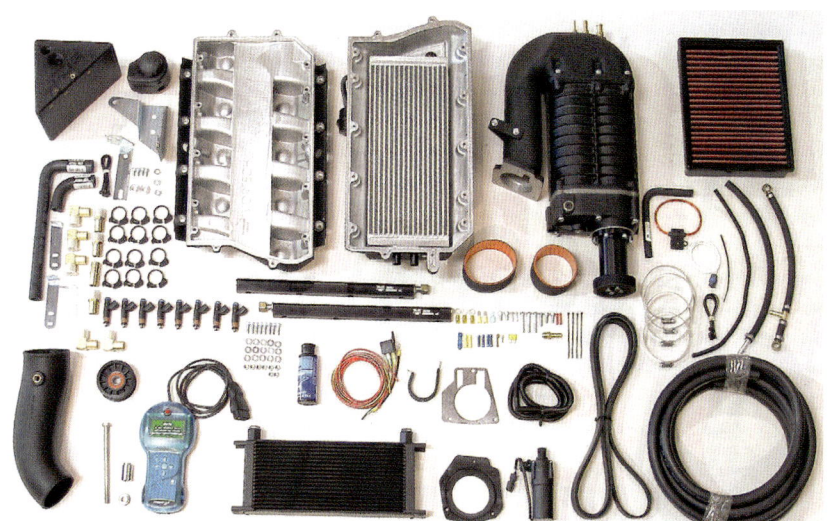

Lysholm's 5.3-liter GM truck blower kit is typical of many modern supercharging systems for V-8 truck powerplants where there is a fair amount of hood clearance: The air-water intercooler is integral with the custom cast-aluminum supercharger intake manifold, which also mounts the supercharger. In this setup, compressed air exits the bottom of the supercharger and flows through the intercooler and into cross-ram intake runners. Building molds for a custom intake manifold is not for the faint-of-heart, but if you have the woodworking skills, there are foundries that will make the castings (which must then be machined). Note the remote heat exchanger and the upgraded fuel injectors, fuel rail, and programmer module used to reflash the stock ECU with a blower calibration. *Lysholm*

supercharger cannot improve low-end performance—and cannot even improve mid-range performance without overboosting significantly at peak power. At this point, switching to a positive-displacement supercharger requires not only buying a completely different supercharger but a different intercooler, because a replacement positive-displacement supercharger cannot be intercooled in your application without constructing a brand-new *air-water* intercooler system in which the air-cooler unit is sandwiched inline between the manifold-mounted supercharger and the intake runners. So you're forced to live with a supercharger that only adds power at high rpm and, thus, only improves performance when you rev the hell out of the engine and drive the vehicle like you're mad at it. Even worse would be if your vehicle is a boat and your application requires a large custom prop to achieve top-speed performance goals, but the centrifugal supercharger you deployed cannot muster the torque to get the boat up on plane without overboosting tremendously at higher engine speeds—in which case the supercharger system is literally useless.

Yet another type of design error is that you build a supercharger system that works but has fatal flaws that hurt the reliability to the extent that parts fail, requiring supercharger system rework to prevent the same thing from happening again and again in the same way. Perhaps you locate delicate rubber or plastic components too near the exhaust. Perhaps mechanical components repeatedly break or the drive system repeatedly breaks or throws supercharger or accessory drive belts.

Still another class of mistake is that you design a system that does not perform well or has no headroom for future performance improvement. Perhaps your Roots-type blower is too small to deliver additional boost with a faster drive ratio without heating the charge so much that the density ratio falls faster than the pressure ratio rises. Perhaps increasing the drive ratio to make the blower pump more air per engine rpm forces you to lower the engine redline to keep from over-speeding the supercharger.

Also avoid used blowers. A dirt-cheap used supercharger can sound like a bargain, but there will be no technical support if you need hand-holding during development—and you will need it. Keep in mind that junkyard blowers may have been abused and damaged from dirt, overheating, or infrequent oil changes. Some people have designed beautiful supercharging systems around used blowers or even rare vintage superchargers that required something more akin to restoration with custom-machined parts than ordinary rebuilding. It can be done and it can be rewarding for the right person, but keep in mind that buying a used supercharger is often false economy.

Overall, the way to avoid fatal errors is with careful modeling, analysis, planning, and mocking-up before you start fabricating and buying parts. Kind of a grandiose version of "measure twice, cut once." In other words, plan ahead.

Whipple's GM Envoy blower kit takes the design approach of locating a large twin-screw supercharger remotely from the main V-6 or V-8 intake manifold and ducting compressed air to the intake manifold or intercooler. Note the throttle body and air intake at the rear passenger side of the engine. *Whipple Superchargers*

PRACTICAL SUPERCHARGER SELECTION

It is critical that anyone sizing a supercharger understand the application clearly and know what performance characteristics are essential and which can be sacrificed, if necessary. What are you trying to do? Are you optimizing performance for low-end torque, mid-range, or high-speed power? Is it a street car, drag car, all-out street car, road-racer, top-speed racer, or something else? What elements of performance are the most important?

Selecting a supercharger solely on the basis of peak power will not get you where you want to go, though it is a good place to start. Fortunately, the task of a supercharger system designer is not to design a new supercharger for the application, but to choose the best supercharger for the application from a finite number of options. Even huge automotive companies rarely scratch-design a new supercharger for a particular engine application. The trick is to hone in on one or more candidate compressors for your application by modeling the application mathematically and then working with the compressor maps of candidate superchargers. It is not rocket science, but it is critically important.

There are virtually always tradeoffs when teaming up a particular supercharger with a particular engine and vehicle, so the right match is critical to the success of a particular application. The wrong supercharger can make an engine sluggish, or peaky, or even catastrophically unstable. It could stifle top-end power or reduce the maximum boost you can run without damaging your engine or requiring super-high octane racing fuel. There is not just one size supercharger that will work for a given application, but there is one that will work *best*.

The modeling process starts with defining the immediate performance objectives and constraints. How will the engine and vehicle be used? How heavy is the vehicle? How fast must the vehicle accelerate in various segments of the power band? How long will the engine need to operate at maximum power and torque? Ultimately, what are the power and torque requirements at various engine speeds and what percentage increase in horsepower is required? What is the redline? Beyond that, to what extent are you willing to modify the engine, drivetrain, and suspension to accommodate high-pressure supercharging? Are you willing to modify the stock compression ratio and upgrade the strength of internal engine reciprocating parts such as the crankshaft, connecting rods, and pistons? Beyond these basic performance and strength constraints, must the vehicle meet emission requirements? What type of fuel and octane are available? How willing are you to modify internal engine components and external engine compartment components and component locations? Do the performance requirements mandate a particular type of supercharger with a particular form factor? Are there important appearance goals? What are the cost constraints? Is there headroom in the design for future performance upgrades?

Size the supercharger in a realistic manner. Too often people get crazy in their horsepower aspirations or focus on selecting a compressor with vast amounts of headroom for future hot rodding. In some cases they end up with a supercharger that could, in theory, support huge horsepower and flow but is unsuited for say, a daily driven street car. It's very easy to make a lot of power with superchargers, so the "bigger is better" mentality creeps in. Be realistic with your intentions and you will be happier in the end.

In the end, the process is the same for a supercharger upgrade or overboosting project as it is for a scratch supercharger system design: You'll generally have to choose between several feasible alternatives with an eye to picking the best one for your specific application, and one that *fits* within the constraints of the engine compartment. In some cases the best alternative for pumping up the boost may be the supercharger you already have, turning faster to deliver more boost and mass airflow into the engine. But you have to run the numbers.

The process of selecting a supercharger and system components with mathematical modeling is shown in Chapter 5 of this book.

BUILDING THE SUPERCHARGER SYSTEM

The first thing to build is the mounting system for the supercharger. It is a great idea to mock up the entire system first, including intercooler and plumbing (if applicable) and throttle body or carburetor, if you're relocating, before you fabricate any parts so you don't paint yourself into a corner by locating the supercharger in a position that makes something else difficult or impossible. All supercharger manufacturers publish engineering drawings with dimensions that allow you to scope out installation constraints before you acquire a particular supercharger. It is critically important to make sure that not only is a supercharger conversion functional, but that routine maintenance is feasible without heroic measures. (You don't want to remove the engine or supercharger system to change a spark plug or oil filter.)

Positive-displacement superchargers are particularly heavy and awkward to handle, but even if you're considering a smaller, lighter centrifugal supercharger, plan to build a mock supercharger and related parts out of lighter materials such as Styrofoam, cardboard, wood, or plastic. This will allow you to easily test the viability of various locations for clearance and drive-belt geometry without risking damaging the finish of the blower or engine parts—not to mention your hands. When working with the supercharger itself, it is a good idea to duct-tape vulnerable surfaces so they are protected as you wrestle the supercharger into various positions to test viability and fabricate supercharger mounts and plumbing.

If you are using a positive-displacement Roots or twin-screw supercharger, there is probably no way to install it in a crowded modern engine compartment without moving or redesigning something major—typically the intake manifold. Items that can be relocated without too much pain include the battery, air cleaner housing, coolant recovery system, windshield washer reservoir, and vacuum tank. You may be able to create space by relocating or reworking the power steering pump or engine water pump (or substituting an electric pump) and replacing the alternator with something more compact—though, obviously, these are serious projects. Supercharger conversion-system designers have replaced, reworked, or redesigned exhaust headers, motor mounts, strut mounts, radiators, and radiator fans and shrouds, and they've installed heat shields and insulation to allow supercharger components to be located closer to hot exhaust or engine components.

Many supercharger vendors offer a selection of intake manifold adapters. This BDS 2-inch adaptor plate is designed to weld to an aluminum intake manifold to mount a 10-71 Roots-type supercharger. *BDS*

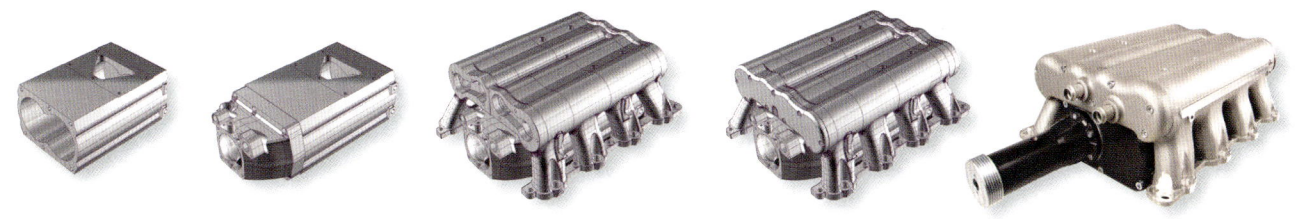

The ideal way to fabricate supercharging components is on a computer. This composite image shows the subassemblies of a RENNtech supercharging system for the Mercedes V-8, including supercharger case and end plates, intake manifold with integral air-water intercooler, and intercooler housing end plates. *RENNtech*

In the days of huge, old-school Roots blowers installed on huge, old-school carbureted big-block V-8s (when intercooling was unheard of in automotive applications and superchargers typically ran low-pressure boost), a manifold-mounted Roots was a simple proposition: carb(s) mounted atop the blower intake manifold (or an adaptor plate welded or bolted to a standard aluminum intake manifold), with a giant hole cut in the hood to accommodate this massive pile of components. With the advent of advanced compact twin-screw and Roots superchargers able to provide pressure ratios as high as 2.5, intercooling is mandatory and the traditional configuration became obsolete.

You will still most likely be mounting a positive-displacement supercharger directly to the stock intake manifold with some kind of adaptor, or attaching the supercharger directly to (or *inside*!) a scratch-built, redesigned intake manifold. The need to intercool today's high-pressure supercharging systems typically now means that a compact *liquid-cooled* heat exchanger must be sandwiched into a plenum integral to the supercharger/intake manifold assembly, with air entering the compressor inlet through a throttle body attached to one end and compressed air discharging *upward* into a liquid-cooled heat exchanger sandwiched between bolt-together manifold halves, from which air exists from one or both sides into intake runners that deliver air to the cylinder head(s).

It is not unheard of to locate a positive-displacement supercharger remotely from the intake manifold (in a few cases gear-driven off the front of the crankshaft) with the compressor discharge ducted to the intake manifold, but the need to locate the throttle body upstream of a positive-displacement supercharger makes this type of system problematic and therefore rare (positive-displacement superchargers have zero ability to tolerate backflow when attempting to pressurize the cul-de-sac formed when the throttle closes, and older Roots-type blowers require rotor-cooling wet air-fuel mixtures).

It has become rather common to integrate a positive-displacement supercharger case and custom intake manifold into a single aluminum casting machined to house the guts of the compressor rotating assembly. The entire assembly bolts to the cylinder heads of a Vee engine like a stock intake manifold; in the case of inline engines where the supercharger is not triangulated between two cylinder banks, the supercharger/manifold assembly will require support braces whether or not the stock intake manifold had them.

Smaller positive-displacement superchargers are sometimes mounted on brackets like a centrifugal. Large, old-school Roots superchargers invariably mount directly on the manifold of a V-8 engine due to the escalating stiffness requirements of mounting systems robust enough to limit vibration of such a large mass far from the center of gravity of the engine. The original diesel engines with Roots blowers were inline eights, sixes, or fours, and over the years a few large inline-6 gasoline powerplants have been supercharged with Roots blowers mounted directly on the cylinder head or block.

If you're interested in building custom supercharger parts, and have the patience and woodworking skills to take on building custom molds, there are foundries willing and able to cast one-off aluminum or iron parts from your molds (after which critical surfaces can be precision-machined). Mold pattern-making is beyond the scope of this chapter but there are books that describe the process of building and coating wood-and-filler patterns (search for books about sand casting and rapid tooling).

Alternatively, you could design parts with CAD solids modeling software, which will output data sets machine-ready to direct a five-axis CNC mill to fabricate the design(s) from aluminum or steel billet (search for books about CNC machining, programming, and implementation). CAD output can be used to direct rapid-prototyping equipment to fabricate molds for lost-foam or other methods of destructive casting in the case of difficult parts. Or you might elect to manually fabricate a "sheet-metal" manifold with supercharger mounts by cutting and grinding metal plate, tubing, pipe, or rod and welding together the fabricated parts.

Where a new blower manifold is not available and it's not feasible to scratch-build one, you might choose radical manifold-ectomy and reconstructive surgery: Amputate a section of the stock intake manifold (say, with a band saw) and weld on an adaptor plate or fabricated plenum machined to accept fasteners that mount the supercharger.

One advantage of using a more compact centrifugal supercharger is that it is usually not necessary to disturb the stock intake manifold and throttle assembly. Centrifugal compressors will permit excessive charge air pressure at low airflow to surge backward through the compressor wheel when, say, a throttle closes suddenly, permitting this type of compressor to safely pressurize throttle bodies and carburetors.

Centrifugal superchargers typically hang off the engine on a bracket like a large alternator, somewhere near the timing cover. In some applications long driveshaft extensions have been used to transmit power to the opposite end of the engine. Another advantage of centrifugal superchargers is that there is often a selection of different "trim" compressor wheels that may be installed within a given compressor housing. Swapping or machining the discharge housing to accommodate even larger compressor wheels is also common.

Before finalizing supercharger selection, you'll need to take a steel-eyed look at the practicality of the installation. Some questions worth considering include:

- Is there sufficient space in the engine compartment for a positive-displacement supercharger? A centrifugal supercharger? Is it possible a turbocharger would be more practical (thereby eliminating the need for a mechanical supercharger drive system)?
- How critical is low-rpm boost in supercharger selection? Do you need a positive-displacement supercharger or will additional low-rpm torque simply smoke the tires?
- If pre-supercharged low-end performance does need improvement, could a centrifugal supercharger with transient pulsed nitrous injection augment low-end performance to acceptable levels?
- Are there obvious advantages to the feasibility of implementing a suck-through versus a pressurized throttle in the application (thereby determining whether or not you're using a centrifugal)?
- Are you willing and able to fabricate a custom intake manifold?
- Would it be feasible to locate the supercharger rotor assembly *inside* a custom replacement manifold that functions as the supercharger housing?
- What engine components can be moved to create space without too much pain? (Battery? Airbox? Intake manifold? Throttle body?)
- What lengths of blower pulley extensions are available to position the supercharger body closer or farther from the plane of the drive belt?
- Could a stock serpentine-belt accessory layout be expanded with a longer belt to accommodate a supercharger?
- Instead of being driven directly from the crankshaft, might a supercharger be driven from an auxiliary pulley installed next to the stock pulley on an accessory?
- Might it be possible to drive a supercharger from gears (or pulleys) on the flywheel, distributor drive, camshaft (or crankshaft)?
- Is it worth considering a Corvair-type V-belt arrangement in which a V-belt twists to engage intermediate pulleys turned 90-degrees from the drive pulley?

MOUNTING THE SUPERCHARGER

When it comes to mounting a supercharger, the goal is always to do the job with the fewest compromises to the following constraints:

- Access to convenient, widely spaced mounting points that rigidly anchor the supercharger in all three dimensions.
- Unencumbered access to a plane passing through the crank pulley, all driven and idler pulleys, and a tensioner for the supercharger drive belt.
- Accommodation with existing belt-driven engine accessories.
- Clearance from fixed surfaces when the engine and transmission flex during applications of high torque.
- Ease of attaching air ducting to the compressor inlet and discharge.
- Ease of relocating the throttle assembly upstream of the air inlet of Roots and twin-screw compressors.
- Accommodation for oil feed and drain lines, if required.
- Access for normal engine servicing (oil filter, dipstick, power steering fluid reservoir, spark plugs, fuel filter, air filter, and so on).
- Supercharger mounting system provides the flexibility for charge cooling. In the case of most modern positive-displacement superchargers, it is effectively mandatory that the air-cooler section of the intercooler be integral with a custom supercharger intake manifold, which becomes the foundation of the supercharger mounting system.

In reality, some of these constraints may override selecting a supercharger that optimizes performance. If it turns out installing the ideal compressor is impractical or impossible, you'll have to select a compromise supercharger that will fit.

It is fairly common for positive-displacement supercharger system designers to create space for a bulky blower by replacing the stock intake manifold. A positive-displacement blower will alleviate the VE cost of shortened runners by replacing high-velocity low-rpm air with low-end boost pressure. This custom manifold was built by GM Racing for the forced-induction 2.0-liter I-4 Ecotec drag-race and land-speed record I-4 powerplant.

If you are working with a Vee-type engine, it may be possible to create hood clearance by locating the supercharger underneath the intake manifold, deep within the valley between the cylinder banks. PES's G4 blower manifold for the Audi 4.2-liter V-8 incorporates a bottom-fed integral brick-type air-water intercooler core pressurized by an Eaton M90 Roots-type supercharger. Compressed air from the blower exits the intercooler core into a plenum and turns 180 degrees to enter the intake runners. *PES*

Supercharger Mount Design Criteria

To control vibration, the *stiffness* of supercharger mounting brackets is the critical design objective, because vibration can destroy supercharger bearings and damage rotor lobes or other high-speed rotating components. Vertical inline four-cylinder engines without balance shafts may need additional bracing in a vertical plane to deal with vibration from inherent imbalances. (Stiffness is a measurement of how far something will bend when loaded in a certain way, which is totally different from how far something can be bent until it breaks.)

Vibration resulting from the added mass of a heavy supercharger will be minimized if the supercharger is mounted as close as possible to the engine's center of gravity. This will minimize problems resulting from changes in the center of gravity.

Engine rocking from increased supercharged torque and supercharger mass torture tests the hose connections in supercharger ducting; this can be minimized by locating the supercharger as close as possible to the engine mounts.

Supercharger mounts should be based far apart in *three separate planes* unless a mount is so broad-based and short that it intrinsically provides two- or three-dimensional support. Ideally, the supercharger should be braced as close as possible to the driven pulley such that belt tension exerts the least possible leverage against the supercharger.

There are advantages to using heat-treated aluminum ("T" suffix) for fabricating supercharger mounts:

- Aluminum's softness makes it very easy to cut, drill, and mill.
- It has good efficiency of strength-to-weight ratio.
- It can be welded to aluminum intake manifolds (except 7000 series, which is harder to machine and not suitable for welding).

Aluminum must be 150 percent thicker than steel to achieve the same stiffness with respect to bending because a given thickness of aluminum deforms three times as much as it would were it made of steel. Aluminum loses 50 percent of its strength when bent, and heat-treated aluminum should never be bent to build parts. Because aluminum is built thicker, aluminum structures typically have much greater resistance to thermal distortion during welding. Built to the same standards, an aluminum structure weighs 35 to 45 percent less than a steel structure (though aluminum structures are often built to be *higher* in overall strength because aluminum reaches its endurance [failure] limit sooner than steel in terms of flexure). Therefore, the rigidity of structure (deflection) becomes the limiting design criteria for an aluminum structure, which forces a higher than necessary overall yield and tensile strength. Whatever the basic strength of a metal, doubling thickness increases strength as the cube of the increase, such that something twice as thick is eight times as strong. As long as the a structure is being designed to standards of stiffness that keep it far from the ultimate failure point, aluminum is quite efficient when it comes to absorbing bending loads without deforming, making it the material of choice for structures subject to bending. One weak point in aluminum structures is the "as-welded" strength; to compensate for the loss of strength in the weld zone, all butt joints should be designed to allow backing bars and extra longitudinal reinforcement. The other weak point is aluminum fastening points: The width of aluminum lugs should invariably be 250 to 300 percent the diameter of the fastener, and with lug thickness at least equal to the fastener's diameter. Aluminum is more readily subject to fatigue failure (referred to as its endurance limit) than mild steel.

DRIVE BELTS

Supercharger drives typically take the form of ribbed-serpentine or toothed rubber belts, direct drive from the nose of the crankshaft, or by gears. Flexible composite belts are ubiquitous, but it is worth noting that supercharger system designers have sometimes used other technologies to drive superchargers. People have employed chain drives to power superchargers, and there have been some fairly recent attempts to do the job with ultra-strong drag-bike chains. Chains are efficient because they bend easily, but because they don't stretch, chains have little or no ability to dissipate shock loading. Chains can be massively strong, but if they break the result can be mayhem. Gear drives are historically more common, with some Gatsby-era luxo-cruisers equipped using them to power centrifugal superchargers. The giant centrifugal aviation supercharging systems installed on piston engines during World War II like the Rolls-Royce Merlin exclusively employed one- or two-speed gear drive systems to run the supercharger. The Roots blowers essential to the functioning of two-stroke diesel engines were direct-driven. Some modern drag cars are boosted with massive centrifugal superchargers powered by gear-drive systems from outfits like The Supercharging Store that run off the front of the crankshaft. Hydraulic and electrical drives have been deployed to drive superchargers with some success, but so far none of these alternative drive technologies is common in today's world of automotive supercharging, where belts rule.

Modern high-tech materials have greatly increased the strength and longevity of flexible mechanical drive belts made from composites ranging from fabric-reinforced rubber to metal- or Kevlar-reinforced carbon. Drive belts waste some of the power they transmit through bending and flexing the belt—work that turns into heat that shortens the life of the belt. There are many types of power-transmission belts, some of which work well to drive superchargers. See the other sidebar in this chapter for more details about these different types.

The tensile strength of supercharger belts varies from about a ton for some thin, six-rib fabric-rubber belts to more than 12 tons for some super-duty carbon-Kevlar belts up to 5 inches wide. Obviously, Godzilla 12-ton belts are not very flexible, meaning there is going to be a lot more horsepower wasted just bending the belt around the pulleys. The increased power wastage of stronger belts is a good argument for not overdoing it with a lot more belt than you need. All things being equal, longer belts are more robust than shorter belts because they have more ability to stretch to absorb sudden heavy loads.

When it comes to belt loading, one fact of life that may seem counter-intuitive is that the faster a belt is moving when transmitting horsepower, the lighter the loading on the belt. This is a result of the fact that the faster something is turning, the *less* torque is required to deliver a certain amount of horsepower. The relationship between torque and horsepower and speed is defined by the equation:

$$\text{Torque (ft-lb)} = \frac{(\text{Horsepower} \times 5{,}250)}{\text{rpm}}$$

This equation explains why the spindly looking shaft connecting the turbine and compressor in a turbocharger can transmit rather large amounts of power with absurdly low torque due to the tremendous rotating speed of the turbine and compressor. For example, the twisting force of an exhaust turbine turning at 120,000 rpm and delivering 100 horsepower the opposing compressor wheel is less than 5 pound-feet torque:

$$\text{Torque} = \frac{(100 \times 5{,}250)}{120{,}000} = 4.375 \text{ ft-lb}$$

Note: Not 437.5 ft-lb or 43.75 ft-lb, but 4.375 ft-lb! Keep in mind that some small turbochargers are capable of running safely at 300,000 rpm. In any case, fast-turning blower belts require less strength because they're transmitting less torque.

Belt manufacturers build a safety margin into the published belt-duty specs, but it's human nature to be optimistic when plugging numbers into mathematical models, so it's fairly common to need more boost than you expected to achieve a specific amount of engine horsepower with a supercharger conversion. Unless you are working with numbers on a specific compressor map (as opposed to calculated numbers), it's also fairly common to need more supercharger rpm than calculated to achieve a given level of boost.

Most automotive supercharger belts live a relatively easy life, particularly compared to the sort of environment belt manufacturers consider heavy or "severe" duty, which is running most of the time near the strength limits of the belt. (This certainly does not include the belts on Top Fuel draggers, which may absorb 900 to 1,000 horsepower delivering the extreme boost required to make 8,000 horsepower at the crankshaft as well as the inertial loading from accelerating engines capable of revving from idle to redline in less than a tenth of a second.) Modern street superchargers are equipped with bypass mechanisms or clutches that allow the supercharger to essentially freewheel when the engine is lightly loaded, at which time drag on the belt is somewhere between 0 and 1/2 horsepower. Because automotive street supercharger belts do not normally work hard, during the relatively brief bursts of maximum blower-belt loading that occur when a light vehicle is under maximum load delivering boost as well as accelerating the supercharger (inertial loading on the belt you didn't include in the calculated horsepower number required to drive the supercharger), most belts can tolerate as much as 50 percent overload without permanent damage. This is an excellent thing, because the inertia involved in accelerating a supercharger could easily increase transient belt loading 50 percent above the steady-state loading required to deliver maximum boost. As always, build in some drive system headroom for future hot rodding, since there is a nonsuperficial chance the initial power boost from a supercharger conversion will not suffice permanently.

Compared to aluminum, mild steel has several advantages:

- High strength for a given size structure
- Weld-able with an oxy-acetylene torch, arc welder, heli-arc welder, or through brazing
- Plasticity for bending and flexing without failure

The yield point of mild steel is about 36,000 psi, while the ultimate tensile failure point is about 60,000 psi, meaning the plastic range is approximately 24,000 psi, or about 40 percent of the ultimate strength. By comparison, aluminum, with a yield point of, say, 34,000 psi, has an ultimate strength of 45,000 psi, providing a plastic range of only 11,000 psi. A steel structure has considerable ability to absorb energy and endure deflection without failure; aluminum has about 40 to 50 percent greater structural efficiency compared to mild steel in terms of strength versus weight. When it comes to providing stiffness in the face of compression or tension loads, the structural efficiency of aluminum disappears under the requirement that aluminum have three times the cross-sectional area of steel to provide equivalent stiffness. Mounting structures that must endure compression or tension without deforming are better made from steel. Because the goal of supercharger mounts is extreme stiffness (far below the point of failure), ultimate strength is not an issue and there is little advantage of using high-strength alloys like Core-Ten or stainless steel, which are significantly more difficult to cut and machine than mild steel and vastly more difficult than aluminum.

Mild steel will corrode without a protective coating. What's more, dissimilar metals touching in the presence of an electrolyte like water can amplify corrosion problems due to galvanic corrosion (sometimes called electrolytic corrosion—which is the principle behind batteries). A surface coating of cadmium or chromium plating is a fairly effective measure to protect mild steel from corrosion, as is powder-coating or zinc-chromate paint.

Lugs and welds are the weak point of supercharger mounting structures. Lugs should be overbuilt as much as practically possible. Additional layers of reinforcing can be welded to the basic structure to strengthen it, and fasteners should be supported by thick steel washers that distribute the clamping load over a larger area. All structural welds should be reinforced if there is the slightest doubt regarding strength.

Supercharger mounts should be fastened with grade-8 bolts and locknuts or nuts with interference-type lock washers (and it doesn't hurt to reinforce the locking mechanism with high-strength thread-locker, such as Loctite Red). Keep in mind that spring-type lock washers and thread-locker will not remain functional if subjected to exhaust heat—an environment that essentially *requires* eccentric (slightly oval) locking nuts (*not* Nylock nuts with a nylon locking mechanism that will melt). If it is not possible to use discrete through-bolts with nuts, the next-best option is a stud torqued into a threaded receiver until it bottoms out. If it's not feasible to use a stud (say if a structure must slide sideways into place due to overhead clearance issues), keep in mind that bolts torqued into a treaded receiver have a high probability of working loose because there is virtually no way to simultaneously achieve optimal clamping force against the structure being fastened while bottoming out the bolt in the receiver with appropriate torque. In aviation applications—where a loose bolt can kill you—the mandatory solution is pre-drilled bolts secured to other pre-drilled bolts with stainless-steel safety wire or cable.

BUILDING A MECHANICAL DRIVE SYSTEM

Building the drive system for a supercharger must, to some extent, proceed in parallel with mounting the supercharger, as the supercharger must be mounted in a place that permits constructing a high-performance mechanical drive system that functions with complete reliability. In most cases this will be a belt drive, but people have made it work with gear, chain, and electrical drives.

INDUSTRIAL BELTS

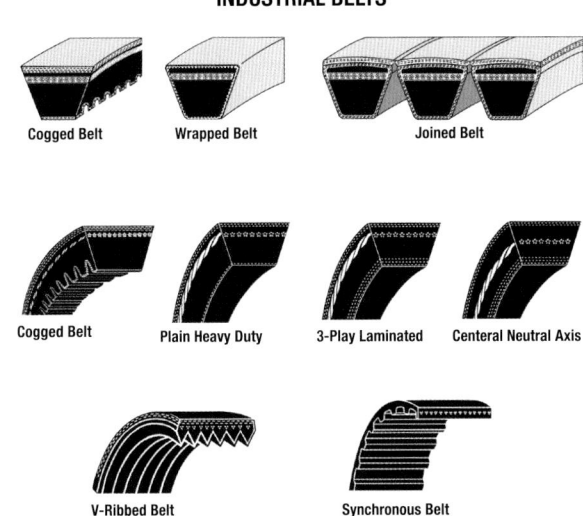

Cogged Belt | Wrapped Belt | Joined Belt

Cogged Belt | Plain Heavy Duty | 3-Play Laminated | Centeral Neutral Axis

V-Ribbed Belt | Synchronous Belt

Supercharger belts are a subclass of industrial belt that is actually a light-duty application compared to situations where an industrial belt works most of the time at nearly full capacity. Modern superchargers mostly use V-ribbed and cogged belts, though single and multiple V-belts are sometimes still found driving superchargers. Cogged belts cannot slip (until they fail), while ribbed belts will slip (which is better than wrecking a blower or shredding a belt) and are capable of shorter-radius turns. *Gates*

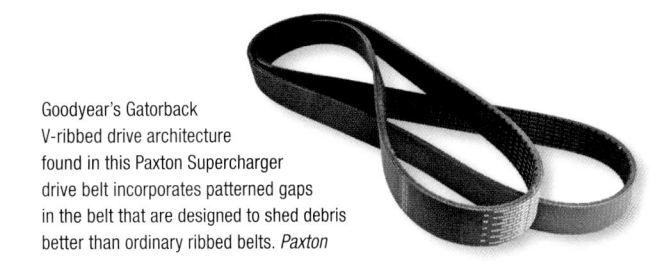

Goodyear's Gatorback V-ribbed drive architecture found in this Paxton Supercharger drive belt incorporates patterned gaps in the belt that are designed to shed debris better than ordinary ribbed belts. *Paxton*

COMMON BELTS USED IN MODERN SUPERCHARGING

The *V-belt* was invented in 1917 by John Gates of the Gates Rubber Company, which is still in the business of supplying a vast array of belts for OE and aftermarket automotive applications (including supercharger drive belts). V-Belts were once *the* belt in engine compartments, driving generators, fans, water pumps and power-steering systems. They are quiet and provide a large contact area between the belt and pulleys in a narrow package. V-belts do not bottom out in the pulley, and heavy loading causes a V-belt to sink more deeply into the pulley groove, increasing friction when it's most needed.

V-belts have been supplanted as accessory drive belts on many engines because they are less efficient than ribbed serpentine belts at transferring power, which saves fuel, and because replacing a single serpentine belt is faster than sequentially removing multiple V-belts to service the engine. Due to their thickness, V-belts tend to require larger-radius pulleys, though some V-belts have been manufactured with notches along the narrow side so that they are able to drive smaller-radius pulleys on driven accessories without excessive heat buildup. V-belts are limited in their ability to bend in a concave direction to negotiate the short-radius belt-tensioner and idler pulleys commonly used to increase the amount of belt wrap around supercharger drive and driven pulleys. A single V-belt is thus limited to linking one, two or, at the most, three pulleys before the maximum average belt wrap around any one pulley becomes too short for good friction without running twin belts.

In some cases automotive engineers do specify multiple belts to drive certain accessories, but in other cases they've handled the belt-wrap problem by running dedicated belts from a multi-groove crank pulley to drive individual accessories. Multiple belt drives take up precious space in tight modern engine layouts, however, and exert more fuel- and power-wasting drag on the engine. Bottom line: V-belts may not be sexy, but they are quiet and they work. But they are no longer commonly used in supercharger drive systems, you can still obtain V-belt pulleys for superchargers and the crank drive (typically equipped to run *twin* V-belts).

It is worth noting that V-belts have been successfully "ganged" in heavy-duty multi-belt applications, such as the Robinson R-22's light helicopter rotor drive system, which uses four V-belts to continuously transfer 160 horsepower with fail-safe redundancy such that the failure of a single belt is not catastrophic. It is also worth noting that multi-belt pulleys for double- or even triple-belting, or perhaps heterogeneous belt types—can be swapped onto engine accessories in place of the stock drive pulley and used to transfer power to a satellite belt that drives. This technique can be used to drive an add-on supercharger in tight engine situations when it is difficult or impossible to extract drive power directly from the crankshaft.

Ribbed belts are essentially flat belts with ribs. They are more efficient than V-belts at transmitting power and produce little or no noise. Multiple V-shaped longitudinal ribs running the length of the belt mesh with receiver grooves in the pulley like mini V-belts to provide a much greater contact area between the belt and pulley than a flat belt of the same width. Under heavy loading, the ribs squish harder into the pulley grooves, like a V-belt. Ribbed belts are easily bent backward to form a concave wrap against idler and tensioner pulleys or, in some cases, to drive low-torque accessories that run in reverse. Although some ribbed belts are double-sided. Goodyear's Gatorback architecture segments individual ribs into multiple sections, with the breaks offset from adjacent ribs in patterns intended to reduce noise and mitigate damage caused by debris caught between the belt and pulley.

A thin, 3/16-inch ribbed belt will handle about 10 horsepower per rib, and a thicker 3/8-inch belt will handle about double that. A 6-rib 3/16-inch belt will thus handle 60 horsepower; whereas, a 3/8-inch belt can safely transmit 120. The precise strength of particular ribbed belts varies according to the reinforcing used in the backbone of the belt, the stiffness of the belt, and the rib design. Thicker belts require somewhat larger pulley sizes because the mandatory minimum bend radius is longer.

A crucial advantage of ribbed belts is that there is nothing but friction to prevent the belt from slipping, which they sometimes do. What, you don't think that's an advantage? Many people assume the perfect supercharger belt drive system not only has the strength to deliver the necessary power and torque to the supercharger without breaking a sweat but the friction to transmit the power and torque without ever slipping, screeching, shuddering, vibrating, or losing boost under any circumstances. True, you never want a drive system that vibrates and shudders, but belt slip can actually be a blessing as a kind of safety valve. Vendors selling centrifugal superchargers usually prohibit installing toothed belts or free-revving the engine with no load because attempting to accelerate a centrifugal supercharger too fast can overload and damage its internal gear-up mechanism.

Overloading a centrifugal supercharger's internal transmission when there's no capacity for external belt slip is like equipping a really powerful car with ultra-sticky tires when you've got a transmission insufficient to handle maximum torque under worst-case loading. With tires that always hook up, the transmission's living on borrowed time. There may be better methods of protecting a supercharger than a slipping drive belt, but belt slippage works and it's free. A belt that *will* slip with heavy enough loading is good supercharger life insurance.

The one and only advantage of a *straight-toothed belt* is that this type of belt positively cannot slip unless it fails. Teeth in the belt engage teeth in the pulley like a cam belt engaging the cam sprocket such that slippage is impossible unless the belt fails and teeth are literally ripped from the belt. Straight-toothed belts tend to be noisy due to the fact that at high speed individual teeth on the belt impact the pulleys like felt hammers impacting piano strings, which can produce a growling noise with variable pitch according to the belt speed.

Competition engines that rev and accelerate hard and run a lot of boost pressure may need toothed belts to overcome extreme horsepower and inertial loading in order to achieve the boost and power required to win races. Toothed belts cannot slip until they fail, but failure to slip could cause the belt to fail catastrophically under shock loading if the combination of horsepower required to drive the supercharger and horsepower required to overcome the inertia of the supercharger loading exceeds the strength of the teeth. It is worth bearing in mind that a centrifugal supercharger experiencing inertial loading that's extreme enough to require a toothed belt drive system will almost definitely live a shorter life unless you build in some auxiliary inertia-absorbing device such as a clutch. Note that a number of vendors sell supercharger pulleys with built-in sprag-type overrun clutches that allow the blower to freewheel when the engine loses speed rapidly on throttle close. This will lessen the likelihood of belt failure, reduce the loading on internal centrifugal gearing, and help improve responsiveness on shifts when the throttle opens again by lowering inertia.

Straight-toothed belts have the disadvantage that there is nothing inherent in the design that provides side-to-side alignment. This makes the alignment of straight-toothed belts especially critical to keeping the engine from throwing the supercharger belt and mandates a pulley with flanges that help to guide the belt onto the crank pulley. That said, a toothed belt with pulley alignment that is constantly pushing it against the flanges is living on borrowed time.

Herringbone toothed belts embody some of the advantage of both ribbed and straight-toothed drive belts. Like straight-toothed belts, they cannot slip unless they fail. They are quieter than straight-toothed belts because the angled teeth mesh with the receivers in the pulley gradually rather than all at once. The diagonal teeth of herringbone belts prevents the belt from slipping sideways, resulting in a belt with the self-aligning capability of a ribbed belt.

If space is tight, it may be possible to locate the supercharger rotor assembly inside the intake manifold, as Neuspeed did with this supercharger assembly for the 2.0-liter VW inline-4. The rotor assembly is an M-series Eaton with a 60-degree helix. *Neuspeed*

The components of a simple supercharger drive belt system include crankshaft pulley, belt, supercharger pulley, and tensioner and idler pulley. This is a Vortech Power Pulley setup to increase the boost on a Mustang with a higher drive ratio that spins the blower faster than stock. *Vortech*

Drawing of twin V-belt accessory drive system. V-belts are not sexy but they work, and in multi-belt systems they offer redundancy.

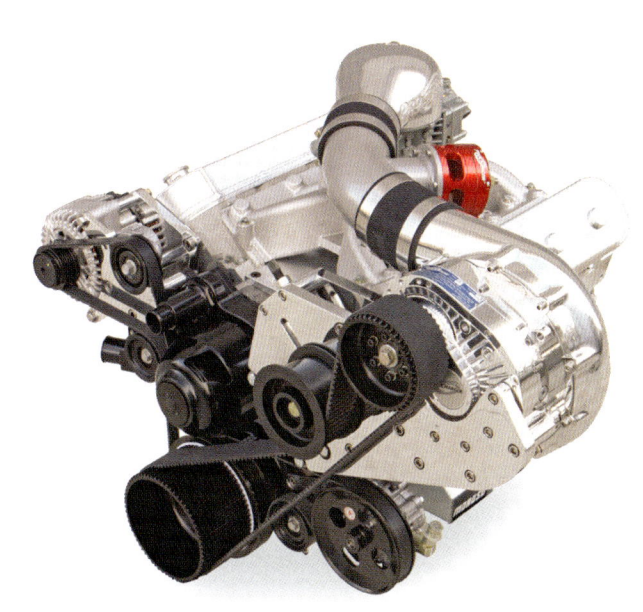

Procharger's LSx carbureted supercharger kit includes a cogged belt drive system that eliminates any possibility of slip in competition conditions at the cost of increased stress on the centrifugal supercharger's speed-multiplication gears during drag-race conditions. *Procharger*

From the get-go you'll need to know how much horsepower the supercharger itself will consume (and waste) delivering the required airflow and boost pressure, as well as how much horsepower will be wasted in the drive system getting power to the supercharger input shaft (most of the waste energy is spent flexing the drive belt as it bends around the pulleys). Supercharger manufacturers typically provide power graphs that plot the horsepower (or kW) energy required to achieve a particular airflow and pressure ratio, and in some cases manufacturers plot horsepower consumption lines on the compressor map (some don't like to publish maps at all, much less maps showing power consumption to avoid losing business from people fixated on individual numbers as opposed to the big picture). If you don't have access to the manufacturer's published data for a specific compressor, you can generically calculate the horsepower requirement based on the equations shown earlier in this chapter:

Required crankshaft supercharger drive power = ((boost × airflow) / 229 hp) / (drive power efficiency × compressor adiabatic efficiency)

Armed with calculated numbers for the supercharger's horsepower requirement and belt speed at peak loading, you'll be able to determine (1) torque loading on the supercharger drive belt, (2) minimum width of the belt, and (3) worst-case loading on the drive, driven, idler, and belt-tensioner pulley bearings.

Previously we calculated that using an Eaton R1900 TVS supercharger to boost a 290-horsepower 5.0-liter V-8 to 400 horsepower (a 38-percent power boost) requires 25 to 30 horsepower at the crankshaft to drive the blower, and that future hot rodding to 500 horsepower would require approximately double the drive power. To protect the drive design for an *additional* future engine horsepower increase of 25 percent above 400 horsepower, we should build a drive system able to accommodate pulleys wide enough to handle a belt that will easily transmit 60 horsepower. Although a thin, 3/16-inch, 6-rib belt should safely handle the 60 crankshaft horsepower required to deliver 50 lb/min air at 16-pi boost, the belt would be operating at the upper end of its power rating.

SUPERCHARGER PULLEYS

Engine pulleys are manufactured from mild steel, stainless steel, aluminum, and in some cases plastics like nylon. At this time of writing, supercharger drive and driven pulleys were still machined from metal, though plastic is suitable for idlers if loading is not too heavy or concentrated in one direction, as is the case when belt wrap angle begins to approach 180 degrees.

The same softness that makes aluminum easy and quick to machine makes it problematic as a raw material for a drive pulley: Friction from the belt can erode aluminum to the point that it's worn out in as little as 20,000 to 30,000 miles. If you plan to use an aluminum pulley, the surface should be hard-anodized to make it more resistant to wear. Anodizing is an electrolytic process that vastly increases the thickness of self-passivation oxidation on the surface of aluminum for increased hardness and decreased thermal conductivity. Anodizing, which can be dyed several colors for appearance, will resist corrosion. Google "anodizing," "metal finishing," or "coatings" to find a source.

Some suppliers market plain-aluminum R&D test and development supercharger pulleys. The idea is that developers start with a conservative boost pressure defined by the aluminum pulley and then use a lathe to turn the pulley smaller to incrementally pump up the boost pressure. After this, the production pulley would be manufactured from steel.

Steel is much harder than aluminum and will last much longer before it is too worn to be serviceable. Like brake rotors, mild steel pulleys may form rust when wet (until the belt polishes off the rust), but do not even think about chrome-plating steel drive or driven pulleys. Chrome is hard but extremely slippery, which is definitely not what you want on the drive surface of a pulley. Stainless-steel pulleys (with at least 10.5 percent chromium content) do not rust and are extremely hard and wear-resistant, but the high chrome content of stainless steel gives it a lower coefficient of friction than mild steel. 41XX steel alloys made with chromium and molybdenum are strong but chromoly steel is pointless as a raw material for pulleys. The additional strength is not required in a pulley, the material is harder to machine and more slippery than mild steel, and it will rust.

Supercharger suppliers market pulleys prefabricated in discrete sizes selected to increase or decrease boost 1 to 2 psi per change to the next larger or smaller pulley. Machine shops and custom pulley specialists will build whatever custom size pulley you need.

You might assume "a pulley is a pulley is a pulley" when it comes to the exact specification of the ribs or teeth (or the crown on smooth idler or tensioner pulleys). Some manufacturers, however, have attempted to develop arcane proprietary tricks designed to simultaneously maximize traction between the pulley and belt and minimize belt wear by subtly varying the angles of ribs and teeth, the width and height of their crests, and the radius of edges. In other cases the "advantages" of a particular pulley may be hype designed to sell product.

Putting a minute radius into the edges of ribs or teeth can help to protect the belt from premature wear compared to sharper-edged crests. A relatively wide crest on a rib or tooth can improve belt traction by fitting ribs or teeth tightly into the receiver grooves deep in the belt close to the reinforcing backbone. This may simultaneously improve belt longevity by transferring the load immediately into the backbone, relieving the belt teeth or ribs of having to absorb heavy shear forces that occur when a narrower pulley crest fits more loosely into the belt (which will definitely result in the belt living a life that is nasty, brutish, and short). Pushed to the limit, traction and longevity may be a zero-sum game: A pulley will grip the belt better if teeth or ribs are machined slightly large or slightly farther apart than the receiving structures in the belt, which produces outstanding traction at the expense of significantly shortened belt life. Which is fine for competition where no one is concerned about longevity beyond the length of time it takes to win, but it's not so great for the street.

If a machine shop has never previously built a custom supercharger pulley, you might not want to be the customer that pays them to learn the tricks. The safest bet is to buy prefabricated pulleys from the supercharger supplier or ask your supplier to recommend a source experienced in building excellent custom pulleys. As always, cut-rate engine parts are false economy.

If you have the space, larger diameter pulleys of any kind are always better because the bearings turn slower, the increased radius bends the belt less (for improved drive efficiency and, therefore, less belt heating), and the increased circumference of the pulley increases the contact area between pulley and belt for improved traction. Keep in mind that contact area can also be increased by using idler or tensioner pulleys to wrap the belt farther around whatever size pulley is viable in the application, thereby increasing the *wrap angle* of the belt. If there is too little pulley area in contact with the belt, ribbed or V-belts will slip. If there are too few pulley teeth in contact with a cogged belt, a toothed belt will soon be shorn of its teeth. Because traction is a function of both friction and pressure, increases in contact area do not produce commensurate increases in traction, but instead deliver increases equal to the *square root* of contact area increases.

For maximum longevity, the surface of idler and tensioner pulleys should always match the surface of whichever side of the belt is in contact with the pulley (smooth, ribbed, toothed, and so on). Some serpentine belts are available double-sided. Smooth idler/tensioner pulleys are often manufactured with a slight crown, which helps keep the belt centered. Tensioner and idler pulleys are often flanged to make sure the belt is not thrown if alignment is questionable.

Unless space is so tight an 8-rib drive will not fit, an 8-rib drive is preferable to protect the design for substantial future power increases, versus a thicker 3/8 belt with lower efficiency.

Note: If the supercharger is sharing the same drive belt with other engine accessories, *you need a belt with the strength to handle the combined load of all engine accessories at once*—combined with the inertial loading when you are accelerating all the accessories and the supercharger is producing heavy boost. How much horsepower does it take to drive an alternator, power-steering pump, water pump, smog pump, mechanical fan, and so on? To some extent this depends on what electrical devices happen to be running (such as headlights), whether you're working the power steering pump by turning the wheels, how many cfm a mechanical fan is pushing, and so forth.

Power wasted driving engine accessories was an important component of the difference between "gross" and SAE net horsepower in the original musclecar era of the 1960s (the other aspect was the open exhausts used on OE engine dynos), an indication that the number is not trivial. To calculate the horsepower loss to drive the engine accessories, you'll need to research your particular accessories, keeping in mind that any alternator has a maximum number of amps it can deliver, at which point additional current draw will begin to deplete the battery. When it comes to evaluating horsepower draw from electrical systems, we start with the fact that 1 horsepower is equal to 745.69 watts (0.745 kW). Then, 15 horsepower is equal to

745.69 watts × 15 = 11,185.35 watts

Since **Current = Watts / voltage**

11,185.35 watts / 13.7 volts = 816.45 amps (assuming a typical automotive electrical system delivers 13.7 volts when the engine is running).

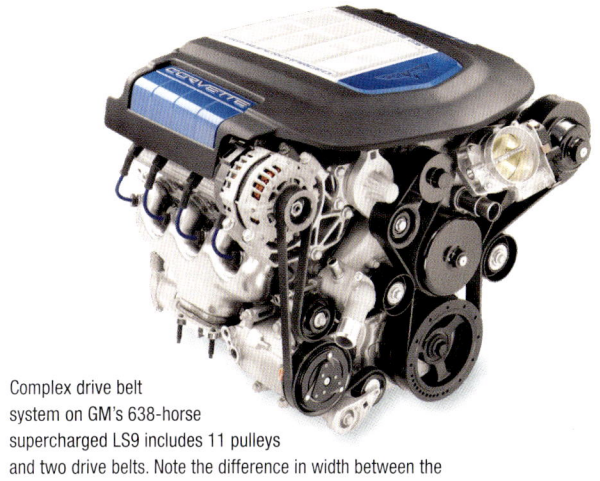

You can also calculate the inertia of engine accessories if you know the rotating weight, at which point you can calculate the power required to accelerate the mass at a certain rate, which is how inertial chassis dynamometers like the Dynojet calculate engine horsepower.

We calculated earlier in this chapter that an Eaton R1900 supercharger turning at 10,400 rpm to force 44 pounds per minute of air at 9.5 psi into a 5.0-liter engine needs to run at a pulley ratio of 1.53 times crankshaft speed if the engine is running at 6,800 rpm. Because Roots and twin-screw superchargers have no internal transmission to increase rotor speed, if the R1900 is equipped with the smallest standard 72-millimeter (2.8-inch) diameter pulley, we'd need a crank pulley with a diameter of a little more than 110 millimeters (4.3 inches) to make the required boost. On the other hand, running the largest 96-millimeter Magnuson blower pulley, we'd need a larger 147-millimeter (5.8-inch) crank pulley.

Well, in theory. When you are developing a new supercharger conversion system there is a good chance that boost and horsepower delivery will not be exactly as modeled. Even if they are, detonation problems could effectively force you to scale back on the boost pressure. If you're using prefabricated pulleys, keep in mind that starting with a crankshaft (drive) pulley that delivers the calculated pulley ratio with the smallest or largest off-the-shelf supercharger pulley gives you less freedom to change boost by swapping blower pulleys than if you started somewhere in the middle. Off-the-shelf driven supercharger pulleys are typically less expensive than acquiring or custom-building a new drive pulley to change boost pressure.

Custom-building pulleys provides some ability to customize the pulley offsets for alignment purposes if alignment is not achievable purely by selecting the right supercharger mounting location, but keep in mind that many superchargers are available with optional extension housings that relocate the supercharger pulley as much as 18 inches from the standard position next to the main body of the supercharger. Some extension housings provide a few tenths of an inch of fine adjustment for optimizing pulley alignment at installation time.

Complex drive belt system on GM's 638-horse supercharged LS9 includes 11 pulleys and two drive belts. Note the difference in width between the 6-rib alternator drive and the 10-rib blower drive. *GM Media Archive*

A simple ribbed supercharger drive on a big-block Chevrolet with Vortech supercharger. Long belts generally have increased durability because of their increased ability to absorb sudden shock loading. It is always better to tension the belt inward because doing so increases traction by increasing the wrap angle around pulleys.

Supercharger suppliers like Vortech offer many options for supercharger drive systems. Note the smooth and ribbed idler pulleys. Drive and driven pulleys should match the surface of the traction side of the drive belt, while idler pulleys in serpentine-belt drive systems must match the pattern on whichever side of the belt they are contacting (which might be the front or back side of the belt). It is not unheard of for low-torque engine accessories to be driven from the smooth side of a ribbed belt. *Vortech*

Thirty-tooth cogged driven pulley on Vortech centrifugal supercharger. The blower's internal gearing must be factored into the effect on blower speed of changing external pulley sizes. *Vortech*

Idler and tensioner pulleys provide flexibility in routing belts around obstacles and enable blower system designers to increase belt traction by increasing the angle of belt wrap around drive or driven pulleys. Note spring-loaded tensioner pulley on the left, which provides automatic belt tensioning and allows easy pulley removal *Tork Tech*

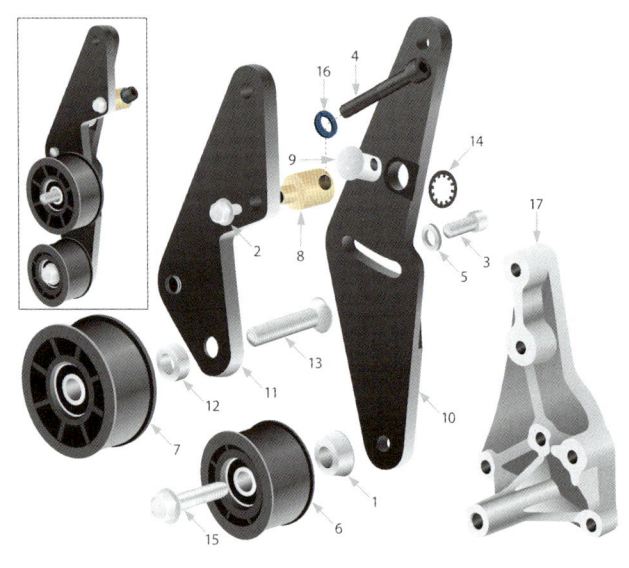

This is the right way to build a manually adjustable supercharger drive pulley. Jackson Racing tensioner pulley is adjustable via an Allen bolt (4), which pivots a bracket (11) to tighten or loosen the pulley (7). After the supercharger drive belt is tight, the bracket must be clamped in place with a bolt (3). *Jackson Racing*

Perhaps there's space to install a prefabricated offset pulley that bolts onto the crank damper with the same bolts as the stock accessory drive pulley. With this you can drive an add-on supercharger belt in an entirely new plane, farther from the timing case (a little like the outer rear wheel on a dually truck). Or you may be able to use a prefabricated dual-drive pulley that replaces the existing crank pulley to drive both belts. If not, it may be necessary to fabricate a custom add-on or replacement pulley (or even a crank damper with pulley grooves built in). Where adding an entirely new drive belt and pulleys for the supercharger is not feasible, it may be possible to mount the supercharger such the pulley lines up with a pre-existing serpentine belt setup, making it possible to install a longer serpentine belt that drives the supercharger along with the existing engine accessories (perhaps with add-on idler pulleys that route the belt around obstacles on its way to and from the blower pulley). Many supercharger and kit vendors sell an extensive array of blower, crank, idler, and spring-loaded tensioner pulleys, or will refer you to machine shops that can machine custom drive or driven supercharger pulleys.

When designing the supercharger drive, keep in mind that centrifugal and inertial forces will tend to fling the belt outward in a path that does its best to approximate a circle—a phenomenon referred to as orbiting. In a worst case, orbiting can lift a slightly loose belt enough as it approaches the pulley that the belt could be thrown if any of the pulleys is permanently misaligned or transiently pulled out of alignment, or if shock forces or vibration bend the belt far enough out of line. If at all possible, it is preferable to install idler or spring-loaded tensioner pulleys such that they are pressing *inwardly* against the *outside* of the belt in a concave direction, which not only helps to control orbiting to reduce the chance of a thrown belt but increases the amount of belt wrap around the pulleys for improved traction. Idler or tensioner pulleys pressing in a concave direction against the smooth outside of a belt should have a smooth surface (unless the belt is a double-sided ribbed or toothed belt). Idlers or tensioners pressing outward against the ribbed or toothed side of a belt should be machined with receiver grooves or teeth exactly like the drive and driven pulleys. In all cases a larger pulley diameter is better, both from the point of view of improved traction and because the belt will run cooler when it is negotiating longer-radius curves.

Idler pulleys should ideally be located a distance of at least twice the idler diameter from the nearest pulley in order to provide (a) time for the belt to cool as it travels through open air and (b) distance for the belt to stretch to compensate for imperfect pulley alignment. The alignment of a tensioner/idler pulley directing the belt onto the drive pulley is critically important, more so the closer together the two pulleys are to each other. Spring-loaded tensioner pulleys must be installed so they are pressing against the unloaded, slack side of the drive belt, where the belt is moving away from the crank (drive) pulley toward the supercharger, rather than on the tension side of the circuit, where the belt is being yanked from the supercharger toward the crank pulley under full torque. If a tensioner pulley absolutely cannot be installed on the slack side of the belt, you'll have to install a manually adjustable tensioner pulley on the loaded side of the belt with bearings appropriate to the heavy loading—ideally adjustable via a threaded bolt that turns to pull the tensioner pulley tight by pivoting the mounting plate to shorten (or lengthen) the path of the belt. Once adjusted, this type of tensioner mechanism must be clamped in position by tightening (1) the pivot bolt and (2) at least one additional locking fastener located in a slotted hole that permits the plate to pivot. Some idler mounting plates are machined with ridges to help prevent slippage.

Beware over-tensioning supercharger belts, which in theory could lead to excessive side-loading on supercharger bearings and premature bearing or belt failure. Correct supercharger belt tension is similar to that of any normal correctly tensioned engine accessory belt; if there is any question, acquire a tensionometer and use it to make sure belt tension is set in accordance with recommendations from the supercharger manufacturer.

A spring-loaded tensioner must always be installed on the slack, unloaded side of the belt. The spring is selected so there's sufficient power to take up slack in the supercharger belt as the belt is stretched by torque or aging and maintains the proper amount of pressure between pulleys and belt, not to overcome belt torque on the loaded side to tension the belt.

It is always wise to verify that idler pulley bearings are robust enough to handle the temperature, rpm, and load encountered driving the supercharger.

Tork Tech crankshaft drive pulleys illustrate that supercharger belts may be driven directly from the crankshaft via slotted pulleys with Woodruff key or from add-on auxiliary pulleys that bolt to directly driven pulleys. If there is space it is better to build a supercharger drive system with its own belt and drive pulley rather than extending a factory serpentine drive system, because an auxiliary drive allows you to change the diameter of the crank pulley to achieve required supercharger speed and boost without affecting the speed of other engine accessories. *Tork Tech*

Underhood temperatures are commonly as much as 100 degrees F above ambient temperature. This means supercharger system bearings could easily be running in an environment of more than 200 degrees F on a hot summer day in Texas or Arizona. If you are lubricating any bearings with crankcase oil from an air-cooled engine, the oil could be still hotter. Oil coolers are a wonderful thing for any forced-induction engine, but in any case make sure that any bearings you install in a supercharger drive system can handle the heat (see Chapter 7, which talks about heat management).

All bearings have a redline. To determine whether an idler pulley will overspeed its bearing, you need to know how much the crank pulley will overdrive the idler, based on the pulley ratio between the idler and the crank pulley (assuming the supercharger belt is driven directly by the crankshaft rather than indirectly from some other accessory; if not, in

ELECTRIC AND HYDRAULIC SUPERCHARGER DRIVE SYSTEMS

Others mechanisms sometimes used to transmit drive power from an engine to a supercharger are hydraulic and electric drives.
People have designed effective continuously variable drive systems that have been used to power superchargers. The most common is the wastegate-regulated exhaust turbine used to power millions of turbochargers. The biggest problem with harnessing exhaust gases as a power source is that exhaust turbines need to be operating at thousands of rpm before the low torque produced by the energy in exhaust heat and pressure can deliver the horsepower needed to drive a compressor to an effective speed. To drive a positive-displacement compressor operating at 10,000 rpm with an exhaust turbine, you'd need a gear-reduction system, and the whole idea would defeat the advantage of positive-displacement superchargers, which is low-rpm boost.

The appeal of using electric and hydraulic motors powered by alternators or crank-driven hydraulic pumps to drive superchargers is that (1) these types of motors do not need to be turning fast to deliver plenty of torque; (2) there is more than enough torque available at the crankshaft at speeds down to idle to power a supercharger via alternator or hydraulic pump; (3) it is easy to regulate voltage or hydraulic pressure to vary to a motor driving a supercharger; and (4) the geometry of wires or hoses transmitting power can be vastly more flexible than mechanical and belt or gear drive systems.

One problem with electric and fluid drives is that they are less efficient. Converting the chemical energy in gasoline to mechanical energy in the crankshaft, to electrical energy in the alternator to mechanical energy in the electric motor for driving the supercharger is *not* efficient because energy is lost every time it changes form. (Turbines have their own efficiency problems, but in the case of turbochargers, vast amounts of heat are going to be lost out the exhaust anyway.)

One advantage of an electric drive is that it is possible to store electrical energy in a battery during deceleration or times of light engine loading. This offloads the work of driving the supercharger at maximum engine load to the battery so that all of the engine's power can be devoted to doing useful work moving or accelerating the vehicle.

At the time of this writing, the biggest thing standing in the way of electrical drive systems for superchargers (or low-speed electrical *assists* for turbochargers) is that the electrical systems still found on most vehicles operate at voltages that are too low to provide the required power without tremendous current load, which adds greatly to the cost of the motor, wiring, and variable-speed electric motor controllers.

step one calculate the rpm of the intermediate pulley based on the ratio of the first two pulleys and then in step two modify intermediate rpm to account for the effect of the ratio between pulleys two and three). The pulley-to-pulley calculation goes as follows:

$$\text{Idler rpm} = \text{Engine rpm} \times \frac{\text{(drive pulley diameter)}}{\text{idler pulley diameter)}}$$

Check with the bearing or idler supplier to verify that the bearings will not overspeed before the engine hits redline. If the idler bearing would turn too fast, slow it down by installing a larger idler pulley. Or upgrade the bearing to one that will handle the speed.

The load on idler bearings in the supercharger drive system will be a function of the force—belt tension in this case—multiplied by the belt speed in feet per second, multiplied by a constant of up to 2, depending on the amount of belt wrap around the idler pulley:

Force = Power / Velocity

We're going to need to know the velocity of the belt in feet per second, which we can calculate from engine rpm and crank pulley circumference. To get the result in feet per second, we'll need to convert rpm to revolutions per *second* and we'll need to convert pulley circumference from inches to feet:

Revs/sec = RPM / 60
Feet = Inches / 12
Minute = 60 seconds
Circumference = Diameter × π [3.14159265]
Velocity = Circumference × engine rpm
Force = Power / velocity
550 = Pounds 1 horsepower can lift 1 foot in 1 second (converts horsepower to pounds)

The velocity of the belt in feet per minute is thus:

Velocity ft/min =
$$\frac{\text{(Pulley Diameter (inches)}}{12)} \times 3.14159265 \times \frac{\text{(rpm}}{60)}$$

= rpm × Pulley diameter / 229

Power lb/ft/sec = **Horsepower / 550** [lb-ft / hp-sec]

Force pounds = Power / Velocity

= (Horsepower / 550) / ((rpm × pulley diameter) / 229)

Load pounds = **Force** × **[A number greater than 0 and less than 2.0]**

Because the belt loads the idler pulley (in fact, all pulleys) in both directions, load is often greater than force (though it can also be less, depending on the change in the angle of the belt as it moves pass the idler). Load cannot be more than 2x force, with the heaviest load occurring when the belt wraps 180 degrees around the idler pulley and the lightest load occurring when the belt is nearly tangential to the idler pulley. Actual load is typically about 150 percent of force. Static load when the powerplant is stopped will depend on the angles of the belt to the pulley, the type of belt, the distance between pulleys, and the supercharger. Check with the supercharger supplier for recommendations.

Tensioner pulleys in particular require robust mounts that are very stiff to prevent vibration than can accelerate belt wear and hasten the fatigue of the mount or fasteners. The mounts must be thick, broadly based, and supported by triangulating braces if the mount is extended to locate the pulley any distance from the base of the mount. Bending moment on the bearings can be greatly eliminated by supporting the pulley from both faces, which can be accomplished by supporting a shaft running through the tensioner bearing from either end. The distance between a pulley and the base of an extended mount (or a triangulating support brace) will amplify the bending moment on the mount by giving whatever load there is in the belt more leverage.

Every X inches of mount extension increases bending moment against the mount by **belt loading × distance = inch-pounds of force**. If the belt loading on an idler pulley is a total of 130 pounds, and the pulley is 3.5 inches from the base of the mount, bending moment is **3.5 × 130 = 455** inch-pounds, or **455 / 12 ≈ 40** pound-feet. Suppose that a sudden application of throttle instantaneously doubles loading on a supercharger belt because of (a) the inertial loading accelerating the blower and (b) the sudden application of load *turning* the supercharger to make boost as a bypass valve closes. Bending moment on a 3.5-inch extended mount is suddenly **3.5** inches × **260** pounds = **910** inch-pounds or 76 pound-feet torque, which is like yanking on the mount with a breaker bar using the kind of force you'd use to tighten some head bolts.

Vibration or resonation from any source and load oscillation in the blower belt caused by the pulsed airflow of positive-displacement superchargers may be amplified by a flexible idler mount, which may accelerate belt wear and

It is possible to build (or have built) extension housings of custom length as seen in this CT Engineering Roots-type supercharger for the V-6 Honda Accord and Acura TL, a good illustration that bulky Roots-type blowers need not be mounted directly on the intake manifold. *CT Engineering*

in a worst case result in the belt being thrown. It's easy to see why stiff idler and tensioner mounts are critical to a reliable supercharger drive system. Obviously, it is critical to use Grade 8 (noncounterfeited!) through-bolts or studs with locknuts everywhere in the blower drive system. Given the potential for wildly destructive consequences caused by the failure of fasteners that secure moving parts like pulleys, there is a good argument to be made for using not just Grade 8 but aviation-grade fasteners.

BUILD THE INTERCOOLER SYSTEM

With the supercharger mounted and the drive system squared away, the next major task is to get after the intercooler.

For virtually all modern positive-displacement superchargers that run more than about 5.5-psi boost, intercooler design (if applicable) is usually going to be integral with the supercharger mounting system. This is because intercooling is required to fight detonation (especially in states like California where premium gasoline is limited to 91 octane), and positive displacement superchargers are usually mounted directly on the intake manifold with an liquid-cooled air-cooler unit inline between the compressor discharge and the intake plenum/runners. The air-cooler section of the intercooler system is effectively *in* the intake manifold assembly (which may also house the supercharger rotor assembly).

An excellent example of this type of architecture can be found in the ZR1 Corvette. In this type of integrated design, the supercharger assembly mounts between the Vee-banks of a V-6, V-8, V-10, or V-12 powerplant, bolting directly to the block. The throttle mounts on the compressor intake housing, which is located on the front or rear of the supercharger unit. The supercharger discharges compressed air *upward* into a plenum that contains a water-cooled heat exchanger. Cooled charge air exits the intercooling chamber directly into intake runners at either side that deliver supercharged air to the intake ports of the cylinder heads.

Assuming you've built the air cooler into the supercharger manifold and mounting system, what remains is to build the intercooler water-cooler unit and coolant pumping system. The chapter in this book about heat management explains how to size and design intercoolers that are effective at cooling charge air to the degree necessary without introducing a large pressure drop through the air cooler.

If you are using a centrifugal supercharger, you have the option to use a liquid-cooled inline air cooler, but you may also have the option of air-air intercooling. Direct air-cooled intercooling is more efficient than cooling charge air on the way into the engine with a water-cooled inline air cooler and then cooling the liquid in a remote air-cooled heat exchanger. Air-water intercoolers have to first move heat from charge air to liquid coolant and then from the liquid coolant (which is relatively cool) to road-draft air. Another advantage of air-air intercoolers is that there are no moving parts (unless you install an auxiliary electric fan to help cooler the intercooler).

Water-cooled intercoolers do have the advantage that it is far easier to move heated water through a small pipe or hose to a remote water-cooler unit than it is to duct large amounts of charge air to a remote air-cooler unit, or to duct large amounts of road-draft air to cool an air-air intercooler in the engine compartment. Air-water intercoolers also offer the possibility that ice water or refrigeration or dry ice can amplify the cooling power of the air cooler. Water has tremendous power as a heat sink, meaning that even if the water-cooler section cannot keep up with heating that occurs under heavy boost, heavy boost in light street vehicles tends to be very transitory, after which the heat can be removed from the liquid coolant at leisure by the water-cooler unit *and* by unboosted ambient temperature air entering the engine when the supercharger is freewheeling and negative pressure (vacuum) exists downstream of the throttle.

One disadvantage of an air-water intercooling system is that hot engine compartment air will tend to heat-soak the air-cooler unit unless it is well insulated, and of the power of the water cooler will be used to remove heat from the engine compartment rather than charge air. It is particularly important to make sure that components of any intercooler be well isolated from hot exhaust components. Best case, this would mean geographical isolation; worst case, it could mean building heat shields around hot components and wrapping cold intercooling components (see Chapter 7 of this book, Heat Management).

BUILD THE AIR CLEANER/AIR INTAKE SYSTEM

You're going to want an air cleaner that is large enough to do the job with minimal pressure drop, but do not automatically reject the stock system: Depending on the power boost and the stock air intake architecture, it may be possible to use the stock cold-air intake system with a supercharger conversion, or perhaps with modifications to increase the size of the air

Blower discharge housing for the Eaton supercharger sends air to Jackson Racing's intercooler kit for the Mazda Miata. If you are diverting compressed air from a positive-displacement supercharger to a remote intercooler, you need a way to duct the air out of the supercharger discharge. *Jackson Racing*

filter. At all costs try to use a cold air intake. By that I mean not just any low-restriction intake, but a *real* cold air intake with a pickup that ingests 100 percent of its air from outside the engine compartment. Unless an engine requires heated intake air in very cold weather to improve fuel vaporization during warm up or to prevent throttle icing (virtually all piston engine aircraft are still equipped with "carb heat" systems that divert exhaust-warmed air into the throttle), hot intake air is a bad deal in all respects. The car companies understand this. Ever since carburetors (with potential icing problems) became extinct in the United States in 1988 on roadgoing vehicles, OE vehicle manufacturers have made sure their vehicles exclusively ingest cool, dense air from the fenderwell, cowl, or hood scoop and through plastic ducting that helped to insulate intake air from heat soak from the hot engine compartment.

The fact is, a low-restriction aftermarket air intake system—designed to mitigate the pressure drop that occurs when the enhanced engine airflow of a supercharger conversion exceeds the capacity of the stock air cleaner and intake plumbing—can be worse than useless if the air intake kit uses an exposed underhood air filter. The problem is that if the air intake *can* pick up heated air, it *will* pick up air that's at least partially heated. Air intake kits with exposed open (K&N-type) air cleaners breathing air from the engine compartment are ingesting air heated by (1) the radiator fan (160–200 degrees F), (2) hot engine surfaces (160–220 degrees F), and (3) exhaust headers (up to 1,000 degrees F). If ambient temperature air is 70 degrees F, air in the engine compartment could easily be 200 degrees F, and is at least 50 to 65 degrees F hotter than ambient, depending vehicle speed and the quality of the engine ventilation architecture. The consequences of 150 to 200 degrees F intake air are significant, more so if the supercharger system is not equipped with an intercooler. Supplying hot air to a supercharged engine at full atmospheric pressure from the heat-soaked engine compartment instead of cooler, 100 percent ambient air at reduced pressure can be a "one-step-forward, two-steps-back" solution that in a worst case can destroy your supercharger and engine.

What's so bad about hot air? Hot air kills power, mandates anti-detonation countermeasures that kill still more power and damages superchargers.

Testing by Kenne Bell compared a 700-horsepower '03 Cobra with an isolated fenderwell air filter to the same vehicle with an open engine compartment filter. Even with a huge fan blowing at the engine to simulate 90 miles per hour, the open underhood air filter delivered ambient air that was 45 degrees F hotter than the isolated filter, which can be equivalent to about 4-psi boost. Opening the hood helped mitigate the problem, but could not eliminate it. The '03 Cobra made 30 more horsepower on the Kenne Bell chassis dyno than it did making a run with the hood closed due to the hotter intake air.

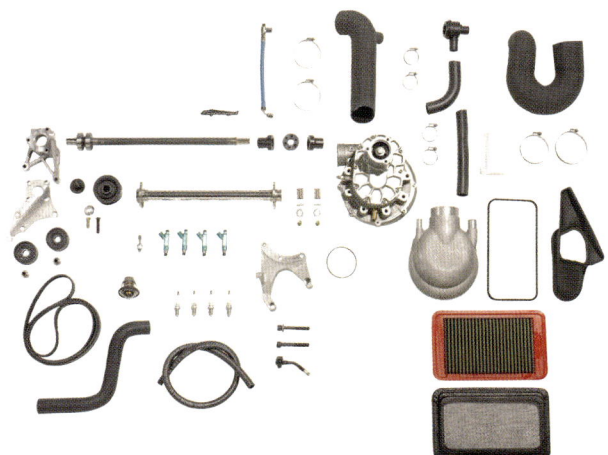

When Toyota Racing Development developed a supercharger kit for the Scion tC, engine space constraints were daunting. The intake manifold is behind the engine. The serpentine accessory drive belt is squeezed between the engine and the frame on the passenger side of the engine, leaving no space for an auxiliary supercharger drive. The solution was an extended serpentine belt driving a remotely mounted centrifugal blower with a long driveshaft plus a tight 90-degree bend on the supercharger air inlet ducted to a relocated MAF sensor. Note that although the production version of the kit provides a molded air intake, the preproduction system used welded-metal intake ducting. *Toyota Racing Development*

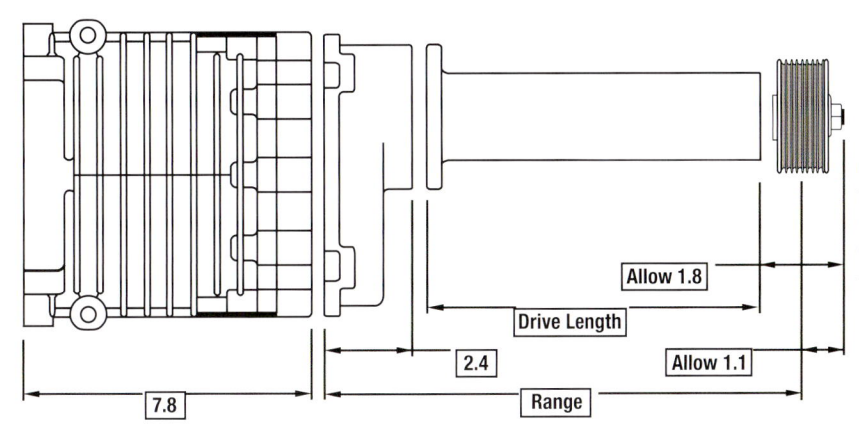

Magnuson Products offers extension housings of varying lengths that allow the supercharger to be relocated certain fixed distances in relation to the plane of the drive belt, with a small amount of ad-hoc final adjustment. *Magnuson Products*

Testing determined that the installation of a shroud between the fan and an open air cleaner in the engine compartment did nothing to reduce the temperature of air entering the supercharger. Kenne Bell makes notes that the trick of removing a headlight and installing an open filter behind it also does not succeed in supplying ambient temperature air to the supercharger because to heat-soak and hot-air mixing. The point is not that low-restriction air cleaner systems are not a good idea, just that you need one with an air intake that is *100 percent isolated* from the engine compartment so it can only breathe cool ambient air (pointing a blast of road-draft air in the general direction of an exposed air cleaner in the engine compartment and hoping for the best is not going to work). It is also worth noting that metal air ducting from an isolated ambient-air filter that heat soaks will raise the temperature of air on its way to the engine—a great reason to consider wrapping all air ducting that passes through the engine compartment with good insulation.

Beyond the immediate effect of heat on air density, hot intake air increases combustion temperature by the amount of the intake temperature increase, which can cause detonation. Because virtually all supercharger conversion engines are knock-limited, and because detonation under heavy loading will destroy an engine in short order, tuners are forced to deal with the problem by lowering peak combustion pressure by either lowering boost or retarding ignition timing. In either case, the solutions amplify the first-order power loss of hot intake air. Not that it's exactly a power *loss* problem: The net effect of the supercharging system is to add power, so it's more a case of power you didn't know you could've had.

The Mountain Performance supercharging system for the Yamaha RX-1 snowmobile was designed to extract power from the lower left engine case with a cogged pulley, route power upward to a driveshaft running to the middle of the engine, and send drive power downward through a second cogged belt to the far side of a Rotrex supercharger. *Mountain Performance*

DESIGNING AND BUILDING A SUPERCHARGER SYSTEM

197

Hot air is bad for superchargers exactly the way hot coolant is bad for engines. Each 10-degree F increase in manifold air temperature is equivalent to the thermal loading of the heat of compression of an additional 1 psi of boost. By this reckoning, an increase in intake air temp of 130 degrees F increases thermal loading as much as an additional 13 psi of boost. Feeding a supercharger 200-degree F intake air and boosting the pressure to 10 psi boost would thus have the same effect on intake temperature (and detonation) as would a supercharger breathing 70-degree air but pressurizing it to 23-psi boost.

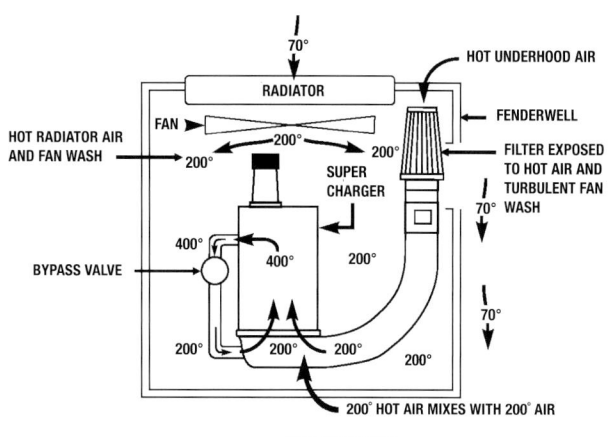

HOT AIR KIT
A 10 DEG RISE IN AIR CHARGE TEMP. RESULTS IN A 1% LOSS IN HP.
(example: 50 DEG = 5% = .05 x 300HP = 15HP)
THAT'S HOW THE WORLD CALIBRATES DYNOS FOR VARYING AMBIENT TEMPERATURES. SAE IS THE MOST COMMONLY USED CONVERSION.

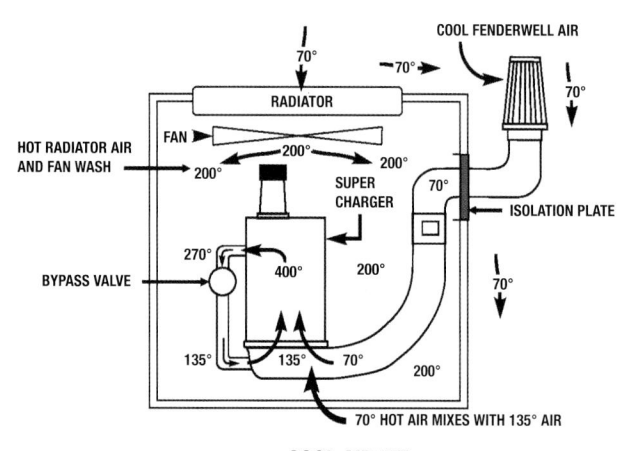

COOL AIR KIT
NOTE: SUPERCHARGER AIR ASSUMED TO BE 200 DEG FROM 20-PSI BOOST (~10 DEG PER POUND OF BOOST) FOR COMPARISON.

When you are building a supercharger system, it is worthwhile to provide 100 percent cold air to the supercharger intake and to insulate engine compartment intake ducting to protect against heat soak. Many people want their hot rod parts to look fabulous rather than race-ugly, but you will not know the cost you are paying for heat soak and hot air intake unless you datalog air temperature as it moves through the supercharging system.—*Kenne Bell*

Everyone knows that overheating an engine is not good for it, but some people have a hard time understanding that the same is true of a positive-displacement supercharger. Too little piston-cylinder clearance caused by loss of coolant will cause the pistons in a powerplant to seize and ruin the engine by breaking rings, scoring cylinders, and damaging pistons; pistons seize in the bores and the engine is dead. The thing is, piston engines and superchargers are both air pumps, and both have internal clearances that are critical to healthy functioning. The engine has pistons, while Roots and twin-screw compressors have rotors, but both are aluminum and both expand with heat, and in either case too much thermal expansion can cause damage.

Overheated intake air flooding the supercharger—heated further as the blower makes boost because of the isentropic heat of compression—can cause the rotors to expand to the point that they contact each other or the case, typically ruining both and maybe necessitating a complete rebuild. Twin-screw blowers, which are always squeezing (and heating) the air as it moves through the compressor, may heat and *reheat* intake air if the bypass valve is open to re-inject a portion of the compressed output of the supercharger downstream of the throttle body when the throttle is closed or nearly closed. Some of the heat of compression is lost when compressed air is expanded, but the net effect of bypass valves can be to heat and reheat the rotors. Rotor heating is so bad for superchargers that old-school Roots blowers require a wet air-fuel mixture through the rotors to cool the rotors with fuel vaporization.

BUILD THE LUBRICATION SYSTEM

Some superchargers require an external supply of pressurized motor oil from the engine to lubricate the bearings by separating metal surfaces with a hydrodynamic film, after which the oil drains downhill out of the supercharger and back into the crankcase. Others are equipped with a self-contained lubrication system that splashes or wicks oil from an on-board reservoir to the surfaces that require lubrication, typically using synthetic fluid found in aircraft-type gas turbine lubricants that perform well from -40 degrees F to 400 degrees F or higher. Others manage with permanently lubricated, sealed bearings.

When a supercharger lubrication system uses pressurized motor oil supplied by the engine's oiling system, it is critical that the bearings continuously receive clean oil at normal temperature and pressure through a restrictor orifice that prevents excessive amounts of oil from being diverted out of the block through the supercharger bearings. A common practice is to tap into the engine oil system by removing the engine oil pressure sending unit and replacing it with a T-fitting that accommodates both the sending unit and a braided-steel hose connected to the supercharger oil supply fitting. It is important to make sure that the oil supply hose is not routed close to anything really hot, such as any part of the exhaust system.

Key
A Oil feed to tee piece
B Oil feed to supercharger
C Oil drain from supercharger
D Oil cooler
E Oil filter with 'sandwhich' plate

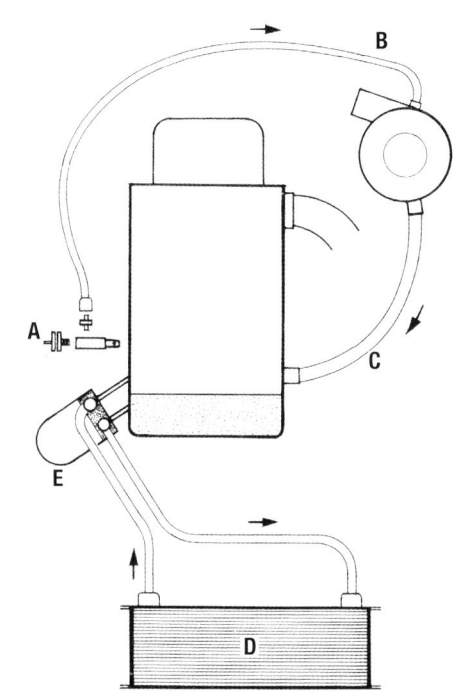

A schematic for a supercharged engine oiling centrifugal blower that requires external oiling. (A) The oil-pressure sending unit at filter reinstalls on a T-fitting that allows oil to travel at full engine oil pressure through a restrictor orifice to (B) the supercharger, where it lubricates the bearings and drains via gravity through (C) a high-volume hose to the engine sump. The oil-cooling circuit at the filter diverts pressurized oil to (D) an air-cooled heat exchanger, from which it returns to (E) the oil filter and on to the engine oil supply system.

On this type of system, oil flowing out of the supercharger bearings leaves the supercharger through a larger hose and drains downhill back to the engine sump via gravity. The high operational speed of some types of superchargers whips oil into a foam that requires some tricks that keep oil from backing up in the drain hose. This can get to the point that oil finds it way past seals designed to keep oil out of the air stream and burns in the combustion chambers, causing mild-to-severe exhaust smoking. Countermeasures include (1) a large-diameter oil drain hose, (2) a drainage pathway to the sump that runs continuously downhill as steeply as possible, and (3) a drain connection to the sump that's "above water" such that foamy oil enters the crankcase above the oil level with as little restriction as possible. Obviously, aerated oil is much more of a problem with centrifugal compressors, some of which have operating speeds above 100,000 rpm.

In some cases the supercharger must be oriented within a certain range of horizontal or vertical for the internal reservoir to supply oil as it should or for the gravitational aspects of an engine-fed lubrication system work properly. The above factors have the potential to cause serious trouble if you mount the supercharger without giving due consideration to getting oil to and from the blower. If you anticipate difficulties with supplying engine oil to a supercharger, this could influence supercharger choice. Some suppliers offer superchargers that can be lubricated externally or from an internal oil reservoir filled with special synthetic lubricant.

Insufficient vertical elevation above the oil sump for good drainage can be dealt with by pumping the oil back to the sump with a dry-sump-type mechanical or electric pump, or by *lowering the oil pan and oil pump pickup* so that foamy oil (which can be the consistency of whipped cream in extreme cases) has a better path to the sump. Sometimes lowering the sump level an inch or two can make all the difference. This is a more common problem with turbochargers, which may be located below the exhaust manifold, but some difficult engine compartments make it extremely desirable to locate a centrifugal supercharger in a position where there is insufficient vertical elevation for good oil drainage.

One way to lower the oil pan is to build a spacer plate that matches the oil pan gasket on both sides and weld or bolt it to the pan. You'll need to find an extended (deep) oil pump pickup or to amputate the lower part of the stock oil pickup and extend it by welding in a new section of tubing that puts the pickup at the bottom of the extended oil pan. If something makes it impossible to lower the entire pan, you could amputate the deepest part of the sump (say, with a band saw), tack-weld on jigs that anchor the two pieces of oil pan to each other separated by the distance you're extending the bottom piece, and then weld or braze in a sheet-metal plate to join the two pieces. If you're running a common performance engine, there may be off-the-shelf deep sumps available, but keep in mind that the point is to *lower* the oil level, not increase the oil capacity, so you'll need an extended dipstick or some other method of adjusting the target height for oil in the deepened sump. This might seem obvious, but a deep sump should be protected by a bash-plate if there is any possibility that an inch or two (or whatever it is) of reduced ground clearance will ever bring the deep pan into contact with something evil.

TEST AND TUNE

When you've finished constructing a roll-your-own supercharger conversion system, it's time to check the tightness of everything and then install temperature and pressure instrumentation to test and tune the system. You'll be measuring efficiency and pressure drop at the air cleaner and throttle body, pressure at the compressor discharge, intercooler inlet and outlet, and temperature at the compressor discharge, I/C inlet and outlet, and intake plenum, and back pressure in the exhaust system upstream of the cat and muffler and just downstream of the muffler. For detailed information about testing and tuning, see my book *How to Tune and Modify Engine Management Systems*.

Chapter 10
Overboosting

There are a number of ways to increase boost pressure on a supercharged engine, whether it is a factory system or a supercharger conversion:

1. If the existing air cleaner or air intake system is causing a pressure drop at the compressor inlet, eliminating the pressure drop allows the compressor to deliver a higher psi boost above ambient pressure.
2. Similarly, eliminating pressure drop through an intercooler will result in higher manifold pressure for a given pressure ratio from the compressor.
3. Overdriving a supercharger by installing a smaller supercharger pulley or a larger crankshaft pulley, causing the supercharger to run at a higher multiple of engine rpm, will cause the compressor to pump more air by increasing the amount the supercharger rotates per crankshaft revolution, also known as the drive ratio. If the supercharger is a Roots or twin-screw type, the final drive ratio of the blower is the same as the ratio of the diameters of the drive and driven pulleys, also known as the *pulley ratio* (which you can determine with careful measuring and a calculator). If the supercharger is a centrifugal type, to get the final drive ratio you have to factor in the *internal drive ratio* of the supercharger, since the pulley ratio will not be the same as the final drive ratio. Keep in mind that increasing boost by overdriving the blower will almost definitely generate more heat in the compressed charge and more parasitic drag on the crankshaft, and will probably change the compressor's thermal and volumetric efficiency at peak boost (and other points as well), though, depending on where you started,

Neuspeed Power Pulleys

Modern centrifugal compressor wheels typically incorporate reverse-curved exducer blades for improved thermal efficiency, an effective strategy for engines where boost pressure will not reach levels much over 1 atmosphere. Every other inducer blade is truncated to maintain high-boost performance without restricting the effective flow area for air entering the impeller. The state-of-the-art in centrifugal compressors is billet compressor wheels made from forged blanks. The Turbonetics HPC compressor wheel is machined from aluminum billet. For high pressure ratio applications permanently running at pressure ratios as high as 5.0:1, the Turbonetics HPR wheel can be made from aluminum or titanium billet. *Turbonetics*

RIVA XXX-charger high-boost compressor upgrade for Sea-Doo 215/255/260 watercraft engines with centrifugal supercharger. Changing to a compressor wheel with a more aggressive trim (trim = inducer versus exducer ratio) results in the supercharger delivering more aggressive airflow and boost. In some cases an existing centrifugal supercharger or turbo compressor can be machined to accept the larger compressor wheel, while in other cases the compressor housing must be changed. The RIVA XXX-Charger features a 140-millimeter Vortech impeller, billet spacer, machined front and rear housings, and RIVA heavy-duty clutch washers. The XXX package was designed to deliver 14-psi boost at 8,100 rpm and 15.5-psi boost at 8,500 rpm. Increased interior volume produces performance gains 15.5 psi at 8,500 rpm. *RIVA Racing*

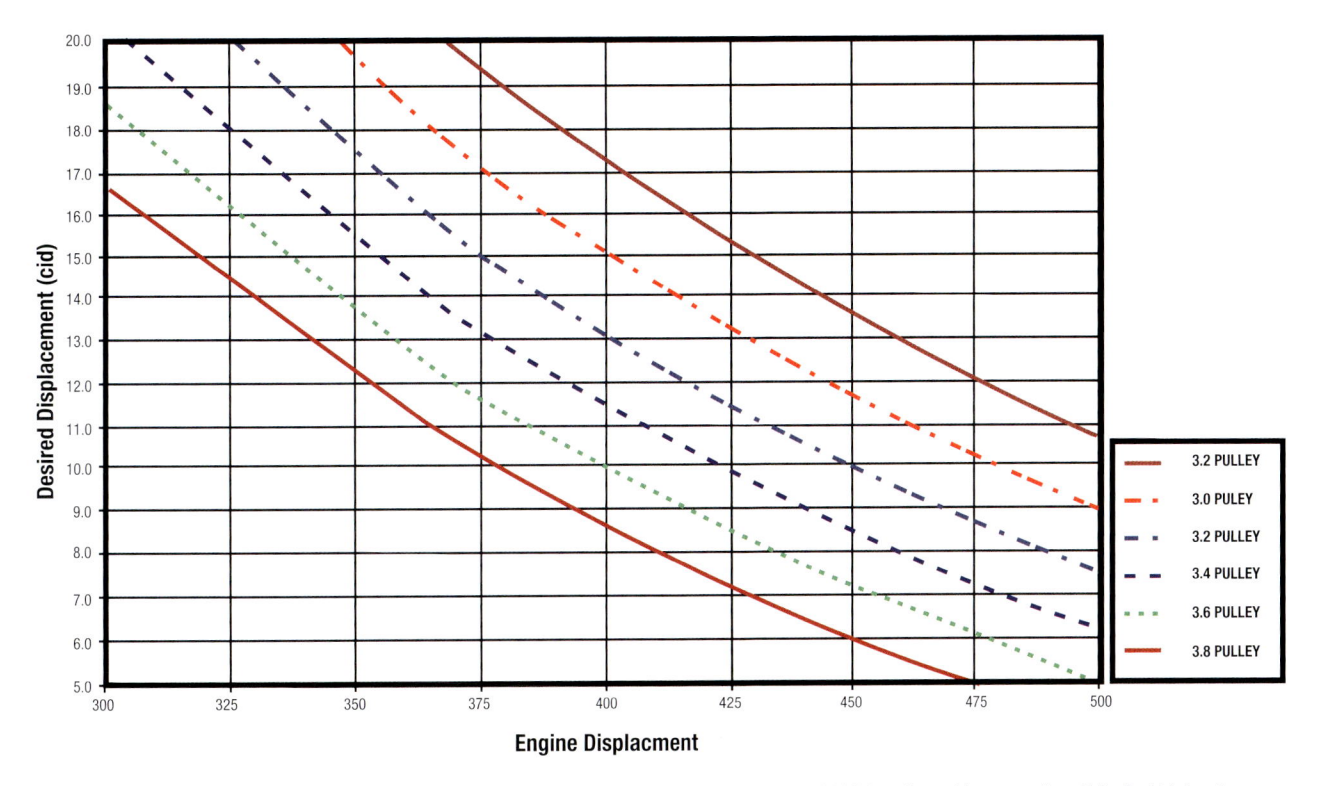

A pulley selection guide for an overdriven Magnuson 2300, based on a 7.35-inch stock 'Vette crank pulley and 36/30-tooth overdrive rear pulleys. Note: For high boost applications, it may be necessary to upgrade to an 8- or 10-rib serpentine ATI balancer to prevent slippage. Find the point where your engine displacement and desired boost level meet, then select the colored line closest to that point. Look up the colored line in the key on the right. *This chart is a guide only. All boost levels are approximate and should be verified on engine. Magnuson Products*

these could *increase*. If you push the supercharger far enough out of its peak thermal efficiency envelope, what you'll get from adding boost is a lot of heat, pressure, potential detonation, and little or no additional power.

4. There is another way to increase boost pressure, and it explains why installing a bigger cam can actually *reduce boost pressure*. If you *lower* the basic volumetric efficiency of an engine, the engine will act as more of a bottleneck to the blower, forcing a fixed-displacement supercharger to build more boost pressure in the intake manifold as it works harder to cram a certain amount of air into the engine. This will tend to heat the air, which is definitely not a good thing. On the other hand, this kind of boost increase is not always as dysfunctional as it sounds. For example, if high off-idle torque and low emissions are critical, you could decide to install a small cam and long intake runners, which would produce excellent cylinder filling at low engine speed. Of course, the basic normal-charged volumetric efficiency of the engine would be down at higher rpm, which would automatically force a positive-displacement supercharger to generate more boost pressure as it relentlessly pushes a fixed amount of air

in the engine. Yes, the supercharger will generate a little more parasitic drag making more boost, and, yes, you may stress the intercooler a little more from cooling off the charge, but letting the supercharger do the work of making high-end power can be a great strategy toward producing a really great torque curve.

OVERBOOSTING WITH PULLEY CHANGES

The section of this book that tells how to mathematically model a roll-your-own supercharger system makes use of pulley ratio to select crank and supercharger pulleys that will convert engine rpm at maximum boost to the blower rpm needed to achieve a certain airflow and pressure ratio. The equation is: **Pulley ratio = Blower rpm / (Engine rpm [* supercharger internal drive ratio])**. To achieve the required pulley ratio, we chose sizes for the two pulleys such that the diameter of the crank pulley divided by the diameter of the blower pulley equaled the ratio of the blower and engine rpm. The supercharger drive ratio is assumed to be 1.0 except in the case of centrifugal superchargers with internal gear or pulley ratios that provide additional supercharger speed multiplication.

When it comes to overboosting, we employ pulley ratio a different way. Let's say all we know is that the current pulley ratio delivers a boost pressure of 5 psi at a certain engine rpm and we want to try running the engine with 7-psi boost. If we are running a factory-supercharged engine in good health with no modifications, or we have a turnkey supercharger kit installed on a factory-stock engine, we may be able to find out exactly what size blower or crank pulley we need to overdrive the supercharger to make specified boost increase just by asking someone who's already done it. If not, a new pulley ratio is required to make the new target boost based on the existing boost pressure and existing pulley ratio, as shown below. Keep in mind that for this formula to work perfectly, we'd need a supercharger and engine with perfectly linear increases in pump capacity, and we'd need to keep the manifold temperature precisely where it was at the old boost pressure, meaning that in the real world the actual boost might not be exactly as predicted.

$$\frac{\text{Pulley ratio}}{\text{old pulley ratio}} = \frac{\text{target boost}}{\text{current boost}}$$

With a little algebra this formula can be rearranged as follows:

$$\text{Pulley ratio} = \text{old pulley ratio} \times \frac{\text{target boost}}{\text{current boost}}$$

Let's say a supercharged engine was making 7.5-psi (pressure ratio of about 1.5) boost at 5,000 engine rpm at a compressor speed of about 10,000 rpm with a pulley ratio of 2.0 using a 190-millimeter crank pulley and a 95-millimeter blower pulley. Let's say we want to know what pulleys we could use to increase the boost to 9-psi boost, which is about a 1.6 PR, a 20 percent increase.

$$\text{Pulley ratio} = \text{old pulley ratio} \times \frac{\text{(target boost)}}{\text{current boost)}}$$

$$= 2.0 \times (9 \text{ psi} / 7.5 \text{ psi})$$
$$= 2.0 \times 1.2$$
$$= 2.4$$

The calculated new pulley ratio to achieve 9-psi boost instead of 7.5 psi is thus 2.4 versus the original 2.0. If we decide to retain the existing 190-millimeter crank pulley, we'll need to change blower pulleys from a 95-millimeter unit to a smaller, 80 millimeter one. Alternatively, if we want to retain the original 95-millimeter blower pulley, we could increase the crank pulley from 190 to 230 millimeter. If, on the other hand, 230 is larger than will fit and 80 millimeter is smaller than we want to go on the blower side to keep pulley area as large as possible, we could split the difference: A 210-millimeter crank pulley would do the job with an 87.5-millimeter blower pulley.

If you increase the crank pulley diameter, it is important to consider the impact of this on the speed of other engine accessories, because the alternator, water pump, power steering pump, and any other driven accessories will turn faster, which could potentially overspeed the bearings at redline and lead to early failure. You should verify that this will not happen, or stick to overdriving the supercharger by decreasing the blower pulley size. Keep in mind that reducing the blower pulley size will decrease traction by reducing the contact area between the belt and pulley (and possibly the angle of belt wrap). The reduced radius of the pulley will amplify the increased thermal loading on the belt of the added horsepower required to turn the blower at higher boost by bending the belt more as it turns the supercharger.

BASED ON 90 TOOTH CRANK PULLEY AND 36/30 TOOTH OVERDRIVE REAR PULLEYS

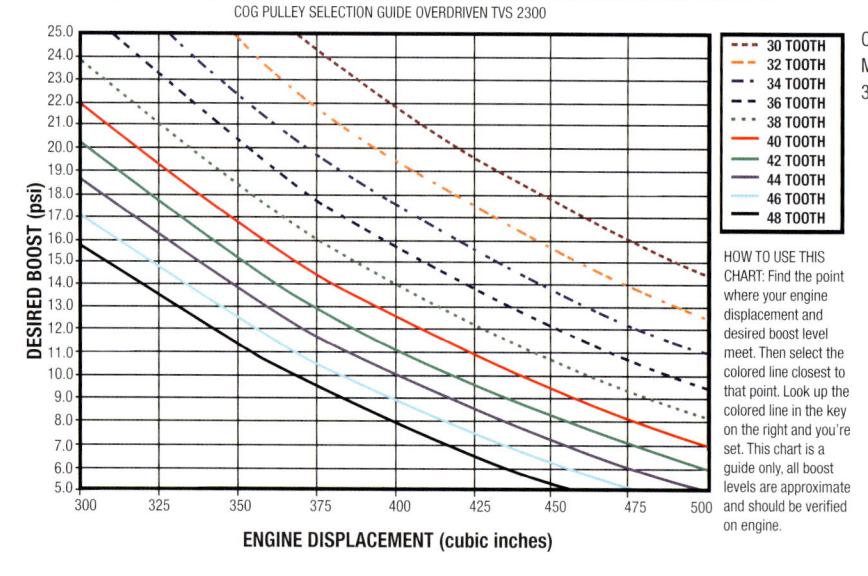

Cog Pulley Selection Guide for Magnuson Products MP2300 supercharger, based on 90-tooth crank pulley and 36/30-tooth overdrive rear pulleys. *Magnuson Products*

HOW TO USE THIS CHART: Find the point where your engine displacement and desired boost level meet. Then select the colored line closest to that point. Look up the colored line in the key on the right and you're set. This chart is a guide only, all boost levels are approximate and should be verified on engine.

CravenSpeed's MINI supercharger overdrive consists of a two-piece hub and pulley. *Terry Sayther Automotive*

Here's the engine:

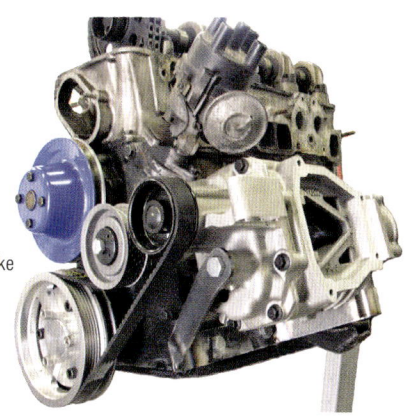

This 1.6-liter 16-valve MINI engine shows the Eaton Roots-type supercharger. Access to the blower looks simple on the engine stand, but changing pulleys will take a good chunk of a day. *Terry Sayther Automotive*

CHANGING PULLEYS

Swapping supercharger or crank pulleys can be a process that's short and sweet or a complicated nightmare. Contact the supercharger manufacturer or factory shop manual for the pulley removal procedure if it's an OEM supercharged vehicle, or contact the kit manufacturer for an aftermarket blower conversion kit.

In the case of a 2001–2004 Roush-supercharged Mustang, overboosting can be as simple as:

- Remove the blower pulley bolt with a socket wrench while you immobilize the pulley with the aid of the belt and a channel-lock pliers wrapped in cloth.
- Remove the belt by relieving pressure on the spring-loaded tensioner pulley.
- Lightly tap off the pulley with a rubber mallet.
- Apply anti-seize compound to the shaft.
- Reverse the process to install the new pulley, which is smaller but usually does not require a shorter belt.

In the case of a supercharged MINI S, overdriving the supercharger with a pulley change is a more complex process that will burn up most of a Saturday. Here's the car:

MINI Cooper S models have been boosted with both superchargers and turbos. If you have a 2002–2006 supercharged model you may be interested in overboosting. *MINI*

- The supercharger is buried deeply in the engine compartment, so R&R of the pulley can easily take twice as long as you expected, even if you're a pessimist.
- You're going to need a special puller tool to remove the stock MINI supercharger pulley.
- Remove the right front wheel and RF plastic inner fender liner (which may require new plastic screws unless you're super careful).
- Remove the right upper motor mount bolts and bracket.

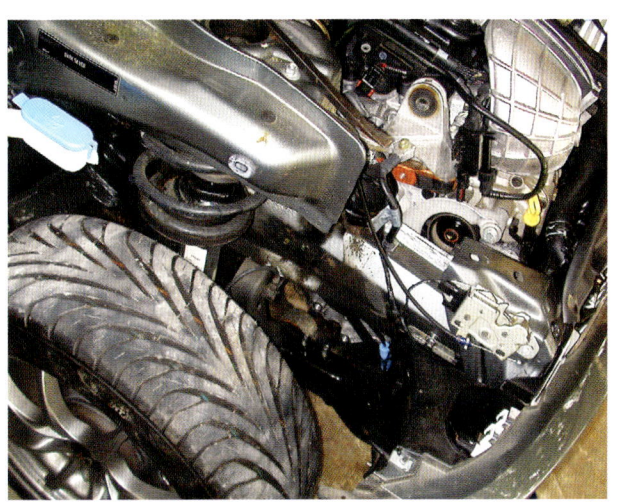

Here's a MINI with fenders and left inner fenderwell removed, showing blower pulley to the left of the yellow dipstick. With the engine cowling removed, the blower is still well hidden, tucked under discharge ducting. *Terry Sayther Automotive*

- Support the engine with a trolley jack.
- Loosen the bottom right motor mount bolt and jack the engine until it's high enough the compressor pulley almost clears the frame.
- Make sure you have the compressor belt routing diagram or draw one yourself for reassembly.

OVERBOOSTING

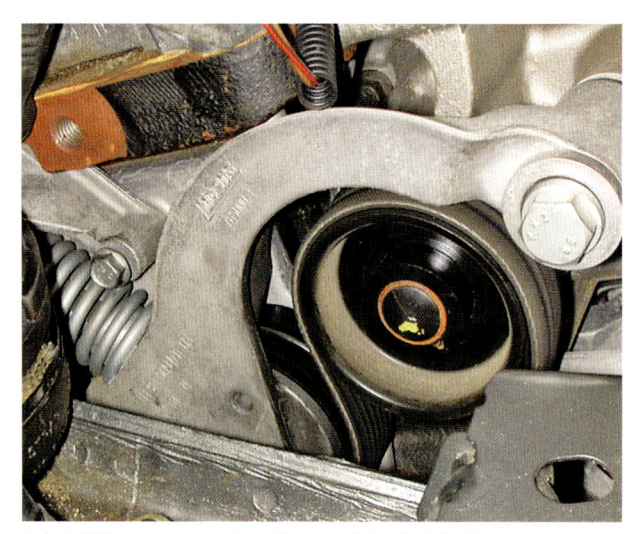

A stock MINI supercharger pulley with drive belt installed after the engine's been jacked up. There's still not much clearance between the pulley and frame. *Terry Sayther Automotive*

- Compress the belt tensioner with a large screwdriver or other lever and insert a small rod or screwdriver to immobilize the tensioner in the compressed position.
- Remove the belt and belt tensioner.
- Install the puller tool and remove the supercharger pulley.

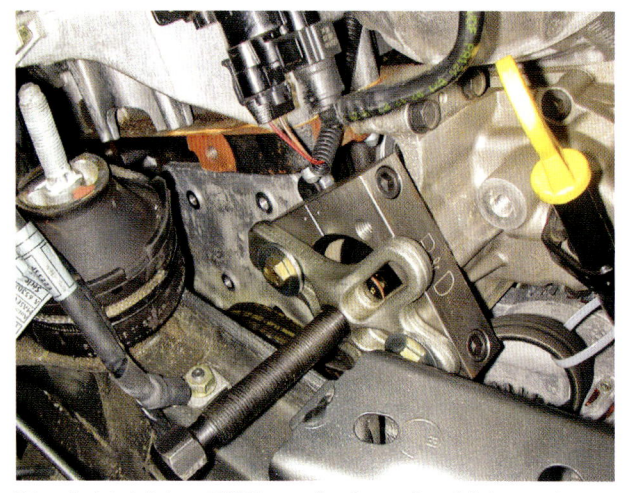

This puller is installed on a MINI blower pulley. Remove it carefully to prevent damaging the stock pulley in case you ever need it again. *Terry Sayther Automotive*

- This is a two-piece pulley. Tap the new pulley hub into place until it is about 1/8 inch from the aluminum supercharger case.
- Immobilize the new pulley by wrapping the old belt around it and grabbing the belt with a locking pliers.
- Install the outer pulley to the new hub with supplied bolts (using thread-locker compound) and torque to specs.

- Lower the engine and reinstall engine-mounting hardware.
- Reinstall the tensioner pulley assembly.
- Install a new blower belt, and relieve the pressure on the tensioner spring so you can remove the screwdriver/rod holding the tensioner spring compressed.
- Reinstall the fender liner and right front wheel.
- Prepare yourself for tire smoke at any time and place.

Or, there's always this:

New Craven Speed supercharger pulley installed on MINI. *Terry Sayther Automotive*

If you attempt to remove a pressed-on blower pulley with the wrong tool—for example, a steering-wheel or gear puller that is not up to the job, it is almost certain that you will damage the pulley. Outfits that sell overdrive pulleys often sell the special tool required to extract that original pulley. In most cases you can increase clearance enough to slide on a new pulley by hand by warming the new pulley in an oven while you ice the blower shaft, which increases the clearance between the two parts. Lubricate the shaft with anti-seize compound and once the pulley is on the shaft (and true!), slide it home by hand or pull it all the way on with its own bolt and torque to specs. Never pound directly on a pulley with a hammer, which could damage the pulley and might damage the guts of the supercharger. In general, if a steel damper or pulley needs persuasion, *tap* on it with a rubber mallet or cushion the blow from a metal hammer with a piece of wood. Heat and ice should do the job with no trouble.

A CravenSpeed MINI overdrive pulley with the belt installed and engine de-jacked.
Terry Sayther Automotive

The Crank Shop wanted to build "a small car with a big engine that hadn't been done before." Larry Audette's 2003 MINI is equipped with a FAST fuel-injected, 11.5:1 compression 392 Chrysler Hemi, which is supposedly "very mild." A BDS two-lobe supercharger, underdriven to 85 percent crank speed, delivers 6-psi boost; overdriven 50 percent the blower delivers 12-psi boost. The engine has dynoed at 687 horsepower at 5,500 rpm and 728 pound-feet at 4,000 rpm. According to his wife Paula, "Larry says the MINI is a little bit front heavy, so it spins a lot. He has fun though." *The Crank Shop*

EXTREME IGNITION

Throwing a miniature lightning bolt across a spark gap–filled supercharged air-fuel mixture requires a powerful, high-amp ignition and, typically, a spark plug gap reduced into the .025–.030 range or sometimes below .020. Unless rules prohibit it, competition-type nitrous powerplants should run a fully digital ignition that permits adjusting global ignition timing in any increment as well as individual-cylinder trim.

Overheated spark plugs are a serious risk on boosted powerplants. When it comes to spark plugs, plan on going at least one heat range colder for each 100 horsepower of boost, and know that it is common for high-boost supercharged engines to require spark plugs that are two to three heat ranges colder than stock. Avoid platinum plugs with their more delicate fine-wire center electrodes, which tend to break off at the first sign of detonation. Some experts recommend avoiding extended or projected-nose plugs, which bring an increased risk of detonation on boosted engines. Avoid resister-type spark plugs. Steer clear of split-electrode or other gimmick spark plugs. Extreme high-boost engines have run well with purpose-built racing plugs from Champion, Autolite, and NGK.

In general, copper-core plugs with copper-alloy electrodes tend to be more forgiving of variations in operating temperature and will tolerate higher temperatures without the center electrode overheating. If spark plugs are overheating, a temporary fix is to reduce combustion temperatures by increasing fuel enrichment during boost, but keep in mind that many turnkey supercharger kits with fuel enrichment are already calibrated rich out of the box, and additional fuel enrichment to fight knock will inevitably reduce power.

In some cases the center electrode will run cool enough but the ground-strap electrode is still overheating, in which case a colder plug may not help. In this case you may need a plug with a shorter ground strap, meaning the length of the electrode from the weld to the tip. In this case, projected-nose plugs could actually help, due to the fact that the ground strap is typically shorter, with a short, straight electrode that runs directly from the weld toward the center electrode. Some people have had good luck modifying the ground strap electrode on a standard plug by cutting it shorter and bending it more directly toward the center electrode.

Some extreme boosted engines with extreme plug overheating and surface ignition/detonation problems have had good luck with "retracted-nose" or even "Surface-fire" plugs, in which the center electrode essentially fires directly to the plug casing from a well formed below the bottom threads, where the lip of a casing bends inward to form a circular ground that essentially runs at cylinder head temperature. The main problem is that lighting off the charge from inside a hole introduces combustion inefficiencies and requires a powerful ignition. Some tuners have found that big old traditional full-bodied 13/16th spark plugs resist overheating better than the smaller plugs that are used in modern applications (especially "shorty" plugs, which may be easier to remove but have less porcelain on the back of the plug). Some tuners have successfully machined the cylinder head(s) to handle the 13/16th threads found on many older plugs from years past. This is also likely to get the plug threads closer to the coolant jacket.

Chapter 11
Extreme Supercharging

You could say "extreme" is in the mind of the beholder, but for the purposes of this discussion, any supercharging system shall be deemed "extreme" if it's not conventional—conventional being a belt-driven power-adder on an automotive engine capable of running on pump gas, which is theoretically capable of being street legal. Let's expand that definition a bit to include any supercharging system that boosts power by the lesser of 250 to 300 horsepower or more than about 50 percent (many of which also would require race fuel or large amounts of octane-booster).

I'm talking about supercharged race cars, extreme-power "streetable" cars, trucks with blowers, supercharged bikes, watercraft, sleds, ATVs, boats and aircraft, supercharged off-road vehicles of all types, supercharged engines running on alternative fuels (such as methanol, ethanol, propane, natural gas, nitromethane, nitropropane, or a combination of fuels), multi-stage supercharging systems, supercharged engines with nitrous, and engines that are "twin-charged" with both a supercharger and turbocharger.

TOP FUEL DRAGSTERS AND FUNNY CARS

Top Fuel drag racing is the extreme of the extreme. You already know about Top Fuel drag cars blasting through the quarter-mile in 4.5 seconds at 335 miles per hour with so much power and acceleration that a 200–mile-per-hour supercar flashing past a fueler stopped at the starting line as the lights turned green would lose the race to the quarter. These cars have nitro-fueled engines equipped with supercharging systems capable of delivering enough air to make 8,000 to 10,000 horsepower from 500 cubic inches of V-8 displacement—more power than *two* heavy railway locomotives pounding the ground at Notch 8 (well, for *part* of 4.5 seconds). Top Fuel dragsters are so radical they literally give their own earthshaking roar a run for its money as they approach half the speed of sound in the 1,320-foot race. If you don't turn your head fast enough when one explodes off the line, a fueler will remove itself from your field of vision.

Top Fuel drag racing is old-school hot rodding raised to the Nth power, and it stays old-school because fuelers are already insanely fast and powerful and no one wants to take risks that could get someone killed. Well, and because powerful people have a vested interest in keeping the established gravy train on track. The technologies currently outlawed in Top Fuel racing include almost everything that's happened in the last 50 years: electronic engine management, electronic injection, overhead cams, four-valve pentroof combustion heads, traction control, turbochargers, twin-screw superchargers, centrifugal superchargers, modern axial-intake Roots superchargers with high-helix rotors, and so on. Top Fuel is a testament to the ingenuity human beings can bring to stealing fire from the gods (in 1960) and engineering it to within an inch of its life. And it's a testament to what can be accomplished with supercharging and nitromethane.

BME's Top Fuel dragster lights it up with 8,000–10,000 ground-shaking horsepower as extreme-duty Roots 14-71 supercharger generates up to 70-psi boost pressure. Its exhaust generates 800 pounds of thrust, which is approximately 30 percent of the thrust produced by early turbojets. *Bill Miller Engineering*

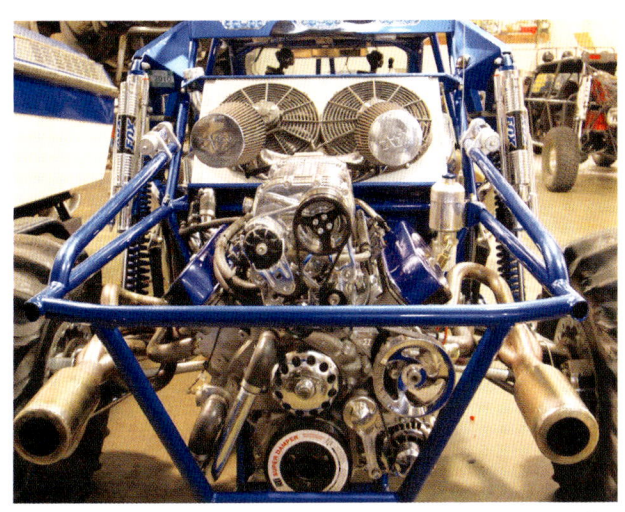

Whipple-charged V-8 sand rail. The rear-engine layout puts the drive belts behind the engine, where there is less chance of debris getting between the pulleys and belts. *Whipple Superchargers*

Lowering a new Gibson-Miller Roots-type supercharger onto the BME "Blower Dyno" to verify performance before racing. The instrumented test-bed is a methanol-fueled 502 Hemi engine with higher compression to maximize performance on alcohol. *BME*

A Top Fuel engine is a robust aftermarket alloy evolution of the 1960s-vintage 426-cubic-inch Chrysler Hemi, a 16-valve pushrod V-8 stuffed full of the strongest parts millennium metallurgy can forge from Unobtainium and send to hell. One thing the NHRA didn't outlaw in Top Fuel is space-age metallurgy. And for good reason: These 496-inch Elephant engines redline at 8,400 rpm, where piston speed is nearly 6,000 feet per minute, and the main job of the engine is to hold together for a few seconds of pure hell as flaming nitro hammers the pistons with 25,000-psi peak cylinder pressure at 10,000 horsepower. There is a moment when each 4.5-inch piston groans under the unimaginable load of almost 400,000 pounds of pressure (about the weight of an EMD freight locomotive!), and at 8,000 rpm on average there's almost 6,600 pound-feet of torque doing its best at all times to twist an 8,620 carbon-steel crank into spaghetti.

And what of the supercharger that's force-feeding one of these nuclear monsters with the oxygen in 5 atmospheres of air pressure? The Gibson-Miller Mark II supercharger is a good example of a modern Top Fuel supercharger: A triple-lobe, quad-gear, 994-cubic-inch (14-71) Roots-type monster designed to achieve the maximum performance and longevity possible while complying with NHRA rules. Bill Miller Engineering, which manufactures the G-M blower, targets Top Fuel Dragster and Funny Car teams, plus additional applications as diverse as monster trucks, drag boats, tractor-pulling, dry lakes racing, the endurance racing engines driving offshore powerboats, and "any other applications using large-displacement, supercharged engines which require Roots-type blowers capable of high-performance, excellent consistency, rock-solid reliability, and long-term durability."

A BME dragger engine, ready to rumble. NHRA rules prevent the Gibson-Miller Roots-type supercharger from using the latest supercharger airflow and efficiency tricks, but it certainly reflects state-of-the-art technology with respect to robustness. Note the containment blanket and straps to protect the driver and control shrapnel in case of a blower explosion. *BME*

EXTREME SUPERCHARGING

207

The Gibson-Miller Mark II Roots-type supercharger flows 3,750 cfm (285 lb/min mass airflow) at 12,500 rpm, a 10- to 12-percent improvement in airflow over the previous G-M model. A mass airflow of 285 lb/min air will burn enough gasoline to make 2,850 horsepower; although nitromethane has significantly less energy per gallon (specific energy) than gasoline, the brake-specific fuel consumption of nitromethane is 0.7–0.8 pounds/horsepower hour. This means a pound of air can burn 7 to 12 times as much nitromethane as gasoline assuming an air-fuel ratio of 1.0–1.7:1 versus gasoline's MBT AFR of 12.0:1 (keep in mind that in 2011 NHRA rules have generally forced Top Fuel racers to dilute nitromethane with at least 10 percent methanol).

At blower redline, air is leaving the supercharger at 250 miles per hour, and you might expect an old-school Roots blower would be red-hot making 65 pounds of boost. But with multiple gallons of nitro blasting through the blower in one Top Fuel pass, according to Bill Miller, the Mark II is barely warm.

Despite the prodigious pumping capacity of an overdriven, 1,000-cubic-inch blower, Top Fuel racers like Bill Miller find it advantageous to lean out the air-nitro ratio above peak torque as a countermeasure against the performance-negative effect of displacing too much air in the supercharger and forcing too much nitromethane to combust as a monopropellant with no oxygen (a process with lower energy yield than burning nitrous with air).

A big-block dragger designed around front-mounted gear-driven centrifugal blower. The Supercharger Store

Gibson and Miller developed the Mark II using BME's Top Fuel engine dyno, which is apparently the world's only dyno capable of fully loading a Top Fuel race engine that generates up to 8,000 horsepower. It is a piece of reworked vintage equipment that was used in the 1940s and 1950s to measure the power of heavy bomber engines and tugboat clutches and their ilk. The dyno is thus nicknamed, "Tugboat Annie," by Dale Armstrong, who adapted it to test blown alcohol and blow fuel engines circa 1970 and refined the dyno while working for NHRA Top Fuel and Funny Car champion Kenny Bernstein in the 1980s and 1990s. BME acquired the dyno in 2004 for the Mark II effort, refurbished the power-absorption unit, and installed a 4:1 gear-reduction unit and a pair of gigantic mufflers that allowed BME to test Top Fuel motors in Carson City, Nevada, without upsetting Homeland Security 450 miles away at LAX.

In addition to delivering improved airflow and boost consistency while complying with NHRA Top Fuel rules, the Gibson-Miller Mark II was designed to reduce the cost of Top Fuel racing. It delivers improved durability such that one blower can make more passes before the Nylatron rotor apex seals and the carbon-impregnated Teflon rotor end seals had to be changed. Rotor and case flexing is a big problem in Top Fuel superchargers because clearances that are too tight will destroy expensive rotor seals, and clearances that are too loose will leak. To reduce rotor twist and flex, in the Mark II design Bill Miller Engineering stiffened the G-M blower case and ends 30 percent, in part by manufacturing the case ends from aerospace aluminum rather than magnesium. The Mark II's airflow consistency stayed within 1 percent for 6 to 10 passes, which is considered excellent in Top Fuel racing even though the life of the apex seals is still only 30 to 60 seconds at full throttle! Meanwhile, BME touts that the Mark II's rotor shafts are 12 times more rigid than other drag-racing

"Maxx Kakl," triple big-block unlimited pulling tractor unleashes with three supercharged big-block automotive-type engines. Pulling tractors drag a "sled" consisting of an 18-wheeler flatbed trailer with wheels at the rear and a slide at the front that lowers to the ground for pulling competitions. A massive weight crawls forward on the sled as the pull proceeds, moving from the wheel area at the rear to the slide area at the front such that the sled offers progressively more resistance to the pulling vehicle. Unlimited modified tractors must weigh no more than 8,000 pounds with a driver, and they may run as many motors as that weight will allow, each no more than 640 cid. Turbos and superchargers are allowed, running on gas or alcohol, and no nitro is allowed. The wheelbase limit is 14 feet. Rear tires are limited to 30.5 inches wide with a rim diameter of no more than 32 inches. Unlimited tractors ultimately run out of traction rather than power and begin to dig themselves into the ground, but horsepower builds momentum early on when the sled is light.

superchargers (the better to resist deflection while enduring 7,000 pounds of force when manifold pressure reaches 60 psi in a blown-fuel race engine).

The Mark II was designed with high-speed, low-friction front and rear gear drives with zero rotor backlash indexed to 0.001 inches for extremely accurate rotor timing in the effort to maximize longevity and performance. The cases are sealed with double-lip rotor shaft seals to keep oil in and the boost out, for improved off-line response due to faster manifold pressure buildup at launch. Even with heavier aluminum ends, the redesigned G-M blower weighs in at just under 86 pounds.

To authenticate performance, BME validates and tests each newly manufactured G-M Mark II on a "blower dynamometer" that subjects the supercharger to loading and stress comparable to what it would sustain when force-feeding a nitro-burning race engine in competition, but without incurring the cost and complexity of a nitro fuel delivery system or the risk of engine durability problems endemic to supercharged nitro-burning race engines. The "dyno" is a Top Fuel engine modified to run on methanol with increased compression, a single magneto, and a blown-alcohol fuel pump providing sufficient neat methanol to make 1,580 pound-feet torque at 6,500 rpm and 2,020 horsepower at 7,100 rpm (at which point the supercharger is absorbing something like 500 to 1,000 horsepower).

ALTERNATE FUEL VEHICLES

When it comes to fueling supercharged engines, oxygenate fuels such as methanol and ethanol not only have a higher octane rating than most gasolines (methanol's octane is 107, ethanol's 113), but the powerful cooling effect of vaporizing alcohol lowers combustion temperatures to the extent that the *octane number requirement of the engine is reduced*. Although nitromethane is very prone to detonation, the heat required for vaporization is quite high. Gaseous fuels such as propane and natural gas (methane, with 0 to 20 percent ethane) have such a low heat of vaporization that they vaporize below room temperature, so there is no cooling effect as there is with fuels that enter the air stream as a liquid and steal heat to vaporize.

On the other hand, the octane rating of natural gas can be as high as 120, depending on the proportion of ethane, with propane motor fuel typically rated at 110, depending on the concentration of butane. All of these fuels are relatively clean burning and have no difficulty meeting or exceeding gasoline-powerplant emissions standards (which doesn't necessarily mean such alternative-fuel vehicles are automatically street legal). Ethanol and methyl tertiary butyl ether (MBTE) mix well with gasoline. Methanol does not, nor does nitromethane. Alcohol fuels make more power than gasoline for a given amount of air ingested by an engine, while propane and natural gas make less, but that matters more for normal-charged engines than powerplants with superchargers, which can normally provide whatever amount of air is required to meet the horsepower target (particularly

Dallas supertuner Bob Norwood built this front-engine "308" drag car 25 years ago by stuffing a flat-12 Ferrari Boxer engine in the front of a custom space frame. He then supercharged the engine with a huge centrifugal compressor built from a modified mammoth locomotive turbocharger—long before the days of modern centrifugal superchargers from Vortech, Procharger, and others. Like many radical Norwood creations, race officials didn't like it a bit.

Art Whipple's drag-racing experience of winning the NHRA U.S. Nationals taught him that the hemispherical, or "Hemi" head, allowed more boost with less detonation. Whipple decided to start with Mopar Performance's 528 Hemi engine to design Marine-ready supercharged EFI crate Hemi engines. Whipple worked with Ross Pistons to create a lightweight, low-compression piston for high-boost levels and high, sustained rpm, and the worked with Crane Cams to build custom hydraulic camshafts. Whipple quad-rotor EFI supercharger package includes a ribbed serpentine belt-drive system, a custom set of Imco Power Flow Plus exhaust manifolds, and a complete MSD ignition system with 6M-2 ignition box. On the dyno, the Whipple marine Hemis are good for 1,200 horsepower at 5,900 rpm and 1,200 pound-feet of torque across a broad range. *Whipple Superchargers*

when the fuel has a lot of octane). All of these alternative fuels have been used for supercharging with great success, though keep in mind that gaseous fuels cannot be used with old-school Roots-type superchargers that require wet air-fuel mixtures to cool the rotors.

BIKES, WATERCRAFT, SLEDS, AND SMALL ENGINE SUPERCHARGING

Supercharging four-stroke motorcycle, snowmobile, watercraft, ATV, and other small engines involves the same principles associated with larger automotive engines, though some of the problems are unique. Many of these vehicles have an excellent power-to-weight ratio without forced induction, but there have been a number of factory-turbocharged motorcycles and watercraft, and a number of vehicles have been equipped with factory centrifugal superchargers.

In general, small-bore engines are more resistant to spark knock because the distance the flame front must travel to burn all the charge is less. Whatever the temperature, pressure, and air-fuel ratio in the combustion chamber, normal combustion completes faster in an equivalent small engine and is thus much more likely to be finished before there is time for detonation (in which pockets of air-fuel mixture furthest from the spark plug spontaneously explode as pressure and temperature increase from the combustion process).

On the other hand, many small engines are air-cooled. Air-cooled engines tend to run hotter cylinder head temperatures than liquid-cooled engines, and overheated combustion chambers can quickly lead to detonation and preignition, either of which can kill an engine in a matter of seconds. Air-cooled engines can also generate colder temperatures (particularly in the case of aviation engines). Shock-cooling an air-cooled powerplant can warp heads and even cylinder barrels via uneven cooling in very cold air if you throttle back too much at high speed at little or no engine loading. The problem may then be compounded by sudden application of high power.

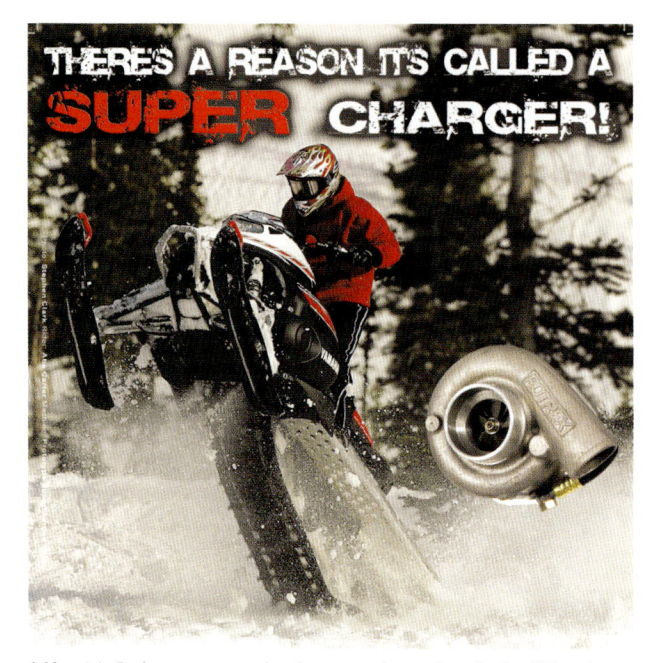

High-output air-cooled turbo engines under heavy load will generally require richer-than-normal air-fuel mixtures to cool combustion, so the brake-specific fuel consumption of an air-cooled turbo powerplant tends to be higher.

The additional thermal loading from the power boost of a supercharger can be a serious problem for small air-cooled engines. It is always a good idea to install an oil cooler on a supercharger-conversion bike or other small engine, and to upgrade the oil cooler if the engine already has one that was sized for the stock, pre-supercharged horsepower. The amount of engine oil diverted to lubricate a supercharger of a type that requires pressurized external lubrication is insignificant to an automotive engine, so it is rare that any automotive engine would require an oil-pump upgrade purely to lubricate an add-on supercharger. However, small motorcycle, sled, watercraft, and ATV engines are a different story because (1) the sump capacity is small enough that there may not be enough oil to adequately absorb the increased thermal loading of higher horsepower, piston-cooling oil squirters, and the isentropic heat of compression

A Mountain Performance supercharging conversion package for the 998-cc four-stroke five-valve Yamaha RX-1 performance sled. The packages uses a Rotrex centrifugal supercharger to provide a 60 percent power gain from 145 to 230 horsepower at 10-psi boost on a mixture of premium fuel and race gas. Mountain Performance

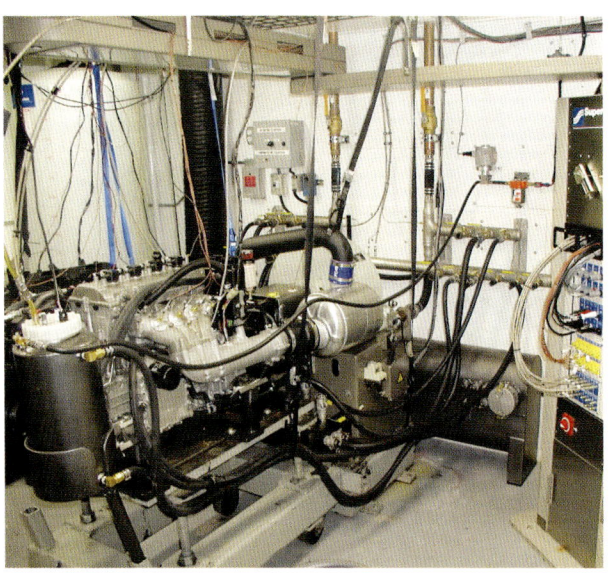

RIVA's hot-rod overboosted Sea-Doo watercraft powerplant on the Superflow torque-cell engine dyno. Note the EGT probes in the exhaust ports, which permit tuners to optimize a forced-induction calibration for peak power while keeping combustion temperatures safe. Supercharged engines make more and more power as you lean them out until they burn up.

of a supercharger, and (2) the half-gallon per minute of oil diverted to lubricate a (centrifugal) supercharger could reduce oil pressure to the rest of the engine to unacceptable levels. All superchargers lubricated with engine oil require a restrictor orifice not only to maintain engine oil pressure at acceptable levels but to keep from inundating oil seals in the compressor to the extent that oil leaks from of the compressor or enters the intake air stream (which can significantly reduce fuel octane).

To verify whether or not there is an oil-pressure problem, supercharger system designers should always install one or more gauges to monitor oil pressure in the engine and possibly at the compressor oil inlet for initial startup and road-testing. If there is not enough oil pressure, you have three options: (1) upgrade the engine oil pump, (2) build a standalone oiling system for the compressor, or (3) use a supercharger with self-contained lubrication system.

Many small powerplants use a "waste-fire" ignition system in which individual coils fire pairs of cylinders near the top of both the compression stroke and the exhaust stroke. This works great on normal-charged engines but may, in rare cases, be problematic on supercharged engines where the intake pressure is higher than exhaust pressure. If there is significant valve overlap toward the top of the exhaust stroke that blows charge into the combustion chamber, it may be ignited by a waste-fire ignition system. You'll know if this is happening because the symptoms are severe backfiring and loss of power. If this problem occurs, you'll need to change over from a waste-fire system to a coil-per-cylinder ignition system, or rephase twin cams, or install a camshaft with less overlap.

Twin-charged Olds Aerotech Quad-4 by Feuling Engineering. Feuling produced its special methanol-fueled version of the Quad-4, with boost by twin turbos and a second-stage positive-displacement supercharger (to right and turn twin turbos). The package delivered massive power on a Feuling's Southern California engine dyno. Without balance shafts and fueled with methanol, the engine was a scary-sounding, cold-blooded beast that rattled and vibrated until it was fully warm.

Centrifugal superchargers in particular can sometimes be problematic on engines with one or two cylinders because there may be 360 degrees or more (in the case of a V-twin or a single-cylinder engine) between intake strokes. The total amount of intake stroke on a twin is less than 180 degrees, which means that air between the compressor and intake valve is stagnant half the time, which could lead to compressor surge if manifold pressure gets too high at too low an airflow and air is forced backward through the compressor wheel.

A&A blown ZX-10R Kawasaki with Rotrex C15-60 Centrifugal Supercharger delivers 8-psi peak boost at sea level running on 93-octane pump gas for a 40 to 50 percent power gain. Fuel enrichment is required, and the recommended weapon of choice is the Power Commander III piggyback fuel controller, which is not included in the basic kit. Note that A&A warns, "If sustained high-rpm riding will be encountered on a regular basis (or for periods of longer than 10–15 seconds at a time), a thicker head gasket, forced induction pistons, octane booster/race gas, and/or water/methanol injection should be employed to keep cylinder temperatures in check due to the high compression ratio of the stock internals." *A&A Performance*

What's more, when the intake valve opens at high engine speeds, the instantaneous engine demand could exceed the mass airflow of the supercharger even if the compressor's average airflow is perfectly adequate. To overcome these problems supercharged twins should have an intake plenum chamber that is at least twice the volume of an individual cylinder. A single-lung powerplant that is supercharged with a centrifugal blower does better with an intake plenum that's three times the volume of the cylinder.

Two-stroke engines, which generate a power stroke from every piston each revolution, have historically had a much better power-to-weight ratio than four-strokes, which makes them useful for powering ultra-light aircraft and light terrestrial vehicles, and indispensable to powering human-wielded appliances such as chainsaws and weed-whackers. At this time of writing, two-stroke powerplants had long since disappeared as a power source for motorcycles sold in the United States, but were still widely found in outboard motors, watercraft, and sleds (with the exception of Yellowstone Park, where two-stroke snowmobiles were banned due to the horrible air pollution).

In recent years, the availability of computer-controlled direct injection-gasoline technology, fortified by 10-micronatomizing technology such as Orbital's Air-Assist, made it possible to accomplish injection in the short interval between exhaust port closure and ignition. It is highly possible that we will see the reemergence of two-stroke engines in U.S. vehicles, including cars, and at this time of writing GM had introduced a two-stroke GDI version of the XV8 world V-8 powerplant.

Depending on the architecture, two-stroke powerplants typically have some or all of the following advantages:

* *Low friction* due to a simplified or eliminated valve mechanism
* *Reduced pumping losses* compared to four-strokes at part-throttle due to nearly equal pressures acting above and below the pistons
* *Reduced parts count* due to simplicity of design
* *Compact engine height* resulting from having no valve mechanism above the cylinder head
* *Naturally low emissions of NOx* resulting from decreased combustion temperatures due to the two-stroke's unavoidable "natural EGR" that dilutes fresh charge with residual exhaust gas
* *Faster combustion* in a geometric combustion chamber uncluttered by the presence of poppet valves

Depending on the particular two-stroke engine architecture, a two-stroke powerplant can be problematic or even impossible to supercharge. One reason for this that may not be obvious is that two-stroke architectures commonly address engine lubrication with oil added to the fuel or misted into the crankcase in lieu of a normal sump-type lubrication system (which is not feasible where the crankcase is being used to pressurize the air-fuel charge mixture on its way into the engine). The lack of a wet sump means there is no readily available method for lubricating superchargers that need an external source of pressurized motor oil. What's more, oil has a low auto-ignition temperature, which tends to lower the octane rating of fuel when oil gets in the combustion chamber. This is not helpful on supercharged engines that typically need all the octane they can get. It is possible for a carefully designed injection-mist crankcase lubrication to prevent most oil from being carried into the combustion chamber with the air charge, at the risk of interfering with ring lubrication.

Large two-stroke engines such as the 6-71 Detroit Diesel have used positive-displacement blowers in place of crankcase charge pressurization, which freed designers to use conventional sump-type four-stroke lubrication, but in general, adding a positive-displacement supercharger to a small engine is self-defeating if the appeal of a two-stroke was a high power-to-weight ratio.

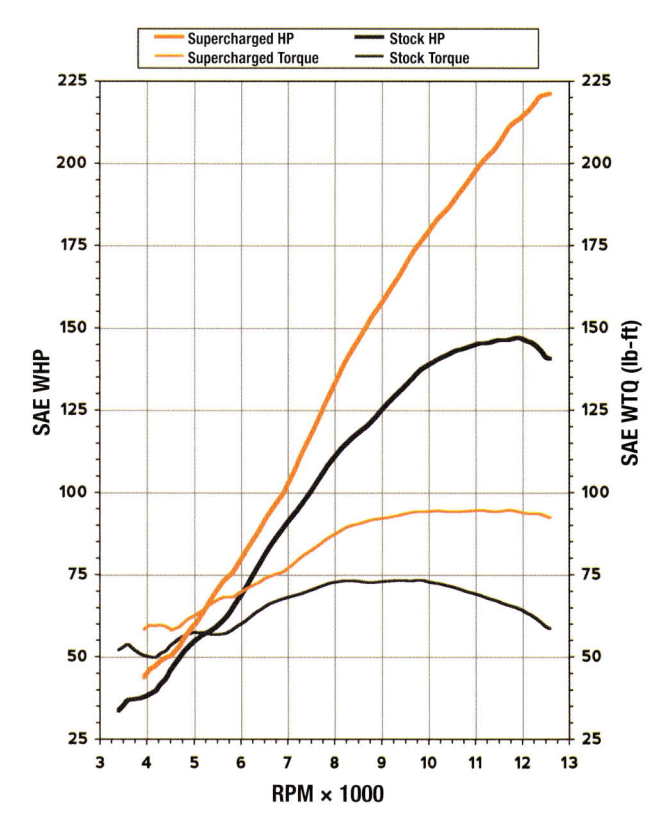

Supercharged Kawasaki ZX-10R dyno graph before and after installation of the A&A Performance supercharging conversion system. Note that although early ZX-10R superbikes are generally considered to have 175 crankshaft horsepower, on the chassis dyno a healthy ZX made just less than 150 stock rear-wheel horsepower and 220 with supercharging. *A&A Performance*

Supercharged Harley with Procharger intercooled supercharger system. Harleys need cool air too—in fact, *especially*, given that air-cooled engines have less reserve capacity for thermal loading than liquid-cooled powerplants. *Procharger*

The other major problem with supercharging two-stroke powerplants is intrinsic to the architecture of basic two-cycle powerplants. Intake pressure is used to simultaneously scavenge combustion gases and charge the cylinder in a precisely choreographed interplay of intake and exhaust pressures and velocities. During this process the intake and exhaust ports are simultaneously open part of the time. Maintaining subtle pressure and velocity specifications is critical to achieving good volumetric efficiency and preventing excessive exhaust contamination with unburned hydrocarbons and excessive charge contamination with exhaust gases.

To understand why this is so, it is worth reviewing the basic two-stroke cycle. In the simplest two-strokes, vacuum under a piston that's rising on the compression stroke sucks intake air through a carb or throttle body into the crankcase through a port low on the cylinder. Following ignition, expanding combustion gases push the piston down the bore with the intake and exhaust ports both covered until the piston descends enough to uncover the exhaust port, which allows cylinder pressure to vent into the exhaust system. Meanwhile, the downward movement of the piston has covered the crankcase port in time for the underside of the piston to compress that intake charge that was sucked into the crankcase. When the intake port opens above the piston, the compressed charge rushes out the crankcase transfer port to the intake port and begins to push combustion gases out the exhaust as it begins to fill the cylinder with fresh air (and, until the advent of GDI, fuel and a certain amount of oil), with a carefully designed aerodynamic baffle in the surface of this piston crown critical to maintaining VE and controlling charge/exhaust contamination.

In this simple two-stroke architecture, excessive crankcase charge pressure will simply blast through the combustion chamber and out the exhaust, which is why mechanically driven superchargers are worse than useless. That said, some two-strokes are equipped with intake valves in the form of reed or flapper check valves on the crankcase instead of the crankcase port, or a rotary valve in the crankcase port. In all cases, however, the exhaust port opens before the intake port and closes after the intake port, which suggests why managing exhaust back pressure with expansion chambers is so critical to

Supercharged Harley V-Rod with a Sprintex blower. Most Harleys are supercharged with centrifugal blowers because of their small size and weight and because Harleys have tons of low-end torque and lack top-end power compared to rice-burner bikes. This compact package was designed to deliver 150 rear-wheel horsepower with 7–11-psi boost and no required internal engine changes. *Patrick Racing*

EXTREME SUPERCHARGING

two-stroke performance. It also illuminates why turbocharger-induced back pressure changes and a pressurized intake can wreak havoc with the volumetric efficiency of two-strokes by wasting intake charge out the exhaust and causing exhaust gases to re-enter the combustion chamber after the intake port is closed. Yes, some two-strokes have been turbocharged by harnessing backpressure through the turbine to prevent excessive exhaust contamination, but getting it to work right is a serious R&D project that demands precise control of compressor and turbine trim and turbine A/R and exhaust housing size, with ample opportunity to create a system with dreadful performance.

The two-stroke architecture most amenable to supercharging is found on Uniflow-scavenged two-strokes, which regulate flow out the exhaust valve with a cam-actuated poppet valve, exactly like a four-stroke. This was the system found on two-stroke Detroit Diesels, which used the Roots blowers to improve intake VE and exhaust scavenging by pushing air into the intake port. These later offered the option to increase power with the addition of a turbocharger that pressurized the blower so that more fuel could be burned while maintaining the required diesel air surplus for clean exhaust and low EGT.

It is interesting to note that the innovation that reinvigorated the two-stroke cycle as a viable technology for emissions-controlled vehicles in the 1990s was similar in concept to what was found on old two-stroke diesels. Direct injection of fuel into the combustion chamber of a two-stroke diesel or gasoline powerplant can eliminate exhaust contamination by timing the fuel injection event such that it occurs after the exhaust port is closed (by an exhaust valve closing or a piston covering an exhaust port). This has the potential to totally eliminate fuel wastage out the exhaust. Of course, unless it's a Uniflow system, you would need some exhaust back pressure to prevent boost from leaking out the exhaust, which is where the exhaust turbine of a turbocharger could prove essential rather than unfortunate.

If you do decide to take on two-stroke forced induction, keep in mind when sizing the compressor that with a power stroke every revolution, two-strokes consume twice as much air as a four-stroke engine of the same displacement. And not only do you need to take lubrication for the supercharger into account, but anything that modifies normal two-stroke crankcase airflow could have disastrous consequences for cylinder lubrication in the engine.

People have developed workable supercharged two-strokes and have used them in aviation diesel applications where a high power-to-weight ratio and high altitude performance is critical. The pre–World War II German Junkers Jumo is one example. Another is the Zoche Aero-Diesel, currently in development in Europe using a four-cylinder-per-row, air-cooled, radial two-stroke diesel configuration with electronically controlled injection and a scavenging supercharger pressurized by a primary-stage turbocharger.

TWIN-CHARGING

Blowing turbo boost into a positive-displacement compressor that is supercharging an engine (whether diesel or spark-ignition) is sometimes called "twin-charging." Twin-charging combines the low-rpm boost capability of a positive-displacement supercharger with the high-rpm efficiency of a turbine-driven centrifugal supercharger. Twin-charging is a special case of two-stage supercharging, which is effective in achieving extremely high pressure ratios with good thermal efficiency by allowing both compressors to be sized and selected to operate at an efficient mass airflow and pressure ratio.

It is important to recognize that regardless of the pressure delivered by an upstream turbocharger, a positive-displacement supercharger will still deliver a fixed pressure ratio unless you change the drive ratio (which makes sense because the blower and the engine are volumetric rather than mass-airflow devices). Any supercharger with displacement and speed calibrated to exceed the pumping capacity of the engine will boost the pressure of whatever air is drawn into the supercharger by forcing charge into the engine at a rate that increases the pressure.

The RDP SRT8 Challenger uses twin Harrop TVS superchargers and nitrous injection to escalate the SRT8's 6.1-liter Hemi from 425 stock horsepower to... well, apparently 1,000 horsepower. RDP-installed Kooks headers and a custom-built RDP exhaust and made extensive modifications to the car to handle the onslaught of power, including (1) a new rear end with custom shafts, (2) Quaife limited-slip differential, and (3) a 3,800-rpm high stall converter to allow the beast to launch with more available torque. *RDP*

The author's twincharged 3.0-liter Toyota 1MZ-FE V-6. Supercharging delivered an instantaneous 5.5 psi of boost pressure, but the additional heat and exhaust pressure translated into quick turbo boost amplification into the 15- to 30-psi range. Excellent air-water intercooling with a large reservoir was designed to absorb tremendous amounts of heat with a low temperature rise to prevent turbo heat from overheating the Eaton/TRD blower. The intercooler circulation system continued to remove heat to a heat exchanger at the front of the car when the car was not under boost.

One downside of twin-charging is that, in the absence of excellent intercooling, compressed air from the turbo will not cool the supercharger rotors like ambient air. A positive-displacement blower designed with clearances upon the assumption that the rotors will be cooled continuously by fresh ambient-temperature air could sustain damage if hot compressed air from a turbocharger causes thermal expansion that reduces rotor clearances below the minimum, causing the rotors to clash.

SUPERCHARGING AND NITROUS

The best reason for installing nitrous oxide injection as a second power-adder on a supercharged engine is to (intermittently) correct for the deficiencies of the supercharging system. For example, the exponential airflow characteristics of a centrifugal supercharger mean that a blower sized to deliver target boost at maximum power will do nothing for the engine's low end. That is fine where the engine and transmission deliver more than enough low-end torque in typical high-performance driving without a power boost. But if there are occasionally times when low-end torque does not make the grade, nitrous injection—perhaps with proportional, pulse width-modulated control rather than all-or-nothing nitrous/fuel delivery—can be configured to deliver the required low-rpm torque onslaught and fade or switch off as the supercharger begins to make boost, or as normal-charged torque builds to a level that will deliver the required performance.

Because nitrous injection is independent of engine speed, the torque and power boost is proportionally greater the slower the engine is turning, which makes nitrous ideal for enhancing low-rpm performance (which is why it is critical to make sure that nitrous delivery does not overstress the engine by coming in at too low an rpm and with more cylinder pressure than the engine can safely handle). Similarly, nitrous can be used to enhance the high-end performance of a flat-torque, stock-type powerplant where an old-school Roots-type supercharger without intercooling provides more than enough low- and midrange performance but cannot realistically deliver enough boost without frying the air to achieve target maximum power. Nitrous, by the way, has a *tremendous* intercooling effect when it vaporizes, significantly increasing air density and offering the potential to cool a supercharger. For much more detail read my book *Nitrous Oxide Performance Handbook*.

MARINE SUPERCHARGING

The effectiveness of supercharged marine engines is evident from the number of factory-supercharged powerplants available for various applications. Supercharging a boat can be at once easier and more challenging than supercharging an equivalent engine in a road-going vehicle.

As with piston-engine aircraft, marine engine speed is not limited by gear ratio and instantaneous vehicle speed as it is with a road-going vehicle. Except in the case of drag boats, as long as an engine can approach maximum power rpm regardless of hull speed, extra power available at low hull speeds has little or no utility. Because marine engine speed is not limited by hull speed, the right combination of supercharger size and drive ratio, and propeller pitch and size, has the potential to provide increased engine longevity by delivering the required maximum hull speed at much lower rpm than a normal-charged engine of the same horsepower. Supercharging can improve efficiency by matching the power curve of the engine more closely to the power required to push the hull through the water at various speeds. The lack of a fixed correlation between engine rpm and hull speed and the relative unimportance of engine horsepower at low hull speeds, when there is normally a large horsepower surplus,

Spiderman, an offshore powerboat, runs twin 1200-horse big-blocks with Vortech centrifugal superchargers. *Vortech Marine*

215

means that a smaller engine with less internal friction can be boosted with a centrifugal supercharger that provides a power graph that more closely matches the horsepower requirement of the hull, which tend to increase exponentially with speed.

The ready availability of an infinite supply of cool or cold water and the superior thermal transfer properties of water make it possible to achieve extremely effective intercooling. The potential exists to down-speed marine engines with relatively high boost such that they function effectively with a narrower powerband at lower rpm. Given that high rpm stresses internal engine components more than boost, trading rpm for increased boost and prop pitch is almost always a good deal because a slower-turning engine will outlast a higher-revving powerplant in race-type conditions.

In general, a marine supercharger does not need to deliver the broad torque curve that is desirable in a road-going automobile engine and can be selected to provide a linear or even exponential power increase with rpm. Because marine engines rarely have a high-torque requirement at midrange, a supercharger can be selected to provide maximum compressor efficiency in the higher part of the power band. (There are, however, hulls that have a nonlinear power requirement graph, such that the engine needs extra power to get the hull "over the hump" in order the reach a more efficient higher speed, which obviously must be taken into account when selecting supercharger size and drive ratio if lower-rpm boost is required to get over the hump.)

One downside of supercharged marine engines is that they typically must endure fairly heavy, continuous loading when navigating at cruise speed from Point A to Point B. Like boosted automotive powerplants, virtually all supercharged marine engines require high-octane fuel, but unlike road-going automotive vehicles, a boat that is low on fuel and cannot find high-octane gasoline on the high seas almost certainly will not have the option to refuel with regular fuel like a car and drive carefully to the next gas station at throttle settings that keep the engine loaded lightly enough that the supercharger does not make enough boost to cause detonation. In fact, throttling back drastically to prevent detonation would not allow many boats to plane, which would curtail maximum speed to an extent that could, in some instances, be dangerous. Knock sensor algorithms that drastically retard timing as an anti-knock countermeasure are not usually a viable option for extended running because of the possibility of damage from increased EGT and stress on the cooling system (not to mention drastically reduced fuel economy). In this situation you need a way to limit boost so you can run at moderately reduced horsepower for as long as necessary until high-octane fuel becomes available. Except in the case of a supercharged engine equipped with suck-through carburetion or mass-airflow engine management, a pressure-actuated mechanical or electronically actuated blow-off valve armed by a "low octane" switch can be installed between the compressor and intake manifold to safely limit boost.

HIGH-ALTITUDE SUPERCHARGING

When it comes to aircraft, the overwhelming supercharger of choice in modern times is a centrifugal compressor driven by a turbine (i.e., a turbocharger), which provides a variable-speed drive regulated by a wastegate that diverts exhaust gases around the turbine to whatever extent is required to make sure that manifold pressure remains below a threshold level of boost. More recently, electronic boost controllers have allowed turbochargers to target *absolute* manifold pressure rather than boost above ambient pressure (which diminishes with altitude) by regulating reference manifold pressure seen at the wastegate. This allows aircraft to maintain full power to the *critical* altitude where the wastegate is fully closed and delivering the maximum pressure ratio achievable without changes to the turbine or compressor.

Thousands of Merlin V-12 engines supercharged with two-speed centrifugal compressors were used to power P-51 Mustangs, Supermarine Spitfires, and multi-engine bombers in World War II, but turbochargers of the day were still problematic and short-lived due to the high exhaust gas temperatures of gasoline-fueled powerplants and the metallurgy of the day.

Because a compressor failure can bring down an aircraft, forced induction conversion systems for aircraft require fail-safe design, aviation-quality machining, special heat treatments, flaw-detection procedures, and radically expensive FAA certification testing. This kind of project is beyond the competency and resources of many people who could design perfectly good power-adder systems for terrestrial or marine vehicles, but turbocharger conversion kits certified by the FAA have been developed and marketed for many popular light aircraft.

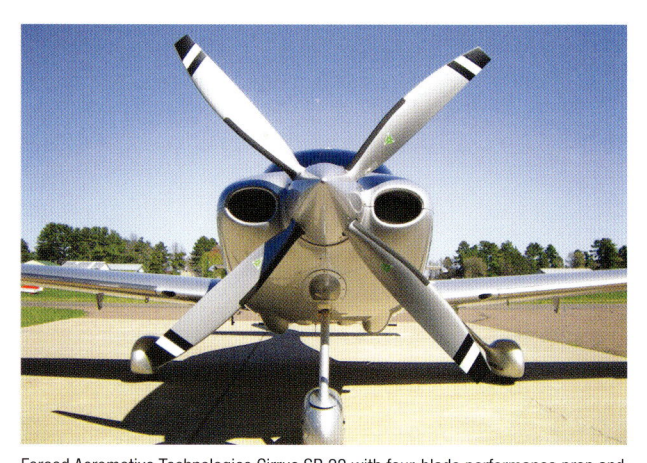

Forced Aeromotive Technologies Cirrus SR 22 with four-blade performance prop and Vortech centrifugal supercharger. A four-bladed prop instead of just two or three blades allows the engine to push plenty of air with reduced risk of a ground strike on landing. The supercharging package was designed to raise the service ceiling 7,000 to 8,000 feet and deliver an additional 15 knots airspeed at 15,000 feet, plus an extra 500 feet per minute climb performance over stock normal-charged aircraft powerplants. *Vortech*

For most people reading this book, high-altitude supercharging refers to vehicles operated on high mountain roads and lakes and trails, including competitions like the Pikes Peak Hill Climb, where vehicles begin the race at Mile 7 on the Pikes Peak Highway at 9,390 feet and race upward for 12.42 miles while negotiating 156 turns and gaining 4,721 feet in elevation. Both the land-speed record trials at Bonneville, Utah, (elevation 4,219), and the hydroplane and offshore powerboat competitions on Lake Tahoe (elevation 4,580) take place at altitudes high enough to have a significant impact on the performance of powerplants without forced induction and high enough to have a significant impact on the optimal design of a supercharging system.

High altitude lowers air pressure and air density in a manner precisely equivalent to a restrictive air cleaner or intake system, discussed in detail in the chapter of this book about modeling supercharger systems. Reduced compressor inlet pressure at higher elevations requires a supercharger to deliver a higher pressure ratio to achieve a target manifold absolute pressure than it would at a lower elevation, which will heat the air more and require that the compressor turn faster, which might or might not result in changes to the thermal and mechanical efficiency of the compressor. The pilot of a P-51 Mustang powered by a Rolls-Royce Merlin could manually shift the centrifugal supercharger gear-drive from a ratio of about 6:1 to 8:1 (a 33 percent increase in overdrive ratio) to maintain power at altitude

Supercharged C/BGMR (Blown Gasoline Modified Roadster) GM LS1 Kugel speed record engine was equipped with a parachute and all the safety equipment required to go 250 miles per hour, plus safety strapping designed to keep the MP2300 TVS supercharger on the engine in case of explosion. *Magnuson Products*

EXTREME SUPERCHARGING

217

using a switch-activated planetary-type friction clutch—or an aneroid-type pressure switch would automatically switch to high-blower mode between 14,500 and 19,000 feet, depending on the pressure contribution from intake ram air.

Engines that will always be operated at high altitude can easily be equipped with a supercharging system optimized for the home altitude. In most cases, however, engines are supercharged for maximum horsepower at sea level, with design decisions optimized where possible with the intention that there should be as little power loss as possible at higher elevations. Note that although an engine that was supercharged to 10 psi at sea level will still be supercharged to 10 psi at 10,000 feet, full boost gauge pressure at high altitude is not an indication that the powerplant is operating with full performance, as gauge pressure only indicates the *differential* between manifold and ambient air pressure. What's more, ambient air density and temperature changes could combine to adversely impact the effectiveness of an intercooling system. When it comes to manifold absolute pressure, an engine receiving 10-psi boost from a supercharging system at sea level is working with 24.7-psi absolute pressure. An engine receiving 10-psi boost at 10,000 feet (where ambient pressure is 10.15-psi absolute) is working with 20.15-psi absolute pressure. The supercharged engine will only deliver 20.15 psi / 24.7 psi = 81.5 percent as much power at 10,000 feet as it did at sea level. On the other hand, a naturally aspirated engine is typically down to about 75 percent power at 10,000 feet.

Other than driving the supercharger faster, there is nothing that can be done about the pressure and horsepower loss. It is worth noting that even without an electronic wastegate controller, a turbocharger that is boost-limited by a wastegate at sea level will compensate for altitude to some extent because the reduced ambient pressure means there is a greater pressure drop through the *turbine* at higher elevations that translates into higher turbine energy, which causes the turbocharger to spin about 2 percent faster per 1,000 feet increase in altitude.

The bottom line is it is critical to understand the effect of altitude on the performance of a supercharged engine, and why you can't necessarily simply drive a compressor faster to compensate for altitude. Many Bonneville racers have learned this the hard way. In one example a turbocharged engine that worked great at sea level surged horribly on the Salt Flats as it turned faster at relatively low mass airflow to deliver the higher pressure ratio needed to deliver full sea-level power. The car could not make enough boost to push the vehicle fast enough to allow engine rpm to increase to a higher airflow range where compressor surge would not have been a problem. Shifting to a lower gear resulted in hitting the rev limiter.

Other than building a variable-speed blower drive system, the only way to "have it all" with the advantages of low-speed boost at sea level and automatic altitude compensation at higher elevations is to twin-charge an engine with a positive-displacement supercharger with a primary-stage turbocharger feeding it air.

If you're modeling supercharger performance at altitude, it is not realistic to assume air temperature will remain where it would be at sea level. This will generally affect supercharger performance in a positive way, since standard air temperature tends to decrease about 3.5 degrees F per thousand feet, and colder temperatures "shrink" air, which increases density. Temperature has a large effect on engine performance, which is why pilots sometimes work with a concept called density altitude, which essentially describes height in terms of air density rather than distance to sea level. Turning a

Rod Sage and his company, Forced Aeromotive Technologies (FAT), received FAA certification for a supercharging conversion package for the Continental IO-550-N flat-6 aircraft engine that makes 310 stock horsepower at 2,700 rpm in Cirrus Design SR 22 aircraft. Manifold pressure was limited by a FAT electronic boost controller to 29.6 inches Mercury. "The Vortech unit has been tested for thousands of hours on jump aircraft for more than five years in taking off and holding full power through 12,000 feet, making several flights per day without failure," Sage said. "This system brings increased performance and reliability to general aviation without the engine heat and maintenance headaches of turbocharger systems." *Vortech*

blower faster at high altitude to maintain sea level power via increased compressor pressure ratio has the adverse effect of increasing compressor discharge temperature, which, in turn, increases the risk of detonation and dangerous high EGT. But lower ambient temperature not only lowers compressor inlet temperature, which helps to reduce peak combustion temperature, but it increases the effectiveness of air-cooled charge-cooling systems.

If you were boosting an engine to 10 psi at sea level with forced induction and wanted to increase the pressure ratio to deliver the full 24.7-psi manifold absolute pressure at 15,000 feet, where ambient pressure is only 8.3 psi, you'd need to increase boost pressure to 24.7 − 8.3 = 16.4-psi boost, which means that pressure ratio increases from roughly 1.7 to 3.0. A 75 percent efficient compressor working at a 1.7 pressure ratio at sea level will raise air temperature 113 degrees F and discharge air at 183 degrees F, and a 60 percent efficient intercooler will lower the temperature 67.8 degrees to 115.2 degrees F. On the other hand, at 15,000 feet, where standard air temp is 15.5 degrees F, the same compressor working at just 70 percent efficiency at a pressure ratio of 3.0 will raise air temp by 240 degrees F and discharge it at 245.5 degrees F; an intercooler with 60 percent efficiency cooled by 5.5-degree F air will lower the temperature 144 degrees to 101.5 degrees F.

The continuously-variable alternative to mechanical supercharging: The M20 turbo conversion modifies engines in Mooney aircraft from naturally aspirated to turbo-normalized, intercooled turbocharging that enables aircraft to carry sea level induction air pressure to higher altitudes. This is accomplished without changes to the original fuel flows, power settings, flight characteristics, or life limits. Turbo-normalizing permits flight into thinner air for higher speeds, fuel economy, and longer distances. Aviation turbochargers are not simply ordinary turbos bolted on aircraft. Certification of a device that could kill you or damage the engine if it fails is expensive and difficult. Aviation turbines are built from aircraft-quality materials such as Inconel, rather than cast or ductile iron. *M20-Turbos*

Dodge Challenger with modern Hemi V-8 and twin Paxton Novi centrifugal blowers. Note the cowl cold air intake system. *Paxton*

EXTREME SUPERCHARGING

219

Index

A&A Performance, 212
absolute temperature, 93
Acura
    Integra, 53
    NSX, 23
    TL, 194
air cleaner/air intake system, building, 195–198
airflow sensors, 115
Allis-Chalmers, 12
alternate fuel vehicles, 209–210
ATI, 22
Auburn, 10
Audi S4, 25

B&M Automotive, 22
BDS, 64 68 172 182, 204
BEGi, 71, 121, 123, 177
    S2000, 144
Behr, 42
Bell Intercoolers, 153, 163
Bentley Motors 4 1/2 Litre, 10
Bill Miller Engineering, 111
Blower Drive Service, 21
BME, 206, 209
BMW, 25
    318ti, 122
    M3, 71, 175
    M20, 219
Bosch, 20, 121
Buchi, Alfred, 6–7, 15
Buick, 16, 21–22
    Grand National, 22–23
    Park Avenue Ultra, 24
    Regal Turbo, 21

C&S carburetors, 110
Cadillac, 16, 51
    Northstar, 43, 65, 154
    STS-V, 25
carburetor selection, 131
Carroll Supercharging Company, 52
Chadwick, Lee, 5–6
Champion, Lieutenant C. C. Jr., 8
Chevrolet, 17
    502 Rat engine, 54
    1956, 20, 40
    Camaro SS, 41, 141, 173–174
    Cobalt SS, 24–26, 33, 49
    Corvair, 18–19, 78
    Corvette, 16, 22–23, 50, 57, 116, 122, 141
    Z06, 177
    ZR1, 5, 25–26, 42, 65, 97, 195
Chrysler, 86
    300C, 16
    Hemi, 17
combustion cooling, 149

compressor
    axial fan, 71–72, 75
    centrifugal, 5–8, 10, 13, 15–16, 22–24, 35, 40, 61–62, 71–79, 84, 99, 152, 168, 183–184, 199–200, 209, 216
    electric-vane, 71
    reciprocating-piston, 71
    sliding-vane, 71
    trim, 75
Comprex, 61, 71–74, 77
Comptech, 84
controller area network (CAN), 110, 119, 121, 124
Crane Cams, 209
Crank Shop, The, 204
CravenSpeed, 205
Crower, Bruce, 17
Crower Cams and Equipment, 52
CT Engineering, 24, 175, 194
Cummins, 15
Curtis D-12F engine, 7

Daimler-Benz DB600, 9
Denso, 22
DiabloSport, 116
Dobeck Performance, 117
    PowerCard Pro, 117
Dodge
    Challenger, 40, 214, 219
    Charger, 21
    Colt, 21
    Hemi, 39
    Ram, 52
    SRT-10 engine, 171
    Viper, 171
Drake Engineering, 15
drive belts, 186
drive systems, 187
    electric and hydraulic, 193
Dryer's Machine Service, 21
Duesenberg, 9–10, 15
    J series, 10, 12
    SJ series, 10
Dutwiler, Ken, 21

Eaton Corporation, 21–22, 24–26, 37, 39, 50, 64–66, 68, 100, 189, 195, 203, 215
    M90, 185
    R1900, 100, 102, 189
    R2300, 64, 97
    TVS superchargers, 25–26, 36, 58, 64, 68–69, 80, 97
Edelbrock, 25
eForce, 58, 67, 116
electric control units, 116
Elliott Company, The, 12
emission-control hardware, 118

engines
    cooling systems, upgrading, 137–168
    emission-compliant, 57
    evaluating health of, 54
    gasoline direct injection (GDI), 115
    management and management systems (EMS), 44, 51, 57, 106–134, 170
        auxiliary modifiers, 125
        calibration (tuning) and testing, 107–111, 133–134, 179, 199
        hardware problems, 113
        OBDII systems, 116–122
        pre-OBDII factory digital systems, 116
        strategies for, 119
            wide-range closed-loop system, 112–113
            preparing cylinders, 59
            raising compression ratio, 59
            sealing head blocks, 58–59
Eurosport, 175

Garlits, Don, 17–18
Garrett-AiResearch, 25–26
GT2871R, 75, 104–105
GT4508R, 103–105
GT5533, 103
Gates Rubber Company, 188
General Electric, 8–12, 14
General Motors (GM), 5, 11–12, 17, 20–22, 24, 34, 49–56, 59, 61, 887, 121, 166, 184
    502 HO engine, 45
    Detroit Diesel, 5, 10–12, 16, 62, 67, 212, 214
    Ecotech, 24, 33–34, 49–55, 58, 60, 88, 143, 184
    Envoy, 181
    Hydra-Matic 5L40/50 engine, 47
    L18, 166
    LS1 engine, 52, 141, 217
    LS3 engine, 106, 116, 175
    LS9 engine, 42–43, 110
    LT1 engine, 49
Gibson-Miller, 68–69, 207–209
Great Chadwick Six, 6

Ferrari, 43
    Boxer, 209
Fiat, 9
Forced Aeromotive Technologies (FAT), 216, 218
Ford, 17, 26, 126
    Boss 429, 20
    Edsel, 17
    Fairlane, 17
    Festiva, 25
    GT, 25–26
    Mustang, 17, 21, 58, 107, 203

California Special, 19
Cobra, 25
GT, 163
    SVO, 21–22, 162, 166
    Thunderbird, 17, 24
    Windsor V-8, 86
fuel
    enrichment, 129–130
    injection, alternate or dual, 132
    management unit (FMU), 125
    pressure regulators, 106, 114–116, 118, 121, 123, 125, 129, 131, 170, 176, 178
    system considerations, 131
Fueling Engineering, 211

Hampton Blowers, 21
Harley-Davidson, 213
Harrop, 214
heat
    exchangers, 136, 138–139, 141
    management, 135–168
Hennessey Performance, 26–27
Hill, Eddie, 18
Holley Performance Products, 22, 110, 124, 127–129
Hollywood Graham, 10, 15
Honda, 21, 25, 53, 60, 111
    Accord, 173, 194
    CBR600RR, 4
    CRX, 23
    Del Sol, 106, 146
    Fit, 164, 176
Hondata S3000, 53
    iVTEC, 35
    S2000, 30–31, 36, 48, 82, 84
    VFR800, 176
horsepower, flywheel vs. wheel, 85
HPC, 144
HPS, 153

ignition
    extreme, 205
    high-voltage components, 117
    timing, 111–112
IMA Motorsports, 156
intake manifold temperature, 83, 85
intercoolers, 22, 82, 98, 103, 137, 139, 141, 146, 151–154, 165, 173, 175, 177, 179, 180
    air-air (air-cooled), 139, 162–164
    air-water (liquid-cooled), 42, 156–161, 164–165, 167, 195
    building a system of, 195
    design tradeoffs, 153–155
    determining the right size, 102–103, 147–149, 151
intercooling
    affect on air density and horsepower, 161

    staging, 103–105
    thermal effectiveness, 150
    two-stage, 160

K-Jetronic, 121

Jackson Racing, 53, 64, 179, 195
Jacobs, Eastman, 12
Jaguar, 39
    I-6 engine, 118
    XFR, 25
    XJ6, 49
    XJR, 25
    XJR-6, 23
    XKE, 118
Jeep Grand Wagoneer, 126
Jet-Hot, 144
John Kasse Racing Engines, 20

Kawasaki ZX-10R, 212
Keiser, 17
Kenne Bell, 22, 40, 143, 167, 196–197
knock sensors, 117
Koenigsegg
    CC8S, 71
    CCR, 71
Kraftwerks, 30, 165, 176
Kugel '32 Hiboy Roadster, 67, 145

Latham, 16, 18
Liberty V-12 engine, 6, 9
Littlefield Blowers, 21
Lotus Turbo Esprit, 21, 25
lubrication system, building, 198–199
Lysholm, Alf, 11, 21
Lysholm Technologies, 22, 24, 26, 61, 69, 71, 180
    3300AX compressor, 71
    LYS1200A, 70
    LYS3300AX, 97

Magnuson Products, 21, 25, 39, 100–101, 107, 170, 173, 197
    Gen1E "Magnacharger," 28
    Magna Charger systems, 171
    MP2300, 175, 201–202, 217
    R2300, 67
    TVS2300, 150
Maserati
    Bi-Turbo, 21
Mazda, 74
    626, 74
Miata, 177, 195
Millenia S, 71
McCulloch, 16–17
McCulloch, Robert Paxton, 16–17
Mercedes-Benz, 25–26, 77, 74, 153, 183
    28/95 engine, 9
    M271, 25

    SLR McLaren, 71
Mercury Marine, 26, 46, 71, 83
MINI, 25, 203–205
    Cooper S, 203
Modern Atkinson Cycle, 37
Mooneyham Blowers, 21
Moss, Sanford, 8, 10
Motech, 120
    M800, 120
Mountain Performance, 49, 79, 134, 176, 197, 210
    ProLogger, 132
    RX-1, 175, 210

NASCAR, 17, 126, 135, 140
Navarro, Barney, 15, 17
Neuspeed, 189, 200
Nissan
    300ZX, 21, 25
nitromethane, 17
nitrous oxide (NOx), 30, 34, 42, 50–51, 57, 59, 77, 83, 117–118, 132–133, 151, 162, 165, 178, 184, 205, 212, 215
Norwood Autocraft, 50, 55, 63
Norwood, Bob, 49, 209

Offenhauser, 19
    I-4, 15
Offenhauser, Fred, 10
oil coolers, 142–144
Oldsmobile, 15, 16, 166
    Aerotech Q-4, 211
    F-85, 18–19
    Jetfire Turbo Rocket, 18–19, 166
Opcon Autorotor, 22, 24–25, 61, 69, 71
Orbital Air-Assist, 212
overboosting, 200–205
    with pulley changes, 201–202

Packard, 17
Paxton, 15–17, 19, 22, 29, 74, 77, 86, 130, 163, 187, 219
    N2500, 74
    Novi SL, 72
    Windsor, 109
Peltier, Jean, 167–168
Perkins, Michael, 146, 167–168
PES/Setrab, 138, 185
pistons
    cooling and heating, 141
Pontiac, 49
    Firebird, 49, 141
    Grand Prix, 25
    Solstice, 49–50, 52–53, 143
    Turbo Trans Am, 21
Porsche, 39, 51
    911, 25–26, 39, 46, 57
    930, 19

933, 156
977, 26
Can Am, 19
Carrera, 26, 46
Porsche, Ferdinand, 9
Powerdyne, 22
Pratt and Witney Model A Wasp engine, 8
Procharger, 41, 61, 110, 155, 213
Pro-Jection, 120, 189
pulleys, 191–193, 200
    changing, 203–204
pulley ratio, 200

radiators, 138–139
Range Rover Sport, 25
Renault, 20
Renault, Louis, 5
RIVA, 200, 210
Rolls-Royce, 10
    Merlin V-12 engine, 8, 13, 216–217
Roots and Roots-type blower design, 5, 8–9, 11–12, 14–18, 21–22, 24, 26–27, 61–62, 66–68, 84, 127, 175, 181–183, 185, 200, 206, 215
    M62, 68
Roots, Philander and Francis, 5
Rotrex, 23–24, 30–31, 73, 78–79, 98, 176, 210
Roush Performance Products, 25
    402IR, 28
    428R, 29
Ruf, 46

Saab, 49
Saturn, 49
    Ion, 24–25, 33
Scania, 15
Shelby American
    Cobra, 19, 196
    Mustang 289, 19, 22
    GT350, 19, 29
    GT500, 70
Shelby, Carroll, 17–18
Sprintex, 21–22, 213
SRM, 22
Stromberg carburetors, 15
Studebaker, 17
    Avanti, 17
Sunbeam Grand Prix engine, 9
Super Charger Store, 76
superchargers, 29–30
    designing and building your own system, 177–199
        common errors, 180
    dynamic, 71
    early attempts to build, 5–13
        compatibility with diesel engines, 6, 11
        conversion components, 178
    heating affects of, 35
    kits, 16–17, 22, 39, 41–42, 45, 49–50, 52, 54, 57, 68, 116, 127, 169–177, 179–180, 189, 196, 202, 205

installing, 170–176
mounting, 184–187
selection of, 80–105, 181–184
sizing, 86–90
staging, 103–105
types of
    centrifugal, 6–9, 13–14, 17, 23, 78, 81, 83–84, 110, 184, 200
    positive-displacement, 63–64
    pressure-wave, 62, 72, 74, 77
    turbo-driven, 8
    twin-screw, 20–22, 24–25, 27, 40, 69–71, 84, 97, 121, 167, 169, 175, 191, 200
use in aircraft, 7–8, 10–12, 14
supercharging
    affects on piston engines, 29–32, 34, 46–48
    bikes, watercraft, sled, and small engine, 210–214
    carburetion, 125–130
    choosing an engine for, 41–79
    common belts used in, 188
    extreme, 206–219
    high-altitude, 216–219
    marine, 215–216
    two-stroke engines, 58, 212–214
Superflow, 210
Svenska Rotor Maskiner (SRM), 11

Thompson, Mickey, 17
Top Fuel drag racing, 5, 9, 17–18, 27, 67–70, 111, 186, 206–209
Tork Tech, 176, 193
Toyota, 38, 56, 144, 153, 196
    1MZ-FE engine, 45, 215
    3S-GTE, 84
    FJ Cruiser, 65
    MR2, 22, 25, 36, 45, 61
    Prius, 37
    Scion tC, 196
    Supra, 25
TPC Racing, 57
turbochargers, 6–8, 10–11, 15, 20, 23, 26, 30, 37–39, 42, 71, 73, 77–79, 98, 216
    fuel economy, 36
    variable nozzle turbine, 76
Turbonetics, 200
twin-charging, 214–215

Volkswagen (VW), 189
    Golf GT, 25
Volvo, 15
Vortech, 22, 55, 61, 75–76, 81, 97, 109, 145, 151, 177, 189, 191–192, 215–216, 218
    Mercruiser, 153
    Power Cooler, 151

water pumps, 140
Weber carbueators, 16, 118
Weiand Air Systems, 22, 61, 124, 129–130, 141
Wenko AG, 74

Whipple, Art, 24, 209
Whipple Superchargers, 20, 22, 26, 40, 61, 106, 181
Whittle, Frank, 75

Yamaha
    Phaser, 49
    Rhino, 47, 79
    RX-1, 175–176, 197, 210

Zytek, 120

MOTORBOOKS WORKSHOP

The Best Tools for the Job.

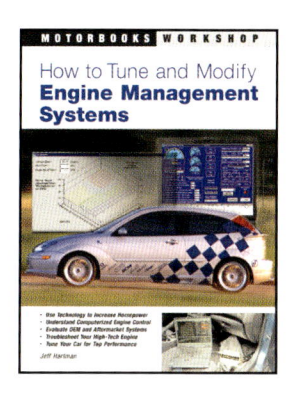

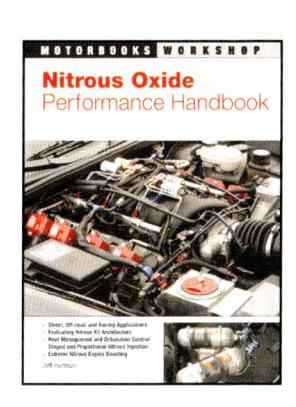

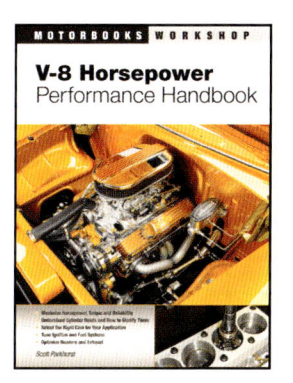

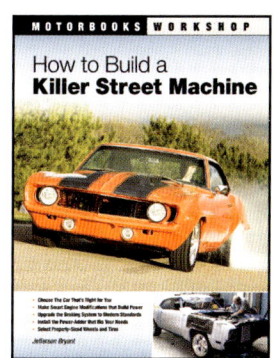

Other Great Books in This Series

How to Tune and Modify
Engine Management Systems
136272 • 978-0-7603-1582-8

Turbocharging
Performance Handbook
144219 • 978-0-7603-2805-7

Nitrous Oxide
Performance Handbook
140442 • 978-0-7603-2624-4

V-8 Horsepower
Performance Handbook
145833 • 978-0-7603-3552-9

How to Build a Killer
Street Machine
145830 • 978-0-7603-3549-9

1993–2002 Camaro and Firebird
Performance Handbook
147260 • 978-0-7603-3709-7

Ultimate American V-8
Engine Data Book
147242 • 978-0-7603-3681-6

GM LS-Series Engines:
The Complete Swap Manual
147150 • 978-0-7603-3609-0

How to Build and Modify
GM LS-Series Engines
145825 • 978-0-7603-3543-7

Chevy Small Block V-8
Interchange Manual
145418 • 978-0-7603-3166-8

Water-cooled VW
Performance Handbook
147258 • 978-0-7603-3766-0

Wheel and Tire
Performance Handbook
145390 • 978-0-7603-3144-6

Engineer to Win
108170 • 978-0-8793-8186-8

Porsche 911 Performance
Handbook 1963–1998
145389 • 978-0-7603-3180-4

How to Rebuild and Modify Porsche
911 Engines 1966–1989
135124 • 978-0-7603-1087-8

101 Projects for Your
Porsche Boxster
145835 • 978-0-7603-3554-3

How to Build a High-Performance
Mazda Miata MX-5
147269 • 978-0-7603-3705-9

Mazda Miata MX-5
Performance Projects
136332 • 978-0-7603-1620-7

Performance Welding Handbook
139436 • 978-0-7603-2172-0

Autocross Performance Handbook
144201 • 978-0-7603-2788-3

101 Performance Projects for Your
BMW 3 Series 1982–2000
143386 • 978-0-7603-2695-4

How to Diagnose and Repair
Automotive Electrical Systems
138716 • 978-0-7603-2099-0

Sheet Metal Fabrication
144207 • 978-0-7603-2794-4

Visit **www.motorbooks.com**